ESSAYS IN THE HISTORY OF CANADIAN LAW
VOLUME X

A Tribute to Peter N. Oliver

PATRONS OF THE SOCIETY

The Osgoode Society is supported by a grant from
The Law Foundation of Ontario.

THE LAW
FOUNDATION
OF ONTARIO

The Society also thanks The Law Society of Upper Canada
for its continuing support.

ESSAYS IN THE HISTORY
OF CANADIAN LAW

VOLUME X
A TRIBUTE TO
PETER N. OLIVER

Edited by

JIM PHILLIPS, R. ROY MCMURTRY,
AND JOHN T. SAYWELL

Published for The Osgoode Society for Canadian Legal History by

University of Toronto Press

Toronto Buffalo London

ISBN 978-0-8020-9911-2

∞

Printed on acid-free paper

Library and Archives Canada Cataloguing in Publication

Essays in the history of Canadian law / edited by David H. Flaherty.

Includes bibliographical references.

Contents: v. 10. A tribute to Peter Oliver / edited by Jim Phillips,
Roy McMurtry and John T. Saywell.
ISBN 978-0-8020-9911-2 (v. 10 : bound)

1. Law – Canada – History and criticism.   I. Baker, G. Blaine.
II. Flaherty, David H.   III. Girard, Philip.   IV. Phillips, Jim, 1954– .
V. Osgoode Society.

KE394.Z85E88   349.71   C81-095131-2

University of Toronto Press acknowledges the financial assistance to its
publishing program of the Canada Council for the Arts and the
Ontario Arts Council.

University of Toronto Press acknowledges the financial support for its
publishing activities of the Government of Canada through the
Book Publishing Industry Development Program (BPIDP).

Peter Oliver (courtesy of the family of Peter Oliver)

Contents

Contents   ix

Foreword

THE OSGOODE SOCIETY
FOR CANADIAN LEGAL HISTORY

This collection of essays in Canadian legal history honours Professor Peter Oliver, who led the Osgoode Society as editor-in-chief from its establishment until his death in 2006. The essays are written by Osgoode Society authors and/or by students and colleagues of Peter's at York University, and include almost all the major figures working in the field of Canadian legal history today. Reflecting Peter's own scholarship and his encouragement of a wide variety of approaches to legal history, the essays are diverse in nature, covering topics from nineteenth-century prison history to the judiciary, the legal profession, and the impact of the 1815 Treaty of Paris. The introduction provides a history of the Osgoode Society and Peter's role in it, as well as an analysis of the Society's publications program, which produced sixty-six books during his tenure. The volume represents, we believe, a fitting tribute to an extraordinary life and career, as well as a significant contribution to Canadian legal history.

The purpose of the Osgoode Society for Canadian Legal History is to encourage research and writing in the history of Canadian law. The Society, which was incorporated in 1979 and is registered as a charity, was founded at the initiative of the Honourable R. Roy McMurtry, former Attorney General for Ontario and former chief justice of the province, and officials of the Law Society of Upper Canada. The Society seeks to stimulate the study of legal history in Canada by supporting researchers, collecting oral histories, and publishing volumes that contribute to legal-historical scholarship in Canada. It has published seventy books on the courts, the judiciary, and the legal profession, as well as on the history of crime and punishment, women and law, law and economy, the legal treatment of ethnic minorities, and famous cases and significant trials in all areas of the law.

Current directors of the Osgoode Society for Canadian Legal History are Robert Armstrong, Attorney General Chris Bentley, Kenneth Binks, Patrick Brode, Brian Bucknall, David Chernos, Kirby Chown, J. Douglas Ewart, Martin Friedland, John Honsberger, Horace Krever, Ian Kyer, Gavin MacKenzie, Virginia MacLean, R. Roy McMurtry, Jim Phillips, Paul Reinhardt, Joel Richler, William Ross, Paul Schabas, Robert Sharpe, James Spence, Mary Stokes, Richard Tinsley, and Michael Tulloch.

The annual report and information about membership may be obtained by writing to the Osgoode Society for Canadian Legal History, Osgoode Hall, 130 Queen Street West, Toronto, Ontario, M5H 2N6. Telephone: 416-947-3321. E-mail: mmacfarl@lsuc.on.ca. Website: www. osgoodesociety.ca.

R. Roy McMurtry
President

Jim Phillips
Editor-in-Chief

Introduction
Peter Oliver and the Osgoode Society
for Canadian Legal History

JIM PHILLIPS, R. ROY MCMURTRY, AND JOHN T. SAYWELL*

This volume is a tribute to the late Peter Nesbitt Oliver, professor of history at York University for more than forty years and, for twenty-seven years, from 1979 to 2006, editor-in-chief of the Osgoode Society for Canadian Legal History. The contributors are mostly authors or editors of Osgoode Society books, plus others who were colleagues or students of Professor Oliver at York University. All would also count themselves as his good friends, for friendship with those he worked with came naturally to Peter Oliver. Although Peter Oliver contributed in many ways to the Canadian academic world – as a teacher and colleague and through his association with the Ontario Historical Society – his work as editor-in-chief of the Osgoode Society represents his most substantial professional achievement. During his tenure, the Society published sixty-six books on Canadian legal history, a remarkable attainment, and the lion's share of the credit for that record must go to the editor-in-chief.[1]

   This introductory essay is principally a history of the Society's publishing program and an analysis of that program's contribution to the field of Canadian legal history. But there was more to Peter Oliver than the Osgoode Society, and a little more to the Osgoode Society than Peter Oliver. Hence we begin with sections on the man, and on the founding and history of the Society. The final section of this chapter introduces the rest of the essays in this collection.

Peter Nesbitt Oliver, 1939–2006

A crowd of more than 250 people filling the room at a memorial for Peter Oliver at old Osgoode Hall in Toronto on 8 June 2006 testified to the numerous friendships that he developed during his rich life and to the great admiration of colleagues for his many achievements. He was born in Kitchener, Ontario, in November 1939, and died in May 2006 in Toronto, less than a year after his retirement from York University. He entered the University of Toronto in 1957, and soon developed a reputation among faculty and fellow students as a conscientious and determined student of history. In 1960 he enrolled in John Saywell's honours research seminar on Canadian political parties, and at Saywell's suggestion went to work on the papers of premier George Howard Ferguson. The paper Peter Oliver wrote for that course eventually grew into his doctoral thesis and a book.

After earning his BA in history from Toronto, Peter went to Harvard for an MA and then returned to Toronto for his PhD, again studying under Saywell, and continued his work on Ferguson. When Saywell left Toronto to join the still-fledgling York University (founded in 1959) as Dean of Arts, Ramsay Cook became Peter's supervisor. Just a few weeks into his new job, Saywell hired Peter as a part-time instructor – the first of many of Saywell's graduate students to join him at York. From 1965 Peter was a full-time lecturer at York, while working on his doctorate. Once the dissertation was completed he became a professor and was given tenure, spending the rest of his university career at York.[2]

Peter Oliver's own primary area of historical interest and research, in his doctorate and through most of his subsequent career even after he joined the Osgoode Society, was the history of Ontario, particularly its political history. In 1967 Saywell asked him to write the annual survey of Ontario for the *Canadian Annual Review*, and he did that for the next decade. During the same period he published his first two books on Ontario political history: a biography of Howard Ferguson, which received a special mention in the Canadian Historical Association's Sir John A. MacDonald Prize competition, and an examination of the province's pre-war political history and culture through a series of sketches of leading politicians and important political issues.[3] Another biography – of conservative politician Alan Grossman – came a few years later.[4] His most recent project, *The Dynasty*, uncompleted but immensely thoroughly researched, would have profiled the provincial Tories in their heyday of the 1960s and 1970s under John Robarts and

Bill Davis.[5] Perhaps not surprisingly the two books he produced for the Osgoode Society were also about Ontario – an account of the province's nineteenth-century prison system and an edited edition of Chief Justice Robert Harrison's nineteenth-century diaries that provides remarkable detail about the social and professional life of Harrison and his contemporaries.[6] His work on the Ontario prison system also produced four contributions to the *Dictionary of Canadian Biography*, on prison officials John Langmuir, Michael Lavell, Thomas McCrosson, and James Moylan.[7]

Given his area of expertise, Peter Oliver was a natural choice for the Ontario Historical Studies Series Trustees to turn to when in 1971 a substantial government grant was allocated to the production of a 'comprehensive history of Ontario.' Professor Goldwin French served as editor-in-chief, and Peter was appointed associate editor. Between 1971 and 1993 that series grew to thirty-one volumes.[8] One of those books, John Saywell's biography of Mitch Hepburn,[9] provided Peter with a chance to get a measure of scholarly revenge on his mentor. Peter's first drafts of articles for the *Canadian Annual Review* were invariably said by Saywell to be too long, and amicable disputes about how to cut them down followed. Peter delighted in telling the story that when Saywell's book on Hepburn came before the board of the Ontario Historical Studies Series he had the pleasure of relaying the message that it needed to be cut. This kind of genteel battle was repeated many times over during Peter's years at the Osgoode Society, with Peter frequently asking authors for cuts (including asking that Saywell's Osgoode Society volume *The Lawmakers* be reduced)[10] and yet getting the same message from reviewers with both of his own books for the Society!

Through his own writing and his work on the Ontario Historical Studies Series Peter Oliver became, in the words of York colleague Marc Egnal, 'one of the pre-eminent historians of this great province.'[11] He won the Cruikshank Medal of the Ontario Historical Society in 1971, for his contributions to 'professional historical writing.' His history of prisons and punishment in nineteenth-century Ontario won the J.J. Talman Award of the Ontario Historical Society in 1998, and his biography of Howard Ferguson was short-listed for the Canadian Historical Association's MacDonald Prize. For his commitment to Ontario history and to Canadian legal history, discussed below, he won the Guthrie Award in 1997, given by the Ontario Law Foundation for 'outstanding public service' and 'excellence in the legal profession,' and the Queen's Jubilee Medal in 2002. In 2001 he was made a member of the Order of Ontario.

In his teaching Peter stressed research in primary sources, and many in his graduate seminar caught the research bug. As a member of the history department he did not relish the ideological and methodological battles that invariably seem to afflict academic departments at some time, and largely stayed away from them. But he was on more than one occasion asked to take on difficult and divisive tasks because he was widely trusted. He made no enemies in the department, evidenced by the presence at his memorial of colleagues from all fields and all approaches to history.

While we are principally concerned here to chart and celebrate Peter Oliver's professional achievements, we cannot resist an additional, more personal paragraph. As Marc Egnal eloquently put it at the memorial for Peter, he not only wrote about the Ontario past but also, in charming and admirable ways, seemed at times to embody its major achievements while embracing to some extent the world of the past. A true 'red Tory,' his Ontario was a society that valued its roots but had become more open, tolerant, and compassionate through the twentieth century, and he passionately believed in the social improvement he chronicled and through which he lived. That appreciation for advancement did not, however, carry over into technology. He used neither computers nor email; his manuscripts were written by hand or on a trusty manual typewriter.[12] Clinging to the past, in more senses than one, while embracing the future, Peter Oliver could not have been anything but a historian, and was perhaps most suited to a social institution, the law, that is both rooted in history and self-consciously aware of its past.

The Origins of the Osgoode Society for Canadian Legal History

The Osgoode Society (the phrase 'for Canadian legal history' was added in 1993) was founded in 1979 at the initiative of Roy McMurtry, then Attorney General for Ontario in the government of Premier Bill Davis.[13] Peter Oliver's entry into the world of Canadian legal history was serendipitous, the result of McMurtry's desire for reading material during a convalescence in 1977. He was given G. Howard Ferguson and Public and Private Persons and, shortly afterwards, concerned about the dearth of legal history writing in Canada and convinced that he could and should so something about it, asked Oliver, whom he had never met, to provide the necessary professional historian's expertise to guide the society he was forming to encourage and promote the writing of Canadian legal history. Surely not knowing where it would all lead, Peter Oliver agreed with alacrity to do so. The rest, as they say, is history. As a recent article introducing Canadian legal history to an Australian audience states, the 1980s were 'a decade of take off in research and interest' in Canadian legal history, and the founding of the Osgoode Society was 'a highly significant event in providing momentum' for that take off.[14]

There are a number of parallels between the Osgoode Society and the Ontario Historical Studies Series discussed earlier in this essay. The latter was created to fill a void in scholarly writing devoted specifically to Ontario history, especially for the post-Confederation period.[15] McMurtry and others believed that there was an even greater problem with Canadian legal history. There was a Canadian Society for Legal History, founded in 1974, but lack of institutional support meant that it did not survive.[16] The Ontario Historical Studies Series had a substantial oral history component, with Peter Oliver as the director of the Oral History Programme, which carried out almost one hundred interviews.[17] This feature was also carried into the work of the Osgoode Society. Indeed, Peter Oliver was one of the earliest Canadian proponents of the use of oral history by historians of the modern period, writing and lecturing on the topic in a variety of forums well before the formation of the Osgoode Society.[18]

The Osgoode Society has always been a membership organization, modelled after a combination of two similar historical membership societies, the Champlain Society and the Selden Society.[19] It still derives its strength and a good deal of its income from its 900 plus members. In its early years it was also funded by the Ontario Ministry of the Attorney General and the Law Foundation of Ontario. The Law Society of Upper Canada has always provided support in kind. Since the mid-1980s the Society's principal source of revenue, apart from memberships, book sales, and donations, has been the Law Foundation. Although the recession of the early 1990s meant lean years for the Foundation and consequently for the Society,[20] the latter has been increasingly generous in the last decade or so and now provides stable funding with substantial three-year grants. Overseen by a board of directors,[21] and administered from the beginning by the indefatigable Marilyn MacFarlane, it has had just two presidents – the late Brendan O'Brien from its founding to 1989, and Roy McMurtry from 1990 to the present. Both have been actively engaged in the Society and its publications program rather than merely ornamental executives.

The Society has employed a variety of techniques over the years to promote Canadian legal history. In its early years it sponsored a lecture at Ontario law schools. For much of the 1980s it had the funds to provide fellowships to academics which bought out some of their teaching time, but that program was cut in the recessionary early 1990s.[22] The two constant and principal activities during Peter Oliver's tenure were the collection of oral histories of the legal profession and a publishing programme. By the time he died, the oral histories encompassed interviews with over 450 individuals, and had yielded approximately 65,000 pages of transcript. Although some of that collection is closed to researchers on the insistence of the interviewees, most of it is available at the Archives of Ontario and many of the oral histories have been used by authors, including a good number of the Osgoode Society's own contributors.[23] The publishing program, the most visible of the Society's activities to the wider world, merits a more extended treatment.

The Osgoode Society and the Writing of Canadian Legal History: A Review and An Appreciation

The Society's initial major ventures into scholarly publishing were the first two volumes in the series *Essays in the History of Canadian Law*.[24] The existing but limited work in the area, almost all of it in article rather than book form,[25] made producing a comprehensive general history impossible, yet Peter Oliver wanted to make a statement about the field, to provide a resource on which others could build. The solution to that dilemma was an essay collection, one that drew together people working independently in a variety of areas, some of whom may not have realized that they were doing 'legal' history. A closed conference in 1980 sponsored by the Osgoode Society and organized by Professor David Flaherty of the University of Western Ontario helped to take stock of existing scholarship and to lay out the basic shape of the project. The original intention was to publish one volume, but the response of potential contributors was sufficient that the plan changed very quickly to include two books – although some essays submitted for volume two were not ultimately published there.[26]

If the *Essays* project was indeed the 'birth of Canadian legal history,' one that 'propell[ed] the writing of Canadian legal history into the modern world,' in the words of one enthusiastic reviewer,[27] then the midwife was Flaherty, a historian of colonial America with appointments in both law and history at the University of Western Ontario who had published extensively on the legal history of the American colonial period. His edited collection of *Essays in the History of Early American Law* remains a classic,[28] and of course also provided a title template for the Society's first volume. Flaherty thus brought to the Osgoode Society's project a breadth of experience and an expertise in legal history, as well as formidable organizational and editorial skills. He saw the project as 'a chance to illustrate the possibilities of research and writing in Canadian legal history,' not as an attempt to provide a 'coherent history' of all of it – a judgment that remains as correct in hindsight as it was at the time. He and Peter Oliver also insisted on a rigorous review process. In contrast to the current practice of having volumes assessed as a whole, each of the essays was individually reviewed by more than one reader, and many went through substantial revisions.[29]

The result was two volumes of essays collections that demonstrate the range of subjects which this field of history can encompass. The law and economic development, master and servant law, the origins of the criminal code, and nineteenth-century custody law were among the topics treated in the first volume, while the second contained studies of the origins of workers' compensation in Ontario and histories of subjects as diverse as Ontario legal education, rape law, and riparian rights. The authors included two pioneers who had worked in the field before 1981 (Richard Risk, with an essay in each volume, and Graham Parker) and a number of then junior scholars who were just starting their careers and who have since become mainstays of the Canadian legal history community: Constance Backhouse and Paul Craven had an essay in each volume, while Blaine Baker, Jamie Benidickson, Hamar Foster, and Paul Romney were contributors to one of the collections. The volumes were very favourably received, with a common theme of reviews being that the field had come of age with their publication.[30]

Those first two volumes of *Essays in the History of Canadian Law* launched the Society on its way to becoming a serious participant in the writing and publishing of scholarly legal history – indeed, almost the only serious Canadian participant. They also provided the general title for a series that has now reached (with this book) ten volumes. In addition, sixty-three more books were published over the twenty-three years in which Peter Oliver was editor-in-chief. In the 1980s and early 1990s the Society published one or two books a year, which was in line with its initial ambitions and belief in what could be achieved; as is stated in the first volume of *Essays in the History of Canadian Law*, the Society intended to publish books 'at the rate of about one a year.'[31] One

testament to its success in engendering interest in the field is that a substantial expansion occurred from the mid-1990s. Three books were published for the first time in 1994, and the following year the total went to
four. Since then, with one exception, each year saw no fewer than three,
and usually four, books produced.

How considerable an achievement this is can be made apparent by
comparing the Osgoode Society to similar organizations elsewhere. The
best-known legal history association in the Anglo-American world is
the British Selden Society, founded in 1887. Like the Osgoode Society it
is a membership organization. Its publishing program runs to some 130
volumes, or roughly a volume a year. Its focus is very different from the
Osgoode Society – the vast majority of its books are edited documentary
collections, and most of them deal with the medieval or early modern
period, reflecting the much greater interest among English legal historians in the more distant than the recent past, and in 'internal' legal history.[32] Across the Atlantic, the Studies in Legal History Series published
by the University of North Carolina Press in association with the American Society for Legal History, is not dissimilar to the Osgoode Society
in its concentration on scholarly monographs. The first volume in that
series was published in 1981, the same year as our first volume of *Essays*,
and the list now has almost fifty titles in both American and British history.[33] It highlights the Osgoode Society's success to observe that a similar series in the much more populous and resource-rich United States
produces slightly fewer books than it does, and that the Selden Society
brings out far fewer volumes. In a country of more similar size to Canada, the Australian Francis Forbes Society was founded in 2002 with
similar objectives to the Osgoode Society. To date it has produced just
five books.[34] In short, this brief review of cognate organizations shows
that they vary in their objectives and organizational structures; but it
also demonstrates that Peter Oliver left the Osgoode Society among the
premier, if not the most successful, legal historical organization in the
common law world.[35]

Five principal points can be made about the Society's publication
program under Peter Oliver's leadership. First, in tune with his historian's sensitivity to context, and following the invocation of Flaherty in
his 'Introduction' to the first volume of *Essays*, the Society's publications have, with a few exceptions, eschewed what has been termed narrowly 'internal legal history,' the history of law and legal institutions
written without a sense of the relationship between law and the wider
society.[36] The emphasis has been on the converse, 'external legal his-

tory,' history that charts the relationships between legal and broader
societal developments. This is not to say that a good deal of what the
Osgoode Society has produced, and continues to produce, has not been
about what one author has called 'the box of distinctive-appearing legal
things.'[37] That, presumably, is the purpose of writing legal as opposed
to some other form of history. Hence the history of courts, judges, lawyers, and legal doctrine has been a very notable presence. There are five
volumes of court history, fifteen judicial biographies or memoirs, nine
books devoted to the legal profession (biographies of lawyers, books on
the history of the profession and law firms and legal education), six
books about the development of the substantive law, and one other
which we would put in this category, Paul Romney's *The Attorney General for Ontario in Court, Cabinet and Legislature, 1791–1899*.[38] That makes
for a total of thirty-six books, more than half of the Society's list as
of 2006. In addition, the various national and regionally based essay
collections contain a substantial amount of material on these kinds of
topics. The first volume of *Essays in the History of Canadian Law*, for
example, contains two articles on private law doctrine and the economy, and other chapters on labour law, chancery and law reform in
mid-nineteenth-century Ontario, and the Criminal Code. Similarly,
volume six of the series, devoted to British Columbia and the Yukon,
looks at, among other subjects, ecclesiastical law, family courts, and the
legal profession.

Such work has been extremely valuable in establishing a basic knowledge of the history of our legal system, institutions and personnel, an
area largely ignored by mainstream Canadian historians during the
twentieth century. But importantly, and testament to Peter Oliver's
guidance, that *oeuvre* is not 'internal legal history' written in a vacuum.
It typically links changes in law and legal institutions to social, economic, and political developments. Two examples should suffice to
make the point. Brian Young's examination of the origins of the Lower
Canadian Civil Code of 1866 intimately links the revision of private law
to large changes in Quebec society. Codification, he demonstrates, was
'a political act,' and 'part of a larger process ... marking the transition in
Lower Canada from a pre-industrial condition in the late eighteenth
century to one dominated by capitalist relations a century later.'[39] Similarly, Philip Girard's biography of that giant of twentieth-century
Canadian law, Bora Laskin, is not only an account of a judge and his
decisions but also of an extraordinarily rich pre- and extra-judicial
career, of Jewish life in twentieth-century Ontario, of struggles to

reform university governance, of the effects of the depression on Canadian intellectual culture, and much more.[40]

A second aspect of the publications program worth noting has been the Osgoode Society's desire to make it a pan-Canadian enterprise. Attention to regional variation is a long-standing feature of Canadian historical writing – indeed of Canadian life and politics – and Peter Oliver recognized the importance of that variety in understanding Canada's legal past. Despite the naming of the Society after Ontario's (then Upper Canada's) first Chief Justice (and a man who later become Chief Justice of Lower Canada), and despite his own scholarship being Ontario-based, Peter Oliver sought to make the publication program national in scope. That ambition was difficult to realise initially, as revealed by the contents of the first two volumes of *Essays in the History of Canadian Law*. Fully eleven of the eighteen essays in the two volumes (excluding the introduction to volume one) are about Ontario, while four of them have national or comparative themes and only three concentrate on places outside Ontario.[41] Ontario-based monographs are also prevalent in the books published in the first decade or so: 72 per cent (eight of the eleven, excluding the two volumes of *Essays*) published before 1990 are about Ontario.

The explanation for this early trend has mostly to do with the fact that little non-Ontario legal history was being written in the 1980s.[42] As Flaherty noted in the first volume of the *Essays in the History of Canadian Law*, the focus on Ontario was the 'result of happenstance rather than editorial design,' with invitations having been 'extended from the Atlantic Provinces to British Columbia.'[43] There was a marked shift from 1990 onwards, a year that saw the Society's two books being a collection of essays on law firms from across the country and another one about Nova Scotia.[44] This geographical diversification resulted from more manuscripts becoming available from outside Ontario, and the period from 1990 onwards shows a distinctly different profile. Rather than 72 per cent of the books being substantially about Ontario, only 33 per cent of the post-1990 books can be so categorised (eighteen of fifty-three). Monographs and essay collections that are national in scope became much more prevalent than before and outnumbered Ontario books – there have been twenty-two of them, or 42 per cent of the total. A significant minority of the post-1990 books have been about other provinces or regions (thirteen, or 25 per cent of the total).[45] *Nova Scotia Essays* was the first non-Ontario and non-national volume published by the Osgoode Society, but the list now includes five books on Quebec,

two on Newfoundland, three on Nova Scotia, and three on the west and
the north. Probably more a result than a cause of this shift in the geographical scope of the publications, 1993 saw the addition of the words
'for Canadian legal history' to the name of the Osgoode Society.

While the last two decades have still seen more Osgoode Society
books about Ontario than about the other provinces and regions
combined, it must be recalled that the various collections of essays organized around specific subjects embody substantial geographical diversity and tend to have more to say about places outside Ontario than
about Canada's most populous province. *Crime and Criminal Justice*,
for example, the fifth volume in the *Essays in the History of Canadian
Law* series, has eight essays that are on regions outside Ontario, six on
Ontario, and one that is national in scope.[46] Perhaps ironically, there
is neither a general legal history of Ontario nor an essay collection
devoted to the province. It goes without saying that the current editor-
in-chief of the series would welcome such an addition, as well as an-
thologies treating other regions of the country that have not yet been
highlighted by the Society.

In short, from its beginnings as a somewhat Ontario-centric enterprise, the Osgoode Society's publishing program has diversified substantially in the last decade and a half, testament to the encouragement
and interest of its editor-in-chief in unearthing the richness and variety
of the Canadian legal past. Certainly Peter Oliver was extremely receptive to the proposal from Philip Girard and Jim Phillips for the volume
on Nova Scotia, a book that turned out to be the first of three volumes
devoted to particular provinces.[47] There was no suggestion that a book
about one of Canada's smaller provinces did not fit the Society's mandate, even though Peter was dealing with an out-of-the-blue inquiry
from two tyros in the field of whom he had surely never heard. And
throughout the pre-publication process, which inevitably involved a
few bumps in the road, he remained steadfast in his commitment.
As the acknowledgments to that volume state, Peter Oliver was 'an enthusiastic supporter of this enterprise from the outset' and 'provided
much encouragement, useful criticism, and practical support.'[48] He was
equally keen about publishing a volume on the history of the same
province's Supreme Court on the occasion of its 250th anniversary.[49] A
similar enthusiasm was manifested for Jerry Bannister's book on the
legal history of early Newfoundland, published by the Society in 2002.
According to Bannister, Peter Oliver 'treated my research on Newfoundland as if it were as important to Canadian legal history as a study

of any other jurisdiction ... I always had the sense from him that he was sincerely committed to a truly national legal history.'[50]

A third feature of the Osgoode Society's publications list is that it replicates the diversity of approaches to doing good history that marks the contemporary historical profession at large. At the risk of drawing too simplistic a set of distinctions among genres, and acknowledging that many of the books fall into more than one of the categories delineated here, it is nonetheless useful to observe that, under Peter Oliver's guidance, the Society's publications came to include quite different forms of historical writing. Standard monographs detailing large developments over time abound, such as Peter Oliver's own magisterial account of the development of penal policy in nineteenth-century Ontario or Sid Harring's analysis of the various ways in which Euro-Canadian law interacted with Aboriginal law and societies in the same period.[51] They are joined by judicial memoirs, such as Quebec Court of Appeal judge Fred Kaufman's compelling story of his life and involvement in a number of highly significant events.[52] In between we find, in addition to the essay collections already discussed, biographies of judges and lawyers, case studies, two documentary collections, and even two 'picture' books!

Peter Oliver was also always keen to publish different kinds of work, giving the Osgoode Society's list a much more diverse appearance than that of, for example, the Selden Society. He was similarly willing to be persuaded of the value of work that did not immediately appeal to him. When Bruce Ziff pitched the idea of a monograph on the Leonard Foundation case, Peter was sceptical that it could support a book. But he was willing to read a draft manuscript, and once he did he appreciated how well that case study linked a legal document to its broader context. He became 'exceedingly positive, and went full steam ahead for me.'[53] While there are no doubt some observers who would decry what at times seems an eclectic approach to legal history, the fact is that the Osgoode Society has done no more than reproduce in microcosm the very considerable variety of ways of usefully doing history that have for decades marked the historical profession generally. Adhering to high standards of scholarship – an issue discussed below – is what counts, not the choice of genre. Understanding the past requires both a sense of the broad sweep of historical change and examinations of the minutiae of lives and events. Indeed in publishing case-in-context studies relatively early in its history, the Society somewhat presaged what has now become quite a popular genre of historical writing.[54]

A fourth point about the Osgoode Society's publication program, which in some ways relates to our earlier discussions of internal and external legal history and diversity of approaches, is that it has not been without a critical edge. Some twenty-four of the Society's volumes focus on what can be termed socio-legal history, and a good many of those are far from positive about the role played by law, legal institutions, and legal actors in our past. Those twenty-four books include volumes on the social history of crime and punishment (nine books), women's history (three), the history of the relationships among racial and ethnic groups and classifications and the legal system (four), the use of law to control and punish political dissent (four), and other topics (four) in which the theme is often the way the law has been used by one social group to marginalize and repress another. Those subjects, and the adoption of a critical stance, are also consistently represented in the essay collections. Peter Oliver's personal politics and historical interests were very different from those of some of his authors, but he believed in publishing good and provocative historical work whether or not he agreed with the authors' interpretations. As one of his former doctoral students and a contributor to this volume stated, while Peter did not agree with his leftist approach to penal and asylum history, he was a 'tolerant and fair' supervisor.[55] Hence the Osgoode Society has put out class analyses of the establishment of penitentiaries in the nineteenth century, feminist critiques of law, and denunciations of Tory disdain for political dissent.[56] Peter Oliver, it might be said, operated in the best tradition of academic tolerance for the views of others. He believed in and supported scholarly diversity – even if he did not always like the particular form it took!

Finally, and this is a related point, that the Osgoode Society under Peter Oliver's leadership produced different kinds of books is in part a reflection of the fact that its authors have been drawn from the profession and the academy, and within the latter from both legally trained academics and those whose formation has been in other disciplines – mostly, but not exclusively, in history. Peter Oliver did not play favourites in this regard; he wanted good work, be it from lawyers with academic interests, from historians who took law seriously, or from other legal academics who understood the importance of history. The list of Osgoode Society authors during his tenure includes seventeen people with appointments at Canadian law schools, twenty-four academics from some other discipline, sixteen lawyers and judges, and two 'others.'[57] That total of fifty-nine individuals is fewer than the sixty-five books they have collectively produced, because a good number of them have written and/or edited more than one volume.[58]

In some ways what is surprising about this summary is the relatively small role played by academics based in law schools. The reasons for their absence are complicated and perhaps controversial: the low priority given by law school administrators to history, especially in the last decade or so, and the fact that legal history is a relatively time-consuming discipline compared to others are possible causes. And it must be acknowledged that not all Canadian law schools have failed to accord an appropriate weighting to legal history, even if the largest (by faculty size) seems mostly uninterested in the Canadian legal past. But whatever the reasons, the fact remains that in a law school world in which legal historians play a limited role, especially compared to the one they occupy at the elite law schools in the United States, the Osgoode Society during Peter Oliver's editorship filled the gap. Indeed we would venture to say that the Society has been a much more important institution for the development of Canadian legal history than the law schools collectively. Deferring to a non–university-based organisation has not characterised any other aspect of Canadian legal scholarship in the modern era.

Peter Oliver's legacy is as much in the quality of the publishing program as its quantity and diversity. From the beginning he insisted on the usual scholarly procedures of blind review by outside assessors, and he himself read and commented in detail on all the manuscripts that eventually made it into print (and many that did not). The many favourable reviews in scholarly journals, too numerous to cite here, are testament to the excellence of the scholarship. In some ways an even more sterling measure is the winning of prizes, and in that respect the Osgoode Society has done remarkably well. Five of its books won four different Ontario Historical Society awards. One prize winner was Peter Oliver himself, who in 1999 was awarded the J.J. Talman Award of the Society for the best book on any aspect of Ontario history in the previous three years.[59] Others have been the Fred Landon Award, given to the best book on regional history in Ontario published in the previous three years,[60] the Joseph Brant Award, for the best book on the province's multicultural history,[61] and (twice) the Alison Prentice Award for the best book in women's history in the preceding three years.[62] The Society has also twice garnered another Ontario-based prize, the Floyd Chalmers Award, given annually by the Champlain Society for writing on Ontario history.[63]

Outside of Ontario the John Wesley Dafoe Book Prize for distinguished writing on Canada and/or Canada's place in the world has been given to two Osgoode Society books.[64] Brian McKillop's *The Spinster & The Prophet: Florence Deeks, H.G.Wells, and the Mystery of the Purloined Past* won the City of Toronto Book Prize and the Arthur Ellis Award for the best non-fiction book, both for 2000, and it was a finalist for the Governor General's Non-Fiction Award. Don Fyson's *Magistrates, Police and People* won the Canadian Law and Society Association Book Prize for 2006 and the Priz Lionel Groulx of the Institut d'histoire de l'Ámerique française, awarded for the best book on the history of French America. Perhaps the two most notable achievements have been awards from leading scholarly associations in Canada and internationally, and Osgoode Society books have garnered two of them. Constance Backhouse's study of *Women and the Law in Nineteenth-Century Canada* won the J. Willard Hurst Prize of the Law and Society Association in 1992, given for the best book in English on socio-legal history for any country. The John A. MacDonald Prize, awarded annually by the Canadian Historical Association for the best book in any field of Canadian history, went in 2003 to Jerry Bannister for *Rule of the Admirals.* Other Osgoode Society books have been given honourable mentions by juries for both of these prizes.[65]

The Peter Oliver Festschrift

The essays in this volume have been contributed mostly by the authors of Osgoode Society books, and also by a colleague (Paul Craven) and two former students (Rainer Baehre and Joseph Berkovits) of Peter Oliver at York University. Our solicitation of contributors did not limit them beyond one, very broad theme – Canadian legal history. Although there might have been some value in restricting authors to a subtheme or themes within that, we believed that such a limitation would not do justice to the ways in which Peter Oliver himself valued and encouraged work in all areas of legal history from all regions of the country. As it happens seven of the contributors gave us essays about subjects that Peter Oliver himself wrote extensively about – criminal justice and the judiciary. The essays are nonetheless an eclectic collection, but we see eclecticism as a mark of his own intellectual curiosity and tolerance for a broad approach to the subject. The essays in this volume look at the legal history of Ontario, Alberta, Quebec, Nova Scotia, and Newfoundland, as well as at 'federal' subjects. They examine judges and lawyers, theorists and practitioners, politicians, litigants, defendants, and convicts; they focus on areas as diverse as labour, criminal, family, land,

and international law. They are about what legal historians have in recent years come to call 'high' and 'low' law. The former refers to law at the elite level – judges, reported cases, legal doctrine and theory and the like; the latter to law on an everyday level, as it was administered in myriad small contexts and affected the lives of ordinary people.[66] We believe Peter Oliver would have appreciated the eclecticism represented here, and that he would have enjoyed the fact that there were so many interesting ways to write about the law, its practitioners, and its subjects.

The first section comprises four essays dealing in diverse ways with the history of crime and punishment, long a central interest of Peter Oliver.[67] Constance Backhouse, a pioneer and the best-known exponent of writing about the history of women and the law in Canada,[68] provides a fascinating case study of a 1929 rape trial in which the defendant was a member of Parliament. Although relatively few rape victims have historically seen their cases effectively prosecuted, this case resulted in five trials (three for rape, one for seduction, and one for perjury) and two appellate judgments. Backhouse weaves together a variety of legal issues, especially the rules on corroboration, with sociopolitical ones, including the francophone defendant's ethno-cultural and religious background. She argues convincingly that extra-legal considerations played a determinative role in securing a conviction for seduction, if not for the more serious rape charge.

Joseph Berkovits, a former student of Peter Oliver's, gives us an innovative essay on aspects of prison culture in late-nineteenth- and early-twentieth-century Ontario. Canadian historians know a good deal about the broad parameters of policy shifts and institutional developments in corrections, much of it, of course, from the work of Peter Oliver himself. Berkovits' work supplements this by looking at the internal workings of prisons, at the culture of these unique institutions, in particular in this essay at the role of prison wardens and their relationships with inmates. Some of his findings are not surprising – wardens needed to be disciplinarians, to be fearless, strict, and uncompromising. But their authority depended not just on their ability to use coercive physical force and other punishments, it also relied on their moral authority. Such moral authority had to be earned; prisoners came to respect, not just to fear, their wardens. Berkovits also shows us that wardens had other ways of managing their captive populations, sometimes binding men to them by displays of mercy, at other times assuming the role of what he calls 'social worker,' solicitous of prisoners' welfare. Finally, in an intriguing section towards the end of his essay, he shows us wardens as advocates, interceding with the outside world on inmates' behalf for remission of sentences or post-release employment. The world of the prison, even the 'maternal' women's prison, was never a pleasant one, but it did at times involve the better human feelings and actions motivated by kindness and sympathy.

Just as the application of the criminal law has at times been subject to a variety of social factors, so too can the making of the law reflect particular political and social contexts. Windsor, Ontario, lawyer Patrick Brode's essay on why Parliament added sexual psychopath provisions to the Criminal Code in 1948 illustrates this point very effectively. The legislation created a new kind of 'status offender,' the 'criminal sexual psychopath,' who could be given an indefinite sentence and be required to undergo medical treatment. Brode's principal question is why this legislation was brought in when it was. He demonstrates that it was not the result of any increase in sexual assaults or other sex-related crimes, but rather reflected both post-war Canadian society's broader concerns about social and sexual order and the newly enhanced status of the psychiatric profession, which was then claiming to be able to 'cure' homosexuality. The new legislation was also a response to a small number of highly publicised incidents, a classic example of a 'moral panic' in which elevated concern about a pre-existing social phenomena results first in a belief that the problem (in this case, of attacks by and on homosexuals) was much larger than it was, and then in draconian new laws to combat the perceived problem.

Paul Craven of York University is well known for his extensive writing about labour and the law in Canadian history, and we are delighted to be able to include in this volume his essay on liability for injuries caused on the railways of mid-nineteenth-century Ontario. Craven weaves together a complex story, one that involved two distinct, but overlapping, bodies of law, and shows, among many other things, the limited reach of the criminal law. On the one hand the law of negligence determined when a worker and/or the railway company could be held liable for injuries. Craven shows that juries invariably held railway companies civilly liable. Yet criminal prosecutions of workers for manslaughter or criminal negligence were generally unsuccessful, juries frequently evincing sympathy for the worker and ignoring judicial directions that strongly encouraged them to indict and/or convict. At the same time, railway workers were subject to employment law, both generally and specifically. Railway companies' rule books were effectively enforced in court, and statute law deemed breach of a company rule a sufficient basis for a conviction for manslaughter when a worker's disobedience resulted in death. These two systems of law overlapped in some respects; as noted, the companies' own demarcated obligations became those used to establish whether there had been a breach of duty. Yet the two systems also competed, in the broad sense that which law governed was representative of whether the railways were effectively regulated by the state or given managerial autonomy. For Craven the answer is clear: companies were insulated from judicial review of their managerial practices and given a free hand in matters of labour discipline, because in turn that meant that they could make the economics-based operating decisions they needed to make. Damages in civil suits were the trade-off, what Craven calls a 'license fee for managerial autonomy.' Craven's essay very effectively reminds us that 'law' operates at many levels, including in the everyday relations between employers and employees, and that the line between the abstract legal categories of public and private action has often been blurred. Railway companies were private corporations imbued with 'public' power to regulate and able to invoke state institutions like courts to enforce their dictates.

The judiciary is another topic that will always be associated with Peter Oliver,[69] and three essays here examine aspects of the Canadian judicial experience. Dalhousie University law and history professor Philip Girard's essay on Sir Wilfrid Laurier's judicial appointments takes on an enduring topic of debate within the Canadian legal system, the influence of patronage on judicial appointments. This is, regrettably, not a subject about which we have a systematic historical understanding; individual judicial biographies sometimes discuss it in microcosm, but Girard's is one of only a small handful of large-scale accounts of patronage and appointments. Laurier made 151 appointments to superior courts during his tenure as prime minster, and while patronage certainly had a role to play in his selections, it was by no means the only factor. Particularly with regard to places on the higher courts, professional assessments of suitability and independence, and the need for strong leadership in the often newly formed provincial courts of appeal, were key considerations. Laurier's approach was the more remarkable in that it followed a long period of Conservative near-monopoly on power, and the temptation to reward political supporters must have been considerable. Girard demonstrates the enduring value of looking at almost any subject historically – unthinking assumptions about what the past must have been like, often based on current practices, are shown to be incorrect, the world a more complicated place than many think it to be.

Jon Swainger also looks at judicial appointments, but in a rather more indirect way, concentrating on the effects of the overwhelming use of patronage by Sir John A. Macdonald and his successors. The result was that many men were appointed to superior courts in the early years of Confederation who turned out unsuitable, and Swainger's essay examines many of the controversies that ensued. The disputes are drawn from Nova Scotia, Quebec, and Ontario. Some were internal battles within parties over who should get the political plums, some were allegations of gross incompetence and/or unsuitability for the bench, and some were about personal and professional rivalries. All were debilitating to the nation's benches, especially the long-running set of allegations and counterallegations that Quebec's judges were variously too old and infirm for their jobs, immoral, or ignorant of the law. Collectively, Swainger argues, the various judicial scandals undermined the administration of justice in the crucial early years of the new Dominion and produced courts unable to put their stamp on the nation by enunciating a distinctive Canadian jurisprudence.

Jim Phillips takes on a rather different aspect of judicial history, examining aspects of the court structure and the use of the judges in support of political authority in early Nova Scotia. One of the challenges facing all Canadian colonies in their early decades was delivering the machinery of justice across long distances to thinly dispersed populations. Phillips' essay shows that in the early years of settlement the Halifax-based Nova Scotia Supreme Court used a variety of techniques to bring criminal justice to the hinterland, but that civil litigation was all conducted in the capital. Demands for more accessible justice led to the establishment of circuits some twenty years after the founding of the court. But circuits were more than an administrative response to the need to deliver justice to far-flung communities. With the winds of revolution blowing across British North America in the mid-1770s, sending the Supreme Court judges out from the capital was seen as a way to enforce the authority of the King's law, and hence of the King himself, to potentially disloyal citizens. Drawing on Douglas Hay's famous thesis about the way the law operated as ideology in the eighteenth century, Phillips argues that certain officials saw the 'majesty' of the law, represented by the judges, as an important bulwark of royal authority.

The third section contains two essays that consider aspects of legal thought and the history of the legal profession in the nineteenth-century Canadas. John McLaren of the University of Victoria examines early

Ontario legal culture through the life and ideas of William Warren Baldwin, doctor, lawyer, judge, treasurer of the Law Society of Upper Canada, and politician. He was also, although he did not live to see it attained, one of the leaders of Upper Canada's movement for responsible government. McLaren shows that Baldwin's commitment to the rule of law and a responsible executive were derived both from his Irish whig background and his education and practice as a lawyer. Certainly no republican, indeed a believer in the virtues of aristocracy, Baldwin nonetheless deprecated the corruption of the Family Compact and its hold on administrative power, especially its abuse of that power and of the justice system in silencing political opponents.

William Baldwin was one of the province of Ontario's best known early lawyers. Less well known, though he clearly deserves better, is William Badgley. Blaine Baker of McGill University has written a good deal about the history of Canadian legal ideas and the legal profession, and here he combines these two topics in a study that charts the relationships among criminal law codification, state building, and the desire of the elite bar of mid-nineteenth-century Canada to enhance its professional status and to play a leading role in the political and social life of the colony. At the centre of Baker's essay is Badgley, lawyer, judge and assemblyman, and his efforts to legislate codes of criminal law and procedure in the 1850s. But his explanations of this phenomenon take us well beyond Badgley himself, and well beyond criminal law codification. Badgley's codes, he argues, were an expression of many things, among them a desire to unify the law of the United Canadas and a commitment to Benthamite principles of coherence, simplicity, and clarity. Most of all he argues that Badgley's codes were symptomatic both of the turn to and faith in legislation that characterised the Province of Canada, and of the elite legal profession's understanding of the leadership role that it could play in politics and society. He identifies the mid-nineteenth century as a unique period in the way elite lawyers in the Canadas thought about their role. Before the rebellions they served an executive not yet responsible to the assembly, and from the later nineteenth century the courts and judge-made law became their focus. In this interim period their gaze was most firmly fixed on what legislation could do to transform society and consolidate the local state.

We have entitled the final section 'New Directions in Legal History,' because the four essays here are all about topics that have received very little attention within Canadian legal history, and all deserve to be more fully integrated into our understanding of what constitutes that history.

This is, indeed, a fitting way to conclude a volume devoted to celebrating a scholar who did a great deal to put the field 'on the map.' International law is the subject of Rainer Baehre's essay on the law and politics of treaties, a welcome addition to a sparse literature. Baehre is a professor at Sir Wilfred Grenfell College of Memorial University and completed his doctorate in history under Peter Oliver's supervision at York University. He examines the provisions of the post-Napoleonic Wars settlement of 1815 and of the Anglo-American Convention of 1818, which involved French and American fishing rights off the coasts of Newfoundland. While debates about the meaning and content of international law contributed to the treaty-making process in both cases, broader strategic and political concerns played a larger role and determined the extent of 'foreign' rights that were recognised. The concessions made to France and the United States harmed Newfoundland's economy, which was in effect sacrificed to Britain's desire to ensure good relations with other powers. Newfoundlanders complained and protested, but could do little to alter the terms – treaty-making was a forum available only to nation states, and dependent territories were excluded from any real influence.

Lori Chambers looks at the operation of 'everyday law,' or 'low law,' in twentieth-century Ontario. Chambers, a historian principally of women and law and a professor at Lakehead University, analyses the operation of the province's *Children of Unmarried Parents Act* of 1921, which provided machinery by which unwed mothers could invoke the aid of the state, through its proxy the Childrens' Aid Society (CAS), in suing the fathers of their children for support. However, the CAS also had the discretion to decide which cases it would advance in court, and Chambers' chapter is thus principally an examination of how that body, effectively an arm of the bureaucracy by virtue of the power delegated to it, exercised discretion. She demonstrates that CAS workers' decisions were fundamentally shaped by their moral disapproval of unwed motherhood, so that only a small proportion of women who applied to the CAS received that organisation's backing in taking the father to court. The women were often disbelieved, and invariably pressed either to marry the father or to release their child for adoption. Thus what appeared on paper to be a valuable legal right granted to a powerless and often despised group was, in practice, substantially reduced by the work of administrators. Chambers also notes the inherent conflict of interest in the system; the CAS was also responsible for arranging adoptions, and fulfilling this mandate was made easier by persuading

unmarried mothers not to seek support to bring their children up themselves, but to give up their babies.

Ian Kyer, a Toronto historian turned lawyer who has written about
legal education as well as law firm and corporate law history, provides
us with a detailed and revealing study of one of the province's most
famous and wealthy twentieth-century lawyers, David Fasken.
Although Kyer has a lot to tell us about how Fasken made his money
and about his contacts with other leading lights of the profession in the
early twentieth century, such as appeal court judges William R. Riddell
and Cornelius Masten, the article is principally concerned with two
other aspects of Fasken's life. In part it is a compelling if at times bitter-
sweet social history, a tale of a family life far from the idyllic. In part –
and in this sense it is a near-unique contribution to Canadian legal history – it is an examination of the techniques of early estate planning.
Kyer shows how Fasken used a variety of measures, especially *inter
vivos* and testamentary trusts, to minimize the payment of succession
duties.

The final essay in this volume by Bruce Ziff and Sean Ward of the University of Alberta takes on a central aspect of Canadian legal history, the
law of the land, but looks at it from the perspective not of official land-
granting but of the informal or customary law of squatters' rights. One
of the ways in which European settlement in Canada was different from
many other British colonies in the nineteenth century was in the relative
absence of squatting and the consequent conversion of informal rights
to officially legal ones. For the most part the Canadian West was
divided up after 1870 by land sales from the Crown, not by individuals
simply establishing themselves on the soil. Yet there were exceptions,
even if unsuccessful and short lived, and Ziff and Ward recount one of
these, the staking of claims around Edmonton by those whose claimed
'right' rested on nothing more than physical possession. Perhaps not
surprisingly, squatting led to more of the same, or claim jumping, and
in turn to vigilante acts to defend apparent rights. And, also not surprisingly, the squatters' claims ran up against official land-granting
policies. In the end many of the squatters had their titles confirmed, a
familiar enough nineteenth-century tale. This essay demonstrates the
complexity of our legal history and, in the process, demolishes widely
and perhaps too easily held assumptions, in this case about the fact that
Western settlement always took place in accordance with established
government policy.

NOTES

* We thank a number of people who provided us with information about, and observations on, Peter Oliver. Marilyn MacFarlane, administrator of the Osgoode Society for the bulk of Peter Oliver's tenure as editor-in-chief, was unfailingly helpful. Ramsay Cook, Martin Friedland, Roy McMurtry, and, especially, Marc Egnal offered remarks at the memorial service for Peter Oliver that we have drawn on here in discussing his professional life. Anne Hodgson and Kevin, Michael, and Tony Oliver also spoke about their father and brother on that occasion, and their comments helped us to understand the man better. We also thank those colleagues in the Canadian legal history community who responded to a request for anecdotes about Peter; we have used only some of them, but appreciate all the responses we received. Blaine Baker offered very useful comments on an earlier draft of this introduction, as did two anonymous reviewers for the Osgoode Society. Readers may have noticed the third-person reference to Roy McMurtry in this note. When referring to ourselves we have done so in the third person, to avoid the awkwardness of phrases such as 'one of the authors of this essay.'

1 The total of sixty-six books includes the three published in 2006 after Peter Oliver's death, that bear the name of Jim Phillips as interim editor-in-chief. Each of those books was chosen by Peter Oliver, and he worked with the authors to bring the volumes almost to completion. We therefore consider the 2006 books to be part of Peter Oliver's legacy as editor-in-chief. For a list of the Osgoode Society's publications, see the last few pages of this volume.

2 See 'The Making of a Provincial Premier: Howard Ferguson and Ontario Politics, 1870–1923' (PhD diss., University of Toronto 1969).

3 *G. Howard Ferguson: Ontario Tory* (Toronto: University of Toronto Press 1977); *Public and Private Persons: The Ontario Political Culture 1914–1934* (Toronto: Clarke, Irwin 1975). For the special mention see the note from Audrey Livernois of the University of Toronto Press to Peter Oliver, 19 June 1978, on file with Jim Phillips.

4 *Unlikely Tory: The Life and Politics of Allan Grossman* (Toronto: Dennys 1985).

5 Peter Oliver's papers contained a very large amount of material for *The Dynasty*.

6 *'Terror to Evil-Doers': Prisons and Punishments in Nineteenth Century Ontario* (Toronto: Osgoode Society for Canadian Legal History and University of Toronto Press 1998); *The Conventional Man: The Diaries of Ontario Chief Justice Robert A. Harrison, 1856–1878* (Toronto: Osgoode Society for Canadian

Legal History and University of Toronto Press 2003). In subsequent notes all books published by the Osgoode Society *and* the University of Toronto Press will be referenced only by date of publication; those brought out by other publishers will be footnoted with their full citation.

7 See *Dictionary of Canadian Biography*, online at www.biographi.ca.

8 For details, see www.ontariohistoricalsociety.ca and an unpublished 1987 paper by Peter James, 'The Making of History: The Ontario Historical Studies Series,' located in Peter Oliver's papers and on file with Jim Phillips.

9 *Just Call Me Mitch: The Life of Mitchell F. Hepburn* (Toronto: University of Toronto Press 1991).

10 *The Lawmakers: Judicial Power and the Shaping of Canadian Federalism* (2002).

11 Remarks of Professor Marc Egnal, Peter Oliver Memorial, 8 June 2006, on file with the authors.

12 Taken from ibid.

13 This section on the history of the Society is derived from, in addition to the specific sources noted, the files preserved in the Society's office in Osgoode Hall (hereafter Society Files). For the origins of the Society see also 'The Osgoode Society,' *Law Society of Upper Canada Gazette* 13 (1979), 156–7, and 'Osgoode Society Gathers Legal History,' *CBA National*, April 1981, 11.

14 J. McLaren, 'In the Northern Archives Something Stirred: The Discovery of Canadian Legal History,' *Australian Journal of Legal History* 7 (2003), 75. Similar encomiums for the leading role played by the Society appear in a number of review articles: see, for example, J. Phillips, 'Recent Publications in Canadian Legal History,' *Canadian Historical Review* 78 (1997), 236–57.

15 See *Ontario Historical Studies Series: A Progress Report* (1984), 2–3.

16 For that society see L. Knafla, ed., *Proceedings of the Canadian Society for Legal History 1977* (Calgary, 1977), with accompanying newsletters. See also G. Parker, *Now and Then*, a circular for Canadian legal historians published irregularly during the later 1970s and early 1980s.

17 James, 'The Making of History,' 11. This collection is housed at the Ontario Archives.

18 See P. Oliver, 'Oral History: One Historian's View,' *Journal of the Canadian Oral History Association* 1 (1975), 13–19; 'Oral History,' lecture delivered to Ottawa Local History Workshop, 1975, in Oliver papers, on file with Jim Phillips; 'Book Review Article of Four Books on Oral History,' *Archivaria* 7 (1978), 164–8.

19 'The Osgoode Society,' 156.

20 See the article in *Law Times*, 28 March–3 April 1994.

21 Three of the original directors remained on the board throughout Peter Oliver's tenure as editor-in-chief – Roy McMurtry, the late Brendan O'Brien, and the late Mr Justice Archie Campbell. For a full listing of current directors see the Society's website at www.osgoodesociety.ca.

22 See generally Society Files. See also P. Oliver, 'The Osgoode Society: A Progress Report,' *Law Society of Upper Canada Gazette* 18 (1984), 77, and *Law Times*, 28 March–3 April 1994. Fellowship recipients included many of the best-known practitioners of Canadian legal history, such as Desmond Brown, Constance Backhouse, Hamar Foster, Richard Risk, Paul Romney, and Carolyn Strange.

23 See, for example, P. Girard, *Bora Laskin: Bringing Law to Life* (2005); R. Sharpe and K. Roach, *Brian Dickson: A Judge's Journey* (2003); E. Anderson, *Judging Bertha Wilson: Law as Large as Life* (2001); and I. Bushnell, *The Federal Court of Canada, 1875–1992* (1997). Scholars other than Osgoode Society authors have also used the collection: see, for example, C. Moore, *The Law Society of Upper Canada and Ontario's Lawyers, 1797–1997* (Toronto: University of Toronto Press 1997).

24 D.H. Flaherty, ed., *Essays in the History of Canadian Law*, vol. 1 (1981) and D. H. Flaherty, ed., *Essays in the History of Canadian Law*, vol. 2. These were not the first two volumes the Society produced. Volume I was the first, but in 1982 there appeared M. MacRae and A. Adamson, *Cornerstones of Order: Courthouses and Town Halls of Ontario, 1784–1914* (1982).

25 For English Canada the principal, almost the only, scholar working seriously in the field was R.C.B. Risk: see G.B. Baker, 'R.C.B. Risk's Canadian Legal History,' in G.B. Baker and J. Phillips, eds., *Essays in the History of Canadian Law*, vol. 8, *In Honour of R.C.B. Risk* (1999). See also R.C.B. Risk, 'A Prospectus for Canadian Legal History,' *Dalhousie Law Journal* 1 (1973), 27–45. Otherwise the bulk of the legal history that was written – by people like W.R. Riddell for Ontario; E. Lareau, G. Doutre, and B.A.T. de Montigny for Quebec; C.J. Townshend for Nova Scotia; and W.F. Bowker and R. Stubbs for Western Canada – tended to be anecdotal and largely concerned with judges and lawyers as individuals. An exception is D. and L. Gibson, *Substantial Justice: Law and Lawyers in Manitoba, 1670–1970* (Winnipeg: Peguis 1972). A review of the field written in the early 1970s for the *University of Toronto Law Journal* had nothing to say about Canada; the approaches discussed were all British or American: see G. Parker, 'The Masochism of the Legal Historian,' *University of Toronto Law Journal* 24 (1974), 279–317. Quebec was somewhat better served: see A. Morel, 'Canadian Legal History – Retrospect and Prospect,' *Osgoode Hall Law Journal* 21 (1983), 159–192, and

V. Masciotra, 'Quebec Legal Historiography,' *McGill Law Journal* 32 (1987), 712–32. For an account of an abortive early attempt to write the history of Canadian law, see P. Girard, 'Who's Afraid of Canadian Legal History,' *University of Toronto Law Journal* 57 (2007), 727–53.

26 See Society file on Flaherty Essays.

27 D.G. Bell, 'The Birth of Canadian Legal History,' *University of New Brunswick Law Journal* 33 (1984), 317.

28 (Chapel Hill: University of North Carolina Press, 1969).

29 See Society file on Flaherty Essays.

30 See Bell, 'The Birth of Canadian Legal History,' and the reviews by B. Wright, J. McLaren, D. Hay, A.W.B Simpson, L. Kealey, and D. Kettler in, respectively, *Osgoode Hall Law Journal* 22 (1984); *Canadian Bar Review* 62 (1984); *Canadian Historical Review* 44 (1983); *University of Western Ontario Law Review* 19 (1983); *Social History* 17 (1984); and *Journal of Canadian Studies* 3 (1984).

31 'Foreword,' in Flaherty, ed., *Essays*, vol. 1, ix. Ironically this phrase continued to appear in the preface to Osgoode Society books until 1996, a year in which three books were published and a year after four had been produced. It disappears from 1997 onwards.

32 The meaning of 'internal legal history' is discussed below. For more details on the Selden Society, see www.selden-society.qmw.ac.uk. Interestingly, most of the Selden Society's membership is resident in North America.

33 Information on the Series can be accessed at www.h-net.msu.edu/~law/ASLH.

34 See www.forbessociety.org.au.

35 See Christopher Moore's similar assessment, reviewing Sharpe and Roach, *Brian Dickson*. He states: 'The Osgoode Society may be the most successful legal history society around.' *Law Times*, December 2003.

36 For the distinction between 'internal' and 'external' legal histories, see R.W. Gordon, 'J. Willard Hurst and the Common Law Tradition in American Legal Historiography,' *Law and Society Review* 10 (1975), 325–33, and D. Flaherty, 'Introduction,' in Flaherty, ed., *Essays*, vol. 1, 12–19. A recent article uses the terms 'lawyers history' and 'historians law' to make the same distinction, and also charts the emergence of the divide between the English academic and legal worlds as occurring at the end of the nineteenth century: see R. A. Cosgrove, 'The Culture of Academic Legal History: Lawyers' History and Historians' Law, 1870–1930,' *Cambrian Law Review* 33 (2002), 23–34.

37 Gordon, 'J. Willard Hurst,' 11.

38 (1986). While we are confident that almost all of our categorisations are
unexceptionable, we acknowledge that some readers might quibble with a
few of our decisions. For example, we included R. Fraser, ed., *Provincial Justice: Upper Canadian Legal Portraits from the Dictionary of Canadian Biography*
(1992) in the judicial biography list because it contains a good many of them,
but whether it belongs there or under the legal profession heading is debat-
able – and irrelevant as it certainly should be among the total of thirty six
volumes about 'distinctive appearing legal things.' In the 'legal doctrine'
category we include, in addition to the obvious books, both B. Ziff, *Unforeseen Legacies: Reuben Wells Leonard and the Leonard Foundation Trust* (2000)
and P. Brode, *Courted and Abandoned: Seduction in Canadian Law* (2002).

39 *The Politics of Codification: The Lower Canadian Civil Code of 1866* (Toronto:
Osgoode Society for Canadian Legal History and Montreal: McGill-Queen's
University Press 1995), xiii.

40 See *Bora Laskin*.

41 A point made by a reviewer in 1984: see Bell, 'Birth of Canadian Legal History,' 317.

42 There were exceptions, most notably L.A. Knafla, ed., *Law and Justice in a
New Land: Essays in Western Canadian Legal History* (Toronto and Calgary,
1981); T.G. Barnes et al., eds., *Law in a Colonial Society: The Nova Scotia Experience* (Toronto 1983); L.A Knafla, ed., *Crime and Criminal Justice in Europe
and Canada* (Waterloo: Wilfrid Laurier University Press 1981); vol. 21 of the
Osgoode Hall Law Journal; and vol. 32 of the *McGill Law Journal*, on Quebec
legal history.

43 'Preface,' in *Essays*, vol. 1, xiii.

44 C. Wilton, ed., *Essays in the History of Canadian Law*, vol. 4, *Lawyers and Business in Canada 1830–1930* (1990), and P. Girard and J. Phillips, eds., *Essays in
the History of Canadian Law*, vol. 3, *Nova Scotia* (1990).

45 As with the discussion of internal and external legal history above, not all
of the Society's publications are easily categorized and some might question our decisions on what to include where. Biographies of Supreme Court
judges pose a particular problem. We have included Girard, *Bora Laskin*, as
an Ontario book, but Anderson, *Judging Bertha Wilson*, as a national one.
The former is substantially based in Ontario and Laskin's time on the
Supreme Court of Canada is only part of the life detailed by Girard. Con-
versely, although Wilson was an Ontario appointment to the Supreme
Court of Canada, Anderson's account of her life deals more with her years
at the Court, a national institution. We have for similar reasons counted
Sharpe and Roach, *Brian Dickson*, as a national book, not a Manitoba one. In
a few other cases we have categorized books in ways that do not reflect

their title. For example, Brode, *Courted and Abandoned*, is largely about Ontario law and cases.

46 J. Phillips, T. Loo, and S. Lewthwaite, eds., *Essays in the History of Canadian Law*, vol. 5, *Crime and Criminal Justice* (1994).

47 H. Foster and J. McLaren, eds., *Essays in the History of Canadian Law*, vol. 6, *British Columbia and the Yukon* (1995); C. English, ed., *Essays in the History of Canadian Law*, vol. 9, *Two Islands, Newfoundland and Prince Edward Island* (2005).

48 Girard and Phillips, *Essays*, vol. 3, *Nova Scotia*, ix.

49 P. Girard, J. Phillips, and J. B. Cahill, eds., *The Supreme Court of Nova Scotia, 1754–2004: From Imperial Bastion to Provincial Oracle* (2004).

50 J. Bannister to J. Phillips, email correspondence, 27 December 2006. This was in reference to Bannister's *Rule of the Admirals: Law, Custom, and Naval Government in Newfoundland, 1699–1832* (2003).

51 *White Man's Law: Native People in Nineteenth-Century Canadian Jurisprudence* (1998).

52 *Searching for Justice: An Autobiography* (2005).

53 B. Ziff to J. Phillips, email correspondence, 28 December 2006, on file with the authors. The book is Ziff, *Unforeseen Legacies*.

54 See M. Friedland, *The Case of Valentine Shortis: A True Story of Crime and Politics in Canada* (1986); R. Sharpe, *The Last Day, the Last Hour: The Currie Libel Trial* (1988); B. O'Brien, *Speedy Justice: The Tragic Last Voyage of His Majesty's Vessel Speedy* (1992); and P. Brode, *The Odyssey of John Anderson* (1989).

55 R. Baehre to J. Phillips, email correspondence, 12 June 2007.

56 The references are to R. Baehre, 'Prison as Factory, Convict as Worker: A Study of the mid-Victorian Saint John Penitentiary, 1841–1880,' in Phillips, Loo, and Lewthwaite, eds., *Crime and Criminal Justice*; C. Backhouse, *Petticoats and Prejudice: Women and Law in Nineteenth-Century Canada* (Toronto: Osgoode Society for Canadian Legal History and Women's Press 1991); and F.M. Greenwood, *Legacies of Fear: Law and Politics in Quebec in the Era of the French Revolution* (1993). Compare the first article to Oliver's account of the origins of the Kingston Penitentiary in *'Terror to Evil-doers,'* chap. 2, and the Backhouse book to his chapter on the Mercer Reformatory in Phillips, Loo, and Lewthwaite, eds., *Crime and Criminal Justice*.

57 This count is only of those who were either authors or editors of monographs, and does not include writers of individual chapters in essay volumes. It also excludes McRae and Adamson, *Cornerstones of Order*. The 'others' are Barry Cahill, an archivist, *The Thousandth Man': A Biography of James McGregor Stewart* (2000); Girard, Phillips, and Cahill, *The Supreme Court of Nova Scotia*; and Beverley Boissery, an independent writer, *A Deep*

Sense of Wrong: The Treason, Trials and Transportation to New South Wales of Lower Canadian Rebels After the 1838 Rebellion (1995), and, with Murray Greenwood, *Uncertain Justice: Canadian Women and Capital Punishment 1754–1953* (2000) – both Osgoode Society for Canadian Legal History and Dundurn Press. We have included Robert Sharpe twice because he wrote one book (*The Currie Libel Trial*) while an academic and another as a judge (*Brian Dickson*, with K. Roach). William Kaplan is on the law school academics list because, at the time he wrote *Bad Judgment: The Case of Mr. Justice Leo Landreville* (1996), he taught at the University of Ottawa law school. The 'other academics' category includes some individuals – Robert Fraser, Susan Lewthwaite, Paul Romney, and Carol Wilton – who hold PhDs in history but who work outside university history departments.

58 Those authors who have written more than one monograph and/or edited more than one collection include Peter Oliver himself, with two. The others are Constance Backhouse (3), Blaine Baker (2), Beverly Boissery (2), Patrick Brode (4), Barry Cahill (2), David Flaherty (2), Philip Girard (3), Murray Greenwood (4), Jim Phillips (5), Robert Sharpe (2), Fred Vaughan (2), David Williams (2), Carol Wilton (2), and Barry Wright (2).

59 That prize was for '*Terror to Evil-Doers*.'

60 J. Honsberger, *Osgoode Hall: An Illustrated History* (2004), won the award in 2006.

61 C. Backhouse, *Colour-Coded: A Legal History of Racism in Canada, 1900–1950* (1999), won in 2002.

62 L. Chambers, *Married Women and Property Law in Victorian Ontario* (1997), won the award in 2001, and Anderson, *Judging Bertha Wilson*, won in 2004.

63 L.S. McDowell, *Renegade Lawyer: The Life of J.L. Cohen* (2001), won for 2001, and Girard, *Bora Laskin*, won for 2005.

64 Saywell, *The Lawmakers*, won in 2002, and Sharpe and Roach, *Brian Dickson*, won in 2003.

65 D. Fyson, *Magistrates, Police and People: Everyday Criminal Justice in Quebec and Lower Canada, 1764–1837* (2006) was an honourable mention for the Hurst Award in 2007, and both Fyson and Philip Girard's *Bora Laskin* were honourable mentions for the MacDonald Prize in 2006 and 2007, respectively.

66 For an excellent recent discussion of this distinction, see D. Hay, 'Legislation, Magistrates and Judges: High Law and Low Law in England and the Empire,' in D. Lemmings, ed., *The British and their Laws in the Eighteenth Century* (Woodbridge, UK: Boydell Press 2005).

67 In addition to his seminal '*Terror to Evil-Doers*,' see also four other articles by him on punishment: 'A Terror to Evil-Doers: The Central Prison and the

Criminal Class in Late Nineteenth-Century Ontario,' in R. Hall et al., eds., *Patterns of the Past: Re-interpreting Ontario's History* (Toronto: Dundurn Press 1988); 'From Jails to Penitentiary: The Demise of Community Corrections in Early Ontario,' *Correctional Options* (1984), 1–10; 'To Govern By Kindness: The First Two Decades of the Mercer Reformatory for Women,' in Phillips, Loo, and Lewthwaite, eds., *Crime and Criminal Justice*; and, with M. Whittingham, 'Elitism, Localism, and the Emergence of Adult Probation Services in Ontario, 1893–1972,' *Canadian Historical Review* 68 (1987), 225–58. Peter Oliver also taught a history of crime and punishment course at York University for many years, which had large enrolments.

68 Her fourth Osgoode Society book, *Carnal Crimes: Sexual Assault Law in Canada, 1900–1950*, is being published at the same time as this volume.

69 See Oliver, *The Conventional Man*, and 'Power, Politics, and the Law: The Place of the Judiciary in the Historiography of Upper Canada,' in Baker and Phillips, ed., *Essays*, vol. 8, *In Honour of R.C.B. Risk*.

PART ONE

Criminal Justice: Law, Policy, and the Limits of the Criminal Sanction

1

Rape in the House of Commons: The Prosecution of Louis Auger, Ottawa, 1929

CONSTANCE BACKHOUSE*

Seventeen-year-old Laurence Martel mounted the massive marble stair-case of the House of Commons and made her way toward Room 417. The former convent pupil had been boarding with an aunt in Ottawa for the past five months. A Franco-Ontarian from Alfred Township near Hawkesbury, Martel had her sights on a secretarial career. In September, she had enrolled at Henry's Shorthand School, a business college on Bank Street. She was two weeks away from completing her course, and hoped to obtain a clerical position with the federal government.[1]

It was Friday afternoon, 15 February 1929. Prime Minister William Lyon Mackenzie King headed a Liberal minority in Parliament.[2] The government that Laurence Martel hoped to work for was overwhelmingly male. Agnes McPhail, elected in 1921, was the first and only woman in the House of Commons. There were no women in the Senate, although the 'Famous Five' had already launched their legal challenge to declare women 'persons' and eligible for appointment.[3] Women had made little progress within the civil service. The first female federal public servants, hired in 1870, had been the matron and deputy matron of the Kingston Penitentiary. By 1885, the number had risen to only twenty-three. Occupational segregation brought more women into government stenography positions by the early twentieth century. But after 1921, many were forced to resign upon marriage. Laurence Martel was aspiring to admission into a very male workplace, and one that was predominantly anglophone as well.[4]

Laurence Martel was on her way to see her member of Parliament, Louis Mathias Auger, on the advice of her father. An impoverished, practically illiterate labourer who knew little of the ways of the civil service, Jean Baptiste Martel had told his daughter to ask their MP to help her find a position. Laurence Martel's aunt, Bertha St Pierre, had followed up to make the appointment for her niece. When Laurence Martel reached Auger's fourth-floor office, she knocked. Louis Auger opened the door and invited her to enter.[5]

The interactions that ensued between Louis Auger and Laurence Martel would eventually spawn one of the most scandalous moments in Canadian legal history. Louis Auger would face five trials for rape, seduction, and perjury before he was finally convicted and sentenced to two years in Kingston Penitentiary. Although sexual assault was commonplace in early twentieth-century Canadian society, women rarely found vindication in the courtroom. The crime was infrequently reported and often indifferently prosecuted. The scepticism with which judges and jurors generally viewed the testimony of female complainants was buttressed with strict legal doctrines such as corroboration and recent complaint, and defense counsel were given wide license for cross-examination regarding the victim's reputation and prior sexual history. The resulting rates of conviction were low.[6] Louis Auger's case was to prove exceptional on many levels, as a determined group of anglophone prosecutors and judges demonstrated their willingness to alter customary presumptions, legal rules, and procedures to ensure they made an example of the young Franco-Ontarian MP. Auger's public office and his ethno-linguistic heritage combined to alter the traditional application of the law of sexual assault in this notorious and controversial proceeding.

Born in Contrecoeur, Quebec, on 3 April 1902, Louis Auger had moved to Hawkesbury at the age of ten, when his father, a grocer, resettled the family in eastern Ontario. Auger had obtained a Bachelor of Arts and a Bachelor of Philosophy at the University of Ottawa, a bilingual Roman Catholic institution, where his stellar academic performance brought distinction and medals. He began teaching French, history, mathematics, and penmanship at the University of Ottawa in 1925, and during the fall of 1926, he contested the federal seat for the riding of Prescott. Unable to secure the Liberal nomination, Auger ran as an Independent Liberal and handily defeated the sitting Liberal member. This in itself was not extraordinary. Prescott was 'so strongly liberal' that Liberal candidates often competed with each other at the

Louis Auger, circa 1924
Graduating Class Mosaic, Bachelor of Arts, Seventh Form, 1923–4
Archives of the University of Ottawa

polls. What was more unusual was Auger's youth. The day after the election, the *Ottawa Journal* published Auger's photograph on the front page, declaring that the twenty-four-year old MP was the 'Youngest in House.'[7] The press took to calling him the 'Baby of Parliament,' while back home his proud constituents dubbed him the 'Boy Orator.' In 1928, Auger enrolled as a student-at-law at Osgoode Hall. The ambitious Auger was articling with a lawyer in L'Orignal, Ontario, attending part-time law lectures at Osgoode Hall, and simultaneously trying to carry out his functions as a sitting MP in Ottawa.[8]

Martel had seen Auger in Hawkesbury once, but had never spoken to him. Somewhat timidly, she handed the politician her application form for the federal public service. Although her English was improving, Laurence was confused by the unilingual form. The two filled out the application, and on Auger's prompting, Martel listed as her references the Hawkesbury parish priest, the mayor, and Auger himself. Then they reached the line that asked the applicant's age. Martel told Auger that she was seventeen years old, and Auger replied that candidates had to be at least eighteen. He told her to wait until her next birthday before submitting the application. What transpired next was a matter of great controversy. Beyond dispute, whatever ensued ruined the reputations of both.

Laurence Martel's Testimony

Testifying in the Ottawa Police Court on 5 March 1929, Martel explained that after they completed the application form, Auger told her that he had grown up with her father and knew him well. He said that despite her age, he might be able to find her a temporary position. He said he would phone her. He asked Martel to take off her coat and hat, which she did. 'He made me sit on the sofa,' she told the court. Then he 'started to kiss' her, and she pushed him back, telling him to let her go. The Crown attorney asked why she didn't 'scream and screech.' 'I was so nervous I could only cry and tell him to let me go,' replied the young woman. The examination continued:

Q: What happened then?
A: Then he took off my bloomers.
Q: Why didn't you prevent him doing that?
A: I could not. I tried everything but I couldn't prevent him. He was holding me and was too big for me and too strong.

Q: When he took off your bloomers, what happened?

A: He was trying to do things but I was struggling hard.

Q: When doing these things to you on the sofa what was the condition of his clothing after he had taken off your bloomers?

A: He didn't take off his trousers, he just unbuttoned them.

Q: Did he have connection with you?

A: No, he tried but he could not succeed. I kicked at him and ...

Q: How did you get away from him?

A: After I yelled at him to let me go, he got up and I got up too. Then I put on my bloomers and my coat and hat.

Laurence Martel made a quick escape, traces of tears covering her face. Embarrassed and confused, she took the streetcar home through the blustery, snowy streets to her aunt's residence.

The next day, Saturday at noon, Auger telephoned Martel. He told her that she should come back to his office at 2:00 p.m., adding: 'You won't be sorry if you come.' Martel was dubious about Auger's intentions, and she also had an appointment at a beauty salon that afternoon to have her hair 'marcelled.' When Auger telephoned a second time at 1:30 p.m., she had left for the salon. He phoned back a third time about an hour later, leaving insistent messages with Martel's aunt. When Martel got back, she took the messages and decided to return to Auger's office. Martel tried to explain her decision to the court: 'Well, I thought that as he knew my father so well he might be sorry. I thought he might apologise and say he was sorry for what he had done. He hadn't gone very far ...' In later proceedings, she would also explain that she thought Auger might have wanted to discuss her prospective employment. The Crown also asked Martel if she had told her aunt what had happened the day before. Martel replied she had not. The Crown asked her why she didn't take Mme St Pierre with her when she went to see Auger a second time. 'I didn't want anybody to know what had happened,' explained Martel.

When Martel arrived at Auger's office later that afternoon, the House of Commons seemed deserted, with only a few elevator operators and security guards on duty. Auger was alone in his room. The curtains were down. Martel entered and asked what was so important that it necessitated her return. Auger laughed and locked the door. He took off her hat. He took off her coat. 'I was trying to prevent him, but I couldn't,' testified Martel. The telephone rang, and when Auger answered it, Martel took her hat and coat and tried to leave, but she could not unlock the door. Auger terminated the phone call, removed her hat and coat a second time, and angrily pushed her onto the sofa. Martel testified:

Q: In what condition were your clothes?
A: He had taken off my bloomers.
Q: Why didn't you scream and yell and call for help?
A: I did yell 'let me go' and I was crying.
Q: Did you yell out loud?
A: Yes, but there was nobody there. I didn't know they didn't work on Saturday afternoons.
Q: Why didn't you scratch his face?
A: I could not move. He was holding my hands. All I could do was to kick him.
Q: When he had you down on the sofa and he on top of you, what happened then?
A: He had connection with me.
Q: Had any man or boy, previous to that, ever had connection with you?
A: No, never.

When Auger released the young woman, her underclothing and dress were bloody. He instructed her to go to the bathroom on the floor above and wash up. Dazed and discomposed, she did so. When she had cleaned up, she went back to the office to get her purse. Auger escorted her out of the building, and then walked with her towards the train station, where he boarded the late afternoon train to Hawkesbury. Martel caught the streetcar in front of the Chateau Laurier Hotel. When she got home, her appearance startled her aunt, who asked what was the matter. Embarrassed, Martel disappeared into her room, muttering, 'the Auger business is finished as far as I am concerned.' Mme St Pierre followed her niece, her anxiety aroused. 'Did he try to get near you?' she queried. 'He did worse than that,' responded Martel. 'Did Auger kiss you?' pursued the aunt. Martel broke down and confessed everything. Bertha St Pierre wrote to tell Martel's father in Hawkesbury. Criminal charges were laid against Louis Auger on 25 February 1929.

Louis Auger's Version

Louis Auger told the press that the charge was 'absolutely unfounded,' and that he would 'vindicate himself' on all counts.[9] The picture he painted of Laurence Martel was far from that of a naive country girl. He depicted Martel as an ambitious schemer, determined to exploit his political connections to secure a civil service appointment. Although he had told her to wait another year, he claimed that Martel had boasted that she would conceal her age and sit the civil service examinations 'under false pretences.' Auger had cautioned her against this. He advised that her best hope was to check the classified advertisements in the Ottawa papers, and escorted her to the door. When she returned again on Saturday, she came because she and her aunt had decided that Auger could do much better with the application form. Auger denied having promised Martel any job, insisting that he had 'a higher conception of his position as a member of parliament.' His accuser 'voulait le forcer à lui faire obtenir une position dans le service civil.'

Auger also spoke of Martel as coquettish, anything but what her strict convent education might have led one to expect. He claimed that she had flattered him, talking about how the young people in Prescott County followed all his political meetings. The MP alleged that she told him that all the girls were fighting over who would 'have' him. Martel had demanded to know whether he had 'many girls in Ottawa.' She had gossipped about her boyfriends and said that she participated in 'auto parties.' She had asked to ride in Auger's 'pretty' car, and he had offered to drive her to Hawkesbury 'when the roads got better.' She had asked to be introduced to Auger's male friends, particularly the one who had telephoned while she was in the office, because she 'liked' the way his voice sounded. Auger portrayed Martel as a girl-about-town, akin to the daring young flappers of the 'Roaring Twenties' who smoked, shortened their skirts, bobbed their hair, and pursued sex in the rumble seats of motor cars.

As for himself, Auger claimed that despite his 'eligible bachelor' status, he was aloof from the loosening sexual mores, and 'too busy to bother with girls.' He conceded that he had agreed to call for Martel at her business college to have supper next week, but claimed that this was only to introduce her to the young man who had telephoned. He admitted having quipped rather jocularly at the train station that he was off to see his 'girl' in Hawkesbury. But he denied caressing Martel or using terms of endearment. He had not 'laid a finger on the girl.' She was either 'lying or imagined it.'

This was not the first time that Auger's sexual reputation had occupied the press. In 1927, Ottawa physician Duncan A. MacGregor brought a lawsuit against him for unpaid medical fees. The treatments had been for a malady that physicians had to report 'to the health authorities' in order 'to comply with provincial regulations,' as the press described it, using veiled language to refer to venereal disease. According to Dr MacGregor, Auger had sought treatment under the assumed name of 'Joseph Tremblay of the Department of Public Works' between Christmas and New Year's Day in 1926, and then skipped on the bill. When the doctor later recognized Auger from a Toronto newspaper photograph, he served him with the outstanding account at the House of Commons. Auger refused to pay. He defended the claim by calling his relatives and friends to testify that he had spent the holidays in Hawkesbury and Montreal, and could not have obtained medical services in Ottawa. The doctor called the elevator girl of the medical office block, the janitor, the electrician, and several other physicians, all of whom testified that they had seen Auger in Dr MacGregor's office. The presiding judge suggested that a medical examination of Auger might settle the matter, but both sides objected. Dr MacGregor argued that the results might not be definitive, and Auger's lawyer complained that it would subject his client to 'unnecessary humiliation.' In the final result, the court characterized the situation as one of 'mistaken identity,' and dismissed the doctor's claim, before a courtroom 'filled with more than 100 friends of the interested parties, including many residents of Hawkesbury,' who swarmed the defendant with their congratulations. The *Ottawa Journal* advised that this had 'completely removed any stigma the charge may have laid upon the character of Canada's young parliamentarian.'[10]

Auger's portrayal of himself as a man too busy for female liaisons may have jarred readers' perceptions further when the press leaked another scandalous item. The day after charges had been laid with respect to Martel, the *Ottawa Citizen* reported that 'police officers changed the lock and barred the Prescott MP from his room as the result of some discovery not related to this case.' The *Ottawa Journal* added that 'the young member had his room in the House of Commons taken away from him' after he was 'found in a very compromising situation in his room at seven o'clock in the morning.'[11] Later reports confirmed that the Speaker of the House cancelled Auger's room privileges because he had repeatedly entertained different women overnight in his office. After parliamentary security personnel stumbled upon Auger's amorous escapades for the third time, sanctions issued. According to two sergeants, they had removed Auger's Do Not Disturb sign and entered Room 417 with a master key on the morning of 15 February, only to discover Auger and an unidentified naked female lying on the couch. Women's clothes were strewn about the room. This was just hours before Laurence Martel arrived to meet with Auger for the first time. Auger would later admit that he had gone to a cabinet reception with 'a lady' who had 'spent the night with him in his room,' but insisted that this had occurred on the 13th and not the 15th of February and denied that security officers had ever confronted them in the office.[12] Whatever the truth was, the events cast a pall over Auger's efforts to characterize himself as morally circumspect, too busy to have dalliances with women.

A Politician Under Indictment: 'We Don't Get Many of Them Here'

Prosecutions for sexual assault in twentieth-century Canada were complicated by issues of gender, class, and ethnicity. Judges expressed scepticism about women who made allegations of rape, endlessly quoting seventeenth-century English jurist Sir Matthew Hale, who warned of the many innocent men falsely accused.[13] Where the complainant was working class and belonged to a minority racial or ethnic group, her testimony was even more suspect. Under ordinary circumstances, a working-class Franco-Ontarian woman's charge of rape against a male of higher status would have lacked credibility, even when the accused was also a francophone. This was particularly so where she had not raised an outcry, heroically resisted her assailant, or suffered substantial physical injury during the attack.[14] However, the Auger case was further complicated by an overlay of politics. It was unsettling for Canadians to witness an elected official, responsible for overseeing the law of the land, put on trial for rape. Although his situation initially provoked amazement, the legal authorities soon turned on Auger, singling him out for tenacious prosecution and retributive justice. He found his status as a middle-class, male parliamentarian to be of little protection; in the end it worked to his considerable disadvantage.

Louis Auger was arrested late on the evening of 25 February 1929, as he left Parliament Hill. Members of the police morality squad had to wait for hours, unable to execute their warrant within the precincts of the House.[15] The guard who booked Auger at the jail asked him to list his occupation. When the accused replied, 'Member of Parliament,' the guard repeated the phrase, and then mused sardonically, 'We don't get many of them here.' Startled officials released Auger on a bail bond of $1,000 around 3:00 a.m., only to discover that neither police magistrates nor county judges had the power to grant bail in such serious cases. Auger was brought back to court the next morning, but the authorities hesitated to lock him up in the Nicholas Street jail with the other prisoners. Auger was held in the police station, while he waited to hear whether a higher court would grant bail. The officer on duty arranged to have a restaurant deliver bacon, eggs, and coffee to the accused man.

Front-page headlines characterized the arrest as 'sensational,' adding that the charges were 'the most serious ever laid against a member of parliament.' Some newspapers forecast that it was unavoidably 'calculated to reflect on the dignity of parliament.'[16] The *Ottawa Journal* reporter underscored the anomaly of a man of Auger's stature facing criminal prosecution. He described Auger's reluctance to hand over his personal belongings, right down to his money, watch, fountain pen, letters, papers, and the 'usual male effects.' 'Do I have to put everything I have in there?' complained the prisoner. 'I'm afraid you do,' replied the guard. The reporter added that newspapers and tobacco were banned due to prison regulations, and noted the 'crude jail furniture,' upon which Auger sat, 'exhausted after the ordeal he had passed through since his arrest.' The daily deprivations in Canadian jails were rarely chronicled by crime reporters. Ordinary prisoners were stripped down and consigned to numbingly barren quarters without apparent reflection or concern. But when the detainee was a man of education and prominence, the routine jail procedures suddenly seemed inexplicable and onerous.

When Auger announced that he would not sit in the House of Commons while the charges were pending, it fuelled speculation over his political career. The press reported that Parliament had complete discretion to oust a member who had been charged or convicted of a criminal offence. This was not entirely accurate. Parliamentary privilege permitted the House to expel its members 'for such reasons as it deemed fit.' It had done so only twice, when Louis Riel was thrown out in the 1870s and when Thomas McGreevy was expelled for contempt for refusing to answer parliamentary committee questions about profits he had extracted from unlawful contracts in 1891.[17] However, the matter was not wholly discretionary. The Criminal Code stipulated that anyone holding public office, convicted of an indictable offence, and sentenced to more than five years, must be removed from a position of public trust. The indictable charges facing Auger were rape and seduction. The first carried a maximum penalty of death or life imprisonment; the second, a maximum of two years.[18] Cognizant that an accused was innocent until proven guilty, Auger's parliamentary colleagues decided to wait and see.

The Prosecutions and the Protagonists

The prosecution of Auger was remarkable for the single-minded perseverance with which the Crown pursued the charges. When the extraordinary saga concluded in June 1930, some sixteen months after charges were laid, the matter had consumed five separate trials and two appeals. Auger was victorious in more than half. The first trial, on the charge of rape, resulted in a conviction and a sentence of nine years. The conviction was reversed by the Ontario Court of Appeal, which sent the case back for a new trial. Crown attorneys often chose not to prosecute the original charge again in such circumstances, provoking Ottawa's Le Droit to comment that the decision to retry Auger for rape was 'quite rare.' The second trial foundered with a 'hung jury,' when the jurors were unable to reach a unanimous verdict, with seven opting for conviction and five for acquittal. Undaunted, the prosecution retried Auger for rape a third time. This time the jury unanimously voted for acquittal. Most cases would have sputtered out there, and Montreal's La Presse predicted that the Crown would likely retire the outstanding seduction charge, terminating 'toute l'affaire.'[19]

But Auger was brought back to face trial for seduction, convicted, and sentenced to two years. The politician's next appeal to the Ontario Court of Appeal failed. And still the authorities did not desist. Auger faced a fifth and final trial, on charges of perjury stemming from his earlier testimony denying that security guards had caught him with a naked woman in his parliamentary office. By this time, Auger's finances were severely depleted. He could no longer afford the illustrious defence counsel he had retained earlier: Gordon Smith Henderson, Raoul Mercier, Arthur Graeme Slaght KC, Moses Doctor, and Roydon A. Hughes. Although reduced to acting as his own counsel, Auger's litigation skill caused observers to marvel. He secured an acquittal on the perjury charge. Many seemed astonished at the relentlessness of the prosecution. Judge Colin O'Brian, presiding over the final perjury trial, exclaimed: 'Mr. Auger's trials have cost the county a lot of money. They have not done the public any good, and the sooner they are over, the better.'[20]

Reporters probed the demeanour of the central protagonists, detecting shifts as the case wore on. 'On the verge of collapse' during the first trial, Martel 'broke down and began to weep' when cross-examined 'severely regarding the details of the Saturday attack.' Her 'tones became lower and lower' as she spoke. She fled Ottawa for her parents' home near Hawkesbury, where the *Citizen* recounted that she was exhausted from the 'severe strain' of the trial. She appeared 'very pale' with 'eyes downcast' in the second trial. During the third, she 'walked very slowly into the court' looking 'weak.' She kept her 'eyes averted from the prisoner in the dock.' By the fourth trial, Martel seems to have gained greater composure, buoyed up perhaps by the tenacity with which the authorities were pursuing Auger. The *Citizen* noted that the young woman testified 'clearly and without hesitation,' adding: 'Her experience in the box during the previous hearings has evidently had its effect, and her voice was much stronger, while her manner was more confident.' When Auger insisted on cross-examining Martel himself, despite the disapproval of his counsel, the young woman 'squared visibly and faced him with flashing eyes.' She 'stood erect' and 'replied with vigour' and 'a determined air.' Reporters described her as 'smartly attired in a long black coat with fur cuffs and a pullover hat to match.' Her frock was 'light-coloured,' set off by 'silk stockings with dark shoes.' In later proceedings, she wore a 'blue dress, light grey fur coat, hat and overshoes.'[21]

In contrast, Auger seems to have become more haggard and tentative over time. His first day in court, he arrived 'smartly dressed and clean shaven,' and seated himself at the counsel table with the other lawyers. Reporters made much of his optimism, noting that he 'smiled at friends in court,' 'appeared quite cheerful and confident,' and 'tilted back in his chair with both hands in his pockets' while he 'chewed gum.' The stylish young man was turned out in a 'navy blue suit with white soft collar and dark necktie' and 'carried a grey fedora hat.' He followed the proceedings 'with keen attention,' and 'repeatedly passed messages to his counsel.' Reporters added that he was still 'in good physical condition' by the second trial. He had been refused bail, and the press marvelled that jail had taken so little toll. 'Close confinement for the last seven months' had not 'affected' him, claimed the *Ottawa Journal*, emphasizing that the politician had not 'lost any weight.' By the third trial, Auger had become 'a bit paler than usual,' and 'looked thinner' and more 'anxious.' The *Citizen* reported that he seemed 'nervous,' and 'frequently twisted in his seat.'

After his acquittal in the third trial, the *Journal* described Auger cheerfully 'walking the streets for the first time since his arrest nearly a year ago' accompanied by counsel and bondsmen, and 'smoking a pipe.' Reporters followed him by train to L'Orignal, where he travelled by sleigh across 'snow-covered country' to greet his aged parents, three brothers, and one sister at their farm house in Prescott County. He boasted to reporters that he was writing a book about his arrest, trials, and time in prison. Asked for the likely title of the publication, he r-torted sarcastically: 'My Trip to California.' By the fourth trial, the *Citizen* noted that Auger was 'wan and worried in appearance,' and that he 'wilted perceptibly under the judge's remarks.' When sentence was pronounced, he 'wore a harassed expression,' and according to the *Journal*, departed 'dejectedly from the court.'[22]

Legal historians rarely have access to information about the psychological frame of mind of parties to litigation. In this unusual case, the newspapers offered a glimpse of the toll that criminal proceedings could take on the complainant and the accused both. Equally remarkable was the psychological connection between the two. Auger's initial bravado gave way at the same time that Martel's timidity diminished. As one grew in stature and self-confidence, the other faltered and was overwhelmed.

The Doctrine of Corroboration: An Aberrant Application

Louis Auger had good reason to be confident initially. Rape trials have historically garnered one of the lowest conviction rates of any criminal offence.[23] In part, this was attributable to the unusual evidentiary rules that applied. Under English common law, the evidence of female rape complainants was considered to be 'of little weight' and judges cautioned juries that it was dangerous to convict upon their 'uncorroborated' testimony.[24] Canadian courts insisted that it was a 'miscarriage of justice' to 'put the prosecutrix on the same footing as an ordinary witness.'[25] There was no empirical foundation for this concern, and it was a marked deviation from the general common law rule that the testimony of a single witness, if believed beyond a reasonable doubt, was sufficient to prove a criminal case. The decision to ask for corroboration was an example of masculinist paranoia, attached primarily to claims involving sexual violence, exploitation or immorality made by women and children.[26]

In this case, the prosecution could offer only two potential items of corroboration. Ottawa jail physician Dr J. Fenton Argue, who had conducted a medical examination of Martel ten days after the alleged rape, told the court that her hymen was inflamed and swollen, and that it had been 'lacerated by a blunt instrument – probably a man's penis' ten to fourteen days earlier. But even uncontested medical testimony was not always accepted as corroboration in law. A few judges found it corroborative, but most dismissed it as failing to identify which man had actually accomplished the intercourse.[27]

The second potential item was Martel's 'recent complaint' to her aunt. Mme St Pierre testified that her niece had returned home from the Parliament Buildings on 16 February and told her the details of the sexual assault, a narrative that matched perfectly with Martel's sworn testimony in court. The difficulty here is related to the restrictions on the admissibility of recent complaint evidence. If the complaint was not made at the 'first reasonable opportunity,' if it was not 'spontaneous and voluntary,' it could be excluded.[28] Auger's defence counsel objected that Martel could have alerted a police officer or a passer-by on her way home. He also insisted that the complaint had been elicited under questioning by Martel's anxious aunt. Equally problematic, most courts rejected recent complaint evidence as qualifying for full 'corroboration,' holding that it merely 'confirmed' the complainant's consistency.[29]

Vast numbers of sexual assault prosecutions went down to defeat for lack of corroboration. The Auger trials stand out as anomalous, for the majority of the judges who ruled on the case took a comparatively lax approach to corroboration, with several expressing criticism of the doctrine. The first such decision came at the initial rape trial, when Ontario Supreme Court Judge William Henry Wright cited both the medical evidence and Martel's complaint as facts to 'support' the theory of the Crown. He instructed the jurors to 'test and weigh her story and her conduct before and after and all round,' but he did not offer the standard cautionary formula that it was risky for juries to convict in the absence of corroborating material.[30]

When the defence appealed the guilty verdict, the issue divided the Ontario Court of Appeal. The three judges in majority quashed Auger's conviction, adopting a traditional analysis of corroboration. Judge William Edward Middleton, supported by Chief Justice Sir William Mulock and Judge David Inglis Grant, insisted that the failure of the trial judge to 'caution the jury as to the danger of convicting in the absence of any corroboration,' was a 'very serious matter' that had potentially 'caused a failure of justice.' The three judges dismissed the medical testimony and the recent complaint as insufficiently corroborative of Martel's lack of consent. Their decision to quash the conviction was fully in line with Canadian legal authority.[31]

In an unprecedented dissent, using language that had never been used in any previous Canadian sexual assault decision, Judge James Magee claimed that the doctrine of corroboration ought not to apply as a blanket prescription to all cases of sexual offences.[32] While there were circumstances where the warning might be appropriate, it struck him as unnecessary to require one in every situation:

I cannot agree that any such direction should be called for in the case of a woman who is attacked any more than in the case of a man who is robbed or wounded when alone ... Here there were no circumstances calling for the singling out of the young girl attacked as one whose evidence should be dealt with differently from that of any other witness testifying to an offence of personal violence and who was practically uncontradicted.

Judge Frank Egerton Hodgins, also in an unprecedented dissent, took issue with the requirement that a formal warning ought to be required in every rape trial. 'If this rule exists, which I doubt,' he wrote, 'its application in this case must be a common sense one.' He claimed that the 'so-called rule,' which was founded on the 'words of Sir Matthew Hale,' only required a warning where there was no evidence of corroboration on the record, something that he felt far from true in the present case.[33] Other situations that might warrant the caution arose when the accused had taken the stand to deny the charge, thus raising a 'real issue as to which story is to be accepted.' Here, Auger had 'trusted his reputation and fortune to the hazard of a rather relentless cross-examination instead of pledging his oath':

The essence of the case was her story; there was no other, and the warning to use due care in considering it ... was fully performed if the trial Judge dealt fairly with the suggestions against its entire acceptance and reminded the jury that the prisoner was entitled to the benefit of any reasonable doubt. If the Judge had a duty in addition to this, it would weigh down the scales unfairly against the woman in that the warning would apply only against her being believed in her accusation and would leave any inconsistency or slip in full force in favour of the man. The rule cannot be used so as to produce injustice.[34]

Auger's prosecution for seduction also showed the doctrine of corroboration applied very loosely. The corroboration rules for seduction were set out in the Criminal Code, rather than under the common law as for rape. The Code provided that no one could be convicted of seduction 'upon the evidence of one witness,' unless such a witness were 'corroborated in some material particular by evidence implicating the accused.'[35] Canadian courts interpreted this to require more particular corroboration than under common law, insisting that the corroboration not only 'implicate the accused,' but also that it be 'independent' of the complainant, something which stood apart from her testimony.[36]

Despite the rigorous statutory requirements, Carleton County Court judge Edward J. Daly held that corroboration existed in Auger's case. He noted that the 'demeanour of the girl,' was corroborative, although this was not independent of Martel's testimony, and other courts would reject such analysis.[37] Daly also accepted the recent complaint as additional indication of veracity: 'How the story first came out, the girl's account, the actions of her aunt ...' Judge Daly listed the medical evidence of Dr Argue and the blood stains discovered on the stairway. Finally, there was evidence that Louis Auger had filled out Martel's application form and then telephoned her repeatedly the next day. The majority of the appellate court had earlier rejected much of this as corroborative, yet Daly gave no reasons for his differing opinion.[38] To describe Daly's corroboration analysis as cursory would be generous.

When the seduction conviction was appealed, Ontario deputy attorney general Edward J. Bayly KC represented the Crown before a different set of five appellate judges.[39] He reviewed the testimony that Judge Daly had found corroborative, and then demanded: 'What more corroboration could be asked? Can anyone suggest microphones in the room? Are these things done publicly with a free hand?' This time, the full bench agreed. Chief Justice Francis Robert Latchford stated that corroboration was required in two areas: the commission of the crime and the prisoner's connection with that commission. Without further discussion, the court ruled unanimously that there was 'independent testimony indicating sexual connection by some person with Laurence Martel' and also that there was 'some independent testimony tending to connect the prisoner with the crime.'[40] The judges made no attempt to explain why their ruling was so different from the earlier appellate outcome.

Two trial judges, Wright and Daly, applied the corroboration rules to Auger's rape and seduction prosecutions in an almost desultory manner. Two dissenting judges at the court of appeal, Magee and Hodgins, offered the first gender-based judicial critique of corroboration expressed in a Canadian courtroom. Five appellate judges in Auger's seduction prosecution accepted as corroborative evidence that would have been flatly rejected by other Canadian courts. While some trial and appellate judges followed the traditional analysis in this case, the majority of the judges who presided over the Auger proceedings issued rulings that were observably different from earlier Canadian corroboration judgments. Nor was their reasoning a sign that wider legal reform was on the way in the near future. Similar rulings were not issued prior to 1975, when sexual assault law began to undergo major legislative reform.[41]

That such unusual decisions were delivered in the context of the notorious Auger proceeding is cause for reflection. Did the status of the accused man figure in these opinions? Was it easier for Judges Magee and Hodgins to give voice to these unprecedented opinions in the case of a man who had shocked their sensibilities through an arrogant abuse of the public trust? Was the atypical nature of the case one of the reasons why no other judges afterwards picked up on their reasoning to explore its potential applicability on a wider basis?

The Question of Linguistic, Ethno-Cultural, and Religious Discrimination

Prescott County, home to both Martel and Auger, represented a geographic point of junction between English and French Canada that has been described as 'la boucle de la ceinture bilingue' and the birthplace of 'l'identité franco-ontarienne.' Waves of French-speaking immigrants crossed the border into eastern Ontario in the 1880s, as part of an 'immense diaspora' that saw nearly one million French Canadians leave Quebec for English Canada and the United States. Their arrival in Prescott radically transformed an Anglophone farming and forestry frontier into permanent rural settlements dominated by francophones. The influx inspired panic among the political and intellectual elites of Ontario and provoked the enactment of Regulation 17, which imposed English language instruction on all Ontario elementary schools between 1912 and 1927. Francophone resistance interfered with enforcement and intensified the battle lines. With the repeal of Regulation 17, the open confrontation diminished, but hostilities simmered below the surface.[42]

Both Laurence Martel and Louis Auger were attempting to make their way in the English-speaking labour market, Martel at an anglophone business college, and Auger at Osgoode Hall. Nevertheless, they seem to have been uncomfortable over the predominantly unilingual trial. Although the complainant, the accused, and the majority of witnesses were francophones, the lawyers and judges spoke nothing but English, and Judge Wright commanded a hesitant Laurence Martel to 'speak English as far as possible.' There were no francophone judges in the provincial superior court system, and not one of the judges who presided over Auger's multiple trials spoke French. The first Franco-Ontarian judge, appointed in 1936, inspired the *Fortnightly Law Journal* to note that the profession was 'not enamoured' of such encroachments 'in a traditional Anglo-Saxon province.'[43] There were no Franco-Ontarian Crown attorneys until 1935. The first appointment of a francophone assistant Crown attorney in Ottawa was vigorously opposed by a group of anglophone lawyers from Carleton County, who objected to the candidate's linguistic and religious background.[44]

The Crown attorney who prosecuted Auger's rape trials was Colonel John Andrew Hope KC, an anglophone native of Perth, Ontario, a birthplace of the Orange Lodges. A man not noted for his sensitivities towards Roman Catholics or Franco-Ontarians, Hope would later chair a controversial Royal Commission on Education that recommended the abolition of Ontario separate schools for children older than twelve.[45] It was Hope who chose to commence the second rape trial after the first conviction was quashed, and even more surprisingly, a third after the hung jury failed to deliver a verdict.

The changing linguistic composition of the Auger juries was also worthy of note. The Criminal Code made some provision for francophone jurors in Quebec and Manitoba, but not in Ontario.[46] *Le Droit* reported that the overwhelmingly anglophone jury pool in Auger's first trial was composed of three 'canadiens-français' and fifty-seven 'de langue anglaise.'[47] In that proceeding, Hope used his prosecutorial discretion to excuse all the French Canadians from the final roster. Hope's first all-anglophone jury was the only jury that voted to convict Auger. A number of Auger's supporters registered complaints with the Crown about the absence of French Canadians, and by the second rape trial, the publicly embarrassed Hope allowed three French Canadians to be sworn. However, the trial continued primarily in English, and when translators were permitted for French-speaking witnesses, the assistance was offered grudgingly.[48] By the third rape trial, Hope did not challenge any of the potential jurors, and four francophones were selected. Reflecting on the shifting jury composition, *La Presse* noted that the convicting jury was 'exclusivement de langue anglaise.' The hung jury was 'mixte.' The third jury, which would vote to acquit, was composed of 'un tiers de Canadiens français.'[49] Montreal's *Le Petit Journal* also noted Auger's preference for a judge and jury from Prescott County: 'Si j'étais dans mon comté, parmi les miens, les choses se passeraient autrement.'[50] All three factors, ethnicity, language, and religion, appear to have operated to Auger's detriment.

'Such a Crime Within the Precincts of the House': A Politician's Reckoning

Upon his first conviction, Auger pre-empted his expulsion from the House of Commons by filing his formal resignation with the Speaker. *Le Droit* reported that the prime minister read the letter, that the news was 'reçue par la Chambre au milieu d'un profond silence,' and that the unprecedented event terminated the day's proceedings. The *Ottawa Citizen* canvassed other sitting members, and reported that there was 'no sympathy for the young member' given his conviction for a 'particularly grave crime,' but that many expressed regret 'that a public career of potential promise now comes to such a tragic termination.'[51]

Auger linked much of his trouble to his political career. He complained that the contents of the parliamentary security officers' reports about the overnight escapades in his office had been delivered 'at once to his political enemies in Hawkesbury' and then leaked to the press. The security officers denied this.[52] He intimated that 'political enemies' in Hawkesbury and Ottawa were 'responsible for his plight.' Auger never divulged names, and it is impossible to know whether he meant adversaries within the Conservative opposition or disgruntled colleagues within his own party. Midway through the proceedings, Auger again complained that he was a 'victim of his political foes' but this time that Martel's aunt, Bertha St Pierre, was the 'arch fiend' and 'master mind of the whole affair.'[53] It was a common defence strategy to allege that sexual assault complainants or their family members were out to blackmail the accused. Evidence to support such assertions was rarely produced, and true to form, no details were ever disclosed about Mme St Pierre's alleged connection to Auger's 'political foes.' Even if she had such connections, it seems odd that she would have conspired to bring down false charges that would impact so terribly upon her young niece.

Given Auger's compromised sexual reputation, there must have been other means to discredit the politician that would surely have brought less disgrace upon her own family. Indeed, Auger might have made more of the fact that Hope, the prosecutor who so tenaciously pursued the case, was an active Conservative.[54]

Although it is difficult to draw firm conclusions about whether improper political influences affected Auger's prosecutions, there is no doubt that his political position was a liability at sentencing. At first, Auger's counsel tried to use his client's political career in mitigation. Speaking to sentence at the first rape trial, Raoul Mercier described Auger as 'a young man who had spent the greater part of his life behind scholastic walls, and who was suddenly thrust into the limelight which was inevitable from his quick rise politically.' Upon his election, Auger had 'received world-wide congratulations and scores of letters from female admirers' culminating in 'many new temptations.' Mercier reminded the court that Auger had already paid dearly for his error. He had 'voluntarily' resigned his seat in parliament, and his 'ambitions and his future' were 'clouded.' Mercier advised that Auger had 'worked hard' to purchase a $12,000 farm for elderly failing parents, and that they would lose the property without their son's continuing assistance. Auger also rose to speak to sentence. The first words out of his mouth were: 'I wish to say to my friends that the verdict against me condemns an innocent man. Before God, I am innocent and by mere perjury I am convicted. The girl perjured herself ...'

Judge Wright interrupted to lecture that it was 'very bad grace' for Auger to be casting aspersions upon the complainant at this point:

The crime for which you have been convicted is one of the most serious known to law. It is a most unusual spectacle to find a member of the Commons committing such a crime within the precincts of the House. It is unparalleled. Some features of your crime aggravate it very much. You are a man of education and prominence. The crime was committed against a young innocent girl of seventeen years of age, the daughter of one of your constituents. It is inconceivable how you could commit such an offence ... The womanhood of this country must not be subjected to assault by those in position to compel them to submit. I sentence you to nine years in prison.[55]

The prisoner's former glory as the youngest Member of Parliament did little to shield him from the full force of the law; if anything, it had provoked the court to pronounce harsher terms. Auger was led out of the courtroom 'weeping,' holding his handkerchief to his eyes, supported by the wardens of the court.

The nine-year term was overturned when the conviction was quashed, but Auger came up for sentencing again upon his conviction for seduction. Judge Daly asked Auger if he had anything to say for himself before judgment was passed. Having learned nothing about the utility of a public demonstration of remorse, Auger stood up once more and declared: 'I am innocent, My Lord.' 'Too late to say that now,' retorted the judge, continuing:

Auger, I understand you are a university graduate and when twenty-four years of age you were elected a member of parliament for Prescott county. You knew the father of this girl and promised to get her a position. She came to you to fill out her application form, feeling that your name would aid her in getting an appointment. You knew she was under eighteen. You ravished her; took advantage of the daughter of one of the men who put you in parliament. You are not entitled to consideration ... Considering the attitude you have taken, I have no sympathy for you. The sentence of the court is that you go to prison for two years.[56]

This was an extraordinary sentence, the maximum permissible. The reporter for the *Citizen* asked the judge whether this meant that Auger would have to serve his time in Kingston Penitentiary. 'Yes,' replied Judge Daly, the sentence 'was for two years, not for two years less one day.' Clearly aghast, the reporter stressed for his readers that Judge Daly had decided not to 'allow any time off for the accused's incarceration in jail while awaiting trial.' Given Auger's imprisonment for almost a year between his arrest and his final conviction, this was no small oversight.

The Aftermath

The termination of the prosecutions probably brought little comfort to Laurence Martel. Crown attorney Hope told the jurors that the 'girl's whole life' had been 'injured,' and her 'prospects for marriage blasted.'[57] Martel's testimony regarding her sexual victimization had been blazoned across the press for more than a year. Even though the court rejected the unsavoury allegations that Auger's lawyers had made about Martel's prior sexual history, the aspersions had been paraded before the public in prurient detail. The stress caused Martel to drop out of Henry's Shorthand School two weeks before graduation. Her chances of securing that coveted secretarial appointment to the federal civil service must surely have been dashed. Whether she managed to reconstruct her life, obtain employment, and reconfigure her social position are all a subject of mystery.

As for Auger, his conviction for seduction was duly brought to the attention of the Law Society of Upper Canada. On 18 September 1930, the benchers ruled that his behaviour amounted to 'conduct unbecoming a barrister and solicitor,' and struck his name from the rolls. His promising legal career was ended before it began.[58] If he carried through on his boastful plan to write a book about his experience, no record of any publication survives. After his release from the penitentiary, Auger tried unsuccessfully to run for the Prescott provincial seat in 1934 and for the federal seat in 1935.[59] He served a one-year term as mayor of Hawkesbury in 1936.[60] He moved to Montreal the next year, and tried unsuccessfully to contest the federal seat for the Saint-Henri riding in 1939.[61] During the 1930s and 1940s, he seems to have worked as a teacher, a bookseller, a munitions inspector, and a newspaper editor.[62] He married Bernadette Goyer, a woman ten years older than himself in 1934, but his extramarital sexual liaisons seem to have continued undaunted, and he fathered at least two children out of wedlock during his first marriage.[63] After Bernadette's death in 1946, Auger moved to Chambly where he married Marie-Berthe Villemaire in 1947, and fathered another four children.[64] Never one to let political ambitions lie, Auger successfully ran for mayor of the parish of Saint-Joseph-de-Chambly from 1955 to 1959, and also served as the president of the local branch of the Société Saint-Jean-Baptiste, an organisation that promoted the French language and French-Canadian culture.[65] Louis Auger died in Chambly on 6 March 1966 at the age of 63.[66]

Conclusion

The multiple prosecutions of Louis Auger represent one of the most publicised, most controversial sexual assault trials in Canadian history. Unlike many early twentieth-century rapists, who carried out their crimes unscathed, Auger was charged. He was prosecuted not once but five times. The traditional rules regarding the doctrine of corroboration were bent by a series of judges who glossed over deficiencies that would have produced acquittals for other men. Louis Auger, a professional man of high political stature, was convicted and sentenced to the highest punishment permitted. This was astonishing within a criminal justice system that more often than not rejected the testimony of women who complained of sexual assault. It was as if the customary gender assumptions had been turned on their head.

Auger's political status and his Franco-Ontarian identity may help to explain this. The dramatic eclipse of the 'Baby of Parliament' reflected deep anxiety over the deportment of Canadian politicians. The retributive sentiments that laced the majority of the judicial opinions reflect the desire for public denunciation of a political figure who had been caught in the act of abusing his office. Louis Auger was undoubtedly not the only male of prominence who was engaged in multiple sexual partnering, some consensual and some coercive, during the Roaring Twenties. But he had demonstrated a brash arrogance that made it difficult to ignore his notorious escapades. Lines had to be drawn to preserve decorum and restore some dignity. That the rogue was an upstart, young Franco-Ontarian made it easier to single him out. Certainly, history would bear out that Franco-Ontarian lawyers who aspired to elite positions could attract more than their share of critique.[67] The authorities went after Louis Auger with zeal until they pinned him down, catapulted him from office, and locked him up in Kingston Penitentiary. That Auger's accuser was a working-class, seventeen-year-old Franco-Ontarian, the daughter of an illiterate labourer, receded from view. When the gender, class, and ethnic bias that framed the law of sexual assault in early twentieth-century Canada confronted the prospect of a young politician apparently guilty of raping an underage constituent, all but his public office and Franco-Ontarian heritage melted away.

The cause of women's rights inched forward in tandem with the Auger case. On 18 October 1929, the Privy Council issued its decision in the 'Person's Case.' Women were found to be 'persons' eligible for appointment to the Canadian Senate. The press reported the jubilation of the Canadian feminist movement over its victory on the same page that it headlined the news of Auger's hung jury in his second rape trial.[68] The ironic juxtaposition serves to remind us that one of the critical elements in the Auger case was indeed the question of gender. Laurence Martel was ultimately vindicated. Her word was believed. She was actually deemed credible by a Canadian court, in an era when achieving credibility was an extraordinary event for a francophone, working-class, sexual assault victim. The tragedy is that it took the collective venom of the legal elite, anxious to censure an unruly young MP, and the pervasive discrimination against Franco-Ontarians, to achieve the conviction.

NOTES

* I am delighted to participate in a volume designed to celebrate the contribution that Peter Oliver has made to the development of legal history scholarship in Canada. As one amongst an entire generation of legal historians, I remain greatly indebted to Peter's leadership and for his superb editorial guidance. I have chosen the story of Louis Auger as my contribution to the volume, out of respect for Peter's important research into the lives of Ontario politicians, and his remarkable expertise in the field of penological history.

I would like to thank the following individuals for their assistance: Monda Halpern, Pascal-Hugo Plourde, Marie-José Blais, Ian McDonald, Michelle McLean, Chad Gaffield, Ruby Heap, Judith Emery, Susan Lewthwaite, Sanda Rodgers, Diana Majury, Michel Morin, Robert Choquette, Pierre Mercier, Father Roland Leclaire, Sonia Blouin, Danielle Pilon, Michel Lalonde, Barry Stead, Martin Perron, Sophie Grenier, Pierre Louis Lapointe, Veronique Larose, Mireille Rolland, and the Centre de Recherche en Civilisation Canadienne-Française at the University of Ottawa. My research assistants, Megan Reid and Sabina Mok, have provided invaluable information. Financial assistance from the Social Sciences and Humanities Research Council of Canada, the Bora Laskin Human Rights Fellowship, the Jules and Gabrielle Léger Fellowship, the Trudeau Fellowship, and the Law Foundation of Ontario is gratefully acknowledged.

1 The facts recounted in this essay are drawn from the reported court decisions in *Rex v. Auger*, *Canadian Criminal Cases* [hereafter *C.C.C.*] 52 (1929) 2 and *Rex v. Auger*, *C.C.C.* 54 (1930) 209, as supplemented by *Rex v. Auger*, Archives of Ontario, Record Group [hereafter RG] 22–392–0–998, box 26 and the press coverage in the *Ottawa Citizen*, *Ottawa Journal*, *Montreal Standard*, *Quebec City Chronicle-Telegraph*, *Toronto Telegram*, *Ottawa Le Droit*, *Montreal La Presse*, *Montreal Le Devoir*, *Montreal Le Petit Journal*, *Montreal La Patarie*, *Montreal Le Nationaliste*, and *Le Devoir*. For a more detailed account of the trials published in French, see Constance Backhouse, 'Attentat à la dignité du Parlement: Viol dans l'enceinte de la Chambre des communes, Ottawa 1929,' *Ottawa Law Review* 33 (2001–2), 95–145. Marguerite Anderson, *Doucement le bonheur* (Sudbury: Prise de parole 2006), short-listed for

the Trillium Book Award in Ontario, offers a fictionalized account of these trials based upon the research in the French essay, and an imaginative prediction of the future lives of the central protagonists. I want to thank Tinnish Andersen, Marguerite's daughter, who while a law student at the University of Ottawa put her mother in touch with me regarding the possible fictionalization of the research. Subsequent to the publication of Andersen's novel, a descendant of Auger contacted both of us from France to provide additional information regarding Auger's later life. This allowed me to pursue further research into Auger's later personal, political, and employment history. A brief summary of this appears at the end of this essay.

2 The distribution on 24 December 1928 was Liberal 117; Conservative 89; Progressive 12; United Farmers of Alberta 11; Liberal-Progressive 9; Labour 3; Independent 2. *Canadian Parliamentary Guide, 1929* (Toronto: A.L. Norman 1929).

3 *Ottawa Evening Citizen*, 14–15 February 1929.

4 Graham S. Lowe, *Women in the Administrative Revolution* (Toronto: University of Toronto Press 1987); Kathleen Archibald, *Sex in the Public Service* (Ottawa: Public Service Commission 1970); Nicole Morgan, *The Equality Game: Women in the Federal Public Service (1908–1987)* (Ottawa: Canadian Advisory Council on the Status of Women 1988), 1–11; Janet Smith, 'Equal Opportunity in the Public Service,' *Labour* 20 (1975), 13–15. In 1947, the proportion of francophones in the federal public service totalled 12.25 per cent: *Les Obstacles à L'Égalité Des Femmes Dans La Fonction Publique Fédérale* (Ottawa: Canadian Advisory Council on the Status of Women 1979), 60. At the outset of the Trudeau era, only one of more than three dozen top-level bureaucrats was francophone, and only 6 of the 163 civil servants who received $14,000 a year or more were from Quebec. See Peter C. Newman, 'A Shining Political Season,' *National Post* (Toronto), 29 September 2000.

5 Martel's parents were Jean Baptiste Martel and Espérance Carriere. The father's occupation was listed on Laurence's birth certificate. Most labourers in Alfred Township were tenants who worked as agricultural employees. The declining rural economy in the late nineteenth century intensified the francophone proletarianization when many anglophones left to seek prospects elsewhere. Chad Gaffield, *Aux Origines de L'identité Franco-Ontarienne: Education, culture, économie* (Ottawa: University of Ottawa Press 1993), 119, 154; Chad Gaffield, 'Schooling, the Economy, and Rural Society in Nineteenth-Century Ontario,' in Joy Parr, ed., *Childhood and Family in Canadian History* (Toronto: McClelland and Stewart 1982). Although Lau-

rence Martel referred to Bertha St Pierre as her 'aunt,' she was actually a distant cousin.

6 For a more detailed description, see Constance Backhouse, *Carnal Crimes: Sexual Assault Law in Canada, 1900–1975* (Toronto: Irwin Law 2008, forthcoming).

7 *Ottawa Journal*, 15 September 1926.

8 *Ottawa Evening Citizen*, 21 March 1929; *Ottawa Evening Journal*, 26 February 1929, 21 March 1929; *Canadian Directory of Parliament 1867–1967* (Ottawa: Public Archives of Canada 1968), 15; *Canadian Parliamentary Guide* (1928); Paul-François Sylvestre, *Nos Parlementaires* (Ottawa: Les Éditions L'Interligne 1986), 79; Law Society of Upper Canada Archives, Osgoode Hall, Toronto. Auger's parents were Louis Auger and Alphonsine Cusson. He attended Hawkesbury Separate School, and obtained his Bachelor of Philosophy in 1923, and Bachelor of Arts *avec grande distinction* in 1924. He was awarded a gold medal in 1920 by the Association Saint-Jean-Baptiste du Canada, a bronze medal in 1922 by La Société Saint-Jean-Baptiste de Montréal, and a gold medal in 1923 by the Association Canadienne-Française d'Éducation d'Ontario. He became the assistant prefect of discipline at the University of Ottawa in 1924, a professor in 1925, and taught for two years before leaving his academic position: *Calendar of the University of Ottawa*, academic years 1918–27. Gaffield, *Aux Origines de L'identité Franco-Ontarienne*, 169, notes the frequency with which multiple Liberal candidates contested provincial elections in Prescott. In the 1926 election, three Liberal candidates competed against one Conservative, with Auger heading the poll with 3,846 votes, over Evanturel (Liberal: 3,134), Kirby (Conservative: 2,504), and Labrosse (Independent: 635). *Canadian Parliamentary Guide, 1929* (Toronto: A.L. Norman 1929), 293, 269. Auger was articling with Edmond Proulx, a former Prescott County Liberal MP and provincial member of the legislative assembly. Auger's legal ambitions resulted in many absences from the House, and observers criticised him as 'detached and aloof,' 'inconspicuous' and 'not much of a mixer.' The *Ottawa Journal*, 5 May 1928, took a jibe at the 'Baby Member': 'Louis Auger, Liberal member for Prescott, and the "baby" of Parliament, evidently believes that youth should be seen and not heard. He hasn't made a speech this session. Mr. Auger is 26 years old and a bachelor.'

9 These and Auger's following quotations are taken from press interviews and coverage of his courtroom testimony: *Ottawa Citizen*, 26 February 1929, 18 October 1929, 27 January 1930, 29 January 1930, 14 June 1930; *Ottawa Journal*, 26 February 1929, 21 March 1929, 17–18 October 1929, 29 January 1930; *Montreal Le Devoir*, 26 February 1929; *Montreal La Presse*, 26 February 1929.

10 *Ottawa Journal*, 28 April 1927; *Ottawa Journal*, 11 May 1927.

11 *Ottawa Citizen*, 26 February 1929; *Ottawa Journal*, 21 March 1929.

12 Testimony given during the perjury trial, as covered in the *Ottawa Citizen*, 2 June 1930, 4–5 June 1930; *Ottawa Journal*, 4–5 June 1930; *Ottawa Le Droit*, 4–5 June 1930.

13 Matthew Hale, *Historia Placitorum Coronae*, vol. 1 (London: Nutt and Gosling 1734), 635–36, posthumously published.

14 Backhouse, *Carnal Crimes*.

15 The rules of Parliament provided that a member was immune from civil suit or action while inside Parliament: *Ottawa Citizen*, 26 February 1929; *Ottawa Evening Journal*, 26 February 1929.

16 *Ottawa Citizen*, 26 February 1929; *Ottawa Evening Journal*, 26 February 1929.

17 *Ottawa Citizen*, 26 February 1929; *Ottawa Evening Journal*, 26–27 February 1929, 6 March 1929, 21 March 1929. James R. Robertson, *Criminal Charges and Parliamentarians* (Ottawa: Library of Parliament, Research Branch 1994).

18 Criminal Code, *Revised Statutes of Canada* [hereafter *R.S.C.*] 1927, c.36, s.1034, later amended by *An Act to amend the Criminal Code (Sentencing) and other Acts in consequence thereof, Statutes of Canada* [hereafter *S.C.*] 1995, c.22, s.750(1) to oust office holders who were sentenced to imprisonment for two years or more. On the penalties for rape and seduction, see Criminal Code, *R.S.C.* 1927, c.36, s.211, 299.

19 *Ottawa Le Droit*, 7 May 1929; *Montreal La Presse*, 31 January 1930.

20 *Ottawa Citizen*, 17 January 1930, 5 June 1930.

21 *Ottawa Citizen*, 18 March 1929, 20 March 1929, 16–17 October 1929, 27 January 1930, 31 January 1930, 10 March 1930; *Ottawa Journal*, 20 March 1929, 16–17 October 1929, 28 January 1930, 31 January 1930, 7 February 1930.

22 *Ottawa Citizen*, 26 February 1929, 16 October 1929, 27 January 1930, 30–31 January 1930, 12–13 March 1930, 5 June 1930; *Ottawa Journal*, 26 February 1929, 16–17 October 1929, 27–28 January 1930, 30–31 January 1930, 7 February 1930, 12 March 1930.

23 Nation-wide data compiled in 1930 showed rape convictions at 34 per cent, compared with burglary at 91 per cent, theft at 85 per cent, robbery at 75 per cent, and assault at 75 per cent. Convictions on charges of murder (including offenders detained for insanity) registered at 44 per cent. *Annual Report of Statistics of Criminal and Other Offences* (Ottawa: Canada, Dominion Bureau of Statistics 1930). For additional data, see Backhouse, *Carnal Crimes*.

24 *Halsbury's Laws of England*, vol. 9 (London: Butterworths 1909), 388; Edward Hyde East, *Pleas of the Crown*, vol. 1 (1803; reprint, Abington, Oxon: Professional Books 1987), 445.

25 *Rex v. Mudge*, C.C.C. 52 (1929) 402.

26 The requirement for 'corroboration' was attached to criminal proceedings
for sexual offences and civil proceedings for affiliation, breach of promise
to marry, and divorce. The unsworn testimony of children 'of tender years'
also attracted the need for corroboration, as did the evidence of accom-
plices, claims against estates of deceased persons, and criminal prosecutions for perjury, treason, blasphemy, forgery, and personation. *The
Dictionary of English Law*, vol.1 (London and Sydney: Sweet and Maxwell
and the Law Book Co. of Australia 1959), 504; Audrey A. Wakeling, *Corroboration in Canadian Law* (Toronto: Carswell 1977), 1–3. For discussion on
the absence of justification with respect to sexual offences and children's
testimony, see Backhouse, *Carnal Crimes*.

27 *Rex v. Hyder*, C.C.C. 29 (1917) 172 accepted medical evidence of a ruptured
hymen as corroboration on a charge of carnal knowledge. *Rex v. Arnold*,
C.C.C. 87 (1947) 236 accepted medical evidence as corroborative of rape. In
contrast, *Rex v. Silverstone*, C.C.C. 61 (1934) 258 dismissed medical evidence
as insufficient on a charge of indecent assault on a male child because it
showed only that a crime had been committed, not that it had been committed by the accused. *Rex v. O'Hara*, C.C.C. 88 (1946) 74 dismissed medical
evidence in a trial for carnal knowledge of a girl between fourteen and sixteen years, because although it affirmed the credibility of the complainant,
it did not implicate the accused. The second approach would eventually
become the accepted rule.

28 On the importance of promptness, see *The Queen v. Riendeau, Les Rapports
Judiciaires de Québec: Cour du Banc de la Reine* [hereafter *B.R.*] 9 (1900) 147;
The King v. Akerley, New Brunswick Reports 46 (1918) 195; *The King v. Trenholme*, B.R. 30 (1920) 232; *Rex v. Proteau, British Columbia Reports* [hereafter
B.C.R.] 33 (1923) 39; *The King v. George Hubley, Nova Scotia Reports* 58 (1925)
113; *Rex v. Hall*, C.C.C. 49 (1927) 146; *Rex v. Elliott*, C.C.C. 49 (1928) 302. On
voluntary and spontaneous disclosure, see *The King v. Bishop*, C.C.C. 11
(1906) 30; *Rex v. Dunning, Saskatchewan Law Reports* 1 (1908) 391; *Rex v.
Stonehouse and Pasquale*, B.C.R. 39 (1927) 279.

29 The admission of such evidence was described as an exception to the hear-
say rule, a survival of a rule from more than a century earlier that admitted
evidence of previous statements of a witness not under oath similar to his
or her testimony in court, for the purpose of confirming that testimony:
Hopkinson v. Perdue, C.C.C. 8 (1904) 286. For cases refusing to take recent
complaint as corroboration, see *The King v. De Wolfe*, C.C.C. 9 (1904) 38; *Rex
v. McMillan, Western Weekly Reports* [hereafter *W.W.R.*] 9 (1916) 1181; *Rex v.*

Everitt, C.C.C. 45 (1925) 133; *Hubin v. The King*, C.C.C. 48 (1927) 172; *Rex v. Mudge*, C.C.C. 52 (1929) 402; *Rex v. Stinson*, C.C.C. 61 (1934) 227; *Rex v. Tol-hurst*, C.C.C. 73 (1939) 332.

30 As discussed in *Rex v. Auger*, C.C.C. 52 (1929) 2.

31 *Rex v. Auger*, C.C.C. 52 (1929) 2. See Seymour F. Harris, *Principles and Practice of the Criminal Law*, 14th ed. (Toronto: Carswell 1926), 156–7; Sidney L. Phipson, *The Law of Evidence*, 6th ed. (Toronto: Carswell 1921), 487.

32 I have found no similar critique of the doctrine of corroboration in my review of all reported judicial decisions for rape, carnal knowledge of girls under the age of consent, indecent assault on females, seduction, incest, corrupting children, indecent acts, gross indecency, buggery, unlawfully defiling women, abduction of women, procuring, communicating venereal disease, and carnal knowledge of women with disabilities in Canada prior to 1929. For further description of the sample and findings, see Backhouse, *Carnal Crimes*.

33 For a case explicitly rejecting this proposition, see *Rex v. Reeves*, C.C.C. 77 (1941) 89, quashing a conviction because the trial judge had failed to warn of the danger of convicting upon uncorroborated testimony in a case in which corroborative evidence had already been adduced. The court specified that the rule applied whether or not there was corroborative evidence on the record.

34 *Rex v. Auger*, C.C.C. 52 (1929), 4–9.

35 Criminal Code, R.S.C. 1927, c.36, s.1002. It was not until 1954 that corroboration became a mandatory statutory requirement for rape: Criminal Code, S.C. 1953–54, c.51, s.134.

36 The 'independent' requirement appeared first in Canada in *Hubin v. The King*, C.C.C. 48 (1927) 172, citing an English decision, *Rex v. Baskerville*, *Law Reports, King's Bench* 2 (1916) 658, as the source of the analysis. Eventually, these rules were fused, and the legislative corroboration requirements were pronounced applicable to common law as well. The fusion is often traced to the earlier *Baskerville* decision, which stated that 'the test applicable to determine the nature and extent of the corroboration is thus the same whether the case falls within the rule of practice at common law or within that class of offences for which corroboration is required by statute.' The first application of the 'independent' principle to a prosecution of rape in Canada was *Rex v. Stern*, W.W.R. 3 (1932) 688, where the complainant's identification of the accused's car and a blanket inside were found insufficiently 'independent' to constitute corroboration. *Thomas v. The Queen*, C.C.C. 103 (1952) 193 reversing *Rex v. Thomas*, C.C.C. 100 (1951) 112, was the

first Canadian sexual assault decision to stipulate that there was no distinction between cases where corroboration was a statutory requirement and those that fell into the 'rule of practice' at common law.

37 *Rex v. Stern*, W.W.R. 3 (1932) 688 held that 'the way in which the complainant told her story in the witness box' was a 'matter of demeanour' and 'while an intrinsic test of her credibility,' it was not 'corroboration properly so called, which it has been held must be independent testimony which affects the accused by connecting or tending to connect him with the crime.'

38 *Ottawa Citizen*, 10 April 1930.

39 Francis Robert Latchford, Cornelius Arthur Masten, John Fosberg Orde, Robert Grant Fisher, and William Henry Wright. The latter had been elevated since presiding over Auger's first rape trial; the accused and his counsel did not object to his hearing the case.

40 *Rex v. Auger*, C.C.C. 54 (1930) 209; *Ottawa Citizen*, 10 April 1930.

41 The judges who used a more conventional approach were the three who signed the majority appellate decision in the first rape appeal, and trial judges Hugh Thomas Kelly and William Edward Raney, who presided over the second and third rape trials. Judges Magee's and Hodgins's unprecedented judicial critique was not duplicated in any reported decision in Canada up to 1975. For a discussion of the sample of cases reviewed, including selected archival decisions from the Northwest Territories, British Columbia, Alberta, Saskatchewan, Manitoba, Ontario, Quebec, and Nova Scotia, and further analysis of the traditional strict application of the doctrine of corroboration, see Backhouse, *Carnal Crimes*.

42 Gaffield, *Aux Origines de L'identité Franco-Ontarienne*, 16–17, 27, 54–7, 62, 84; Robert Choquette, *L'Ontario français, historique* (Montreal: Éditions Études Vivantes 1980), 178–96; Robert Choquette, *La Foi Gardienne de la Lange en Ontario, 1900–1950* (Montreal: Les Éditions Bellarmin 1987); Mason Wade, *The French Canadians 1760–1967*, vol. 2 (Toronto: Macmillan 1968), 627–8, 634; Ramsay Cook, *Canada and the French-Canadian Question* (Toronto: Macmillan 1966), 35–9; Marc Cousineau, 'Belonging: An Essential Element of Citizenship – a Franco-Ontarian Perspective,' in William Kaplan, ed., *Belonging: The Meaning and Future of Canadian Citizenship* (Montreal: McGill-Queen's University Press 1993).

43 On Ottawa practitioner E.R.E. Chevrier's appointment, see *inter alia, Fortnightly Law Journal* 6 (1936), 1, as quoted in William Kaplan, *Bad Judgment: The Case of Mr. Justice Leo A. Landreville* (Toronto: Osgoode Society 1996), 39.

44 Ironically, the appointee was Raoul Mercier, reputed to be 'l'un des grands défenseurs des droits des Canadiens français' as well as a promoter of 'la bonne entente entre les deux groupes ethniques qui composent le Canada,'

who had acted as counsel for Auger in a number of these trials. (Mercier spoke English throughout the Auger proceedings.) His son recalled that a delegation of anglophone Ottawa lawyers travelled to Toronto to meet with Premier Mitchell Hepburn to register their objections. They argued that Mercier was in debt, and that he was Catholic and French. The premier, predisposed to support Mercier because of party affiliations and his active campaigning for Hepburn in the previous election, dismissed the first argument by saying that in the Depression, many good people were in debt. He apparently told the group he would not countenance the other objections. Interview with the Hon. Justice Pierre Mercier of the Superior Court of Ontario, 22 January 2001, notes on file with the author.

45 Hope was born in 1890 to Peter Hope, a merchant, and Jane L. Holmes Hope. He was educated at Perth Public School and Perth Collegiate Institute, and was called to the bar in 1914. Hope served in France during the First World War, and then practised with the Perth law firm of Stewart, Hope, and O'Donnell, serving as Ottawa Crown attorney from 1923 to 1933. He was appointed to the Ontario Supreme Court in 1933 and to the Court of Appeal in 1946. He chaired the Royal Commission from 1945–50. 'Hope, Lieut.-Colonel John Andrew, D.S.O., M.C., V.D.,' in *Who's Who in Canada, 1928–29* (Toronto: International Press 1929), 818; *The Canadian Who's Who, 1936–37*, 523–4; *Ottawa Citizen*, 8 February 1955; Law Society of Upper Canada Archives, Past Members Files.

46 Criminal Code, *R.S.C.* 1927, c.36, s.923–4.

47 *Ottawa Le Droit*, 18 March 1929, 21 March 1929.

48 *Montreal La Presse*, 17 October 1929. Joseph Lamoureux sought the services of an interpreter when he could not understand the lawyer's questions. Judge Kelly complained that the witness 'appeared to understand English,' and warned Lamoureux 'not to trifle with the court.' In the second and third trials, witnesses had to beg to give their evidence in French. When witness Mlle J. Latreille claimed she could not explain as well in English as in French, Judge Raney quipped: 'I wish I could speak French as you speak English,' before relenting and allowing a court interpreter to participate.

49 *Montreal La Presse*, 17 October 1929, 28 January 1930.

50 *Montreal Le Petit Journal*, 2 February 1930.

51 *Ottawa Citizen*, 21–22 March 1929; *Ottawa Le Droit*, 22 March 1929.

52 Testimony from the perjury trial as covered in the *Ottawa Citizen*, 2 June 1930, 4–5 June 1930; *Ottawa Journal*, 4–5 June 1930; *Ottawa Le Droit*, 4–5 June 1930.

53 These allegations were made during the third rape trial, covered in the *Ottawa Citizen*, 16 October 1929, 6 November 1929, 27 January 1930, 29–30

January 1930; *Ottawa Journal*, 29–30 January 1930; *Ottawa Le Droit*, 18 March 1929, 21 March 1929, 4 June 1930; *Montreal La Presse*, 17 October 1929, 28 January 1930.

54 Hope was president of the South Lanark Progressive Conservative Association, whereas many of Auger's defence counsel were active Liberals. Raoul Mercier served as president of the East Ottawa Liberal Association, Gordon Henderson was a 'successful stump speaker' for the Liberals, and Arthur Slaght ran unsuccessfully for the Liberal Party in a Temiskaming by-election in 1919, and was the Liberal MP for Parry Sound from 1935–45. *Ottawa Journal*, 7 June 1958; 'Henderson, Gordon Smith,' in Henry James Morgan, ed., *The Canadian Men and Women of the Time* (Toronto: William Briggs 1912), 523; *St Thomas Times-Journal*, 24 January 1964; Law Society of Upper Canada Archives, Past Members Files.

55 *Ottawa Citizen*, 22 March 1929.

56 *Ottawa Citizen*, 11 March 1930; *Ottawa Journal*, 11 March 1930.

57 *Ottawa Citizen*, 18 October 1929.

58 Family descendants appear not to have known that Auger was never admitted to the bar. His son, Louis III Auger, would later describe his father as an 'avocat et journaliste' – lawyer and journalist – in 'Famille Louis Auger,' n.a., *Chambly, 1655–1900* (Sherbrooke, QC: Éditions L. Bilodeau 1990), 84. The Law Society of Upper Canada confirmed that Auger was never called to the bar: correspondence from Susan Lewthwaite, research coordinator, Corporate Records and Archives, 13 May 2007. The Barreau du Quebec confirmed that he was not registered in their archives: correspondence from Martin Perron, Gestion de l'information, 8 May 2007.

59 I was unaware of the details of Auger's life after prison at the time of publication of the French version of this essay. I apologise to Marguerite Andersen whose fictional presentation of Auger's and Martel's stories was written without the benefit of the information that follows. Her fictional imagining provides a marvellous counterpoint to what I have been able to discover about his actual life. There are no surviving prison records regarding his two-year term in the Kingston Penitentiary: see correspondence 7 June 2007 from Barry Stead, senior analyst, Library and Archives Canada, after a search of Kingston Penitentiary Inmate History Description Ledgers, RG73 Accession 1985–86/163, boxes 19, 20, 21; Attendance Register, RG73 Accession 1980–81/013, box 80; Remission Register, RG73 Accession 1987–88/013, box 55; Discharge Register RG 73 Accession 1987–88/013, box 141. Reference to Auger's campaign for the Ontario legislature in the June 1934 election is found in 'Voting Charges Against Liberal are Dismissed,' *Globe and Mail*, 9 January 1935, where he is listed as the independent Liberal who

ran second (4,766 votes) after the Liberal candidate Aurelien Belanger (5,033 votes). Auger forwarded a petition to have the election results set aside, charging that Belanger was guilty of 'irregularities, fraud and corruption.' The petition was dismissed by an Ontario court because the petitioners were 'not prepared to proceed' when the case was called. Auger ran again in the 1935 federal election in the Prescott riding as an independent Liberal, and came second (3,620 votes) to Liberal candidate Elie Oscar Bertrand (6,034 votes). Auger listed his occupation at the time as 'teacher.' Parliament of Canada, History of Federal Ridings since 1867: Prescott, Ontario (1867–1952), retrieved 26 March 2008 from Parliament of Canada website, www.parl.gc.ca/information/about/process/house/hfer/hfer.asp? Language=E&Search=Det&Include=Y&rid=563.

60 N.A., 125 *Hawkesbury, 1859–1984* (booklet held in Hawkesbury Library, book amicus #20132561). While mayor, Auger became embroiled in a public dispute with the Ontario minister of welfare, David Croll, over the working conditions of Hawkesbury men seeking relief in government-run lumber camps: 'Failed to Accept Bush Jobs Offered,' *Globe and Mail*, 4 November 1936; 'Others in Camp Now Ask Return to Hawkesbury,' *Globe and Mail*, 14 November 1936.

61 He ran again as an independent Liberal, his 229 votes dwarfed by Émile Boucher, the successful Liberal candidate (6,261 votes.) Assemblée Nationale du Québec, *Les Résultats Électoraux Depuis 1867: Montréal – Saint-Henri*, retrieved 26 March 2008 from Assemblée Nationale du Québec website, www.assnat.qc.ca/FRA/patrimoine/resultatselec/m2.html.

62 Auger is listed at 174b Principale Ville St-Laurent from 1937–47: annual volumes of *Lovell's Montreal City Directory* (John Lovell and Sons: Montreal 1937–47). He is listed as an 'instituteur' – teacher – in the registration of his first marriage in 1934 (see note 64 below). Mireille Rolland advised that Auger was running a bookstore in the late 1930s and early 1940s (see note 63 below). The city directories list him as an inspector for the Canadian Munitions in 1943 and a 'rédacteur' – editor – for *La Patrie*, a Montreal newspaper, between 1944 and 1947.

63 Information about this came from Mireille Rolland, who wrote to Marguerite Andersen and me from France in March 2007, to identify herself as the daughter of Louis Auger. Her mother, Germaine Rolland (neé Cloutier), married to François Rolland, gave birth to Marie Lise Rolland on 8 September 1939 and Marie Simone Rolland on 7 August 1941, in Saint-Laurent, Quebec (now Montreal). Both girls were registered as children of Germaine and François Rolland, and it was not until the 1960s that Mireille learned from her mother that Louis Auger was actually the biological father of her-

self and her sister. In the late 1930s, Germaine and François had rented an apartment from Auger, and the couple used to socialise with the Augers. Germaine and Louis became lovers and Germaine left her husband and moved in with Louis Auger as his paramour, leaving behind all her belongings, including her sewing machine, with François. Mireille, who was still a young child at this time, recalls the relationship between her mother and Auger as a difficult one. When her mother later left Auger, and took some of his belongings, Auger brought (unsuccessful) legal proceedings against her. Correspondence between the author and Mireille Rolland, 24 March 2007–18 April 2007.

64 The first Auger-Goyer marriage took place on 4 September 1934 (paroisse Saint-Laurent, ville Saint-Laurent), and ended on Bernadette's death on 2 August 1946. The marriage to Marie-Berthe occurred on 18 October 1947 (paroisse Saint-Enfant-Jésus de Montréal.) *Index consolidé des mariages du Québec (1926–1996)* and *Index consolidé des décès du Québec (1926–1996)*, Min. de la Santé et des services sociaux et société de généalogie de Québec (June 2000). Marie-Berthe and Louis's four children were Françoise, Anne-Marie, Hyacinthe, and Louis (III): 'Famille Louis Auger,' *Chambly 1665–1990*, 84–5.

65 Ville de Carignan *Index des Rues de Carignan*, retrieved 26 March 2008 from Ville de Carignan website, http://villedecarignan.org/upload/villedecari-gnan/editor/ass et/215_1_IndexRuesCarignan.pdf; 'Famille Louis Auger,' *Chambly 1665–1990*, 84.

66 Obituary, *Montreal La Presse*, 7 March 1966.

67 Kaplan, *Bad Judgment*, 100, 127, 147, notes that the Franco-Ontarian heritage of Superior Court Justice Landreville went some distance towards explaining the persistence and venom of the campaign to remove him from the bench in the 1960s. Landreville, born in Ottawa, practised law in Sudbury while serving as its mayor prior to his elevation to the bench in 1956. Kaplan described Landreville as an 'outsider at a time when the legal establishment was dominated by insiders' and as someone whose 'flamboyant manner and extravagant lifestyle' affronted those who 'expected' the Franco-Ontarian to 'know his place.'

68 *Ottawa Citizen*, 18 October 1929.

2

Wardens and Prisoners: Aspects of Prison Culture in Ontario, 1874–1914*

JOSEPH ASHLEY BERKOVITS

There is now an extensive literature about the origins and purposes of the penitentiary and reformatory institutions. The early histories of the penal institutions are also well known to us, as are the philosophies of many of the reformers and government officials who helped create and shape them.[1] For Ontario, Peter Oliver's *'Terror to Evil-Doers'* provides a definitive account of the many components that made up the province's early penal system.[2] But while the narrative of the prison as an institution is well documented, we still know little about what daily life inside that institution entailed, nor do we know as much as we would like about the details and nuances of incarceration. The harshness of the prison experience has also been well chronicled,[3] but while we know a great deal about prison conditions, we have little understanding of how prisoners and prison staff felt about them, and how they interacted with each other. One important aspect of the prison experience was the role that the office of the warden played, and the focus of this essay will be the warden–convict relationship, which has much to reveal about the unique culture that was created inside the prison.

In the late nineteenth and early twentieth centuries, wardens[4] were expected to be not only prison administrators but also fearsome symbols of moral authority within the prison. Wardens were given an arsenal of disciplinary tools to secure the obedience of prisoners. Prisoners were dressed in drab uniforms, were told to be silent, were assigned numbers, and were subject to a litany of other indignities, all designed to mortify them into rehabilitation. But prisoners did not lose their essential individuality, and wardens did not descend into absolute despotism. The prison's inexorably grim repertoire of deterrence, deprivation, and punishment was often tempered with the many gestures of kindness that wardens were able to offer their prisoners at an individual level.

The relationship between prisoners and wardens could be as surprisingly personal as it was because the prison was still a relatively new institution, and the role of the professional warden was still being defined. At Ontario Central Prison, Andrew Mercer Reformatory for Women, and Kingston Penitentiary – the three institutions discussed in this essay – wardens and their families intermingled with the prisoners. And because wardens knew virtually each inmate by name, their relationship with the prisoner was as much personal as it was bureaucratic. The warden of this era willingly, of necessity, and with varying degrees of success, played many roles: that of fearless leader, disciplinarian, social worker, legal advocate, and, in a more general sense, surrogate parent. Wardens aspired to fulfill such an ambitious agenda partly because the safe and orderly functioning of the prison demanded that they earn the esteem, or at least the obedience, of their inmates. But they also did so partly because they came to understand that these convicts were not just faceless criminals, they were at times a quite engaging group of individuals, many of whom were worthy of their concern. It is in those moments that wardens and inmates were able to transcend the prison environment.

The many dimensions of this relationship found their reflection in the way prisoners interacted, and were expected to interact, with their wardens, who, by virtue of their comparatively elevated social standing, and obvious position of power over the prisoners, often viewed and treated the inmates as surrogate children. Wardens were also often old enough to be the parents of their inmates.[5] The way prisoners and wardens regarded each other affected their very language. Prisoners at Mercer Reformatory were openly encouraged to call their superintendent 'mother.' Maternal feminism allowed women, in their accepted role as sustainers of the family, to enter the spheres of health care, education, poor relief, and finally the reformatory prison. The total environment of the reformatory prison was an ideal place for activists to attempt to recast errant members of the lower class into the role of dutiful daughters, ready to serve their middle class mothers. The maternalistic warden was at turns religious, genuinely motherly, and also very much a captive of her own class interests. Nobody expected the warden at Central Prison or Kingston Penitentiary to play the official role of 'father' to their inmates, but quietly and with less fanfare he often did. Less overt forms of familial address were often used at the male institutions. Male prisoners were unfailingly designated, by staff and by themselves, as the warden's 'boys.' In addressing a note to Warden Gilmour, for example, prisoner AE Mc signed off as 'one of the Boys.'[6] As public figures, male wardens lived up to their role as disciplinarians, but they were actually more well-rounded individuals, capable of kindness as well.[7]

Despite this, prisoners and wardens did not always understand each other. It was by no means an equal relationship, and interactions between wardens and inmates were replete with misunderstandings, manipulations (by both sides), deceptions, and self-deceptions. Ultimately, the distinction between the paternal and the paternalistic, and the maternal and the maternalistic, was forever being blurred by the wardens. Class differences often created an insurmountable divide. The interaction between wardens and prisoners was also marked by their differing goals. While wardens strove for order, obedience, and rehabilitation, individual prisoners wished for better conditions and an earlier release. In the process, there was much manipulation by both sides.

The roles that wardens and prisoners played were needed not just for reasons of expediency and power, but also as a means of injecting a note of humanity into an otherwise grim association. Kindness could lead to self-affirmation for both sides. It is largely because of the uniquely personal connection that was established between the warden and the inmate that the story of the prison in this period is not an entirely dismal one. Even though wardens presided over and condoned regimes that imposed unwholesome diets, unsanitary accommodation, and corporal punishments, wardens were not essentially cruel people and prisoners were not always victims.

This essay will begin with a brief portrait of the three institutions discussed above. The focus will then shift to the warden–prisoner relationship. I shall illustrate how, as the price of the approachability and personal leadership style that they cultivated and desired, wardens often exposed themselves to physical danger. This potential for attack in turn enabled them to demonstrate their fearlessness and served to enhance their moral authority. A warden who was tough was also capable of dispensing tough discipline, and in a section that follows, I analyse the important role that corporal punishment played in the warden's relationship with the prisoners. The essay also focuses on the warden's role as advocate and social worker on behalf of the prisoner, both while the inmate was in prison and when he or she was out on probation.

Ontario Prisons: 1870–1910

The period between 1870 and 1910 represented a watershed in the history of the prison. It was an era in which the ideology of reform and the urge to punish converged. By the late nineteenth century, the reformed prison was still new enough to inspire citizen activism, and religious and scientific luminaries were keen to shape penal institutions as Ontario witnessed an explosion of new theories, maturing perspectives about the limitations of the prison, energetic activists, and a booming economy. At the provincial Central Prison, as many as 445 men were supposed to be transformed into skilled workers who, once morally reconstituted on the factory line, would develop a work ethic and earn the government a profit at the same time.[8] At its counterpart for women, Andrew Mercer Reformatory, about 120 female convicts were to be remade into dutiful daughters of the province, their criminality washed away in the suds of the laundry room.[9] And at the federal fortress of limestone that was Kingston Penitentiary, an average of some 600 prisoners found their lives dominated by the ubiquitous stone which surrounded them. They were set to mindlessly quarry and assemble it, block by block, into the silent and solid walls that entombed them, spiritually and physically, and in the process were supposed to remould themselves.

While late-nineteenth-century prisons were marked by rehabilitative idealism, the public increasingly wanted them to also set an example of terror and deterrence. Activists groups such as the Toronto Prisoners' Aid Association expressed their faith in the capacity of the criminal to be rehabilitated, and in the new theories that would facilitate this transformation, while at the same time insisting that he or she be more severely treated. Prisoners paid the price for this dual ambition. At Central Prison, the impossibility of running a prison profitably turned life into a daily horror of drudgery and reproach. At Mercer Reformatory, the numbing reality of laundry work overshadowed many of its good maternal intentions. Male administrators and reformers also regarded any concessions to female sensibilities with suspicion, and their concerns underlined the difficulty of creating a nurturing atmosphere in a custodial setting. Prisoners at Kingston Penitentiary lived in a prematurely aging facility with any desire for innovation having already been spent. Kingston's emphasis on custody alone underlined the desire of many of its inmates to break out of the penitentiary. Convicts spent their time there dreaming of escape, or dreaming of nothing at all.

Opened in 1874, Central Prison was an institution built in partnership with private industry, designed not only to rehabilitate criminals through skilled labour but also to make the province a profit. Capitalism and idealism were meant to go hand in hand. But it failed on both counts. It was never a true reformatory, nor was it ever a viable business. No amount of money, creativity, or ideology could overcome all the depressing realities of incarceration: poor food, confinement, sickness, and punishment. And no amount of investment could make a prison profitable, or prisoners into good workers. While convict labour at Central Prison was meant to be more than meaningless drudgery, to teach trades, and to provide skilled industrial labour so that inmates would be prepared for well-paying jobs on the outside, it failed in this also. For all the prison's impressively complex and expensive machinery, costly free labour still needed to be brought in to supplement and supervise the inmate workers.

Andrew Mercer Reformatory for Women was a revolutionary institution. Opened in 1880, it was the first separate facility for women in Canada. It was run almost entirely by women, and it usually housed no more than 120 inmates. Priding itself on being more a reformatory than a prison, Mercer attempted to break away from a punitive identity, instead abiding by a maternalistic ideology. Mercer referred to itself as a home, facilitated by 'attendants,' not guards, populated by 'residents' rather than prisoners, and in the charge of middle-class women who purportedly saw themselves more as surrogate mothers than as superintendents. Housing mostly prostitutes, vagrants, public drunkards, and not many violent or property criminals, it was geared to the treatment of moral offenders, and, as such, it was a place that emphasised a profoundly moral agenda. The maternal duties of the female wardens extended beyond the walls of the prison. When orphaned young women were suspected of dabbling in prostitution, they were often shipped off to Mercer Reformatory by their concerned communities. These motherless girls were placed in the care of the Mercer superintendent who was, in effect, given the mantle of 'moral mother' of the province. For example, Ada V was an eighteen-year-old servant convicted under the *Vagrancy Act*, who, in the opinion of the county Crown attorney, was desperately in need of a proper authority figure. 'I hope under your care and instructions,' he wrote Superintendent O'Sullivan, 'the girl may grow physically and mentally strong and resist evil.'[10] The unsavoury pasts of these women, all their sins from the outside world, would be 'washed away,' in the endless purgatory that was the laundry room.

At Mercer, there was never much soul-searching over what labour the convicts would perform, or much thought about equipping them with skilled vocations to take to the outside world. Women at Mercer were treated to home life, Mercer Reformatory style. But it was a household with a lot of dirty clothes. 'Experience has proved that, for many reasons,' Superintendent Mary Jane O'Reilly reflected near the end of her career, 'laundry work is one of the most suitable employments for our women.'[11] All able-bodied women, more than 60 per cent of the total inmate population, were expected to work in the laundry room, where an awesome annual average of 240,000 pieces of washing were completed.[12] But washing, much like everything else at Mercer Reformatory, was never as benign as it seemed; it was as exhausting as breaking stone, taxing and brutalizing at every turn.[13]

At Kingston Penitentiary, there was no complex machinery. Inmates were surrounded by stone – in the physical sense, by the stone that made up the walls of the institution, and the stone they worked with perilously and unremittingly every day; and in the spiritual sense by the stone-hearted attitude of the officials who had placed them in captivity. There was precious little desire for reform. The institution's experimentation with the ideas of the nineteenth-century Irish prison reformer Sir Walter Crofton represented perhaps its only dalliance with prevailing ideology. Crofton believed in the importance of distinct stages of classification, each with an increasing degree of freedom and privileges. With an initial 'penal' stage of isolation, followed by a 'reformative' stage, and with four classes of increasing privilege, culminating in a stage of 'semi-liberty' consisting of probation and training, Crofton's system was ambitious, expensive, and difficult to implement.[14] Over time, the penitentiary preferred to concentrate on the initial isolation aspect of the Crofton system, and to treat it as a disciplinary end in itself rather than an initial phase of rehabilitation. As Oliver has commented, by the 1890s, 'Kingston's soon notorious prison of isolation was nothing more than a unit designed to deal with recidivists and trouble-makers. It was never used as a mechanism through which all prisoners must proceed as they worked their way up the classic Croftonian ladder.'[15] Cells remained tiny, classification came to naught and new types of labour were scarcely thought of. Self-consciously isolated from the reformist experimentation of the 1870s and beyond, there was nothing new or forward-looking about Kingston Penitentiary. It was a time capsule wrapped up in stone and, for the roughly 700 inmates within, it remained a tomb of isolation from the outside world.

The Warden as Fearless Leader

Both compassion and cruelty in prison were dispensed face to face. Prisoners and their keepers did not regard each other in the abstract, but came to have feelings for each other on a personal level. Through a combination of ruthlessness, charisma, courage, and personal charm, wardens made themselves into larger-than-life figures within the prison walls, and in the process, they were able to shape the prison in their own image. Wardens were dauntless and strong because they knew that the prisoners would not fear or respect them if they were otherwise, and because they knew that the orderly function of the prison itself needed someone who could personify such attributes. It was more realistic to expect prisoners to be obedient to a warden, than to an abstract or remote prison bureaucracy. The pivotal role that the warden played in the convict's life also underlined his or her status as the most important proxy for outside society: no one from the external world was to make contact with the prisoner without going through the warden, who decided how much outside information and interaction the convict was entitled to receive.[16] In this sense, the warden's power over the prisoner extended beyond the walls of the prison.

Life in a total institution,[17] where a comparatively small group of people were thrust together in a relatively small space twenty-four hours a day, meant that people had no choice but to interact with each other on a level more intense than could be contemplated in a non-custodial setting. Stripped of their liberty and families, inmates became dependants of the warden, and by extension, the warden often fell into the role of their emotional protector, or abuser. On one hand, the warden meted out punishment, an unpleasant pseudo-parental role, but on the other, he or she was often also an advocate for the prisoner, communicating with families, securing jobs upon release, and at times arguing for pardons and paroles. Some inmates bonded sufficiently to correspond with their wardens after release. Thus, far from stripping away individuality, the closed environment of the prison served to highlight the importance of personality.

The warden, therefore, was not a removed figure. His or her presence was an essential feature of daily life. Despite the inherent risks, wardens chose to walk freely among the prison population. He or she was available for personal interviews, often dined with the inmates, and delivered the Sunday sermons. The superintendent of Mercer did not even bother to lock the door to her apartment. Wardens knew that this kind of accessibility put them in jeopardy of bodily harm, but they were willing to take the chance. Braving the assaults of angry inmates earned the respect of prisoners. Families of the wardens lived inside the institution as well and were well known to the convicts and their families.[18] There were few boundaries between the personal and professional lives of the wardens. By putting a face to their position they were able to both reassure and impress the prisoners with a commanding persona. They were also able to show everyone, staff and prisoners alike, that they were personally in charge. But wardens paid a price for their availability. One very real risk was contracting that scourge of all prisons, typhoid. Central Prison's Warden Gilmour, for example, was out of commission with the disease for the summer of 1900.[19]

More prevalent was the danger of physical attack. Central Prison's Warden Massie made a habit of being personally accessible to the inmates. He moved among them with minimal guarding, sometimes with no escort at all. Every Sunday at 11:00 a.m., after drill exercise, prisoners who wished to speak to Massie on any topic were given the right to file into the dining hall and put their case to him directly. Usually thirty to forty, and sometimes as many as eighty men would take advantage of this privilege. Only one guard was posted in the hall to help the warden keep order. It took Massie between twenty minutes and an hour to hear the prisoners out, meaning that a convict could typically expect to receive about a minute or so for the warden to summarily render his judgment. 'My practice,' Massie explained, 'is to give all the prisoners who wish to consult with me about anything, or desire any special privilege,' to do so.[20]

One such session in July of 1891 started out badly and quickly deteriorated. A group of twenty prisoners headed up the line, complaining volubly about misconduct reports. Massie was flustered and took considerably more time to deal with their objections than usual. Word spread of the warden's difficulties, and before long lengthy line of prisoners formed in the hall. Impatiently waiting his turn was a thirty-one-year-old recidivist 'D.' D had a violent history, and had frequently fought with other inmates. For one such outburst, he had recently stood six hours in irons. When Massie finally gave him his attention, D started out in 'an overbearing manner,' complaining about his removal from the kitchen brigade. Massie curtly explained that it was the prison's policy to put trained chefs in the kitchen whenever possible and that one such qualified prisoner had recently arrived, necessitating D's replacement. Having concluded his explanation, Massie brusquely turned to the next prisoner, only to find D blocking his way. D refused to budge, and threatened him. Without asking for help from the guard, Massie took the prisoner by the arm and led him towards the north wing. D took a few steps, but then 'turned short round' and gave Massie 'a violent kick between the thighs, and broke from [him]. In following him up he kicked [Massie] a second time in the same place.' Finally, the lone guard interceded and caught D from behind. With the help of others he was removed to his cell. Massie was in no condition to hear any more cases. 'I had to dispense the others,' Massie wrote, 'without giving them the privilege of saying what they wanted, and suffered from the pain all the afternoon.' As for D, he was soon to suffer from pain as well, being recommended for either a strapping of ten strokes or a flogging with the 'cat,' 'to the extent permissible.'[21]

Why did the warden subject himself to such danger? Why was the room not better watched, and why was the lone guard standing so far away? The lack of protection was probably deliberate. Having the guards standing too close would have implied that the warden was afraid to stand up to his inmates. The presence of prison employees would have also diminished the prisoners' capacity to speak freely to the warden, especially if complaining or informing about particular guards. Paradoxically, too much security could also hinder security. Prisons were not particularly trusting places, and wardens were no different. Massie and his colleagues never held much faith in their employees. The Sunday sessions were one opportunity for the warden to exercise pure power, to stand alone, without the focus being on anyone else but him. It was also a chance to play an appealingly paternalistic role, like a feudal lord dispensing small favours to his impoverished peasantry. The risk was there, but there were many practical reasons for keeping relations on a personal and direct level.

Above all, it was most important for Massie and his colleagues to exhibit personal bravery. As Kingston's Warden Creighton stated, a warden should never give in to fear of an inmate under any circumstances.[22] Prisoners respected strength in each other, and likewise admired that same quality in their leader. Hence, when Massie was assaulted, his first act was not to call for help, but to physically apprehend the offending inmate himself. He took the convict on, even though he knew that he was no match for him. Direct contact with the inmates and possible injury was a chance that the warden was willing to take if he or she was to secure their regard and cooperation. It was a risk a warden took, but not an unreasonable one. These attacks happened only rarely in Ontario and, unlike in prisons in the United States, were never fatal. This relative immunity of the wardens to danger was a testament to both the respect that their office inspired, and to the comparative civility of the prisoners.[23]

At Kingston Penitentiary, Warden Creighton was always prepared to demonstrate his bravery. On one occasion, in front of 500 convicts assembled in the dining hall, he single-handedly battled a notorious troublemaker. Arrangements at Kingston were much more formal than at Central Prison. Inmates were required to make an appointment to see the warden and he would see a maximum of only eight per day.[24] With reduced access, inmates who wished to make a point sometimes had to take drastic measures. A few weeks prior to the fight, convict Maurice B had emerged from more than a year of confinement in the dungeon. It was rumoured that he was now looking to establish himself as 'the hero of the penitentiary.' After breakfast, it was Creighton's practice to dismiss the Catholics to chapel and to read a biblical passage to the Protestants who remained seated. B, a Catholic, defiantly left his place before he was supposed to, and loudly proceeded to exit. Creighton cautioned him to remain seated and to await his turn. 'Must I?' he replied, while advancing toward the warden with a fork raised in his hand. Creighton related what happened next:

[I] instantly grasped [the convict's] two arms, and bore him back a short distance, and finally to the ground. During this time [the prisoner] was making desperate efforts to stab me with the fork, saying, 'take that – take that' and no doubt he would have killed me if he could – but I held him so tightly that he had no power except from the waist, and only succeeded in pricking me slightly in the neck and abdomen – just sufficient to draw blood.

Two guards, apparently the only ones on duty in a room filled with hundreds of prisoners, finally rushed to Creighton's aid and removed the prisoner. Meanwhile, in a remarkable display of respect for Creighton, the convicts remained impassive. Sitting speechless and motionless for the duration of the struggle, not one inmate took advantage of the situation. On the other hand, in a telling example of the inmate 'code,' not one inmate rushed to the warden's defence, either.

Despite the 'painful wounds' he had just received, Creighton remained cool. 'I immediately returned to the desk ... and proceeded ... as if nothing had happened – although I must admit that the struggle with B took away some of my wind. But to make as little of the matter as possible, and to prevent excitement, I took no notice of the blood trickling down my neck, nor did I examine the prick in my abdomen till after the men had gone off to work.' Creighton looked back on the incident with satisfaction. Prisoner B may well have killed him, if not for the intercession of the guards, but what was important to Creighton was that he had stood up to him. 'Any Warden who wishes to maintain his authority over the class of men I have to deal with, must never show the white feather. My motto is "Be Just, and fear not" – and God helping me I will carry out that motto to the best of my ability in this Penitentiary.' More than anything else, Creighton was glad that he had not 'lowered' himself 'in the eyes of the other convicts.'[25]

Warden Lavell, Creighton's successor, would have his character tested in similarly tense situations. During the noontime meal, 'convict George [illegible]' approached Lavell and 'in a very loud and exciting tone' defied him to punish him for an 'unjust' misconduct report. Lavell ordered him to his seat. The prisoner turned away from the warden, but then impulsively jumped up and pulled a guard off his stool. Practically all of the convicts instantaneously rose to their feet, hissing and cheering. Lavell immediately shouted at them all to 'sit down!' His firmness had the required effect: they did so at once. The incident was over in seconds, but for a few terrifying moments, when the prisoners had reacted more from instinct than from reason, a riot could have ensued. In those fleeting moments there was no time to call for more guards, to employ rational arguments, or even apply force. It was up to the warden to draw on the strength of his own personality, and all the emotions of fear and respect that his position inspired. Like Creighton and Massie, Lavell emphasised the importance of not appearing to be frightened. 'I coolly asked the officers on duty in the hall to report the names of convicts who acted in the manner they did. I did this in the presence of all the convicts. I was perfectly collected, and it was plainly seen we were ready to suppress any mutiny ... I find always the advantage of being cool and firm in emergencies and I will not be taken by surprise.' Lavell's need to repeatedly assure his superiors that he was not anxious strongly suggested that he was not as calm on the inside as he appeared to be on the outside. He admitted that he had faced these types of emergencies too many times before and pressed for the abolition of congregate dining. Shortly after, his wish was granted.[26]

In an era when guards were greatly outnumbered and generally un-armed, there were times when the sheer force of a warden's personality was all that kept a prison from falling apart. It was a terrific burden which demanded that the warden manifest a certain charisma and inspire deference. Massie, Creighton, and Lavell were part of a tradition of larger-than-life wardens in the nineteenth and early twentieth centu-ries, with reputations that were frequently nourished by myth-making and legend. Elam Lynds, an infamously fierce warden at the Auburn Penitentiary in New York, had heard about a plot of a certain inmate barber who planned to cut his throat. Lynds immediately ordered the inmate to shave him. 'When the prisoner had complied with the order without carrying out the plot, Lynds is supposed to have told him, "I am stronger without a weapon than you are when armed."' Such tales, Lewis argues, fed into the 'popular stereotype' of the nineteenth-century warden as strongman.[27] In fact, in the early nineteenth century, American wardens frequently paid for their accessibility with their lives. At Charleston State Prison, for example, Warden Walker was stabbed to death in the chapel, the third warden in a row to be killed at that institution.[28] Facing up to danger made wardens look tough in the eyes of their inmates.

The Warden as Disciplinarian

Ontario officials were convinced that the warden had not only to con-vey an aura of strength, but to establish terror as well. Inspector Moylan reported with favour a case where it was the 'painful duty' of Warden Creighton to order the flogging of a group of troublemakers recently transferred from Quebec's St Vincent de Paul Penitentiary, which had been run by a weak warden. 'It is fatal,' Moylan urged, 'to manifest any weakness or indecision of character, or to allow convicts to see or think they have gained the upper hand.'[29] Moylan's successor Inspector Stew-art concurred, arguing in a paper given to a National Prison Congress that too many wardens were naive and indulgent.

It delights [the neophyte warden's] heart to meet the seemingly harmless demands of his wards, and he congratulates himself on the ease with which an institution can be administered when new methods are adopted. It is only after a few months of experience that he realizes that every special privilege granted by him has been abused, that the abuse has been established by his own author-ity and cannot be eliminated without admission of his previous incompetence. If he is superior to his own weakness, he will admit his error and by self stultification endeavour to bring back discipline to the point where he found it, but in doing so he is apt to incur the antagonism as well as the contempt of his wards.[30]

Keeping discipline in the prison was the warden's most important and pressing duty. Without an orderly prison, nothing could be accomplished, and no one could be safe: not the staff, nor the other prisoners. However, when a warden's moral authority was not enough and punishments had to be carried out, the warden also knew that his or her power to forgive was a useful disciplinary tool in itself, and an opportunity to show some kindness, not to mention a chance to earn some goodwill from inmates who were deserving of a second chance. When it came to dispensing punishment, the warden's role of surrogate parent was at its most overt, and his or her control over the prisoner was at its most complete. Corporal punishments, often carried out in view of the other inmates, were infantalising and brutal to the recipient, and could be terrifying to the rest of the prison population. Wardens were therefore acutely aware of the psychological effect of punishment, and they often used their power to inflict or reserve it with great effect. An incorrigible prisoner was summoned by Massie to witness a beating and was told that he would be next. At the sight of the other man's agony, the prisoner 'had sunk down into himself on the floor, limp and abject in animal terror, his face an ashen gray, his eyes round and staring from his head in wild, staring fright, and his lower jaw moving up and down with incredible rapidity.' The spectacle had had the desired effect. 'You will not be flogged,' the warden announced. 'You will be taken back to your cell. I advise you to think over what you have seen and to decide that you will mend your ways.'[31] On another occasion, one prisoner was in such as state of apprehension over a court-ordered lashing, that Warden Gilmour wrote the sentencing judge asking for clemency. The prisoner had already received the first of his two whippings and, he observed, was appearing 'to have a nervous breakdown.'[32]

Even though male prisoners were expected to bear their punishments bravely, for their very masculinity depended on that ability, many of them could barely conceal their terror of them. Prisoner RHW was confined to a punishment cell. It was not clear if he was about to receive or had just received a thrashing, but he wrote the warden to complain that he would 'only be a fit subject for the Hospital when my sentence expires.'[33] Indeed, punishment inside the prison was not only meant to deter, but was calculated to break the spirit of resistance. At the Kingston Penitentiary, for example, whippings were given by alternating guards in sets of twelve lashes. The pause between each new set was designed to give the convict a chance to beg for mercy. The rotation also ensured that the guards remained fresh, and that each set of blows would be delivered with maximum force. For his assault on guard Birmingham, Elmer B was given a dozen strokes each by Keepers Brennan, Mills, and Arthurs.[34] William H attacked a guard and was also given three dozen lashes of the 'cats,' twelve each from Officers Milk, Money, and McLean.[35] If the warden was satisfied that the convict was sufficiently contrite during the short break between the sets, the rest of the punishment would be suspended. Convict John A, an otherwise model prisoner and a skilled engineer, got into a violent altercation with a guard. Warden Creighton sentenced him to three dozen lashes. 'After receiving one dozen,' Creighton recounted, 'he called me to him and begged off, as he said he could not take any more. Since that time I have not had any more cause of complaint against A.'[36] Warden Metcalfe often gave convicts a chance to repent after the first twelve lashes, but promised more if the conduct did not improve.[37] But many convicts made no request for mercy or immediately reversed their pleas. Convict George L, who had punched a guard, took two sets of the 'cats,' and when it came time for the third guard to resume the punishment, 'he begged off and promised good conduct in the future.' Creighton remitted the final dozen, but the moment L was released from the triangle, he regretted his contrition and cursed the keepers who had flogged him.[38]

At Mercer Reformatory, the female superintendent's role as disciplinarian was complicated by the presence of a male surgeon. If O'Sullivan was the undisputed 'mother,' she also had to contend with the presence of a 'father.' Surgeon King was dedicated and outspoken, authoritative and often authoritarian. While American reformatories for women were replacing male doctors with female ones, Dr King remained. The presence of male surgeons, Freedman has argued, 'contradicted the theory that women's problems, whether medical or emotional, could best be treated by members of the same sex.'[39] Dr King's status as the only senior male officer in an institution otherwise run by women gave him more power than any of his counterparts in the men's prisons. This fact could not help but colour his role as surgeon, and govern his relations with his colleagues and the convicts. More than any other surgeon, King was intimately involved with the disciplinary regime of the reformatory. While the duties of his counterparts would extend to examining prisoners for their fitness to withstand punishment, and taking issue with the appropriateness of certain punishments in general,[40] King would actually advocate punishments. Granted, surgeons were figures with authority, but in a male-run institution, it was the warden's pre-rogative to make punishment decisions, not the surgeon's. In a female-run institution, however, a male officer could have more latitude, and King exercised it.

Effie L was a resident of the Mercer's syphilitic ward, which was, along with the laundry room, one of the most miserable places in the prison. To make matters worse, the hated laundry room attendant, Mrs Mick, officiated there part-time as well.[41] There were seven inmates in the ward, and Effie L was one of the most vexatious. Surgeon King had a difficult time maintaining order there, and wrote the superintendent a long memo describing his problems. He singled out Effie L who was 'not only noisy, curses, swears, uses bad language, pretends to be lame or sick or unable to do anything she is asked to do, but is extremely vin-dictive towards not only [Attendant Hunter] but the inmates of the ward ... Attendant Mick in addition believes her to be dangerous and terribly treacherous.' King then proceeded to go on a fact-finding mis-sion, interviewing all the other residents of the ward for their impres-sions of Effie L's behaviour. Each of them, he reported, confirmed the fact 'that she refuses to work, refuses to sit at the table and eat with them, picks up her dish with food and repairs to her own room, makes herself willfully troublesome, has the girls in fear, tells lies, is noisy nearly the whole time, pretends to be lame but when she thinks she is not watched has been seen standing and walking ... she refuses to be amenable to discipline.' Effie L's fellow inmates were prepared to share information about her to the authorities. They no doubt happily informed the hypersensitive Dr King that she 'designates' him '"a son of a bitch" though not to himself.' More seriously, inmates also divulged that L was planning to use her infection as a weapon against other inmates of the ward, as well as against staff members. She 'threatened to put stuff in the tap, in their food or drink on their dishes and if possible on the person of Mrs Hunter and when I asked what they meant by stuff they told me fluid or solid excreted or discharged from her own body (which is syphilitic) for the purpose of inoculating or poisoning Atten-dant Hunter, and as a vindictive act make the girls eat or drink it.'

King, having concluded his personal inquiry, had each of the other six inmates and the two staff members endorse his report. He thereupon made his recommendations: 'I cannot too strongly advise that there are only three solutions in sight; 1st is absolute isolation continuous during her term; 2nd the efficient use of the spanker, to be repeated if there should be a recurrence of the improper actions and language; and 3rd a trial before the Police Magistrate for the threatened determination on her part to infect or poison the Attendants with whom she comes in contact with syphilitic poison of her own body; and secondly for expressed threats of compelling the other girls to eat or drink the syphilitic poison of her own body.' He deemed a 'long sentence in the penitentiary' as the most desirable response.

Superintendent O'Sullivan's report to the inspector was a little less impassioned, infinitely more practical, and far more tempered with mercy. She worried about the fact that Effie L had lain in bed refusing to work for so long that she had developed bedsores. The other inmates were afraid to come near her, and so hers remained the only cell they had not whitewashed. Placing her in the isolated cells in the dungeon would only put her health at risk, as it was too cold. A bread and water diet had failed to change her behaviour or curb her vocabulary. The attendants were 'worn out with her conduct.' Unlike the doctor, she did not request the authority to punish Effie L any further. Rather, she asked for the ability to transfer her back to jail. King had been free to make his recommendations, but in the end, it was O'Sullivan's opinion that counted most.[42] And in this case, it was 'mother,' not 'father,' who made the decision that further punishment, at least for this prisoner, was not necessary.[43]

The Warden as Social Worker

While being tough and having the power to dispense discipline was essential to earning respect, the wardens' position as religious leaders also gave them a commanding air of authority, and a genuine desire to be helpful to others. Many American reformers and wardens believed that 'God was the great reformer of sinful men.'[44] Their Christianity and deep personal faith gave them the assurance to talk to individual prisoners without fear or personal doubt, and the conviction to deliver thundering sermons to inmate assemblies. This devotion was shared by their counterparts in Ontario, where most wardens acted as unofficial clergymen, giving daily sermons at meal times and leading prayers on religious occasions.

There was, therefore, a softer side to the paternalism of male wardens and maternalism of female ones. It was marked by personal dedication and a sense of religious and moral responsibility. These were endearing qualities that helped make prisons more harmonious places. This kindness was especially apparent where young inmates were concerned, as evidenced indirectly by what some released inmates wrote back to wardens. 'According to promise,' Robert W, who was seventeen years old, wrote Warden Massie to assure him that he arrived home safely to Ottawa, 'the train being 1 1/2 hours late.' He added that he was spending his first week home all day long at the Exhibition, and seeing a show every night. He closed by wishing him 'all the pleasure the season can afford.'[45] Warden Gilmour wrote a sentimental and passionate letter to the federal minister of justice in an attempt to avert a court-ordered whipping of a fifteen-year-old boy, who in the warden's opinion, 'does not look more than thirteen.' 'B. is only a child in knickerbockers and to think of baring his little back for the lash would be a foul blot upon Canadian penitentiaries.' He also doubted the veracity of the charge of indecent assault found against him. Gilmour arranged to have the young man transferred to a children's institution under the care of J.J. Kelso.[46] Massie took a similar interest in Robert W, a sixteen-year-old convict. Writing to the boy's family clergyman, Massie described, 'How much I desired to do more than it is possible for me at present for the young lads placed under my charge, I cannot tell you. I love my work and its responsibilities, presenting as it does such vast possibilities for helping them ...' Massie observed Robert at work in the machine shop, 'unsettled, boy-like, giving to his work very indifferent attention ... being more occupied with what was going around him than with his duties.' After some days, he called him into his office. Massie had a fatherly chat with the young convict and the warden was clearly charmed. Robert 'spoke very pleasantly' to Massie, who found him to have 'a bright pleasant face ... He is not a criminal in his make up; all he requires is a knowledge of a trade.' After six months of close supervision and encouragement, Massie confidently applied for a pardon. It was denied.[47]

Wardens frequently concealed their often quite genuine feelings of parental fondness behind an intentionally gruff exterior. By taking the younger prisoners in hand, they claimed they would only be providing the proper discipline and direction that the prisoners' own parents had neglected to provide. 'I hold that nothing tends so much to produce criminals,' Warden Massie wrote one young inmate's parents, 'as the want of proper control in the family, which allows boys to grow up without any fixed purpose for their future. They continue indolent habits, which lends to their being either of little use in any station in life, or they become criminals, and I realize it is to be my duty as long as they are under my charge, to inculcate habits of activity, and strict obedience to the rules and regulations laid down for their observation.' Massie assured the parents of Edward S that such severity, however, did not mean the absence of affection. Thanks to frequent conversations, he found the 'lad' to be 'quite cheerful' and 'bright' and was making sure that he was receiving proper instruction from the officers in the field of engineering. Over time, however, the warden noticed that Edward was no longer robust and was growing pale. Satisfied with his character, he arranged for his early release, some two months short of his one year sentence. Edward's father wrote Massie a note of thanks. 'You have granted to him some privileges to which, from what my son says, he was not strictly entitled. Thank you very much.' And then he added touchingly, 'I have delayed a few days in writing, but the first days of my son's return were so short, that I did not find time to write. My son who had occasion to know and appreciate you has the best of souvenirs, and for my wife's and my own part, although we are not favored with your acquaintance, we nevertheless may say that we know how kind you are, and if ever I pass through Toronto, I will stop and make it my duty to call on you.' The next month Edward's father wrote to Massie to inform him that his son had secured a job at a sash and door factory. Massie replied with delight, but reluctantly revealed that as Edward was leaving the prison, he stole some tobacco from the conservatory and distributed it to the prisoners. Massie warned that there was still more parenting to be done. The boy had 'to guard against a bad trait of character which needs to be eradicated.'[48]

Warden Creighton's comment on one teenage convict was, 'if he had been as obedient to his Parents as he is to me I do not think he would have been here.' 'I treat the Convicts with ... kindness,' Creighton continued, 'but not with too much indulgence, and that is where I think his Parents have failed in their duty – by not controlling their sons in their childhood and youth.' Nevertheless, Creighton had taken a personal interest in ensuring that this convict learned a trade that would earn him a good living upon release.[49] Often, wardens helped younger inmates and many elder inmates, for that matter, because they liked them, and the rhetoric of proper parenting was merely a justification for their efforts.

Not all attempts at parenting, however, were successful, or applauded. Warden Gilmour 'very strongly' advised the father of William C not to pay his son's fine, and let him instead remain under his care. 'The way to prevent him from drinking is if possible to break his appetite and nothing will do that so effectually as keeping him entirely away from liquor for some months.' But William's father would have none of Gilmour's pseudo-paternalism and decided to inject a note of reality. 'I ask a favour of you but not your advise,' Mr C replied angrily. 'I want advise from no man ... If you want to blame anybody blame the Magistrate for sending him there for it is an outrage to send anyone to the Central for a simple drunk. I will be up at Central Prison about 1 P.M. to pay his fine.' In a separate letter to his son (which was impounded by the management), Mr C revealed that he had little faith in the warden's sanguine depiction of the prison. 'I have heard in court that prisoner[s] are not safe in the central prison for every few months we hear of knifing or some mudderous [sic] affair or the whipping machine, it seems that there is brutality both by the convict and the warden.'[50]

On another occasion, Massie appeared to be taken with a particularly charming young convict named George D, alias B. Writing to the sentencing judge, Massie echoed a sentiment oft repeated by convicts that 'all the great criminals are not behind prison bars.' '[M]any get there,' he philosophized, 'who by a very slight divergence at one time of their lives, from the line which circumstances laid for them, would have changed their whole course of life, and they would have been very different men.' In a letter to his parents, George described how Massie had been delighted with his essays on prison reform, which the warden was promising to publish. George had also given Central Prison and Massie himself a glowing report. Indeed, Massie enjoyed George's letters to his parents so much that he had his secretary copy them out before allowing the originals to be sent off. According to George, Central was 'well and nicely constructed, and perfect order and cleanliness abounds every where about the prison.' The cells were large, well ventilated, and clean. Amazingly, this convict found that the food was 'good, well prepared.' To top it all off, the 'officers from the warden down are polite gentlemen.' He saved most of his praise for the warden himself. 'The Warden takes special pains and interest in the welfare of the prisoners. I have had one of two conversations with the warden and find he is a perfect gentleman and scholar and any prisoner who behaves himself and is worthy he will do anything he can to assist him.' Four months later, while Massie continued to petition rigorously on his behalf, the prisoner successfully escaped. In an earlier letter to the sentencing judge, Massie had written, 'I have sometimes been badly taken in and deceived, but against that I have assisted many who have proved worthy.' The remark proved truer, and more prophetic, than Massie realized.[51]

Wardens who were seen as approachable and wise were also in a better position to control the prison. The more inmates confided in them, the more their wardens were not only able to help them, but also to gain insight into their inadequacies and vulnerabilities. Inspector Moylan observed that Creighton always made an effort to 'converse in a free and friendly manner' with convicts. 'Bad as some convicts are, there are but very few who will not appreciate a favor; and any indication of kind feeling or assurance of sympathy on the part of those who rule over them, is not only elevating to their depressed spirits, encouraging their hopes, but in itself, is a controlling power.'[52] When Creighton was dying, Moylan remarked that the convicts showed their esteem to the old warden by 'their exceptionally good conduct' for the duration of his illness, taking care 'to do nothing that would, in the least degree, disturb or annoy him.'[53] Creighton's successor, Dr Michael Lavell, aimed to have an equally personal relationship with the convicts, striving to know 'every prisoner and secure his confidence.'[54] Lavell's background as surgeon at the penitentiary for the previous twelve years had made him a familiar figure, and was given as a reason for his engagement as warden, owing to his 'thorough acquaintance with the character of the prisoners.'[55]

Prisoners also knew that if they had any complaints, it was better for them to make their case directly to the warden than to try to go over his or her head. The warden may have been a stern and imposing figure, but he or she was never a remote one. The inspector, on the other hand, rarely took inmate protests seriously, for he had not developed any sort of relationship with them. This was a dependence that the warden guarded jealously. In the words of one ex-inmate, during his visits, the inspector would

go around with the governor, and in a pompous lordly fashion, stops at a cell door and with terrible words shouts as if he was Jehovah's vice-regent upon earth: 'I am Her Majesty's Inspector of Prisons! Have you any supposed cause of complaint?' The governor is there with him; the poor fellow addressed in this awe striking manner, looks through the bars of the cell, and knowing that the truth would bring him bread and water diet and lodgings in the dark cell and certainly no redress from the inspector, the crushed mortal without lifting his head pronounces a guttural 'no.'[56]

When, for example, Inspector Stewart once came to the prison to question convict K about his previous escape, K refused to speak to him, claiming that he did not know who he was and that he could therefore not trust him. He would only speak to the warden.[57]

This emphasis on being approachable meant that wardens came to believe they knew their charges well enough to bestow upon some extraordinary favours. The process of familiarisation was facilitated by the personal contact that wardens entered into with inmates' families and circumstances. The demands of the families of convicts kept prisoners and officials alike grounded in reality, and ensured that the prisons maintained an uneasy dialogue with the outside world. The prison could never be sealed off from society, and no warden, no matter how parental, could ever replace a real parent. But for a while, the warden, thanks to the powers of his or her office and his or her human sympathies, was in a position to play a surrogate role. The more the warden knew about a prisoner's external family, the more effective he or she could be in this endeavour. Since wardens read most incoming correspondence and met virtually all incoming visitors, they were able to make a quick study of each convict and his or her situation.

Warden Creighton was impressed with the loyalty that prisoner James S inspired in his wife, who, in order to live closer to her husband, moved away from Waterloo and took up a position as a domestic in Kingston.[58] Warden Platt sympathised with Robert Y's nervous mother sufficiently to urge Robert to write to her more often.[59] Warden Foster wrote one prisoner's sister requesting her to stop writing him about local robberies, and to another convict's girlfriend to remind her that he was a legally married man.[60] Warden Massie and his successors never hesitated to wade into the personal lives of convicts. Massie in particular was dauntless. He tried many times to put a stop to extramarital affairs by writing ferocious letters to mistresses, and routinely withheld letters to inmates from girlfriends whom he thought were bad influences. When he did not have faith in the suitability of the partners prisoners had chosen themselves, he advised against marriage, even in the case of pregnancy, and he had no qualms about getting involved in complicated and sometimes violent family disputes.[61] Sometimes families had to be persuaded to simply back off. Warden Gilmour wrote thirty-three-year-old convict Henry F's sister, imploring her to convince the family to stop writing so many sentimental letters. Henry was enough of a 'baby' as it was, and Gilmour was 'in hopes he may get a little manhood put into him while here.'[62]

If prisoners' families and all their problems did not intrude through their letters, they came in person. Prisoner John McD's sister was a particularly disruptive, though not uncommon kind of visitor. Warden Gilmour grumbled to the inspector that she never failed to create a disturbance in the prison by her 'arrogance and domineering proclivities ... Mrs. J. never makes a request, it is always a command, and if her overbearing, domineering troublesome propensities continue we should be compelled to debar her from the Institution as her visits result in an outburst from McD. that makes this place a hell on earth.'[63]

While wardens could be moved to anger over difficult prisoners with their troublesome families and friends, they just as quickly grew sentimental over what they considered to be the worthier cases. Massie wrote to an inmate's brother to request that he send some cloth to the prison which could be made up free of charge into a respectable discharge suit. Otherwise, James V would have nothing to wear upon release but rags.[64] Warden Gilmour was concerned enough about the fate of convict Samuel S's wife and eight children that he took the initiative to write to the inmate's pastor to request that he check and make sure the family was not lacking in the necessities of life.[65] In another case, Gilmour asked the sister of an inmate to look after his wife and family while he was inside.[66]

In other cases, it was the job of the superintendent to protect inmates from their own families and friends, particularly exploitative and cheating husbands. O'Sullivan quickly came to the conclusion that Mary C's husband was a disagreeable man and a liability. Not much of a provider, he seemed to depend upon her earnings as a prostitute to get by, and had developed serious financial problems upon her incarceration. He was constantly writing to her at the Mercer asking for money to pay for childcare and various medical problems stemming from an ingrown toenail, and then from an abscessed tooth, both of which he described in far too much detail. Finally, he issued an ultimatum: either she commit to coming back to him, or he would commence selling the furniture. Meanwhile, he expected O'Sullivan to help effect a reconciliation between the two of them. O'Sullivan swung into action. She arranged for the baby to be taken in by a respectable woman in town. O'Sullivan also made her sympathies clear, frostily writing the husband that she was tired of his 'impertinent' inquiries. 'You have not contributed to the support of your child, leaving it dependent entirely upon strangers ... It is difficult to reconcile your letters. I do not intend to advise your wife in this matter nor to ask her any questions ... I see no object in your addressing yourself to me in this matter.'[67] Prisoner Maud K's husband, John, wrote Superintendent O'Sullivan from his cell at Central Prison wondering if she would allow his wife to receive his letters. He had written her before, but had received no response, postulating that it was 'probably owing to jealousy on the part of a girl' at Mercer whom he 'used to keep company with.' O'Sullivan did not appear to dignify his request with a reply, and neither, apparently, did his wife.[68]

These contacts led wardens to believe that they understood their prisoners as whole persons. O'Sullivan asked for the early parole of a favourite convict so she could take her along on a family vacation, a request that was flatly refused.[69] When eighteen-year-old prisoner Hattie F absconded from her parole with another former prisoner, O'Sullivan sent her several cajoling letters, assuring her that she was not angry at her and hoping that she would return to custody, so she could 'begin once more and be the good little girl we all liked so well here.' Hattie F replied that, 'every time I get a letter from you I am more ashamed of my self.' After numerous messages back and forth, Hattie F agreed to come back, but not until the superintendent promised to take her holidaying to her new cottage in Lafontaine.[70] O'Sullivan worked very hard to get Sarah D, who, like the majority of inmates, had a drinking problem, a position as a domestic at the home of a 'respectable' Toronto woman that she knew. She was therefore able to press for a ticket of leave, rather than a full discharge for this inmate, enabling her to keep a 'hold on her' which 'will probably be the means of her leading a better life.'[71] These exceptional gestures of faith would not have been possible without the wardens' determination to get to know their inmates.

The Warden as Advocate

When prisoners turned to the wardens for help in getting jobs after their release, they frequently put their personal reputations on the line to help them. Warden Massie did not hesitate to write letters of recommendation to his own friends urging them to hire ex-prisoners. For example, he wrote to the wife of a bed frame manufacturer he knew, asking her to persuade her husband to give prisoner William B a position at his factory. 'I will be very pleased if your husband will give him employment,' he wrote, 'if not continuously, at least till he gets a start ... He is very impressible, and if you speak a word of encouragement to him when opportunity presents, it will go a long way towards overcoming difficulties.' Massie urged William B's family not to give up on their son. After all, he assured them, it was the middle of an economic depression. He sent them two dollars of his own money for Christmas. He promised to visit them when he next travelled to Rochester, where the family resided. On another occasion, Massie not only successfully campaigned for a pardon for twenty-six-year-old Alexander O, but he also offered him a job as a guard.[72] To help a former convict along with his new fruit-growing business, Massie placed a large order of peaches from the recently liberated Stephen F, only to be disheartened by their poor quality when they arrived. Massie even lent prison tools along with ten dollars to discharged prisoner Albert S, to help him get a start in the pattern-making trade in Peterborough.[73]

One way of helping an ex-prisoner, as well as extending the relationship, was for the superintendent of Mercer Reformatory to secure her a job with one of her relatives. Lizzie B, a former prostitute, was posted at O'Sullivan's son's house as a domestic. The house was within walking distance of the Mercer.[74] Rose B, a twenty-one-year-old convicted under the *Vagrancy Act*, was another ex-prisoner placed with a member of O'Sullivan's family. But alas, for Rose B, the transition from prostitute to domestic was too difficult. 'The girl herself seemed satisfied and happy, but without a moment's warning left the house, doors open, taking only with her what she wore and no word or trace of her have we had since.'[75]

Warden Gilmour regularly wrote letters of recommendation for prisoners who were about to be released. 'Louis P. goes out on the 28th inst.,' Gilmour wrote to one prospective employer. 'Had he been working on salary, he could not have been a better man. Can you do anything for him by way of employment on the C.P.R. ? I hope you may.' Charles P wondered if Gilmour would be willing to bend the truth a little bit in his letter of reference. 'I am sure of the job,' P wrote to Gilmour, 'if you don't have to state in the recommend that I was in the Central.' Knowing that a criminal record was not exactly an asset in the job market, the warden was happy to oblige. On a blank sheet of paper with his home address typed at the top, Gilmour wrote: 'Charles P. has applied to me for a reference, and I beg to say that P. was in our employ for a considerable time over a year. He is a competent brush hand, enameling beds. We found him steady, industrious and temperate, and I can cordially recommend him to anyone requiring such help. I might say,' he added with delightful irony, 'that he left on his own account ... J. T. Gilmour, Manager.'[76]

Male and female wardens were by turns fierce and terrible, paternal and affectionate – but they were always approachable. They were determined to get to know their inmates, and in the process, they let the prisoners into their lives as well. While they subscribed to the harsh criminology of their era, they were also the product of a time when the barriers between one's professional and one's personal life were not sharply delineated. Being a warden was more than a job for these men and women, it was a vocation. Family, friends, and personal contacts were all solicited to help these idealistic matriarchs and patriarchs go about their job.[77]

Indeed, where certain favourite inmates were concerned, wardens would stop at nothing, particularly in the pursuit of early releases and pardons. Warden Gilmour engaged in exhaustive correspondence with the lawyers of John F, in an effort to overturn his conviction, even going so far as to inform them (off the record, he hoped) of certain 'unfair methods of warfare,' which he had learned that the prosecuting constable was known to employ.[78] Gilmour entered into a similar exchange of letters on behalf of convict Robert C. In one letter to the minister of justice, Gilmour urged for a ticket of leave. 'Unless he is at liberty and in a position to protect himself, I am afraid he may suffer serious financial loss.' After talking to locals in C's hometown of Cayuga, he was able to assure the minister of his 'inoffensive' character; as he himself had observed, C was 'not bright mentally.'[79] Judge John Ardagh of Simcoe County wrote to the federal minister of justice, protesting Gilmour's interference in his sentences, particularly in the case of convict Norman S. This convict would be finishing a two years less a day term at the Central Prison, and was on route to serve another two years, two months at the Kingston Penitentiary. Gilmour had submitted that the additional time at the Kingston was cruel, and sarcastically attacked the 'peculiar' thinking of the judge in devising such a sentence. 'The tendency in rural localities,' Gilmour had commented sweepingly, 'is to be too severe on young men.' 'His criticism of my "fine process of reasoning,"' Ardagh retorted furiously, 'I might expect to find in some irresponsible newspaper, but coming from an official who holds the position he does, (and knowing very little of the facts he undertakes to write about) – and offered moreover to the head of the Department of Justice for the whole Dominion ... is objectionable.'[80] The minister of justice, too, was growing weary of Gilmour's explosive language. 'Let me say,' the minister warned him,

that I think the language you use in your letter is rather vigorous. No doubt you have written exactly as you feel about the case, but when you cry out so emphatically for 'Justice! Justice!' do not forget that in exercising any authority I may have in the matter of releasing prisoners, I am not carrying out the decree of 'Justice' but interfering with them.[81]

In response to another one of Gilmour's increasingly feverish crusades for an early release, Deputy Minister of Justice David Mills apparently felt the need to help the warden to regain some perspective. 'If there is any modification of the sentence,' Mills impatiently explained,

it is a matter of grace and not of right on the part of the convict, and so action is never urgent in order that justice may be done. The party is in confinement due his own misconduct ... I do not know precisely what you mean by hoping that the future may have something better in store for you, unless you assume that it is my duty to act upon your recommendations at once, and without inquiry, and so substitute your judgment for my own.[82]

In response to another case, Minister of Justice A.B. Aylesworth wrote to Gilmour, 'I do not see how I can properly apply a different rule to prisoners who have been sentenced to the Central Prison from the course of practice which obtains in other similar institutions throughout the country.'[83] In yet another vigorously argued plea for clemency, Gilmour seemed to be haranguing the minister: 'Where is the justice? If Mc. is treated justly, M. is treated unjustly, and vice versa. Which is it?' Aylesworth tried to be as diplomatic in his reply as possible. Gilmour was letting his emotional feelings for certain inmates overrule his objectivity, and if Gilmour did not see it, the minister did: 'We should always like to have the opinion of the head of the institution in which a prisoner is incarcerated as to the effect ... the imprisonment has had on him and whether his conduct generally entitles him to a Ticket of Leave; but I am sorry to say that in the case of the Central Prison, Toronto, reports on prisoners are in almost all cases limited to the words 'premature to make a recommendation.'[84] In his impassioned and often unprofessional efforts to spare selected inmates, Gilmour was compromising his duty to the others, and unwittingly, tarnishing his image in the criminal justice community. It would have impossible for him to extend the same amount of effort to all the inmates. A combination of charm, youth, and sheer luck enabled certain prisoners to capture his attention. The warden knew the price – to his time and to his reputation – which that these petitions entailed. That he was willing to proceed with them demonstrated his paternal feelings towards many of his inmates.

At Kingston Penitentiary, the warden often used his power to petition as a disciplinary tool. If an inmate was well behaved and industrious while inside, the warden would frequently campaign for early release regardless of the inmate's relative guilt or innocence. 'The fact that my recommendations generally receive attention at headquarters,' Creighton wrote, 'has an excellent effect upon the Convicts; inciting them to good behaviour and industry. They all know very well if they are not deserving nothing will be done for them by me.' Creighton did not seem overly concerned with the veracity of a particular charge. He perfunctorily cited a convicted rapist's claim to innocence and added rather lamely and more as a justification than a defense, that 'the young woman has been since married.' What mattered most to Creighton was the convict's good behaviour inside. '[The prisoner] has always been honest and truthful here. He has not been reported for any offenses during the whole term of his imprisonment.'[85] Alfred W ran a sewing machine in the tailor shop, and was 'very industrious at that.' His few reports were chiefly for talking, and hence, his early release was recommended.[86] Convict Robert B, a carpenter, was convicted of setting his wife's lover's property on fire. The lover was now dead, so in Lavell's mind, B was no longer a threat to society. Besides, he added, he 'fully believe[d] the man has repented of his [rash] act.' Most importantly B had performed valuable work for the prison.[87] Prisoner L had made himself useful as a handyman around the prison, having 'spared no pains' to perform his work with diligence, Warden Metcalfe petitioned in a letter to the minister of justice.[88]

But like their counterparts in other prisons, wardens at Kingston Penitentiary would often let their sentiments overrule their discernment, turning them into overzealous advocates. After conducting an exhaustive amateur investigation, Creighton not only felt ready to conclude that convict Thomas G was innocent of an assault conviction, but was sure he could prove who really was culpable for the crime.[89] In another case, Creighton urged the early release of convict John W. so that he might take up a job as sales agent for 'fruit evaporators.' 'We have now 774 convicts,' Creighton reminded the minister of justice. 'Two months imprisonment in a case of this kind is of little consequence ... for the want of ... immediate employment is the greatest difficulty discharged convicts have to contend with.'[90] As for prisoner William H, a man sentenced for multiple rapes, Creighton was sure that the women accusing him of the crime were prostitutes.[91] Warden Platt asserted that there were 'grave doubts' as to the guilt of convict Charles B, for the man testifying against him was 'a scoundrel.' Plus he had aged parents in Germany to take care of. 'Pardon him,' Platt wrote to the minister of justice, 'and let him go home.' The next month, B was pardoned.[92] Platt even arranged for a lawyer to represent a convict charged with assaulting one of his own officers.[93] One former prisoner felt sufficient faith in the powers of Warden Foster, as well enough confidence in their relationship, to ask him for legal advice some time after his release. Foster assured him that he would do what he could.[94]

For many prisoners, the warden's apparent power to pardon took on magical properties. The warden basked in the appreciative glow of desperate convicts hoping to secure favour. Inspector Moylan worried that the incoming prisoners became fixated on the idea, not realising that the warden could not always deliver on his promises. As a result, inmates, he observed, became 'uneasy and irritable.' For wardens, the promise of early release became a disciplinary tool only effective in the short term. 'Neither the Warden nor any other officer has the power over the mind and action of the convict that he ought and would have if it were not for the continual idea of pardon ... While one may be made happy by clemency being extended to him, hundreds are made miserable because they think, and, in most cases, know that they are as much entitled to pardon as the one who received it.'[95] Those rejected for pardon 'consider themselves martyrs; they become dissatisfied, restless and give no small share of trouble.'[96] Even Warden Platt, one of the most enthusiastic of advocates to hold the office, wondered if the petitioning was starting to get out of hand. 'As the practice now is, friends and relatives of some of the worst and most undeserving succeed in getting petitions for parole before the minister, and the consequence is that every man in the prison thinks he has an inalienable right to petition.' To cut down on the 'scores' of petitions, Platt recommended that only first-class convicts be given the right to apply, except upon special recommendation by the warden.[97] Platt also voiced concern about the incitement of visiting lawyers, and wished to curtail their access as 'they tend to destroy the discipline of the place.'[98] Lawyers' interviews with convicts, Platt reiterated, were expressly forbidden except in the warden's presence or that of an officer of his choosing.[99]

Officials and wardens alike could complain of the workload and discipline problems all they wanted, but wardens cherished the power and prestige their role as petitioners brought them, as well as the information about convicts' backgrounds that the procedure afforded. One prisoner made the mistake of going over the warden's head, and had a former employer apply directly to the Governor General for a remission. He had perhaps correctly thought that he would have had a better chance of succeeding if he had a person sponsoring him who did not come from the prison service. Warden Lavell was most perturbed, and promptly took control of the case. Henceforth, Lavell assured Inspector Moylan, the petition would be sent through 'the proper channel,' namely, the office of the warden.[100] And that is where successive wardens ensured that it remained.

Probation: The Twilight of the Relationship

For wardens like Superintendent Emma O'Sullivan, being the 'moral mother' of her charges was more than just an act, and ultimately more than just a responsibility. It was something she truly wanted to do. An obviously affectionate woman, she made heartfelt attempts to create lasting relationships with the prisoners. But there was a practical side to her devotion, too. O'Sullivan believed that the greater the emotional bond she could establish with the inmates, the greater chance she would have to continue to influence their rehabilitation. Nowhere was this desire on her part manifested more powerfully, and poignantly, than in the months following release. Jennie O wrote the superintendent about a year after her release to tell her 'friend,' as she addressed O'Sullivan, that she had gotten married, as she knew she would have hoped to hear. 'I wasn't very long after getting out was I?' she proclaimed proudly, adding her new married name. O'Sullivan was delighted, but countered with some practical concerns and homespun advice: 'Did you not tell your intentions to your parents until after you were married? I judge from your letter that you did not. Write and tell me what your husband's occupation is and where you are going to live. You ought to be an expert housekeeper, but one must be a home maker as well. A husband must find a happy and contented wife as well as a neat house.' She concluded by asking her former inmate to write her soon, 'with further particulars,' but there was no response.[101]

The chance to correspond with women who no longer resided at Mercer, and help them with their problems, was for O'Sullivan the ultimate verification of her role as parent. But the cold fact was that these communications would have in most cases never existed had they not been a condition of parole.[102] Nevertheless, while the former prisoners followed regulations and wrote, many indulgently sent her letters that were far more detailed and vastly more tender than the letter of the law dictated, often signing them sentimentally, and much to O'Sullivan's delight, with 'daughter.' But when parole was over, so too, inevitably, was the exchange of letters. O'Sullivan arranged for twenty-one-year-old Ruth W to be placed at the home of a reliable middle-class matron in Penetanguishene, while she worked as a hospital cleaner. 'I am doing real well now Mrs. O'Sullivan. I am quite happy up here ... My little sister in the Holland Landing was very much surprized indeed to hear I was out but she said she laughed about me being in Penetanguishene as she knows a little song by that name.' She listed her daily schedule, as well as the Christmas gifts she was given, consisting of a box of hand-kerchiefs, a dollar, a pair of leggings, a box of chocolates, a vase of flow-ers, four cards from home, and some homemade candy. As arranged, she was using a pseudonym at work. Soon, however, Ruth W was homesick. She relocated to Barrie to be with her parents, but was appre-hensive about O'Sullivan's reaction to her abrupt move. 'There will be no scolding from me,' O'Sullivan replied, 'as long as you do what is right, and it is gratifying to read what you say that you are determined to be a good woman, that nothing will tempt you to be any different.' Several letters later, Ruth W wrote O'Sullivan to inquire whether since her parole was set to expire in a few days, she would be required to report any more. When she discovered that she would not have to write any more, after almost ten months of detailed and friendly correspon-dence, she tried to take her leave from O'Sullivan as gently as possible. 'If you do not hear from me again Mrs. O'Sullivan I hope you will not think I have gone back to my old ways because I will never do that. But I don't want to become a nuisance to you for the rest of my life. I feel very grateful for the trouble you have taken with me already and I thank you very much Mrs. O'Sullivan.' At least on the surface, O'Sullivan took Ruth's tactful display of modesty at face value. 'Don't think I shall ever consider hearing from you or good news of you a "nuisance." I shall be more than pleased to hear from you and shall endeavor to answer your letters promptly.' But there were no more letters.[103]

Claudia M was a twenty-year-old ex-prostitute who signed all her parole reports to O'Sullivan as her 'faithful child,' but the mother–daughter relationship between these two was often strained. O'Sullivan arranged for her to be sent to as prison-like an atmosphere as possible, employing her as a domestic on an island in Muskoka, a truly isolated place, far away from corrupting city influences. The former prisoner continually talked of her loneliness, her fatigue, and the swarms of mos-quitoes. 'All you can see every place you look is islands.' She also found the job of cooking and cleaning for a family of ten, with only one other servant to work with, to be endless and tiring. 'Every place I go,' she wrote, 'I seem to have such a lot of dirt to clean ... I don't seem to ever get rested,' she continued, 'I always feel sleepy I don't know why I go to bed pretty early & never get up before half past 7.' With disarming and childlike openness, she listed her daily experiences in minute detail, even mentioning a time she cut her finger, which her employers treated with Listerine. She later described a rash on her hand. O'Sullivan showed her concern by having Dr King prescribe an ointment for it, and had it mailed up to Muskoka.

Despite her confinement on a secluded island, Claudia tried to make her life as unfettered as possible. The one thing that the former convict made the best of was the outdoors, and the freedom from enclosure and cells. Her employer gave her a bathing suit, and she soon took vivacious delight in spending her recreational time in it and doing housework outside clad in her new costume as much as possible, going fishing and even doing the washing in it by the riverside. O'Sullivan countered with some concern, ostensibly about her spending too much time close to the water. 'Muskoka lakes are notoriously treacherous,' she warned the girl, but it was clear that she did not like the idea of the parolee parading about so scantily clad. O'Sullivan was sure that she was proud of her new bathing suit, but did she remember to attend to her prayers? But after donning a grim uniform for so many months, Claudia was determined to wear her cheerful bathing suit as much as she could.

Soon her reports became more obtuse, and hinted, sometimes tauntingly, at less childlike activities. She boasted to O'Sullivan that a wealthy young man from a neighbouring island had taken to rowing her about, while she sported her cherished bathing costume. But O'Sullivan was not to worry, Claudia assured her, because her gentleman caller came highly recommended from a respectable family. Furthermore, the girl who worked with her often came along to chaperone (but not always, in fact maybe only once, if at all). She was a Salvation Army girl, who was 'always talking about God' and was 'always singing hymns' and 'playing a small harp,' no doubt serenading the young couple with prayers as they went rowing down the river (on the admittedly rare occasions when she did accompany them). O'Sullivan was not impressed. 'Under no consideration would I go alone boating with any man.' The entire Mercer 'family' continued to pray for her, O'Sullivan wrote, and suggested that she do more of the same herself. Claudia's last letter was full of similarly 'innocent' news that seemed calculated less to delight and more to subtly torment the superintendent. There was a distinct element of hostility underlying this mother–daughter relationship. In her final letter, sensing that her parole was soon over, Claudia inquired, 'Mrs. O'Sullivan may I ask you how long I have to report?' Apparently not any longer, because the letters stopped.[104]

Other former prisoners sincerely wished to extend the emotional bond they had with the superintendent. Matilda C wrote the superintendent about how busy she was at her new job in Montreal, and hoped that she would extend her regards to O'Sullivan's 'lovely family,' whom she apparently got to know well during her stay in prison. O'Sullivan responded with news about her son's marriage and her recent vacation. She promised to come and visit her when she next travelled to Montreal. These letters could well have been written by two long-time friends.[105] Ethel B wrote O'Sullivan, asking her if she could come and stay with her for a while, since she was very lonely. O'Sullivan responded that that would be against regulations, but enclosed 'a little Xmas card similar to those given here ... I shall always be glad to hear from you,' she concluded, 'and hope your next letter will not be so despondent.'[106]

O'Sullivan complained many times that the sentences at Mercer were not nearly long enough. She despaired over the fact that the average sentence was for only six months and twenty-eight days.[107] But she also recognized that parole would give her a chance to exercise more influence over many prisoners than she could in prison, by giving them an incentive to give up their bad habits, particularly alcohol.[108] She saw prisoners, even the habitual drunkards and recidivists, as valuable, capable people who 'usually manifest a desire to reform.'[109] Becoming a surrogate mother was not only a way for O'Sullivan to offer these women some affection, but was an attempt, on her part, to establish a bond with them. She hoped that she could exercise a reformatory influence that would extend beyond their brief period of incarceration and parole. It was difficult for O'Sullivan to let go, but usually not so hard for the inmates. The mother–daughter relationship, so beautifully acted out by both sides for a time, would inevitably come to a close.

Conclusion

The warden–inmate relationship was far from ideal, but apart from being a vehicle for creating order within the prison, it existed for other reasons. For, even when wardens failed to measure up to their own standards, when their physical weakness became apparent during attacks, or when their absolute power was diluted by parole, convicts, at least begrudgingly, respected them for their character and tenacity. Through their unstinting efforts, wardens won a small measure of unconditional love from the convicts. The respect that each warden earned brought not only order but also a measure of civility to the prison. The compelling personalities, sad circumstances, and personal appeal of many of the inmates often fascinated and charmed the wardens and frequently motivated them to help convicts when they could, and when it came to disciplinary matters, to be a little forgiving. As Peter Oliver observed, 'Neglect and a sense of hopelessness, however, did not constitute the whole story. In some important ways, achievements were made in the penal enterprise which rebounded to the benefit of all, and there were many examples, some of which became institutionalized, of benevolence, humanity, and efficiency.'[110] The warden–prisoner relationship, although often fraught with difficulties and misunderstandings, also demonstrated that the prison experience was not entirely dehumanizing. Even though the prison environment was a harsh one, there still remained some room for kindness in that otherwise dreadful place.

NOTES

* I first attended one of Peter Oliver's history classes as a child, accompanying my mother who was Professor Oliver's student. Some years later, Peter Oliver became my history professor, too, and since that time graciously advised me throughout my studies in the field. This essay is based upon my doctoral thesis, 'Us Poor Devils': Prison Life and Culture in Ontario: 1874–1914,' Department of History, University of Toronto 2000. I thank my thesis supervisor, Professor Jim Phillips, for his many years of patient guidance as my thesis supervisor. I also thank the members of my thesis committee: Professors Ian Radforth, Carolyn Strange, and Peter Oliver. I also thank the Department of History at the University of Toronto and the Social Sciences and Humanities Research Council for their financial support during my years as a graduate student.

1 See the pioneering work of Richard B. Splane, *Social Welfare in Ontario: 1791–1893, A Study of Public Welfare Administration* (Toronto: University of Toronto Press 1971). For the classic interpretation of British prison administration, see Leon Radzinowicz and Roger Hood, *The Emergence of Penal Pol-*

icy in Victorian and Edwardian England (Oxford: Clarendon Press 1990). For the origins of the modern prison system, see J.M. Beattie, *Crime and the Courts in England, 1660–1800* (Oxford: Clarendon Press 1986). See also, David Garland, *Punishment and Welfare: A History of Penal Strategies* (Brookfield, VT: Gower 1985), and Garland, *Punishment and Modern Society: A Study in Social Theory* (Chicago: University of Chicago Press 1900). For a Marxist analysis, see Dario Melossi and Massimo Pavarini, *The Prison and the Factory: Origins of the Penitentiary System*, trans. Glynis Cousin (London: Macmillan Press 1981). For revisionist histories that have much to say about the founders of the modern prison, see Michel Foucault, *Discipline and Punish: The Birth of the Prison*, trans. Alan Sheridan (New York: Vintage Books 1979); Michael Ignatieff, *A Just Measure of Pain: The Penitentiary in the Industrial Revolution, 1750–1850* (London: Penguin Books 1975); David J. Rothman, *The Discovery of the Asylum: Social Order and Disorder in the New Republic*, rev. ed. (Boston: Little, Brown 1990). For a re-evaluation of the revisionist analysis, see Michael Ignatieff, 'State, Civil Society and Total Institutions: A Critique of Recent Social Histories of Punishment,' in Stanley Cohen and Andrew Scull, eds., *Social Control and the State* (London: Basil Blackwell 1983).

2 Peter Oliver, *'Terror to Evil-Doers': Prisons and Punishments in Nineteenth-Century Ontario* (Toronto: Osgoode Society for Canadian Legal History and University of Toronto Press 1998).

3 For an account of the brutality at Central Prison as well as a history of the institution, see Peter Oliver, 'A Terror to Evil-Doers: The Central Prison and the "Criminal Class" in Late Nineteenth-Century Ontario,' in R. Hall et al., eds., *Patterns of the Past: Interpreting Ontario's History* (Toronto: Dundurn Press 1988). See also Joseph Berkovits, 'Prisoners for Profit: Convict Labour in the Ontario Central Prison, 1874–1915,' in Jim Phillips, Tina Loo, and Susan Lewthwaite, eds., *Essays in the History of Canadian Law*, vol. 5, *Crime and Criminal Justice* (Toronto: Osgoode Society for Canadian History and University of Toronto Press 1994). See also Rainer Beahre, 'Prison as Factory, Convict as Worker: A Study of the Mid-Victorian St John Penitentiary, 1841–1880,' in *Essays in the History of Canadian Law*, vol. 5. For accounts of Mercer Reformatory, see Carolyn Strange, 'The Velvet Glove: Maternalistic Reform at the Andrew Mercer Ontario Reformatory for Females' (MA thesis, University of Ottawa 1983), 84. See also Strange, '"The Criminal and Fallen of Their Sex": The Establishment of Canada's First Women's Prison, 1874–1901,' *Canadian Journal of Women and the Law* 1, no. 1 (1985). For a more positive portrayal of life at Mercer Reformatory, see Peter Oliver, '"To Govern by Kindness": The First Two Decades of the Mercer Reformatory for

Women,' in Jim Phillips et al., eds., *Essays in the History of Canadian Law*, vol. 5, *Crime and Criminal Justice* (Toronto: University of Toronto Press and Osgoode Society 1994). For a depiction of life at Kingston Penitentiary, see W.A. Calder, 'Convict Life in Canadian Federal Penitentiaries, 1867–1900,' in Louis A. Knafla, ed., *Crime and Criminal Justice in Europe and Canada*, rev. ed. (Waterloo: Wilfrid Laurier University Press 1985). For an analysis of all three institutions within the context of the administration of the criminal justice system, see Oliver, 'Terror to Evil-Doers.'

4 By warden, I also mean superintendent. At Central Prison, the warden was later called a superintendent. At Mercer Reformatory, the head of the institution was always called a superintendent. Wardens may have played many roles in the prison, but they were not the only important actors. Guards, the prison surgeon, the prison inspector, visiting missionaries, and the prisoners' own families and friends all made a significant contribution to the prison dynamic, and each group, in varying degrees, shared a different dynamic amongst themselves and with each other. The warden's relationship with his or her staff, for an example, is a separate topic. This article will only focus on the wardens' specific relationship with the prisoners, however.

5 Roughly 50 per cent of the prisoners in the three institutions were under the age of thirty. See Kingston Penitentiary, *Annual Reports*. In fact, 57.4 per cent of the inmates at Central Prison and over 61.7 per cent of the inmates at Mercer Reformatory were under the age of thirty. Oliver, 'Terror to Evil-Doers,' 450.

6 Central Prison, [CP] Case File [CF] #23040. This prisoner was requesting a parole recommendation.

7 Two of the wardens of this era, Michael Lavell of Kingston Penitentiary and John Gilmore of Central Prison, were also medical doctors, providing a masculine parallel to the nurturing model offered by their maternalistic counterparts. Lavell was surgeon at Kingston Penitentiary prior to becoming warden, and after his retirement, is remembered for certifying Louis Riel, then under sentence of death, as mentally competent. See entry on Lavell by Peter Oliver, *Dictionary of Canadian Biography*, vol. 13 (Toronto: University of Toronto Press 1994), 580–2. See also entry by H. Pearson Gundy on Kingston Warden John Creighton in the *Dictionary of Canadian Biography*, vol. 11 (Toronto: University of Toronto Press 1982), 216–17.

8 For a detailed statistical analysis of the population profile of both Central Prison and Mercer Reformatory, see Oliver, 'Terror to Evil-Doers,' chap. 11.

9 Mercer Reformatory could hold some 200 inmates, but did not operate at full capacity. At Mercer Reformatory, Central Prison, and Kingston Peni-

tentiary, the numbers of inmates fluctuated from year to year during this period, so any number given is a rough estimate. I have also been guided by population figures on Central Prison and Mercer Reformatory given by Splane, *Social Welfare in Ontario*, 180–1.

10 Mercer Reformatory, [MR] Case File [CF] #2159. Ada V, a resident of Salem, Ontario, was sentenced to one year and ten months on 22 June 1896 from the Police Magistrate's Court in Guelph under a charge of vagrancy.

11 Annual Report, [AR] MR, 1898, 7.

12 See for example, AR MR, 1890, 102.

13 It has been said that laundry work was the hardest work of all in prison. Philip Priestley, *Victorian Prison Lives: English Prison Biography, 1830–1914* (New York: Methuen 1985), 141.

14 Kingston Penitentiary, [KP] Annual Report [AR] of Inspector Moylan, 1881, ix–xv.

15 Oliver, 'Terror to Evil-Doers,' 313.

16 Indeed, prisoners at Kingston Penitentiary, for example, were typically not even allowed to speak to their lawyers without the warden or a member of the warden's staff being present. See Warden's Letter Book [WLB], 11 August 1901, where Warden Platt writes to the deputy minister of justice: 'The rule observed here is to allow no interview with convicts except in my presence or in presence of an officer selected by me.'

17 See Erving Goffman, *Asylums: Essays on the Social Situation of Mental Patients and Other Inmates* (London: Penguin Books 1977).

18 Convicts at Central Prison and Mercer Reformatory frequently referred to the children of their respective wardens by name.

19 CP CF #16963, 15883.

20 CP CF #11514, 13 July 1891.

21 Ibid.

22 KP WLB, 15 November 1883.

23 Unlike the violent atmosphere that prevailed in American institutions, particularly as described in W. David Lewis, *From Newgate to Dannemora: The Rise of the Penitentiary in New York, 1796–1848* (Ithaca, NY: Cornell University Press 1965).

24 KP WLB, 1 December 1897.

25 KP WLB, 18 May 1876, Warden Creighton to Inspector Moylan.

26 KP WLB, 6 February 1896. The prisoner was to be flogged and to be placed in the prison of isolation.

27 Lewis, *From Newgate*, 88–9.

28 Brockway, *Fifty Years of Prison Service*, 36–40.

29 AR KP, 1876, Inspector Moylan, 10.

30 Inspector Douglas Stewart, chairman of the Committee on Prison Discipline, paper given at the National Prison Congress, October 1905. Appendix to AR KP, 1905, 10–11.

31 *Manitoba Free Press*, 14 and 16 April 1917. The reporters were reflecting on a whipping they had witnessed at Central Prison many years ago, probably in the 1880s.

32 CP CF #22366.

33 CP CF #16787. Inspector Noxon authorised Warden Gilmour to apply only ten strokes at a time until the prisoner's refusal to work came to an end. It is not clear whether the R.H.W. wrote the letter to the warden before or after the strapping.

34 KP WLB, 28 September 1891, Acting Warden Sullivan to Inspector Moylan. Guard Birmingham's sworn statement of the assault appeared in 22 September 1891.

35 KP, Punishment Register, 20 March 1890.

36 KP WLB, 21 November 1878, Warden Creighton to Z.A. Lash, assistant minister of justice. Creighton was requesting an early release for the convict due to his poor health.

37 KP WLB, Warden Metcalfe to Inspector Stewart, 31 January 1898. Three convicts, including the incorrigible Elmer B were about to receive twenty-four lashes each.

38 KP WLB, 2 March 1876, Warden Creighton to Inspector. Creighton does not reveal whether the inmate was placed back into the triangle to receive his final dozen lashes.

39 Estelle B. Freedman, *Their Sisters' Keepers: Women's Prison Reform in America, 1830–1930* (Ann Arbor: University of Michigan Press 1981), 71.

40 Dr Aikins, the surgeon at Central Prison, had argued against the punishment of bread and water for lengthy periods of time at the Royal Commission investigating Warden Massie. Ontario, *Sessional Papers*, 1886, 'Royal Commission Appointed to Enquire into Certain Charges Against the Warden of the Central Prison and into the Management of the Said Prison.'

41 There is some information available that suggests that scholarly research on Mick's life might be worthwhile. A Wikipedia entry on Mick cites evidence that she was killed in 1925 by escaping prisoners at an institution she later worked at, the Toronto Municipal Jail Farm. See 'Margaret Mick,' *Wikipedia: The Free Encyclopedia*, 6 December 2007, retrieved 12 April 2008 from http://en.wikipedia.org/w/index.php?title=Margaret_Mick&oldid=176087193. The Wikipedia entry has links to an entry about Mick on the 'Officer Down Memorial Page,' www.odmp.org/canada/officer/729-jail-matron-mrs.-margaret-mick, as well as a link to *Debates of the Senate (Han-*

sard), 1st Session, 38th Parliament, vol. 142, Issue 70, 14 June 2005, where Senator Lorna Milne makes a speech about the life of Mick, naming her the first female peace officer to be killed in the line of duty in Canada.

42 MR CF #3771, 1910.

43 Nevertheless, on many other occasions, the superintendent would not hesitate to order corporal punishment on any particular inmate. The superintendent was not opposed to corporal punishment, she was just not in favour of it when she felt that it would do no good.

44 Blake McKelvey, *American Prisons: A History of Good Intentions* (Montclair, NJ: Patterson Smith 1977), 55, 74–5.

45 CP CF #9282, 28 September 1898.

46 CP CF #25071, 27 September 1911.

47 CP CF #14321, 1 August 1895.

48 CP CF #13880, 1884–5.

49 KP WLB, 15 December 1877, Warden Creighton to Z.A. Lash, deputy minister of justice, Ottawa. This convict had an older brother in the Central Prison.

50 CP CF #18830, September 1902.

51 CP CF #11026, February–June 1891.

52 AR KP, Inspector Moylan, 1881, xxiii–xxiv.

53 AR KP, Inspector Moylan, 1885, xi–xii.

54 AR KP, Warden Lavell, 1886, 6.

55 AR KP, Inspector Moylan, 1885, xiii.

56 'Our Penal Institutions: Article IV,' *The Labour Union*, 10 March 1883.

57 KP WLB, 23 April 1896, Warden Lavell to Inspector Stewart. Lavell tried to apologise for the inmate.

58 KP WLB, 21 April 1882.

59 KP, Convict's Letter Register, 20 June 1905.

60 KP WLB, 15 May, 9 May 1899.

61 CP CF # 13754, 14336, 14250, 13719, 19276, 19465, 8095, 13682, 24424, 13788, to name but a few.

62 CP CF #20108, August 1904.

63 CP CF #26225, April 1913.

64 CP CF #7710, May 1886.

65 CP CF #25060, August 1912.

66 CP CF #16207, December 1898.

67 MR CF #3052. Mary C was twenty-one years old and convicted at the Belleville Police Court on 11 March 1904 of prostitution for a term of six months.

68 The warden or superintendent in each institution would personally read most of the incoming correspondence, ostensibly for security reasons. His

or her deputies or occasionally the guards would read the mail when their superiors were ill or out of town. MR CF #3658. Maud K was a thirty-eight-year-old domestic and had been sentenced to a six-month term to Mercer from Bracebridge for the crime of 'obscene and abusive language.'

69 MR CF #2978, December 1903. Prisoner Elizabeth C was twenty-three years old and was sentenced for two years less a day for child abandonment. She was Cree. O'Sullivan had her working in her personal apartment.

70 MR CF #4112.

71 MR CF #3093, May 1905.

72 CP CF unknown. Prisoner Alexander O, received 9 November 1889, released on pardon 24 February 1890.

73 CP CF #11202, 12935, and 13379.

74 MR CF #3389.

75 MR CF #3835, Superintendent O'Sullivan to Dominion Parole Officer, 19 November 1912.

76 CP CF #15436 and 15115.

77 While no great fan of the patriarchal system, Jacobs holds it in grudging esteem and in particular laments the emergence of 'emotionally detached management' and 'detached bureaucratic administration' in the prison service. James B. Jacobs, *Stateville: The Penetentiary in Mass Society* (Chicago: University of Chicago Press 1977), 73–104.

78 CP CF #15518, February 1899.

79 CP CF #19063, May 1904.

80 CP CF #15246, December 1898. For another war of words with a sentencing judge, see also CF #21677.

81 CP CF #21403, February–March 1907. The convict finally was granted a ticket of leave.

82 CP CF #17501, 22 October 1901.

83 CP CF #23593, 15 August 1911.

84 CP CF #21360, February 1907.

85 KP WLB, 23 January 1879, Warden Creighton to Z.A. Lash, deputy minister of justice, Ottawa.

86 KP WLB, 3 March 1879, Remission Report of Warden Creighton.

87 KP WLB, 13 July 1891, Warden Lavell to Inspector Moylan.

88 KP WLB, 28 May 1898, Warden Metcalfe to Hon. David Mills, minister of justice, Ottawa.

89 KP WLB, 1 October 1877, Warden Creighton to Z.A. Lash, deputy minister of justice, Ottawa.

90 KP WLB, 6 March 1879, Warden Creighton to Z.A. Lash, deputy minister of justice, Ottawa.

91 KP WLB, 9 October 1882. Remission Form signed by Warden Creighton.
92 KP WLB, 19 July 1900, Warden Platt to David Mills, minister of justice.
93 KP WLB, 1 June 1900, Warden Platt to John McIntyre, QC, Kingston, Ontario.
94 KP WLB, 27 March 1899.
95 AR KP, 1881, Inspector Moylan, xvi–xvii.
96 AR KP, 1891, Inspector Moylan, xvi–xvii.
97 AR KP, 1902, Warden Platt, 26.
98 KP WLB, 6 October 1899, Warden Platt to G. Martin, barrister at Law, Chatham, Ontario.
99 KP WLB, 11 August 1901, Warden Platt to the deputy minister of justice, Ottawa.
100 KP WLB, 13 November 1890, Warden Lavell to Inspector Moylan.
101 MR CF #3300. Letters 1 January, 15 January 1909. This prisoner was convicted at the age of seventeen for 'vagrancy.'
102 Before her release on parole, Convict May O was required to write a and sign a pledge to, among other things, 'promise to report once a month to the Superintendent.' MR CF #3938.
103 MR CF #3451. Ruth W was sentenced on 12 December 1907 to a term of six months as well as a fine and costs for vagrancy.
104 MR CF #3583. Correspondence from July 1910 to December 1911.
105 MR CF #3505, March–September, 1909.
106 Ethel B alias Jane Smith was sentenced by Police Court, Ottawa, 27 June 1908, for a term of six months for vagrancy. She was twenty-three years old and pregnant. She gave birth to a female child while in prison, and contrary to the superintendent's advice, did not agree to give up her child but took her back with her to Ottawa. O'Sullivan remarked that Ethel was 'somewhat weak-minded ... I know that she cannot look after herself.' At the time of writing her letter, Ethel was in a house of industry at Perth, Ontario. MR CF #3514, 13 January 1910.
107 AR MR, Superintendent O'Sullivan 1902, 73.
108 MR CF #3661. O'Sullivan argued in the case of Prisoner Alice P that parole would help her cure herself of drink better than prison.
109 AR MR, Superintendent O'Sullivan, 1901, 48.
110 Oliver, 'Terror to Evil-Doers,' xxvi.

3

'Perverts a Menace': The Development of the Criminal Sexual Psychopath Offence, 1948

PATRICK BRODE

In 1948, the Canadian Parliament enacted one of the most remarkable criminal statutes of the twentieth century. In a piece of legislation that contained several amendments to the Criminal Code, the 1948 act defined an entirely new kind of offender – the 'criminal sexual psycho-path.' These were individuals who, through a 'course of misconduct in sexual matters,' had displayed an inability to control their sexual im-pulses, and as a result were liable to 'inflict loss, injury, pain or other evil' on another person.[1] Once identified by proper psychiatric evi-dence, offenders could be subject to an indeterminate sentence and, in addition to disciplinary punishment, were to receive 'reformative treat-ment.' For the first time, the Criminal Code embodied the idea that an offender could have a medical as well as a criminal problem. It fol-lowed that these persons required medical care in addition to simple incarceration. There was general support for this change. As Progres-sive Conservative justice critic John Diefenbaker remarked, not only would this 'have the effect of punishing wrongdoers and protecting the public at large ... it will restore many of these wrongdoers, after treat-ment, to a place in society.' But above all, this was timely legislation, for 'this provision represents the first action on the part of the parliament of Canada to meet a type of offence that is becoming general, a type of offence that creates fear in the minds of mothers and fathers ...'[2]

This was legislation based upon fear, but was it based upon reality? This essay will examine the origins of the sexual psychopath laws and what various trends and uncertainties of the post-war world led up to this legislation. It is a lesson in how criminal law standards can trace their development to sources as diverse as medicine, journalism, the influence of other jurisdictions, and public opinion.

There have been few examinations of how the sexual psychopath laws originated. One writer notes that the legislation resulted from a 'mounting moral panic,' but provides no further discussion of the foundation for such a significant change.[3] In his monumental study of the history of homosexuality in Canada, Gary Kinsman suggests that the 1948 act was intended to 'regulate homosexuality' and that 'this legislation participated in constructing homosexuality as a criminal sexual danger.'[4] Kinsman discusses some of the sources of such a repressive change, he cites numerous American state laws that were passed on this subject, and points to media focus on violent crimes by men against children that seemed to give a sense of urgency to the amendment. Elise Chenier has written a thorough account of the medical and psychiatric developments that led many to conclude that the bill would ultimately prove to be a worthwhile remedy.[5] However, it is also useful to have an understanding of the concerns of the time and the immediate incidents that led to the creation of a law that sought to understand 'deviant' male behaviour as conduct that should be subject to medical regulation and correction.

Prior to 1930, most concern with 'abnormal' sexual behaviour centred on females who, either as prostitutes or cross-dressers, defied the norms of society. With the avowed intention of authorities to stamp out the 'social evil' of prostitution, it was women who engaged in illicit sex who were the focus of campaigns for social purity.[6] Periodically there were hysterical press allegations (invariably unsubstantiated) that there existed a vast 'white slave' network selling respectable young women into forced prostitution. This concern for vulnerable women, as well as a fervent evangelism, resulted in the social purity movement of the 1880s, that made the seduction of a young woman a criminal offence. Moral panics had a tendency to come and go, and from 1909–14 Canada underwent another wave of dread of 'this awful traffic in procuring the daughters of our goodly homes for the vile and shameless social evil ...'[7] The safety of young women and their potential contamination was a shrill but sporadic concern.

By the 1930s criminologists and journalists became increasingly focused on male sexual abnormality and its consequences. All men who deviated from accepted sexual practices were considered a potential threat to children and to the social order itself. As Estelle Freedman observes, 'the male sexual deviant became the subject of special attention, particularly if he was inadequately masculine (the effeminate homosexual) or hypermasculine (the sexual psychopath). Both categories of deviant males were thought to attack children, thus simultaneously threatening sexual innocence, gender roles, and the social order.'[8] The male homosexual was considered to be an aggressor and a potential predator to children. According to a 1924 report from Indiana State Prison, 'The sexual perverts are at any rate an exceedingly dangerous and demoralizing class which should be permanently isolated to prevent their mingling with others.'[9]

From 1937 to 1940, American newspapers and magazines tended to sensationalise any incident of child molestation or rape and thereby concluded that there was a vast contagion of crime being perpetrated by deviants. In 1937, J. Edgar Hoover, the director of the Federal Bureau of Investigation, called for a 'War on the Sex Criminal' or the 'sex fiend, the most loathsome of all the vast army of crime, [he] has become a sinister threat to the safety of American childhood and womanhood.'[10] Isolated incidents such as two or more murders of children in succession could result in public hysteria and the passage of a state law. Michigan passed the first law concerning sexual psychopaths in 1937.[11] Any person convicted of a sex crime (rape or child molestation) could be ordered to undergo psychiatric tests, and if found to be a 'psychopathic personality' could be committed to a state hospital for an indeterminate period. As one commentator on this new law stated, 'Though the need is real, it is doubtful whether there is an actual increase in crimes of this type. Any apparent increase may be explained by publicity. The notoriety attached to each new offence has produced a vociferous agitation for new and stringent laws'[12] A similar statute was enacted in Illinois in 1938. One observer felt that this 'hasty legislation was a result of present popular uneasiness on the subject (of sex crimes) and popular belief that the danger is growing. Such a belief arises periodically as a result of lurid newspaper fanning.'[13] Prior to the Second World War, five states – Michigan, Illinois, Ohio, California, and Minnesota – passed sexual psychopath laws. All of this was done in the absence of any reliable statistical indication that sex-related offences were increasing.

There is no evidence that during the late 1930s Canada was experiencing the same level of anxiety over alleged deviant behaviour. There could be local outbreaks of moral panic, as occurred in Oshawa,

Ontario, in 1927, when H.W. Elliott, the superintendent of the Children's Aid Society was charged with molesting boys in his care. When he appealed his conviction, the Crown attorney wrote to the deputy attorney general, 'I do certainly hope that you will be successful in the appeal, as the public opinion in the City and locality is very much riled.'[14] Such panics were restricted in their impact and were usually of limited duration. Parliament rarely considered the Criminal Code, and no proposals were made to control sex-related offences.

The first concerns about dealing with the psychiatric problems of prisoners surfaced in 1938, in the Royal Commission to Investigate the Penal System (the Archambault Commission). That commission recommended that instead of simply warehousing all prisoners, there should be a comprehensive system of classification. Those inmates with identifiable psychiatric problems should be separated. Still, even the Archambault Report could not envision any rehabilitation, and it proposed that habitual offenders be segregated, for 'the purpose of the prison is neither punitive nor reformative but primarily segregation from society.'[15] With the coming of the Second World War, no action was taken on the report. Indeed, media fascination with sex crimes fell off during the war years (even though in the U.S. the rate of those crimes rose during the war) as journalists concentrated on the international conflict.

In the immediate post-war period, interest was renewed in sex crimes as a social problem. A variety of factors combined to focus the public mind on the supposed threat of the sexual psychopath, to make the 1948 act possible. In both the United States and Canada there was an impulse to return to 'normalcy,' with men going back to their former jobs, and women forsaking the factories and returning to domestic life. The onset of the Cold War, with its emphasis on cultural conformity, only served to intensify, 'efforts to control deviant behavior. Nonconformity – whether political, social or sexual – became associated with threats to national security.'[16] Montreal was a prime example of a city that had tolerated a high level of prostitution and illegal gambling during the war years. However, in 1946, Montreal residents formed a 'Concerned Citizens League' to crush the vice trade.[17] But it was the effect that homosexuals could have on vulnerable women and children that gathered the most publicity, and during the post-war years a new sex crime panic began to gather momentum.

This was brought about by a series of well publicised attacks on children. Six-year-old Donnie Goss was killed in Calgary in July 1946. Before his killer was executed, he also confessed to murdering an eleven year-old in Vancouver.[18] Winnipeg had been undergoing a nightmare since the fall of 1945. Three little boys had been assaulted by a pedophile there, and in January 1946, the same individual killed thirteen-year-old Roy McGregor. Winnipeg police reported that, 'sex perverts are being brought to police headquarters for grilling.'[19] The presumption was that the murderer had to be a homosexual. However, all suspects were released for want of evidence. In September 1946 another boy was slain, and Winnipeg Police still maintained that the killer had to be a 'sex pervert.'[20] In Winnipeg, any man who had any record of a gross indecency conviction for having had consensual sex with another man could expect to be considered a suspect in any attack on a child. Neither these newspaper reports nor the wider public discussion made any real distinction between homosexuals, pedophiles, and sexual psychopaths. All of them were lumped into a larger group of 'sex maniacs' who were abnormal and therefore a danger. In 1947, it was reported that a molester in the Maritimes was caught after having attacked several children. One mother pleaded, 'Within a few years the same man, or someone like him, will be free again to repeat the same crime. Is there nothing that can be done to protect us?' Early in 1945, nine-year-old John Benson was murdered in Montreal. The immediate reaction of the Montreal police was 'to question 1,500 previously convicted sex perverts in the Montreal area.'[21]

One of the most shocking incidents occurred in Windsor, Ontario, where a serial killer emerged shortly after Victory in Europe day. One man was attacked and two were butchered to death near public parks. The last attack was against a soldier recently returned from overseas and, according to the coroner, the victim had likely bled to death as the killer watched. A few days later, a note was scrawled in a public washroom warning that a woman would be the next victim. The murders were so horrific that they were widely reported, and the *Globe and Mail* featured the headline 'Maniacal Knife Killer Threatens Girl to be Fourth Windsor Victim.'[22] According to the local newspaper, the killer must be 'someone with a perverted mind' and a 'blood-lusting maniac'[23] who was a threat to all women and children. There was a massive, but futile roundup of all derelicts and unusual characters in an effort to find this 'Slasher.' After August 1945 the terror abated, but returned in July 1946 when the attacks began anew. One man staggered into police headquarters with an ice pick embedded in his back and another was stabbed and almost killed in a park. Once again, all the victims were men. It slowly came to the police that these attacks were being directed against men, and specifically against homosexuals. When he was finally apprehended, the murderer, Ronald Sears, confessed that he had been molested by a pedophile when he was nine and he had resolved to conduct a one-man crusade against homosexuals.

While no women or children had been at risk during this murder spree, the newspaper reaction to the killings was instructive. In a series of articles the *Windsor Daily Star* proclaimed that sexual offences against women and children were commonplace and little was being done to stop them. After doing its best to whip up a sensation, the newspaper quietly conceded that the real number of sex related crimes were few, and that they had only been able to identify twelve such offences.[24] Despite the statistical fact that assaults against women and children were uncommon, and that there was no accusation that any homosexuals had committed the attacks, the newspaper launched into a vitriolic crusade against homosexuals. Gay gathering areas were 'hot beds of sex perversion' and the favoured site for the 'stabbings which have come to be part of the habitual pastime of certain of the degenerates.'[25] On 8 July 1946, the newspaper ran a particularly chilling editorial:

'Perverts a Menace'
How about gathering in the sex perverts in Windsor as one definite step toward ending these crimes of violence? If that were done, people could feel more at ease. As long as these perverts are allowed to run free, they are a menace to everyone. One suspect is under arrest, but others are at large. With so many persons being slashed, Windsor will have another couple of murders on the sheet before long. To save human life, it would be advisable to round up all the perverts and hold them for observation.[26]

This corrosive rhetoric would continue throughout the course of the Slasher hysteria. The following day the *Star* suggested:

With the arrest of the youth accused of five stabbings, two of them fatal, the task of the authorities is far from ended. There must be a concerted drive to round up 'queer' persons of the sort who were responsible for the young man's plight. And we're not too ready to believe that the public would object to some good old-fashioned strong arm tactics in the process.[27]

The extreme homophobic nature of these pronouncements is all the more remarkable given that homosexuals had been the victims, not the perpetrators, of the Windsor Slasher attacks. Yet, with an almost

Gestapo-like enthusiasm, the newspaper was calling for the elimina-
tion of those who did not sexually conform. The ultimate effect of these
editorials is difficult to gauge, but they did seem to reflect the view that
all homosexuals were a dangerous element in society that should be
put away for the protection of the innocent.

This attitude was not limited to the newspapers. Sears' trial and sentence of death was carried by the press across Canada and there were
several requests that he be shown mercy. The one feature of the case
that caught the public's attention was that Sears himself had been the
supposed victim of a pedophile when he was a child. This had 'contam-
inated' him, and caused him to fight back against those who had vio-
lated his innocence. One writer from London, Ontario, best exemplified
the popular attitude towards this serial killer of homosexuals when she
advised the minister of justice, 'In my opinion they (homosexuals) need
stabbing.'[28] The Windsor Slasher case was perhaps the most glaring
instance of the tensions that could be raised in the post-war sex crimes
panic. Moreover, it was a panic that was fed by the media. John Loughery observed the same phenomenon in the United States, saying, that
'the press had adopted a calculated, inflammatory stance out of proportion to the known facts about modern levels of crime. Even more
important, they note, the terms sexual psychopath, sex criminal, deviant, and homosexual came to be used almost interchangeably in discussing the situation.'[29]

The renewal of the sex crime panic is all the more unusual, considering that in the United States, arrests for rape and sexually related
offences fell after the war. In retrospect, the late 1940s were one of the
safest and most peaceful in urban American history.[30] Neither did
Canadian cities report any increase in sex-related crimes. In the two
years following the war years, the rates of arrest for crimes such as
indecent assault, rape, and indecent acts declined.[31] The annual reports
of chiefs of police, which would surely have reported a noticeable
increase in attacks on women and children, do not deal with this topic
or cite any such concerns. Vancouver police chief W.H. Mulligan had
reported a significant increase in crime during the war years, which by
1947 had declined significantly. In Toronto, the chief attributed a more
peaceful society to the easy availability of jobs. The chiefs usually
expressed dismay over the lifting of wartime restrictions on gasoline,
which lead to substantial increases in traffic fatalities. But there is no
mention of any plague of sex crimes. The Dominion Bureau of Statistics
reported in 1947 that the rate of indictable or serious offences had only

increased 1 per cent from the rate in 1938. The increase in population over the same period was fourteen per cent.[32]

Despite the reality that there was no surge in crimes against women or children, the media's fascination with singular cases helped generate a tidal wave of concern. In addition to this, Canadians were avid readers of the American press. In 1948, the *Saturday Evening Post* featured a lead article entitled 'What Can We Do About Sex Crimes?' which proclaimed that sex offences, both reported and unreported, were sweeping the country. According to this inflammatory report, America was under siege by men who 'cannot control the dark impulses which are latent in all of us' and that 'at least tens of thousands of them are loose in this country today.' The magazine seemed a bit at a loss as to how to answer its own question but listed castration or exile as possibilities. One thread that ran through the article was the urgent need to identify psychopaths as soon as possible and segregate them.[33] In July 1947, FBI director J. Edgar Hoover published an article entitled 'How Safe is Your Daughter?' in the *American* magazine. The introductory photograph to the article featured a trio of little girls fleeing from a menacing male hand and a quote from Hoover that 'the nation's women and children will never be secure ... so long as degenerates run wild.'[34] Ironically, these views were being propagated by a man whose fondness for cross-dressing and homosexuals would (had they been publicly known) have made him one of the degenerates he sought to entrap.

In Canada as well, the post-war years seemed ones of anxiety instead of relief. Newspapers reported growing international tensions, and that the Soviets would soon have atomic weapons. 'The Atom Bomb Race is Officially Open' the *Ottawa Journal* gloomily reported in 1948.[35] The Canadian press also mimicked the sex crime panic articles of the American media. In July 1947, *Maclean's* magazine ran an article entitled 'The Truth about Sex Criminals' in which it pointed to 'the growing problem of sex criminality.' The magazine advised its readers that during the war, medical officers were astounded at the number of men who had been refused enlistment because of their perversions. Obviously, this condition was far more widespread than most people were aware, and 'the truth is that sex deviates act under an overpowering compulsion. Normal people regard their acts as ugly and sordid; the psychiatrist sees them as the product of diseased, ailing minds in need of extensive treatment.' The lash and periods of confinement were no solution and, if anything, the existing prisons were hothouses for encouraging this kind of behaviour. The article cited a case in which one of the most eminent jurists in the country, Ontario chief justice J.C. McRuer, had been forced to sentence a seventeen-year-old sex offender to prison. 'If he is curable he should be treated by doctors or psychiatrists ... It is with regret that I send him to an institution where his condition will be ignored,' wrote the chief justice. The *Maclean's* article concluded by suggesting that the Criminal Code be amended to provide for indeterminate sentences where in special institutions 'half hospital, half jail' they would receive medical treatment.[36] A series of articles in the *Winnipeg Tribune* had already suggested that a medical option be pursued. They noted that there had still been no action to implement the Archambault Commission's recommendations on separating various types of prisoners. The Reverend W.R. Wood, Protestant chaplain at Stony Mountain Prison in Manitoba, declared that homosexual rings operated within the prison. Far from offering treatment, the prison was a place where 'older men prey on younger, good-looking fellows ... One after another, young irresponsibles were caught in the net, and became members of the crew.' Chaplain Wood concluded that the problem was that there was no 'scientific classification of inmates and the segregation of the various classes of offenders.'[37]

The post-war sex crime panic found its leader in a former Montreal Crown attorney, J. Alex Edmison, described as a 'former Montreal lawyer and alderman, who turned his back on a lucrative law practice to devote all his time to prison reform.'[38] After he moved to Toronto in 1947, he began to agitate for stricter laws against sex offenders and a compliant press gave him the publicity machine he needed to reach a broad audience. In a series of articles published in October 1947, the *Globe and Mail* informed the public of the imminent threat it faced from deranged sex offenders. These criminals were dramatically portrayed as a small but malevolent group who passed unnoticed among the general public, 'but they are subject to brutal impulses such as never enter the minds of ordinary men.'[39] With funding provided by Toronto's Kiwanis Club, Edmison organized the Canadian Penal Association to lobby for stricter laws to counter this threat. The resulting 'Committee on the Sex Offender' featured an impressive cross-section of officials from both enforcement and welfare branches. Supporting Edmison was Toronto's police chief, John Chisholm, as well as the deputy commissioner of penitentiaries, Dr L.P. Gendreau. Also a part of the movement was Murdoch Keith of Toronto's School of Social Work, Dr D. Kelly of the Canadian Medical Association, and D.C. Draper of the John Howard Society of Ontario. This was an impressive array of important figures, drawn not only from law enforcement but also from those agencies that hoped to treat and rehabilitate the offenders.

The Canadian Penal Association received substantial press coverage in late 1947. At the heart of Edmison's message was a warning that the current sentencing system was inadequate. He recounted to audiences how, as a Crown attorney, he had seen a man who had assaulted no less than ninety-six small boys receive only three months imprisonment and no treatment. The Canadian Penal Association's campaign was not based on any statistical rise in crime or offences against women, but on those unique and newsworthy cases that had captured the public's attention. After one speech, Edmison talked with reporters and commented, 'the situation in Windsor was admittedly serious ... it has been given a lot of publicity since the Sears case.'[40] After a series of reports on Edmison's movement, the *Globe and Mail* published a glowing endorsement:

What is required, then, is a change in the Criminal Code, which will provide for detention of proved sex deviates, to give them medical or psychiatric treatment. If this treatment is effective it will be a decided gain for society. If it is not, continued detention will remove the danger of a repetition of the offence. What would be the best and soundest method for handling this question is the goal being sought by the committee called together by Mr. Edmison. The people of Canada owe him a great deal for the initiative and energy he has shown ...[41]

Coinciding with these widely publicised reports and the media concern over a renewed sex crime menace, was the rise in public estimation of the psychiatric profession. In the era after the invention of the atomic bomb, it seemed there was little that modern science could not do. With advanced treatment methods, perhaps the sexual deviant could be changed back into a normal, conforming member of society. During the Second World War, psychiatrists had played a prominent role assisting the Canadian military. All personnel had been subject to mental testing, and homosexuals and lesbians had been counted among the 'psychiatric disorders' that rendered them subject to discharge. Significantly, instead of being labeled simply in a same-sex category, they were assigned to the more sinister category of 'psychopathic' personality.[42]

The war had been a boon to the psychiatric profession, and hundreds of doctors with no previous experience in the field were assigned to assist psychiatric casualties. Far more psychiatrists were required to attend to those traumatised by combat. After the war, there would be standardised psychiatric training in medical schools, and the number of specialists in the field would grow significantly. In the United States, Dr William Menninger, the president of the American Psychiatric Association, did his best to encourage this growth to deal with 'the formidable problems awaiting psychiatry in the postwar period ...'[43] After the experience of war, 'a faith developed that psychiatry could promote prevention by contributing toward the amelioration of social problems that allegedly fostered mental diseases.'[44] In 1947, there was an alteration to the Canadian prison system to provide for a commissioner and two deputy commissioners. Significantly, one of the deputies was Dr Louis Philippe Gendreau, formerly the chief psychiatrist at Manitoba General Hospital, and later to be a member of Edmison's committee.[45] Still, there appeared to be something self-serving about the profession's interest in these new laws, for 'since the sexual psychopath laws usually specify that the diagnosis for the court shall be made by psychiatrists, they have an economic interest in the extension of this procedure.'[46]

Almost all concerned citizens carried a faith in a better, more scientific world. In 1947, citizen groups in Edmonton and Calgary had been sending urgent petitions to Justice Minister J.L. Ilsley requesting the government to consider some means of treating and curing sex criminals.[47] To jurists and non-medical experts, it seemed that treatment was the obvious resort. Even at the time the Windsor 'Slasher' Ronald Sears was being sentenced, the trial judge felt compelled to publicly state he wished there was someplace where he could send this disturbed young man 'where [he] could be treated, and where, if possible, [he] could be cured.'[48] If the public wanted action, there was a ready example in what was being done in many of the American states. Since the end of the war, four more states had enacted sexual psychopath laws to hold sex offenders for indefinite periods. Typically, they were generated by a sensational case or cases. In 1947 there were four sexual attacks against children in Indiana, in which two of the children had been murdered. Before the year was out, the state legislature had enacted a sexual psychopath law. The diffusion of these laws in the post-war period was 'evidence of a feeling within certain segments of the public that still further measures need to be taken to "put away" sex offenders.'[49]

Whatever the merits, the Canadian Parliament was receptive to passing similar legislation. In fact, it is remarkable how little debate there was on the issue, which, for the first time, criminalised a kind of personality rather than a specific act. The first step occurred in 1947 when a category of 'habitual offender' was introduced into the Criminal Code. Justice Minister Ilsley told the House of Commons that modern psychiatry had changed the world, and 'it might be that we should construct certain institutions which would be more in the nature of hospitals than prisons, (and) staff them with psychiatrists.'[50] Both government and opposition accepted it as a given truth that there existed a class of habitual offenders that should be put away. David Croll of Toronto thought it a rude awakening to Canadians to learn that such a criminal underclass actually existed. When the first habitual offender was given an indeterminate sentence in Vancouver in 1947, the local newspaper thought this kind of sentence was long overdue.[51]

The following year, the government introduced a further series of amendments to the Criminal Code, which included a special designation for criminal sexual psychopaths. Now, any person who by a course of misconduct in sexual matters had shown 'uncontrollable desires' to the extent that he might injure others could face prison for an indeterminate period. Yet, before an individual could even be considered under this section, they first had to commit a 'triggering' offence, such as rape, indecent assault, or carnal knowledge of a child. After a person had been convicted of one of these violent offences, a judge, with the consent of the Attorney General, could order a hearing into whether or not the convict should also be declared to be a psychopath. At this hearing, the judge could hear evidence from two psychiatrists as to the extent of the danger the person posed. If the court found that he fit the definition, then he could be sentenced to the penitentiary for not less than two years and for an indeterminate term thereafter.

On the eve of the debate on this bill, Edmison's Committee on the Sex Offender released an interim report at a public reception at Toronto's King Edward Hotel. In his subreport, Dr L.P. Gendreau thought that developmental factors created the sexual delinquent and that these factors could be remedied by treatment. However, Dr J.D.M. Griffin challenged many of these premises and instead suggested that there existed many varieties of sexual behaviour, which did not indicate any mental illness, nor lead to violent crime. While the interim report contained conflicting medical comments on the nature and treatability of sex offenders, it did focus public concern on the issue.[52] In a newspaper account given only days before Parliament debated the amendment, John Diefenbaker, the justice critic for the Progressive Conservatives, pronounced that something drastic had to be done, for 'we in parliament should meet this problem. It is one which affects in a very considerably increasing measure the moral welfare of the children of this country.'[53] The impetus to create a treatment plan for sex psychopaths was now irresistible.

However, the subsequent debate frequently bogged down over details. Diefenbaker thought that the definition of 'psychopath' was too vague. Ilsley responded that similar wording had been used in American statutes. Indeed, he noted that eight American states already had similar laws, and that parliamentary draftsmen had used the Massachusetts statute as an example for the Canadian bill. Nevertheless, at Diefenbaker's suggestion, the definition was altered to read that any person who had 'a lack of power to control his sexual impulses' was a psychopath. While they could quibble over wording, there was no question on the need for the legislation. The premise of the legislation was that accused persons with these personalities, whatever their previous record of convictions, posed a threat of future sexual violence. In its way, it was pre-emptive legislation to catch and cure a criminal before he committed an act. One enthusiastic proponent of the bill, Vancouver Member of Parliament Howard C. Green, drew his inspiration from a series of resolutions from parent-teacher associations. He read into the record the resolutions from these associations, decrying the 'light sentences imposed on moral degenerates' and demanding that they be retained in custody and forcibly treated until they were safe to return to the streets.[54]

In the charged atmosphere of the time, with the media bombardment on the 'pervert menace' such as the Windsor Slasher, and the potential of modern medical science to cure psychopaths, there was general support for the proposition. As Ilsley explained, 'it enables certain of these persons to be taken out of circulation ... and to be given curative treatment which will lead to their release without their being a menace to society.' The opposition had no reservations about this bill. A Calgary member abhorred 'the great increase in crimes of this kind, and by the brutality and bestiality of them.' In his riding parents were loath to let their children leave the house during non-school hours. This bill would be welcome news to these parents. John Diefenbaker also accepted at face value the stories propagated by the U.S. and Canadian media that there was an epidemic of attacks against children. The evil hand was reaching out to grasp the little girls, and this bill would lock these monsters up indefinitely. He agreed with the government that this 'type of offence ... is becoming general ... ultimately, I believe this section will have the effect of punishing wrongdoers and protecting the public at large.' As well, it might result in the curing of these offenders and putting them back in control of their sexual desires.[55] As the parliamentary debate illustrates, the criminal sexual psychopath law was a flowering of both anxieties and sympathies. Elise Chenier has commented that the act was 'a legal, medical and cultural phenomenon that dominated public safety concerns at mid-century' and, that in addition to being a manifestation of middle-class anxieties, '[i]t was equally part of a long-standing tradition of moral reform.'[56]

If social deviants were to be reprogrammed, they would have to be given medical treatment somewhere. However, there was nothing in the government's proposal to match their good intentions with the money necessary to build and staff treatment facilities. 'I think the legislation has to precede the establishment of such facilities,' Ilsley explained to the House. No one questioned him on this point nor was there any further comment on whether the government ever seriously intended to fund such institutions. Neither was there any comment on the constitutional inconsistency that, while the federal government controlled the penitentiaries, medical treatment facilities were provincial institutions. No one had consulted the provinces to enquire if they would support the proposed changes.

In their enthusiasm to show the public that they were dealing with this urgent dilemma, these problems were swept aside. The only note of doubt came from the justice minister himself, who mentioned in passing that 'I am told that the results (curing psychopaths) in the United States are not the least bit conclusive.'[57] Two weeks later, Ilsley noted the comments of a British medical specialist, Dr W. Norwood East in the *Journal of Nervous and Mental Diseases*, that medical experts disagreed on the nature of sexual offenders and whether or not they could be cured. In light of the scientific uncertainty it seemed premature, in Ilsley's view, to be introducing legislation 'when we are not prepared to state for sure that we can say why they (sexual psychopaths) should be released again.'[58] On this point, the opposition seemed to have more confidence in the new law than the government, for Diefenbaker cited the recidivism rate in the United States, notably New York State at 9 per cent which demonstrated the effectiveness of treatment programs. Ilsley remained sceptical but thought the amendment a worthy experiment. With this less than ringing endorsement, Canada's sexual psychopath law received royal assent on 30 June 1948.

If anything, the public felt that these new laws designating criminal personalities did not go far enough. The *Toronto Telegram* regretted the need for triggering offences and further psychiatric hearings. In their view, it was unfortunate that these criminal designations and indefinite sentences were not automatic.[59] Not long after Canadians had begun this test, some Americans were beginning to express their misgivings. Writing in the *American Journal of Sociology*, Professor Edwin H. Sutherland noted that there was no difference in the trend of sex crimes between states that had sexual psychopath laws and those that did not. Above all, there was no connection between these laws, which were based on the notion of treating individuals as if they were sick, with medical facilities. Some of the Midwest states that had passed these laws did not provide for treatment. However, New York State, which did not have a sexual psychopath law, provided extensive treatment for psychopaths. Even if the sexual psychopath laws were an indication of a social movement towards the treatment of criminals as sick individuals or 'patients,' they were still the fruit of specific hysterical outbreaks. Sutherland found that the states which had enacted these laws had done so as a direct result of some infamous case; that they were 'customarily enacted after a state of fear has been aroused in a community by a few serious sex crimes committed in quick succession.'[60] Just how reliable was a law that had its basis in hysteria? Americans were also beginning to criticise laws which criminalised a class of individuals simply because of their sexual inclinations. In Nebraska, a review of their 1949 statute found that three persons who had engaged in consensual homosexual acts and eight exhibitionists were committed as dangerous psychopaths. Eight years after this statute, commentators wondered 'whether persons who practice homosexuality with adults of like desires and who do not proselytize among children present a danger to the community.'[61]

Over time, it became apparent that the intention in Canada was to treat all homosexuals as sexual psychopaths. While the general crime rate may have declined in the post-war years, the arrest rates for homosexual-related offences such as gross indecency had risen in cities such as Vancouver and Toronto. These may well have mirrored organised police crackdowns on gay gathering areas. In major American cities the police became even more focused on homosexuals, for 'vice squads consisted of officers wholly devoted to ferreting out sex crimes, and (judging from annual police reports) their productivity was measured by the number of prostitutes, sexual perverts, and drug dealers they arrested.'[62]

A further indication of the change in focus from child protection to controlling same-sex relationships was an amendment to the criminal sexual psychopath provision in 1954. In the omnibus changes to the legislation that year, buggery and gross indecency became triggering offences for a hearing on whether or not a person was a criminal sexual psychopath.[63] As a result, all homosexual activity, even that of a consensual, non-violent nature, could trigger a hearing under the provision. In a society in which all gay sex was illegal, gay men now also faced the prospect of being declared psychopaths and given indefinite terms in prison. There had been no debate on this change, and it was simply inserted during the 1953 parliamentary session as part of an overall reform of the Criminal Code. Yet it was a significant alteration for the 1948 law, which had been designed to protect children against violence, had now metamorphosed into a provision designed to control homosexuals for simply being homosexuals.

It is possible that justice department officials inserted this amendment as part of a general crackdown on homosexuals in the early Cold War period. At almost the same time this was being added to the Criminal Code, the *Immigration Act* was being amended to add homosexuals to the list of persons barred from entry to Canada as security risks.[64] A 1950 U.S. report had identified homosexuals as having deviant personalities that could easily be subverted, and Canadian officials were quick to mimic this approach. The RCMP was monitoring the civil service and possessed hundreds of files on gay or possibly gay men. Many officials were confronted with proof of their homosexuality and forced out of the civil service. As for this specific change, the thrust of the Criminal Code amendment had little to do with actually protecting the public. As Gary Kinsman observed, by adding consensual homosexual acts to the triggering process for the criminal sexual psychopath hearing, 'this section could be used in a more severe fashion against men having sex with other men and with adolescent boys than against people engaging in heterosexual acts that may in contrast have involved violence and force.'[65]

Yet the 1948 provision was used exceedingly sparingly. In 1954, the then justice minister noted that there were only sixteen criminal sexual psychopaths in Canada's penal system.[66] The McRuer Report noted that between 1948 and 1955, twenty-three people received this designation and about two-thirds of these were heterosexuals.[67] If anything, this miniscule number of committals might have triggered some introspection that there was no vast contagion of sex crime, but a few, incorrigible offenders. While the original purpose of the act may have been to protect children and to provide treatment to men who could not control their sexual impulses, both laudable objectives, since 1954 the provision existed as a condemnation of all homosexuals and a declaration that their existence posed a threat to society. This became apparent in the case of a high school teacher, Sidney Keith Neil.

Neil was convicted of having had sex with two young men from his Calgary school in 1955 and 1956, and upon his conviction on two counts of gross indecency, the Crown attorney sought a finding that he was a criminal sexual psychopath. Psychiatric evidence was called and while the doctors stated that they considered Neil a homosexual and a psychopath, they conceded that he was not mentally disturbed and could control his impulses. The evidence of his seductions revealed that Neil had been a homosexual since the age of about thirteen. He had taught since 1937, and beginning in 1954 he had attempted to persuade older male students to join him in same-sex activities. Whenever a boy demurred, Neil immediately stopped his advances. At no time had he ever used force. Nevertheless, the trial judge found that he came under the definition of a dangerous psychopath. After all, he was an admitted homosexual and had committed gross indecencies on at least two occasions. Neil was sentenced to two years in prison for each of the convictions and to an indefinite period of detention as a criminal sexual psychopath. The Alberta Court of Appeal overturned the later finding and the Crown appealed to the Supreme Court of Canada.

The *Neil* case would be the opportunity for the Supreme Court to give form and substance to the bare wording of the 1948 act and the 1954 amendment. 'The purpose of the enactment,' wrote Justice Cartwright, was 'to protect persons from becoming the victims of those whose lack of power to control their sexual impulses renders them a source of danger,' but this evil did not necessarily include 'merely the persuading or seducing of another to participate in sexual misconduct.'[68] Considering that a finding of criminal sexual psychopath could result in a person being imprisoned for life, Cartwright was of the view that it required 'coercive conduct resulting in the active infliction of pain, injury or other evil on the victim, not merely the persuading or seducing of another to participate in sexual misconduct.' Similar in tone were the comments of Mr Justice Rand, that the term criminal sexual psychopath was 'intended to describe a condition of impulse that in certain circumstances of normal control would become uncontrollable.'[69] The evidence before the Court was that Neil was controllable and that his acts were not violent or a general threat to the community.

While the majority of the Supreme Court agreed with this conclusion, Chief Justice Kerwin added, 'the disease (homosexuality) is a terrible one and requires treatment, but the penalty imposed is severe.' He assumed that a homosexual seduction would inevitably lead to corruption. Academic writers took note of the *Neil* decision, and Alan Mewett commented that it reflected the general view that 'homosexual contacts tend to corrupt the victim and make him as depraved and perverted as the corrupter.'[70] Therefore, sanctions against homosexuals were justified in order to prevent tainting others. In effect, psychopaths 'were visualized as a small group of men that suffered from a lack of power to control their sexual impulses. The ideological framing of homosexuals as sex crazed melded easily with this sexual psychopath frame.'[71]

It is beyond the scope of this essay to detail the later amendments to this provision and its consideration by the McRuer Commission in 1958. However, it is safe to generalise that as the hysteria ebbed, Canadians became more concerned about violent acts, which endangered the public, instead of conduct, which offended morality. In due course, the attention of the law would be on habitual violent offenders rather than socially unacceptable personalities.

In the final result, laws do not come about in a vacuum, and the 1948 criminal sexual psychopath law illustrates how a series of a few violent acts in several Canadian cities, most notably the Goss killing in Calgary, the attacks on boys in Winnipeg, and the Slasher killings in Windsor, could create a general climate of fear. This moral panic, which had no basis in any statistical increase in violence, was fostered by the newspapers and magazines that churned out articles and editorials describing the nature of the alleged threat to society. This moral crusade was given form and substance by a few outspoken leaders such as J. Alex Edmison, who could rally wide support for a new approach towards sex offenders. In the unease of the post-war years, it was felt that there were enemies in our midst and that something had to be done to put them away. Modern psychiatry seemed to offer the most scientific way to identify and segregate deviant individuals, and hopefully reform them. Lastly, the example of the United States, where aggressive action was being taken by many states to curb this menace, made Canadians feel that they were remiss if they did not follow suit. American examples would be cited several times in the Canadian Parliament as the best way to protect children from this contagion. Widespread fears were accepted without question, and the result was a law that labelled a type of behaviour as a dangerous criminal personality. The resulting law was not widely applied. Yet it eventually it became a tool to control non-violent offenders who did not conform to the post-war code of morality. Ultimately, the criminal sexual psychopath law was one born of fear, and was not one responsive to justice or society's long-term needs for protection.

NOTES

1 *Criminal Code Amendment Act, Statutes of Canada 1948*, c.39, s.43.
2 *House of Commons Debates* 6 (14 June 1948), 5196.
3 David Kimmel and Daniel Robinson, 'Sex Crime, Pathology: Homosexuality and Criminal Code Reform in Canada, 1949–1969,' *Canadian Journal of Law and Science* 16 (2001), 152.
4 Gary Kinsman, *The Regulation of Desire: Homo and Hetero Sexualities*, 2nd ed. (Montreal: Black Rose Books 1996), 183.
5 Elise Chenier, 'The Criminal Sexual Psychopath in Canada: Sex, Psychiatry and the Law at Mid-Century,' *Canadian Bulletin of Medical History* 20 (2003), 75–101.
6 William N. Eskridge Jr, 'Law and the Construction of the Closet: American Regulation of Same-Sex Intimacy, 1880–1946,' *Iowa Law Review* 82 (1996–7) 1007–135: 'The main phenomenon, eclipsing all others, was the expansion of prostitution and a middle-class recoil from that expansion' (1018).
7 On the social purity movement of the 1880s, see Patrick Brode, *Courted and Abandoned: Seduction in Canadian Law* (Toronto: Osgoode Society for Canadian Legal History and University of Toronto Press 2002), chap. 6, 'Virtue by Statute'; on the white slavery panics, see Mariana Valverde, *The Age of Light, Soap, and Water: Moral Reform in English Canada, 1885–1925* (Toronto: McClelland and Stewart 1993), chap. 4, 'The White Slave Panic,' especially the quote at page 89 from the Annual Report of the Methodist Church, 1911.
8 Estelle B. Freedman, '"Uncontrolled Desires": The Response to the Sexual Psychopath, 1920–1960,' *The Journal of American History* 74 (1987), 89.
9 Eskridge, 'Law and the Construction of the Closet,' 1063.
10 Freedman, '"Uncontrolled Desires,"' 94.
11 *Michigan Public Act* (1937) No. 196. The act was declared unconstitutional in 1938; it was re-enacted without the offending provisions.
12 William K. Jackson, 'Constitutional Law – Validity of Sex Offender Acts,' *Michigan Law Review* 37 (1939), 614.
13 'Notes on Recent Illinois Legislation,' *University of Chicago Law Review* 5 (1937–8), 91.
14 As quoted in Steven Maynard, '"Horrible Temptations": Sex, Men, and Working-Class Male Youth in Urban Ontario, 1890–1935,' *Canadian Historical Review* 78 (1997), 221.

15 *Report of the Royal Commission to Investigate the Penal System in Canada* (Ottawa: King's Printer 1938), 223.

16 Freedman, '"Uncontrolled Desires,"' 97.

17 'Montreal's Abortive Vice Probe,' *Canadian Bar Review* 24 (1945), 813; and Montreal *Le Devoir*, 14 December 1945, that the immoral state of the city's streets had been accepted during the war but that 'la protection accordée au vice' had to stop.

18 *Globe and Mail*, 'P.O.W.s Hanged,' 18 December 1946.

19 *Winnipeg Tribune*, 10 January 1946.

20 Ibid., 20 September 1946.

21 Sidney Katz, 'The Truth About Sex Criminals,' *Maclean's*, 1 July 1947, 12.

22 *Globe and Mail*, 20 August 1945.

23 *Windsor Daily Star*, 20 August 1945.

24 Ibid., 'Prosecutions Few For Sex Crimes,' 31 August 1945.

25 Ibid., Editorial, 8 July 1946.

26 Ibid., 'Now' column, 8 July 1946.

27 Ibid., Editorial, 9 July 1946.

28 Amy Taylor to Minister of Justice, 1 December 1946, in Library and Archives Canada, Record Group 13, vol. 1659.

29 John Loughery, *The Other Side of Silence: Men's Lives and Gay Identities – A Twentieth-Century History* (New York: John Macrae 1998), 168.

30 Freedman, '"Uncontrolled Desires,"' 97; Philip Jenkins, *Moral Panic: Changing Concepts of the Child Molester in Modern America* (New Haven: Yale University Press 1998), 53–4.

31 See annual reports of the chiefs of police for Windsor, Vancouver, Ottawa, and Toronto for the period 1944–8. I am grateful for the assistance of Hariette Fried of the City of Ottawa Archives, Mike Fish of the Windsor Municipal Archives, and Norina D'Agostini of the Toronto Police Museum.

32 *The Canadian Year Book, 1950* (Ottawa: King's Printer 1950).

33 David G. Wittels, 'What Can We Do About Sex Crimes?' *Saturday Evening Post*, 11 December 1948.

34 *American* magazine, July 1947.

35 *Ottawa Journal*, 1 April 1948.

36 Katz, 'The Truth about Sex Criminals,' 12.

37 *Winnipeg Tribune*, 'System Dooms New Prisoners,' 2 November 1946.

38 Katz, 'The Truth about Sex Criminals,' 46.

39 'Study Launched to Curb Sex Criminals,' *Globe and Mail*, 16 October 1947; and subsequent articles, 'Sadistic Psychopath Peril to Society,' 17 October 1947; 'Prison No Cure,' 18 October 1947.

40 *Windsor Daily Star*, 'Hope for Curbing Sex Criminals,' 17 October 1947.
41 *Globe and Mail*, 'Valuable Step Forward,' 20 October 1947.
42 Kinsman, *The Regulation of Desire*, 150.
43 Bernard H. Hall, ed., *A Psychiatrist for a Troubled World: Selected Papers of William C. Menninger M.D.* (New York: Viking 1967), 564.
44 Mark S. Micale and Roy Porter, *Discovering the History of Psychiatry* (New York: Oxford University Press 1994), 273.
45 *Toronto Daily Star*, 22 August 1947.
46 Edwin H. Sutherland, 'The Diffusion of Sexual Psychopath Laws,' *American Journal of Sociology* 56 (1950), 146.
47 Katz, 'The Truth about Sex Criminals,' 12.
48 *Rex v. Sears*, in Archives of Ontario, Record Group 22, file 1890, 375.
49 Domenico Caporale and Deryl F. Hanann, 'Sexual Psychopathy – A Legal Labyrinth of Medicine, Morals and Mythology,' *Nebraska Law Review* 36 (1957), 321.
50 *House of Commons Debates* 5 (3 July 1947), 5033.
51 See *Vancouver News-Herald*, 21 November 1947: '... at long last the authorities are prepared to seek a substitute for the stupid and ineffective in-again-out-again-in-again prison system.'
52 Chenier, 'The Criminal Sexual Psychopath in Canada,' 92.
53 *Globe and Mail*, 4 June 1948.
54 *House of Commons Debates* 6 (3 July 1948), 5031.
55 *House of Commons Debates* 6 (14 June 1948): Diefenbaker, 5196; Smith, 5198.
56 Chenier, 'The Criminal Sexual Psychopath in Canada,' 77.
57 *House of Commons Debates* 6 (14 June 1948), 5195–8.
58 *House of Commons Debates* 6 (3 July 1948), 5033–4.
59 'Half-Hearted Attempt to Deal with Habitual Criminals,' *Toronto Telegram*, 30 June 1947.
60 Sutherland, 'The Diffusion of Sexual Psychopath Laws,' 143.
61 Caporale and Hanann, 'Sexual Psychopathy,' 324.
62 William N. Eskridge Jr, *Gaylaw: Challenging the Apartheid of the Closet* (Cambridge, MA: Harvard University Press 1999), 63. Increased police action against homosexuals after the war did increase in some Canadian cities – for example, Vancouver, nine arrests for indecent acts in 1944, but between 1945 and 1947, they averaged thirty a year; in Toronto the number of indecent acts went from one in 1945 to nine in 1947.
63 *Criminal Code Amendment Act*, Statutes of Canada (1953–4), c.51 s.659.
64 Philip Girard, 'From Subversion to Liberation: Homosexuals and the Immigration Act 1952–1977,' *Canadian Journal of Law and Society* 2 (1987), 1.

65 Kinsman, *Regulation of Desire*, 184.
66 *House of Commons Debates* (11 March 1954), 2898.
67 *Report of the Royal Commission on the Criminal Law Relating to Criminal Sexual Psychopaths* (Ottawa: Queen's Printer 1958), 8.
68 *The Queen v. Neil* (1957) 1 Supreme Court Reports, 699.
69 Ibid., 691.
70 Alan W. Mewett, 'Morality and the Criminal Law,' *University of Toronto Law Journal* 14 (1961–2), 217.
71 Kinsman, *The Regulation of Desire*, 184.

4

The Law of Rules: Prosecuting Railway Workers in Mid-Nineteenth-Century Ontario*

PAUL CRAVEN

One July evening in 1860, Charles and Elizabeth Ham were returning by wagon from Toronto to the farm they rented near Pickering. As Elizabeth told it later, they took especial care as they approached the Kingston Road railway crossing, for they had narrowly escaped being run down there that very morning. A deep cut obscured their view of the line as they approached from the west, but as they entered the crossing they saw an eastbound locomotive gaining rapidly on them. Charles leapt up and whipped the horses, but the train was upon them before the wagon cleared the track. He was thrown out and killed. A few days later a coroner's jury concluded that Ham came by his death 'through the negligence of those whose duty it was to give the required signal of alarm on engine No. 35 at the crossing of the Kingston Road.' Had the inquest named names, it would have amounted to an indictment for manslaughter.[1] The accused could have been arrested and lodged in jail to await their trial. The same would have resulted from an information laid with a magistrate. This did not happen, for when the Toronto fall assizes convened on 8 October, Mr Justice William Buell Richards remarked that there were twenty-two prisoners awaiting trial, two for arson and the others for simple larceny. The following day, however, the grand jury came into court with a true bill against David Preston, engine driver of the Grand Trunk Railway, on a charge of manslaughter.[2]

The assize calendar was a full one, and it was not until a week later that Preston was arraigned and put to his trial for having negligently caused the death of Charles Ham.[3] The essence of negligence was the breach of a legal duty, in this case one imposed by statute. The Crown attempted to prove that Preston had failed to sound the locomotive's whistle or ring its bell as he approached the Kingston Road crossing, in contravention of section 104 of the *Railway Act*:[4]

The bell shall be rung, or the whistle sounded at the distance of at least eighty rods from every place where the Railway crosses any highway, and be kept ringing or be sounded at short intervals, until the engine has crossed such highway, under a penalty of eight dollars for every neglect thereof, to be paid by the Company, who shall also be liable for all damages sustained by any person by reason of such neglect, one half of which penalty and damages shall be chargeable to and collected by the Company from the Engineer having charge of such engine and neglecting to sound the whistle or bell as aforesaid.[5]

Preston was prosecuted by the county counsel, R. Dempsey, and defended by two leaders of the bar, the Honourable John Hillyard Cameron, QC, of Toronto, and John Bell of Belleville. Dempsey called ten witnesses, but from the beginning his case was weak. Three men who had been mowing in a field near the railway could not remember hearing the bell or whistle as the train approached but, as one of them said, 'I live in the neighbourhood and become accustomed to the sounds and may not observe it.' On cross-examination he admitted that 'if persons on the engine will swear that the bell was rung and the whistle sounded at the proper place, I will not say I could contradict them.' Most of Dempsey's witnesses explained that they had not been paying attention and could not be sure that there had been no warning. Only Elizabeth Ham was definite in her evidence that her husband had approached cautiously, watched carefully, and listened for bell or whistle before entering the crossing. 'I am positive there was no bell rung or whistle sounded at all ... If the bell had been rung or whistle sounded we would have heard it as we were looking out for it.' But she also denied hearing the two short sharp whistles for 'down brakes' just before the collision, the only whistles that the other prosecution witnesses had heard.

The defence called Preston's fireman and another employee who had been riding on the locomotive. They testified that the fireman had rung the bell and Preston had blown the whistle all along the approach to the crossing. This was corroborated by a brother of one of Dempsey's mowers. After examining five more witnesses, all of whom had heard the whistle, Cameron considered he had made his point:

At this stage of the defence the prisoner's Counsel asked His Lordship whether he thought it necessary to proceed further. He had several witnesses to call who would prove to the same facts, namely, the signals given by the steam whistle.

His Lordship said that was a question for the Jury.

Mr. Cameron said that he would not offer any further evidence, nor would he take up the time of the Court by addressing the Jury, he felt the Jury would not return a verdict which would consign the prisoner to the Penitentiary.[6]

The jurors acquitted Preston without leaving their seats.

This, however, was not the end of the matter. Preston was acquitted on 16 October; on 27 October, the eighteenth day of the Toronto assizes, Cameron and Bell filed appearances to defend his employer in Elizabeth Ham's suit against the Grand Trunk Railway Company, for 'carelessly and negligently driving, conducting, and managing a locomotive engine' so that it killed her husband.[7] Before 1846 in England and 1847 in Canada, no one could sue for damages arising out of a wrongful death. Thereafter, *Lord Campbell's Act* gave such a right of action to the families of persons killed by the defendant's wrongful act, neglect, or default.[8] Elizabeth Ham went to law to make the Grand Trunk compensate her and her husband's five minor children for his death.

The testimony from Preston's criminal trial was read to the civil jury, and most of the same witnesses gave additional evidence. Ham called six new witnesses; the Grand Trunk, five.[9] The evidence for the plaintiff was similar to that of the prosecution at the criminal trial, but there was a subtle shift in emphasis away from the warning signals and towards the speed of the train and the impaired visibility at the crossing. The conductor was called to testify that his train had left the Don station fifteen minutes late and was running five to ten minutes behind its time when the accident occurred. He claimed not to know whether the train passed through the cutting at more than ordinary speed, but his evidence did establish that the train usually ran at twenty-eight miles per hour on average, 'including stoppages.' Other witnesses for the plaintiff remarked that the train was going fast, and one of the mowers made up for his uncertainty about the bell or whistle by insisting that it went 'very fast; fast as I ever saw it, faster than it usually goes there.' A number of witnesses called attention to the dangerous layout of the crossing, where eastbound trains ran down a steep grade and around a sharp curve obscured from view by the depth of the cutting. Both elements had been hinted at in the criminal trial, but now they were elaborated just as the conflicting evidence about the bell and whistle was played down.

Among the new defence witnesses was David Preston, testifying over the objection of plaintiff's counsel that he was 'not competent.'[10] He insisted that the proper warning signals had been sounded. More importantly, given the new twist in the plaintiff's case, he testified that 'there is a heavy down grade there; we were travelling between 30 and 35 miles per hour ...' Preston claimed that he first saw the wagon and whistled for 'down brakes' as he came around the curve, when Ham was still some thirty or forty feet from the track.[11] The defence evidence was concerned almost exclusively with whether the warning signals had been given properly.

Judge Richards must have agreed that the bells and whistles formed the crux of the case, for as he planned his summation he emphasized the statutory duty:

I shall tell the Jury that the ground on which this action lies is that the Company's Servants in the managing of the train have been guilty of negligence. If death was caused by the want of care and negligence of the deceased then of course they should find for Defendant. The Statute prescribes the duties to be performed by the Company and their Servants and if they did their duty as so pointed out they cannot be liable.[12]

The jury did as juries in suits against railway companies were usually wont to do: they found for the plaintiff, awarding £200 to Elizabeth Ham and £100 to each of the five children. However disappointed the Grand Trunk's lawyers may have been, they would not have been surprised. The Canadian jury was a well-understood obstruction on the main line to justice. John Bell's report to his client was laconic and assured: 'In this suit damages were given for $2800.00 ... It is considered that the verdict will either be set aside or a new trial granted.'[13]

The Grand Trunk applied for a new trial, 'the verdict being against law and evidence, and the judge's charge; for there was no evidence of negligence on the part of the defendants or their servants to warrant the verdict.' In making the application, Cameron put forward Preston's acquittal 'as a strong circumstance to shew the accident was not the result of negligence.'

Early in the new year, Chief Justice (Common Pleas) William Henry Draper ruled on the application. He noted that while much of the evidence at trial had turned on whether proper signals had been given, Ham's declaration had charged the Grand Trunk with negligence generally. So far as the signals were concerned, Preston's acquittal was not conclusive: 'On the mere conflict of evidence as to the ringing of the bell or the sounding of the whistle ... the jury may have given him the benefit of a doubt, which the jury in this instance did not feel themselves in any way bound to extend to his employers.' But if the company had complied with the statutory requirements, they might still be held responsible for damages:

I do not interpret these provisions to mean that if the company have on their locomotive a bell or whistle, and ring the one or sound the other as is set forth, they are consequently freed from responsibility for damages that may be occasioned by the use of their locomotives upon the railway ... There may be many other acts of negligence which will entitle a sufferer to compensation, though these requirements are exactly fulfilled.[14]

Neither side had cited authority, but Draper reached back to a decision of his illustrious colleague, Sir John Beverley Robinson, to elaborate this point:

What we constantly find done upon railways where the track crosses a public highway which is unenclosed, is a sufficient proof that caution is deemed to be necessary, *for we usually see the speed slackened*, and the train going at such a rate that in case of any thing unexpected being found to be upon the track, it could be stopped in time to prevent mischief, *and it is surely the most reckless folly not to observe this caution*, for how can it be known what people or animals may be wandering or loitering along a highway which is accessible to every thing.[15]

Here, Draper pointed out, the evidence showed the train to have been running fast, and its speed had not been slackened as it approached the crossing. The jury in Preston's criminal trial 'may have considered that he was not proved to be responsible for the rate of speed at which the train was travelling, 35 miles an hour on a heavy down grade, and approaching the main travelled road between Toronto and Kingston; that it was for others rather than for him to have provided that, on approaching a crossing so very dangerous as this is described to be, the speed should be materially diminished.' But this could not exculpate the company in an action for damages on a general claim of negligence in managing the locomotive. If trains should ordinarily be slowed as they approached crossings, it was more than ordinarily careless not to do so at so hazardous an intersection. Indeed, Draper continued, the claim might include negligence 'in construction, and in using a road so dangerously constructed and laid out.' While the company might succeed at trial on the latter claim, 'I do not readily see how they could do so on the point of not slackening a speed so apparently dangerous under the circumstances.' The application for a new trial was refused.

Negligence as Nexus

Charles Ham's demise at the Kingston Road crossing was an unexceptional example of a fairly common sort of mishap in an unremarkable year for railway accidents. There were no major disasters in 1860: nearly half of the fifty-four fatalities involved trespassers on the track; four-fifths of the non-fatal injuries involved railway workers. Nor was there anything particularly unusual in its legal aftermath. Coroners regularly convened inquests over the victims of railway accidents. Trainmen were not infrequently sent to trial for manslaughter and then acquitted. Civil juries usually found for the plaintiff in suits against railways. Railway companies often appealed the jury verdicts, sometimes successfully and sometimes not. Charles Ham's misadventure was so ordinary in both its causes and its consequences that it is tempting to consider it less a unique event bound in its specific web of contingency and facticity than an ideal type.

There is a surprising amount of law in this ideal type. The central category is *negligence*, attracting punishment or redress for injuries resulting from the failure to perform a legal duty. Negligence emerged as a distinct tort precisely when changed transportation technologies and social patterns resulted in an overwhelming increase in 'running-down' accidents and a corresponding volume of litigation.[16] When railways displaced stagecoaches, so that running-down fatalities displaced mere injuries, the common-law doctrine that there could be no recovery for tortious death came to be seen as at best an anomaly, at worst a barbarity. *Lord Campbell's Act*, which extended to relatives of the deceased the same right of recovery available to injured persons, was a creature of the railway age.[17]

As the Ham litigation showed, the law about negligence intersected with the law about employment in at least three important ways. First, the common-law contract of employment imposed duties of care upon worker and employer. Employees owed it to the employer to exercise skill and care in their work; employers owed it to their employees to provide a safe working environment. Injured workers quite frequently sued their employers for negligence in breaching the contractual duty to provide a safe working environment. Their claims were typically upheld by trial juries, then reversed on appeal due to the broad range of legal defences available to employers. I know of no nineteenth-century Ontario cases in which an employer sued an employee for negligence, although such an action was theoretically possible.[18] Employers had other more effective and certain remedies, in self-help and at law. Beyond the duty of care, the employee owed obedience to the employer's lawful commands, and the railway company employer had the legal authority (and perhaps, per Draper, the legal duty) to adopt rules and regulations for the conduct of employees. The making and enforcing of railway company rules was bolstered by a number of regulatory and punitive statutes. In these circumstances, employee disobedience was *prima facie* evidence of negligence.

This brings us to the second point at which the law about negligence intersects with the law about employment: the principle that an injured party could recover damages from the employer for the negligence of the employee. Whether this is theorized as the master's personal tort (on the basis that the master acts through the servant so that the servant's wrongful act is the wrongful act of the master), as mere vicarious liability (on the basis that the master should have supervised the servant more closely, so that liability passes back to the master at one remove), or just as a convenience for ensuring that damages once assessed are likely to be paid, this liability was one more reason for employers to enforce the terms of the employment contract closely.

The third point to be made here about the intersection of the law about negligence and the law about employment is bound up as well with the emergence of railway corporations as private bodies with public purposes. The nineteenth-century state supplemented – and even substituted itself for – the employer's not inconsiderable power to enforce employment obligations. This was true in a general sense, of course, with the *Master & Servant Act*[19] and the complementary legislation about apprenticeship, but there the state merely gave the employer an effective means of enforcing its own contracts. In the case of negligence by railway employees, however, the state seems (with some reason, as will later appear) not to have trusted the employer to prescribe or to enforce terms of employment in the public interest: hence the *Railway Act* provisions requiring signalling at crossings and proscribing employee drunkenness.[20] So, too, we have the public power to prosecute railway workers for breaches, not only of the common-law and statutory requirements but also of the employer's own rules.[21] The object here was less to strengthen the disciplinary authority of the employer – separate provisions empowered railway companies to enforce their rules – than to provide the state with a means of punishing workers in circumstances where the employer might be inclined to deal with them leniently, if at all.

The Law of Rules

It is an interesting legal–historical question when it became accepted at common law that company rules were binding on employees who did not choose to treat their promulgation as repudiation of the terms of their pre-existing employment contracts.[22] However, the railway managers did not have to rely on a common-law right to make and enforce workplace rules. Railway companies received express legislative grants of rule-making authority in their acts of incorporation. The Canadian legislature provided for the enforcement of employer rules generally under the *Master & Servant Act*, and, in the special case of railway workers whose inattention to duty resulted in fatality, through criminal proceedings for manslaughter.

The very early Canadian railway charters, like those of the London & Gore (1834)[23] and the Erie & Ontario (1835),[24] empowered their directors to make rules and regulations, but made no provision for public or private enforcement, or for legislative supervision of the rules. These early charters were stillborn as economic conditions precluded successful railway promotion until the late 1840s. By the time of Canada's first railway construction boom in the early 1850s, Canadian railway legislation was directly influenced by developments in Britain, where a system of state supervision of railway rules and employee discipline began in 1840, and general terms of incorporation came into effect in 1845.[25]

The imperial Board of Trade cooperated with the Colonial Office in vetting colonial railway legislation, and encouraged colonial legislatures to follow the English example. Canada adopted general railway legislation on the English model. By the late 1850s, this legislation required companies to institute codes of operating rules for employees, which could be enforced by stoppages of wages. Breaches of operating rules became misdemeanours punishable in the courts by fine or imprisonment. Rulebooks were to be filed with the government, but after a brief fling at proactive regulation, this became a purely formal requirement. The model of industrial discipline emphasised private lawmaking backed up by public enforcement.

Although Lord Stanley had earlier withheld imperial consent pending changes in the colony's St Lawrence & Atlantic railway bill, it was Gladstone's brief sojourn at the Colonial Office that established the framework for Canadian railway legislation. Gladstone's experience in railway regulation as vice-president of the Board of Trade (1843–5) and author of the abortive English legislation of 1844–5 informed his circular despatch on colonial railways, issued in January 1846.[26] Accepting that a single rigid formula could not be made to apply everywhere in the Empire, Gladstone nevertheless maintained that English experience 'has ascertained some general principles on the subject, the application of which is neither transitory nor local, but which, it may now be presumed are applicable in various degrees to the legislation of every country.' These included the reservation of unfettered legislative authority to amend or repeal railway legislation, and provisions for prepayment of one-tenth of the capital, for carriage of mails and the military, for public safety, and for governmental oversight of railway tolls and accounts. There were ten conditions in all, and while none of them was always indispensable, Gladstone promised that the imperial government would assent to colonial legislation that met all of them. 'On the other hand, any Railway Law framed in neglect or disregard of them must be so reserved.'

Upon receipt of the circular, the Canadian legislature hastened to amend one pending railway bill to comply with its terms, and sent out an Address to Her Majesty, praying that she would not withhold assent from the session's railway bills. While the Select Committee found difficulties with several of Gladstone's conditions, the legislature was particularly worried by the requirement for paid-up capital.[27]

When Grey succeeded Gladstone as Colonial Secretary later the same year, he endorsed the policy of the colonial railway circular. Five Canadian bills were confirmed despite their non-compliance, but, in conveying the royal assent, Grey warned that the legislature should revise and amend them. A second despatch imposed similar conditions on two additional bills. In 1847 and 1848, the Colonial Office referred nine Canadian railway bills to the Railway Commission of the Board of Trade for comment. The commissioners' lengthy critiques of these bills seem to have been inspired in approximately equal proportions by profound experience of railway working and chauvinistic regard for the perfection of the English acts. Among their particular concerns, the commissioners noted the lack of uniformity in Canadian railway bills, and suggested that the colony should adopt general railway incorporation legislation along the lines of the English clauses consolidation act.

In 1845, a Select Committee of the Canadian legislature had begun to consider 'what general provisions ought to be introduced into such railway bills as may come before the House during the present or future Sessions, for the advantage of the public and the establishment of a sound Railway System.' Within a few months of the receipt of Gladstone's circular, it reported a bill based on the English act, but substituting the executive government for the Board of Trade. The principles of the English legislation were incorporated in the Canadian railway clauses consolidation act of 1851.[28] The act was amended the following year to avoid the risk that the imperial government would disallow the Grand Trunk incorporation statute.[29] After the passage of the amended clauses consolidation act, which was to form the basis of the Dominion *Railway Acts* from Confederation on, the imperial government withdrew from direct supervision of Canadian railway charters.

The consolidation act made few substantive provisions governing railway operations and the conduct of railway employees. Railway workers were to wear identifying badges; engine drivers were to sound a bell or whistle at railway crossings; it was made a misdemeanour to be intoxicated while in control of a train. The making of detailed rules and regulations was silently delegated to the companies, without the benefit of even the model code which had been in place in England for more than a decade. The companies' rule-making powers derived from their power to make by-laws, subject to government approval. Fines imposed by such by-laws could be collected by summary proceeding before a magistrate.

The Baptiste Creek and Desjardins Bridge disasters of 1854 and 1857 concentrated public attention on complex questions of railway safety. They produced over-simple, although highly expedient, solutions. Fifty people died at Baptiste Creek in a gruesome collision between a Great Western mail express and a construction train. After two inquests, a grand jury investigation, three criminal prosecutions, several civil suits, and a commission of inquiry,[30] Baptiste Creek engendered *An act for the punishment of the officers and servants of railway companies contravening the by-laws of such companies, to the danger of persons and property.*[31] The title says it all: breach of the domestic rules of railway companies could now be prosecuted as a criminal offence. Contraventions involving actual or potential injury to persons or property were punishable by a fine of up to £100 and imprisonment for up to five years.[32]

Three years later, the Great Western locomotive *Oxford* crashed through the floor beams of a defective swing bridge, plunging two carloads of passengers into the icy waters of the Desjardins Canal. The fifty-nine dead included some of the province's most prominent citizens, not least the railway's principal contractor, Samuel Zimmerman. Although worker misconduct played no part in the catastrophe, the *Act for the better prevention of accidents on railways*, which it inspired, continued the criminal provisions.[33] It required railway companies to make rules for the governance of their employees, which could be enforced by fines of up to a month's wages. In addition, it extended the powers of the Board of Railway Commissioners, a dormant creature of the Grand Trunk's 1852 statute. The board was now charged with regulatory responsibilities similar to those of the English Board of Trade, including general powers of inspection. Headed by Samuel Keefer, an experienced public works engineer, the reinvigorated board attacked its function with unprecedented ardour. Keefer actively promoted safety standards, the codification of rules, the improvement of equipment, the collection and publication of statistics, and measures for enforcing all of these.[34] Whatever its immediate impact, Keefer's proactive style had no long-term effect. Less than two years after its revivification, the Board of Railway Commissioners was put back to sleep. After this short-lived experiment with English-style administrative regulation, Canada returned to the expedient of 1851, giving the executive government – typically a cabinet committee – responsibility for overseeing the railway industry.[35]

The new *Railway Act* was an updating and further consolidation of the clauses consolidation act and the railway accident acts of 1856 and 1857. Section 178 reconstituted the Board of Railway Commissioners as a cabinet committee consisting of the receiver general, the minister of finance, the commissioner of public works and the postmaster general. Sections 158 through 164 continued the penal provisions of 1856. At the request of the railway companies, the act was amended in 1860 to provide for the appointment of company police and to make it easier to punish pilfering. What had begun with imperial concern that the local government should be able to control its railways, and continued with public outrage over the industry's abysmal safety record, had resolved itself by the end of the decade into governmental deference to the employer's right to manage the enterprise as it saw fit, with the aid and encouragement of the public purse and the public courts.

This legislative scheme essentially abandoned the state's role in regulating railway operations to coroners, magistrates, and high court judges. Instead of ongoing public supervision of operating practices by administrative regulation or inspection, work practices in the industry were scrutinized on an ad hoc, piecemeal basis, and then only when something went drastically wrong. Judicial interpretation generally narrowed the issue in such investigations to the simple question of whether the accused railway worker had disobeyed a company rule. As one Canadian judge put it,

The public generally were interested in seeing the rules of the railway company properly observed, because they had no control themselves over the cars by which they travelled. The Legislature, therefore, in order to enforce strict obedience to the rules, had not made their violation a common breach of contract, but had made it an indictable offence.[36]

Framing the issue in this way removed employee conduct from its context of work practices and workplace relations, and virtually guaranteed that the broader social, economic, and technical causes of railway accidents went unexamined. The primacy of management discretion was unquestioned. Nevertheless, railway managers were ambivalent at best about public prosecutions of misconducting workers, preferring their own exclusive control over workplace discipline. Public prosecution of railway workers did more to preserve the illusion of a state role in ensuring safety and the reality of unfettered management rights, than it did to control worker behaviour. For petty offences, workers had more to fear from their employers than from the courts. At the other extreme, trial juries almost never agreed to convict workers for manslaughter in railway accident cases.

Workers could be held to account for deaths caused by their carelessness or inattention to duty even without the provisions of the 1856 statute. By the mid-nineteenth century, it was well accepted at common law that people could be prosecuted and punished for the consequences of their negligence. 'If the circumstances indicate a wanton and malicious disregard of human life, the killing may amount to murder,' instructed a Canadian coroner's manual, 'if they indicate negligence only, the killing will be manslaughter; and if they show an absence of even negligence, the killing will then be merely by misadventure or accident.'[37] There could be no negligence where there was no legal duty, but railway workers were caught in a web of obligations – by their employment contracts at common law, by their employers' charters, by the substantive provisions of the railway acts – so there should have been no difficulty on this account. When workers were indicted for manslaughter in railway accidents before the passage of the 1856 act, criminal negligence was the legal concept underlying the prosecution. 'The principle of criminal responsibility for accidents, fatal to human life in the prosecution of lawful pursuits, is negligence.'[38] Negligence was a two-edged sword, however. It was sharp enough to puncture the blanket of discretion that had been so carefully wrapped around the rights of railway management. This may help to explain why the blunt instrument of 1856 had to take its place.

There were at least two ways in which reliance on criminal negligence threatened the evolving scheme of management rights. First, it raised the spectre that the corporation, or its principal officers personally, might be made criminally responsible for failing to observe safety regulations or other legal duties. The question whether a railway corporation or its officers might be guilty of manslaughter was considered at length by Chief Justice Macaulay in the wake of the Baptiste Creek disaster.[39] Emphasising the distinction between murder and manslaughter, rather than the breach of legal duty underlying the theory of negligence, Macaulay argued that since manslaughter did not admit of accessories before the fact, the corporation or its officers could not be indicted when the immediate cause of the accident was the inattention or misconduct of someone on the scene. Macaulay's method linked fault, at least in the sense of criminal blame, to proximate cause rather than reasonable forseeability. His logic prevailed. While there were occasional attempts to indict corporate officials for manslaughter in railway accidents, none came to trial.

Nevertheless, an emphasis on negligence as the foundation for criminal prosecution threatened the scheme of management rights in another way. Compensation for injuries and deaths suffered by passengers and others in railway accidents was based in the tort of negligence. In almost every case, the negligence was alleged to have been the fault of railway workers. The railway company paid compensation not because it had done anything wrong, but because as master it was vicariously liable for its servants' wrongdoing. Thus, the fiction of employee negligence served a dual purpose: it ensured compensation to injured

third parties, while preserving the companies' right to manage operations without effective public supervision. However, an emphasis on
common-law negligence as the foundation for criminal prosecution
threatened to explode the fiction that sustained this system of compensation. The Ham trials make a good example: after Preston was acquitted by one jury, another found the railway company liable in damages
for the death. The Grand Trunk appealed on the ground that Preston's
acquittal showed that there had been no negligence on the part of its servants. This argument failed, and the court suggested in effect that while
Preston may not have broken any rule, the company may have been
negligent in failing to make an appropriate rule. Chief Justice Draper's
observation that this could go further to include negligence 'in construction, and in using a road so dangerously constructed and laid out,'
invited far-reaching investigations of company policies and practices. If
admitted, how could the line between the master's vicarious liability
and the servant's criminal responsibility be preserved? Cases like this
one showed that employee negligence was a necessary fiction if the privacy of management rights was to be preserved. Draper's obiter comments aside, by making breach of a company rule the nub of the matter,
the 1856 legislation made more searching inquiries unnecessary and
irrelevant.

Railway Labour Relations

To say this is to invite consideration of the labour relations context
within which employers established rules and disciplined workers. In
approaching this topic we might begin with some speculation about the
interests of the various principals in the Preston–Ham trials. Elizabeth
Ham, clearly enough, wanted compensation for her husband's death;
she may also have been seeking retribution against her husband's kill-
ers. Had he been convicted of manslaughter, David Preston could have
been sent to the penitentiary for five years and would have been liable
for a £100 fine, half the Grand Trunk's civil damages, an additional fine
to be levied by the company, and summary dismissal. Preston, we may
infer, wanted to keep his job and stay out of jail.

What, though, were the Grand Trunk's interests in the Preston trial?
At first blush it might seem that the company would welcome the prosecution, which socialised labour discipline and emphasised the duty of
obedience. (The Grand Trunk had a domestic rule about bells and whistles to the same effect as the *Railway Act* provision.) On closer examina-

tion, the railway company's interest appears less clear cut. Were Preston to be acquitted of manslaughter, the railway could draw the inference that there had been no negligence, thereby undercutting Ham's claims for damages. From this point of view, it was better that Preston be tried and acquitted than that he not be tried at all. Moreover, the manslaughter charge represented an outside interference with management rights and thereby threatened, in its small way, the whole elaborate structure of railway labour relations policy. There is an inference to be drawn about Grand Trunk management's perception of its interests from the fact that the company organised and paid for Preston's defence.[40] Indeed, not only did it retain Preston on the payroll as an engine driver, but in 1869 it promoted him to locomotive foreman, a position he held until 1878, when he joined the Toronto, Grey & Bruce as its master mechanic.[41]

To appreciate the delicate balance the railway companies aimed for in making and enforcing work rules, it is necessary to understand the constraints they faced as employers in the middle years of the nineteenth century. Not surprisingly, the central concern of railway labour relations strategy was cost control. The major railways were by far the country's largest employers, with enormous payrolls that they sometimes had difficulty meeting. Until well into the 1870s, though, the companies found it all but impossible to reduce wage rates or achieve significant employment economies through layoffs. The Grand Trunk had fired a retrenchment-bent general manager in 1859 when his attempt to impose a 10 per cent wage cut led to a strike threat.[42] Both the Grand Trunk and the Great Western adopted substantial manufacturing programs, in part to provide slack-time work for the shopcrafts. Running trades workers were assigned shop duties during slack periods in order to avoid the necessity of layoff.[43] This emphasis on the retention of labour and the maintenance of wage rates reflected a scarcity of skilled workers and the railways' interest in preserving their often-substantial investments in recruitment and training. It also reflected the fact that for the railways, more than any other nineteenth-century industry, a competent, obedient, and loyal workforce was the critical element in cost control.

One reason for this was the inherent danger of many railway jobs. Of course much nineteenth-century work involved risks that would be considered unacceptable today, but many of the hazards of railway operations applied not only to the workforce but also to the public at large. Railway accidents threatened workers, passengers, and casual bystanders, not to mention expensive equipment and valuable freight. Moreover, it was in the nature of the industry that much of the riskiest and most sensitive work could not be supervised directly. Obedience and application had to be enforced indirectly. Premium wages and job security were set off against strict obedience and watchfulness.

Many of these dangers were inherent in the hard and soft technologies of the industry. For example, the industry's reliance on frangible iron rail until well into the 1870s contributed heavily to accident rates. Derailments due to track damage accounted for only part of the problem, although rail breakage occurred frequently, especially in winter. Iron rail took its toll indirectly in a variety of ways: excessive wear and tear on locomotives and cars, resulting in wheel and axle breakage; the presence of many track repair gangs, increasing the risk of human error in setting switches and signals; delays, stoppages, and temporary schedule changes, resulting in employee fatigue and uncertainty, contradictory orders, and a frightening number of collisions. The widespread adoption of steel rail in the 1870s had an immediate and salutary effect in reducing all these causes.[44]

An obvious example of the industry's 'soft' technologies was timetable-based train control, where momentary carelessness or minor infractions could not only disrupt schedules and wreck expensive equipment but also cost the company tens of thousands of dollars in damage claims. The technology of mid-nineteenth-century train control on single-track railways relied almost exclusively on the crew's strict observance of signals, the clock, and written instructions. Like the potential for accidents locked into the 'hard' technology of iron rails, the dangers associated with train control began to diminish with double-tracking and the adoption of block signals in the 1880s.

Other examples of accident-prone technologies abound: link-and-pin couplings and hand-operated brakes were notoriously dangerous, especially for their operators; while innovations intended to overcome the limitations of existing equipment, like the cars with extensible axles introduced to avoid unloading and reloading through freight at interchange points with narrow-gauge roads, often brought new dangers with them. (The change-of-gauge cars' axles tended to change gauge in transit.) The point is that many accidents were technological in origin. To this extent the companies' rulebooks substituted obligation for engineering.

The problem of indirect supervision extended not only to workers charged with the maintenance of schedules, the preservation of expensive equipment, and the safety of life and limb, but also to the security of cash and cargo. Station agents and passenger conductors handled large sums of the companies' money; trainmen, station, and warehouse employees handled valuable freight; stores employees, clerks, and even sectionmen had access to a variety of assets. Despite the valiant efforts of the companies' audit departments and police forces, employee carelessness, misappropriation, and theft were constant threats to the railways' precariously balanced accounts. It was as important to the railways to foster employee obedience, care, and fidelity in these respects as in those affecting scheduling and safety.[45] A similar point can be made in connection with practically every aspect of railway operations, for in all of them the demands for efficiency and economy conflicted with other pressures and temptations.

To keep employees on the straight and narrow, to habituate them to their work requirements, to retain their skills and loyalties, and to ensure their prompt obedience, the railway companies constructed elaborate moral economies of corporate paternalism, compounded of rewards and punishments, incentives and deterrents, benefits and expectations, symbols and substance. Railway employment was a world unto itself, its separateness not just a product of the special demands of the work, but an intentional creation of the employers. In the great railway centres, the railway community was institutionally complete. The Grand Trunk sponsored schools and churches; rowing, cricket, snowshoe, and rifle clubs; horticultural, literary, and benefit societies; it even had its own militia regiment commanded by the general manager and his ranked subordinates in proper military array. In lesser places, where the handful of railway employees necessarily involved themselves in the social and institutional life of the general community, the companies kept them on the move, rarely allowing a station master or a freight agent to stay long in one place. Dependence was the companies' guarantee of the obedience, care and loyalty from their employees, upon whom their own success so intimately depended.[46]

While the whole structure of railway life was oriented to labour discipline, retention, and reproduction – trains tended to run in families – the most characteristic instrument of specific indirect control was the railway rulebook. Once a railway company adopted its rules, it filed them with the government and printed them for distribution to all employees. On most roads, the workers signed for the books and were required to carry them at all times on pain of a fine or dismissal. In format and even to some extent in content, the rulebooks resembled modern collective agreements. In their nineteenth-century context, they seem sometimes to have been accorded the same status as the family Bible: one Great Western baggageman recorded the birthdates of his six children on the flyleaf of his rulebook. Although some of the earlier examples were quite rudimentary, by the 1860s railway rulebooks were elaborate codes of conduct and expectation, often amounting to more than a hundred pages of closely printed instructions. They constituted the positive domestic law of the railway companies, and as with the general law, ignorance of their terms was no defence.

In addition to the rulebooks, railway companies issued 'special regulations,' often in connection with timetable changes, and posted or distributed circular letters interpreting the rules and explaining their application. For example, in 1874, the Grand Trunk's traffic department published extracts from its circulars in book form: they ranged from warnings to station agents not to overlook their subordinates' misconduct – 'Agents who fail in this ... may expect trouble to result sooner or later, and when they least expect it' – to advice about how to avoid unnecessary words in telegrams; from first-aid instructions to be followed in the case of men having an arm or leg run over by a car to the proper mode of filling out train cash-box report forms. A surviving example of the circular book has subsequent letters pasted in, each countersigned by the book's owner to certify receipt. The last of these, a circular to telegraph operators at roundhouses dated January 1878, suggests just how captious hair-splitting railway officials could be in exercising supervision via the written word: 'In giving train orders I observe you use the words "all trains due are in." This is rather indefinate [*sic*], and for the future you will please use the following words, "all trains due **have arrived**" – Please note.'[47]

The companies did what they could to enforce their regulations, and while in many cases this must have meant leaving employees to the tender mercies of foremen and local superintendents, there was generally a right of appeal to a higher authority. A fascinating glimpse of railway disciplinary procedures is afforded by the surviving Great Western 'Advises of Officers Minutes,' reporting the regular meetings of the railway's department heads in the winter of 1873–4.[48] The agenda for these meetings ranged widely over every aspect of operating detail, and included the final disposition of disciplinary cases. The discipline items range from the abrupt '4 Coal Cars off Switch at Suspension Bridge –

Switchman dismissed' to trial-like investigations leading to the appor-
tionment of penalties among the transgressors:

Collision between No. 6 Day Express East, and No. 5 accommodation West
between Merritton & St Catherines 3d Nov. The General Manager and General
Superintendent having been present shortly after the Collision and then examined all parties concerned, and having conclusive evidence that the Holding
Flag was exhibited on the Switch Tower at Merritton in time to stop No. 5 which
was unnoticed by the Driver, and being satisfied that Driver Anderson of No. 5
was under the influence of liquor this examination was held to hear Anderson's
defence. His fireman and Engine Driver Temple of No. 6 were also examined.
    Anderson is discharged (1) for having a passenger (an ex-Fireman) on his
Engine contrary to rule (2) although not drunk, undoubtedly from having
taken drink being unfitted for the proper discharge of his duty, causing him to
overlook the Flag at Merritton and failing to prevent the collision which
occurred on a perfectly straight Track. Engine Driver Temple was commended
for his good look out, and the judgment he displayed in stopping and backing
his Train, otherwise a very serious accident must have been the result.
    MacKenzie a boy pupil in the Operator's Box at Merritton was also exam-
ined, and proved that having been sent by the Signalman to hold No. 6 at Merritton Station he had told the Brakeman of that train of his message (which
Brakeman admitted to the General Superintendent) who grossly neglected his
duty in not informing his Conductor. The Brakeman to be discharged.[49]

Railway punishments were intended to be exemplary. First-time offenders might be let off with a warning of dire consequences should
their misconduct – which might be anything from 'carelessness in giving train orders' to 'irregular living' – recur. The officers' committee
considered the problem of 'small pilferings' in station yards, and decided to 'make an example or two.' Industrial capital punishment was
publicised for exemplary effect, as in this Grand Trunk circular:

I regret to say that operator 'A. Woods' of Dickinson's Landing, has been summarily dismissed from the Company's service, and criminally prosecuted, for
carelessly disobeying Special Rule No. 20 and the Note to Rule 18; and reck-
lessly disregarding the important instructions given in Circulars Nos. 4, 5, and
6, small book.
    A special crossing was arranged between No. 18 and an 'up' special freight
train at Dickinson's Landing. The Operator received and replied to the order,

and forged the Switchman's signature to it!! He neglected to raise the danger signal, and subsequently gave No. 18 a clearance order! The Trains met but, fortunately, the Enginemen saw each other in time to prevent a collision. No punishment can be too severe for such culpable neglect, and operator 'Woods' will be criminally prosecuted for contravening the Company's Regulations.

I would seriously advise all hands to keep the Rules and Regulations, and the Traffic Department instructions in small Circular Book, fresh in your memory, by carefully reading them over occasionally.[50]

Disobedience as Practice

'Inattention to these plain directions,' the circular concluded, 'must sooner or later result in disaster.' Sooner or later disaster did strike, and its victims more often than not were the trainmen themselves. Surely a sense of self-preservation should have accomplished what rules, rewards, and punishments apparently could not: strict obedience and consequent safety. However, as a review of railway work practices reveals, things were not quite so simple as all that.

Workers cut corners and committed technical infractions, just to get the work done. Engine cleaners might stop up the smoke holes in fireboxes to get the locomotive in steam, because 'any air over the fire made us work harder.'[51] One Great Western fireman recalled how he used to steal a few blocks of coal from the shop fuel supply to power his wood-burning engine up the steep Copetown grade.[52] Personal safety or comfort might motivate rule-breaking: few conductors would insist that their brakesmen remain on the car roofs in a February blizzard. Often the press of time led to short cuts: in the wake of an 1864 accident in which three trainmen lost their lives when an axle-tree broke and they were unable to signal the engine driver to stop the train, it was reported that freight conductors frequently neglected to reattach the communication cord when there was shunting to be done.[53]

The clock was the primary regulator of railway work. The major Canadian railways were trunk roads whose passenger business often depended on making connections with American lines. The Grand Trunk traffic department's Circular 14 insisted that 'running passenger trains on time is of the greatest importance, and everything consistent with safety must be done to secure the connections East and West.' The mechanics of train control meant that if a train failed to keep to its time it was liable to collide with an oncoming or following train. The pres-

sures on conductors and engine drivers to cut corners were immense. In
order to keep to time, it might seem necessary to skimp on other pre-
cautions. In 1865 the Toronto *Globe* published the letter of a mail conductor, employed by the post office to make three trips a week on the
Grand Trunk between Toronto and Kingston, complaining that trains
were run at dangerous speeds, especially in winter:

Ask the drivers and they will tell you it is not their fault – Mr Spicer's orders
are, 'Make your own time.' The fact is they are given a time bill to run on, which
at this season they cannot accomplish. By referring to it you will see that to be
'on time,' they have to run at the rate of 26 miles an hour between Kingston and
Toronto going west. This necessitates their frequently running at forty miles an
hour to make up for lost time by snow, trains off the track and other obstructions.[54]

Many accidents were attributed to trains running fast for this reason: as
one widely distributed folksong put it, 'Many a man has lost his life /
trying to make up lost time.' On the evening of Charles Ham's death,
David Preston's train left Toronto fifteen minutes late but reached the
Kingston Road crossing only five to ten minutes behind time: it was
catching up to the timetable by running fast. Fifteen years after the Ham
accident, a correspondent complained in the press that passenger trains
were approaching that same Kingston Road crossing at thirty miles per
hour, a more dangerous practice than ever since recent building in the
area had reduced visibility even more.[55]

   Commenting on an 1874 accident, the Toronto *Globe* remarked that
railway companies often condoned employee disobedience, and quoted
a report of the British Board of Trade suggesting that railway rules were
often more honoured in the breach than in the observance:

Railway work is a description of work which must be *got through*. When it cannot be performed without risk the risk is incurred. The officers and servants of
the company are too frequently induced, if not compelled, in the absence of
necessary means, appliances, or accommodation, to disobey printed rules, or to
adopt hazardous methods of working, and, in the course of their daily work, to
become habituated to operations which they would themselves, in the first
instance, see to be objectionable. They are often unduly blamed when accidents
actually occur because their difficulties in these respects are not sufficiently
known or considered.[56]

Shifting the Blame

Inasmuch as they were often reproved and sometimes indicted by coroners' juries investigating deaths on the railway, employees may indeed have often been blamed for accidents. But at least as often, railway workers received the benefit of the doubt. Even passengers affected by an accident could be magnanimous. One October day in 1859, a Grand Trunk conductor forgot a train order and allowed his express to collide with a freight train. Far from blaming him, his passengers called a meeting and unanimously resolved to ask the railway to deal leniently with the conductor's dereliction, because he was urbane and attentive and had only forgotten the order because of 'the hurry and confusion attending the departure of the train from Kingston.'[57] The best evidence of the public generally giving employees the benefit of the doubt was the almost complete reluctance of juries to convict railway workers of manslaughter by negligence.

This was not for want of judicial encouragement. From Chief Justice Macaulay's charge in the Baptiste Creek disaster forward, judges emphasised the breach of the rule and the lack of prior intent as the ingredients of manslaughter. They also stressed the individual, decontextualised responsibility of the prisoner. As Judge Wilson told switchman Lawrence Ryan after a grand jury ignored the bill against him, 'It had been said, probably with some degree of truth, that the man who was killed was driving into the station yard at too great a rate of speed; but that did not make Ryan the less culpable for not obeying orders. He recalled this to Ryan's mind, that he might not triumph in getting off.'[58] But like most others in his situation, Ryan did get off – and thereby hangs a tale.

Charges to the Perth County grand jury by three different judges of assize illustrate the view from the bench. In 1860, an engine driver and conductor were to be tried for manslaughter in a collision that caused the death of a railway labourer. Judge Hagarty instructed the grand jury that, 'if a person in charge of a railway train by the non-observance of the rules and regulations of the Company, which were made binding by act of Parliament, allowed the train in his charge to run into collision with any other train, – if done designedly would of course be murder, – but if otherwise, – if through neglect and without design, then it was manslaughter.'[59] Five years later, switchman Ryan was to be tried for failing to set a semaphore, thereby allowing a train to run into the station, causing a collision that killed its engine driver. Judge Wilson began his charge by drawing the familiar distinction between murder, an act of human malignancy, and manslaughter, an act of human frailty. He went on to stress what he saw as the policy of the legislation:

... it was not to be tolerated that men should take and hold situations where the lives of persons were entirely entrusted to them and not be made responsible for the consequence of their neglect. The safety of society required that they should be held strictly to it. They were not to trifle with their duties so as to cause the death of other people ... the case was one which must be investigated with great care, seeing that many people without hesitation placed themselves on railway cars, and had no control whatever over, nor were allowed to give directions in regard to, the working of the trains.[60]

In 1869, Judge Richards presided over the assize where engine driver Whittaker and another member of his train crew were to be tried for failing to sound a bell or whistle at a railway crossing, where a teamster was run down and killed. Like the others, he stressed the distinction between murder and manslaughter, going on to suggest a test of reasonable care and drawing an analogy between locomotive drivers and people who fired guns into crowds. 'The law cast upon all persons having the control and management of dangerous instruments – as a gun, a locomotive, a steam boiler, any of those machines, in fact, which were likely to produce injury to others – the responsibility of possessing a reasonable amount of knowledge as to how these machines should be managed.' Whittaker was well liked locally, and his prosecution was unpopular. Richards seems to have bowed to this sentiment by hinting that the prisoner's fault was somehow diminished by the contributory negligence of the victim: the test, he said, was 'whether the driver of the engine caused death, or whether death was caused from the want of a reasonable amount of care on the part of the person killed.'[61]

The lengthiest and most pointed account of the grand jury's duty in such cases was laid down by Judge Morrison at the Middlesex spring assizes of 1874. Three Great Western trainmen were to be tried for manslaughter in a case that had shocked the country: an oil lamp had spilled in a passenger car, which caught fire. The trainmen had neglected to fit up the bell cord, despite the plain language of the *Railway Act* and the company rulebook, so the passengers had no means of communicating with the engine driver to stop the train. Several passengers died. Judge Morrison patiently led the grand jury through the statutory provisions about communication cords and the binding effect of company rules.

'But *independent of these provisions*,' he continued, 'so highly does the law value human life, that when life has been lost through the carelessness or negligence of any person, whether by an act of omission or otherwise, such neglect may be so criminal as to be the basis of an indictment for manslaughter; and generally, it may be laid down that when one, by a neglect of duty, has contributed to the death of another, such person is criminally responsible, and such neglect admits of no justification.'[62] There was more in this vein before the judge hammered in the last nail:

It may be that others besides the accused were also guilty of neglect. If that appears it will not excuse the neglect of the parties charged ... It does not lie in the mouth of one to say as a justification that another was negligent also. They cannot divide the negligence so as to exonerate them from the effect of their own wilful or negligent conduct.[63]

It is difficult to see what more he could have said to set the grand jury on the right path. Not only did it ignore the bill, though, but it was complimented by the press for seeing the matter 'in its proper light.'[64]

At least twenty-two Ontario railway workers were charged with manslaughter in railway accidents between 1854 and 1879. Outcomes are known for twenty of them. Grand juries ignored half the bills. Of the remaining ten, eight were acquitted by trial juries, often despite the presiding judge's charge. The contrast between the apparent readiness of coroners' juries to indict and the reluctance of assize juries either to uphold the indictments or to convict is readily explained. Coroners' juries were involved in wide-ranging investigations of engineering and work practices to determine how a death came about, while assize juries were exposed to a narrower range of facts focused on the question whether the accused was criminally liable for the death. By the same token, coroners' juries convened over the mangled remains of the victims, amid the shock and horror of the community; the attention of assize juries was focused not on the victims, now buried and unseen, but on the accused, who often appeared to them as involuntary proxies for rich, impersonal, and despised railway corporations.

The local communities from which juries were drawn rallied in support of railway workers who were prosecuted for manslaughter. The 1855 commission to investigate accidents on the Great Western heard that track foreman David Beamer, whose neglect to set proper signals before removing a set of rails contributed to the deaths of some first-class passengers, was acquitted despite the chief justice's strong charge against him. 'It is not for us to express any further opinion on the subject,' the commissioners wrote. 'We conceive it, however, to be very desirable for the safety of the public ... that all cases (affecting Railroad Companies) should be removed to the jurisdiction of tribunals remote from the operation of local or personal influences.'[65]

When a London stationmaster was dismissed by the Great Western and prosecuted for manslaughter by negligence in collision, the local magistrates reluctantly committed him for trial. On the eve of the assizes, a sympathy meeting, numerously attended by railway workers as well as the leading citizens of the town, organised to support him. The prosecuting counsel 'frankly expressed the great regret felt by the Company in prosecuting so efficient a servant as Mr Manby had hitherto proved.' He was convicted nonetheless, but when it came time to deliver sentence, Judge McLean, remarking 'that the testimony on his behalf was very strong, and the presentation of a numerously and respectably signed petition ... went to show it,' imposed a small fine to general applause.[66]

When a coroner's jury committed engine driver David Whittaker to trial for manslaughter in a crossing accident, for having failed to sound his bell or whistle, a correspondent told the local newspaper that the guilty verdict was

the only one that a conscientious jury could render; but it seems hard that a man of the highest moral character, the oldest and most careful driver on the line, and who has run an engine for 13 years without an accident, or ever having been reported for a fault, should find himself placed in such an unfortunate position by the neglect of a simple duty, the non-performance of which has become almost a standing rule with the drivers of the G.T.R. ... That Mr Whittaker has the sympathy of the whole community with him in his unfortunate position, was evidenced by the fact that when led away in arrest by the constable, more than one strong man was fain to turn aside to hide a falling tear, and to console himself with the hope that the penalty might be as light as the fault was unpremeditated. [67]

The grand jury showed its sympathy by ignoring the bill.[68]

When a Guelph jury disregarded 'conclusive evidence' of a switchman's neglect of duty and ignored Judge Macdonald's unambiguous direction to convict, he told them that 'a greater perversion of justice could not be made; and the public had no safety if such verdicts were given.'[69] When the bill against switchman Lawrence Ryan was ignored, the Toronto *Globe* theorized that the grand jury was unduly influenced by local feeling against the Grand Trunk. Judge Wilson left Ryan in jail overnight, then delivered a stern lecture before discharging him.[70] Popular juries, it appears, had a different conception of justice than the lawyers. They were not satisfied with formal proof that an employee had disobeyed the rules. The worker may have been at fault in some way, but the burden of blame lay elsewhere; on the company's silent condonation of rule-breaking, on the pressures of the job, on the system of working. According to the judges, if the accused was negligent, the negligence of others was no defence. Juries consistently refused to see the world that way.

While the Great Western prosecuted Beamer for manslaughter in 1854, and offered a reward for conductor Twitchell's apprehension the same year, railway companies appear not to have initiated manslaughter prosecutions under the 1856 act. In several cases they arranged and paid for legal representation for workers facing manslaughter charges. In at least one case, a railway solicitor vociferously objected to the legality of a coroner's inquisition and refused to cooperate in producing the impugned employee for trial, responding that 'he is pursuing his avocation as usual.'[71] Workers who were prosecuted for manslaughter were not automatically fired or demoted: David Whittaker was still a Grand Trunk engine driver in 1874, while David Preston was promoted to locomotive foreman in 1869.

Nevertheless, railway companies did initiate prosecutions for neglect of duty in non-fatal accidents. In 1866 the Grand Trunk prosecuted engine driver Jeremiah Austin for being intoxicated while in charge of his engine, in breach of the *Railway Act*. This was apparently the first trial of its kind under that legislation, and the railway's counsel opened the case by observing that it was necessary for the company to bring it up, 'for if it was suspected that they were harbouring persons incapable by reason of their habits of life of attending to their duty, they would be subject to serious charges.' Despite the Recorder's charge that the Grand Trunk should have 'no servants in their employment in whom they had not perfect confidence, and hence the question raised as to his being a man with a large family was one not to be considered,' the jury acquitted Austin.[72]

Prosecutions under the *Railway Act* differed from prosecutions for disobedience under the *Master & Servant Act* because the former was by indictment and involved a jury trial, while the latter was a summary proceeding. In 1865 the Grand Trunk brought their night telegraph operator at Stratford station before the local magistrates, charging him with criminal neglect of duty resulting in a collision costing more than $10,000. When the bench found the evidence insufficient to commit him for trial under the *Railway Act*, the railway proposed to lay an information under the *Master & Servant Act*. The magistrates declined to proceed since the evidence would be the same.[73]

In 1873–4, the Grand Trunk prosecuted engine driver William Pelling for disobeying orders, causing about $7,000 worth of damage in a collision. The company proceeded under the *Master & Servant Act*. When police magistrate MacNabb observed that the offence seemed out of proportion to the maximum penalty – a $20 fine or 30 days in jail – the Grand Trunk's counsel explained that it was 'on account of the severity of the punishment which prisoner would be liable to on a conviction – he would be sent to the Penitentiary ... And whilst the Company did not wish the prisoner to be excessively punished, yet they desired the men in their service should know that for disobedience of orders they would be punished.' Over the objections of Pelling's counsel that he lacked jurisdiction since the offence should be prosecuted under the *Railway Act*, MacNabb, who gave it as his private opinion that Pelling and his fireman had been asleep, fined the prisoner $20 and costs.[74]

A few weeks later, the Grand Trunk prosecuted two more employees involved in a collision for breach of orders under the *Master & Servant Act*. The conductor pleaded guilty and was let off with a $1 fine; the brakesman, who refused to admit his wrongdoing, was remanded in custody for a couple of days and then fined the maximum $20, after a lecture from MacNabb about his 'reprehensible carelessness.'[75] The following week, the Northern Railway prosecuted one of its brakesmen in similar circumstances; he was fined $5 and costs.[76] Evidently, the railway companies were finding summary proceedings before a willing magistrate preferable to jury trials in disciplining their workers. The spate of prosecutions was short lived, however, and, in July, MacNabb sent a Northern Railway conductor and engine driver to trial at the assizes for breach of rules in a collision.[77] In December, the magistrate said that he 'could not try' a brakesman who had been brought up for neglecting his duty, but would have to commit him for trial.[78] This suggests that Robert Harrison, who had defended Pelling, had been right in maintaining that such actions should be brought under the *Railway Act*.[79] In 1878, when the Grand Trunk prosecuted engine driver John Berry for disobedience resulting in a collision, the case went to the assizes, where he was acquitted on a directed verdict.[80]

Unlike prosecutions for manslaughter, nearly all of which originated in coroners' inquisitions, disobedience prosecutions were almost completely within the control of the railway companies themselves. The chief exceptions were a few police prosecutions of trainmen for running at excessive speeds contrary to municipal bylaws. Disobedience prosecutions became an extension of the railway companies' domestic disciplinary powers, to be used or avoided as the needs of the moment required.

If employees typically received the benefit of the doubt from jurors, the companies did not. The idea that railway companies accepted accidents as a normal cost of doing business was widely held. It even found voice in the *Transactions* of the Canadian Society of Civil Engineers:

Accidents which are caused by defective track, defective bridges or trestles, inefficient fences, low bridges, buildings too close, &c., &c., are in by far the greater number of incidents preventable accidents. And yet many railway corporations prefer to run the risk of accident, and pay the damages when they arise, rather than be at the expense of removing the apparent cause. There are railways which could easily be named (running through long settled country) where there are no fences to speak of, and where the management prefers to pay for cattle killed or passengers injured rather than fence the track, and laughs at legislative enactments that no one ever undertakes to enforce. There are railways, where the low overhead bridge counts more than one or two victims, and yet continues to exist; and there are numerous examples to be found, of weak, rotten and unguarded trestles, patiently waiting the time when they will spring into notoriety as the cause of a 'frightful accident.'[81]

Juries are an index of popular allocations of blame. It was not only that they awarded vicarious damages to accident victims, but that they often seemed to hold the companies directly responsible. They almost always found against the railway companies in personal injury cases. This propensity was notorious. 'Every person of any experience in courts of justice knows that a scintilla of evidence against a railway company is enough to secure a verdict for the plaintiff,' Baron Bramwell once said, and in his testimony before an English royal commission he expressly made the connection with employment law: 'There are cases in which juries go wrong; for instance, in an action against a railway company, they generally go wrong there; in actions for discharging a servant they generally go wrong ...'[82]

This point about juries is an important one, because it reminds us that even within the four corners of the paradigmatic legal process – the trial – there were practices in contestation. Decision-making by judges and decision-making by juries were not just different processes; they could be opposing processes. Such considerations may encourage us to view 'law' itself as a practice, or a complex of practices, and indeed there is much to be said for placing the lawyers and judges on the same ground as the enginemen and conductors for historical scrutiny. But there are dangers on the other side. The practices of judges and juries are not 'the law.' Nor are ideas about justice or duty. 'The law' is something more concrete, the *effective* expression of norms of decision, power clothed with right. This is what distinguishes 'the law' from other institutions and processes. The practices of judges and courts may vary widely across the centuries and from place to place, but law is everywhere and inevitable. Law is hegemonic; among competing normative processes, it is the one that rules.

In mid-nineteenth-century Canada, with the rapid development of the railways, two quite distinct and competing, although certainly over-lapping, rule-based systems grappled with the circumstances of the new industry. The law dispensed by judges, fed from the sources of the common law and by the efforts of legislators, changed to accommodate the railway age. At the same time the sheer operational reality of the industry produced its own disciplinary institutions and practices. It should come as no surprise that the two systems were in many respects very much alike – after all, they were the necessary creatures of the same economy and society. That there were two systems at all was the prod-uct of an underlying sameness: on the one hand, judicial deference to the rights of property; on the other, railway managers' insistence on the right to manage their own (and their employees') affairs. The two sys-tems were deeply intertwined: on the one hand, railways could enforce their rules in the public courts; on the other, the courts would rely on those rules to establish legal duties. They were also locked in contesta-tion, the underlying fracture being precisely about private rights and public interest. In this sense, the trial of David Preston was an exercise in hegemony and symbolism. It asserted the public's right to supervise railway operations without challenging actual work practices or the arrangements that necessitated them. Elizabeth Ham's civil action was no less symbolic an exercise because she succeeded. The Grand Trunk's damages were a license fee for managerial autonomy.

Railway corporations were the preeminent nineteenth-century exam-ples of the delegation of public purposes to private bodies. In Canada, they were also prime recipients of public largesse. Despite this, and despite the public interest in safety of operations, the state foreswore regulatory supervision of the industry. The state gave railway managers an unfettered discretion to make operating rules and criminalised employee disobedience. This scheme was ineffective in regulating workers' conduct, since juries were notoriously unwilling to lay the sole blame for accidental deaths on railwaymen. At the same time, by insulating railway managers and operating practices from judicial or regulatory scrutiny, the scheme helped to perpetuate the industry's poor safety record. The criminalisation of railway worker misconduct had less to do with disciplining the workforce, or ensuring public safety, than with protecting corporate management's private right to control the enterprise.

NOTES

* This essay is a reworking of two papers originally presented in 1988 and 1989 but not published. They were intended for a monograph about law and railway accidents, an attempt to draw together my writing (much of it with Tom Traves) on railway industrial history and my interest in the legal history of labour relations. Peter Oliver was a significant source of encouragement for all this work. He participated in the Advanced Seminar on Law and History, which I convened at York University and to which the 1988 paper was presented; he recruited my piece on master and servant law for the Osgoode Society's first collection of essays; and as a member of the editorial board of the Ontario Historical Studies Series, he commissioned me to prepare *Labouring Lives* which contains my study of labour relations on the Great Western railway. As editor-in-chief of the Osgoode Society, he encouraged me to plan the railway accidents book and wrote one of his famously glowing letters of recommendation endorsing my application for teaching release. This nevertheless failed to sway the keepers of the purse strings; the project had to be put on hold; other projects intervened (including my current work on petty justice in New Brunswick, which Peter promoted with funds and enthusiasm up to the time of his last illness); and so it is fitting that it should be revisited here, not only as a contribution to the legal history of nineteenth-century Ontario, in which Peter's own scholarship has been so valuable, but also as a tribute to his curatorial energies in making that field one in which many varied flowers might bloom.

1 W.F.A. Boys, *A Practical Treatise on the Office and Duties of Coroners in Upper Canada* (Toronto: W.C. Chewett 1864), 185; see also *R. v. George Dowey*

(1869), *Prince Edward Island Reports (Haszard & Warburton)* 1, 292; *Ex parte The Grand Trunk Railway Company and ex parte C.J. Brydges* (1874), *Lower Canada Jurist* 18, 141. Some of the spectators at the inquest, who included several neighbourhood magistrates, urged the jury to name specific wrong-doers. The township reeve called on a Toronto lawyer, R.M. Allen, to express a view. Despite Allen's opinion that the names of the persons on the engine should be inserted in the verdict, the jury declined to alter it. *Spectator* (Hamilton), 24 July 1860, copying *Globe* (Toronto).

2 The foreman of the grand jury was a music professor; the other jurors included four merchants, four farmers, three gentlemen, a manufacturer, a broker, and a builder. *Leader* (Toronto), 9 October 1860.

3 For Preston's criminal trial, see Richards' benchbook, Archives of Ontario [henceforth AO], RG 22 series 390, box 90, 57–68, and a press report in the *Leader* (Toronto), 17 October 1860 (republished in *Patriot* [Toronto], 24 October 1860).

4 Canada (Province), 22 Vict. (1859) c.66, *An Act Respecting Railways*.

5 Compare the provision in the Grand Trunk's *General Regulations applicable to all Servants*, adopted in April 1857:

The bell is always to be sounded when approaching a tunnel, cutting, station or a junction, and engine drivers are to take care the whistle be sounded 150 rods before reaching every level crossing of a public road, and that the bell be rung from 80 rods before reaching such crossing, until the crossing be passed ...

GTR Canadian Board Minutes, Library and Archives Canada [henceforth LAC], RG30 v. 1000, 139–54.

6 *Leader* (Toronto), 17 October 1860.

7 The plaintiff's declaration is set out in the appellate report, *Ham (admx) v. The Grand Trunk Railway Company* (1862), *Upper Canada Common Pleas Reports* 11, 86. For the trial at first instance see Richards' benchbook, 243–57, and two very brief newspaper accounts: *Globe* (Toronto), 29 October 1860 and *Leader* (Toronto), 29 October 1860.

8 The English (9&10 Vict., c.93) and Canadian (10&11 Vict. c.6) statutes (both known to contemporaries as *Lord Campbell's Act*) were substantively identical, with one exception: the Canadian version expressly gave a cause of action to the families of persons killed in duels (s.3).

9 According to the *Leader*'s account of the civil proceedings, 'the evidence, as taken on the trial of the engineer for manslaughter, was read from His Lordship's notes.' The *Globe* remarked that 'the circumstances attending the accident had already been partially investigated on the trial of the engine driver, Preston, for manslaughter,' and went on to record that the

civil jury gave its verdict 'upon hearing the case fully investigated.' Richards' benchbook shows that all eight of the defence witnesses from the previous trial were recalled, and against their names he marked 'sworn ante' with the page numbers of their earlier testimony, suggesting that it was read out to the jury. Most of them gave additional evidence at the civil trial. Five of the prosecution witnesses from the criminal trial appeared again, but only one of them was 'sworn ante' and she gave new evidence at the civil trial.

10 The benchbook records the objection without explaining it. The appellate decision states that Preston's evidence 'was objected to, but received, his name being endorsed on the record. Though not strictly proved it was notorious that he had been indicted for manslaughter in killing the deceased, Charles H. Ham, and had been tried and acquitted at the same assizes about ten or twelve days before.' Endorsing Preston's name on the record would ensure that the objection could be relied upon as a ground for appeal.

11 Preston said that on hearing the whistle, Ham stopped his horses and looked at the train before entering the crossing. This conflicted slightly with his fireman's evidence at the criminal trial, read to the jury at the civil trial, that when he first saw Ham, 'he was standing looking at us, the horses not moving; he struck the horses and then the alarm [was] given for brakes. The alarm whistle was made when [Preston] first saw the man.'

12 Richards' benchbook, 257. The defence maintained that the accident was caused by 'want of proper care and diligence' on Ham's part, and that he, 'by his conduct in crossing the said highway and by his carelessness materially contributed to the happening of the accident.' In ruling on the application for a new trial (discussed below), Chief Justice Draper concluded 'that the deceased was wholly taken by surprise when he was just crossing the railway track, by perceiving the engine closely approaching, and I refer to the evidence of the defendants' engineer as confirming and not shaking this conclusion.'

13 John Bell, Record of legal work done for Grand Trunk Railway, 13 January 1858 – 31 March 1861, Toronto Public Library, Baldwin Room manuscript collection.

14 *Ham (admx) v. The Grand Trunk*, 90.

15 *Renaud v. The Great Western Railway Company* (1853–5), *Upper Canada Queen's Bench Reports* 12, 408 at 424. The emphases are Draper's.

16 C.H.S. Fifoot, *History and Sources of the Common Law: Tort and Contract* (London: Stevens 1949), 164

17 Legal writers had some initial misgivings about this innovation, chiefly because they mistrusted juries. In the first (1847) edition of his treatise on

railway law, for example, William Hodges worried that 'the liabilities thus imposed appear to be of a very weighty description. If a deceased person should leave children and grand-children, and also a father, mother, and wife, the damages which a jury may think to be proportioned to the injury resulting from the death to each of these persons, might, under certain circumstances, amount to a very large sum of money.' It was not long before the courts significantly restricted the scope of damages, however, so that in his 1855 edition Hodges replaced his earlier remarks with the observation, 'that the responsibilities of railway companies ... have been greatly extended by Lord Campbell's very beneficial Act.' *The Law Relating to Railways and Railway Companies* (London: S. Sweet 1847), 466; *A Treatise on the Law of Railways, Railway Companies and Railway Investments* (London: S. Sweet 1855), 622. Throughout the 1870s, though, a series of papers read by lawyer Joseph Brown to the Social Science Association, beginning with 'The evils of the unlimited liability of masters and railway companies for accidents arising from the negligence of servants, especially since Lord Campbell's Act' (1870), caused extensive comment, in Canada as well as in Britain. See, for example, 'Liability for accidents' 6 *Canada Law Journal*, new series, 6 (1870), 197; 'Proposed alterations in the law of master and servant,' *Canada Law Journal*, new series, 15 (1879), 174.

18 In *Frontenac Lead Mining Co. v. Kilshaw*, tried at the Kingston fall assizes in 1878, the employer sued the superintendent of its smelter for damages to the business caused by his misconduct. The case seems to have turned on breach of the duty of fidelity (concerning which there was a special covenant in the contract) rather than carelessness.

19 Paul Craven, 'The Law of Master and Servant in Mid-Nineteenth-Century Ontario,' in D.H. Flaherty, ed., *Essays in the History of Canadian Law*, vol. 1 (Toronto: Osgoode Society for Canadian Legal History and University of Toronto Press 1981), 175–211; Douglas Hay and Paul Craven, eds., *Masters, Servants and Magistrates in Britain and the Empire, 1562–1955* (Chapel Hill: University of North Carolina Press 2004).

20 For example, (Canada) 31 Vict. c.68 (1868), s.20(10) and (11). The intoxicated conductor provision seems to have appeared first in (Canada) 16 Vict. c.99 (1853), *An Act to increase the capital stock of the Great Western Railroad Company, and to alter the name of the said company*, s.12.

21 The *Railway Act* provided for company rules and regulations (s.50 of the 1868 revision), penalties of not less than a month's pay to be imposed by the company (s.51), enforcement by the courts in infringements that put person or property at risk (s.78) and by a justice of the peace in less serious cases (s.79).

22 A related and still more complex question is whether employers were entitled at common law to discipline employees for breach of company rules,
or were entitled only to treat the breach as repudiation of the contract by
the employee, thereby justifying summary dismissal.

23 (Canada) 4 Wm. 4, c.29 (1834): s.15 gave the directors power 'to make and
subscribe such rules and regulations as to them shall appear needful and
proper ... touching the duty of the officers, clerks and servants ...'

24 (Canada) 5 Wm. 4, c.19 (1835).

25 See generally, R.W. Kostal, *Law and English Railway Capitalism, 1825–1875*
(Oxford: Clarendon Press 1994); Henry Parris, *Government and the Railways
in Nineteenth-Century Britain* (London: Routledge and Kegan Paul 1965);
and (with an emphasis on amalgamation) Edward Cleveland-Stevens,
English Railways: Their Development and Their Relation to the State (London:
G. Routledge 1915).

26 *Colonial Gazette* (London, UK), 24 January 1846.

27 *Debates of the Legislative Assembly of United Canada* [henceforth *Debates*] V (2),
1846, 1599–1602. For the British perspective, see *Colonial Gazette* (London,
UK), 6 December 1845.

28 (Canada) 14&15 Vict. (1851) c.51.

29 *Debates* XI (1852–3), 786–95.

30 'Report of the Commissioners appointed to inquire into a series of accidents and detentions on the Great Western Railway' [henceforth Accident
commission], *Journals of the Legislative Assembly of United Canada*, 18 Vict.
App. YY, 1855.

31 (Canada) 19 Vict. (1856) c.11.

32 Paul Craven, 'The Meaning of Misadventure: The Baptiste Creek Railway
Disaster of 1854 and Its Aftermath,' in Roger Hall et al., eds., *Patterns of the
Past* (Toronto: Dundurn 1988).

33 (Canada) 20 Vict. (1857) c.12.

34 Board of Railway Commissioners of Canada, *Report of Samuel Keefer Esq.,
Inspector of Railways, for the Year 1858* (Hamilton: Gillespy and Robertson
1859).

35 Paul Craven, 'Regulating Railway Accidents: The View from Desjardins
Bridge,' paper presented to the 3rd Canadian Business History Confer-
ence/37th Annual Business History Conference, Toronto, March 1991.

36 *Beacon* (Stratford), 3 November 1865, quoting Wilson J at Perth assizes.
Although the grand jury had ignored the bill charging switchman Ryan
with culpable negligence (at common law), Wilson asserted that he could
nevertheless be indicted for rulebreaking (under the statute). However, 'it

would look like persecution to indict him for not obeying orders, and the learned counsel conducting the Crown business had exercised a proper discretion in proceeding no further.'

37 Boys, *Coroners*, 53, quoting a judgment of Pollock C.B. in *R. v. Swindall*, 2 C&K 230.

38 *Globe* (Toronto), 8 November 1854. Chief Justice Macaulay distinguished between the civil liability of individuals and corporations, 'as for wrong or careless acts committed by their agents or servants in the prosecution of their business,' and 'other acts of negligence, amounting to gross and wilful neglect, and evincing a wanton disregard of consequences' for which individuals are criminally responsible, 'when their tortious acts endanger human life, and loss of life ensues.'

39 Ibid.

40 Bell, Record of legal work. Bell was the Grand Trunk's solicitor for Canada West from 1858 until his retirement in 1904. When Grand Trunk engine driver George Walker was tried for manslaughter (and acquitted) at Kingston in 1864, he was defended by Grand Trunk solicitors John Bell and Mathew Crooks Cameron.

41 See Preston's evidence in the case of *McLaren v. Central Canada Railway Co.* tried at the Toronto assizes in January 1880: AO, RG 22 series 390, Cameron benchbooks, box 212, file 2, 58–9.

42 For the GTR strike, see Paul Craven and Tom Traves, 'Dimensions of Paternalism: Discipline and Culture in Canadian Railway Operations in the 1850s,' in Craig Heron and Robert Storey, eds., *On the Job: Confronting the Labour Process in Canada* (Kingston: McGill-Queen's University Press 1986); for parallel developments on the GWR, see my chapter, 'Labour and Management on the Great Western Railway,' in Paul Craven, ed., *Labouring Lives: Work and Workers in Nineteenth-Century Ontario* (Toronto: University of Toronto Press 1995).

43 Paul Craven and Tom Traves, 'Canadian Railways as Manufacturers 1850–80,' Canadian Historical Association, *Historical Papers* (1983); reprinted in Douglas McCalla, ed., *Perspectives on Canadian Economic History* (Toronto: Copp Clark Pitman 1987) and in Michael J. Piva, ed., A *History of Ontario: Selected Readings* (Toronto: Copp Clark Pitman 1988).

44 Paul Craven, 'Maintaining the Way: Iron, Rolling Mills, and the Transition to Steel Rails in Canadian Railway Operations, 1850–80,' paper presented at the New History Society, Toronto, October 1986, and to the Symposium in Canadian Economic History, University of Ottawa, November 1986.

45 Paul Craven, 'Faithful Servants,' paper presented at the Legal History Workshop, University of Toronto, November 1989.

46 Mutual dependence is in the eye of the beholder; this discussion is not intended to imply that employees saw things the same way as the companies (although sometimes they did), that there was no resistance to company authority, or that railway workers did not create their own institutions, subvert those created by the companies, or ally themselves with class and other institutions outside the railway community. For a discussion of these topics, see Paul Craven, 'Labour and Management on the Great Western Railway.'

47 LAC, RG30 v. 12477.

48 LAC, RG30 v. 8.

49 Ibid.

50 LAC, RG 30, v. 12477.

51 University of Western Ontario, Spriggs Collection, box 4312: Baines to Spriggs, 13 April 1934.

52 Ibid., 13 February 1934.

53 *Globe* (Toronto), 10 February 1864.

54 Ibid., 18 February 1865.

55 Ibid., 21 September 1875.

56 Ibid., 25 March 1874.

57 *Transcript* (Montreal), 4 October 1859.

58 *Beacon* (Stratford), 3 November 1865.

59 Ibid., 2 November 1860

60 Ibid., 3 November 1865.

61 Ibid., 2 April 1869.

62 *Free Press* (London), 6 May 1874. Emphasis added.

63 Ibid.

64 Ibid., 9 May 1874.

65 Accident commission, 22, 72.

66 *Free Press* (London), 6, 7 November 1857; *Beacon Weekly* (Stratford), 11 November 1857.

67 *Beacon* (Stratford), 2 April 1869.

68 Ibid.

69 *Globe* (Toronto), 17 June 1867.

70 Ibid., 31 October 1865.

71 AO, RG 22 series 392, box 83, Donnelly case file, Aemilius Irving to Rolland Macdonald, 11 March 1861.

72 *Globe* (Toronto), 4 September 1866.

73 Ibid., 13 May 1865.

74 Ibid., 7 January 1874.

75 Ibid., 17 January 1874; *Leader* (Toronto), 17 January 1874.

76 *Leader* (Toronto), 26 January 1874.

77 *Globe* (Toronto), 10 July 1874.

78 Ibid., 24 December 1874.

79 For Harrison, see Peter Oliver's introduction to his edition of Harrison's diaries: *The Conventional Man: The Diaries of Ontario Chief Justice Robert A. Harrison 1856–1878* (Toronto: Osgoode Society for Canadian Legal History and University of Toronto Press 2003). Oliver did not include Harrison's brief account of Pelling's case: in the typescript diary at AO, the *Toronto Leader*'s coverage of the trial is pasted in.

80 *Globe* (Toronto), 29 October 1878.

81 *Minutes of the Transactions of the Canadian Society of Civil Engineers*, 2:1, 1888; comment by discussant Cunningham on a paper by A.T. Drummond, 8 March 1888.

82 In *Cornman v. The Eastern Counties R.R. Co.*, as quoted by F.F. Heard, 'Curious Law Extracts,' *Canada Law Journal*, new series, 11 (1875), 272; 'Baron Bramwell's Opinion of Trial by Jury,' *Canada Law Journal*, new series, 5 (1869), 589.

PART TWO

The Judiciary: Ideology, Legitimacy, and Politics

5

Politics, Promotion, and Professionalism: Sir Wilfrid Laurier's Judicial Appointments

PHILIP GIRARD*

The controversy in early 2007 over the Harper government's alteration of the composition of judicial selection committees reminds us that the manner of appointment of superior court judges is a perennial issue in Canadian political and legal history. Two examples, a century apart, will suffice. When the defeated Alexander Mackenzie appointed several 'midnight judges' in October 1878, the day before he handed power back to Sir John A. Macdonald, an outcry erupted, but nothing could be done. When Pierre Trudeau injudiciously showered judgeships on friends and faithful as he left office in 1984, however, he saddled his successor with an election issue skillfully exploited by Brian Mulroney. Even with the addition of advisory committees to the selection process, appointments to the higher judiciary in Canada remain essentially a matter of prerogative.[1] With neither the *deus ex machina* of the Lord Chancellor to distance judicial nominations from party politics, as in Britain, nor the legitimacy that direct election or confirmation hearings provide (sometimes) in the United States, judicial appointments in Canada have often been the subject of cynical critique as a result of their lack of transparency.

The calculus of patronage has long been the most significant element in judge-making, but as Jonathan Swainger has observed in relation to the immediate post-Confederation period, 'portraying judicial appointments ... as simple matters of partisanship badly distorts the difficulties involved.' The process of appointment 'involved navigating a course between partisanship, the politics of public appointments, professional qualification, and the sensibilities of those schooled in the law.'[2] Existing work does not provide us with much of a sense of how this matrix of factors changed over time, or how a particular government might try to use judicial appointments to achieve goals – such as nation-building, for example – beyond those of rewarding supporters and ensuring that the administration of justice is carried on competently.

The centralisation of section 96 appointments in the federal cabinet means that the most fruitful way to study them is by individual administration, but the secondary literature disappoints on this score. Prime ministerial biographers feel they have more important topics to explore, and prime ministerial memoirs are usually silent or misleading on the subject. Joseph Pope began this trend with his highly inaccurate observation that 'when Sir John A. Macdonald came to select a man for the judicial office, he knew neither Friend nor Foe. His sole inquiry was who, by high character, legal attainments and expertise is best fitted to uphold the prestige and dignity of the Bench.'[3] Decades later, Lester Pearson's comments on his own judicial appointments take up the same mantra, equally inaccurate in his case: 'A bad judge can do a lot of damage. Thus, in the appointment of judges, my first and exclusive concern was judicial quality and capacity.' [4] The literature on judicial biography is less forthcoming than one might hope. Collective biographies of the judges of a particular court tend to focus on the characteristics of the judges appointed, as opposed to the actual process of appointment.[5] Individual biographies and autobiographies often gloss over the subject.[6]

In this essay, I examine all section 96 appointments of Sir Wilfrid Laurier during his fifteen years in office, from 1896 to 1911, although the focus is primarily on the provincial supreme courts and the Supreme Court of Canada, rather than the county courts. I chose Laurier for several reasons. He had a sufficiently long tenure for patterns to emerge clearly. The addition of two new provinces and one new territory required the elaboration of the Canadian judicial apparatus, and the Laurier years also saw the creation of the first two courts of appeal outside Ontario and Quebec: Manitoba's in 1906 and British Columbia's in 1909.[7] And aside from the relatively brief tenure of Alexander Mackenzie in 1873–8, Laurier was the first prime minister faced with an existing bench comprising almost exclusively judges appointed by the opposing political party. He thus had a choice, either to promote incumbent (mainly Conservative) judges when appellate or chief justice positions opened up, or to appoint his own (Liberal) candidates directly from the bar (a process called 'parachuting').

Existing scholarship on the dynamics of patronage under Macdonald and Laurier has stressed a 'remarkable similarity' between the two administrations, and as a generalization that is probably correct.[8] It has also been suggested that Macdonald treated judicial appointments almost exclusively as a reward for political service, with a couple of prominent exceptions (Oliver Mowat and Samuel Hume Blake) used primarily as a fig leaf to legitimate the essentially patronage-driven nature of the process.[9] No similar study of Laurier's judicial patronage has been conducted,[10] but my own previous research on the Nova Scotia Supreme Court revealed that Laurier promoted one of John A. Macdonald's appointees to be chief justice, even though his Nova Scotia cabinet ministers opposed such a promotion, and even though there were suitable Liberal candidates clamorously lobbying for the position.[11] I wanted to see whether that tantalising example of seniority trumping partisanship was replicated elsewhere during the Laurier years. In other words, did Laurier's use of judicial patronage differ from Macdonald's in the extent to which it relied on past political affiliation?

The final reason for choosing Laurier was the quantity and quality of correspondence on the topic of judicial appointments available in his papers. Laurier was not a micromanager: he left the balancing of the minutiae of local patronage considerations to his regional ministers, but inserted those results into a broader calculus. A thematic analysis of the concerns revealed in his correspondence demonstrates the complexity of the factors at work: political patronage, professional ability and reputation, conventions relating to judicial promotion, ethno-religious considerations, and the overall public interest in a bench characterized by impartiality, integrity, dignity, and competence. The papers also reveal Laurier as a consummate politician, able to balance 'all the troubles of judge making' with skill, grace, and even humour.[12]

Initially, I planned to make judicial independence a large theme in this study, but ultimately decided that a more comprehensive research strategy would be required to provide a proper treatment of that topic. A strand of contemporary opinion voiced concerns about the impact on judicial independence of frequent recourse to judges as royal commissioners, and expressed alarm at the threat to judicial impartiality evident in the sometimes overly cozy relationship between large corporate interests and some judges.[13] The Laurier papers shed light on other issues touching on judicial independence, such as how to deal with possibly alcoholic judges and how to put a stop to internecine judicial warfare. These are dealt with only in passing here. Instead, I will concentrate on two themes: judicial promotion, for the reasons discussed earlier, and nation-building. How did Laurier, as the first French-Canadian prime minister, balance religion, ethnicity, and region in his judicial appointments to all levels of courts?

I like to think that Peter Oliver would have enjoyed this essay. He had an abiding interest in the Upper Canadian judiciary in particular, as revealed in his sensitive and balanced study, 'The Place of the Judiciary in the Historiography of Upper Canada,' and his last labour of love, the edited diaries of Ontario chief justice Robert A. Harrison.[14] Indeed, the naming by the Liberal Mackenzie government of Harrison, a lifelong Conservative and protégé of John A. Macdonald, as chief justice of Ontario directly from the bar, shows just how unpredictable the whole process of judicial appointment could be. And that is perhaps the central message of this offering. When analyzed globally, Laurier's judicial appointments reveal certain patterns of interest to students of Canadian politics, law, and history, but unforeseen events and the hazards of timing also played their role in the case of many an individual candidate.

Laurier's Appointments: Numbers

There were 256 vacancies in section 96 courts filled by the Laurier government, 105 in the county courts and 151 in all courts above the level of the county court[15] (see table 5.1). I defined 'vacancy' as the opening up of an existing judicial post by the death, resignation, or promotion of the incumbent, or the creation of a new position. Thus, the 256 vacancies represent rather fewer than 256 individuals, as a given person may have filled more than one 'vacancy' during his life as he climbed the rungs of the judicial hierarchy. Of the 151 vacancies above the level of the county court, which I will call 'supreme court appointments' for convenience,[16] 96 were at the trial level and 55 at higher levels.[17] The latter comprised the following positions:

1 the chief justice of a trial court such as the four divisions of the Ontario High Court of Justice (Queen's Bench, Chancery, Common Pleas, and after 1903, Exchequer), the Quebec Superior Court, Manitoba's Court of King's Bench (after 1906), and British Columbia's Supreme Court;
2 the chief justice of provincial Supreme Courts possessing no separate

appeal court (all provinces except Ontario, Quebec, Manitoba pre-1907, and British Columbia pre-1910);

3 chief justices of those provinces possessing appeal courts, who were styled chief justices of their respective provinces;[18]

4 the chief justice of the Northwest Territories Supreme Court until 1907;

5 puisne judges of a provincial court of appeal; and

6 all members of the Supreme Court of Canada.

Laurier's Appointments: Process

The minister of justice played a highly significant role in judicial appointments. In replying to a judicial aspirant from British Columbia, Laurier begged his correspondent 'to remember that in all judicial appointments my word is not the supreme and last one, but the Minister of Justice is the man who finally decides.'[19] Laurier had four ministers of justice: Oliver Mowat (1896–7), David Mills (1897–1902), Charles Fitzpatrick (1902–6), and Allen Aylesworth (1906–11), none of whom was exactly a shrinking violet. Nonetheless, his statement cannot be taken at face value. Even if the minister of justice was responsible for formally proposing candidates to cabinet for appointment, the Laurier papers show the prime minister's active personal involvement in many files. In fact, Laurier seldom referred to the minister of justice in his correspondence with judicial aspirants, and sought out directly the opinions of a variety of influential figures as part of the process of filling judicial vacancies. I have felt justified in referring to all the judges appointed during these years as 'Laurier appointments' because in spite of the involvement of a variety of people in the process, the buck really did stop on Laurier's desk.

The views of the senior regional minister from the province in question were also important. In replying to a judicial aspirant from Ontario, Laurier noted that 'these appointments are to be left to my colleagues who represent each province in the Cabinet, and in [your] case, it has to be left to my colleagues from Ontario.'[20] Once again, though, this overstates the case. The opinion of W.S. Fielding, as Nova Scotia's cabinet representative and minister of finance in all four of Laurier's governments, was highly important in all judicial appointments for that province, but he did not always get his way.[21] Fielding did not agree with Laurier's decision to promote Charles Townshend to the chief justiceship of Nova Scotia in 1907, for example, nor did Frederick Borden, the

Table 5.1: Appointments to Supreme and County/District Courts, July 1896–October 1911

Court	Vacancies above trial level	Number filled by promotion	Vacancies at trial level	Vacancies at Co/Dist Ct
Supreme Court of Canada	12	7	N/A	N/A
Exchequer	–	–	1	N/A
Ontario	11	6	12	55
Quebec	11	8	43	N/A*
Nova Scotia	2	2	5	8
New Brunswick	1	1	4	3
PEI	–	–	1	3
Manitoba	8	6	8	6
Northwest Territories	1**	1	***	N/A
Yukon	–	–	4	N/A
Saskatchewan	1	1	5	8
Alberta	2	1	5	7
BC	6	3	8	15
Totals	55	36	96	105

Notes: Total vacancies 1896–1911 (excluding county courts): 55 above trial + 96 trial = 151. Proportion of vacancies above trial filled by promotion = 36/55 (65%).
*Quebec had no county courts, hence the larger size of the Superior Court.
**Laurier appointed two chief justices of the Northwest Territories Supreme Court (NWTSC), but the second became the chief justice of Alberta and is counted there.
***Five judges appointed to NWT SC later shifted to Saskatchewan SC (3) and Alberta SC (2), and are counted in SK and AB totals; one of these later shifted from SK to MB KB and is counted again there.

other cabinet member from the province. And when Laurier learned that Arthur Lewis Sifton was stepping down as chief justice of Alberta in order to become premier of the province, in addition to asking for Sifton's own views as to a successor, he said 'of course I must consult Oliver.'[22] He meant Frank Oliver, MP for Edmonton, successor to Sifton's brother Clifford as minister of the interior and Alberta's representative in the cabinet. But in the end, Laurier did not agree with either Sifton or Oliver's proposed candidate for the puisne judgeship opened up by Horace Harvey's promotion to the chief justiceship.[23] Rather, he placed 'a good deal of reliance generally on [the] judgment and advice of ... our good old friend [Alberta] Senator Peter Talbot,' and in the end preferred Talbot's candidate for the position, William Simmons. In addition to political figures, the opinions of Catholic bishops were sometimes sought (or provided unsolicited at the behest of the candidate) where a Catholic candidate was in the running for a particular vacancy. With so many potential sources of advice, the dynamics of judicial appointment provided Laurier with ample scope to rise above ministerial preferences and shape the bench as he wished.

County Court vs. Supreme Court

Laurier observed in 1906 that it was 'more than a tradition, but almost the invariable rule of the Department' that county court judges were never to expect promotion to a higher court.[24] I have not found the reason for this policy clearly articulated anywhere, but one may speculate that the minister of justice did not wish to be plagued by constant demands from county court judges for promotion, and thus decided it was easier to create a strict rule barring the same. English precedent may also have been influential, although it is not invoked in Laurier's correspondence. In the 125 years of the county court's existence in England, only eleven of its judges were ever promoted to a higher court, and none before 1920.[25] The effect was to create a very clear status demarcation between the supreme and county courts, and thus to enhance the prestige associated with the appointments to the higher courts. Again, this mirrored attitudes in England, where 'the county court bench never carried anything like the same prestige as the superior courts – it was not so much a lower division as a lesser league.'[26] Higher salaries and a more generous pension plan for supreme court judges also reinforced this distinction, as did the fact that in 1903 the Laurier government legislated compulsory retirement for county court judges at the age of eighty (provincial supreme court judges held office for life until 1961).[27]

County court appointments were straight patronage appointments, apt for rewarding men who had been modestly useful to the party and had either modest ambitions or modest talents, or both. They provided financially secure positions which accorded the holder some level of local or regional prestige, whereas supreme court judgeships were associated with talent and reputation on a provincial or national scale. Of the 105 appointments made to the county courts during the period under review, only two went on to be promoted, proving the accuracy of Laurier's observation. James Emile Pierre Prendergast, named first to the Manitoba county court in 1897, was translated to the Northwest Territories Supreme Court in 1902, and in 1907 to the Supreme Court of Saskatchewan after it was erected as a province; and the constitutional law scholar William Henry Pope Clement, first named to the BC county court for West Kootenay in 1905, was promoted a year later to a puisne judgeship on the BC Supreme Court.

In Quebec, the absence of a county court meant that the Superior Court of Quebec was much larger than its counterparts in other provinces. By the end of Laurier's tenure it had forty judges, including a chief justice, whereas the High Court of Justice for Ontario had only twelve spread across its four divisions. As table 5.1 shows, Laurier had just twelve trial level vacancies at the supreme court level to fill in Ontario (along with fifty-five county court positions), while he had no fewer than forty-three to fill on the Superior Court of Quebec. Quebec thus offered over three times as many 'high quality' patronage posts as did Ontario in the judicial field; in Ontario, the competition for a much smaller number of posts was correspondingly more intense. In Quebec, the competition centred on the location of appointment. Unlike the High Court in Ontario, whose judges all resided in Toronto but went on circuit periodically, the Quebec Superior Court was geographically decentralized. About half its judges sat in Montreal, five in Quebec City, two each in Sherbrooke and Trois-Rivières, and one each in a dozen or so districts across the province.

Those judges appointed to the outlying districts typically wanted to sit in the district where they had family ties. There was a good deal of lobbying to achieve this end, and the shuffling around of sitting judges to accommodate these needs could get a bit dizzying. When Philippe-Auguste Choquette was thinking of leaving politics in 1897, he told Laurier that

je suis informé par M. le juge Plamondon, [who had just retired from the district of Arthabaska] que le Juge Larue [then at Rimouski] n'aurait pas d'objection à aller à Arthabaska, ... lorsque le salaire du Juge de Sherbrooke sera voté & qu'alors l'ami Lemieux [who had just been appointed to succeed Plamondon] sera transféré là; de sorte que si je sors de la politique, je prendrai tout aussi bien, si non mieux, la place de Larue que celle de Billy [then at Gaspé] & je vous laisse ça en mains ...

In the end, Choquette had to settle for Arthabaska, but his campaign for a transfer to Rimouski became moot when he was named to the Senate in 1904 and resigned his judgeship.[28]

The county court/supreme court distinction was not totally avoided even in Quebec, however, as the metropolitan judges tended to deprecate those appointed to hinterland seats. 'In some of the country districts the judges have not half the work they can do,' wrote Norman Trenholme of the Court of King's Bench, while Laurier confided to his former law partner Joseph Lavergne that while some judges merited a pay increase, 'il y en a d'autres qui sont déjà trop payés avec le salaire qu'ils ont aujourd'hui pour la satisfaction qu'ils donnent.' [29]

The inferior position of county and district court judges was constitutionally entrenched in the sense that section 99 of the *British North America Act* provided that judges of the 'Superior Courts ... shall be removable by the Governor General on Address of the Senate and House of Commons,' whereas the government could and did provide a less onerous method under the *Judges Act* for the investigation and removal of county and District Court judges. On at least one occasion the Laurier government invoked this process, in order to investigate complaints about James F. MacLean, the first judge named to the newly created district court of Battleford, Saskatchewan. Unfortunately, within months of his appointment in May 1909, complaints reached Ottawa of the novice judge presiding while intoxicated. Sir Wilfrid was not amused to receive a letter declaring that 'the habits of the man were such as to bring disgrace and contempt upon the administration of justice,' and grumbled that if the complaints were correct, 'some one is responsible for having given us very bad advice.' In writing to Justice John Henderson Lamont of the Supreme Court of Saskatchewan to inform him of his appointment as a commissioner to investigate the conduct of Judge MacLean, Laurier observed that 'the administration of justice in the North West is a thing as to which we cannot be indifferent. We must maintain at all cost the prestige of British justice.' [30] The Laurier government had invested much political and ideological capital in its role of 'opening up' Western Canada as a free and democratic part of the Canadian polity, which would prosper under the rule of law. The symbolism of the very first appointee to the court at Battleford proving to be unfit was intolerable, and Laurier's government moved quickly to try and address the problem.

Lamont duly held a hearing, but in the end his report was equivocal. One incident of drunkenness was not proved, and although a second incident was proved, there were some extenuating circumstances. The cabinet apparently decided this was not sufficient to proceed with removal, and Judge MacLean (reformed, one hopes) remained on the bench until his death in 1917. If the incident reveals Laurier as initially somewhat trigger-happy where judicial independence was concerned, it also shows his ability to negotiate the delicate balance between judicial independence, judicial accountability, and broader concerns about the administration of justice in the West.

Promotion vs. Parachuting

With regard to appointments to the fifty-five positions above trial level, the evidence is clear that Laurier relied heavily on promotion to fill them: thirty-six of these positions (65 per cent) were filled by promotion from a lower court rather than appointment of a man who had never served as a judge. This in itself was not a change. The Conservatives had twenty-six vacancies above the trial level to fill between 1878 and 1894, and also promoted sitting judges to them at exactly the same rate (seventeen promotions, or 65 per cent). What does mark a change is that of the thirty-six judges promoted by Laurier, thirteen were originally Conservative appointees. Thus, of those positions filled by promotion of a sitting judge, more than one-third (36 per cent) went to men who were owed nothing by the Laurier government. In virtually all these cases, the man promoted was the senior puisne judge on the court in question, or the court below. In other words, an emerging convention favouring seniority regardless of pre-appointment political affiliation was at work. Examples can be found from all across Canada, except Alberta and British Columbia. The convention seems to have originated in Ontario and Quebec, where it was widely practised under John A. Macdonald, and then to have radiated outwards during the Laurier years.

Under Macdonald, however, promotion usually meant promoting a judge appointed by a previous Macdonald administration, so that the demands of partisanship and professional norms were not necessarily in conflict, while under Laurier, promotion was more likely to mean promotion of a Conservative appointee. To the extent that a seniority-based convention gained strength under Laurier, it functioned simultaneously to restrict the wide ambit for patronage formerly provided by the most prized judicial appointments, and to assist in the advancement of judicial independence from the executive branch. In the Canadian context, where the 'Baconian' nature of the judiciary has been extensively documented, this is an important change.[31]

The emergence of this convention was also home-grown, as there certainly was no such practice in England. The office of Lord Chief Justice was usually reserved for the Attorney General, and almost never given to a sitting judge. Charles Abbott (later Baron Tenterden) was promoted to Lord Chief Justice of the King's Bench in 1818 after two years on Common Pleas, but there was no similar example for over a century.[32] Judges appointed to the High Court were very seldom appointed to the Court of Appeal or as Lords of Appeal in Ordinary, the higher posts typically going to members of the government until well into the twentieth century.[33]

It is not clear how and when they emerged, but ideas about entitlement to promotion appear to have become well entrenched by 1900. Snell and Vaughan have noted that 'the senior puisne justice in the provincial appeal court was [seen as] the candidate ex officio best suited and most favoured by the profession' for a Supreme Court of Canada vacancy in the first decade of the twentieth century.[34] Similar views prevailed in provincial supreme courts as well. When the chief justice of the Manitoba Court of King's Bench retired in 1909, Justice Thomas Graham Mathers reminded Laurier that he was 'the senior puisne Judge and as such, ha[d] ... a claim to promotion.'[35] And when a vacancy opened up on the Quebec Court of King's Bench (i.e., the appeal court), Chief Justice Henri-Thomas Taschereau and Justice Norman Trenholm both begged Laurier to send them Justice John Archibald, a judge with fifteen years' experience on the Superior Court, not someone appointed directly from the bar.[36] Mathers was duly appointed chief justice in Manitoba, but rather than promote Archibald (who had been appointed by the Conservatives), Laurier named Alexander Cross directly from the bar to the Quebec Court of King's Bench.

The promotion of incumbents to leadership positions within an organisation is a double-edged sword. Promotion can be a powerful incentive to excel at one's work in the lower ranks. But when promotion becomes too regularised, it can stifle initiative, exclude innovative ideas from outside the organisation, and create a self-perpetuating club. Arguably, this has happened with the Supreme Court of India, where the government has respected the judges' desire to see promotion to the court determined by seniority in the state high courts, and promotion to the chief justiceship determined by seniority on the court itself. This has resulted in no fewer than thirty-three chief justices serving in only fifty-four years, some with tenures measured only in weeks.[37] Promotion by seniority has excluded politics from the process of appointment, but at the risk of making strong judicial leadership impossible.

In the patronage-driven environment of nineteenth-century Canadian politics, it is not surprising that recourse to the idea of promotion based on seniority should emerge as a way of trying to reduce direct political influence on the judiciary, thus advancing judicial independence. While in the English context the possibility of promotion itself being used as a reward by government has sometimes been advanced as a reason to oppose it, promotion by seniority is less open to such objections. In Canada, the entitlement of the Attorney General to the chief justiceship of Canada or a province was also much less secure than in England, allowing a different pattern of appointment to emerge. That Laurier should have fixed on seniority as a way of reducing patronage considerations at higher court levels was of a piece with other reforms adopted by his government. Patronage lists for purchasing supplies (though not services) were abolished in 1907. In 1908, a permanent Civil Service Commission was appointed with a view to ensuring respect for the merit principle throughout the civil service. And the *Election Act* of that year 'forbade corporations to contribute to campaign funds, required publicity of contributions, and set heavy penalties for ballot tampering.'[38]

The emergence of the convention regarding promotion of senior judges is clearly tied to a cluster of ideas about expertise, professionalism, and progress. The convention is not a pure expression of meritocracy – the longest-serving judge is not necessarily the most competent or 'expert' – but is at least consistent with meritocratic ideals. And in this era of nascent civil service reform, reform of professional education, and advancing credentialism, the idea that the government should enhance the quality of the judiciary by appointing and promoting the 'best' people, rather than those who were owed favours, began to gain some traction. Of course the ideal was to find both in the same person. As Laurier frankly explained to judicial aspirant J.T. Brown, 'in making appointments of this kind we must look first to the fitness of the nominee ... The next point is to try and give satisfaction to those upon whom we depend for our support.'[39] That 'satisfaction' continued to be highly important for those appointed to trial level positions, but less so with regard to appellate posts and chief justiceships.

How powerful was the convention under Laurier? Starting in the east, in both Nova Scotia (1907) and New Brunswick (1908), when the chief justiceship fell vacant, a senior judge who had been a Conservative MP in his pre-judicial life was appointed.[40] Charles Townshend was the senior puisne on the Nova Scotia Supreme Court, while Frederick Eustace Barker was third in line in New Brunswick, although the two senior

Table 5.2: Superior court vacancies above trial level 1896–1911: Number filled by promotion and political affiliation

	Vacancies above trial	Number filled by promotion (%)	Political affiliations L = Liberal, C = Conservative, N = no known affiliation
Supreme Court of Canada	12	7 (58%)	L:7, C:2, N:3
Ontario	11	6 (54%)	L:8, C:1, N:2
Quebec	11	8 (72%)	L:9, C:1, N:1
Nova Scotia	2	2 (100%)	L:1, C:1
New Brunswick	1	1 (100%)	C:1
Manitoba	8	6 (75%)	L:6, C:2
NWT	1	1 (100%)	C:1
Saskatchewan	1	1 (100%)	C:1
Alberta	2	1 (50%)	L:2
British Columbia	6	3 (50%)	L:6

to him were only three and twenty months senior, respectively.[41] In Nova Scotia, the senior Liberal on the court was Benjamin Russell, appointed in 1904 after two successful terms in the House of Commons. In spite of a widespread assumption that Russell would succeed to the chief justiceship, Laurier passed him over twice for the top job, once in 1904 on the retirement of Chief Justice McDonald, and then again on Chief Justice Weatherbe's retirement in 1907. On the latter occasion, Russell wrote to Laurier that he was resigned to Townshend's promotion and indeed welcomed it. In such cases, he opined, 'the justice of the case seems to me that either the senior judge or the senior Liberal should be appointed.'[42] Although New Brunswick had had a certain tradition of promoting sitting judges to the top job, Townshend's promotion marked a sea change in the way chief justices were appointed in Nova Scotia: in 1860, Premier William Young appointed himself chief justice, and on his retirement in 1881, Sir John A. Macdonald appointed his cabinet colleague James McDonald as his successor. McDonald's successor Weatherbe, chief justice from 1905 to 1907, was a Mackenzie appointment and hence represented a happy coincidence of 'the senior judge and the senior Liberal.'[43]

In Quebec, the chief justiceship of the Superior Court fell vacant twice, and that of the King's Bench three times: in all five cases Laurier filled the post by promotion, and in all but one of these, the appointee was the senior puisne judge on his court, or very close to it. Twice appointees of John A. Macdonald benefitted from the promotion, one of these being Adolphe Basile Routhier, author of the words to 'O Canada,' who had spent over thirty years on the Superior Court before being named its chief justice in 1904. Two of the Liberals promoted to the chief justiceship of Quebec, Henri-Thomas Taschereau (1907–9) and Louis Amable Jetté (1909–11), had enjoyed tenures almost as long. Only in the case of Jetté's successor was deference to judicial seniority not evident. Horace Archambeault was a relatively junior King's Bench judge when promoted, but had been attorney general of Quebec from 1897 to 1905 and was, as Laurier wrote to him, 'le choix qui était indiqué par le barreau. Je suis très bien renseigné sur ce point là; je connais le degré d'estime et de considération de chacun des juges dans l'opinion de ceux qui paraissent tous les jours devant eux.'[44]

Naming Jetté's successor was nonetheless agonizing for Laurier. His own preference was to appoint his former law partner and long-time friend Joseph Lavergne, whose wife Émilie was assumed by many to be Laurier's former mistress. Laurier had named his friend as a puisne judge of the Court of King's Bench in 1906, and already in 1907 Lavergne was lobbying strongly for the chief justiceship of the province. In addition to emphasizing their long and intimate friendship and his own political contributions, Lavergne added a nasty personal barb: if Laurier were to name Taschereau instead of him, it must be as a reproach for the 'indépendance de mon fils.' Armand Lavergne, whom many thought was really Laurier's son, was a Liberal MP but was about to be expelled from the party as a result of his increasingly vocal espousal of the views of Laurier's enemy Henri Bourassa. Lavergne also tried to argue that taking seniority ('doyennete') into account was contrary to past precedent, a point Laurier did not address in his reply.[45] Again in 1909, Lavergne sought unsuccessfully to become chief justice on the death of 'pauvre Sir Henri,' but by 1911 Laurier, perhaps realizing he would not have another chance, was strongly inclined to accede to his friend's wishes. At the last moment he had to restrain himself, as he told Archambeault with his usual frankness:

Je vous le dis en toute franchise, que si je n'avais consulté que le sentiment personnel, malgré toute l'amitié que j'ai pour vous, j'aurais fait le choix de mon ami Lavergne ... Les circonstances actuelles sont telles cependant que si je n'avais écouté que la voix de ma propre sympathie, il y aurait un tolle général dont l'effet aurait été déplorable.[46]

Laurier's treatment of the top judicial posts in Quebec show that promotion of the senior judge was becoming a strong presumption, but one that could still be overcome by a combination of stellar professional reputation and conspicuous political service, as in the case of Archambeault.

Curiously, in Ontario, where conventions about judicial promotion had been well established under John A. Macdonald, Laurier chose to observe them less rigorously. The Supreme Court of Judicature for Ontario possessed two divisions, the Court of Appeal and the High Court of Justice. The High Court itself had three divisions: Queen's Bench (later King's Bench), Chancery, and Common Pleas, each with its own chief justice; a fourth division was created in 1903, it too with its own chief justice. Laurier had the chance to appoint the chief justice of Queen's Bench in 1900, and duly promoted the senior puisne judge of that division, William Glenholme Falconbridge, a Macdonald appointee. He also promoted another Macdonald appointee, the senior puisne judge of the Chancery Division, R.M. Meredith, to the Court of Appeal in 1905. But four other vacancies on the Court of Appeal he filled with men who had not been judges before. All were conspicuous Liberals, Frederick Lister being an MP at the time of appointment, J. Thompson Garrow an MPP, and J.J. McLaren and Charles Moss having run unsuccessfully for the provincial Liberals. Laurier also promoted one of his own appointees to the Chancery Division to the Court of Appeal, but James Magee was at least the senior puisne in Chancery at the time of his promotion.

The chief justiceship of Ontario fell vacant three times during the Laurier years, and all three times Laurier filled the position via promotion rather than outside appointment. Twice he appointed senior judges, but in 1902 he chose Charles Moss, whom he had just appointed to the Court of Appeal five years earlier; in this case there were two judges senior to Moss on the Court of Appeal, both Conservative appointees, who might be thought to have had superior claims.

The creation of the Exchequer Division of the High Court in 1904 provided Laurier with the chance to appoint its chief justice. This time he succumbed to temptation and appointed his cabinet colleague William Mulock, passing over both a very senior Catholic judge, Hugh MacMahon of Common Pleas, on whom more later, and William Renwick Riddell, the patron saint of Canadian legal history. Riddell's letter to Laurier regarding the post produced what is perhaps the most brusque reply by the normally even-tempered Laurier in all of his correspondence related to the judiciary. Riddell wrote to say that the minister of justice was recommending him as chief justice of the new division, and continued: '[T]his nomination I did not seek and would not have done so under any circumstances – but it having been made I shall feel hurt if it is not approved as tho' I were either not a good enough lawyer or a good enough Reformer.' Laurier replied the next day: 'I beg to acknowledge the receipt of your favour of yesterday. Permit me to say that the tone of it appears to be absolutely unfair and uncalled for, and if you care to further discuss the matter with me, I will be glad to see you at any time that may be convenient to you.'[47] No one could accuse Laurier of holding a grudge however; Riddell was duly appointed a judge of the King's Bench Division two years later.

Moving west, patterns of promoting senior incumbents were fairly strong, but several times Laurier chose to fill chief justiceships directly from the bar with men who had good party credentials and the confidence of the bar. As in Ontario, Laurier had to fill the post of chief justice of Manitoba three times. On the first two occasions (1899 and 1903) he named the two most senior judges, both Macdonald appointees. By the time the second of these men, Joseph Dubuc, retired in 1909, the Manitoba Court of Appeal had been created. The first chief justice of that court, Hector Mansfield Howell, was styled chief justice of appeal until Dubuc's retirement, when he succeeded to the title of chief justice of Manitoba. On Dubuc's retirement, the King's Bench (now in effect the trial division) thus needed a chief justice, and Laurier duly appointed the senior puisne judge, Thomas Graham Mathers, as noted earlier.

Howell had no previous judicial experience, but held an excellent reputation at the bar and had been president of the Manitoba Law Society in 1904; he had paid his political dues by running unsuccessfully for a seat in the provincial legislature. Howell had been a Conservative, but along with his uncle D'Alton McCarthy had joined the Liberal Party in the wake of the Manitoba schools crisis of 1896.[48] There is no correspondence from Howell importuning Laurier for a judicial position, and it appears that Howell was the choice of the local bar in spite of his lack of judicial experience. Later, Laurier would solicit Howell's views on suitable candidates for vacancies in the Manitoba courts, admitting that he knew 'very little of the Bar of the Province, and my colleague the Minister of Justice [Allen Aylesworth] is not very familiar with it either.'[49] Howell was somewhat unusual among Laurier's Manitoba appointments. His continuing commitment to promotion was evident when the Manitoba Court of Appeal was created in 1906: only one of its three puisne judges, Frank Hedley Phippen, came directly from the bar; the other two, William Edgerton Perdue and Albert Elswood Richards, were both Laurier appointees but were then the senior judges on King's Bench.

The judiciary of the provinces of Saskatchewan and Alberta had their origins in the Supreme Court of the Northwest Territories, created by the Macdonald government in 1887. The court as originally constituted had five judges, but no chief justice until the Laurier government provided for one in 1900. The post was not filled until 1902, when one of the original members of the court, Thomas Horace McGuire, was named to it. He retired after only a year, to be succeeded by Arthur Lewis Sifton, whom Laurier appointed directly from the bar. In 1903 the court was enlarged to five puisne judges plus a chief justice; all of them were given commissions to either the Alberta or the Saskatchewan Supreme Court after their creation in 1907, providing a welcome element of stability in the transition to 'home rule.' The first chief justice of Saskatchewan, Edward Ludlow Wetmore, was one of the initial Macdonald appointees and a Conservative. The only correspondence from him in the Laurier Papers is a note stating that 'on my return home yesterday from a holiday trip ... I found a communication from the Under Secretary of State informing me that I had been appointed Chief Justice of Saskatchewan,' and thanking Laurier for an honour he clearly did not expect.[50]

Sifton exchanged his commission as chief justice of the Supreme Court of the NWT for one as first chief justice of Alberta, but he did not remain there long. When he moved into provincial politics in 1910, Laurier chose to pass over the senior puisne judge, David Lynch Scott, in the search for Sifton's successor. Even though Scott was a Conservative whom John Thompson had appointed to the Supreme Court of the Northwest Territories in 1894, one of Laurier's own appointees to the Alberta Supreme Court had advised that he was 'highly respected [and a]ll his brethren on the Bench would like to see him appointed [as chief].'[51] Laurier chose instead the most senior of the judges he himself had appointed to the Supreme Court of Alberta, Horace Harvey. Scott had been Crown counsel in the treason trial of Louis Riel, and it is possible that Laurier felt unable to promote him because of the highly negative views of the Riel trial still held in French Canada. Whatever the reason, the result was that political affiliation seemed more important in promotion decisions in Alberta than in other provinces, but it is difficult to be firm about this because the chief justiceship was vacated only twice during the Laurier years.

In British Columbia the commitment to promotion rather than out-side appointment was distinctly weaker than elsewhere in Canada. This may be related to the uniquely apocalyptic terms in which partisan rivalry is described by Laurier's West Coast correspondents. Archer Martin, an energetic young backroom boy, set the tone for this corre-spondence with a letter written only days after Laurier's first election victory in June 1896. He was not so much concerned to appoint a Liberal to an upcoming vacancy on the Supreme Court, but to ensure that a Conservative was not appointed.

Nothing ... would do so much good to the cause out here as to stop this appoint-ment [i.e., of a Conservative named Eberts] by Sir Charles [Tupper]. It would be the signature to the social clique here that their power had gone and it would further be the end of that judicial tyranny which has terrorized the Bar and made it dangerous for a lawyer to be an active Liberal in the Courts in this City. I have suffered from this influence I can assure you. I know many young law-yers here who would have been liberal had they dared, but with five tory judges they had to succumb.

Martin went on to recommend one Angus McColl for the vacancy: 'McColl is a Liberal though not a prominent or active one, still he is Lib-eral ... He also is a good Canadian and does not share the prejudice of some of our judges against us!' Martin concluded with a rousing call to arms: 'We have fought a hard fight against killer, unscrupulous and arrogant opponents and now we want you to show your power.'[52]

Laurier not only took Martin's advice by naming McColl to the pro-vincial Supreme Court, but then promoted him to chief justice two years later, ahead of three judges senior to him, all of course appointed by the Conservatives. It seems that the West Coast Liberals got the display of power they wanted. McColl died after less than four years in the top job, and little is known about him. His successor, Gordon Hunter, was parachuted on to the court in 1902, ahead of not only two remaining Conservative appointees but also two new Laurier appointees, Paulus Aemilius Irving (1897) and the fervid Archer Martin (1898). Martin was strongly opposed to Hunter, who, he alleged, had gone over to the enemy and was only posing as a Liberal. Hunter portrayed himself as a devout Liberal in his own correspondence with Laurier, to the point of saying that he was opposed in principle to the appointment of 'outsid-ers' (i.e., non-Liberals) to government positions. 'The patronage of the party in this Province is too small as it is to go round without handing out any of it to outsiders however meritorious their claims may be in the abstract.'[53] Martin had made the same point, admonishing Laurier that 'if we go out of our own party to bestow the prizes in our gift we are simply courting a repetition of that disaster which befell our party because of Mr. [Alexander] Mackenzie's neglect to recognize the just claims of its members.'[54]

Archer Martin had an extraordinarily high opinion of himself, and deeply resented the appointment of Hunter as chief justice. The two engaged in some unedifying public contretemps, and Hunter increasingly turned to alcohol as a coping mechanism; predictably his judicial performance suffered. Laurier became so frustrated that he enquired directly of the deputy minister of justice whether the government could appoint a commission to inquire into the administration of justice by the BC Supreme Court. E.L. Newcombe replied in the negative, pointing out that section 99 of the *British North America Act* provided the sole means of bringing judicial misbehaviour by superior court judges to account.[55] Matters came to a head in March 1909, when charges against Hunter were about to be laid before the Senate. Laurier was all for proceeding, but cooler heads prevailed; no charges were laid in the Senate, and somehow the matter was never raised in the House of Commons.[56] The solution was provided by a 1907 BC statute creating a separate court of appeal. Martin would be elevated to that court, which would have its own chief justice, and Hunter would have no power over him.

By the time the court of appeal appointments were made in 1909, there were no longer any Conservatives on the Supreme Court. Irving and Martin, by then the two senior puisnes, were promoted to the new court, and they were joined by William Alfred Galliher, who had been Liberal MP for Kootenay from 1900 to 1908. As in 1902, Laurier appointed the chief justice of the new court directly from the bar: he was James Alexander Macdonald, leader of the BC Liberal Party and leader of the opposition 1903–9. Provincial politics had been officially non-partisan until 1903, when Richard McBride's government clearly identified itself as Conservative; under these circumstances Laurier may have felt that the provincial party needed some assurance its leaders would not be forgotten.

Laurier's British Columbia appointments are unique in the sense that, of the six positions above the trial level that fell vacant between 1896 and 1911, not a single one was filled by the promotion of a judge initially appointed by the Conservatives. Only half were filled by promotion at all, the lowest proportion of any province except for Alberta, meaning that appointment directly from the bar was relied on more frequently.

Finally, we should consider Laurier's dozen appointments to the Supreme Court of Canada. His appointment of Henri-Elzéar Taschereau as chief justice of Canada in 1902 duly observed the convention of promoting the senior puisne judge; Taschereau was appointed to the top court as one of Mackenzie's 'midnight judges' in 1878, but had been a Conservative in the pre-Confederation legislative assembly of the Canadas. When Taschereau retired in 1906, however, Laurier promoted Charles Fitzpatrick, minister of justice in his own cabinet, directly to the post – the only time a chief justice of Canada has ever been appointed from outside the Court. Three other cabinet colleagues would be appointed directly to the Court, Louis Davies in 1901, David Mills in 1902 (also Fitzpatrick's predecessor as minister of justice), and Louis Brodeur in 1911. Wallace Nesbitt was appointed directly from a Toronto practice in 1903; he was said to be a Conservative, but stayed only two years in Ottawa.

The remaining six candidates had all been judges before, and were evenly balanced between those with long judicial experience and those with little. J.D. Armour (1902) had served twenty-five years on the bench in Ontario, while Albert Killam (1903), appointed when chief justice of Manitoba, had served nearly as long. James Maclennan (1905) had been named to the Ontario Court of Appeal in 1888 by Sir John A. Macdonald, in spite of having run three times for Parliament as a Liberal in the 1870s (twice his election was declared void, and the third time he was defeated). The other three men, John Idington (1905), Lyman Poore Duff (1906), and Francis Anglin (1909), had, respectively, one, two, and five years' judicial experience, but they also had long experience at the bar, which most of the political candidates lacked. Idington had few evident political connections, while Duff and Anglin had been highly active in Liberal Party circles.

With such high turnover in these years (half of Laurier's Supreme Court appointees died or resigned after four years' service or less), it is difficult at first to discern much of a pattern in his appointments. Existing scholarship is critical of his record, not without justification, based on the high number of direct political nominations.[57] But Laurier was also trying to make the Supreme Court more reflective of the country's regional and ethno-religious diversity: he appointed the first French-Canadian chief justice in Taschereau; the first Western judge in Killam; reallocated a seat from the Maritimes to British Columbia, to reflect the rise of that province; and appointed two English-speaking bilingual

Catholics to the court, one from Quebec (Fitzpatrick) and one from Ontario (Anglin). The latter appointments gave Catholics equal representation on the six-member court, a novelty considered in the next section. Rewarding political colleagues was clearly a dominant trend, but so was professional reputation (hence the appointments of Armour and Nesbitt in particular), and building a court that fairly represented the major groups in a heterogeneous country. Laurier pursued this mission in other courts as well, but was best able to achieve it in the country's highest court, a matter to which we will now turn.

Religion and Ethnicity

Quebec scholarship on Sir Wilfrid Laurier tends to see him as consumed by the need to placate English-Canadian opinion at every turn, such that he had to ignore or sacrifice French-Canadian interests and ideals.[58] His judicial appointments provide some, but not complete, support for this position. Laurier's attempts to balance the dichotomies of English and French, Protestant and Catholic, East and West, show a certain nation-building agenda at work. As just noted, Laurier named the first French-Canadian chief justice of Canada, and he was also concerned to maintain the tradition of a French-Canadian judge on the Manitoba Court of King's Bench. He went to rather unusual lengths to do so when chief justice Joseph Dubuc retired in 1909, summoning James Emile Pierre Prendergast from the Supreme Court of Saskatchewan to fill the 'French-Canadian' slot. Prendergast was a francophone from Quebec City who had heeded the call to go west in 1882. He flourished in St Boniface, and was named to the Manitoba county court in 1897 before being promoted to the Northwest Territories Supreme Court, as noted earlier. He would remain on the Manitoba court for thirty-four more years, rising to chief justice of the province in 1929.[59]

However, this manoeuvre by Laurier might be characterized as 'robbing Peter to pay Paul.' Once Prendergast had vacated his Saskatchewan position in 1910, he was not replaced by a francophone or a Catholic. Retired judge Thomas McGuire, writing to Laurier in 1909, saw provincial Attorney General W.F.A. Turgeon, a talented young Acadian, as 'obviously ... the next Catholic judge' in the province, but urged Laurier to wait a while, as Turgeon was badly needed where he was.[60] McGuire helpfully suggested he was willing to return to the bench and 'hold the place for him till the time matured for him.' Turgeon was indeed young, at thirty-three, for a Supreme Court position, though

Archer Martin was that age when appointed to the British Columbia Supreme Court, and it is not even clear whether Turgeon wanted the position. Nonetheless, Laurier apparently did not seek out another French Canadian or a Catholic for the position, and appointed the Methodist James Thomas Brown as Prendergast's successor.[61] Nor was a francophone appointed to the Alberta Supreme Court, although one Catholic member (a convert from Anglicanism, as it turned out), Nicholas Du Bois Dominic Beck, was appointed in 1907. The next year Beck recommended to the minister of justice the appointment of another Catholic, saying, 'two Catholics out of six judges would be probably less than the fair proportion.' He was not indulged.[62]

When the chief justiceship of New Brunswick fell vacant in 1908, Laurier did not see fit to promote Pierre-Amand Landry, an Acadian judge appointed to the Supreme Court of New Brunswick by John Thompson, even though he was senior (marginally) to the judge Laurier did in fact elevate. Landry was a Conservative, but so was Frederick Eustace Barker, and in fact relations between Laurier and Landry seem to have been cordial, at least at the epistolary level. It was likely Laurier's assessment that New Brunswick's English-speaking population was not ready for an Acadian chief justice, and in that his political judgment was probably correct.

Laurier did not appoint a French-Canadian judge to a supreme court position in Ontario – it would be another quarter-century (1936) before Mackenzie King dared to appoint Edgar-Rodolphe-Eugène Chevrier. Had Laurier done so, might the whole controversy over French-language education in Ontario after 1912 have played out differently? Could the Ontario government have moved to restrict the educational rights of French-speaking Ontarians so severely with a representative of their community on the Supreme Court of Ontario?[63] Laurier appointed the Franco-Ontarian Albert Constantineau to the county court judgeship of the United Counties of Prescott and Russell in 1900, but in this respect did no better than the Conservatives, who under Mackenzie Bowell had appointed the scholarly Ottawa francophone Joseph Alphonse Valin to the District Court of Nipissing in 1895.[64] And out of twenty-one Ontario superior court judges either appointed or promoted by Laurier, only two, Robert Latchford and Francis Anglin, were Roman Catholic. Latchford spent two terms at Queen's Park and was briefly Attorney General in the dying days of G.W. Ross's Liberal government in 1904–5. Anglin, the son of a prominent Irish Catholic Liberal who had been speaker of the House of Commons, was likewise a recognized leader of the Irish Catholic community of Ontario. Laurier's record was a little better than Macdonald's – there was only one Catholic judge, Macdonald appointee Hugh MacMahon, on the superior court judiciary in Ontario when Laurier came to power – but not significantly better.

Laurier always felt vulnerable to the strong Orange factor in Ontario politics, and revealed it strikingly in a letter to premier G.W. Ross in 1903. In the course of discussing the possible promotion of Justice MacMahon to the chief justiceship of the new Exchequer Division, Laurier agreed that he deserved promotion. MacMahon had had a brilliant career: he built up the largest practice in western Ontario before moving to Toronto in 1883, successfully defended one of the men charged with the notorious Donnelly murders in 1880, and acted as lead counsel for the Dominion in the dispute with Ontario over the province's western and northern boundary. Had he been a Protestant, there seems little doubt that he would have been promoted beyond his position on the bench of the Common Pleas Division. 'But for some reason which I never fully understand, and which always remained a mystery to me,' wrote Laurier, 'I have found, upon every occasion, a determined hostility to any advancements proposed for him ... My impression is that there is a feeling in Ontario, of which my colleagues from there, are eternally reminded, that with a Roman Catholic Premier [i.e., prime minister], Roman Catholicism should not be put too prominently to the front.'[65]

In fact, MacMahon had sought out higher positions before, and had powerful backers, including Bishop Walsh of Toronto, who wanted to see him on the Supreme Court of Canada. He was to be forever disappointed. Oliver Mowat, when minister of justice, told MacMahon in 1897 that it was impossible to put three Catholics on the Supreme Court, although that in fact happened when Francis Anglin was appointed as the first Catholic from outside Quebec in 1909.[66] MacMahon believed Laurier wanted to appoint him as lieutenant governor of Ontario in succession to Mowat in 1903, but was deterred by the Protestant opposition to his nomination. That may well have been the case. In his correspondence with Ross, Laurier confided that he had 'the impression that through the country generally, my religion and my origin are a bar which the Tories have been sedulously keeping up and, which, in the next election, will tell against us, as it did in the past.' Even as a seasoned politician with two strong mandates from the Canadian people behind him, Laurier felt his religion and ethnicity to be a constant liability, and calculated the political cost of every French and Catholic appointment across the country.

One cannot lay all MacMahon's troubles at the feet of Orange intransigence, however. It was, in a sense, his misfortune to be already on the bench, as his promotion would not pack as much political punch as appointing a new Catholic judge to a post. Laurier chose to make his cabinet colleague William Mulock chief justice of the new Exchequer Division rather than MacMahon, and to appoint Francis Anglin to one of the vacancies for a puisne judge. With that, he paid a heavy political debt and also garnered applause (and perhaps votes) in the Irish Catholic community. MacMahon's promotion would have achieved neither of these goals.

With regard to the promotion of Catholics to judicial positions outside Ontario, Laurier's record is somewhat spotty. He had promoted Thomas McGuire to be chief justice of the Northwest Territories Supreme Court in 1902. McGuire retired in 1903, but came to regret it, as he found that 'through the rapid increase in cost of living in the West, my pension is too small for comfort now.'[67] He constantly importuned Laurier, unsuccessfully, for another position or honour – Board of Railway Commissioners, lieutenant governor of Saskatchewan, a return to the bench, a senatorship, a knighthood – always playing up his role as an Irish Catholic representative.[68] The paucity of Catholic appointments in the Prairies has been noted. West of the Rockies, Laurier's record was a bit better. Denis Murphy, appointed to the British Columbia Supreme Court in 1909, seems to have been the first Catholic named to that court since its creation over fifty years earlier.[69] And it was possible to appoint Catholics to the first two positions created on the Yukon Territorial Court. Calixte Aimé Dugas, a Montreal police magistrate, was appointed in 1898, and James Craig, a protégé of Ontario's Robert Latchford, joined him in 1900.[70] The third judge, Charles Daniel Macaulay (1902), was a Protestant.

To round out this consideration of ethno-religious factors in judicial appointments, let us consider again Laurier's Supreme Court appointments. His two innovations there were the appointment of the first French-Canadian chief justice, and equal representation of Catholics and Protestants after Anglin's appointment in 1909. Each of these was significant in its own right, and required some political courage. But this religious balance was achieved at the expense of French-Canadian representation. When Charles Fitzpatrick, an Irish Catholic from Quebec, replaced Chief Justice Taschereau in 1906, the court's French-Canadian complement shrank to one, and there it would stay until Pierre-Basile Mignault joined the court in 1918. There is of course a certain intractability in trying to achieve microcosmic perfection with small numbers. Yet Laurier's record on Supreme Court appointments is quite similar to his record elsewhere in the country. He did not place or promote Catholics or French Canadians on the bench at a much greater rate than John A. Macdonald, and to the extent that he did, English-speaking Catholics tended to do somewhat better than French Catholics overall.

If Laurier used judicial appointments only tentatively in service of a nation-building agenda, his patterns of promotion reveal a more significant break with the past. When he came to power in 1896, the Liberals had been in power only five years in the three decades since Confederation, and the pressure to reward political friends was correspondingly intense. Laurier responded to this pressure by giving trial judgeships, whether in the county or superior courts, to those who had served the party, particularly those who had run for office or had served in provincial assemblies or the House of Commons. In this he followed the Macdonaldian pattern. But where positions above the trial level were concerned, Laurier's fondness for promoting a senior incumbent judge, regardless of past party affiliation, was a clear break with Macdonald.

Laurier pursued this policy at some political cost, and did so more or less uniformly across the country, with the exception of British Columbia. This conclusion sits uneasily with traditional views. Laurier has been criticized for deploying patronage in a manner suitable for the small towns of Canada in which he grew up, but increasingly inappropriate for the more urban and complex society emerging by the turn of the century.[71] This essay has argued that in his higher judicial appointments, at least, partisan considerations were not always the key to advancement. Laurier was responsive to professional opinion and to the needs of a growing judicial hierarchy in which provincial courts of appeal were coming to play a key role; responsive, in short, to the need for a judicial branch appropriate to a modern state, one that was competent, independent of the executive, and impartial.

NOTES

* I would like to thank Daniel Girard for his excellent research assistance, and Ruth Bleasdale, Krista Kesselring, and Tim Stretton for comments received on an earlier version of this essay.

1 Section 96 of the *British North America Act*, 1867 provides, 'The Governor General shall appoint the Judges of the Superior, District and County Courts in each Province.' This essay will use the phrase 'section 96 judges' to include all three types of judges. 'Superior courts' include the supreme court of each province, the Supreme Court of Canada, and the Exchequer Court (later the Federal Court of Canada).

2 J. Swainger, *The Canadian Department of Justice and the Completion of Confederation, 1867–1878* (Vancouver: UBC Press 2000), 99.

3 As cited in G. Stewart, 'John A. Macdonald's Greatest Triumph,' *Canadian Historical Review* 63 (1982), 25.

4 *Mike: The Memoirs of the Right Honourable Lester B. Pearson*, vol. 3 (Toronto: University of Toronto Press 1975), 222–3.

5 Studies of particular provincial supreme courts include Ignace-J. Deslauriers, *La Cour supérieure du Québec et ses juges 1849–1er janvier 1980* (Quebec: n.p. 1980); Pierre-Georges Roy, *Les Juges de la Province de Québec* (Quebec: Imprimerie du Roi 1933); J.W. Lawrence, *The Judges of New Brunswick and Their Times* (1907; reprint, Fredericton: Acadiensis Press 1983), with a new introduction by D.G. Bell; W.J. Klein, 'Judicial Recruitment in Manitoba, Ontario and Quebec 1905–1970,' (PhD diss., University of Toronto 1975); Clara Greco, 'The Superior Court Judiciary of Nova Scotia, 1754–1900: A Collective Biography,' in P. Girard and J. Phillips, eds., *Essays in the History of Canadian Law*, vol. 3, *Nova Scotia* (Toronto: Osgoode Society for Canadian Legal History and University of Toronto Press 1990); R.B. Brown and S.S. Jones, 'A Collective Biography of the Supreme Court Judiciary of Nova Scotia, 1900–2000,' in P. Girard, J. Phillips, and B. Cahill, eds., *The Supreme Court of Nova Scotia, 1754–2004: From Imperial Bastion to Provincial Oracle* (Toronto: Osgoode Society for Canadian Legal History and University of Toronto Press 2004); D. Brawn, *The Court of Queen's Bench of Manitoba 1870–1950* (Toronto: Osgoode Society for Canadian Legal History and University of Toronto Press 2006); L. Knafla and R. Klumpenhouwer, *Lords of the Western Bench: A Biographical History of the Supreme and District Courts of Alberta 1876–1990* (Calgary: Legal Archives Society 1997); David Vercheres, *A Progression of Judges: A History of the Supreme Court of British Columbia* (Vancouver: UBC Press 1988).

6 A pioneering study that examines in detail the backstory to an individual judge's appointment is J.G. Snell, 'Frank Anglin Joins the Bench: A Study of Judicial Patronage, 1897–1904,' *Osgoode Hall Law Journal* 18 (1980), 664–73. Robert J. Sharpe and Kent Roach shed some light on Brian Dickson's initial appointment to the Manitoba Court of Queen's Bench in 1963, but almost none on his promotion to the Supreme Court of Canada a decade later.

Brian Dickson: A Judge's Journey (Toronto: University of Toronto Press and the Osgoode Society for Canadian Legal History 2003). With Bertha Wilson's biographer, it is the obverse: there is fairly detailed coverage of Wilson's appointment to the Supreme Court of Canada but very little of her appointment to the Ontario Court of Appeal. Ellen Anderson, *Judging Bertha Wilson: Law as Large as Life* (Toronto: University of Toronto Press and the Osgoode Society for Canadian Legal History 2001). Samuel Hughes discusses his own appointment rather defensively in *Steering the Course: A Memoir* (Montreal: McGill-Queen's University Press 2000).

7   Prior to the establishment of separate courts of appeal, provincial supreme courts were 'unicameral'; appeals from the trial judge were made to the full bench (hence, the label '*in banco* appeals'). The trial judge was not formally prohibited from joining in the appeal from his own decision until well into the twentieth century.

8   G.T. Stewart, 'Political Patronage under Macdonald and Laurier 1878–1911,' *American Review of Canadian Studies* 10 (1980), 12.

9   Stewart, 'Macdonald's Greatest Triumph.'

10   Klein, 'Judicial Recruitment,' studied Laurier's judicial appointments from 1905 only, in Ontario, Quebec, and Manitoba.

11   P. Girard, 'The Supreme Court of Nova Scotia, Responsible Government, and the Quest for Legitimacy, 1850–1920,' *Dalhousie Law Journal* 17 (1994), 438–9. The matter is further explored in my forthcoming *DCB* entry for Benjamin Russell.

12   The phrase was one used by John A. Macdonald in 1869, as cited in Swainger, *The Canadian Department of Justice and the Completion of Confederation*, 99.

13   The best-known example is John Ewart's 1903 harangue on the topic when he 'welcomed' William Egerton Perdue to the bench of Manitoba on behalf of the bar. Ewart alleged that railway companies offered free passes to judges, and that judicial independence was subverted when the federal government paid handsome bonuses to judges to conduct royal commissions. The *Canadian Law Review* agreed with Ewart's critique, suggesting it was not mere idiosyncrasy on his part. See Brawn, *Court of Queen's Bench*, 179–82.

14   'The Place of the Judiciary,' G.B. Baker and J. Phillips, eds., *Essays in the History of Canadian Law*, vol. 8, *In Honour of R.C.B. Risk* (Toronto: Osgoode Society for Canadian Legal History and University of Toronto Press 1999); P. Oliver, *The Conventional Man: The Diaries of Ontario Chief Justice Robert A. Harrison 1856–1878* (Toronto: Osgoode Society for Canadian Legal History and University of Toronto Press 2003).

15 N. Omer Coté, *Political Appointments Parliaments and the Judicial Bench in the Dominion of Canada 1896 to 1917* (Ottawa: Lowe-Martin 1917). Also useful is the earlier volume of the same name by the same author covering the period 1867 to 1895, published in 1896.

16 The courts included here are the provincial supreme courts, the Supreme Court of Canada and the Exchequer Court of Canada. Appointments as local judges in admiralty were not included in the calculations because these positions were almost invariably given to men who were already provincial supreme court judges.

17 Five judges who were appointed by Laurier to the Northwest Territories Supreme Court were later appointed to the new Supreme Courts of Alberta and Saskatchewan. I treated these as only one set of five vacancies, not two, as the positions on the new provincial supreme courts, except for the chief justiceship of Saskatchewan, were not true vacancies. The chief justice of the NWTSC, A.L. Sifton, became the chief justice of Alberta.

18 In Manitoba and BC the first chief justices of the new courts of appeal were styled 'Chief Justice of the Court of Appeal' until the incumbent chief justice of the province died or retired, and henceforth the chief justice of the court of appeal would assume that title.

19 LAC, Wilfrid Laurier Papers, MG 26 G, ser. A, Laurier to William Galliher, 27 April 1909, 154979 [hereafter, all references to the Laurier Papers will include date and page number only].

20 WL to Roger Conger Clute, 8 July 1900, 47255.

21 P. Girard, 'The Supreme Court of Nova Scotia,' 438.

22 WL to A.L. Sifton, 6 June 1910, 172284.

23 WL to A.L. Sifton, 14 September 1910, 174556.

24 WL to W.H.P. Clement, 31 December 1906, 117066.

25 Patrick Polden, *A History of the County Court, 1846–1971* (Cambridge: Cambridge University Press 1999), 260.

26 Ibid., 242.

27 S.C. 1903, c.29.

28 Choquette to WL, 28 November 1897, 18356a.

29 Trenholme to WL, 28 September 1909, 160346; WL to Joseph Lavergne, 18 May 1901, 56307. Laurier's comment is not necessarily confined to judges residing outside Montreal and Quebec, but is likely aimed mostly at them.

30 WL to John H. Lamont, 17 September 1909, 160117. Lamont later served on the Supreme Court of Canada from 1927 to 1936.

31 F. Murray Greenwood is the scholar most associated with this idea in Canada, but Peter Oliver sums it up succinctly in 'The Place of the Judiciary,' 443. He notes that Sir Francis Bacon, attorney general under James I, 'had

insisted that judges must act as "lions under the throne, being circumspect that they do not check or oppose any points of sovereignty."' This is in contrast to a view of judges as impartial interpreters of the law, even where important state interests are at stake.

32 And even that example proves the rule. In 1921, Alfred Lawrence, a senior judge on the High Court, was named Lord Chief Justice, but he was required by Lloyd George to sign an undated letter of resignation; he held the post for less than a year and was succeeded by Attorney General Gordon Hewart, who then served as chief justice for eighteen years. R. Jackson, *The Chief: The Biography of Gordon Hewart* (London 1959), 126–44.

33 Harold Laski, *Studies in Law and Politics* (1932; reprint, Freeport, NY: Books for Libraries 1968), 171.

34 J.G. Snell and F. Vaughan, *The Supreme Court of Canada: History of the Institution* (Toronto: Osgoode Society for Canadian Legal History and University of Toronto Press 1985), 91.

35 Mathers to WL, 30 October 1909, 161516–19.

36 Taschereau to WL, 6 March 1907, 121044–6; Trenholm to WL, 22 February 1907, 120405–7.

37 Burt Neuborne, 'The Supreme Court of India,' retrieved 10 July 2007 from http://icon.oxfordjournals.org/cgi/reprint/1/3/476.pdf, 482–3.

38 O.D. Skelton, *Life and Letters of Sir Wilfrid Laurier,* vol. 2 (Toronto: McClelland and Stewart 1965), 106. J.E. Hodgetts et al., *The Biography of an Institution: The Civil Service Commission of Canada, 1908–1967* (Montreal: McGill-Queen's University Press 1972).

39 WL to J.T. Brown, 4 March 1910, 167513–14. Brown was duly named to the Saskatchewan Supreme Court in April.

40 There was no vacancy in the chief justiceship of Prince Edward Island during Laurier's tenure.

41 Daniel Hanington, senior to Barker by twenty months, died in office a little over a year after Barker's promotion; he may have been offered the post and declined it on grounds of health.

42 Russell to WL, 11 May 1907, 122259–64.

43 McDonald retired early in 1904 but Weatherbe was not appointed until January 1905. The delay was probably due to the intense lobbying for the post and the fact that Weatherbe was regarded as something of a loose cannon even by the Liberals.

44 WL to Archambeault, 12 August 1911, 188852.

45 Lavergne to WL, 25 January 1907, 118637–45; WL to Lavergne, 26 January 1907, 118658–659; Lavergne to WL, 27 January 1907, 118646.

46 WL to Archambeault, 12 August 1911, 188852.

47 Riddell to WL, 23 March 1904, WL to Riddell, 24 March 1904, 83689–91.
48 H. Morgan, *The Canadian Men and Women of the Time*, 2nd ed. (Toronto: William Briggs 1912), 552.
49 WL to Howell, 30 October 1909, 161582. On the Manitoba judiciary generally, see D. Gibson and L. Gibson, *Substantial Justice: Law and Lawyers in Manitoba 1670–1970* (Winnipeg: Peguis Publishers 1972), and Brawn, *The Court of Queen's Bench of Manitoba 1870–1950*. Neither has much to say about Howell, in Brawn's case because he excluded the Manitoba Court of Appeal from his study.
50 Wetmore to WL, 17 September 1907, 129406–7.
51 Nicholas Du Bois Dominic Beck to Charles Fitzpatrick, 14 March 1908, 137542.
52 Martin to WL, 29 June 1896, 4997–5001.
53 Hunter to WL, 11 June 1900, 46368–71.
54 Martin to WL, 16 July 1898, 21634–5.
55 Newcombe to WL, 28 August 1908, 143979–81.
56 On the rivalry between Hunter and Martin, see D.R. Vercheres, *A Progression of Judges: A History of the Supreme Court of British Columbia* (Vancouver: UBC Press 1988), 127–40; D.R. Williams, *Duff: A Life in the Law* (Vancouver: Osgoode Society for Canadian Legal History and UBC Press 1984), 33–5, 62–3, 80–2.
57 See, for example, Snell and Vaughan, *Supreme Court of Canada*, 82–114.
58 Réal Bélanger, *Wilfrid Laurier: quand la politique devient passion* (Quebec: Presses de l'Université Laval et Entreprises Radio-Canada 1986).
59 Prendergast remained in the position until 1944, when he retired after some forty-seven years on the bench.
60 McGuire to WL, 30 January 1909, 151154–6.
61 Turgeon was appointed to the Saskatchewan Supreme Court in 1921, and became chief justice in 1938.
62 Beck to Charles Fitzpatrick, 14 March 1908, 137542–7.
63 The notorious Regulation 17 of 1912 'limited French as the language of instruction to the first few years of elementary school ... and it restricted the amount of time which could be devoted to French as a subject to one hour per day.' Peter Oliver, *Public and Private Persons: The Ontario Political Culture, 1914–1934* (Toronto: Clarke, Irwin 1975), 94–5.
64 Constantineau seems to have had ample credentials to be a superior court judge. He published *A treatise on the de facto doctrine in its relation to public officers and public corporations* (Toronto: Canada Law Book 1910), which was relied on by the Supreme Court of Canada in *Re Manitoba Language Rights*, [1985] 1 S.C.R. 721 at para. 76–7. Valin achieved a certain notoriety later in

life as one of the provincially appointed guardians of the Dionne Quintuplets.

65 WL to Ross, 7 October 1903, 77572–3.
66 There is a lot of correspondence related to possible appointments for Mac-Mahon in the WLP: Bishop Walsh to Charles Fitzpatrick, 17 May 1897, 14796–7; Fitzpatrick to MacMahon, 26 May 1897, 14978–80; MacMahon to Fitzpatrick, 24 May 1897, 14827; MacMahon to WL, 6 December 1900, 51476–80; WL to MacMahon, 10 December 1900, 51481–2; MacMahon to WL, 6 October 1904, 90507–9; MacMahon to Fitzpatrick, 21 September 1905, 101407; MacMahon to WL, 14 March 1908. In addition, there is a good deal of correspondence between MacMahon and Fitzpatrick in 1896–7 in connection with MacMahon's efforts to assist in the resolution of the Manitoba schools crisis.
67 McGuire to WL, 20 January 1909, 150753–4.
68 See letters from McGuire: 21 April 1902, 64487–8; 30 April 1902, 64754–6; 10 February 1906, 107000–1; 8 August 1908, 143025–6; 20 January 1909, 150753–4; 30 January 1909, 151154–6; 19 July 1909, 159179–80; 23 July 1910, 173203. After his retirement from the bench, McGuire (although presumably a Conservative when appointed to the bench) was keen to point out to Laurier how he travelled around Saskatchewan with Liberal candidates during both provincial and federal election campaigns (letter of 19 July 1909).
69 John Foster McCreight was an Anglican when appointed to the court by Macdonald in 1880, but converted to Catholicism three years later according to his entry in DCB 13 (1994).
70 Latchford to WL, 3 April 1900, 44305.
71 Stewart, 'Political Patronage under Macdonald and Laurier.'

6

'High above the Generality of the People': The Ideological Origins of the Nova Scotia Supreme Court Circuit

JIM PHILLIPS*

Two decades after its founding in 1754 the Nova Scotia Supreme Court (NSSC) first ventured out of the capital of Halifax and visited other communities on circuit. In doing so it adopted a long-established feature of the English court system, the assizes, and, as in many other British North American colonies in the eighteenth and nineteenth centuries, circuits became an important aspect of judicial administration. In pre-Confederation Canada only the Supreme Court of Prince Edward Island did not have some sort of circuit system, and the territories and provinces added after 1867 also made their superior courts itinerant. The Northwest Territories Supreme Court, for example, traversed regular circuits in the second half of the nineteenth century, as did the Alberta and Saskatchewan Supreme Courts, successors to that court.[1] The influence of the English inheritance, and perhaps more importantly limited judicial resources and the imperatives of geography and settlement patterns, made circuit systems the most effective way of bringing superior court judges to the hinterland.

At one level the origins of the *Supreme Court Circuit Act* of 1774,[2] which introduced the circuit, can be told as a straightforward account of the search for an administratively expedient solution to a problem of colonial governance – how to organise the justice system so that it served settlements outside of Halifax. In the first section of this essay I survey the administration of justice in the colony prior to 1774 and situate the introduction of the circuit court within that context. But while circuits would likely have been introduced at some point in order to bring the NSSC to the hinterland and to improve the everyday administration of justice, there is ample evidence that they were a response to political concerns. In the second half of this essay I draw in particular on the writings of two colonial officials, both lawyers and law officers of the Crown, to show that the *Supreme Court Circuit Act* was motivated by the desire to use the colony's highest court as both a bluntly political, and more subtly ideological, instrument of authority in the tempestuous political climate of the mid-1770s. Itinerant high court judges in the mid to late eighteenth century were seen as bulwarks of imperial loyalty, their presence outside the capital a reminder of the power of the state and a counterweight to incipient revolutionary sentiments.

This essay, therefore, in addition to reflecting Peter Oliver's interest in the history and the Canadian courts and judiciary,[3] engages with two important themes in the study of colonial legal history. The first is that of the intimately related topics of the reception of law and a legal system and the concomitant institution-building on the ground. The second is the reception not only of institutions of justice but also of the perceptions and conceptions, explicit and unstated understandings, which underlay those institutions. Nova Scotian officials brought in a circuit system similar to that which operated in eighteenth-century England, and did so in part because they had imbibed the broader ideological understandings of the function of the royal courts that were present in the metropole.

The Nova Scotia Justice System Before the Circuit: Ad Hoc Itinerant Justice

In the 1750s and early 1760s the NSSC, founded in 1754 with English barrister Jonathan Belcher as its sole judge, operated in conjunction with two lower courts staffed by justices of the peace (JPs) with no formal legal training.[4] The Inferior Court of Common Pleas (ICCP) had county-based civil jurisdiction, while the Courts of Sessions, also limited to one county, dealt with minor criminal cases and did much of the administration of local government. Until 1759 there was only one ICCP and one Sessions Court, for the colony was only one county, Halifax. For the first five years of the NSSC civil suits from the outlying communities were therefore litigated in the capital, either as original suits before the Halifax County ICCP, which until 1764 had exclusive original jurisdiction in most cases, or as appeals to the NSSC from the ICCP, which were conducted as trials *de novo*. Criminal cases went either to the NSSC or the Halifax County Sessions, depending on their seriousness and the consequences attaching to conviction. The centralisation of justice in the capital likely caused few problems, because neither the Acadians nor the Micmac used the courts, and the only other substantial population was at German-settled Lunenburg.

The spread of European settlement in the 1760s, much of it from New England to take up the former Acadian lands, saw the establishment of new communities and, more importantly for our purposes, new counties – Annapolis, Kings, Cumberland, and Lunenburg counties were created in 1759 following Governor Charles Lawrence's proclamation encouraging settlement, and Queens was formed in 1762 by dividing Lunenburg after the town of Liverpool was founded.[5] Along with the creation of new counties came the establishment in each of an ICCP,[6] sitting twice a year, and henceforth litigants went there at first instance. By the mid-1760s two related complaints were being voiced about this system. First, increased settlement and more litigation also meant more appeals, which led in turn to complaints about the inconvenience and expense of having to litigate in the capital. Second, concerns were expressed about the quality of adjudication in the ICCPs. As Governor Montague Wilmot put it, local judges' 'want of education' and their 'interests and concerns with the people' precipitated complaints about 'ignorance and partiality.'[7] This concern, of course, fuelled the proliferation of appeals.

In 1764 a change in the NSSC's jurisdiction partially solved the problem caused by amateur local judges, but only exacerbated that of having to litigate at a distance. That year, at the assembly's request, two new 'assistant' (puisne) judges were added to the NSSC. More importantly, the court decided that its commission gave it the jurisdiction of the three courts of common law at Westminster Hall – King's Bench, Common Pleas, and Exchequer. This meant that henceforth the NSSC exercised concurrent original civil jurisdiction with the ICCP, and litigants throughout the colony thus had a choice of using the higher tribunal in almost all cases, and avoiding adjudication by local ICCP judges. Despite the fact that the NSSC sat only in Halifax, most litigants apparently preferred to use the higher tribunal. According to lawyer and future Solicitor and Attorney General Richard Gibbons, 'many Plaintiffs resident in the Most distant parts of the Province commence their Actions in ... [the Supreme] Court, to avoid the danger apprehended from the Partiality, Prejudice and Ignorance of their own County Inferior Courts of Common Pleas.'[8] James Monk Jr, Solicitor General in the mid-1770s, was more precise, asserting that by 1774 'four-fifths of the law disputes arising in the country are sued and tried in the Supreme Court sitting at Halifax.'[9]

The expansion of the NSSC bench and of its jurisdiction therefore exacerbated the problem of long-distance litigation. Predicting this, the assembly had requested that circuits be established when it asked for two new judges in 1763,[10] but despite Governor Wilmot's belief that the circuit proposal was a good one, it was not adopted by his council. The most likely explanation, given his later refusal to travel on circuit, is that Chief Justice Belcher was adamantly opposed and carried the day with his council colleagues. His opposition would have been the more pointed because, resentful of having colleagues forced upon him by his assembly-based opponents who disliked some of the polices he had pursued as the colony's chief executive in 1760–1, he had been able to insist that the new judges' commissions, issued under the prerogative, prevented them sitting without him. A circuit which required a non-travelling chief justice would have been of little practical use.[11] Although some continued to advocate for the introduction of circuits,[12] another decade would pass before they were established.

The prosecution of serious criminal cases presented different kinds of problems, ones that could not be dealt with without the judges travelling or, as we shall see, legislation to allow trials to take place in Halifax. Although the new counties had Courts of Sessions, like the ICCPs staffed by non-legally trained JPs, and although the Sessions theoretically had jurisdiction over all criminal cases, English practice had long required that serious crimes, especially capital offences, be tried before superior court judges.[13] Given the widespread availability of the death penalty a substantial range of crimes therefore had to be tried in the NSSC,[14] and a number of cases were brought to Halifax for trial in the 1750s and 1760s.[15] However, in addition to this being expensive and inconvenient, there was the further problem of legality after new counties were established, for the common law required that felonies be tried in the counties in which they were committed. Some cases could still be tried in the capital, for Halifax County was very large, encompassing the whole of the colony not part of another county,[16] but not all could be.

A variety of solutions were adopted. One was for the court to travel to the locality, for the NSSC was the court for the whole colony and had jurisdiction in each county.[17] Much more commonly the problem of jurisdiction was solved through the use of special commissions of oyer

Jim Phillips

and terminer and general gaol delivery, which authorised those commissioned to try serious criminal offences. The first example of the use
of such a commission outside Halifax dates from 1762, when one was
issued for Kings County in a murder case, and special commissions
were issued on a number of other occasions through the 1760s and early
1770s.[18] An advantage of the special commission system over that of the
NSSC simply travelling to the locality was that Belcher, always reluctant to travel outside the capital, was not required to be present. Anybody could be named to a special commission, and Belcher was not
included on many of the commissions which have survived. Indeed
some of them issued after 1764 omitted all the NSSC judges, and named
the Attorney General instead.[19]

By the late 1760s, however, there was considerable dissatisfaction
with this system. The absence of the chief justice, the only trained
lawyer on the Supreme Court,[20] seems to have caused qualms about
trying capital cases by special commission. Lieutenant Governor
Michael Francklin voiced concerns over entrusting such cases to anyone other than NSSC judges.[21] In addition, as the preamble to the statute which changed the system in 1768 pointed out, the special
commission system was very expensive for the government when there
was no road from Halifax to the local community because all court officials had to be transported by sea. A further, and related, problem, also
noted in the preamble, was that 'the uncertainty of passages by Sea'
made it difficult to know exactly when to summon jurors and witnesses
to court.[22]

The result was a 1768 statute which authorised many, though not all,
offences committed outside the capital to be tried in Halifax – it applied
to felonies 'committed in any county situate on the sea coasts of this
province, or to which there is no communication with the town of Halifax by land.'[23] The immediate cause of this innovation may have been
a 1768 case in which the alleged murderers of Thomas Gordon at Liverpool, Queens County, were first brought to Halifax for trial. Later in the
year, perhaps because of doubts about the legality of this proceeding, a
special commission was instead appointed to go to Liverpool to try the
case there.[24] The statute stayed in force at least until to the 1830s,
although it was not used once the circuit system was complete throughout the colony.[25] It was augmented during the revolutionary years by a
measure that permitted the trial in Halifax of any persons suspected of
treason or other crimes against the state, whether or not there were
roads to the community.[26]

The *Supreme Court Circuit Act*, 1774

Criminal cases were but a small part of the administration of justice, however, and dealing with them did not make the everyday problems of long-distance civil litigation go away. Thus, in the early 1770s, the assembly renewed its efforts to have the NSSC go on circuit. As Governor Francis Legge explained to London, the principal motivations for the assemblymen were twofold and had been around for some time. First, 'the travel and expense of the parties and of their witnesses' in bringing cases to Halifax 'is so burdensome to the suitors ... that the debt recovered is often lost in the expense of the suit.' Second, the 'general inability' of the ICCP judges, combined with 'party differences among them,' meant that cases were often wrongly and/or partially decided.[27] The former was also the assembly's principal stated reason, laid out in the preamble of the *Supreme Court Circuit Act* of 1774.

Although it was rural assemblymen who initiated the circuit proposal in 1774, many in positions of executive power also argued in its favour. Legge was enthusiastic, and both of the lawyers who wrote about the court system in the 1770s, Solicitor General James Monk Jr and future Solicitor and Attorney General Richard Gibbons Jr, advocated it strongly.[28] Their political reasons for doing so are discussed below, but they also advanced arguments that circuits would improve the quality of the administration of justice. Gibbons, for example, deprecated the qualifications and quality of the ICCP judges, and saw Supreme Court circuits as the solution. The NSSC judges would be 'in Station high above the generality of the People,' and therefore 'would in a great measure be unconnected with, and unknowing of, them, and consequently indifferent between the Suitors.'[29] Monk, who claimed credit for getting the *Circuit Act* passed, stressed the poor quality of ICCP judges and argued that trying all cases in Halifax was ruinous to suitors. He also argued that circuits would be better for the administration of criminal justice – in particular they would be considerably cheaper than the system of one-off special commissions.[30]

The circuit bill passed the assembly with little difficulty,[31] and the council also quickly approved the measure, although it amended the bill so that it would not take effect until London had approved it. Legge's reasons for the delay were that he wanted to be sure that it did not 'militate against the practice and usage of England,' but the deferral brought an assembly request that approval be obtained as quickly as possible, as 'the Inferior Courts hitherto established in the several Counties, do not answer the intended purpose.'[32] There was no reason to think London would object, for the English royal judges had long operated with a circuit system, and the home government's approval was received in February 1775.[33] The only opposition to the measure appears to have come from Chief Justice Belcher, who disliked it 'from personal Considerations' – the fact that he did not wish to travel outside the capital.[34] Belcher's formal objection was that the statute was unnecessary because his existing commission as chief justice was sufficient, in Monk's words, 'to warrant the holding of the Supreme Court in such different counties as the governor shall judge fit.' However, even if that were true, as Monk pointed out, Belcher had not gone in the past.[35]

Belcher may not have been able to stop the bill, but he did avoid having a legal obligation to travel, via a provision in the act that while the circuit courts had to be comprised of two judges in accordance with English practice, the presence of the chief justice was not required. The original version of the act had not included this provision. Indeed, perhaps anticipating that such an act would shortly be introduced, in late 1773 Belcher had assented to his assistant judges receiving new commissions permitting them to sit without him.[36]

The *Supreme Court Circuit Act* established circuits to Annapolis, Cumberland, and Kings counties twice a year, meeting respectively at Annapolis Royal, Cumberland (now Amherst), and Horton (now Wolfville). The locations were selected because they were 'those counties into which there are roads, and the court can with ease give its attendance.'[37] In one respect the act did not meet all the hopes of the legal professional critics of the ICCPs, who wanted their abolition. Both Monk and Gibbons argued that the lower civil courts were both unreformable and unnecessary under the new arrangements.[38] But perhaps because their judges, remunerated only by fees from suitors, were powerful men in their localities and would have had the ear of local assemblymen, this change was not made. Also, all assemblymen were wary of eliminating one level of court lest it lead, as Monk proposed, to the appointment of more judges to the Supreme Court bench who would then have to be paid for by the assembly, a measure which Monk indeed advocated because of the workload.[39] A fourth judge was not added to the bench until 1810, the result of circuit workload demands.

The NSSC on Circuit: The Majesty of the Law in a Time of Crisis

The *Supreme Court Circuit Act* obviously filled a gap in the administration of justice. But for the political elite of the colony in the early to mid-

1770s it clearly had other, political, benefits, at a time when the gathering clouds of revolution were worrying all North American colonial administrations. Although Nova Scotia did not become one of the secessionist American colonies, there was certainly concern that it might do so. Pre-revolutionary Nova Scotia was a colony largely settled by New Englanders (following the Acadian expulsion), and one in which there was considerable antagonism between the official and merchant-dominated Halifax establishment and the thinly scattered population in the rural settlements, who brought with them from New England their dissenting religious traditions and preference for township government over the English system of JPs appointed by the centre.[40] As relations between Britain and its colonies deteriorated in 1774, there were meetings in some communities to express support for colonial rights. In retrospect, it is clear that there was no substantial or sustained enthusiasm for revolution, and that protests were much more about Halifax-hinterland relations than large imperial questions. They were also fuelled by the unpopular prosecutions initiated by Governor Legge and conducted by Solicitor General Monk of a number of revenue collectors who were in default, which strained to breaking point relations between executive and assembly; the latter sent a petition to London asking, *inter alia*, 'to be delivered from the Oppression of Practitioners in the Law.'[41]

The prosecution of revenue collectors, however, was a dispute within the governing class, and did not engage wider issues of empire and independence. Nova Scotians' response to the revolutionary tide is typified by the one issue that did generate substantial discontent, the two *Militia Acts* passed by the assembly in the fall of 1775. One of these provided for the recruitment of militiamen in every community and for a fifth of those chosen to be stationed in Halifax; the other taxed local communities to pay for this. Governor Legge's militia policy, a response to concerns about the relatively defenceless state of the colony, seemed to affirm that the authorities cared much more for Halifax than the rest of the colony, and took men, money and defensive capacity away from often impoverished and vulnerable rural communities. It was a disastrous policy, producing 'a universal ferment throughout the whole people' expressed through many protesting petitions, including the famous one from the inhabitants of Yarmouth asking to be allowed to remain neutral in the coming conflict.[42] Ultimately, of course, the colony remained fundamentally loyal, although armed rebellion did occur in the very thinly settled Saint John valley (now New Brunswick but then Sunbury County of Nova Scotia) and in the more populous northern region of Cumberland County. But the fact that Nova Scotians' support for revolution was ultimately both insignificant and short lived did not mean that in 1774 officials, who were, after all, fundamentally ignorant about the outlying communities, were unconcerned that the colony might join a continental movement. Indeed, Solicitor General Monk began his 'Observations' on the court system with a stark assertion of this fact. 'With no small degree of truth it has been said,' he claimed, 'that the ... People in this Colony [are] inclined to search after a Liberty so bordering on Democracy as to weaken and destroy [the] authority of the Crown.'[43] And this suspicion provides the background against which those who advocated circuits most strongly drew the links between itinerant royal judges and imperial politics.

The principal advocates of the *Supreme Court Circuit Act* were Solicitor General James Monk Jr and Richard Gibbons Jr, a future Attorney General. Both were Tory Anglophiles and both avidly sought advancement through official preferment. Monk was the son of James Monk Sr, one of the original Halifax County ICCP judges and Solicitor General of Nova Scotia from 1760 to 1768. Monk Jr apprenticed in his father's law office, served as clerk of the Crown and acting prothonotary in the NSSC, and studied law at the Middle Temple in the early 1770s. While in London he became a protégé of Secretary of State Earl of Hillsborough, whose influence obtained for him the post of Solicitor General in 1772, which he took up two years later. When he returned to Nova Scotia in 1774 he also had a promise from Hillsborough that he would succeed as Attorney General when the ill and aging William Nesbitt was forced to give up the post. In Halifax Monk worked closely with Governor Legge in the prosecution of defaulting revenue collectors, and in the process alienated many in the assembly who had friends among those prosecuted. He left Nova Scotia in 1776 when appointed Attorney General of Quebec, and he later became a Lower Canadian judge.[44] Monk's views on the circuit and its political uses were penned principally in his 'Considerations on a Bill for Directing the Supreme Court,' written in late 1774, and his 'Observations on the Courts of Law in Nova Scotia,' written the following year.[45]

Richard Gibbons Jr was the son of one of Halifax's first settlers, and by 1755 had become a member of the Nova Scotia bar. From 1757 he was clerk to the Halifax County ICCP, a post he held for sixteen years while simultaneously practising in the NSSC. He became a close confidante of Lord William Campbell, governor of Nova Scotia from 1768 to 1773, and when Campbell left the colony travelled with him to England in search of preferment. He was not immediately successful, but he did succeed Monk as Solicitor General in 1777 and four years later became Attorney General. He also became the judge, in 1785, of the newly established colony of Cape Breton. Gibbons' views on the *Supreme Court Circuit Act*, contained in his 'Review ... of the Administration of Justice in Nova Scotia,' were written in 1774 for his patron Campbell, and transmitted by the latter to Secretary of State Dartmouth.[46]

Both men appreciated that a variety of measures were needed to prevent Nova Scotia becoming a rebellious colony, and both saw judicial reform as a crucial part of government policy. No measure 'will be more necessary, or more useful,' claimed Monk, than reform of 'the Courts of Law.'[47] Three principal themes about the relationship between the NSSC circuit and colonial politics emerge from Monk's and Gibbons' writings; the first dominates Gibbons' critique, the other two are drawn principally from that of Monk. First, both men saw political benefits deriving from the simple fact that good government, including impartial and effective judicial adjudication, made for fewer grievances. Gibbons began his 'Review' with a clear statement about the links between impartial and effective courts and political stability:

One of the most essential Principles of all good Government ever was and ever must be the due and impartial Administration of Justice among the People Subject to such Government. It will then necessarily follow that the Government wherein the Administration of Justice is lodged in the Hands of Persons of Learning, Judgement, Independence and Integrity will best answer the purpose of its Institution; and the People under its Influence and protection enjoy the Blessings of Peace, Happiness, and Security, and Honor, Obey and respect public Authority in an incomparable greater Degree than where that Power is lodged with Weak, Ignorant, Illiterate, Contemptible or Unjust Men. A Government and People thus circumstanced must be truly pitiable; the Consequences of such an Administration were and must be, weakness in the Hands of Government, and Oppression, Distress and Disorder among the People.[48]

The absence of able and impartial judges would result in 'Hatred and Contempt' for those in judicial authority, which would in turn produce men 'distrustfull to the Government whose Delegates' the judges were.[49] Gibbons returned to this theme at the end of his pamphlet, arguing that a professional court was needed to replace the inferior civil courts, for professional judges would give a much better quality of adjudication and enhance governmental legitimacy. NSSC judges 'by their

Indifference, Superior Abilities, and Application' would 'hear Causes coolly, discuss them justly, and pronounce Judgement upon true Principles of Law and Reason.' As a result litigants 'would be induced to acquiesce under their determination, and thereby avoid many tedious and very expensive Litigations.'[50]

Monk, who was the harshest critic of the colony's lower civil courts, made the same points as Gibbons about the links between judicial impartiality and settler grievances. Both he and Gibbons were also wont to cite as a major problem the fact that ICCP judges were unsalaried and remunerated wholly by litigants' fees. This made them inclined to foment and encourage litigation.[51] But the larger problems were those of lack of training in the law and the tendency of ICCP judges to be 'trading magistrates,' men involved in business with litigants and whose judgments were influenced by their commercial activities. 'Those Gentlemen who grace those Inferior Seats of Justice are mostly Connected in dealing – in Husbandry and Trade – with the Suitors,' asserted Monk, adding that they frequently 'advised the Suit' – presumably recommended to one party that litigation be resorted to.[52] Gibbons also deprecated the ICCP judges' 'Intercourse and Connections in Business and dealings' with litigants, and their tendency to advise their friends and neighbours on going to law – 'many of them ... act as Counsellors and Solicitors between the Parties.'[53] Like Gibbons, Monk also complained about their lack of legal training – the 'want of Jurisprudent and practical knowledge in the Judges of the Inferior Courts' – which resulted in proceedings being 'ever set aside on Writs of Error brought to the Supreme Court ... whether the judgment be just or not.' Time and money were thus wasted in useless litigation.[54]

The links between the courts and politics ran deeper than the simple fact that good adjudication meant good government, however, and the second theme, prevalent in Monk's 'Observations,' was that the inferior court judges were too often untrustworthy men and the inferior courts themselves operated as a forum for political dissent. Many of the ICCP judges were, Monk argued, 'Characters of Violence and *Patriotic* principles,' whose courts served as forums for 'popular meetings,' giving people ideas above their station. 'Each suitor,' Monk complained, 'is pleased with his Faculty of Reasoning at the Bar – on Equity, Liberty and Constitutional Justice,' so that over time 'in place of the industrious husbandman, the subordinate subject, there too frequently appears a litigious artful, "Law and Liberty" declaimer.'[55] He continued with a flourish:

The Peasantry of a Country, where the rudiments of Knowledge are cheap and easy, beget a Fondness for Reasoning – these Courts cherish and improve a disposition for public declamation – and in a short process of Time many a New England Character has been seen to rise from the Plough, and bear the Laurel of 'smart, Cute, Clever, Man' who understands the Liberties of the People, and fit to become a Speecher, or Moderator of a Town Meeting 'to guard to posterity, the natural Rights of Mankind in Civil Society; and the Constitution of the Province, perhaps, of America.'[56]

Abolition of the ICCPs would therefore remove the opportunity for the disaffected to foment political dissent. It 'would accomplish an alteration in the Character and Conduct of Men now artful, indolent, declaiming and dishonest' but who would become instead 'industrious, quiet, and useful subjects.' Should the inferior courts be abolished, he continued, 'the good Consequences immediately would be that such impolitic meetings of the Multitude so led up and educated; without an Authority of Control, or a disposition for decorum; far less subordination to Government; often heated with Liquor, and at full Liberty to meditate and execute popular, violent measures destructive to good Government – would be Averted.'[57] And of course the benefit of Supreme Court judges was that they would limit themselves to adjudication and support of government. 'They would carry ... a sentiment of tenderness in the Crown' and 'not presume to deal out *Liberty* and Constitutional principles to the Multitude ... to the subvertion of Peace and good Government.'[58]

Gibbons had little directly to say about the political leanings of ICCP judges, but he hinted at something similar to Monk's views in his proposals for a revamped judicial system. He wanted the ICCPs to be abolished and replaced by two 'Superior Courts of Provincial Jurisdiction,' one with the powers of the English Court of King's Bench, the other with those of the Common Pleas and Exchequer. Each would be headed by a salaried and legally trained chief justice, and each would have two other judges, who while they need not be lawyers ought to be politically sound. They should be 'possessed of a Liberal education, Integrity, Honour and Sound Judgment.'[59] In short, they should be men attached to government.

The third political theme in the arguments of those advocating circuits, again one emphasised much more by Monk than any other person, was that in going out to the colony's scattered communities the NSSC would act as what can be called an ideological instrument. To clarify this, I draw on one aspect of Douglas Hay's well-known argument about the law as ideology in eighteenth-century England.[60] Hay argues that the criminal law served not simply as a repressive instrument relying on the terror of the gallows, but as 'an ideological system,' one that 'combined imagery and force, ideals and practice' in sustaining the power of the propertied ruling classes. That ideology combined three elements – majesty, justice, and mercy – and it is the first of these which is relevant here. Hay's analysis of majesty points to both more and less overt ways in which the assizes were used in support of political authority. By more overt I mean those occasions within the criminal trial process which gave the judges the opportunity to deliver lectures on authority and deference – the grand jury address and the sentencing speech.

By less overt I mean the general impression that the entire ritual of the assizes was wont to make. Here Hay argues that 'the assizes were a formidable spectacle in a country town, the most visible and elaborate manifestation of state power to be seen in the countryside, apart from the presence of a regiment.' The well-publicised and escorted entry to the town, the scarlet robes, wigs, and black caps of judicial attire, the elaborate ritual of the proceedings, the learning and eloquence of judges and barristers – all gave the law 'considerable psychic force.' While the address to the grand jury and the death sentence provided special opportunities for lessons about obedience to authority, such education was subtly present in every aspect of the assize proceedings. Hay argues that 'the judges' every action was governed by the importance of spectacle,' and cites Blackstone in support of the salutary effect of such spectacle: 'the novelty and very parade of ... [their] appearance have no small influence upon the multitude.' Although Hay was writing about eighteenth-century England, it is noteworthy that colonial elites frequently reproduced, to the extent that they were able, these outward manifestations of the power and authority of the law and of the political regime that it supported.[61] Indeed, it has been argued that similar uses were made of the U.S. Supreme Court, which also traversed circuits in the early decades of the new republic.[62]

Men like Gibbons and Monk had read their Blackstone, for they both cited him on more than one occasion in their writings, and they had certainly imbibed the unspoken assumptions of eighteenth-century Englishmen about the uses to which itinerant courts could be put, for they clearly believed in the ideological uses of the institutions of the law delineated by Hay. Monk's 'Observations' expressed particularly clearly the need for and uses of 'majesty' in the administration of justice. He argued that the judges of the Supreme Court could provide the people with lessons and examples of appropriate behaviour. They should 'maintain a degree of dignity and Authority that would overawe, punish and prevent any tumulatary meetings' and would provide an effective counter to 'the Attempts of the populous; or the Incendiary.'[63] To this end he wanted all the judges and officers of the Supreme Court, such as the Attorney General, to attend every circuit. When they did so they should 'preserve all degree of Dignity, as well in appearance as Conduct' and not 'wear the Appearance of County Attorneys Sojourning for an Existence.' This would be one means 'to keep the Clamorous and disaffected in quietude, duty and subordination.'[64] Monk also stressed the political importance of the circuits in a memorandum written after the *Supreme Court Circuit Act* had passed the assembly, and designed to persuade London to approve it. The act was a measure that would 'preserve a respect by community to justice, government and courts of law.'[65]

As noted above, after the *Supreme Court Circuit Act* was passed Monk lamented the fact that it did not require the chief justice to travel. His presence would help the NSSC 'become of Real dignity, Power and respect among the Multitude.'[66] In an additional memorandum written after the *Supreme Court Circuit Act*, Monk particularly deprecated Belcher's resistance to a requirement that he travel the circuit, for his presence would have augmented the dignity of court proceedings and inspired, even more than that of his colleagues, a due respect for law and, through that, for properly constituted authority. The key was 'to throw the Judicial Powers of Government wholly into the possession of Men uninfluenced by popular Motives, of Jurisprudent knowledge, Wisdom and attachment to the Crown.'[67] Making the direct link between the inauguration of the circuit and the revolutionary crisis, he insisted that such a measure was particularly necessary 'at a Time when the dignity, the Authority, and Consequence of this Court, should disseminate its Power and Influence among the Multitude, for the preservation of quietude and subordination, to that Government they have so long and so happily lived under ... And which ... at present they are but too ripe to lay aside for the ... Continuance and Support of American Violence.'[68]

Gibbons' 'Review' said little about the ideological uses of the circuit. Nonetheless, intense Anglophile that he was – he insisted that 'no human form of Judicial Administration can be better adapted to [Nova

Scotia] ... than One constructed upon the Principles of that of England'[69] – he clearly saw the ideological benefits of the presence of professional judges in the outlying settlements. 'The Reverence which would attend,' their visits, he asserted in his concluding paragraph, and the 'Confidence that would be placed in Such Judges,' would 'tend to remove or prevent Many great Causes of Discontent, Murmur, Complaint and Confusion among the People.'[70] It also bears note that the link between the majesty of the law, as represented by circuit courts, and colonial politics was understood by others in the colony. In recommending the *Supreme Court Circuit Act* to London, Governor Legge argued that a particular benefit of the measure was that 'the influence of the judges of the Supreme Court who are in general approved and attached to government' would assist in 'quieting the minds of the people [and] ... supporting the authority of government.'[71] Indeed, some half a dozen years before the circuit system was introduced, Lieutenant Governor Michael Francklin saw one of the many advantages of proposed road improvements as being that the NSSC 'can be regularly held in the several counties and the people kept in good order and in subordination to the law.'[72]

Conclusion

I am not arguing that the NSSC circuit system was solely the product of political demands. The fact that the circuit expanded throughout the late eighteenth and nineteenth centuries to the rest of the colony, in response to a desire for its services certainly indicates otherwise.[73] Nor do I suggest that the circuit was always seen by the colonial elite in such an overtly political manner – although sentiments similar to those voiced by Monk, Gibbons et al. continued to be occasionally expressed for another three decades. Echoing the ideological arguments for circuits made in the 1770s, at the end of the century, for example, Lieutenant Governor Sir John Wentworth averred that 'it is of great importance that the Supreme Court should sit in the remote districts, as it makes great Impression on the minds of the people.'[74] Similarly, commenting on the 1805 act to extend the circuit to Lunenburg and Pictou, Wentworth noted that 'the Supreme Court sitting in these places ... establishes decorum and respectability toward all the functions of justice, and impresses the minds of the people with deference to the laws.'[75] But such arguments clearly diminished in frequency as the century wore on, and they disappear in the nineteenth century as the circuit performed what has been termed a more 'utilitarian' role in colonial governance.[76]

Nor, indeed, am I suggesting that the views of men like Monk and Gibbons were widely held in the colony, although they were reflected in all of the evidence that we have about the opinions of those in the governing elite. No doubt for many of the assemblymen, especially those who came from communities outside Halifax, the expense of civil litigation under the pre-1775 system, and problems relating to the quality of adjudication, were sufficient reasons for supporting the *Supreme Court Circuit Act*. But the evidence is clear that at least a small coterie of Nova Scotia's official class, Englishmen temporarily resident in the colony like Legge or Anglophiles like Monk and Gibbons, appreciated very clearly the links between the forms of law and the substance of political authority. In the heated times of the early 1770s they saw the NSSC circuit as working two important changes. It would substantially undermine the local power of ICCP judges and, even more importantly, they would bring the majesty of the law – its elaborate rituals, its grand jury addresses, its processions of royal authority – to the colony's far-flung communities. In doing so the judges were to impress the inhabitants with clear evidence of the tangible reality of royal power, while providing an oratorical counterweight to any talk of resistance to the authorities in Halifax. The *Supreme Court Circuit Act* thus provides an example of not only colonial institutional borrowing but also of ideological transmission across the Atlantic.

NOTES

* I thank Brad Miller for comments on a previous draft of this essay, and the reviewers of this volume for reading it.

1 See L.A. Knafla, 'The Supreme Court of Alberta: The Formative Years, 1905–1921,' in J. Swainger, ed., *The Supreme Court at 100: History and Authority* (Toronto: Osgoode Society for Canadian Legal History and University of Alberta Press 2007). For the other Western provinces, see D. Brawn, *The Court of Queen's Bench of Manitoba, 1870–1950: A Biographical History* (Toronto: Osgoode Society for Canadian Legal History and University of Toronto Press 2006), and H. Foster, 'The Struggle for the Supreme Court: Law and Politics in British Columbia, 1871–1885,' in L.A. Knafla, ed., *Law and Justice in a New Land: Essays in Western Canadian Legal History* (Toronto: Carswell 1986). For the pre-Confederation provinces, see M. Banks, 'The

Evolution of the Ontario Courts, 1788–1981,' in D. Flaherty, ed., *Essays in the History of Canadian Law*, vol. 2 (Toronto: Osgoode Society for Canadian Legal History and University of Toronto Press 1983); N.J. Goudie, 'The Supreme Court on Circuit: Northern District, 1826–1833,' in C. English, ed., *Essays in the History of Canadian Law*, vol. 9, *Two Islands, Newfoundland and Prince Edward Island* (Toronto: Osgoode Society for Canadian Legal History and University of Toronto Press 2005); K. Donovan, 'The Origin and Establishment of the New Brunswick Courts,' *Journal of the New Brunswick Museum* (1980), 57–64; D. Fyson, *The Court Structure of Quebec and Lower Canada, 1760–1860* (Montreal: Montreal History Group 1994).

2 *Statutes of Nova Scotia [SNS]* 1774, c.6.

3 See his *The Conventional Man: The Diaries of Ontario Chief Justice Robert A. Harrison, 1856–1878* (Toronto: Osgoode Society for Canadian Legal History and University of Toronto Press 2003), and 'Power, Politics, and the Law: The Place of the Judiciary in the Historiography of Upper Canada,' in G.B. Baker and J. Phillips, eds., *Essays in the History of Canadian Law*, vol. 8, *In Honour of R.C.B. Risk* (Toronto: Osgoode Society for Canadian Legal History and University of Toronto Press 1999).

4 The discussion of the history and jurisdiction of the Supreme Court in this and subsequent paragraphs is based on J.B. Cahill and J. Phillips, 'The Supreme Court of Nova Scotia: Origins to Confederation,' in P. Girard, J. Phillips, and J.B. Cahill, eds., *The Supreme Court of Nova Scotia, 1754–2004: From Imperial Bastion to Provincial Oracle* (Toronto: Osgoode Society for Canadian Legal History and University of Toronto Press 2004). There were of course courts other than the NSSC and the ICCP, including a small claims jurisdiction reserved for JPs, a Court of Chancery with the governor as chancellor, and a variety of specialised courts – admiralty, marriage, and divorce, and so on. But for current purposes the ones that mattered are the NSSC and its two immediately subordinate bodies for civil and criminal cases.

5 See J. M. Beck, *The Evolution of Municipal Government in Nova Scotia* (Halifax: Public Archives of Nova Scotia 1973), and D.C. Harvey, 'The Struggle for the New England Form of Township Government in Nova Scotia,' *CHA Report* (1933), 15–22.

6 See, for example, Council Minutes, 9 January 1760, Nova Scotia Archives and Records Management [NSARM], Record Group [RG] 1, vol. 188, 101.

7 Governor Montague Wilmot to Board of Trade, 17 December 1764, NSARM, Colonial Office Series [CO] 217, vol. 21, 126.

8 J.B. Cahill, 'Richard Gibbons' "Review of the Administration of Justice,"' *University of New Brunswick Law Journal* 37 (1988), 52 [hereafter 'Gibbons' Review']; see below for a discussion of the genesis of this document.

9 James Monk Jr, 'Considerations on a Bill for Directing the Supreme Court of Nova Scotia to Sit in the Counties of Halifax, King's County, Annapolis, and Cumberland, November 1774,' at CO 217, vol. 51, 71.

10 For the assembly address, which makes it clear that having a circuit was an important motivation for the appointment of additional judges, see *Assembly Journals*, 19 and 24 November 1763 and Assembly to Governor Wilmot, 24 November 1763, CO 217, vol. 21, 9. For Wilmot's attitude, see Wilmot to Board of Trade, 17 December 1764, CO 217, vol. 21, 126.

11 The council did discuss a compromise suggestion that a kind of 'super ICCP,' a court between the ICCPs and the NSSC, be established in Halifax and also travel to outlying communities, 'so that the administration of justice would be similar to that in England,' but nothing came of this. See Wilmot to Board of Trade, 17 December 1764, CO 217, vol. 21, 126.

12 See Lieutenant Governor Michael Francklin to Board of Trade, 30 September 1766, CO 217, vol. 44, 73.

13 For English practice, see J.M. Beattie, *Crime and the Courts in England, 1660–1800* (Princeton: Princeton University Press 1986).

14 For the content of the Nova Scotia criminal law in this period, see J. Phillips, 'Securing Obedience to Necessary Laws: The Criminal Law in Eighteenth Century Nova Scotia,' *Nova Scotia Historical Review* 12 (1992), 87–124.

15 In 1757, for example, an ex-soldier called Wilkinson was tried in Halifax for robbing Harry Leahey at Fort Cumberland. See Council Minutes, 26 May 1757, RG 1, vol. 187, 514–16, and Supreme Court Records, RG 39, Series J, vol. 117.

16 See the trial of Robert Bacon in 1765 for a murder allegedly committed at Louisbourg, RG 39, Series J, vol. 1, 23, and Series C, vol. 4, No 47. In fact this is the only example I have found where an offence committed in the far reaches of Halifax County was tried in Halifax between 1759 and the enactment of a statute in 1768 (see below) which permitted cases from throughout the colony, from Halifax or any other county, to be tried in the capital.

17 Lieutenant-Governor Francklin to Board of Trade, 12 June 1768, CO 217, vol. 22, 231.

18 For the Kings commission, see Council Minutes, 30 January 1762, RG 1, vol. 188, 293–4. For Annapolis, Queens, and Kings, see ibid., 17 October 1767, 16 August 1768, and 27 September 1768, RG 1, vol. 189, 79, 107, 109; Commissions Series, RG 1, vol. 168, 37–8, and vol. 251, 150. Special commissions were used for all criminal trials in Halifax in the early 1760s, because Belcher served as chief executive of the colony for three years and thus could not also preside in the NSSC. See Cahill and Phillips, 'Origins to Confederation,' 58.

19 Attorney General William Nesbitt was one of three named to preside on a special commission to sit at Liverpool in 1768. See Council Minutes, 16 August 1768, RG 1, vol. 189, 109.

20 None of the first four assistant judges – Charles Morris, John Collier, John Duport, and Isaac Deschamps – was a lawyer. The first legally trained assistant judge was James Brenton, appointed in 1781. See Cahill and Phillips, 'Origins to Confederation.'

21 Lieutenant-Governor Francklin to Board of Trade, 12 June 1768, CO 217, vol. 22, 231.

22 *Supreme Court Act*, SNS 1768, Second Session, c.9.

23 Ibid. For its passage, see *Assembly Journals*, 21, 25, and 26 November 1768.

24 See *Nova Scotia Gazette*, 28 July 1768; Council Minutes, 16 August 1768, RG 1, vol. 189, 109; RG 1, vol. 167, 78. The case was tried in Liverpool in September, RG 39, Series J, vol. 1, 61–5.

25 The act was reproduced in Uniacke's 1805 edition of the statutes, which only included the text of statutes still in force and was commented on by Beamish Murdoch in his *Epitome of the Laws of Nova Scotia*, vol. 3 (Halifax Howe, 1832–4), 56.

26 *Trial of Crimes Against Government Act*, SNS 1777, c.13 (in Manuscript Statutes, RG 5, Series S, vol. 5). This statute was only to stay in force 'during the present Rebellion in America.' It was used in April 1777 when Thomas Falconer and Parker Clarke were tried at Halifax for high treason committed in Cumberland County. See E.A. Clarke and J. Phillips, 'Rebellion and Repression in Nova Scotia,' in F.M. Greenwood and J.B. Wright, eds., *Canadian State Trials*, vol. 1, *Law, Politics and Security Measures, 1608–1837* (Toronto: Osgoode Society for Canadian Legal History and University of Toronto Press 1997).

27 Governor Legge to Earl of Dartmouth, 16 November 1774, CO 217, vol. 51, 39.

28 See 'Gibbons' Review,' and J.B. Cahill, 'James Monk's "Observations on the Courts of Law in Nova Scotia, 1775,"' *University of New Brunswick Law Journal* 36 (1987), 131–45 [hereafter 'Monk's Observations']; see below for a discussion of the genesis of this document.

29 'Gibbons' Review,' 57.

30 'Monk's Observations' and 'Considerations on a Bill.' Monk gave his 'Observations' to Board of Trade undersecretary John Pownall before he left for Nova Scotia to take up his post as Solicitor General and to Legge when he arrived, and claimed that it was his arguments that persuaded Legge to support the idea and that he had much to do with the passage of the bill through assembly and council. See Monk to Dartmouth, 16 November 1774, CO 217, vol. 51, 68.

31 *Assembly Journals*, 25 and 28 October, and 3, 4, 5, and 12 November 1774. See also 'Considerations on a Bill,' 72: 'even the judges of ... [the] Inferior Courts have voted for it in the House of Assembly where there was not heard one voice against the bill.'

32 Legge to Dartmouth, 16 November 1774, CO 217, vol. 51, 39–40, and *Assembly Journals*, 5 November 1774.

33 See RG 5, Series S, vol. 4. For London's deliberations and approval, see Opinion of Richard Jackson, Counsel to the Board of Trade, on the Supreme Court Amendment Act, 26 January 1775, in CO 217, vol. 27, 5; Dartmouth to Legge, 27 January and 22 February 1775, CO 217, vol. 51, 75 and 78. For the organisation and operation of the English Assizes, see J. Cockburn, *A History of English Assizes, 1558–1714* (Cambridge: Cambridge University Press 1972).

34 'Monk's Observations,' 143. See also his statement that the cause of opposition was that 'judges of the Supreme Court may be indulged to stay at home, and be excused from a very necessary part of their duty,' 'Considerations on a Bill,' 71. Monk also asserted that Belcher was uncooperative after the act was passed when it came to drawing up rules and procedures for the new circuits. See Monk to Dartmouth, 16 November 1774, CO 217, vol. 51, 69, and 'Monk's Observations,' 143.

35 'Considerations on a Bill,' 72.

36 'Monk's Observations,' 143, and 'Gibbons' Review,' 52n57. For the commissions see RG 1, vol. 168, 346.

37 Monk to Dartmouth, 16 November 1774, CO 217, vol. 5, 67.

38 'Monk's Observations' and 'Gibbons' Review.' Gibbons argued for replacement of the ICCPs by two 'Superior Courts of General Provincial Jurisdiction,' one with King's Bench jurisdiction and the other with that of Common Pleas and Exchequer. 'Gibbons' Review,' 54.

39 'Monk's Observations,' 138. The chief justice of Nova Scotia was a London appointment paid for out of the parliamentary grant. The assistant (puisne) judges' positions were created and paid for by the assembly, even though appointment to the posts was by the executive. For a detailed account of judicial salaries and tenure in this period, see Cahill and Phillips, 'Origins to Confederation.'

40 There is a substantial literature on pre-revolutionary Nova Scotia politics and on the colony's reactions to the American revolution. See in particular for the former, J.B. Brebner, *The Neutral Yankees of Nova Scotia: A Marginal Colony During the Revolutionary Years* (New York: Columbia University Press 1937); J.M. Beck, *The Politics of Nova Scotia*, vol. 1, *1710–1896* (Tantallon, NS: Four East Publications 1995); and Harvey, 'The Struggle for the New England Form of Township Government in Nova Scotia.' For the latter, see especially E.A. Clarke, *The Siege of Fort Cumberland, 1776: An Episode*

in the American Revolution (Montreal: McGill-Queen's University Press
1995); J.M. Bumsted, 'Francis Legge,' *DCB* online; and Clarke and Phillips,
'Rebellion and Repression in Nova Scotia,' 172–80.

41 For the Assembly petition, see J.B. Brebner, 'Nova Scotia's Remedy for the
American Revolution,' *Canadian Historical Review* 15 (1934), 180–92.

42 The Yarmouth petition is Inhabitants of Yarmouth to Legge, 8 December
1775, CO 17, vol. 52, 36–7; the quotation is in Lieutenant Governor Mariot
Arbuthnot to Earl of Sandwich, 14 January 1776, in G.R. Barnes and J.H.
Owen, eds., *The Private Papers of John, Earl of Sandwich, 1771–1782*, vol. 1
(London: Naval Records Society 1932), 116–17.

43 'Monk's Observations,' 135–6.

44 For Monk, see J.H. Lambert, 'Sir James Monk,' *DCB* online, and the introduction by Cahill to 'Monk's Observations,' 131–2.

45 See notes 9 and 28.

46 For Gibbons see R.J. Morgan, 'Richard Gibbons,' *DCB* online, and Cahill's
introduction in 'Gibbons' Review,' 35–6. For the review, see note 8 above.

47 'Monk's Observations,' 136.

48 'Gibbons' Review,' 40–1.

49 Ibid., 41.

50 Ibid., 58.

51 See Monk's assertion that ICCP judges were 'in general needy Men' who
'naturally wish a multitude of Suits.' Monk's Observations,' 138. See also
his similar comments in 'Considerations on a Bill,' 70. Gibbons argued that
the system of remuneration by fees alone was 'a great Temptation' for ICCP
judges 'to become Fomentors of Quarrels and Disputes, and Stirrers up and
Promoters of Law Suits ... to enhance the Profits of their office.' 'Gibbons'
Review,' 50.

52 'Monk's Observations,' 137.

53 'Gibbons' Review,' 47.

54 Ibid., 138, 139.

55 Ibid., 138. Emphasis in original.

56 Ibid., 138.

57 Ibid., 140.

58 Ibid., 137, 139. Emphasis in original.

59 'Gibbons' Review,' 54, 55.

60 D. Hay, 'Property, Authority and the Criminal Law,' in Hay et al., *Albion's
Fatal Tree: Crime and Society in Eighteenth-century England* (London: Allen
1975). The quotations below are from 26, 27.

61 See, *inter alia*, J. Muir and J. Phillips, 'Michaelmas Term, 1754: The Supreme
Court's First Session', in Girard, Phillips, and Cahill, eds., *The Supreme*

Court of Nova Scotia; D. Fyson, *Magistrates, Police and People: Everyday Criminal Justice in Quebec and Lower Canada, 1764–1837* (Toronto: Osgoode Society for Canadian Legal History and University of Toronto Press 2006), chap. 8; and A.G. Roeber, 'Authority, Law and Custom: The Rituals of Court Day in Tidewater Virginia, 1720–1750,' *William and Mary Quarterly* 37 (1980), 29–52.

62 See Glick's evidence of the use of grand jury addresses to lecture the citizenry on federalism and the importance of the central government: J. Glick, 'On the Road: The Supreme Court and the History of Circuit Riding,' *Cardozo Law Review* 24 (2003), 1753–1843. See also K. Newmeyer, 'Justice Joseph Story on Circuit and a Neglected Phase of American Legal History,' *American Journal of Legal History* 14 (1970), 112–35.

63 'Monk's Observations,' 140.

64 Ibid.

65 'Considerations on a Bill,' 71.

66 'Monk's Observations,' 140.

67 This is from 'Observations on the Present Practice of the Circuit Courts, 1775,' in 'Monk's Observations,' 142–3.

68 Ibid., 145.

69 'Gibbons' Review,' 41. See Monk's similar references to the ICCPs being 'inconsistent with the Jurisprudent Constitution of Great Britain,' in 'Monk's Observations,' 139.

70 'Gibbons' Review,' 58.

71 Legge to Earl of Dartmouth, 16 November 1774, CO 217, vol. 51, 39–40.

72 Francklin to Board of Trade, 30 September 1766, CO 217, vol. 44, 73.

73 For the expansion of the circuit and its operation in the nineteenth century, see J. Phillips and P. Girard, 'Courts, Communities, and Communication: The Nova Scotia Supreme Court on Circuit, 1816–1850,' in H. Foster, B. Berger, and A. Buck, eds., *The Grand Experiment: Law and Legal Culture in British Settler Societies* (Toronto: Osgoode Society for Canadian Legal History, and Vancouver: UBC Press 2008), 117–34.

74 Wentworth to John King, 15 September 1800, RG 1, vol. 53, 134–5.

75 Wentworth to William Windham, 14 November 1806, RG 1, vol. 54, 134–5.

76 Phillips and Girard, 'Courts, Communities and Communication.'

7

Judicial Scandal and the Culture of Patronage in Early Confederation, 1867–78

JONATHAN SWAINGER*

In the midst of the political picnic season of late September 1877, Edward Blake addressed a large gathering of Liberal party supporters at a political rally at Teeswater, Ontario. Touching upon the topic of judicial appointments, the former minister of justice declared,

The man who is appointed a judge, and as such may at any time hold in his hands the fate, whether as fortune, freedom, or good name, of any one of us, this man holds his office by a tenure practically not far removed from life. He may be a blessing, but again he may be a curse, to his country for twenty or thirty years; and therefore it is a most sacred duty on the part of a Government to search for the very best men to administer these tremendous responsibilities.[1]

As a piece of electioneering, Blake's claim was a sound principle that national leaders as different as Sir John A. Macdonald, Sir Wilfrid Laurier, Lester Pearson, and Brian Mulroney supported in theory but have often ignored in practice.[2] This is not to suggest that qualified individuals were not sought out for judicial appointment and promotion, but rather, that the measure of what constituted 'the very best men' has been mercurial. As I have argued elsewhere, the process of selecting candidates for the bench demanded skill in weighing legal, social, regional, religious, and intellectual abilities, in concert with a sense of what was 'best' in a given set of circumstances.[3] Not surprisingly, the nominee who might arrive on the bench as a blessing could, in the fullness of time, be revealed as a curse.

Blake's career at the bar and his experience as minister of justice from 1875 to 1877 had provided him with a number of opportunities to witness the circumstances transforming a sitting judge into a curse. Charges of imbecility, deafness, infirmity, partisanship, drunkenness, ignorance, fraud, and pig-headedness were common, not only during Blake's term in office, but as a regular theme of correspondence delivered to the Department of Justice after the ministry was first created in 1868.[4] Although concerns ranged from the trivial to the extreme, the accumulated effect was that, between 1867 and 1878, almost every province provided a setting for judicial controversy or scandal. What follows is less a survey of all the incidents that erupted during the completion of Confederation than it is a series of images capturing how the politicization of judicial appointments proved to be a fertile seedbed for trouble on Canada's benches. Although not every province is featured, there is no question that turmoil was seen in every jurisdiction, ranging from British Columbia's Supreme Court and its squabbles over pensions, judicial rank, and battles over jurisdiction, the lamentable state of Manitoba's judiciary during the 1870s, the deteriorating reputation of Ontario's county courts, the increasing prominence of politics on that province's high courts, the absolute chaos of Quebec's judiciary, the judicial crisis in New Brunswick, the openly political character of appointing judges to Nova Scotia's new county courts, and the Canadian Supreme Court's faltering early years. All signalled that there was something inherently wrong with Canada's judicial culture.[5]

That the nation's judiciary was the subject of a near constant stream of complaints in the aftermath of Confederation could not help but undermine public confidence in the administration of justice. It did not matter that the behaviour of only a small number of judges was involved in the worst cases, since the brushstrokes of public controversy left traces on every bench. And while we must proceed carefully, it is difficult to come away from these incidents without wondering about the extent to which they shaped the sense of what judges did and the roles they played in Canadian society. By treating judicial appointments purely as political patronage, and thus encouraging an environment in which uneven talents were appointed to the bench where some managed to become embroiled in controversy, had the Conservatives and Liberals established too low a standard for the new Dominion's judicial culture? And even when sitting judges were not attracting unwanted attention,

were lesser lights diluting the quality of judicial reasoning and interpretation?[6] Such possibilities suggest that the judicial scandals and controversies of the early Confederation era were not only about a small
collection of individuals suffering from the ravages of time, poor
judgment and, in some instances, alcohol. Rather, these ignoble events
speak, at a more profound level, to a failure to think about judges, judging, and the courts as integral elements in the nation-building enterprise.[7]

During the last week of May 1870, the Department of Justice received
an agitated letter from Halifax lawyer Thomas J. Wallace, complaining
that despite a catalogue of sins, Nova Scotia's chief justice, William
Young, remained on the bench. Although the animosity between the
two men extended back to 1866, when Wallace was disbarred after
authoring an insulting letter to Chief Justice Young, the most recent out-
break of hostility was rooted in the allegation that in one recent case,
Young 'had exhausted every art to bias and warp the judgment of some
of his associates to personal and unworthy ends.'[8] A petition outlining
the chief justice's failings had been presented to Parliament, and that
body's failure to act had, according to Wallace, badly undermined the
dignity of Nova Scotia's bench. Responding on behalf of the government, George E. Cartier indicated that '... the Judges of the Courts of the
Dominion hold office during good behavior and can only be removed in
an address from the Senate and House of Commons and that the Minister of Justice knows of no grounds and has no intention of moving in
any matter affecting Chief Justice Young.'[9] This, from the government's
perspective, ended the issue.

Tepid in comparison with other complaints levelled at judges in the
decade after the union of 1867, Wallace's charge against Chief Justice
Young is nonetheless instructive. Although alleging that Young had
corrupted the bench by unduly influencing his brethren, and that the
law and the dignity of the bench had been undermined, the matter bore
the marks of personal animus. Wallace did not manufacture the complaint, but the strained relations between the two men certainly
coloured the supposed wrongs, and Young's abrasive manner probably
fuelled Wallace's sense, that he had been treated unjustly. In this sense
the conflict between Wallace and Young serves to remind us of the relative size of the legal community in British North America. In a world
as small as was the legal fraternity of the new Dominion, let alone
the bar and bench in one of the provinces, close confines and regular
contact offered a wealth of opportunities to aggravate real and imag-

ined slights.[10] Wallace may have had legitimate grounds for complaint, but given the history between the two men, it took little effort to dismiss the charge as the latest instalment of their ongoing conflict.

Wallace's complaint against Young is also instructive because of an allegation it does not make. Despite the well-established argument in Canada that that judicial appointments had, as Peter Oliver succinctly put it, 'become thoroughly politicized,' the complaint did not claim Young had acted in a partisan manner, either on the bench or in his behaviour towards Wallace.[11] The absence might be attributed to a number of possibilities. Perhaps nothing in what Young had allegedly done resonated with partisan motives, but given the broad sense of what was political in a very political setting, such a possibility seems unlikely.[12] A more compelling explanation may be that claiming a judge had acted in a partisan fashion said everything and nothing; there was little to be gained by such an allegation unless the judge had been particularly blatant. It is beyond question that Confederation era commentators and public figures recognised the political aspect of judicial appointments. John A. Macdonald explained to Timothy Anglin that in the appointment of judges there was a 'true constitutional principle' at play.

Whenever an Office is vacant it belongs to the party supporting the Government if within that party there can be found a person competent to perform the duties. Responsible Government cannot be carried on any other principle. I am not careful however, what a man's political antecedents have been, if I am satisfied that he is really and *bona fide* a friend of the Government at the time of the appointment. My principle is, reward your friends and do not buy your enemies.[13]

As easy as it would be to characterise this as typical of Macdonald, one hastens to point out that Edward Blake claimed that as minister of justice it had been his 'especial duty ... to take care that no man is appointed to the vacancy who is not thoroughly competent to fill the position. In selecting from amongst those who may fulfil this condition, the Government must of course rely largely upon the advice of those of its friends who from local knowledge and intimate political connection have the best means of deciding upon the political aspect of the question.'[14] Despite his discomfort with the seamier side of political life, Blake accepted the 'political aspect' of judicial appointments, and while his colleagues may not have been as skilful (or cunning) as Macdonald, the Liberals nonetheless attempted to keep pace.[15]

As much as patronage was a key element in building a political party and securing victory at the polls, judicial appointments presented a number of challenges to such a system. Obviously, not every party stalwart was qualified to sit on the bench, and those who did possess legal training and judicial aspirations did not always make the best judges. The possibility that middling lawyers could be raised to the bench thanks to political pedigree is all too apparent. The sense that judicial appointments were widely understood to be patronage driven may have encouraged the open criticism of these appointees and their subsequent judicial behaviour, because seats on the bench were akin to any political largess. That neither the Conservatives nor Liberals viewed judicial appointments as fundamentally different than other appointments meant that both parties elevated individuals who lacked judicial mien and fostered an environment in which sitting judges became the subject of public concern and, in some instances, parliamentary petitions.

'Best Fitted for the Position':
The Pictou/Cumberland County Court Appointment

It has been suggested that while professional and personal contacts meant that judicial appointments in Quebec and Ontario were complicated affairs, the politicisation of the nomination process was felt more keenly beyond central Canada, because party leaders were entirely reliant on local political counsel.[16] In Nova Scotia, for example, the province's internal politics turned on the battle for control between those whose interests were tied to Halifax, and those who lived in the outlaying districts. When combined with the often-voiced animus towards central Canada, these internal sectional disputes rendered the business of judge-making all the more fraught. And when Macdonald's Conservatives were swept from office in the wake of the Pacific Scandal, the Liberals reaped a slate of successful candidates lead by A.G. Jones.[17] Fortunately, the establishment of Nova Scotia's county court system in 1874, which came into effect on 21 August 1876, provided the Liberals with a new patronage opportunity to pay the queue of party debts.[18] The slate of judicial vacancies was simply too alluring, and rather than break with Macdonald's model, the Liberals filled every available seat with a devoted party man. But to the extent that patronage appointments were supposed to build party loyalty, the internal battles over nominees were quite divisive and may have caused more damage than good.

The battle over the judgeship of Pictou and Cumberland Counties began with a letter directed to Edward Blake, six months before the county courts were to begin operating. Writing to Blake on 31 March 1876, J.W. Carmichael, one of the few Nova Scotia Liberals who remained loyal during the Macdonald years, recommended the appointment of James Fogo, an established barrister, judge of probate in Pictou County, and a man 'best fitted for the position.'[19] Carmichael reasoned that Pictou's two representatives meant it was more important than neighbouring Cumberland, which had only one, and therefore Pictou's recommendation ought to take precedence.[20] Eleven days later, a divergent opinion appeared when James Duffers urged Blake to appoint W.A. Morse who, in the 1872 general election, stood for the party solely on the hope that his candidacy would prevent a Tory landslide. The idea had been that if Morse ran in Cumberland, prominent Conservative Charles Tupper would be forced to campaign there, and potentially reduce his influence in Pictou. As it turned out, one of the candidates who may have benefited from Morse doing so was none other than J.W. Carmichael. In return for the effort on behalf of the party, Liberal Premier William Annand promised Morse that he had 'first claim on his party to any promotion going to the bench.'[21] By 1876, the political debt was long overdue, compelling Duffers to conclude that 'it is not just ungenerous of Carmichael to pass Morse by as it was in Carmichael's interests that Morse consented to be made a fool of in Cumberland.'[22] Duffers claimed, 'If Morse is now overlooked it will be useless for the Halifax Committee ever to attempt to direct or control any County elections and the whole party will be demoralized.'[23] Clearly, Morse was the candidate that the Halifax faction backed while Fogo was the choice of local party interests in Pictou. Carmichael's appeal to Alexander Mackenzie verified what was at stake, and revealed that Jones' involvement had drawn the ire of local party supporters. 'However great respect I have for Mr Jones, I am not content that he should interfere with appointments which are peculiarly County appointments and not for the County of Halifax.'[24]

Centred as it was on rewarding party service, the argument devoted relatively little attention to whether either candidate was qualified to sit on the bench. Believing that such a discussion favoured Morse, Duffers argued that Morse was 'a young man of good fair abilities and sufficient experience at the bar' while Fogo was 'a perfect fossil' who had not had 'a case in court for the last 20 years.'[25] Further, not only did Chief Justice Young, a former Liberal premier, support Morse as the qualified candidate but the local bar was entirely willing to endorse Morse.[26] Fearing that Fogo would win out because of Carmichael's influence, Duffers lamented to Blake, 'I can't help adding that you will find all the leading names of the party here quite of my opinion as to the capabilities of the two gentlemen and I don't think that Mr Carmichael's personal influence should override that of the whole party.'[27] Ultimately, a letter written by A.G. Jones on 22 April 1876 and sent to Mackenzie settled the case; the debts owed to Morse had to be paid for, if ignored, 'it will cause more discontent and disgust than I can describe.'[28]

A week later, Mackenzie wrote Carmichael in an attempt to clear the path for Morse to be named. Fogo, Mackenzie had learned, was sixty, and thus 'entirely too old.'[29] Further, political allies in Halifax were intimately familiar with the state of affairs, along with the promise to Morse, and failure to act would 'destroy the party in the county.' And given the organisational and financial burden carried by the Halifax portion of the party, 'some consideration is always due them.' It was also certain that in terms of professional opinion, Morse was clearly the preferred candidate. Finally, in the spirit of party harmony, Mackenzie rhetorically asked if it would not be preferable to allow the minister of justice to make the appointment free from constraints, and suggested that a gesture on Carmichael's part 'would greatly facilitate the settlement of the question.' Undaunted, Carmichael continued to battle on behalf of Fogo. Alluding to some unspecified charge against Morse, Carmichael obliquely asserted 'that in almost every case when judges have been appointed, and are to be appointed for Nova Scotia, it would be desirable that the qualifications were of a higher order than exists.'[30] Insisting that the Halifax wing yielded far too much influence, Carmichael refused to yield.

Even if Halifax is entitled to consideration on account of its superintendence, and the expenditure in outside counties, this does not apply to Pictou which manages its own affairs in election matters, much less should Pictou be the county selected to be specially controlled. I have the vanity to believe that Pictou is of quite as much importance to the government as Cumberland and it strikes me as very doubtful policy to have so much consideration for Cumberland a county we have never won and so little for Pictou which we carry now and again. True ours is a very doubtful County and may be lost next time, but most assuredly the course suggested is not one calculated to retain it.[31]

Carmichael closed rather ominously in stating that while 'fully sensible to my small importance to the party farther than being always prepared to give the government an honest support, I do not wish to be placed in the humiliating position before the County and the Country that would be involved in the event of Mr. Morse being appointed County Court Judge.'[32] Morse received the nomination on 21 August 1876.[33]

Although the battle over nominating a judge to Pictou and Cumberland certainly reflected the particular characteristics of politics in Nova Scotia, similar conflicts erupted almost every time a vacancy occurred anywhere in the Dominion. And as was the case in the contest between Morse and Fogo, references to the professional qualities of the candidates unerringly demonstrated that the very best man need not be a particularly good lawyer. The victorious Morse was described as possessing 'good fair ability' and 'sufficient experience,' hardly a ringing endorsement for a judicial candidate. And the fact that Fogo's backers saw little difficulty in nominating a sixty-year-old man to a position requiring a considerable amount of labour, suggests that the ability to fulfil a judicial office was rather low on the list of qualifications. And as a form of patronage designed to build party strength, the evidence indicates that the internal battles over dispensing this largesse actually created internal divisions that left permanent scars. The results, for the quality of judicial personnel and for party unity, left little to recommend the process.

Unparalleled: The Tumult of Quebec's Superior Courts

Although the problems plaguing the Quebec bench preceded the union of 1867, a parliamentary eruption of late March 1868 acknowledged one of the worst kept secrets of the early Confederation era.[34] Sparked by Pierre Fortin, Conservative MP for Gaspé, requesting a parliamentary return detailing the sittings of court at Amherst on the Magdalen Islands in the Gulf of St Lawrence, the House of Commons erupted into a spree of name-calling, accusation, and recrimination.[35] At one point, L.H. Masson, the MP from Soulanges, claimed that the Montreal bench did not enjoy the confidence of the country and that two of the judges were 'a little out of their head,' two lived immoral lives, and a fifth was so deaf as to having given judgment for $100 in a case involving a $10 claim.[36] A.A. Dorion followed up on Masson's claim, and stated that of the twenty-three judges in Quebec, 'six were totally unfit for office from age or infirmity, while one was grossly omitted from his immoral conduct, and a scandal to the bench, and others from ignorance of the law.' Further investigation would reveal that no fewer than thirteen judges were 'manifestly incompetent.'[37] Dorion concluded by claiming that 'the degradation of judicial administration in Quebec had reached an extent altogether unparalleled, but he hoped that the Minister of Justice would, for the honor of his own profession, take care that no future appointments were made except of gentlemen competent for the position.'[38]

Responding to the charges, George Etienne Cartier admitted that while a number of Quebec's judges suffered from declining health and old age, Dorion's charges lacked conviction since he had not named the allegedly incompetent judges. Further, all of the individuals that Cartier had promoted to the bench – men such as Judges Badgley, Drummond, Mondolet, Berthelot, Taschereau, Johnson, Winter, Lafontaine, and Bossé – were all highly qualified.[39] In truth, Cartier had damned himself, for every judge named, save Berthelot and Tashereau, was the subject of either public or private complaint in the ensuing decade. Still, from Cartier's perspective, the problem was attributable to the tiny pension fund that had restricted the means of pensioning old or infirm judges in Lower Canada. As the debate continued, charges targeting Judge Aimé Lafontaine were raised but failed to generate discussion. Prime Minister and Minister of Justice John A. Macdonald brought the discussion to a close in noting that, while the debate had been 'productive of much good,' he hoped it might compel a number of sitting judges to reflect upon their individual situation and retire from the bench.[40]

Reporting the debates on 3 April, the Montreal *Gazette* agreed with Dorion's claims, and added that 'it is quite possible that there is no exaggeration; indeed, it is hardly possible to overstate the inefficiency of the Bench.'[41] True to the underlying political character of the issue, while neither Dorion nor Cartier was blameless, the *Gazette* pointed to the Reform appointments of Justices Loranger, Sicotte, Duval, and Drummond as being especially flawed.[42] Adopting a different tack, the April edition of the Montreal-based *Canada Law Journal* thought the debate was 'painful and personal,' but denied that the problem was the incapacity or immorality of sitting judges. Offering a view that would be echoed in other jurisdictions facing judicial backlogs, the *Journal* emphasised that the issue was one of available judicial personnel; there simply was not 'a sufficient number to carry on the work' of the Superior Court in Montreal.[43] More to the point, it was not 'fair to describe the judges generally as infirm and immoral, because, in the first place, the want of an adequate pension fund, and, in the next place, the absence of a sufficiently powerful public opinion, has permitted several persons to retain seats on the bench whom the epithets infirm or immoral may without injustice be applied.'[44]

To the degree that the debates, manoeuvres, and subsequent enquiries captured the tangle of personalities and politics at stake on
Quebec's bench, few commentators were initially willing to portray
Cartier's *Judicature Acts of 1857* as the source of the chaos.[45] Described by
Brian Young as 'an integral part of the bureaucratization process that
included Lower Canada's educational, municipal, and county institutions,' the act established nineteen judicial districts with judges residing
in Montreal, Trois-Rivières, Quebec City, Sherbrooke, and Aylmer.[46]
Although characterised as 'a great boon to the people of Lower Canada'
by saving 'the trouble and expense of conveying witnesses long distances to Montreal and Quebec, for the hearing and decision of cases'
and making 'litigants feel they were near to the courts and could more
easily have their legal business executed,' within a decade of its creation
there were few who thought the act had succeeded.[47] Rather than creating a rational and ordered structure to support an emerging economy,
the act fashioned a chaotic system that expended a great deal of energy
managing uneven judicial talents.

While the *Judicature Acts of 1857* escaped immediate attention, the
quality of judicial nominees and the politicisation of judicial appointments assumed centre stage. Appearing near the end of a column
addressing English judicial appointments, the editors of Toronto's version of the *Canada Law Journal* referred to criticisms of judicial appointments in Quebec that had been published in *Le Revue Critique:*

Seats on the bench are amongst the prizes offered by political rings for uncompromising support; and it makes very little matter whether *rouge* or *bleu* in the
ascendant, the same principle is acted on by both parties, and generally judgeships are conferred, not on account of fitness for the office, but because it is
necessary to provide for a member of the party in power. The system is radically bad; for in lieu of good lawyers, worn-out politicians are placed on the
bench. If a man is a political failure, *presto* he is made judge; so that there is a
very fair chance of the Bench becoming the receptacle for that favoured class
of the community which, fifty years ago, in England, was said to monopolize
the Church. Thanks to the system, the Bench of Quebec does not command the
respect which is accorded to persons occupying judicial positions in other
countries.[48]

Perhaps guilty of overreaching, the author nonetheless identified the
flawed nature of judicial appointments in Quebec and elsewhere.[49] As
biting as was this salvo, a year later W.H. Kerr unleashed a sustained

attack on the bench and bar in Quebec, arguing that 'the main cause of the present lamentable state of affairs is traceable to politics.'[50]

Reprinted from *Le Revue Critique* and compelling the editors of Toronto's *Canada Law Journal* to state that they 'hope things are not quite so bad as he puts them,' Kerr's description was scathing. Ranging from the intellectual aridness of legal practice in the countryside, the laxity of standards for admission to the profession, the absence of effective policing of professional conduct, the failings of judicial decentralisation, the systemic backlog of the Montreal courts, and judicial ignorance of the Common Law, the assault finally pointed to the politicisation of judicial appointments. The process had lowered the dignity of the bench and impaired 'the respect of the public for the judges.'[51] Although Kerr believed that the bar could aid the cause by restricting professional voting rights to those with at least ten years' practice, and to elect benchers without reference to politics, the greater task fell to the minister of justice to adopt measures to raise the administration of justice 'to a high state of efficiency.' Specifically,

let him choose the best men without distinction of party to fill any vacancies. Let him increase the salaries to members of the Bench, so that judges may cease to feel like criminals, and be able to live respectably. Let him insist upon the retirement of those who are physically incapable of performing their duties. Let him hunt down without mercy the judge who neglects his duties, or is guilty of any act incompatible with his position.[52]

Addressed as it was to John A. Macdonald, the ablest proponent of the politicisation of judicial patronage, Kerr's plea would find an unsympathetic audience.

Kerr returned to the topic three years later when he assumed a leadership role in advocating for changes in the composition of Montreal's bench, where, in the aftermath of Mr Justice Joseph Ubalde Beaudry's death and Mr Justice Mondolet's refusal to sit on cases involving the *Insolvency Act* (1875) and the *Dominion Election Act* (1874), because he viewed them as an unconstitutional intrusion increasing the judicial workload, Judges Berthelot, McKay, and Johnson were all poised to resign in 'dissatisfaction with the existing state of affairs.'[53] Although the structure of Quebec's court system and the means of appointing judges remained the fundamental source of the problem, both the public meetings and the private correspondence crossing Edward Blake's desk as minister of justice revealed how quickly personalities assumed centre stage. Thus, it was Mondolet's stubborn refusal to sit on cases involving the two acts, along with his insistence on receiving a pension equal to his full salary that were identified as the problem and quickly occupied most of the attention. When the Montreal bar convened a special meeting in late October 1876 to discuss the deadlock, it concluded that the province's entire judicial structure required reorganisation 'from beginning to end,' although their resolutions concentrated on short-term responses. First, so that judicial business in the city might be managed more effectively, it was moved that none of the Montreal-based judges attend any business outside of the city. Second, the meeting agreed that the gridlock and inefficiency of the Superior Court in Montreal was largely the result of Mondolet's position regarding the *Insolvent Act* and the *Dominion Elections Act*. Finally, and most significantly, the bar agreed to a petition praying that the Governor General be requested to form a committee to investigate and then take all reasonable actions necessary to alleviate the situation in Montreal. The bar wanted Mondelet impeached.[54] As events would turn out, this was not to occur, for on 31 December 1876, Mondolet died while awaiting a leave of absence.

Obviously, Mondolet's death did not solve any of the fundamental problems in Quebec, although by the late 1870s the passage of time had effected a renovation of sorts. In the decade after the rancorous parliamentary exchanges of late March and early April 1868, almost all of the individuals identified directly or by inference – Badgley, Drummond, Mondolet, Berthelot, Johnson, Lafontaine, Thompson, Winter, Loranger, Duval, and Sicotte – had left the bench or died in harness. In fact, twenty-one judicial vacancies occurred in Quebec between March 1868 and the end of the Mackenzie government in October 1878.[55] The spectacle receded from public view, not because the organisation of Quebec's judiciary had been addressed, or because judicial appointments became less political, but rather, because the most egregious judges had left centre stage. Indeed, it was all too easy to conclude that the problem was a Quebec problem rather than confronting it as a concern affecting the entire nation. And while some commentators were prepared to adopt such a perspective, centred on the supposed peculiarities of Quebec, the occurrence of scandals and controversy elsewhere indicated that the fundamental problem crossed all jurisdictions and was, in fact, thoroughly entwined within the new Dominion's political and legal culture.

A Legal Monkhood: Ontario's Superior Courts

In the midst of the increasingly animated debate on 30 March 1868 over the state of Quebec's judiciary, and in particular reference to charges levelled at Judge Aimé Lafontaine of the Judicial District of Ottawa for Quebec's Superior Court, Ontario premier John S. Macdonald sanctimoniously declared that charges of the nature against Lafontaine '... had never been brought against the judiciary of Ontario.'[56] While no sitting judge had been accused of embezzlement, the inference that Ontario's judiciary was above reproach was hubristic. Only a month earlier, Chief Justice W.H. Draper of Ontario's Queen's Bench had tendered his resignation in anticipation of becoming chief justice of the Court of Error and Appeal, and triggered almost half a decade of simmering controversy embracing the untimely death of Chancellor P.M. VanKoughnet, the courting of Edward Blake, the elevation of J.G. Spragge, the judicial resignation and return to active politics of Oliver Mowat, and the appointment of S.H. Blake as vice-chancellor.[57] While the turmoil in Quebec played out amidst a tangle of personalities, politics, and a flawed judicial system, the events in Ontario were mired in the politicization of judicial appointments, clashes of career aspiration and personality, and the nursing of professional slights. The timing of events, however, meant that until the mid-1870s the turmoil in Quebec provided a screen for the Ontarian controversies and scandals.

When Chief Justice W.H. Draper broached his appointment as chief justice of the Court of Error and Appeal and senior judge for the entire province, the chain of possible appointments and elevations was bewildering.[58] His departure gave rise to the possibility that Chancellor P.M. VanKoughnet, Chief Justice William Buell Richards of Common Pleas, Justice John H. Hagarty of Queen's Bench, or Conservative lawyer John Wellington Gwynne might be raised to the chief justiceship of Queen's Bench. Draper thought that while Chancellor VanKoughnet would be a good choice, 'he would like to have the Chief Justiceship offered to him because that would give him the opportunity to reject it.'[59] Still, VanKoughnet was certainly preferable to either Spragge or Mowat, the former whose 'head is not much better than mine,' and the latter an 'Equity fanatic' inclined to go to 'Equitable extremes' to the detriment of statutes and common law rules. In Draper's estimation, Richards would be disinclined to move and while Hagarty was 'a good lawyer and a man of impeccable honor and character,' the bar would be antagonistic to such a promotion. And while Gwynne was 'at times crotchety,' he would make a good chief justice and a passable chancellor. Tellingly, Draper warned that the combination of Gwynne along with Justices Morrison and Hagarty on any court would take some time to 'settle down.' The hope that the personalities would settle down was ill-founded. Rumours of VanKoughnet's possible elevation compelled Justice Hagarty to state that he would reduce his own workload to a bare minimum and 'leave the Lion's share of the work to the responsibility of the Head.'[60] Hagarty also insinuated that Justice Morrison, with whom he had sat on Queen's Bench for the better part of five years, was party to a cabal. Reporting on the strained relations, Robert Harrison implored John A. Macdonald to do something at once, as without a chief justice in place, Morrison and Hagarty would quarrel endlessly, leaving Harrison caught between the two. From his perspective, Hagarty was ill-suited to be on the bench at all and lacked any ability to be a chief justice.[61]

Hagarty was not alone in viewing VanKoughnet's possible elevation as a harbinger of things to come. Appointed to Chancery in 1864, Oliver Mowat had become restive by 1868 when, thanks to a straitened financial situation created by his own spending habits and a limited salary, he was contemplating resignation to return to professional practice.[62] The appeal of such a move had been underlined by the extended debate over who was to replace Chief Justice Draper and the realization that Mowat would be denied the chancellorship. Still, Mowat decided to stay put, and by July the question of elevating VanKoughnet was stymied by his decision to 'stand committed' with Vice-Chancellors Mowat and Spragge until the new Dominion Supreme Court would provide the opportunity for professional advancement for 'some of the judges here.'[63] To the extent his plans had been rebuffed, Macdonald could retain the hope that VanKoughnet might yet move. Macdonald was annoyed nonetheless, and declared that 'it is too bad that the interests of Justice should be sacrificed on account of the selfish vanity of Mowat and Spragge, who, although they have no chance of being Chancellors themselves would desire to keep VanKoughnet where he is, rather than have a new Chancellor appointed over their heads.'[64]

Macdonald then turned to Chief Justice William Buell Richards of Common Pleas to assume the chief justiceship of both the Queen's Bench and Upper Canada.[65] Despite concerns over his behaviour, Justice Hagarty of Queen's Bench ascended to the chief justiceship of Common Pleas in Richard's place, a move that served to create some welcome distance between the new chief justice and Justice Morrison.

Consistent with Richards' condition for accepting the move to Queen's Bench, Justice Adam Wilson was elevated to that court and John W. Gwynne was appointed to Common Pleas, where he filled Wilson's vacated seat.[66] The new arrangements proved to be short-lived, for a year later Chancellor VanKoughnet died suddenly and threw Macdonald once again 'into all the troubles of judge-making.'[67] Feeling committed to renew the offer of the chancellorship to Edward Blake, Sir John acknowledged that politics rendered such a nomination to be difficult, but it was 'a singular coincidence that the Members of the Equity Bar are very nearly all Grits.'[68] Wishing to avoid the spectacle of 'every Grit newspaper in Western Canada' writing that Blake had 'patriotically sacrificed his own interests by refusing the Office and remaining true to his Country and his party,' Macdonald asked that Judge Morrison confidentially ascertain Blake's feelings about the Chancellorship. The position was his if he wanted it, but if not, 'it should be considered between us as if the offer were not made.'[69] Blake was uninterested in cooperating, and Sir John

was a good deal disappointed at Blake's course. I think he ought to have met the matter in the same spirit in which I made the offer, and which he admits ... It is all very well for him to say that he will justify the offer in case I am attacked, but there would be no occasion for the attack if he would accept my suggestion, – that unless he accepted, it should be considered that no offer was ever made. Under no circumstances can he lose by this arrangement, while by another I may be prejudiced and the Government as well.[70]

Ultimately, Blake declined the seat on the equity bench, and J.G. Spragge, who Macdonald had thought was 'not of heavy enough metal to preside in the Court' and whose health had been suspect for at least a year, was given the opportunity to head the Chancery.[71] S.H. Strong, who 'was pointed out by every leading practitioner at the Equity Bar, without reference to politics, as being the man for the vacancy,' was nominated to fill Spragge's place.[72]

The protracted behind-the-scene enquiries and subsequent nominations concerning the Ontarian high courts receded until 23 October 1872, when Oliver Mowat finally acted upon his intention of resigning his office as vice-chancellor.[73] Mowat had initially been appointed to Chancery in the midst of the negotiations leading to Confederation, and while 'attracted by the prospect of congenial work, security, and serenity' that such a position offered, in hindsight his acceptance seems odd.[74] The demands of political life may have lost their appeal, and the opportunity of spending more time with his large family was undoubtedly a benefit, but when, after less than four years on the bench he broached the topic of resigning, it is clear that the $6,500 salary and the absence of opportunity for advancement had cooled his enthusiasm for judicial life. Had he resigned in 1868 and actually returned to private practice, few would have thought the decision untoward.[75] But when he stepped down and back into public life as Liberal premier of Ontario, and thus accepted a position that paid less than what he had received in Chancery, the response was predictable. Steeped in the politics of the day, Macdonald's reaction to Mowat's decision was to be expected:

My feelings on learning of your return to political life are of a composite character. I am glad, for the sake of Ontario, that you have assumed your present position. With all your political sins you will impart a respectability to the Local Government which is much wanted, and the Country will have confidence that you will set your face against the coarser forms of jobbery which were infecting our country from our proximity to the United States.

At the same time I may venture to say that I regret to see you imitating the American system of judges returning to political life, after having accepted the legal monk hood of the Bench. It is not likely to be extensively followed, the precedent is a bad one, but practically it will not do much mischief. However, you have made the plunge, and there is an end of it.[76]

Following closely on similar lines, Toronto's *Canada Law Journal* published a scathing column criticising Mowat's decision for degrading the honour and dignity of the bench by casting all judges in an unflattering political light. That the Conservative editors adopted such a stance was predictable, while at the same time, Mowat's rejoinder that there were no constitutional reasons barring his move was hardly convincing.[77] The entire debate was rife with hypocrisy. Macdonald's approach to judicial appointments had sullied the judicial culture long before Mowat resigned. And Mowat's decision was entirely rooted in an opportunistic desire to leave the bench, possibly make more money and, if the chance might be had, take on the man who had thwarted his judicial ambitions. The entire controversy can be searched and one will find little that resonates of principle.

Familiar tones echoed through the contest over who would replace Mowat. Macdonald enquired of Chief Justice Draper and Chancellor Spragge for suggestions, noting that a Conservative candidate was preferable.[78] While Adam Crooks and Thomas Moss had both been mentioned, Macdonald thought that 'the Grits would not allow Crooks to go, even if I wanted him for the vice-Chancellorship,' and Moss 'is too young and too ambitious to shelve himself at present.'[79] Having surveyed the field, Macdonald concluded that suitable Conservatives were not to be had and that Edward Blake's younger brother Samuel was to be offered the position. Admittedly, the choice would spark complaints within the party, but as Macdonald cynically wrote Chief Justice Morris in Manitoba: 'Blake will make a good Judge, and I think it is rather a good stroke for the Government to show to the country that the efficiency of the Bench is the first consideration, irrespective of politics.'[80] Having made the most of the situation, Macdonald nonetheless assured D'Arcy Boulton that 'had there been a good Conservative practitioner who could have done the duty as well, he would certainly have been preferred.'[81]

The clashes of personality and politics in and around Ontario's bench signalled a new development for the tattered judicial culture of the early Confederation era. Gone was the sanctimony of John S. Macdonald's declarations heard during the debates over Quebec's judiciary, along with the self-congratulatory observations of the Toronto-based *Canada Law Journal*.[82] For during much of the first five years of Confederation, the *Journal*'s reports and reprints of the scathing attacks on Quebec's judiciary were almost invariably accompanied with none too subtle assurances that such things did not occur in Ontario. After detailing the 1867 contempt of court case involving Thomas Ramsay and the conflicting interpretations offered by Quebec's judiciary, the *Journal*'s editors concluded that

the Bench of Lower Canada is not (with some honourable exceptions) what it ought to be. The conduct of Lower Canada judges has, on more than one occasion, caused Canadians to blush; and we regret to say that people abroad know no distinctions between the Bench of Upper and Lower Canada, and so in their ignorance cast upon the Bench of Canada, the obloquy which appertains to that of the Lower Province alone.[83]

Three months later, the *Journal* reprinted another column on the Ramsay case, and prefaced it with the claim 'that such a case could hardly have occurred in the Upper Province, the Bench there being in the full enjoyment of the esteem and veneration of the Bar.'[84] And by October 1872, statistics generated on the number of appeals to the Judicial Committee of the Privy Council, and details on where those cases originated, provided the *Journal* with further evidence that Ontario's judges were superior to those sitting in Quebec.[85]

But as early as 1871, with the ongoing discussions of the possible fusion of Ontario's equity and common-law courts, and the eventual naming of the Law Reform Commission, the *Journal* became a little more circumspect in extolling the virtues of the province's courts and judiciary.[86] Although the Reform Commission was relatively short-lived and the talk of fusion was subsumed in Oliver Mowat's *Administration of Justice Act* of 1873, the fact that the province was engaged in a searching appraisal of the entire justice system suggested that all was not well.[87] At the same time, the editors of Toronto's *Canada Law Journal* were compelled to admit that Ontario's county court judges were blessed with uneven talents. Specifically, some of those judges 'would appear to have a very hazy idea of their duties in taking down notes of evidence & c., at trials, a most important matter when it is remembered that their rulings are liable to be called into question at any moment by a Superior Court.' And while the *Journal* was prepared to admit that some readers might think the criticism was too harsh, the editors sharply noted that 'even the mild flow of Chancery procedure is disturbed by the strange doings of an occasional County Judge.'[88] The mounting criticism compelled the *Journal* to explain why the situation had deteriorated to the point it had, and, in time, reported on a meeting to discuss the concerns, led by Judge James Robert Gowan, chairman of the Board of County Judges. Four months later, Judge Gowan provided the *Journal* with a lengthy treatment of the range of responsibilities shouldered by the county courts, so as to demonstrate that the county judiciary was overburdened and underpaid.[89] Thus, by the time Oliver Mowat stepped down from Chancery and into the premier's office, few observers in Ontario could have retained the smug confidence that the provincial bench was as spotless as some had once claimed.

To the degree that the first five years of Confederation provided a setting for the spectacle of Quebec's judiciary, the years after Mowat's resignation grew increasingly dark for Ontario's bench.[90] For sheer meanness, few lower points were found than that obtained in the aftermath of *Re Regina v. Wilkinson*, in which George Brown, editor and owner of the *Toronto Globe*, locked horns with Mr Justice Adam Wilson of Queen's Bench. The clash was framed by an application for a leave to prosecute brought by Liberal Senator John Simpson who, as president of the Ontario Bank, had been accused by the Conservative *West Dur-*

ham News of complicity in the alleged electoral corruption implied by George Brown's 'big push' letter of 13 August 1872.[91] Depending on one's politics, the letter was either a legitimate financial solicitation or an invitation to skulduggery at the polls. Although Chief Justice Harrison had indicated that grounds for prosecution did exist, Justice Wilson's endorsement of the ruling shifted focus from the question at hand and singled out Brown's 'big push' letter as one 'written for corrupt purposes to interfere with the freedom of elections. It is an invitation to the recipient as one with some others and the writer to concur in committing the offence of bribery and corruption at the polls.'[92] Neither Chief Justice Harrison nor Justice Morrison knew that the seemingly gratuitous attack was coming, and Harrison later recorded that had they known, both 'would have dissuaded' Wilson.[93]

Within days, George Brown launched an editorial assault on Judge Wilson that was little short of that heard in the turmoil surrounding Quebec's bench. Brown described Wilson's comments as 'an indulgence in assumptions, surmises, and insinuations that we believe to be totally unparalleled in the judicial proceedings of any Canadian Court.'[94] Criticising almost every aspect of Wilson's application of the law and interpretation of evidence, Brown argued that while Conservative newspapers may have spent the better part of a year attempting to elevate the 'big push' letter into a scandal, it was another thing entirely 'when a judge of the Queen's Bench condescends to take up the idiotic howl, and rivals the dirge of the most blatant pot-house politician.'[95] Discussing Brown's response when a number of the senior judges were at Osgoode Hall, both Chief Justice Hagarty of Common Pleas and Chief Justice Harrison of Queen's Bench thought it would be 'more discreet to treat the attack with contempt,' but Justice Gwynne, whose Conservative roots ran deeper than most, thought Brown ought to be prosecuted.[96] As it turned out, a charge of being in contempt of court was laid, and the trial began in earnest in Queen's Bench before Chief Justice Harrison and Justice Morrison on 8 December. After the first day's hearing, Harrison noted in his diary that Brown, who argued the case on his own behalf, 'produced a good impression on the court by his conduct today.'[97] Harrison's hope that Brown would apologise was unfulfilled, and during the week after Christmas, both the chief justice and Morrison authored their rulings.

The penultimate act was disappointing. Harrison and Morrison disagreed entirely, with the chief justice supporting the case for contempt, while Morrison sided with Brown.[98] In a legal sense, the complaint failed and that provided Brown with yet another opportunity of taking a swipe, but this time at Harrison, whom the *Globe* had praised in reporting the West Durham ruling.[99] But having now adopted a position opposing Brown, 'Mr Chief Justice Harrison takes his stand boldly for the despotic power of the Bench, the law of contempt in its extreme form, and the utter wickedness of any journalist who dares to resent the unjust and insolent attack of a judge on the whole profession of which he is a member or on himself individually.' Morrison took 'a much more reasonable view of the powers of the Bench and the rights of the people; and in defining the liberty of the public press he does it in a generous and statesmanlike spirit befitting the age in which we live and worthy of a Canadian judge.'[100] Justice Wilson had refused to enter the court until he was provided the opportunity of reading the judgements, and thereafter, indicated that the court could not proceed until he read a protest. Harrison refused, and proceeded with as much business as was possible, and then adjourned the court owing to Wilson's absence. Later that day when tempers had cooled slightly, Wilson nonetheless indicated that he would be making a statement in court when they reconvened after the new year.[101] Much to his colleagues' relief, Wilson reconsidered and said nothing when he rejoined his brethren on 2 January 1877.[102]

On New Year's Eve, Chief Justice Harrison finally received a possible explanation for what had motivated Wilson. Enjoying a glass of sherry with Ontario's lieutenant governor Donald A. Macdonald, Harrison learned that his own appointment as chief justice had dashed Wilson's hopes for elevation. Further, Wilson blamed Brown for the setback, believing that the editor had counselled strongly against the appointment while enthusiastically backing Harrison. To the extent that this may been true, at the time of Harrison's appointment there had also been significant *party* resistance to raising Wilson, who had criticised both Alexander Mackenzie and Edward Blake.[103] We should be mindful, however, that viewing the conflict between Wilson and Brown as one steeped in personalities and career aspirations should not obscure the environment shaping Wilson's disappointment. Regardless of ability or mien, Wilson's politics trumped any claim to the chief justiceship while the Liberals were in office. And for the reasons that Wilson was unsuitable, Harrison was appealing, for he was one of the stars of the Ontario bar and had fallen out with Macdonald, yet still provided the

Liberals with the opportunity of claiming their appointments were free of partisan motives. Viewed in this sense, although the Wilson–Brown clash resonated with contemporary politics, akin to the scandals on Quebec's bench, the orchestration of judicial seats in Ontario, and the resignation of Oliver Mowat from Chancery, it was another example of how the politicisation of judicial appointments cheapened the nation's judicial culture. It is not that Wilson would have been a brilliant chief justice, or that Harrison had been a dreadful choice, but the options both men faced were more about partisan gamesmanship than a consideration of what qualities the judiciary might bring to the new nation.[104]

Conclusion: 'He May be a Curse'

Why had all this come to pass? A large part of the answer rests with John A. Macdonald and his influence on the nation's early political culture. As the ablest practitioner of employing patronage to build a winning party machine, Macdonald fashioned a system that placed a premium on loyal party service. Judicial patronage was part of that system and whether they liked it or not, all party leaders followed suit.[105] On another front, while this method was hammered into shape during the 1850s and 1860s, Macdonald's approach to politics on the ground subscribed to the notion that disputes, large or small, were best resolved by understandings between gentlemen politicians.[106] Disagreements were to be settled by fashioning a solution offering some form of reciprocity to the various interests at play. The last place to orchestrate these understandings was before a judge. In a broader sense, and in the midst of an era infused with notions of parliamentary supremacy, it was easy for Macdonald, the politician and tactician, to proceed as if the judiciary was relatively unimportant in settling large questions. Essentially, politicians solved contemporary problems, while judges merely applied the law. This perspective, when entwined with his approach to patronage, meant that there was little reason not to place party stalwarts on the bench. The big decisions on building the nation and shaping its character simply were not made by judges. Or, as John Saywell pointed out, 'Macdonald did not see the courts as a potential ally in federal–provincial jurisdictional disputes.'[107]

In his thoughtful examination of Sir Wilfrid Laurier's judicial appointments, Philip Girard concluded that Laurier departed from the Macdonald approach and was disinclined to dispense higher judicial appointments entirely on the basis of partisanship. At the same time, appointments to lower trial courts continued along the lines established by Macdonald and, one might add, Mackenzie. One is left to wonder if Laurier, unable to escape the undiluted partisanship of lower court appointments, was nonetheless motivated to alter course by an awareness of damage done through the method practised since the mid-nineteenth century. For, in truth, that 'old' style of judicial appointments had facilitated a great deal of scandal and controversy, while encouraging endless bickering and divisions within the parties as they wrestled over who deserved elevation.

The consequences were not for the parties alone. For despite Macdonald's disinclination to see the courts as key players in the nation-building enterprise, after the mid-1870s they assumed centre-stage in constitutional interpretation. Indeed, the Canadian Supreme Court, for one, 'was acutely conscious of its nation-building task and, initially at least, seemed to feel that its decisions would be the law of the land.'[108] Unfortunately, its potential to realize the law of the land was undone by its own members' failure to act as a court – as opposed to a collection of individual judges writing individual opinions – and, more gravely, by the continuation of appeals to the Judicial Committee of the Privy Council. Those appeals cultivated 'a palpable sense of fatality on the court ... the judges of the Supreme Court of Canada had concluded that their judgments were of no value at the Judicial Committee.'[109] Influenced as they were by a political outlook and an appointment process that minimized the role of judges and judging in shaping the country's identity, in concert with the looming presence of the Judicial Committee, the Canadian judiciary played its assigned role accordingly. And while it would be inaccurate and unfair to characterise all of the judicial rulings of the late nineteenth century as ill-conceived and inherently flawed decisions delivered by an indifferent assortment of judges, it is true that the jurisprudence of this era was increasingly blinkered, conservative, and uncreative.[110] So while Edward Blake might lament the possibility of a judge becoming a curse – and there were more than a few occasions where individual judges demonstrated all manner of human shortcomings – wayward judges were, in truth, only once piece of a larger picture. For someone such as Blake, who possessed a sharp eye and an intellect to match, a more honest assessment would have acknowledged that when judges became curses, the origins of such transformations were to be found in a political culture and the flawed process of judicial appointment it created.

NOTES

* I would like to thank both Jim Phillips and John Saywell for their comments
and counsel in writing this chapter. Over fifteen years ago Peter Oliver was
the external examiner when I defended my doctoral dissertation. We disagreed about interpretation then and, in the course of the ensuing years, we
managed to disagree about other things as well. Yet throughout it all Peter
remained a steadfast supporter, and while I benefited from a great deal of
his work, including his edited diary of Chief Justice Robert Harrison, it was
his work on the Mercer Reformatory for Women which provided an especially rich occasion. For it was that research that allowed me to inform
Mercer superintendent Mary Jayne O'Reilly's great-granddaughter (who
happens to be my mother-in-law), that she was related to a woman who
spent twenty years in a reformatory housing fallen women and female convicts. Peter relished the story but didn't let it pass without enquiring as
whether any family papers might be had. I know that Peter would have
been intrigued by this essay.

1 Edward Blake, 'The Teeswater Demonstration,' in *Reform Government in the
Dominion – The Pic-Nic Speeches* (Toronto: Globe Steam Book and Job Press
1878), 92–3. Blake had been minister of justice from 19 May 1875 to 7 June
1877.

2 See Philip Girard, 'Politics, Promotion, and Professionalism: Sir Wilfrid
Laurier's Judicial Appointments,' chapter 5 in this volume.

3 Jonathan Swainger, *The Canadian Department of Justice and the Completion of
Confederation, 1867–78* (Vancouver: UBC Press 2000), 99.

4 On the creation of the Department of Justice, see Swainger, *The Canadian
Department of Justice*.

5 See James G. Snell and Frederick Vaughan, *The Supreme Court of Canada:
History of the Institution* (Toronto: The Osgoode Society for Canadian Legal
History and University of Toronto Press 1985), 3–27; Hamar Foster, 'The
Struggle for the Supreme Court: Law and Politics in British Columbia,
1871–1885,' in Louis A. Knafla, ed., *Law and Justice in a New Land: Essays in
Western Canadian Legal History* (Calgary: The Carswell Company Limited
1986), 167–214; Bell, 'Judicial Crisis in Post-Confederation New Brunswick';
Ian Bushnell, *The Captive Court: A Study of the Supreme Court of Canada*
(Montreal: McGill-Queen's University Press 1992), 38–44; Jonathan
Swainger, 'A Bench in Disarray: The Quebec Judiciary and the Federal
Department of Justice, 1867–1878,' in *Les Cahiers de Droit* 34, no. 1 (March
1993), 59–91; Dale Brawn, *The Court of Queen's Bench of Manitoba, 1870–1950
– A Biographical History* (Toronto: The Osgoode Society for Canadian Legal

History and the University of Toronto Press 2006), 47–91. For pre-Confederation controversies in Upper Canada, see Paul Romney, '"The Ten Thousand Pound Job": Political Corruption, Equitable Jurisdiction, and the Public Interest in Upper Canada, 1852–6,' in David H. Flaherty, ed., *Essays in the History of Canadian Law*, vol. 2 (Toronto: Osgoode Society for Canadian Legal History and the University of Toronto Press 1983), 143–99; Paul Romney, *Mr Attorney, The Attorney General for Ontario in Court, Cabinet and Legislature 1791–1899* (Toronto: The Osgoode Society for Canadian Legal History and the University of Toronto Press 1986); Robert Fraser, '"All the Privileges which Englishmen Possess": Order, Rights, and Constitutionalism in Upper Canada,' in *Provincial Justice: Upper Canadian Legal Portraits* (Toronto: The Osgoode Society for Canadian Legal History and the University of Toronto Press 1992), xxi–xcii; and Peter Oliver, 'Power, Politics and the Law: The Place of the Judiciary in the Historiography of Upper Canada,' in G. Blaine Baker and Jim Phillips, eds., *Essays in the History of Canadian Law in Honour of R.C.B. Risk* (Toronto: Osgoode Society for Canadian Legal History and University of Toronto Press 1999), 443–68.

6 For an example of the tension between Ontario's county court judges and those at the appellate level, rooted in concerns about the abilities of the lower court judges, see 'Strictures from the Bench,' *Canada Law Journal*, 8, new series (May 1872), 102–3. At issue was the paucity of notes prepared at the county level and the subsequent inability of the appeal court to ascertain the ground for the decision rendered.

7 The question turns, in part, on whether parliamentary supremacy meant that judicial review was considerably less important than the federal power of disallowance. See Gordon Bale, *Chief Justice William Ritchie: Responsible Government and Judicial Review* (Ottawa: Carleton University Press 1991), and R.C.B. Risk, *A History of Canadian Legal Thought: Collected Essays*, ed. Blaine Baker and Jim Phillips (Toronto: The Osgoode Society for Canadian Legal History and University of Toronto Press 2006).

8 Mr T.J. Wallace, Halifax, to Sir John A. Macdonald, 25 May 1870, Library and Archives Canada [LAC], Record Group [RG] 13, vol. 2034, file 790/1870. For the initial eruption of hostilities, see Philip Girard, 'The Supreme Court of Nova Scotia: Confederation to the Twenty-First Century,' in Philip Girard, Jim Phillips, and Barry Cahill, eds., *The Supreme Court of Nova Scotia, 1754–2004 – From Imperial Bastion to Provincial Oracle* (Toronto: The Osgoode Society for Canadian Legal History 2004), 148. Also see J. Murray Beck, 'Sir William Young,' *Dictionary of Canadian Biography*, vol. 11 (Toronto: University of Toronto Press 1982), 948.

9 Comment dated 4 June 1870 on the back of Wallace's letter and initialled

GC, see RG 13, vol. 2034, file 790/1870. The Department of Justice mail register notes that a letter was sent to Wallace on 17 June indicating that no action would be taken, see RG 13, A1, vol. 441, 790/1870. A month earlier Sir John A. Macdonald had collapsed with a near fatal attack of gallstones and would be absent from public life for four months and Cartier has assumed leadership of the party and the Department of Justice. See Hewitt Bernard to Judge James Robert Gowan, LAC, Manuscript Group [MG] 27, I E 31, vol. 1, 10 May 1870, 47–51, and 14 May 1870, 52–3. Also see Donald Creighton, *John A. Macdonald – The Old Chieftain* (Toronto: Macmillan Company of Canada 1955), 68–72.

10 G. Blaine Baker indicates that in 1880 there were 1,100 practising in Ontario. See G. Blaine Baker, 'The Reconstitution of Upper Canadian Legal Thought in the late-Victorian Empire,' *Law and History Review* 3 (1985), 222. Given this number, it seems unlikely that there were more than 3,000 lawyers in British North America at the time of Confederation.

11 Oliver, 'Power, Politics and the Law,' 462. Also see D.G. Bell, 'Judicial Crisis in Post-Confederation New Brunswick,' in Dale Gibson and W. Wesley Pue, eds., *Glimpses of Canadian Legal History* (Winnipeg: Legal Research Institute of the University of Manitoba 1991), 189–203; Swainger, *The Canadian Department of Justice*, 98–122; Girard, 'Politics, Promotion, and Professionalism.'

12 That in the aftermath of Chief Justice Brenton Halliburton's death on 16 July 1860, Premier William Young appointed himself chief justice demonstrates how thoroughly politicised judicial appointments were in late colonial British North America. Thanks to Jim Phillips for reminding me of the manner in which Young was elevated to the bench. See Beck, 'Sir William Young,' *Dictionary of Canadian Biography*, vol. 11, 948.

13 John A. Macdonald to Hon. T.W. Anglin, 10 Jan 1871, MG 26 A, vol. 574, 70–1.

14 Edward Blake to F. Bechard, 27 Jan 1876, Archives of Ontario [AO], MS 20 (16), 92–3.

15 On Macdonald's use of patronage in building the mid-nineteenth century Conservative party and the Liberal unease with such tactics, see Gordon Stewart, 'John A. Macdonald's Greatest Triumph,' *Canadian Historical Review* 63, no. 1 (March 1982), 3–33. Also see Stewart, 'Political Patronage Under Macdonald and Laurier,' *The American Review of Canadian Studies* 10, no. 1 (Spring 1980), 3–26, and Stewart, *The Origins of Canadian Politics – A Comparative Approach* (Vancouver: UBC Press 1986), 77–82.

16 Bell, 'Judicial Crisis in Post-Confederation New Brunswick,' 193.

17 J. Murray Beck, 'Alfred Gilpin Jones,' *DCB*, vol. 13, 525–9.

18 N. Omer Coté, *Political Appointments, Parliaments, and the Judicial Bench in the Dominion of Canada, 1867–1895* (Ottawa: Thorburn and Company, Printers and Publishers 1896), 363.

19 J.W. Carmichael to Edward Blake, 31 March 1876, AO, MS 20 (5), no. 118 with enclosures. For Carmichael's support of Mackenzie during Macdonald's first administration, see Thomson, *Alexander Mackenzie*, 125. See also L. Anders Sandberg, 'James William Carmichael,' *DCB*, vol. 13, 169–71.

20 Carmichael to Blake, ibid.

21 James B. Duffers to Edward Blake, 10 April 1876, ibid. The promise of a judicial appointment is confirmed in A.G. Jones to Mackenzie, 21 April 1876, ibid. See David A. Sutherland, 'William Annand,' *DCB*, vol. 11, 22–5.

22 James B. Duffers to Blake, 10 April 1876, ibid.

23 Ibid.

24 Carmichael to Alexander Mackenzie, 11 April 1876, ibid.

25 Duffers to Alexander Mackenzie, 20 April 1876, ibid.

26 Ibid. Also see A.G. Jones to Alexander Mackenzie, 26 May 1876, ibid.

27 Duffers to Blake, 21 April 1876, ibid.

28 A.G. Jones to Alexander Mackenzie, 22 April 1876, ibid.

29 The following is based on Mackenzie to Carmichael, 29 April 1876, ibid.

30 Carmichael to Mackenzie, 6 May 1876, ibid.

31 Ibid.

32 Ibid.

33 'Appointments,' *Canada Gazette* 10, no. 9 (26 August 1876), 213. See Henry J. Morgan, ed., 'Morse, William Agnew,' *The Canadian Legal Directory: A Guide to the Bench and Bar of the Dominion of Canada* (Toronto: Carswell 1878), 242–3.

34 The following discussion of the situation is Quebec is based on my longer and more detailed examination in 'A Bench in Disarray.'

35 Fortin's concern was overwhelmed in the debate that followed and was only taken up four days later on 30 March 1868. See 'Address to the House of Commons,' *Journal of the House of Commons* 1 (30 March 1868), 167. The original petition can be found in Secretary of State for the Provinces, LAC, RG c. 1, vol. 310, file 359.

36 L.H. Masson, in *Debates of the House of Commons*, 26 March 1868, 420. The *Newspaper Hansard* notes that the House erupted into laughter following Masson's statement.

37 A.A. Dorion, *Newspaper Hansard*, 26 March 1868. There are a few inconsistencies between the *Newspaper Hansard* and that which P.B. Waite reconstructed from newspaper reports.

38 Ibid.

39 G.E. Cartier, *Newspaper Hansard*, 26 March 1868. Drummond was actually appointed by the Macdonald-Dorion government in 1864.

40 John A. Macdonald, *Newspaper Hansard*, 26 March 1868.

41 'From a Correspondent,' *Gazette* (Montreal), 3 April 1868, 1.

42 Ibid.

43 'Administration of Justice in the Province of Quebec,' *Canada Law Journal* (Montreal) 4, no. 2 (April 1868), 27, and 'Impeachment of Judges,' *Canada Law Journal* 4, no. 3 (July 1868), 53–4.

44 'Administration of Justice in the Province of Quebec.' Macdonald's government introduced a judicial pension scheme in May 1868, which provided for a pension based on two-thirds of an applicant's salary. See *An Act respecting the Governor General, the Civil List, and the Salaries of certain Public Functionaries* (1868), 31 Vict. c.33, s.3.

45 *An Act to amend the Judicature Acts of Lower Canada*, Statutes of Canada, 20 Vict. (1857), c.54.

46 Brian Young, 'Dimensions of a Law Practice: Brokerage and Ideology in the Career of George-Etienne Cartier,' in Carol Wilton, ed., *Essays in the History of Canadian Law: Beyond the Law: Lawyers and Business in Canada, 1830–1930* (Toronto: The Osgoode Society for Canadian Legal History and Butterworths 1990), 103–4.

47 John Charles Dent, *The Last Forty Years: Canada Since the Union of 1841*, vol. 2 (Toronto: G. Virtue 1881), 352, and John Boyd, *Sir George Etienne Cartier, Bart., His Life and Times* (Toronto: Macmillan Company of Canada 1914), 136.

48 'Judicial Appointments,' *Canada Law Journal* 8, new series (May 1872), 107. On the same page of the column, editors William D. Ardagh and Robert Harrison argued that 'no appointment to a judicial office, or to any ministerial office, where professional competence or eminence is required, should be made merely to meet the exigencies of party politics.' But having made that claim, the editors retreated: 'If, however, this must be, (though the confession even of the alleged necessity of this is degrading), let the best men be chosen from the political supporters of the Government which may have the patronage to bestow.' The unqualified view was consistent with that advocated by their fellow Conservative, John A. Macdonald.

49 Although unattributed in the *Canada Law Journal*, it seems likely that the author was William Hastings Kerr, a founding editor of *Le Revue Critique* and dean of law at McGill University from 1881–8. Kerr was one of the most outspoken and principled critics of the administration of Quebec's courts during the 1870s. On the *Revue Critique's* founding principles, see Sylvio Normand, 'Profil des périodiques juridiques québécois au XIXᵉ siècle,' *Les Cahiers de Droit* 34, no. 1 (March 1993), 165.

50 W.H. Kerr, 'The Bench and Bar of Quebec,' *Canada Law Journal* 9, new series (March 1873), 89. Also see 'The Court of Appeals in Quebec,' *Canada Law Journal* 10, new series (February 1874), 32–3.

51 Kerr, 'The Bench and Bar of Quebec.'

52 Ibid.

53 'Bench and Bar – The Deadlock in the Superior Court,' *Gazette* (Montreal), 31 January 1876, 2. Writing to Luther Holton on 27 January 1876, Judge Robert Mackay offered to resign 'to facilitate arrangements for the better administration of Justice in the Province of Quebec.' Mackay to Holton, AO, MS 20 (3), no. 13. A similar offer was made to Holton by Judge Francis G. Johnson on 27 January 1876. See AO, MS 20 (4), no. 21. On Berthelot's willingness to step aside, see Luther Holton to Edward Blake, 31 January 1876, AO, MS 20 (3), no. 14; Holton to Blake, 2 February 1876, AO, MS 20 (3), no. 15; and Blake to Holton, 4 February 1876, AO MS 20 (16), 216–17.

54 'Bar of Montreal – Special Meeting,' *Gazette* (Montreal), 28 October 1876, 2.

55 Coté, *Political Appointments*, 340–59.

56 Swainger, 'A Bench in Disarray,' 67.

57 For a detailed discussion of these events, see Swainger, *The Canadian Department of Justice*, 102–6.

58 On the history and structure of Ontario's courts, see Margaret A. Banks, 'The Evolution of the Ontario Courts, 1788–1981,' in David H. Flaherty, ed., *Essays in the History of Canadian Law*, vol. 2 (Toronto: The Osgoode Society for Canadian Legal History and University of Toronto Press 1983), 492–572. The chief justice of Queen's Bench remained chief justice of Ontario although the chief justice of Error and Appeal was the highest ranked judge in the province. A distinct Court of Error and Appeal did not exist until 1874; prior to that date, the court was composed of the members of the Courts of Queen's Bench, Chancery, and Common Pleas.

59 The following is based on W.H. Draper to John A. Macdonald, 18 February 1868, reel C1567, 65009.

60 Morrison to Macdonald, 20 April 1868, ibid., 65019

61 Harrison to Macdonald, 28 April 1868, ibid., 65025. Harrison's concern probably meant that as a practitioner, he disliked being caught between the battling judges, although the comment might be read as suggesting that Harrison expected an appointment to Queen's Bench. The latter possibility seems unlikely as the published version of his diary for the first half of 1868 does not record any mention of a judicial seat being offered. However, on 18 July, Harrison noted that Macdonald offered a judicial post at the end of Harrison's four-year term in Parliament. See Peter Oliver, ed., *The Conventional Man: The Diaries of Ontario Chief Justice Robert A. Harrison, 1856–1878*

(Toronto: The Osgoode Society for Canadian Legal History and University of Toronto Press 2003), 330. On the rumours of possible appointments and elevations, see 'Judicial Changes,' *Canada Law Journal* 4, new series (May 1868), 105–6.

62 The following is based on Oliver Mowat to John A. Macdonald, 28 May 1868, LAC, MG 26A, vol. 253, 114941–948. Also see A. Margaret Evans, *Sir Oliver Mowat* (Toronto: The Ontario Studies Series and University of Toronto Press 1992), 61.

63 VanKoughnet's allusion to 'the introduction of your bill for a new court' in his letter is unexplained, although he was probably referring to the proposed Dominion Supreme Court. It is conceivable he was also thinking about the possibe fusion of equity and common-law courts in Ontario, although this seems premature in 1868. VanKoughnet to Macdonald, 26 July 1868, LAC, MG 26A, reel C1567, 65031–2.

64 John A. Macdonald to John S. Macdonald, 15 September 1868, LAC MG 26A, vol. 572, 1078–9. The source of Sir John's interpretation of events appears to have been W.H. Draper, see Draper to Macdonald, 7 September 1868, ibid., vol. 160, 65035.

65 The Court of Error and Appeal in Upper Canada became the Court of Error and Appeal in Ontario in 1869 but Queen's Bench, Chancery, and Common Pleas retained the Upper Canada description until 1871. See Banks, 'The Evolution of the Ontario Courts, 1788–1981,' 519.

66 William Buell Richards to John A. Macdonald, 15 September 1868, LAC, MG 26A, reel C1567, 65041. Department of Justice Register, 1868, LAC, RG 13, A1, vol. 437, nos. 391, 393–6. Harrison's diary entry for 16 November records the arrival of the news at Osgoode Hall where the benchers congratulated all the individuals promoted or raised to the bench. See Oliver, *A Conventional Man*, 335. For Draper's elevation, see 'The Chief Justice of Error and Appeal,' *Canada Law Journal* 5, new series (February 1869), 29–30.

67 John A. Macdonald to Hon Joseph Curran Morrison, 26 November 1869, LAC, MG 26A, vol. 573, 580–1. See 'Death of the Chancellor,' *Canada Law Journal* 5, new series (November and December 1869), 281, 309–10. Also see W.L. Morton, 'Philip Michael Matthew Scott VanKoughnet,' in *Dictionary of Canadian Biography*, vol. 9 (Toronto: University of Toronto Press 1976), 803–4. Harrison's diary entry for 9 November recorded that the bar met to pay respects to VanKoughnet, 'who died on Sunday night [7 November] of a broken heart and too much whiskey.' See Oliver, *A Conventional Man*, 366.

68 Macdonald to Morrison, 26 November 1869, LAC, MG 26A, vol. 573, 580–1.

69 Ibid.

70 Macdonald to Morrison, 2 December 1869, ibid., 640–1.

71 John A. Macdonald to John Hillyard Cameron, 15 November 1869, ibid., 425–6, and ibid., 24 December 1869, 791–2. On Spragge's health, see Draper to Macdonald, 18 February 1868, ibid., reel C1567, and 'Illness of the Chancellor,' *The Canada Law Journal* 3, new series (March 1871), 61.

72 John A. Macdonald to John S. Macdonald, 27 December 1869, LAC, MG 26A, vol. 573, 801–6. Spragge's elevation and Strong's appointment are registered in Department of Justice Register, 1869, LAC, RG 13, A1, vol. 439, nos. 1660 and 1661. See 'New Chancery Judges,' *Canada Law Journal* 4, new series (January 1870), 4.

73 Oliver Mowat to John A. Macdonald, 24 October 1872, and Macdonald to Mowat, 25 October 1872, LAC, MG 26A, vol. 253, 114949–50.

74 Evans, *Oliver Mowat*, 54–5. Mowat was appointed to Chancery on 14 November 1864.

75 Such an inference is in 'Resignation of Vice-Chancellor Mowat,' *Canada Law Journal*, 8, new series (November 1872), 264.

76 John A. Macdonald to Oliver Mowat, 25 October 1872, NAC, MG 26A, vol. 253, 114957–8.

77 Evans, *Oliver Mowat*, 63–4. The *Canada Law Journal* pointed out that the practice of judges returning to public life was a practice in line with the politics of the seventeenth and eighteenth centuries. See 'Judges Returning to the Bar,' *Canada Law Journal* 8, new series (November 1872), 291–3.

78 Macdonald to Spragge, 25 October 1872, 26, and Macdonald to Draper, 25 October 1872, 27–8. See 'Who is to be Vice-Chancellor,' *Canada Law Journal* 8, new series (November 1872), 267–8.

79 John A. Macdonald to John Coyne, 30 November 1872, NAC, MG 26A, vol. 576, 207, and Macdonald to Draper, 25 October 1872, 27–8. Moss and Crooks are among the names noted in the *Canada Law Journal* 8, new series (November 1872), 267–8.

80 John A. Macdonald to Chief Justice Morris, 4 December 1972, NAC, MG 26A, vol. 576, 244–5. Sir John also expressed this sentiment to Mr Justice Gray of the British Columbia Supreme Court; Macdonald to Mr Justice Gray, 30 November 1872, ibid., 214–5. Also see Macdonald to John Hillyard Cameron, 27 November 1872, ibid., at 181a, and Macdonald to T.C. Patteson, 7 December 1872, ibid., 256–7.

81 Macdonald to D'Arcy Boulton, 12 December 1872, ibid., 315–16.

82 The self-congratulatory tone had been a part of the *Canada Law Journal's* predecessor – *Upper Canada Law Journal* – almost from its inception; for example, see 'Contempts of Court,' *Upper Canada Law Journal* 4, old series (November 1858), 243.

83 'Contempt of Court in Lower Canada,' *Upper Canada Law Journal* 3, new

series (April 1867), 86. The *Upper Canada Law Journal* adopted the *Canada Law Journal* name at the time of Confederation.

84 'The Judiciary in Lower Canada,' *Canada Law Journal* 3, new series (July 1867), 175. A similar tone is found in 'Conflicting Decisions in Lower Canada,' *Canada Law Journal* 4, new series (June 1868), 135.

85 *Canada Law Journal* 8, new series (October 1872), 233–4. David Bell points to similar statistics as an indication of troubles facing New Brunswick's judiciary.

86 On English developments, see 'Fusion of Law and Equity,' *Canada Law Journal* 3, new series (March 1871), 67–83. On naming the Law Reform Commissioners in Ontario, see 'Appointments to Office,' *Canada Law Journal* 7, new series (October 1871), 283, and 'The Law Reform Commission,' *Canada Law Journal* 8, new series (January 1872), 1. The Law Reform Commission was dissolved in September 1872 by Edward Blake's provincial administration, see Paul Romney, 'John Wellington Gwynne,' *Dictionary of Canadian Biography*, vol. 13 (Toronto: University of Toronto Press and Quebec: Les Presses de l'université Laval 1994), 427–8, and Jamie Benedickson, 'Sir Samuel Henry Strong,' ibid., 994.

87 The debate over the merit of fusion continued in the columns of the *Canada Law Journal* well beyond the *Administration of Justice Act* of 1873.

88 'Strictures from the Bench,' *Canada Law Journal* 8, new series (May 1872), 109.

89 The meeting took place on 24 July 1873 at Osgoode Hall. See 'Meeting of County Judges,' *Canada Law Journal* 9, new series (September 1873), 247–8. James Robert Gowan, 'The Office of County Judge in Ontario,' *Canada Law Journal* 10, new series (January 1874), 6–12. Also see Desmond Brown, 'Sir James Robert Gowan,' *DCB*, vol. 13, 391–5.

90 For a discussion of Liberal judicial appointments and the degree to which that process mirrored Macdonald's approach, see Swainger, *The Department of Justice and the Completion of Confederation*, 106–10, 115–21.

91 On the 'big push' allegations, see J.M.S. Careless, *Brown of the Globe: Statesman of Confederation* (Toronto: Dundurn Press Limited 1989), 340–2, 347–9, and Dale Thomson, *Alexander Mackenzie: Clear Grit* (Toronto: The Macmillan Company of Canada 1960), 246–7. Although the controversy was rooted in a Conservative attempt to create a Liberal counterpart to the Pacific Scandal, Careless' treatment suggests that the actual result was to have Brown struck off the list for royal honours.

92 'The West Durham Libel Suit,' *Globe* (Toronto), 8 July 1876, 2.

93 Oliver, *A Conventional Man*, 551.

94 'Editorial,' *Globe* (Toronto), 8 July 1876, 3. The title of the editorial, which is

obscured but appears to imply that Judge Wilson was on the war path, carries a none-too-subtle reference to the recent front page news of General George Custer's death at Little Big Horn.

95 Ibid.

96 Oliver, *A Conventional Man*, 552.

97 Ibid., 566, and 'In the Court of Queen's Bench – Trial for Contempt of Court,' *Globe* (Toronto), 11 December 1876, 4. Also see Careless, *Brown of the Globe*, 349.

98 Harrison's diary indicates that both he and Morrison actually agreed that Brown's actions in attacking Wilson were objectionable but Morrison may have sided against the complaint because he thought Wilson's actions had been inappropriate in the first instance.

99 'Editorial,' *Globe* (Toronto), 8 July 1876, 3.

100 'The Contempt Case,' *Globe* (Toronto), 30 December 1876, 4.

101 Oliver, *A Conventional Man*, 569.

102 Ibid., 572.

103 Alexander Mackenzie to Edward Blake, n.d., MS 20 (5)-no. 284. The letter's internal context indicates that it was written in 1875, prior to Harrison's appointment and Chief Justice W.B. Richard's elevation to the Supreme Court of Canada. Also see Mackenzie to Blake, 4 July 1876, MS 20 (5)-no. 145, in which the prime minister indicates that Wilson's antipathies towards Mackenzie and Blake were well known.

104 Wilson had not blotted his own copybook in attacking Brown. When Chief Justice Harrison died on 2 November 1878, Chief Justice Hagarty of Common Pleas was raised to Queen's Bench and Wilson became chief justice of Common Pleas. The appointments were amongst the very first completed by John A. Macdonald upon his return to the Prime Minister's Office. When Chief Justice Hagarty became chief justice of the Court of Appeal, Wilson was elevated to chief justice of Queen's Bench.

105 Gordon Stewart, 'The Beginnings of Politics in Canada,' in Alain G. Gagnon and A. Brian Tanguay, eds., *Canadian Parties in Transition* (Peterborough: Broadview Press 2007), 17–32.

106 Swainger, *The Canadian Department of Justice*, 5–7.

107 John T. Saywell, *The Lawmakers: Judicial Power and the Shaping of Canadian Federalism* (Toronto: The Osgoode Society for Canadian Legal History and University of Toronto Press 2002), 92.

108 Ibid., 34.

109 Ibid., 63.

110 Jennifer Nedelsky, 'Judicial Conservatism in an Age of Innovation: Comparative Perspectives on Canadian Nuisance Law 1880–1930,' in David H.

Flaherty, ed., *Essays in the History of Canadian Law*, vol. 1 (Toronto: The Osgoode Society for Canadian Legal History and University of Toronto Press 1981), 281–322; Jamie Benidickson, 'Private Rights and Public Purposes in the Lakes, Rivers, and Streams of Ontario 1870–1930,' in Flaherty, ed., *Essays in the History of Canadian Law*, vol. 2, 365–417; Baker, 'The Reconstitution of Upper Canadian Legal Thought'; Jennifer Nedelsky, 'From Private Property to Public Resource: The Emergence of Administrative Control of Water in Nova Scotia,' in Girard and Phillips, eds., *Essays in the History of Canadian Law*, vol. 3, 326–52; and Risk, *A History of Canadian Legal Thought: Collected Essays*. The gradual departure from this conservative perspective is noted by R.C.B. Risk and explored in a number of essays in Jonathan Swainger, ed., *The Alberta Supreme Court at 100: History and Authority* (Toronto: The Osgoode Society for Canadian Legal History and University of Alberta Press 2007).

PART THREE

Legal Thought and the Legal Profession:
Contested Conceptions of
Law and Lawyers

8

Strategic Benthamism: Rehabilitating United Canada's Bar through Criminal Law Codification, 1847–54

G. BLAINE BAKER*

On Tuesday 21 May 1850, William Badgley introduced to the Legislative Assembly of United Canada at Toronto's Saint Lawrence Hall two private member's bills to codify provincial criminal law and procedure.[1] One of those codes was loosely derived, at least stylistically, from Thomas Babington Macaulay's *India Penal Code* of 1838. The other was modelled after Edward Livingston's unenacted 1826 *Louisiana Code of Criminal Procedure* filtered through David Dudley Field's 1849 *New York Code of Criminal Procedure*.[2] Badgley's *Act to Establish a Criminal Code* and his *Act to Establish a Code of Criminal Procedure* together comprise nearly 400 pages of folio-sized, statutory text in about nineteen-hundred articles. They were given two hesitant and perfunctory readings in the legislature, before referral to a select committee for study.[3] Those bills then disappeared from parliamentary, professional, and public view after the legislature acted on its committee's advice and recommended to Governor General Lord Elgin that he establish a commission 'for the consolidation and assimilation of the Criminal Laws of [the Province of Canada].'[4] The history of legal codification is replete with analogous false starts, evacuations, and failures.[5]

Badgley was an ambitious lobbyist, assemblyman, and statute-draftsman. He has been properly credited with large, extra-parliamentary contributions to leading law-reform initiatives of Canada's post-Rebellion period like land registration laws, bankruptcy statutes, and the ordinance that provided for abolition of seigniorial land tenure on the

Island of Montreal.[6] Elected to the Legislative Assembly in 1847, Badgley served for a year as Attorney General for Lower Canada in the William Henry Draper/Denis-Benjamin Papineau and Henry Sherwood/ D.-B. Papineau administrations of the late 1840s. Most important, he was one of the assembly's more prolific originators and sponsors of private member's bills during his seven years in three parliaments. Although Badgley introduced his codes from the opposition benches two years after the defeat of his Tory Party by the second Robert Baldwin/ Louis-Hippolyte LaFontaine Reform ministry, and allowing for their moderately synthetic or derivative character, the scope of those bills and the time involved elsewhere in nineteenth-century penal-law codifications suggest they were the culmination of a project begun while he was in government.[7]

A few modern commentators have noted, in passing, Badgley's locally unprecedented proposals to 'unify' and 'render scientific' Canadian criminal law and procedure.[8] But the codifier, his legislative texts, parallels with legal-literary developments in other North Atlantic jurisdictions, and professional circumstance have not been the subject of sustained historical examination. Nonetheless, enough is now known about British North American legislative initiatives of the mid-nineteenth century to use Badgley's attempted codification of Canadian criminal justice as a bridgehead to move studies of provincial statutes at-large beyond technical or antiquarian notice onto the terrain of conceptions of legislative and professional action. That change of emphasis should, in turn, help enable Canadian legal historiography to participate in an emerging Anglo-American literature that has taken the implications of late-eighteenth and early-nineteenth-century theories of lawyerly statecraft and professional identity as its principal subject matters.[9]

Badgley's codal legislation offers a suitable catalyst for that historiographical shift by virtue of its draftsman's compulsion to demonstrate the elite bar's indispensability to constitutional stability and parliamentary state-building, and because his codes' indifferent reception by a union government with a locally unparalleled record of legislative law-making is suggestive of uneven, emerging perceptions of the politics, timeliness, and uses of legislation.[10] The assembly's later appointment of less experienced statute-draftsmen like Superior Court Justice Charles Dewey Day, Queen's Bench Justice René-Edouard Caron, Superior Court Justice Augustin-Norbert Morin, and Court of Appeal Clerk Joseph-Ubalde Beaudry to undertake key projects like the codification of Lower Canadian private law and civil procedure also suggests political ambivalence about Badgley's stylistic, strategic, or ideological approach to codal law-making.[11] Another reason for this study is that Badgley's lengthy and formative sojourns in Britain, his acquaintance with Colonial Office policy-makers, and his knowledge of English and United States legal reforms of the day provide explicit, transatlantic, and panamerican links between mid-nineteenth-century provincial and metropolitan statecraft.[12] The three themes introduced in this paragraph will be treated in varying degrees of detail in this essay, working towards Badgley's codes from proposals he made for the legislative restructuring of other aspects of Canadian law.

Brief note should be taken of related developments in the organization of Lower Canadian civil and judicial law. A more-or-less comprehensive code of private law was commissioned by the Legislative Assembly in 1857 and enacted in 1866, and a modified 'Field Code' of civil procedure was promulgated in 1867.[13] Although Badgley lost his seat in the Assembly in 1854, and did not participate in Lower Canada's independent commissions that superintended the codification of private or judicial law, he remained involved professionally and socially with the small clique of legislative utilitarians who undertook, managed, or promoted those projects.[14] Badgley's apparent lack of political and ethnic savvy, together with his conception of the symbolic character of codal legislation, distinguished him from more accommodating but instrumentally oriented members of United Canada's extended parliamentary bar.[15] He thought, distinctively, that the formal dimensions of legal reform, including law's packaging, were often as instrumental to social change as its substantive elements. But he could also behave in a straight-forwardly instrumental fashion when he believed that circumstances warranted the adoption of that posture.

Describing his *Act to Establish a Criminal Code* and his *Act to Establish a Code of Criminal Procedure*, Badgley told the assembly that they were

made up from [Canadian] statutory enactments, as well as from the English law, and the codes of some of the neighbouring States – [they] would apply equally to both portions of the province, because the criminal law in both was the same ... [Canadian criminal law] is composed of a vast collection of subsisting as well as obsolete but unrepealed statutory enactments, and of Judicial opinions frequently conflicting, requiring great and labourous research and study for their discovery and comprehension, even by its Professors, and to the same degree difficult to be known by the large class of official persons who are called upon to carry out its requirements, whilst it is utterly unknown to the great mass of the people who are subject to its penalties. The Bills have been compiled with the view to a removal of these difficulties, and to the condensation into one uniform Code for United *Canada*, of Laws useful and necessary, and at the same time essential to the peace of society, and the security of person and property, communicated in plain and perspicuous language, and comprehended under a regular and systematic arrangement. [The Bills] comprise together a complete body of *Canadian* Criminal Jurisprudence.[16]

Badgley thus commended his codifications of Canadian criminal law and procedure to the legislature by alluding to technical values like economy of expression, comprehensiveness and order, administrative objectives such as ease of doctrinal discovery and application, social aims like heightened popular literacy and public security, and especially political benefits such as institutional assimilation and legal uniformity across the Canadas. Those goals covered the prevailing rhetorical spectrum of formal, bureaucratic, and political justifications for mid-nineteenth-century Anglo-American code reform.[17] But Badgley made no mention to the assembly of substantive legal change. Nor did he reveal why he chose to pursue unprecedented Canadian legal coherence, accessibility, and assimilation through codal renovation of the institutions of criminal justice rather than by that sort of reorganization of any other aspect of official law. Likewise, remarks about the legal profession's mission and expertise were absent from Badgley's parliamentary presentations.

Modern commentators have repeatedly shown that mainstream opinion during the union period routinely identified the law of obligations, the law of land tenure, and successions law as the bodies of Lower Canadian legal doctrine most disturbing for their disorderliness and conflicting or doubtful purposes.[18] Thomas Kennedy Ramsay (soon to be English-language secretary to the Civil Code Commission) and Louis-Siméon Morin (soon to be Attorney General for Lower Canada and French-language secretary to the same agency) captured that sentiment poignantly, if indirectly, in an 1854 review of government proposals to modify local criminal law that were much less comprehensive than Badgley's bills:

we are always disposed to look with favor on amendments, or what purport to be so, when applied to any system [of law] that is palpably faulty; but not so when it is proposed to interfere with the working of an institution so nearly perfect as our criminal law. We are ready to admit that the great English Law

Reformers have done something to simplify criminal procedure, and the humble imitation now before us [John Hillyard Cameron's 'Bill to Amend the Criminal Law of this Province'] follows pretty much their example; but we are disposed to doubt whether the advantages gained by this simplification will compensate for the risk of change.[19]

Criminal justice was generally regarded as United Canada's most internally coherent, procedurally efficient, and geographically uniform body of state law. It was, at least on first inspection, not perceived to be the province's most pressing candidate for codal reorganization.

Another striking feature of Badgley's proposals for codifying mid-nineteenth-century Canadian criminal law and procedure is that, contrary to glowing compliments in the assembly by Solicitor General Lewis Thomas Drummond and Reform Party member Louis-Joseph Papineau, those legislative texts were neither the result of lengthy engagement with the law of crimes nor a product of established commitment to the administration of criminal justice on the part of their draftsman.[20] Criminal law entries in Badgley's 700-page commonplace book are few and superficial, he had little exposure to crimes in law practice, his Attorney Generalship was barely a year in length, he taught Roman and international law at that time rather than McGill College's elective course in penal law, and the District Court on which he sat in the mid-1840s had no significant jurisdiction over criminal matters.[21] Badgley's direct experience of the widespread, Lower Canadian violence many of his professional peers fomented, witnessed, or censured officially during the late 1830s and 1840s was also limited. He watched Canada's Parliament burned by a politically motivated Montreal mob in 1849, and sought unsuccessfully with fellow MLA Allan Napier McNab to save its library. But Badgley was in Britain at the time of the rebellions of 1837 and 1838, and during their immediate aftermath. He also missed Montreal's 'Gavazzi' religious riots of the early 1850s, since he was in the legislature at Quebec City.[22]

Perhaps most telling, Badgley was uninvolved and seemingly uninterested in any of the modest, criminal law reforms implemented by the assembly to enhance protection of property and commerce during his years in elected politics.[23] Excluding the introduction of his own *Act to Establish a Criminal Code*, Badgley's only recorded legislative commentary on criminal law was laconic support for an abortive bill to criminalize duelling. A similar silence prevailed with respect to criminal procedure and the administration of penal justice. Badgley once speculated that Canadian grand juries could usefully be replaced by public prosecutors, and he introduced to the legislature a bill to incorporate the 'Prison Discipline Society of Montreal' (inspired by Livingston's Louisiana *Code of Prison Discipline*), only to withdraw that proposal before its second reading.[24] But he had nothing to say to the assembly about any of the numerous pinpoint laws enacted during his parliamentary tenure treating criminal procedure or the administration of penal justice.[25]

Similarly, Badgley contributed little to the jurisprudence of crimes or criminal procedure through his later work on the Superior Court, the Court of Queen's Bench, or the Court of Appeal. In twenty years, he wrote about 550 reported decisions, but he authored or concurred in a mere handful of criminal judgments, some of which involved what would now be called regulatory or municipal offences.[26] There is, therefore, little evidence that assignors of judicial responsibility saw in Badgley expertise in or enthusiasm for criminal law. Justices Thomas Cushing Aylwin and Charles-Joseph-Elzéar Mondelet were most often posted to criminal trials in Lower Canada's Superior Court or its Court of Queen's Bench during Badgley's time on those tribunals.[27] In short, with the exception of trite remarks about 'the peace of society' and 'the security of person and property' that accompanied introduction of his codes to the assembly, there is scant indication in the available historical record that Badgley was motivated by a substantive interest in criminal justice as a technique of social regulation. Although further sorting of primary sources than was undertaken in the preparation of this essay would be necessary to make definitive observations, Badgley's codes appear to be more like heavily edited and tidy consolidations of existing law tied by marginal references into related international sources than they are pathbreaking doctrinal reforms. But he called them 'codes,' as if to signal seriousness of purpose, scientific rigour, and cosmopolitan cachet.

Badgley did, however, have three attributes that figured largely in the preparation of his penal codes. One such quality was his curiosity about the primary sources and secondary literature of criminal justice elsewhere in the North Atlantic world. References to those texts, printed in his bills but apparently destined for removal when they became law, show that acquisitive disposition.[28] A second and even more relevant quality was Badgley's whiggish commitment to the consolidation of Lower Canada's legal professions. He instigated and ran the province's first permanent, university-related, law-teaching program, and he taught in that school for thirty-five years. Badgley was also a co-founder in the late 1820s of the Advocates' Library and Law Institute of Montreal, and assumed a leading lifetime role in that centre of professional literacy. Similarly, he was an inaugural and active member of Montreal's Society of Brothers-in-Law, a dining club with restricted membership that met bimonthly during the late 1820s and early 1830s to foster social camaraderie and cultural cohesiveness among the local bar's anglophone elite.[29] Most important, Badgley drafted and piloted private member's bills through the legislative assembly in the late 1840s to incorporate Lower Canada's bar and its notariate. Another related statute with which he was associated provided official recognition for university law teaching, and underwrote those schools by offering reductions of apprenticeship time for students enrolled in them.[30] He was thus active on a range of administrative, pedagogical, and social fronts in the mid-nineteenth-century institutionalization of the Lower Canadian bar and the refinement of provincial legal culture. The literature of the law (including legislation) was a major participant in that institutionalization and refinement. Finally, Badgley was a seasoned constitutional trench fighter on behalf of Lower Canada's unificationist British Party.[31] He also experienced, as a working legislator, dramatic transformations of Canada's formal organs of the state that characterized the period between 1837 and 1848. Badgley saw the imperial government suspend Lower Canada's legislative assembly in 1838, and he collaborated closely with the appointed Special Council that replaced it until 1841. He was also Attorney General during the implementation of structural change that rendered the executive branch of the provincial government responsible to the elected legislature in 1848.[32] Badgley's intellectual disposition, his loyalty to United Canada's increasingly insecure legal professions, and his immersion in shifting techniques of constitutional and legislative statecraft therefore offer more promising starting points for assessment of his abortive codifications of criminal justice than are provided by conventional issues of legal doctrine or social control.

Strategic Benthamism

A small but impressive strand of Anglo-American scholarship on the nineteenth-century legal textbook tradition, codification movements, and other signal changes in the way jurisprudential knowledge was acquired and packaged in that period has taken the legitimacy of the legal profession and its role in the state as organizing themes. That writing shows that, although techniques deployed by Anglo-American bars to achieve normative rationality, scientific credibility and professional autonomy varied, a shared goal of their political or intellectual manoeuvring was the attainment for lawyers of positions of heightened importance in the management of social and economic order through state law. In the English rendition of that story, Oxbridge law dons worked through novel treatise literature and a reinvigoration of legal education to insure that judicial independence and the rule of law would be confirmed as central components of the unwritten British constitution, with the result that executive and legislative branches of that state became increasingly reluctant to intrude into the expanding province of the judicially oriented bar.[33] In the United States' version of that transformation, jurists enjoyed a headstart with an entrenched bill of rights that empowered them to challenge or censure governmental action in the courts, and a popular mythology that featured the bar as the bearer of late-eighteenth-century revolutionary banners. Mandarin American lawyers capitalized on those institutional and cultural advantages during the mid and late nineteenth century with more rigorous training, doctrinal systematization, and centralized professional self-government to further a dynamic species of legal science that claimed to be able to manage commercial expansion without compromising established rights.[34]

Many modern North Atlantic jurisdictions also had virulent traditions of anti-legal and anti-lawyer sentiment.[35] The Canadian rebellions of 1837 and 1838 were, in part, a local version of that discontent.[36] The Family Compact and the Chateau Clique, against which those uprisings were directed, were made up largely of lawyers who held appointed office courtesy of the Crown or the unelected local executive branches of government.[37] But criticism and resentment of the bar were not the exclusive prerogative of provincial observers. Colonial Office officials were blunt in their low assessments of the pretensions and skills of Canadian lawyers ensconsed in the pre-union state. Charles Buller thought 'the public officers, to whom the civil administration of affairs in the Canadas has been usually intrusted, have been second-rate lawyers,' and his brother Arthur was less complimentary.[38] Even Lord Durham himself, who listened closely to the political commentary of Canadian jurists, thought they had created and managed a legal regime in Lower Canada that was

a patch-work of the results of the interference at different times of different leg-

islative powers, each proceeding on utterly different and generally incomplete
views, and each utterly regardless of the other. The law itself is a mass of inco-
herent and conflicting laws, part French, part English, with the line between
each very confusedly drawn.[39]

That well-known statement is not only an indictment of a particular set
of legal institutions but also a telling expression of anti-lawyerism on
the part of its author. One interpretive challenge presented to historians
by the Canadian uprisings of 1837–8 and by their local and imperial
aftermath is therefore to explain precisely how elite provincial lawyers
helped to convert anti-legal republican sparks that were among the
causes of those rebellions into a more democratic state in which they
themselves resumed leadership.

A review of Badgley's attempted codifications of Canadian criminal
law and procedure offers a window onto those processes of professional
rehabilitation through lawyerly state formation. Codification of public
or private law has not normally been the result of organized action by
grass-roots interest groups or political lobbyists. It has tended to be the
preoccupation of small and exclusive, often self-interested, legislative
bars. Debates about codification have therefore been lawyers' conversations, not popular ones. So it was with the 1866 Civil Code of Lower
Canada, the Canadian Criminal Code of 1892, and with Badgley's penal
codes.[40] Badgley's codal reforms are thus eligible to be approached as
manifestations of Canadian professional ambition. But unlike most processes of legal professionalization elsewhere in the nineteenth-century
North Atlantic world, that Canadian transformation was required for
an established, administratively oriented bar that had recently been
partially discredited by rebellion, legislative union, and responsible
government to achieve a locally unprecedented niche in a restructured
state.[41] Responsive to that challenge, Badgley envisaged an informally
tripartite constitution, in which lawyers would provide the aristocratic
element of the 'new' regime that he so admired in its British incarna-
tion.[42] The real issue for him was how the provincial legal professions
should insinuate themselves as guardians of social and political order
into an increasingly democratic state.

Badgley's codes and several of his other statutory initiatives will
therefore be treated in this essay primarily as whig administrative reforms intended to help forestall less rigorous legal change, didactic
examples for an emerging legislative bar, and as techniques of state formation designed to depict lawyers carrying forward Durham's consti-

tutional merger of the two Canadas. Those themes have to do with a distinctively Canadian intertwining of mid-nineteenth-century professional culture and state formation, about which local political historians and biographers have been writing obliquely for over a century.[43] But that mutually constitutive process has rarely been labelled as such in political historiography, nor have its students attended to the role of the bar's collective aspirations in mid-nineteenth-century Canadian statism.[44] Whether that intermingling is best characterized as the origins of a legal tradition, as opposed to another kind of cultural event, is a related issue.

Codifier Badgley

William Badgley was born in the walled city of Montreal in 1801, the second of five children.[45] His maternal grandfather, John Lilly, was a successful merchant and justice of the peace who located in Quebec in the wake of the British conquest of New France. His father, Francis Badgley, was part of an established family of London furriers who moved to Montreal in the mid-1780s to become associated with the North-West Company of traders. The senior Badgley later served as Tory member of the Lower Canadian legislative assembly for Montreal East, was an accountant for John Molson's brewery, and the editor of Montreal's conservative *Gazette* newspaper.[46] Little can now be known about William Badgley's early life, except that it was materially comfortable and that he was educated privately by Presbyterian Reverend Alexander Skakel. He was admitted to the bar of Lower Canada in November of 1823, following an oral examination by King's Bench Justices James Reid, Louis-Charles Faucher, and George Pyke.[47] 'Extra-curricular' enthusiasms of the first years of Badgley's Canadian career, which was interrupted in 1830 by an extended visit to England, included the Natural History Society of Montreal, the Society of Brothers-in-Law, and the Advocates' Library.[48]

Badgley apprenticed from 1818 to 1823 with Benjamin Beaubien, a sole legal practitioner who worked out of his home on Saint Gabriel Street in Montreal's old commercial district.[49] Following his call to the bar, Badgley continued to practise with Beaubien until his departure for Britain. Their clients included local stationers Nickless and McDonnell, the Roman Catholic Parish of Saint Antoine in the Richelieu Valley, the unchartered City of Montreal, and at least one prominent merchant mariner.[50] The surviving record of their practice is fragmentary and does not contain any mention of criminal matters. Association with Beaubien also brought Badgley into contact with James Smith, who succeeded him as Beaubien's law clerk in 1823 and who Badgley himself would follow in 1847 when he became MLA for Missisquoi County and Attorney General for Lower Canada. Arch-conservative Smith became one of Badgley's lifelong confidants and his parliamentary mentor.[51]

Details of Badgley's sojourns in England, from 1830 to 1834 and 1836 to 1838, can only be patched together from scattered remarks he later made about those trips. He met and married his wife, Elizabeth Wallace Taylor, in London, and he spent time at the Judicial Committee of the Privy Council and the Colonial Office.[52] Badgley seems to have become intrigued by the Irish *Act of Union* of 1801, and must have observed developing agitation for its repeal. He also witnessed passage of the landmark British *Reform Act* of 1832.[53] And it is reasonable to surmise that Badgley was exposed in England to legislative introduction of 'scientific, colonial-settlement schemes.'[54] That zeal was, in turn, closely related to the emerging British penchant for broader social engineering through land-law reform.[55] Badgley would soon show the Canadian assembly that he knew more about the trans-systemic law of land tenure than most provincial lawyers knew, familiarity presumably acquired in England. Speculation about Badgley's avocations in Britain should also include exposure to the developing imperial yen for comparative studies of legislation. That assumption seems warranted on the basis that Badgley would later move confidently among English, British colonial, and American models in the preparation and publicity of Canadian statutes.[56] In any event, it was not uncommon for well-heeled and professionally ambitious Canadians to spend formative time in Britain. Badgley's younger brother Francis, for example, was admitted to medical practice there and followed that calling in London from 1830 to 1843. His elder brother James was a lieutenant in the Royal Navy.[57]

Upon return from London to Montreal in 1834, Badgley struck out in law on his own, converting the house in which he had grown up on Little Saint James Street into office space to do so. His account book for that period depicts a mixed practice built around the commercial affairs of family members like another brother, forwarder John Thompson Badgley, and his brother-in-law, brewer and banker William Molson. Badgley also acted for leading Montreal business partnerships of the day such as publisher Robert Armour and Company, dry-goods wholesaler Henry Joseph and Company, importer and rentier Peter McGill and Company, foodstuffs forwarder James Gibb and Company, and fur traders and importers Gillespie, Moffatt, and Jamieson (for whom he also worked on a part-time basis in Britain). The only hint of the public character Badgley's career eventually assumed was his counsel work for the Harbour Commissioners of Montreal and Quebec's Trinity House (for the promotion of navigation by regulating river pilots and erecting buoys and lighthouses).[58]

Badgley was made bankruptcy commissioner for Montreal by Governor General Lord Sydenham in June of 1840, a position he held for four years of widespread financial difficulty in Lower Canada. The absence of law-office records for that period, together with Badgley's designation in city directories as a bankruptcy commissioner rather than as an advocate, suggest he treated that quasi-judicial posting as a full-time vocation.[59] Badgley later promoted 'liberalization' of local bankruptcy laws, by sponsoring private member's bills in the assembly to abolish imprisonment for debt.[60] He also adjudicated a disproportionately large number of bankruptcy disputes following his 1855 appointment to the Superior Court, typically applying broad powers of seizure and judicial sale.

Lower Canada's District Court, to which Badgley was promoted in 1844, resembled modern county or small-claims courts to the extent that it had modest civil jurisdiction in litigation involving less than £20, and even more restricted powers in criminal matters.[61] In view of the fact that only two of Badgley's decisions on that court of record seem to have been published, and since access to the judicial archives of Montreal is currently limited, little can now be learned about his tenure on the District Court.[62] It can, however, be said that when a bill was later introduced to the legislative assembly to allow lawyers to charge litigants for representation before that tribunal, Attorney General Badgley opposed that reform and spoke favourably of the speedy, commonsensical dispute resolution provided by that court.[63] As was the case with the Bankruptcy Commission, he was keen to endear the state's newly centralized organs of dispute settlement to their intended constituents in the artisanal and labouring classes.

Badgley was appointed Attorney General for Lower Canada in the Draper-Papineau Executive Council in April of 1847. Two months later, he was voted into the legislature as a Tory member in a by-election in the Eastern Townships riding of Missisquoi. Badgley held that seat for two Parliaments, until he switched to a City of Montreal riding in 1851.[64] He was defeated in a bid for re-election there by Reform candidate Luther Hamilton Holton in 1854, and did not attempt to re-enter elected politics. In addition to his short stint in cabinet, Badgley served for several years in government and opposition as chairman of the Joint Committee of the Legislative Council and the Assembly for Regulation and Management of the Parliamentary Library, chairman of the assembly's Committee on Miscellaneous Private Bills, and as a member of its Standing Committees on Privileges of the House and Railways and Telegraph Lines.[65] Again, neither criminal law nor procedure formed a significant part of those diverse and high-profile assignments.

At the Legislative and Judicial Bars

The main conclusion to be drawn from parliamentary records is that Badgley was one of the union assembly's most prolific brokers, sponsors, and draftsmen of private members' bills. His acts dealt with a potpourri of subjects, including municipal finance, European immigration, patents for inventions, churches and charities, fiscal institutions, and transportation enterprises.[66] But his real legislative passions part out into four categories: constitutional consolidation; land tenure and finance; the administration of civil justice; and, especially, education and professional self-government. Those enthusiasms were anticipated by Badgley's extensive participation of the late 1830s in the Constitutional Association of Montreal, his pamphleteering for land-law reform during the same period, his long involvement with governing organs of the Montreal bar, and his multi-generational administrative and law-teaching affiliation with the Royal Institution for the Advancement of Learning (McGill College).[67] Independent of their subject matter or policy motivation, the regimes Badgley created or refined by statute share the utilitarian features of simplicity, integration, and centralization. His criminal justice codes should be understood as a representative part of that overall legislative initiative, partaking of the epistemological, institutional, and professional aspirations implicit in that larger record.

Badgley's constitutional concern, reflected initially in debating-club speeches and newspaper articles of the 1830s, was the political merger of Upper and Lower Canada. He corresponded regularly with Lord Durham in that connection and, in 1837, travelled with fellow Constitutional Associationists George Moffatt, Peter McGill, and Andrew Stuart to Britain for a year and a half to lobby Whitehall and Westminster for legislative union.[68] Badgley also spoke in the assembly of conversations on those issues with Lord John Russell, colonial secretaries Sir George Grey and Lord Glenelg, and undersecretary James Stephen. He was offered but declined an unsolicited post in the British Colonial Office by Glenelg in 1840, an apparent recognition of his insight into British North American politics and government.[69]

Despite achievement of the *Act of Union* in 1840, Badgley regarded unification of Upper and Lower Canadian institutions as an unfinished aspect of constitutional merger. He routinely vowed to 'do all in [my] power to assimilate the laws of Upper and Lower Canada.'[70] That project was circumscribed to the extent that Badgley 'could not understand that there was any difference between the laws of Upper and Lower Canada, as to the principles which regulated contracts and commercial questions – the difference was only as to [land] tenures and successions.' On another occasion he isolated the remaining mid-nineteenth-century challenge of legal unification by stressing that 'the criminal and commercial laws of Lower Canada were exactly the same as the criminal and commercial laws of Upper Canada – with the exception of the law of primogeniture.'[71] The similarity across the Canadas of those two fields of law remains an open question, but their unlikely linkage as eligible candidates for codification was common among mid-nineteenth-century North American law reformers.

Even the law of immoveable (real) property in Lower Canada was not, in Badgley's view, wholly dissimilar to land law in the upper part of the province. As he said, 'the lands in the Eastern Townships were governed by English law. The Act of 1829 was only passed to validate conveyances made in the French as well as the English form; it did not change the tenure of the land.'[72] Badgley's position was that quit-rent or leader-associate grants in which Eastern Townships lands had been patented after the American Revolution created a comprehensive regime of English-inspired law inside Lower Canada's amalgam of continental European customary norms, decrees of the French Crown, and post-conquest British public law. The constitutional challenge, in Badgley's mind, was to bring seigniorial Lower Canada (about 60 per cent of the superficial land area of that part of the province) into line with the Townships and Upper Canada.[73] Even on the Superior Court of the 1850s and 1860s, Badgley's preoccupation with private-law uniformity (and thus constitutional stability) would routinely be manifested in judgments that limited the applicability of the Custom of Paris in Lower Canada, sometimes dissenting from his court to do so.[74] But economic and imperialistic considerations also coloured Badgley's approach to land-tenure and private-law unification. He was apprehensive that Upper Canada, the Townships, and the lower Ottawa Valley might overtake the Montreal region in commercial prominence if that metropolitan district was not quickly ushered into a 'modern' market economy through the achievement and advertisement of legal uniformity with its transborder hinterlands.[75]

Badgley's 1850 codes of criminal law and procedure were among his most ambitious legislative efforts to further constitutional merger of the Canadas through visible but perhaps symbolic institutional unification. Apparently undaunted by the government's tabling of that project, he served notice to the assembly in November of 1852 of his intention to introduce a 'Bill for the consolidation of the Civil Law of Lower Canada, and the establishment of a practice connected therewith.'[76] The legislature's preoccupation in 1852 and 1853 with curtailing seigniorial land tenure in Lower Canada, and Badgley's defeat in the impending general elections, apparently discouraged him from following through on that notice of motion. Nonetheless, translation of his mid-nineteenth-century vernacular into modern terms of legal art suggests that opposition backbencher Badgley thought, for at least one balmy day in the fall of 1852, that he would be able to codify Lower Canadian private law and civil procedure single-handedly! His plump commonplace book, begun in 1827 and updated assiduously for sixty years, is a uniquely detailed and schematically sophisticated example of that ubiquitous species of nineteenth-century legal literature and would have provided a substantial headstart on private-law codification.[77] Its display of sources, like that of the criminal law codes, was decidedly eclectic in character. In any event, extrapolating from the gradualist approach Badgley sometimes took to law-reform initiatives, it is also reasonable to speculate that he proposed to use his projected Lower Canadian codes of private law and civil procedure as prototypes for reform in the upper part of the province. Indeed, the possibility of a two-step, private-law codification was later embraced by legislators like George Brown, George-Etienne Cartier, Lewis Drummond, and John Alexander Macdonald when the Civil Code of Lower Canada was commissioned in 1857 and when section 94 of the *British North America Act* on uniformity of provincial laws was debated in intercolonial constitutional conferences of the mid-1860s.[78]

It bears emphasis that Badgley was not out of step with emerging Lower Canadian law-reform sentiment when he turned, precociously, to the codification of customary law and judicial procedure. At least one anonymous but influential law journal article, regularly attributed to soon-to-be Tory co-premier and Attorney General Cartier, had recently appeared on that topic. Reformers also included private-law codification in their election platform of 1851, and some of them vetted that project in the assembly.[79] Moreover, 1846 amendments to the constitution of abutting New York had mandated comprehensive codification of that state's private law, and a three-man legislative commission undertook incomplete work on that task from 1847 to 1850. New York law reformer Field also published a well-known and trenchant tract on that subject in 1852, to which was appended American Supreme Court justice and Harvard Law dean Joseph Story's 1837 Massachusetts report in favour of moderate, private-law codification in that state.[80]

Nor is it surprising that Badgley's penchant for institutional merger across the Canadas intensified in the late 1840s. That period saw the abolition of Britain's regime of preferential colonial trade, continuing erosion of Montreal merchants' political power, and the gradual triumph of American trade routes over Canadian ones. It appears that Badgley conceived of institutional forms of empire-building as facsimiles or facilitators of economic modes of imperialism. In so doing, he was following closely the Colonial Office's formula for political and cultural domination in such far-flung corners of the second British Empire as India, Malta, and New South Wales.[81]

On broader constitutional issues, Badgley regarded proposals for political union of Canada with the United States, capped by the Montreal commercial community's 1849 'Annexation Manifesto' (and signed by Badgley's law-firm partner John Joseph Caldwell Abbott, as well as by his blue-chip client George Moffatt), as an 'insane project.' He favoured commercial reciprocity with the Americans in principle, but thought tariffs would be necessary to protect Canadian agriculture and some manufacturing industries in a free-trade arena.[82] Consistent with that sentiment, several of the private member's bills Badgley sponsored to benefit internal improvements and financial enterprises provided Benthamite, statal subsidies like monetary grants, limited liability, tax concessions, gifts of land, and powers of expropriation.[83] That measured economic protectionism echoed Badgley's legal and cultural nationalism and underlay his preference for the continuing development of east-west intraprovincial networks ultimately tied to Britain rather than north-south international links with the Americans.[84] He would later support British North American confederation, primarily out of fear of political absorption into the United States rather than dissatisfaction with the Canadian union of 1840.

Badgley's remarks on statute law related to the Canadian constitution and to legal integration tended to be conclusory rather than explanatory but, as excerpts from his parliamentary and other interventions reproduced in the last seven paragraphs show, substantive justifications for those initiatives were not absent from Badgley's stumping on those issues. That exposition distinguished them from his predominantly formal promotion of the criminal justice codes.

Lower Canadian land-law reform was Badgley's second legislative passion. He was an outspoken supporter of the abolition of seigniorial land tenure, in part on the constitutional grounds that completion of a legislative union of the Canadas required the law and practice of land ownership to be uniform.[85] Although he was, himself, a *censitaire* ('feudal' tenant) on the Roman Catholic Sulpicians' Seigniory of Montreal who waited more than twelve years to take advantage of an opportunity made available in 1840 to commute his lands into freehold tenure, Badgley thought that seigniorial tenure was a 'tax on industry and improvement,' 'a blot on Lower Canada,' 'a mill-stone about the neck of industry – a chain that must drag down the energies of the enterprising cultivator,' 'not a tenure for progress,' and a scheme that imposed 'extortionate conditions' on a *censitaire* whose condition thereby became 'almost that of a serf.'[86] On another occasion, he speculated that the 'extinction' of seigniorialism would immediately increase the market value of land in Lower Canada by 25 per cent.[87]

Seigniorialism was a species of land tenure or, as Badgley characterised it, an 'outmoded settlement scheme' that 'closely resembled English copyhold' and 'the Duke of Wellington's peculiar tenure over Strathfield Sage.'[88] Analogies closer to Lower Canada could have been found in the Colony of New Netherland's and the Province of New York's patroon system of land holding, Prince Edward Island's comprehensive leasehold tenures, or in the latifundian regimes of colonial Latin America.[89] Badgley did not mind seigniorialism's annual 'ground rents,' or object to furtive efforts by seigniors to create oligopolistic markets for land. Nor did he take issue with seigniors' contractual inflation of feudal dues. Indeed, he repeatedly advocated the politically controversial view that, if seigniorial tenure were to be abolished, the 'supereminent principles' of freedom of contract and inviolability of property required seigniors to be compensated on the basis of contractually stipulated *cens* rather than at fixed, sixteenth- and eighteenth-century rates specified in the Custom of Paris and decrees of the French Crown applicable to New France. Liberty and property, and thus freedom of contract, were crucial touchstones of Badgley's whig constitutionalism.[90]

Those values were also played out in heavy reliance on the abstract concept of intent or *mens rea* in his substantive criminal law. The indirect influence of early-modern and modern British political economists like John Locke, John Stuart Mill, and Adam Smith can, again, be seen to have been trickling into a colonial Canadian venue.

By contrast, Badgley railed against the *lods et ventes*, a 'mutation fine' that constituted 'a real draw back on the industry of the country.' He reasoned that that tax, which involved payment by tenants of one-twelfth of a parcel of land's sale price to the overholding seignior, discouraged improvement and transfers of land by penalizing entrepreneurial *censitaires* and benefitting dormant seigniors who skimmed profit off the top of their tenants' speculative and developmental activity.[91] Later, when faced as a judge of the Superior Court or the Court of Appeal with litigation over the scope of the *lods*, Badgley would consistently interpret that seigniorial due narrowly, with a view to minimising its impact.[92]

Piecemeal disassembly of seigniorialism began in Lower Canada with the imperial *Canada Trade Act* and *Canada Land Tenures Act* of the 1820s, and continued with the 'Saint Sulpice Ordinance' and related local statutes of the early union period.[93] Badgley provided aggressive extra-legislative support for those initiatives, and for the spirit of voluntarism in which they were grounded.[94] He also drafted a bill for co-premier LaFontaine in 1850 that closely resembled the milestone *Commutation Act* of 1854. But, by 1852, Badgley was much less sanguine about optional conversions of seigniorialism, noting that in twelve years only five of about 3,400 *censitaires* on the Island of Montreal outside that city had initiated elective commutations. Badgley's prescient solution to the indifference of laity to legislative land-tenure reform, the basic principles of which were adopted for Montreal in the late 1850s and for the rest of Quebec seventy-five years later, was blanket commutation by the state with compensation paid by *censitaires* to a public underwriter in long-term installments.[95] In spite of mixed reception on land-tenure issues in the union assembly, Badgley would go on, by virtue of his elevation to the Superior Court, to become one of twelve Seigniorial Court judges who comprised a quasi-legislative body appointed in 1856 to determine the respective rights of Lower Canadian *censitaires* and seigniors and to recommend a monetary formula for the final capitalization of seigniorial dues. Badgley's ninety-page declaratory judgment on that 'court' is a rich source of information about his conceptions of property, the legal profession's and the judiciary's role in the modern state, and the animating principles of private law.[96] In a nut-shell, he preferred pragmatism, positive law, and legislative supremacy to natural rights, God's will, or historically given norms. Law was thus, for Badgley, a political, official, and technical enterprise. Most important in terms of substantive change, Badgley saluted the demise of seigniorialism on the grounds that it cleared the way for a centralized administrative state by undermining the opposition of pluralistically oriented seigniors to that utilitarian process of institutional rationalisation.

Badgley's enthusiasm for converting seigniorial into freehold tenures was motivated by constitutional and economic factors, and his concern about facilitating land development was represented with equal force in a series of self-motivated measures related to security or publicity of land title and to financing the acquisition and improvement of immoveable property. He published an influential monograph on land-registry systems in 1836, and was delegated responsibility by George Moffatt on behalf of Sydenham's Special Council in 1841 to prepare Lower Canada's first registration law.[97] Badgley later sponsored bills in the assembly to expand or refine his Registration Ordinance and supported legislation to prevent the deterioration of lands charged with hypothecs (mortgages).[98] On a related front, Badgley recognized the utility of judicial chancery power to deal with disputes arising from land-financing contracts, but saw little point in an independent court of equity. He was ready to fuse Upper Canada's legal and equitable jurisdictions in 1853 (as he recalled neighbouring New York had done five years earlier), and did not want to 'await the course pursued in other countries' as Attorney General William Buell Richards preferred to do.[99]

Badgley's 1841 Registration Ordinance substituted a system of public registration of land transactions for Lower Canada's *ancien régime* of unregistered, notarial acts. More to the point, it restricted the custom according to which every deed to land bore an implicit general charge, it abolished the province's traditional system of secret hypothecs, and it established priorities among interests in land on the basis of chronology of registration rather than social statuses such as seignior, woman, or minor.[100] That ordinance was intended by Badgley to facilitate borrowing and lending on the security of immoveables, and especially to help attract British investment capital to Lower Canada. His commitment to those 'progressive' goals can also be seen in his expansive judicial interpretations of the registration law, thought to be necessary by virtue of lay confusion about (and resistance to) its application.[101] Unsurprisingly, Badgley followed up on his Registration Ordinance with a series of statutes designed to create or consolidate local lending institutions.[102] Lawyers at an extended legislative bar were, in his scheme of things, to assume responsibility for economic management of the private sector through positive state law. Causal connections between lawyerly inscription on the pages of statute books and resultant social change were apparently axiomatic for Badgley, or were at least asserted insistently, since his standard cure for social rejections of legal transplants was more legislation.

Finally, with respect to property ownership and development, Badgley was concerned about discrepancies in testamentary practices and inheritance laws between the Canadas. He embraced freedom to dispose of property by wills, made possible in Lower Canada by the formal reception of laissez-faire English principles of succession during the preceding seventy-five years.[103] But Badgley was also a staunch supporter of primogeniture and ultimogeniture, both for intestate estates and as a matter of the testate regimes of popular choice. He protested the continuing legal ability and social tendency of Lower Canadian francophones to defer to the Custom of Paris' provisions for share-and-share-alike successorial distribution. Consistent with that view, Badgley attacked a legislative proposal to abolish primogeniture in Upper Canada, noting that continental European law on equal partibility rather than English practice was used in that bill as the vehicle of institutional assimilation between the Canadas.[104] Standardization was his overriding legislative aim, but that was not a goal to be achieved at any cost in legal forms or social policy. Property ownership and economic sway were, in Badgley's imagination, quasi-constitutional imperatives to be promoted through concentrations or centralizations of wealth. Primogeniture was, however, a political lightening rod in several mid-nineteenth-century North American jurisdictions, widely displaced legislatively due to its aristocratically English pedigree.

Badgley's legislative and other commentary on the reform or repackaging of local law related to landed property was decidedly fulsome, and is thus a good source of his substantive opinions on those subjects. Again, that instrumental candor and sophistication contrasted with his near-formalistic presentations on criminal justice.

The administration of civil justice was Badgley's third legislative preoccupation, played out in refinements of the law of evidence, proposals to restructure juries, and the geographic dispersion of Lower Canada's courts. But that interest in adjectival law was less significant than Badgley's enthusiasm for constitutional consolidation, land development, or professional advancement. It did, however, complement his work on criminal procedure, and it echoed some of what reformer Field was doing with his widely copied New York code of civil procedure. Badgley's reforms that are related to the rules of evidence alone will therefore be canvassed here as representative of his interest in the administration of justice.

Badgley's concern about the law of evidence was a specific one, apparently felt most acutely by him among assemblymen. He prepared and shepherded through the legislature parallel private members' bills, for the eastern and western districts of the province, to provide for local enforcement of foreign judgments, probated wills, and notarized arbitration awards.[105] In one sense, those statutes were merely about streamlining judicial law and proofs and securing procedural uniformity across the Canadas. But those laws also had to do with intercolonial and international comity, of which the reciprocal enforcement of judicial decisions, admission into evidence of foreign laws, and curial notice of statutory instruments had become central aspects in several North American jurisdictions during the preceding quarter century. The facilitation of interprovincial and international commerce was often said to be another benefit of conflicts-of-law provisions like those Badgley wrote into his evidence acts.

However, more complex motives than administrative or diplomatic ones apparently underlay Badgley's evidence reforms. A couple of modern commentators have noticed the prevalence of choice-of-law and choice-of-forum clauses in commercial contracts drafted in the Montreal region during the second quarter of the nineteenth century. The regularity of recurrence to arbitration in Lower Canada, rather than judicial dispute resolution, has also been noted.[106] That reliance on extra-provincial law, foreign courts, or unofficial dispute settlement seems often to have been motivated by a desire to by-pass operation of anti-contractarian rules in the pre-industrial Custom of Paris. Badgley's evidence acts, providing as they did for enforcement by local courts of foreign and unofficial commercial judgments, may therefore be said to be another aspect of his campaign to limit application of *ancien régime*, customary law by making the Canadian state's judicial enforcement mechanisms available in respect of settlements realized through a stop-gap application of alternative systems of normativity.

Badgley's fourth and most noteworthy parliamentary enthusiasm was formal education and professional self-government. He was coun-

sel to McGill College during the 1840s, and later carried numerous petitions from that school to the legislative assembly.[107] Badgley also taught
at McGill from 1844 to 1855 and from 1859 to 1880, and became dean of
its Faculty of Law in 1853. His brother Francis was a distinguished
Canadian medical academic, first at McGill and the Montreal School of
Medicine and Surgery, and later at the Upper Canada School of Medicine. Both Badgleys were heavily involved in professional self-government, especially after incorporation of the Lower Canadian bar in 1849
and that of Upper Canadian physicians and surgeons in the late
1850s.[108]

Badgley prepared private members' bills to create the Saint Lawrence
School of Medicine, to incorporate Lower Canadian medical practitioners, and to institutionalize the notarial and legal professions in Lower
Canada.[109] He also sponsored several private acts for legislative bar
admission.[110] On related fronts, Badgley supported a bill to incorporate
the Toronto Hospital, an act to enable law clerks to shorten their appren-
ticeships on the basis of college study, and an abortive bill to incorporate Upper Canadian physicians and surgeons.[111]

On larger educational issues, Badgley was a promoter of religious
affiliations for Canadian schools who thought that the Prussians, for
example, were 'dreadfully immoral, wholly from the want of religious
teaching in [their internationally pioneering, compulsory] schools.'[112]
Although he was, himself, a practising Anglican with lifelong allegiance
to Christ Church Cathedral in Montreal, Badgley argued forcefully for
the maintenance of a large, official role for organizations like the Roman
Catholic Church, the Seminary of Montreal, and the Christian Brothers
in local cultural matters.[113] That ecumenical view, born as much of pragmatism as devotion, departed uncharacteristically from the secularism
of Durham and Sydenham.[114] Most tangibly, Badgley carried several
petitions from educational institutions to the assembly, and he sponsored a series of major amendments to Lower Canada's newly minted
compulsory school law.[115] Universal elementary education with mandatory municipal property taxation was the result of that bundle of parliamentary initiatives. Finally, Badgley was appointed in 1853 to a select
committee of the legislature 'to inquire into the state of education in
Lower Canada.' Recommendations of that Sicotte Committee led to the
creation in 1856 of Lower Canada's central Council of Public Instruction, the government-sponsored *Journal of Public Instruction*, and three
local normal schools for teacher training.[116] For his commitment to
social reform through legal and administrative boosts to provincial edu-

cation, Badgley was awarded an honourary Doctor of Legal Letters degree by McGill College in 1843, and another by the Episcopal College of Lennoxville (Bishop's University) in 1855.[117] It bears emphasis that one of this essay's themes is that Badgley's legislative statecraft was also meant to provide a pedagogic example to other members of the bar. His educational lexicon was extensive and creative.

Badgley continued to practise law during his time in the legislative assembly. Indeed his practice, sporadic and casual during the preceding quarter century, 'took off' in that period. Badgley expanded his firm in 1849 by engaging future prime minister John Abbott as his first partner and by relocating to larger quarters at 34 Notre Dame Street, Montreal's main land-transportation artery. By the mid-1850s, Badgley and Abbott had moved again into the former's brother-in-law's commercial premises (William Molson's Bank). Symbolising the close linkage of legislature, commerce, bar and college, they shifted McGill's Faculty of Law and the *Lower Canada Jurist* into that bank when Abbott succeeded Badgley as dean of the law school and both partners assumed active editorial positions on the officially sponsored *Jurist* in 1855.[118] Badgley and Abbott also took on a number of promising legal apprentices in that period, like Joel Baker, Samuel Dorman, and future chief justice of Manitoba Alexander Morris.[119] Their firm's growing prominence is further demonstrated, indirectly, by the fact that the well-connected Morris completed the first part of his clerkship in Kingston under rising MLA John A. Macdonald before transferring to Badgley and Abbott and enrolling in their fledgling law school.[120]

Badgley and Abbott's mid-century clientele included mainstays of its senior partner's early practice like the harbour commissioners of Montreal, the extended McGillivray family, retired justice George Pyke, and William Molson.[121] Important new accounts, reflecting Montreal's emergence as a steam transportation and manufacturing centre, were soon added to that established base. Chief among the expanding firm's transportation clients were the Montreal and Bytown Railway Company (which Abbott later bought), and Hugh Allan's international shipping enterprises (which included the Montreal Ocean Steamship Company and would eventually take in the Canadian Pacific Railway).[122] John Frothingham's and William Workman's hardware and iron business, together with Benjamin Lyman's drug manufactory, were the core of Badgley and Abbott's manufacturing portfolio.[123] Badgley routinely pressed his entrepreneurial patrons' interests in the club-like atmosphere of a union assembly populated in growing measure by lawyers with similar clients, and he regularly secured favourable legislative concessions for them.[124] His membership in the legislature's all-important Standing Committee on Railways and Telegraph Lines and his chairmanship of its powerful Committee on Miscellaneous Private Bills presumably enhanced clients' perceptions of his standing at United Canada's legislative bar. But Badgley and Abbott had little to do with criminal justice.

It bears repetition that Badgley was one of the assembly's more prolific sponsors, brokers, and draftsmen of private member's bills during his years in Parliament. That legislative record is, however, also noteworthy for what it does not contain. The enactment of general incorporation laws for transportation, manufacturing, and communication enterprises was probably the most significant Canadian law-reform initiative of the late 1840s and early 1850s.[125] But that was a development in which Badgley took little recorded interest. Similarly, he was silent with respect to other leading, legislative achievements of the day like laws restricting usury and statutes providing free banking and the standardization of Canadian currency.[126] One is therefore left with the image of an energetic and generally effective legislative impresario, operating a cottage parliamentary industry driven by long-standing interests in perfecting constitutional union, facilitating land development, furthering the material interests of his growing law-firm clientele, and consolidating public education and the professions.

Institutions of Canadian Crime

To provide technical context for Badgley's codification initiatives, the institutional genealogy of central-Canadian criminal law down to 1850 should be canvassed, but in short compass. The *Quebec Act* of 1774 confirmed the 1763 reception of the English customary and statutory law of crimes, and an Upper Canadian enactment of 1800 brought forward the date of legal receipt for that jurisdiction to 1792.[127] Imported English penal law of the late eighteenth century routinely has been labelled 'the bloody code' for its inclusion of about 200 capital offences, said to have been designed to enlist terror in service of the promotion of morality and the protection of property.[128] Significant legislative reforms of that metropolitan law occurred in the upper province in 1833, echoed in Lower Canada in 1841.[129] That amalgam of state law was made moderately accessible through a small corpus of locally produced compilations of statutes, student hornbooks, and magistrates' manuals.[130] The combined result of those initiatives was, by the early years of the union period, a sketchy standardization or federalization of Canadian criminal law and procedure, grounded in English tradition modified by progressive legislation based loosely on British and colonial models of the late 1820s and early 1830s.[131] As Donald Fyson, Douglas Hay, and Louis Knafla have demonstrated in recent studies, however, it is important to recognize that neither legislative pronouncements or judicial administration or textbook circulation fully unified or clarified local penal law for legal functionaries or for that law's intended subjects in the popular classes.[132] Nor did those initiatives organize it in a scientific manner.

Perhaps most salient, Canada's neighbouring jurisdictions of New Brunswick, Nova Scotia, Massachusetts, Maine, and New York had undertaken ambitious legislative reforms or consolidations of their criminal law and procedure during the second quarter of the nineteenth century,[133] during which time a British parliamentary commission also produced five tomes on the statutory consolidation of English criminal law.[134] Indeed, co-premier LaFontaine, a supporter of codification knowledgeable about criminal law but no great fan of Badgley, provoked the later's ire in the assembly by alleging (inaccurately) that Badgley had merely cribbed his bills from those English parliamentary papers.[135] Such was the local and international setting, at least the technical and official context, in which the inaugural attempt to codify any aspect of Canadian law occurred.

Despite Badgley's legislative rebuff of the early 1850s, the possibility of criminal-law reform by codal means was kept alive in provincial legal literature for a couple of generations.[136] Completed codification of Canadian criminal law would, however, wait until 1892.[137] But, as contemporary American historian Sanford Kadish has stated, '[James Fitzjames] Stephen's [English criminal] Code [of 1879, that provided a rough basis for the later Canadian code] was far more conservative and less ambitious than Macaulay's, and certainly than Livingston's ... Stephen's Draft Code contains none of the ground-breaking Benthamism of Livingston's or Macaulay's codes.'[138] Stephen himself said of Macaulay's code in 1883, 'A criminal code drawn in the style of the India Penal Code could never be passed through [England's] Parliament, and even if it could I do not think English judges and lawyers would accept and carry out so novel a method of legislating.'[139] Badgley's codes of 1850, derived stylistically from the work of Benthamites like Livingston and Macaulay and remotely from Jeremy Bentham's own proposals for English criminal-law codification, partook more robustly of nineteenth-century utilitarianism than did Minister of Justice John Sparrow David Thompson's enacted Canadian code of the early 1890s. Most important, Badgley's bills were self-consciously linked to the professional rehabilitation of United Canada's leading lawyers, and to assertions of managerial responsibility by the legislative bar for mid-nineteenth-century state formation in ways that Thompson's code was not. Perhaps revealingly, Thompson and his draftsmen George Wheelock Burbidge, Robert Sedgewick, and Charles Masters made no apparent use of Badgley's research base, codal texts, or parliamentary commentary in their later work.

The everyday appreciation and application of criminal law in United Canada remain more or less mysterious. However, it is beginning to appear that, contrary to received lore, the province was not a peaceable kingdom.[140] Ritualized violence in the popular classes,[141] labour riots,[142] religious and ethnic strife,[143] taxpayer revolts,[144] and resistance to governmental authority[145] have begun to be documented in a promising secondary literature on social unrest during the union period. Several recent studies also have focused on treatment by the state's criminal justice mechanisms of particular criminals.[146] Much rarer are examinations of mid-nineteenth-century courts' dealings with general classes of criminals or types of crime.[147] Assessments of elite attitudes towards crime and criminal-law enforcement remain similarly uncommon.[148] Public perceptions of mid-nineteenth-century Canadian criminal behaviour have been more extensively treated in modern secondary literature, but not always on the basis of primary sources that inspire complete confidence in conclusions about those attitudes.[149] Perhaps the best local studies have dealt with institutional appendages of the penal justice system, like prisons and police forces.[150] But that scholarship on penitentiaries and criminal investigation is only remotely relevant to codal storage of substantive law and its relation to constitutional, personal, or corporate professional aspiration. Integrating reflections on mid-nineteenth-century Canadian criminal law 'in action' would therefore impose weighty and slightly irrelevant burdens on historians of union-period institutions or legal codification, in part because accounts of applied Canadian criminal justice for that era remain comparatively few and far between.[151]

Words or phrases commonly associated with codal presentations of nineteenth-century legal knowledge include ones like orderly, comprehensive, internally coherent, stylistically consistent, durable, and centralizing. Perhaps naturally, therefore, Badgley described his penal codes to the assembly as 'complete,' 'perspicuous,' 'uniform,' 'con-densed,' 'plain,' 'regular,' and 'systematic.' In terms of content they are more like 'revisions' or compilations of law, but ones that preceded the first attempt to consolidate Canadian statutes at-large by almost a decade. In that connection, it is worthy of note that Lower Canadian pri-vate-law codifier Caron later opined that the pioneering *Revised Statutes of Nova Scotia* of 1851 (modelled after statute consolidations in New York and Massachusetts) closely resembled a code.[152]

The French, Prussian, and Austrian private-law codes were land-marks but were geographically distant and sometimes regarded as politically controversial examples for mid-nineteenth-century Cana-dian lawyers of contemporary codal technique.[153] Moreover, Jeremy Bentham had recently written a widely circulated self-reflective des-cription of the ways and means of legal codification.[154] That text was predicated on recurrence to inductive reasoning in the framing of codal generalizations from experiential or empirical particulars, application of deductive logic by jurists applying codal principles, rigorous internal classification of legal topics, and the articulation of statements of law in compact, abstract terms. Systematic law reform by legislative means was not unknown to the Anglo-American world before Bentham.[155] Nor did Bentham inaugurate codal technique in that legal tradition.[156] But the mid-nineteenth-century's widely shared methodological imper-atives make readily apparent the relationship of codal presentations of legal knowledge to inductive method and systematization in that era's natural sciences of astronomy, botany, and zoology.[157] Order, coher-ence, and durability were epistemological rather than primarily artistic or substantive imperatives. By way of an aside, there is an important and closely related study of science in law waiting to be written about Lower Canadian legal codifiers like Badgley and Morin who were com-pulsive 'botanizers' and 'natural historians' in their leisure lives. It may be that the discourse of natural science they deployed in legislative settings was, in part, learned and approved in the amateur scientific societies in which they and their contemporaries participated exten-sively.[158]

The key point for present purposes is that codification's magic lay in its most perfect emulation, among alternative legal-literary forms, of empirical and inductive methodologies in the prestigious natural sci-ences that were giving Victorians heightened control over their physical surroundings. Alleged mid-nineteenth-century linguistic slippages such as reference to unwritten private or criminal-law principles as a 'code,' or the payment of codal hommage to consolidations of statutes, are less egregious when appraised from an epistemological standpoint than from an aesthetic or substantive perspective.[159]

Like their New York, Massachusetts, and Pennsylvania contemporaries, legally trained contributors to Canadian periodical and pamphlet literature of the 1840s, 1850s, and 1860s felt increasingly obliged to offer their views on the suitability of codifying state law.[160] The United States' version of that penchant to codify official law has been the subject of so much modern, secondary literature that it has become one of the more pronounced and venerable dimensions of American professional history.[161] But as Robert Gordon, Andrew King, and Perry Miller have observed, that literature traditionally did not treat codification debates as an aspect of the internal politics of the legal profession or as part of the public relations of professionalization.[162] Although Canadian researchers have not yet found a groundswell mid-nineteenth-century 'codification movement,' there are convincing indications that patterns in the production of British North American legal literature were consistent with panamerican and North Atlantic trends of that period.[163] Badgley's abortive criminal codes, the Civil Code of Lower Canada, and the Lower Canadian Code of Civil Procedure can therefore be characterised as pieces of a vanguard of nineteenth-century legal science. It merits repetition that all of those bills should also be understood as integral parts of the unprecedented and fast-paced output of United Canada's legislative assembly, and it bears emphasis that those bills are not radically different in form or epistemic underpinnings from their period's 'near-codes,' namely, privately authored legal treatises.[164] The potential treatment of Lower Canadian legal literature as an aspect of professionalization has, however, been deflected by a prevailing concern in existing scholarship about the pursuit of ethnic nationalism through source-driven state law. Nativism became a powerful force across the North Atlantic world in the decades straddling the turn of the twentieth century, and made deep inroads into legal culture that should provide an organizing theme for social and intellectual histories of that later period. But modern explanations of nativism in local legal thought, and occasional promotion of it, have tended to be analytically and chronologically imperialistic.[165]

Cessare Bonesana Beccaria (1738–94) and Jeremy Bentham (1748–1832) were Europe's best-known theorists of legal codification and criminal-law reform in the late 1700s and early 1800s.[166] In view of their metropolitan prominence, and the derivative character of much of

North America's early penal law, it is unsurprising that monographs by Beccaria and Bentham found their way into Lower Canada, where their presence in original, translated, and edited versions can be readily documented.[167] Those texts also circulated in the antebellum United States.[168] Although neither Bentham nor Beccaria drafted criminal-law codes for legislative enactment, their outlines for codification and their utilitarian justifications for liberalizing penal law supplied the cornerstones for several generations of transatlantic debate on criminal-law reform.[169] Louisiana lawyer and legislator Livingston, from whose codes Badgley and others borrowed, was widely acknowledged as the early-nineteenth-century's leading publicist of Beccarian and Benthamite ideas about criminal-law reform on the North American continent.[170] Again, unsurprisingly, Livingston's texts circulated in Lower Canada.[171] At least two of them were also translated into French and published locally.[172]

More to the point than his general guidelines for legal codification, Bentham produced a *Specimen of a Penal Code* that amounts to a fragment of what he thought a 'comprehensive and enlightened' criminal code should look like.[173] That sample was then used as a calling card in Bentham's persistent and often-parodied pleading with American presidents and state governors, English home secretaries, and Russian emperors to be installed officially as a codal adviser.[174] The historiography of nineteenth-century law reform therefore remembers Bentham as a personification of energy, intellectual credibility and topicality, but mostly as an inspiration to members of the succeeding generation of Anglo-American code reformers such as Thomas Macaulay, Edward Livingston, David Field, Curtis Noyes, Stephen Field, William Howell, Thomas Cobb, and William Sampson.[175] Perhaps revealingly, those names have become 'household words' in the history of American legal thought but, despite those reformers' powerful long-arm influence, they remain more or less absent from Canadian scholarship on nineteenth-century legal culture. Badgley borrowed formally and substantively from the Field, Livingstone, and Macaulay codes, a second set of literary vehicles through which the impact of Bentham and Beccaria was made to be felt on the abortive Canadian codes of 1850.

Ideally, a Benthamite code was presented in broad, normative propositions, systematically and logically related to each other and to more abstract principles of utilitarian political economy, by intellectually oriented and rigorous legal scientists, operating at arm's-length from the hurly-burly of political processes. That formula for legal codification bore the marks of Bentham's overall imperatives for efficient government, namely, reliance on experts, scientific generation of standardized knowledge, simplicity, and uniformity.[176] Badgley repeatedly represented himself to contemporaries as an experienced statute draftsman and non-partisan parliamentarian, he spoke regularly of scientific approaches to the collection, organization, and display of legal information, and he was preoccupied with the use of legislative texts to perfect quasi-constitutional merger of the Canadas.

There are convincing indications that Badgley's adaptations in United Canada – as cabinet minister, governing parliamentarian, member of the legislative opposition, and concerned layman – of scientific and utilitarian approaches to lawyerly statecraft were applauded by their intended constituencies. The codification of criminal law and procedure were, apparently, the fronts on which he enjoyed least success, while greater accolades appear to have come from his pragmatic and entrepreneurially oriented law-office clientele for his work on land-law and legal integration. In those and other projects, however, Badgley was participating in a North Atlantic embrace by elite lawyers of formal and substantive political Benthamism.

The new-found status and economic resources that accrued to Badgley as a result of that embrace led him to engage leading local tailor Benenaiah Gibb and Company to make him fancy cashmere and angora trousers, black silk ties and white cravats, Picadilly collars, and Turkish towels. He bought French silver tea services, gilt finger bowels, crystal champagne glasses, and John James Audobon paintings for his home. Badgley also moved from his Notre Dame Street greystone townhouse to the sprawling Oaklands estate in the outlying village of Côte Saint Antoine, and he hired prize-winning Montreal gardener Etienne Marchant to tend it for him. His children were enrolled in prestigious schools like Lower Canada College and Britain's Royal Military Academy.[177] Modern observers of nineteenth-century legislative statecraft and reorientation or reorganization by the bar should not overlook potential personal motives of the leaders of those transitions like social and economic advancement.[178]

Conclusions

With the law of crimes and criminal procedure, William Badgley chose to work towards path-breaking Canadian legal codification of fields in which he had little personal experience or apparent interest. He also selected departments of law that were thought by his professional and parliamentary contemporaries to be among United Canada's most coherent, uniform, and effective ones. Indeed, Badgley himself made almost no reference to widespread social needs, substantive legal reform, or to the administration of criminal justice in his public glosses or private musings on the codes. Neither the subject matter nor the draftsman was an obvious candidate for codal privilege, except insofar as that task was probably more manageable for criminal justice than other local codification initiatives might have been. Perhaps Badgley had observed from analogous American experiences that comparatively uncontroversial and settled fields of law, like procedure, were the ones in which scientific codal repackaging was most easily achieved. It may seem counterintuitive to characterise nineteenth-century Anglo-American criminal justice as an uncontested field, but prominent United Canadian lawyers routinely did so.

While not quite a one-man codifying or legislating machine as tireless as New York's David Dudley Field, Badgley had a substantial record of statute draftsmanship that was the result of action while in political power, initiatives taken in parliamentary opposition, and delegated lay responsibility or general support for legislative statecraft. His main topical interests were legal unification of the Canadas, land law, the administration of civil justice, and the consolidation of professional culture and authority. Although tangible proposals for comprehensive codification of ostensibly discrete bodies of law did not characterize Badgley's enthusiasm for those subjects, his embrace of legislative utilitarianism placed him in the mainstream of quantitatively unprecedented and subsequently unparalleled statutory lawmaking by Canadian legislators of the 1841–67 period. Unlike many of his contemporaries, however, Badgley seems to have appreciated that the formalism that characterized his criminal code initiatives could often be as instrumental as overt instrumentalism in law.[179]

Badgley also knew as a result of comparative study, and sometimes as a consequence of personal interaction with the relevant lawmakers, about the impact of mid-nineteenth-century utilitarianism on codal initiatives in sibling jurisdictions like New York, Massachusetts, and Louisiana and in the colonies of the second British Empire. Indeed, he typically looked to those Anglo-American venues for formal, strategic, and ideological guidance rather than to continental Europe or to the ancient Mediterranean world.[180] And he did so despite his extensive teaching experience in Roman and international law. That kind of selective and cautious or convenient recurrence to other North Atlantic schools of legal thought was not uncommon among Canadian law reformers of the day.[181] In any case, panamerican and British colonial links provided a veneer of extroversion, currency, and sophistication for Badgley's local projects. He was thus in another vanguard, this time international, of comparative studies of legislation.

Formally, Badgley's statutes and especially his draft codes of criminal law and procedure have Benthamite- and Field-like features such as comprehensiveness, coherence, simplicity, and orderliness. Badgley himself used the adjectives centralizing, assimilationist, and scientific to describe his codes. He was very interested in legal-literary form, personal commendation, and parliamentary prominence but generally less so in substantive law reform, unless it might have led to provincial economic development or to a more perfect legislative union of the Canadas. His emphasis was thus on the scientific presentation of social and economic norms by a central law-making authority reliant on lawyerly statesmen. Badgley's codes can be said to be scientific in a mid-Victorian sense in that they presented legal rules in a systematic and coherent fashion, and because his use of the empirical methods and inductive reasoning anticipated two centuries earlier by Francis Bacon yielded rules expressed abstractly from which solutions to future issues in state law enforcement and litigation could be deduced with professed ease. His metaphors were thus drawn more frequently from the natural sciences than the moral or divine worlds.[182]

But none of those literary or epistemological values was an end in itself for Badgley. They were deployed in service of goals like the assimilation of state law across the Canadas, bureaucratic centralization, and constitutional consolidation. The articulation and achievement of those ends through lawyerly statecraft were, in turn, apparently intended by Badgley to help reverse the rise of local anti-lawyer and anti-legal sentiment, to depict for didactic purposes to the bar at-large a revised form of patrician 'law practice,' and to assist in the resumption by provincial lawyers of positions of leadership in a recently reformed state. Those are the senses in which Badgley's endorsement of legislative utilitarianism and inductive legal science can be said to have been strategic and symbolic. Motivated by shared professional aspirations and in some measure by personal ambition, he can thus be seen to have been keenly concerned about the identity of the bar and its constitutive role in the United Canadian state. The codification of criminal law and procedure presumably became a suitable flagship for those projects in Badgley's calculation because those fields were relatively self-contained, more uniform than many aspects of local law, largely untouched by the vested economic or doctrinal interests of other leading lawyers who tended to focus on successions, incorporation and land-law issues, and because there were credible out-of-province models to provide instruction. Badgley's lack of long experience with or interest in criminal justice was more or less irrelevant because his project was not really about the law of crimes or its administration.

The unequalled footage of shelf-space required to accommodate the legislative production of United Canada for the late 1840s, 1850s, and early 1860s is one indicator of the grip that political utilitarianism achieved on provincial legal culture during that period. That so much of that statutory output was the work of lawyers in elected office or at an extended statutory bar suggests that Badgley's professional ambitions ultimately took deep collective root despite the enigmatic fate of his criminal justice codes. Those codes are, nonetheless, a kind of milestone in the transition of 'ideal types' of provincial legal practice from legal work structured around the 'rule of bureaucracy' during the pre-rebellion period, to an embrace by lawyers of the 'rule of legislation' at mid-century, to the adoption of the 'rule of judge-made law' in the decades straddling the turn of the twentieth century. No doubt local legal culture was not monolithic during any of those periods, and the internal politics of the profession that led to the articulation and pursuit of successive ideal types of practice deserve more careful studies. The rough and tentative periodisation of those transforming cultures suggested here also involves a long reach from one legislator's abortive mid-nineteenth-century codification of criminal justice, but it is intended to provoke further research into the relationship between professional ambition or resilience and shifting conceptions of lawyers' roles in the state. The form, structure, and naming of legal texts can provide potent starting points for that reflection. Focusing on those attributes of law's literature and their rhetorical use by legal publicists would also help to merge accounts of science in mid-nineteenth-century legal thought with mainstream descriptions of reformulated scientific methods, a joinder of intellectual histories that is currently absent from conventional and revisionist assessments of the natural Victorian sciences.[183]

Utilitarianism, parliamentary politics, inductive science, and professionalization appear to have been uniquely fused and popularized by lawyerly Canadian promoters of those distinctively mid-nineteenth-century phenomena. The intelligence that enabled jurists like Badgley to effect that merger and act on it was seemingly strategic and pragmatic, rather than divinely inspired, metaphysically diffident, or theoretically profound. If democratically elected legislators were to be the new political sovereign, natural science the methodological prototype, and utility the preferred ethical standard, formal attributes of legal codification could reasonably have been vaunted as exemplars of those values. Taking a leaf from Badgley's rhetorical book (the Prussians were 'dreadfully immoral'; Canada's annexation to the United States was an 'insane project'; and, seignorialism was 'a blot on Lower Canada'), it might be said that he rushed to the head of mid-Victorian political and scientific parades with his criminal justice codes. Borrowing another page, this time from English legal historian Brian Simpson's book of metaphors, firsts in legal writing are rather like unique achievements in mountaineering. Foreshadowing Edmund Hilary atop Mount Everest, Badgley could have exclaimed 'excelsior' when he presented his locally unprecedented codes to United Canada's legislative assembly. Firsts command attention not only because they are the feats of venturesome and restive spirits but also because the motivation for them is generally high and visible. Badgley may not have gone onward and upward as a codifier following his mid-career adventure with criminal law,[184] but this essay's excavation of that pioneering episode did facilitate observations about a distinctively Canadian intermingling of professional culture and state formation different from those that have been offered in studies of later local codification and treatise-writing initiatives.[185] It also required that attention be paid to the contextually critical omnipresence of utilitarian thought, the curious lack of which in other modern treatments of union period social reform and statism has occasionally been lamented but only recently begun to be addressed.[186]

That body of utilitarian thought, comprised of result-oriented calculation, official law-making by lawyerly experts, wholesale appropriation of the methods and metaphors of the natural sciences, and the assertion of state-law's normative priority, became the 'tradition' that pioneering codifiers like Badgley exemplified. In view of their work's grounding in literate public opinion, which was itself a function of widespread popular participation in informal educational sites like amateur scientific associations, literary societies and debating clubs, it seems misleading to characterise that tradition as a distinctively legal one.[187] That characterisation was one of the possibilities canvassed in the introduction to this essay, and the suggestion that much of what high-profile legal scientists and utilitarians like Badgley were doing was epistemologically and sometimes strategically derivative of other bodies of knowledge rather than distinctive to state law cuts very deeply.

NOTES

* I am grateful to archivists Pamela Miller, formerly of Montreal's McCord Museum, and Robert Michel and Gordon Burr of McGill University for assistance with access to primary sources. Angela Fernandez, Rande Kostal, and Brian Young, as well as the editors of this volume and its anonymous reviewers, provided helpful comments on a draft version of this essay. I also offer kind thanks to the late John Brierley, who originally suggested the subject to me.

1 See E. Gibbs, ed., *Debates of the Legislative Assembly of United Canada, 1841–1867*, vol. 9 (Montreal: Centre d'Étude du Québec 1978), 73–4. See also ibid., at 386, 513–4, 835, 1139–42; vol. 10, at 302–3, 625, 1276, 1631–2.

2 Compare T.B. Macaulay, *A Penal Code Prepared by the Indian Law Commissioners* (London: Butterworth 1838); E. Livingston, *A System of Penal Law for the State of Louisiana* (Philadelphia: James Kay Jr. and Brother 1833), 473–639; New York State, *Fourth Report of the Commissioners on Practice and Pleadings – Code of Criminal Procedure* (Albany: Weed, Parsons and Co. 1849). See generally, J.L. Clive, *Macaulay: The Shaping of the Historian* (New York: Alfred A. Knopf 1973), 427–78; W.B. Hatcher, *Edward Livingston, Jeffersonian Republican and Jacksonian Democrat* (University, LA: Louisiana State University Press 1940), 226–88; D. van Ee, *David Dudley Field and the Reconstruction of the Law* (New York: Garland Publishing 1986), 32–56.

3 McGill University's copies of those bills (hereafter Badgley's codes) were printed and bound by Lovell and Gibson of Toronto for Henry Black in 1850. Black, perennial president of Lower Canada's Vice-Admiralty Court and long-tenured member of the legislative assembly for Quebec City with special interest in criminal justice, was the author of a series of penal statutes that provided the local point of legal departure for Badgley's codes. See Gibbs, *Debates*, vol. 1, 710–3, 727; Province of Canada statutes cited below in note 129. The only other copies of Badgley's codes that have been located were presented by him to the Advocates' Library of Montreal in 1850 and are currently shelved in the Rare Books Room of the Bar of Montreal.

4 The most extensive response to Badgley's legislative texts was written by Collège Sainte-Marie law professor Maximillien Bibaud, and published in Montreal's reform-oriented *La Minerve* newspaper during the spring and

summer of 1851. Bibaud was a devotee of Friedrich Karl von Savigny's German historical school of jurisprudence, anti-code, and anti-Badgley. See F.-M. Bibaud, 'Revue critique du Code Badgley,' *La Minerve*, 19 May 1851 (p. 1, col. 7 – p. 2, col. 7), 2 June (p. 1, col. 2 – p. 1, col. 3), 1 July (p. 1, col. 5 – p. 1, col. 7), 5 July (p. 1, col. 5 – p. 2, col. 1). Minutes of the assembly's select committee on Badgley's codes do not appear to have survived.

5 See generally, J.W. Head, 'Codes, Cultures, Chaos and Champions: Common Features of Legal Codification Experiences in China, Europe and North America,' *Duke Journal of Comparative and International Law* 13 (2003), 1; C. Varga, *Codification as a Socio-Historical Phenomenon*, trans. S. and J. Petrangi and C.Z. Sezeny (Budapest: Akademian Kiado 1991), 91–243.

6 See 4 Vict. (1841), c.30 (LC); 2 Vict. (1839), c.36 (LC); 3 Vict. (1840), c.30 (LC).

7 It took almost five years for Robert Samuel Wright to complete his criminal codes for Jamaica in the early 1870s, about three years for James Fitzjames Stephen to produce his English penal code in the late 1870s (even though he had already reduced British criminal law to digest form earlier in that decade), and nearly three years for Livingston to prepare his Louisiana codes. See M.L. Friedland, 'R.S. Wright's Model Criminal Code: A Forgotten Chapter in the History of the Criminal Law' *Oxford Journal of Legal Studies* 1 (1991), 307, 312; A.H. Manchester, 'Simplifying the Sources of the Law – An Essay in Law Reform II: James Fitzjames Stephen and the Codification of the Criminal Law of England and Wales,' *Anglo-American Law Review* 2 (1973), 527; G.M. Lyons, 'Louisiana and the Livingston Criminal Codes,' *Louisiana History* 15 (1974), 243.

8 See, for example, A. Morel, 'La réception du droit criminel anglais au Québec,' *Revue juridique Thémis* 13 (1978), D.H. Brown, *The Genesis of the Canadian Criminal Code of 1892* (Toronto: Osgoode Society 1989), 84–5; N. Kasirer, 'Canada's Criminal Law Codification Viewed and Reviewed,' *McGill Law Journal* 35 (1990), 841; M. Morin, 'Portalis v. Bentham: The Objectives Ascribed to Codification of the Civil Law and the Criminal Law in France, England and Canada,' in Law Commission of Canada, ed., *Perspectives on Legislation: Essays from the 1999 Legal Dimensions Initiative* (Ottawa: Law Commission of Canada 2000), 125, 166–8.

9 Compare I. Radforth, 'Sydenham and Utilitarian Reform,' in A. Greer and I. Radforth, eds., *Colonial Leviathan: State Formation in Mid-Nineteenth-Century Canada* (Toronto: University of Toronto Press 1992), 64. See also P. Edwards, *The Statesman's Science: History, Nature, and Law in the Political Thought of Samuel Taylor Coleridge* (New York: Columbia University Press 2004), 73–110; D. Lieberman, *The Province of Legislation Determined: Legal Theory in Eighteenth-Century Britain* (Cambridge: Cambridge University

Press 1989), 177–276; G. Drewry, 'Lawyers and Statutory Reform in Victorian Government,' in R. McLeod, ed., *Government and Expertise: Specialists, Administrators, and Professionals, 1860–1919* (Cambridge: Cambridge University Press 1988), 27.

10 Compare B. Young, 'Positive Law, Positive State: Class Realignment and the Transformation of Lower Canada,' in Greer and Radforth, *Colonial Leviathan*, 50; H.V. Nelles, *The Politics of Development: Forests, Mines and Hydro-Electric Power in Ontario, 1849–1941* (Toronto: Macmillan 1974), 1–47; J.M.S. Careless, *The Union of the Canadas: The Growth of Canadian Institutions 1841–1857* (Toronto: McClelland and Stewart 1967), esp. 113–65.

11 See generally, B. Young, *The Politics of Codification: The Lower Canadian Civil Code of 1866* (Montreal: McGill-Queen's University Press 1994), 66–140.

12 Compare B. J. Hibbitts, 'Our Arctic Brethren: Canadian Law and Lawyers as Portrayed in American Legal Periodicals, 1829–1911,' in G.B. Baker and J. Phillips, eds., *Essays in the History of Canadian Law: In Honour of R.C.B. Risk* (Toronto: University of Toronto Press 1999), 241; M.S. Bilder, 'The Lost Lawyers: Early American Legal Literates and Transatlantic Legal Culture,' *Yale Journal of Law and the Humanities* 11 (1999), 47; M.H. Hoeflich, 'Transatlantic Friendships and German Influences on American Law in the First Half of the Nineteenth Century,' *American Journal of Comparative Law* 35 (1987), 599.

13 See 20 Vict. (1857), c.43 (Can.); 29–30 Vict. (1866), c.25 (Can.); 29 Vict. (1866), c.41 (Can.). See generally, J.E.C. Brierley, 'Quebec's Civil Law Codification Viewed and Reviewed,' *McGill Law Journal* 14 (1968), 521; F.M. Greenwood, 'Lower Canada (Quebec): Transformation of Civil Law, From Higher Morality to Autonomous Will, 1774–1866,' *Manitoba Law Journal* 23 (1996), 23 132, 158–82; J.-M. Brisson, *La formation d'un droit mixte: l'évolution de la procédure civile de 1774 à 1867* (Montreal: Thémis 1986), 117–62.

14 See generally, G.B. Baker, 'Law Practice and Statecraft in Mid-Nineteenth-Century Montreal: The Torrance-Morris Firm, 1848 to 1868,' in C. Wilton, ed., *Beyond the Law: Lawyers and Business in Canada 1830 to 1930* (Toronto: Butterworth 1990), 45; B. Young, 'Dimensions of a Law Practice: Brokerage and Ideology in the Career of George-Etienne Cartier,' in Wilton, ed., *Beyond the Law* 92; E. Gibbs, 'William Badgley,' in *DCB*, vol. 11, 40. Over the course of a quarter-century, twenty members of the local bar participated in Lower Canada's commission for the abolition of seigniorial land tenure, its Seigniorial Court, and its commission for the codification of private law and procedure. Of that group, sixteen were also members of the legislative assembly or the special council.

15 Absence from legislative organs did not, however, result in institutional

shunning of Badgley. He was, for example, *bâtonnier* (president) of the Montreal bar from 1853 to 1855, dean of McGill's Faculty of Law during the same period, judge of the Superior Court of Lower Canada from 1855 to 1863, and puisne justice of the Lower Canadian or Quebec Court of Queen's Bench from 1863–4 and 1866–74. See generally, S.B. Frost, *McGill University for the Advancement of Learning, 1801–1895*, vol. 1 (Montreal: McGill-Queen's University Press 1981), 158–61; F.-J. Audet, *Les Députés de Montréal, 1792–1867* (Montreal: Les Éditions des Dix 1943), 68, 295–7; A.W.P. Buchanan, *The Bench and Bar of Lower Canada Down to 1850* (Montreal: Burton's Limited 1925), 98–9.

16 Gibbs, *Debates*, vol. 9, 1141; vol. 10, 1276. Emphasis in original.

17 Compare L. Farmer, 'Reconstructing the English Codification Debate: The Criminal Law Commissioners,' *Law and History Review* 18 (2000), 397; A. Rodger, 'The Codification of Commercial Law in Victorian Britain,' *Law Quarterly Review* 108 (1992), 570; C.M. Cook, *The American Codification Movement: A Study of Antebellum Legal Reform* (Westport, CT: Greenwood Press 1981), 69–95.

18 See, for example, J.E.C. Brierley and R.A. Macdonald, eds., *Quebec Civil Law: An Introduction to Quebec Private Law* (Toronto: Emond Montgomery 1993), 14–45; J.-P. Wallot, 'Le régime seigneurial et son abolition au Canada,' in J.-P. Wallot, ed., *Un Québec qui bougeait: trame socio-politique du Québec au tournant du XIXᵉ siècle* (Trois Rivières, QC: Boreal Express 1973), 255; A. Morel, *Les limites de la liberté testamentaire au Québec* (Paris: Librairie générale du Droit et de Jurisprudence 1960), 19–42.

19 T.K. Ramsay and L.-S. Morin, 'Criminal Law,' *Law Reports and Journal de jurisprudence* [1854], 50. See also Province of Canada, *The Revised Acts and Ordinances of Lower Canada* (Montreal: Armour and Ramsay 1845), ix–x; W.D. Ardagh and R.A. Harrison, 'Codification of the Laws of New York,' *Upper Canada Law Journal* 4 (1858), 125; J.H. Willan, *Some Loose Suggestions for the Improvement of the Criminal Law, in its Present State of Transition* (Quebec: Daily Mercury Office 1867).

20 Papineau, member of the assembly for Saint Maurice and Lower Canada's grand old *patriote*, said of his political nemesis Badgley's codes that 'since the introduction of the representative system [of government in 1791], no man in the legislature had produced a document of equal labour, magnitude, and usefulness' and that Badgley's work had 'been done with great care and research, and accomplished with great precision.' Drummond added that 'he knew no man better able to undertake the labour of codification than [Badgley]. There was no man better fitted for it both from his intelligence, and his habits of labourious study.' Reproduced in Gibbs, *Debates*, vol. 9, 1140–41.

21 Compare 'William Badgley Commonplace Book' (1827–88) [hereafter Commonplace Book] 33, 67, 140, 225, 464, 497, 553, 561, 621, 639, in McCord-Badgley, box 3; 'William Badgley Account Book' (1834–40) [hereafter Account Book], in McGill University Rare Books Room [hereafter McGill RBR], MS 367; D. Mitchell and J. Slinn, *The History of McMaster, Meighen* (Montreal: McMaster, Meighen 1989), 3–29. For indications that some of Badgley's contemporaries in Montreal's corporate-commercial bar were very interested in criminal law, see, for example, Torrance and Morris, 'Commonplace Book,' 121–49, in McGill University Archives, MG 4166, container # 1, file # 00008.

22 See 'John Samuel McCord Diary' (March 1847–April 1852: 27 April 1849), in McCord Papers – McCord Museum of Canadian History Archives (Montreal), M420 [hereafter McCord-McCord]. See generally, E.K. Senior, *British Regulars in Montreal: An Imperial Garrison, 1832–1854* (Montreal: McGill-Queen's University Press 1981), 57–142.

23 See, for example, 10–11 Vict. (1847), c.4 (Can.); 10–11 Vict. (1847) c.9 (Can.); 12 Vict. (1849), c.12 (Can.); 12 Vict. (1849), c.20 (Can.).

24 See Gibbs, *Debates*, vol. 6, 533; vol. 9, 153–5; vol. 8, 558, 1740.

25 See, for example, 10–11 Vict. (1847), c.12 (Can.); 12 Vict. (1849), c.13 (Can.); 12 Vict. (1849), c.21 (Can.); 14–15 Vict. (1851), c.2 (Can.); 14–15 Vict. (1851), c.13 (Can.); 14–15 Vict. (1851), c.95 (Can.); 14–15 Vict. (1851), c.96 (Can.); 14–15 Vict. (1851), c.129 (Can.).

26 Compare *Cartier v. Béchard, Lower Canada Jurist* [hereafter *LCJ*] 1 (1856) 44, (per Badgley, J.) (S.Ct.); *Mountain v. Dumas, Lower Canada Reports* [hereafter *LCR*] 7 (1857), 430 (per Badgley, J.) (S.Ct.); *Regina v. Beaulieu, LCJ* 3 (1858), 117 (per Badgley, J.) (S.Ct.); *Regina v. Croteau, LCR* 9 (1858), 67 (per Badgley, J.) (S.Ct.); A.C. Hooper, *Superior Court, Montreal, 13th, 14th, 15th, and 16th November, 1861, Before the Hon. Mr. Justice Badgley, and a Special Jury: 'Hooper vs. Leslie'* (Montreal: J. Lovell 1861); *Domina Regina, Slack and Bellemare, LCJ* 7 (1862), 6 (per Badgley, J.) (S.Ct.); *Ex parte Mogé v. Roy, LCJ* 7 (1863), 107 (per Badgley, J.) (S.Ct.); *Duval dit Barbinas v. The Queen, LCR* 14 (1863), 52 (per Meredith and Duval, JJ. for the court) (C.A.); *Ex parte Blossom, LCJ* 10 (1865) 35 (per Badgley, J.) (S.Ct.); *Regina v. Paxton, LCJ* 10 (1866), 212 (per Badgley, J.) (S.Ct.); *Dunlop v. The Queen, LCJ* 11 (1867), 271 (per Badgley, J.) (C.A.); *Spelman v. The Queen, LCJ* 13 (1868), 154 (per Duval, C.J. for the court) (C.A.); *Regina v. Downey, LCJ* 13 (1868), 193 (*per curiam*) (C.A.); *Notman v. The Queen, LCJ* 13 (1869), 255 (per Badgley, J.) (C.A.); *Queen v. Lacombe, LCJ* 13 (1869), 259 (per Badgley, J.) (S.Ct.); *Queen v. Fraser, LCJ* 14 (1870), 245 (per Badgley, J.) (C.A.); *Ex parte Edward Spelman, LCJ* 14 (1869), 281 (per Duval, C.J. for the court) (C.A.); *Ex parte Fourquin, LCJ* 16 (1867),

103 (*per curiam*) (S.Ct.); *Regina v. Chamaillard, LCJ* 18 (1873), 149 (per Duval, C.J. for the court) (C.A.).

27 See generally, A. Garon, 'Thomas Cushing Aylwin,' in *DCB*, vol. 10, 24; E. Nish, 'Charles-Elzéar Mondelet,' in ibid., 526.

28 The lack of an available catalogue for Badgley's library makes conclusions about his access to that international literature difficult to demonstrate directly. An auction inventory of the contents of his retirement home on Montreal's McGill College Avenue, together with correspondence between his executor (James Clement Neufville Badgley) and used book purchasers like the American Museum of Natural History, Woodward Rare Books of New York City, and Toronto Public Librarian James Bain, show impressive library holdings in natural history (geology and paleontology) but none in law. Moreover, only one of Badgley's law books turned up in searches of the collections most likely to have acquired them, namely, McGill's Law Library (where Badgley taught for two generations), the Library of the Montreal Bar (modern successor to the Advocates' Library and Law Institute, which Badgley helped to found in 1828), and the library of the Montreal office of the Borden, Ladner, Gervais law firm (modern successor to Badgley and Abbott). Compare McCord-Badgley, box 2, folder 16; G.B. Baker et al., *Sources in the Law Library of McGill University for a Reconstruction of the Legal Culture of Quebec, 1760–1890* (Montreal: McGill University Press 1987), 64–276. The jurisdictionally eclectic, criminal justice holdings of Canada's Legislative Assembly Library, the Advocates' Library of Montreal, the Library of the Quebec Bar, the Law Society of Upper Canada's Great Library, and Montreal's Torrance-Morris law firm, which can be documented were, however, readily available to Badgley. See *Catalogue of Books in the Library of the Legislative Assembly of Canada* (Kingston: Desbarats and Derbyshire 1841); *Catalogue of the Advocates' Library* (Montreal: J. Lovell 1857); *Catalogue of Books Belonging to the Quebec Advocates' Library* (Quebec: John Neilson 1840); J.M. Cawdell, *Osgoode Hall Library Catalogue* (Toronto: H. Rowsell 1841); Torrance and Morris, 'Letterbook' (1848–61) in McGill University Archives, MG 4166, container #1, file #'s 00010–11.

29 See generally, S.B. Frost, 'The Early Days of Law Teaching at McGill,' *Dalhousie Law Journal* 9 (1984), 150; M. Nantel, 'The Advocates' Library and the Montreal Bar,' *Law Library Journal* 27 (1934), 85; G.B. Baker, 'Public Frivolity and Patrician Confidence: Lower Canada's Brothers-in-Law, 1827 to 1833,' in J.E.C. Brierley et al., eds., *Mélanges Paul-André Crépeau* (Cowansville, QC: Yvon Blais 1996), 43.

30 See generally, G.-E. Rinfret, *L'histoire du Barreau de Montréal* (Cowansville, QC: Yvon Blais 1989), 41–54, 169; A. Vachon, *Histoire du notariat canadien, 1621–1960* (Quebec: Presses de l'Université Laval 1962), 86–102 ; R.A.

Macdonald, 'The National Law Programme at McGill: Origins, Establishment, Prospects,' *Dalhousie Law Journal* 13 (1990), 211.

31 See generally, M. McCulloch, 'The Death of Whiggery: Lower Canadian British Constitutionalism and the *tentation de l'histoire parallèle*,' *Journal of the Canadian Historical Association* 2 (1991), 195.

32 See generally, *infra*, text at notes 67–84, 97–106; P.A. Buckner, *The Transition to Responsible Government: British Policy in British North America, 1815–1850* (Westport, CT: Greenwood Press 1985), 205–332; W.G. Ormsby, *The Emergence of the Federal Concept in Canada, 1839 to 1845* (Toronto: University of Toronto Press 1969).

33 See generally, R.A. Cosgrove, *Scholars of the Law: English Jurisprudence from Blackstone to Hart* (New York: New York University Press 1996), 89–178; D. Sugarman, 'Legal Theory, the Common Law Mind, and the Making of the Textbook Tradition,' in W.L. Twining, ed., *Legal Theory and Common Law* (Oxford: Basil Blackwell 1986), 26; P. Stein, 'Legal Theory and the Reform of Legal Education in Mid-Nineteenth Century England,' in A. Giuliani and N. Picarda, eds., *L'Educazione Giuridica II: Profili Storici* (Perugia: Libreria Universitaria 1979), 185.

34 See generally, W.P. La Piana, *Logic and Experience: The Origin of Modern American Legal Education* (New York: Oxford University Press 1994), 79–131; R.W. Gordon, 'The Ideal and the Actual in the Law; Fantasies and Practices of New York City Lawyers, 1870–1910,' in G.W. Gawalt, ed., *The New High Priests: Lawyers in Post-Civil War America* (Westport, CT: Greenwood Press 1984), 51; P. Miller, *The Life of the Mind in America from the Revolution to the Civil War* (New York: Harcourt, Brace and World 1965), 239–65.

35 Compare G. Marquis, 'Anti-Lawyer Sentiment in Mid-Victorian New Brunswick,' *University of New Brunswick Law Journal* 36 (1987), 163; M. Bloomfield, 'Lawyers and Public Criticism: Challenge and Response in Nineteenth-Century America,' *American Journal of Legal History* 15 (1971), 269; G.W. Gawalt, 'Sources of Anti-Lawyer Sentiment in Massachusetts, 1740–1840,' *American Journal of Legal History* 14 (1970), 283.

36 Paul Romney's observations about the role of anti-legal and anti-lawyer sentiment in the Upper Canadian rebellions are suggestive for the lower province and directly relevant to institutional developments in United Canada during the succeeding decades. Compare P. Romney, 'From the Rule of Law to Responsible Government: Ontario Political Culture and the Origins of Canadian Statism,' *Historical Papers* [Canadian Historical Association] 23 (1988), 86; P. Romney, 'From the Types Riot to the Rebellion: Elite Ideology, Anti-Legal Sentiment, Political Violence, and the Rule of Law in Upper Canada,' *Ontario History* 79 (1987), 113.

37 See generally, P. Oliver, 'Power, Politics, and the Law: The Place of the

Judiciary in the Historiography of Upper Canada,' in Baker and Phillips, *Essays in the History of Canadian Law*, 443; A. Greer, *The Patriots and the People: The Rebellions of 1837 in Rural Lower Canada* (Toronto: University of Toronto Press 1993), 87–188.

38 C. Buller, *Responsible Government for Colonies* (London: James Ridgway 1840), 43; A. Buller, 'Appendix D,' in C.P. Lucas, ed., *Lord Durham's Report on the Affairs of British North America*, vol. 3 (Oxford: Clarendon Press 1912), 238–94.

39 Reported in Lucas, ed., *Lord Durham's Report ...*, vol. 2, 116.

40 Compare A. Morel, 'La codification devant l'opinion publique de l'époque,' in J. Boucher and A. Morel, eds., *Le droit dans la vie de famille: Livre centenaire du code civil*, vol. 1 (Montreal: Presses de l'Université de Montréal, 1970), 27; G. Parker, 'The Origins of the Canadian Criminal Code,' in D.H. Flaherty, ed., *Essays in the History of Canadian Law*, vol. 1 (Toronto : University of Toronto Press 1981), 249; Bibaud, 'Revue critique du Code Badgley.'

41 Compare M. Burrage, *Revolution and the Making of the Contemporary Legal Profession: England, France and the United States* (Oxford: Oxford University Press 2006), esp. 207–576; R. Cocks, *Foundations of the Modern Bar* (London: Sweet and Maxwell 1983); G.W. Gawalt, *The Promise of Power: The Emergence of the Legal Profession in Massachusetts, 1760–1840* (Westport, CT: Greenwood Press 1979).

42 Compare P. Mandler, *Aristocratic Government in the Age of Reform: Whigs and Liberals, 1830–1852* (Oxford: Clarendon Press 1990), 44–84, 157–99, 236–74.

43 See generally, M.B. Taylor, *Promoters, Patriots, and Partisans: Historiography in Nineteenth-Century English Canada* (Toronto: University of Toronto Press 1989), 133–51, 161–80, 231–55; C. Berger, *The Writing of Canadian History: Aspects of English-Canadian Historical Writing Since 1900* (Toronto: University of Toronto Press 1986), 2–3, 28, 32–8, 44, 64–6, 120–1, 147–9, 167, 176, 181, 210–29; S. Gagnon, *Quebec and Its Historians*, trans. J. Brierley (Montreal: Harvest House 1985), 81–117.

44 The closest secondary literature has come to those themes is discussion of lawyers' appreciation of patronage opportunities offered by responsible government, and examination of the ways legal practitioners in the union assembly furthered their clients' interests through the achievement of enterprise-specific, legislative concessions. Compare J.B. Brebner, 'Patronage and Parliamentary Government,' *Canadian Historical Review* 19 (1938), 22; J.K. Johnson, 'John A. Macdonald and the Kingston Business Community,' in G. Tulchinsky, ed., *To Preserve and Defend: Essays on Kingston in the Nineteenth Century* (Montreal: McGill-Queen's University Press 1976), 141; B. Young, *George-Etienne Cartier: Montreal Bourgeois* (Montreal: McGill-Queen's University Press 1981), 53–118.

45 See generally, 'The Late Mr. Justice Badgley,' *Legal News* 11 (1888), 410; 'Death of Hon. Wm. Badgley,' *Montreal Daily Star*, 26 December 1888, p. 2, col. 4; 'The Late Judge Badgley,' *Montreal Gazette*, 28 December 1888, p. 3, col. 5; P. Beullac et E.-F. Surveyer, *Le centenaire du Barreau de Montréal 1849–1949* (Montréal: Librairie Ducharme 1949), 34–7; W.S. Wallace, *The Mac-Millan Dictionary of Canadian Biography* (London: MacMillan 1963), 28; J.P. Noyes, 'Hon. Judge Badgley, ex-M.P.P. for Missisquoi,' *Annual Report of the Missisquoi County Historical Society* 4 (1908–9), 47; W.H. Atherton, *Montreal, 1535–1914*, vol. 3 (Montreal: Clarke 1914), 20. No sustained scholarly work on any aspect of Badgley's career has yet been attempted.

46 See generally, J.D. Borthwick, *History and Biographical Gazetteer of Montreal to the Year 1892* (Montreal: J. Lovell 1892), 365; E.K. Senior, 'Francis Badgley,' in *DCB*, vol. 7, 29; H.J. Morgan, *Sketches of Celebrated Canadians, and Persons Connected with Canada* (Quebec: Hunter, Rose and Co. 1862), 492–7.

47 See S.B. Frost, 'Alexander Skakel,' in *DCB*, vol. 7, 809; Library and Archives Canada (hereafter LAC), Record Group 4, box 8, vol. 21, 7649–58; 'Commission Appointing William Badgley Esquire to Practice the Law in all His Majesty's Courts of Justice in this Province' (21 November 1823), in McCord-Badgley, box 1, folder 7; W.S. Johnson, 'Legal Education in the Province of Quebec,' *Canadian Law Review* 4 (1905), 454–6.

48 See Montreal Natural History Society, *Act of Incorporation and By-laws of the Natural History Society of Montreal* (Montreal: A.H. Armour 1833); McCord-Badgley, box 1, folder 7; ibid., folder 8; 'Brothers-in-Law Minute Book' (1827–33), in McCord Museum of Canadian History Archives (Montreal), M21413 [hereafter McCord-Brothers].

49 See T. Doige, *The Montreal Directory* (Montreal: James Lane 1819), 55.

50 Examples of Beaubien and Badgley at work can be found in *Reid v. Porteous* (1825), 8 LCJ 337 (K.B.); *Durocher et al. v. Beaubien and Guy* (1828), *Stuart's Reports* 309 (J.C.P.C.); A. Chaboillez, *Questions sur le gouvernement ecclésiastique du district de Montréal* (Montreal: T.A. Turner 1823); and, A.W.P. Buchanan, *The Buchanan Book* (Montreal: A.W.P. Buchanan 1911), 88.

51 See generally, J.-C. Bonenfant, 'James Smith,' in *DCB*, vol. 9, 728.

52 McCord-Badgley, box 3, contains a collection of Privy Council judgments on appeal from Lower Canada before 1835, in Badgley's handwriting, and Colonial Office correspondence (cited in note 68) that suggest prior acquaintance with those letters' recipients.

53 Badgley's interest in the Irish *Act of Union* can be inferred from analogies he made to that statute in constitutional debate leading up to Canada's 1840 *Act of Union*. His familiarity with the *Reform Act* is supposed on the basis of parallel passages in his criminal justice codes. See generally, *United King-*

dom-Ireland (New York: Greystone Press 1963); J.A. Phillips and C. Wether-
ell, 'The Great Reform Act of 1832 and the Political Modernization of England,' *American Historical Review* 100 (1995), 411.

54 See generally, J.K. Johnson, 'Land Policy of the Upper Canadian Elite
Reconsidered: The Canada Emigration Association, 1840–1841,' in D. Keane
and C. Read, eds., *Old Ontario: Essays in Honour of J.M.S. Careless* (Toronto:
Dundurn Press 1990), 217; W.K. Hastings, 'The Wakefield Colonization
Plan and Constitutional Development in South Australia, Canada, and
New Zealand,' *Journal of Legal History* 11 (1990), 279.
55 Compare J.S. Anderson, *Lawyers and the Making of English Land Law, 1832–
1940* (Oxford: Clarendon Press 1992), 3–84.
56 See below notes 66–106; Anon., 'Society for Promoting the Advancement of
the Law,' *Monthly Law Report* 7 (1844), 110. See generally, A.G. Donaldson,
'The High Priests of the Mystery: A Note on Two Centuries of Parliamentary Draftsmen,' in W. Finnie, C.M.G. Himsworth, and N. Walker, eds.,
Edinburgh Essays in Public Law (Edinburgh: Edinburgh University Press
1991), 99; S.E. Finer, 'The Transmission of Benthamite Ideas, 1820–50,' in G.
Sutherland, ed., *Studies in the Growth of Nineteenth Century Government*
(London: Routledge and Kegan Paul 1972), 11.
57 See E. Desjardins, 'Francis Badgley,' in *DCB*, vol. 9, 16; McCord-McCord,
MS 413, 9 December 1856.
58 See Account Book, note 21 above; 'William Badgley to Gillespie, Moffatt
and Co. (London)' (July 1838), in McCord-Badgley, box 1, folder 10;
R.W.S. MacKay, *The Montreal Directory* (Montreal: Lovell and Gibson
1842), 17.
59 See 'Commission Appointing William Badgley, Esquire to be Commissioner of Bankrupts' (10 June 1840), in McCord-Badgley, box 1, folder 7;
R.W.S. MacKay, *The Montreal Directory* (Montreal: Lovell and Gibson 1843),
18.
60 See Gibbs, *Debates*, vol. 8, 35, 114, 1028–9, 1733; vol. 9, 1485. See also 12 Vict.
(1849), c.42 (Can.); 13–14 Vict. (1850), c.20 (Can.). Those statutes appear to
have been modelled after American federal reforms of the day.
61 See 7 Vict. (1843), c.16 (Can.). See also Province of Canada, *Orders and Rules
of Practice in the Inferior Court of Queen's Bench and in the Circuit Courts* (Montreal: James Starke and Co. 1843); F.F., 'La Cour du Banc de la Reine, au
Terme supérieur, a-t-elle juridiction dans une cause, où une demande
excédant £20 courant et réduite par la preuve, à une somme au dessous de
£20 courant?' *Revue de législation et de jurisprudence* 1 (1845), 153.
62 But see *In the Matter of Vital Gibeau, et al. Bankrupts, Revue de législation et de
jurisprudence* 1 (1845), 188; *Radenhurst v. Macfarlane, Revue de législation et de

jurisprudence 1 (1845), 273 (C.A.) (an appeal from one of Badgley's judgments that reproduces it).

63 See Gibbs, *Debates*, vol. 6, 317.

64 See 'Commission Appointing William Badgley Esquire to be Attorney General for Canada East' (24 April 1847), in McCord-Badgley, box 1, folder 7; 'Commission Appointing William Badgley, Esquire to Her Majesty's Executive Council for Canada' (24 April 1847), in McCord-Badgley, box 1, folder 7; Gibbs, *Debates*, vol. 6, 211. See also, J.O. Côté, *Political Appointments and Elections in the Province of Canada, from 1841 to 1865* (Ottawa: Lowe-Martin Co. Ltd. 1918), 4, 18, 21, 36.

65 See Gibbs, *Debates*, note 1, vol. 9, 827; vol. 10, 66; vol. 11, 21, 748, 2950. See also R. Sage and A. Weir, *Select Committees of the Assemblies of the Provinces of Upper Canada, Canada and Ontario, 1792–1991* (Toronto: Ontario Legislative Library 1992), 233–4, 286, 242.

66 See, for example, Gibbs, *Debates*, vol. 6, 329–30; vol. 11, 664, 2771 (municipalities); vol. 7, 52–3, 56–7, 60, 79–80, 83 (immigrants); vol. 8, 936–7, 1721 (patents); vol. 8, 558, 1043; vol. 10, 437, 510, 660, 1319, 1468; vol. 11, 1976, 2542, 2704 (churches and charities); vol. 8, 2267; vol. 10, 318, 361, 956; vol. 11, 2737, 3111 (financial institutions); vol. 9, 1317; vol. 10, 830; vol. 11, 82, 1878 1885–7, 2908, 2926 (transportation enterprises). See also 11 Vict. (1848), c.1 (Can.); 12 Vict. (1849), c.24 (Can.); 10–11 Vict. (1847), c.35 (Can.); 12 Vict. (1850), c.153 (Can.); 16 Vict. (1852), c.26 (Can.); 16 Vict. (1852), c.56 (Can.); 14–15 Vict. (1851), c.171 (Can.); 14–15 Vict. (1851), c.82 (Can.).

67 For Badgley's work as co-founder and later secretary of the Constitutional Association, see, for example, McCord-Badgley, box 1, folder 9; box 1, folder 10; box 2, folder 21. For his early interest in land-law reform, see, for example, W. Badgley, *Remarks on Register Offices* [hereafter *Register Offices*] (Montreal: Herald Office 1836); W. Badgley, 'Seigniory of Montreal,' in McCord-Badgley, box 1, folder 10; W. Badgley, *Representation against the Title of the Seminary to the Seignory of Montreal; and Objections to the Proposed Ordinance for the Extinction of Seigniorial Dues in the City and the Island of Montreal* (Montreal: Herald Office 1839). On Badgley's work for McGill, see, for example, [W. Badgley], *An Account of the Endowments for Education in Lower Canada, and of the Legislative and other Public Acts for the Advancement Thereof, from the Cession of the Country in 1763 to the Present Time* [hereafter *Account of the Endowments*] (London: Norman and Skeen, 1838); text at note 109, below.

68 See, for example, 'George Moffatt and William Badgley to Lord Durham' (5 April 1838), in NAC, RG 1923, 169; 'George Moffatt and William Badgley to Lord Durham' (9 April 1838), 'George Moffatt and William Badgley to Lord

Durham' (17 April 1838), 'George Moffatt and William Badgley to Lords
Durham and Glenelg' (14 April 1838), in McCord-Badgley, box 1, folder 10;
[Badgley], *Account of the Endowments*.

69 See generally, Gibbs, *Debates*, vol. 11, 41; Morgan, *Sketches of Celebrated Canadians ...*, 495.

70 Gibbs, *Debates*, vol. 6, 528.

71 Ibid., vol. 9, 901. See also vol. 8, 178, where Badgley said, to the same effect, that 'the Civil Law [of Lower Canada] at present [1849] was applied only in cases of real property.' Compare N.B. Doucet, *Fundamental Principles of the Laws of Canada*, vol. 2 (Montreal: N.B. Doucet, 1841), 37–152; H. Des Rivieres Beaubien, *Traité sur les lois civiles du Bas-Canada* (Montreal: L. Duvernay 1832); and, F.-M. Bibaud, *Commentaires sur les lois du Bas Canada* (Montreal: F.-M. Bibaud 1859–61) for suggestions that the issue of legal uniformity may have been larger than Badgley conceded.

72 Reproduced in Gibbs, *Debates*, vol. 8, 1955. The statute to which Badgley referred was 9–10 Geo. 4 (1829), c.127 (LC). See also 20 Vict. (1857), c.45 (Can.).

73 Compare R.C. Harris, ed., *Historical Atlas of Canada*, vol. 1 (Toronto: University of Toronto Press 1987), plate 51. Badgley had, by way of contrast, little to say about the persistence of seigniorial remnants in Upper Canada's Ottawa Valley or its south-western counties. That disinterest presumably had to do with the commercial insignificance of those 'remote' locations.

74 See, for example, *Blanchet et al. v. Blanchet* (1861), 11 LCR 204, 238–53 (per Badgley, J.) (S.Ct.) ; *McGrath v. Lloyd* (1856), 1 LCJ 17, at 18 (*per curiam*) (S.Ct.); *Carden et al. v. Finley et al.* (1860), 8 LCJ 139, at 140 (per LaFontaine, C.J. for the court) (C.A.); *Eastty v. Les Curé et Marguilliers de l'oeuvre et Fabrique de la Paroisse de Saint Nom de Marie de Montréal* (1867), 12 LCJ 11, 17–20 (per Badgley, J.) (C.A.); *Brown v. Hawksworth* (1869), 14 LCJ 114, at 116–24 (per Badgley, J.) (C.A.).

75 Compare D.C. Masters, *The Rise of Toronto, 1850–1900* (Toronto: University of Toronto Press 1947); J.I. Little, *Nationalism, Capitalism, and Colonization in Nineteenth-Century Quebec: The Upper St. Francis District* (Montreal: McGill-Queen's University Press 1989); C. Gaffield, 'Boom or Bust: The Demography and the Economy of the Lower Ottawa Valley in the Nineteenth Century,' *Historical Papers* [Canadian Historical Association] 17 (1982), 172.

76 Gibbs, *Debates*, note 1, vol. 11, 1568.

77 Compare M.H. Hoeflich 'The Lawyer as Pragmatic Reader: The History of Legal Common-Placing,' *Arkansas Law Review* 55 (2002), 114.

78 See Province of Canada, *Journals of the Legislative Assembly*, vol. 15 (Toronto: Lovell and Gibson 1857), 239–40; J. Pope, *Confederation: Being a Series of*

Hitherto Unpublished Documents Bearing on the British North America Act (Toronto: Carswell, 1895), 155, 237; Parliament of Canada, *Journals of the House of Commons* (Ottawa: Malcolm Cameron 1869) 43, 186, 268.

79 See [G.-E. Cartier], 'De la codification des lois du Canada,' *Revue de législation et de jurisprudence* 1 (1846), 337. See generally, P. Poulin, 'Jean Chabot,' *DCB*, vol. 8, 138; J.-P. Bernard, *Les Rouges: libéralisme, nationalisme et anticléricalisme au milieu du XIXᵉ siècle* (Montreal: Les presses de l'Université du Québec 1971), 93; and sources cited below in note 160.

80 See D.D. Field, 'Codification of the Common Law,' in A.P. Sprague and T.M. Coan, eds., *Speeches, Arguments, and Miscellaneous Papers of David Dudley Field*, vol. 1 (New York: D. Appleton 1884), 307. See also M. Reimann, 'The Historical School Against Codification: Savigny, Carter, and the Defeat of the New York Civil Code,' *American Journal of Comparative Law* 37 (1989), 102; R.K. Newmyer, 'Harvard Law School, New England Legal Culture, and the Antebellum Origins of American Jurisprudence,' in D. Thalen, ed., *The Constitution in American Life* (Ithaca, NY: Cornell University Press 1988), 74.

81 Compare D.E. Kirkby and C. Coleborn, *Law, History, Colonialism and the Reach of Empire* (Manchester: Manchester University Press 2001), 9–239; L. Zastoupil, *John Stuart Mill and India* (Stanford: Stanford University Press 1994), 126–207; W.E. Rumble, *The Thought of John Austin: Jurisprudence, Colonial Reform, and the British Constitution* (London: Athlone Press 1985), 144–92.

82 See Gibbs, *Debates*, note 1, vol. 9, 173; vol. 8, 179, 500; vol. 11, 132.

83 See, for example, 12 Vict. (1849), c.178 (Can.); 14–15 Vict. (1851), c.164 (Can.); 16 Vict. (1853), c.103 (Can.). See also Gibbs, *Debates*, vol. 10, 949; vol. 11, 645, 1731.

84 Compare G.J.J. Tulchinsky, *The River Barons: Montreal Businessmen and the Growth of Industry and Transportation, 1837–1853* (Toronto: University of Toronto Press 1977); D. Creighton, *The Empire of the St. Lawrence* (Toronto: University of Toronto Press 1956), 205–385.

85 See Gibbs, *Debates*, vol. 6, 356, 667, 1098, 1102, 1115; vol. 9, 830–1; vol. 10, 1137–8, 1475–6; vol. 11, 2375–8, 2792, 2797-8, 2825, 2991, 2993.

86 Ibid., vol. 8, 179; vol. 9, 811; vol. 10, 1138; vol. 11, 2377.

87 Ibid., vol. 11, 2558–9.

88 Ibid., vol. 11, 2377; vol. 9, 831; vol. 11, 2376. It is noteworthy that Badgley routinely spoke of categories of law like copyhold, or of the law applicable to specific regions like Strathfield Sage, rather than in terms of a uniform English common law. For indications that he could not easily have done otherwise in the 1840s or 1850s, see, for example, A.C. Loux, 'The Persistence of the Ancient Regime: Custom, Utility and the Common Law in the

Nineteenth Century,' *Cornell Law Review* 79 (1993), 183; M. Lobban, *The Common Law and English Jurisprudence, 1760–1850* (New York: Oxford University Press 1991), 257–89; H.W. Arthurs, *Without the Law: Administrative Justice and Legal Pluralism in Nineteenth-Century England* (Toronto: University of Toronto Press 1983), 13–88.

89 Compare S.B. Kim, *Landlord and Tenant in Colonial New York: Manorial Society 1664–1775* (Chapel Hill: University of North Carolina Press 1978), 3–43, 162–234; M.E. McCallum, 'The Sacred Rights of Property: Title, Entitlement, and the Land Question in Nineteenth-Century Prince Edward Island,' in Baker and Phillips, eds., *Essays in the History of Canadian Law*, 358; W.B. Taylor, *Landlord and Peasant in Colonial Oaxaca* (Stanford: Stanford University Press 1972), 111–94.

90 See, for example, Gibbs, *Debates*, vol. 9, 811; vol. 10, 1137–8; vol. 11, at 2375–8, 2792. On the relationship between Benthamite state planning and laissez-faire social theory, see generally, D. Fraser, *The Evolution of the British Welfare State: A History of Social Policy since the Industrial Revolution* (London: Palgrave, Macmillan 2003), 11–123; P. Schofield, *Utility and Democracy: The Political Thought of Jeremy Bentham* (Oxford: Oxford University Press 2006).

91 Gibbs, *Debates*, vol. 9, 811. See also Commonplace Book, note 21 above, 89, 99, 108, 156, 190, 378, 501.

92 See, for example, *Drapeau v. Campeau* (1856), 6 LCR 86, at 87 (per Morin, J. for the court) (S.Ct.); *Les Soeurs de la Charité de l'Hôpital Général de Montréal v. Primeau* (1856), 1 LCJ 13, at 14 *(per curiam)* (S.Ct.); *Drapeau et al. v. Gosselin* (1856), 6 LCR 87, at 88 *(per curiam)* (S.Ct.); *Lamothe et al. v. Fontaine dite Bienvenu et P.A. Talon dit Lesperance* (1857), 7 LCR 49, at 53–5 (per Badgley, J.) (C.A.); *Kierzkowski v. Grand Trunk Railway Company of Canada* (1858), 8 LCR 3, at 4–33 (per Badgley, J.) (S.Ct.).

93 See 3 Geo. IV (1822), c.119 (UK); 6 Geo. IV (1825), c.59 (UK); 3 Vict. (1840), c.30 (LC); 8 Vict. (1845), c.42 (Can.).

94 See, for example, Badgley, *Title of the Seminary*; 'William Badgley to Dr. Gifford' (29 April 1840), McGill RBR CH 302. S262; 'William Badgley to James Somerville' (April 1840), McGill RBR CH 301, S261; 'Duncan Fisher and William Badgley to Peter Redpath' (n.d.), McGill RBR CH 302, S262.

95 See Gibbs, *Debates*, vol. 11, 2377, 2558–9; 22 Vict. (1859), c.48 (Can.); 25–6 Geo. 5 (1935), c.82 (Que.).

96 See 'Commission Appointing the Honourable William Badgley to be one of the Puisne Judges of the Superior Court for Lower Canada' (28 January 1855), in McCord-Badgley, box 1, folder 7; *Lower Canada Reports: Seigniorial Questions*, vol. B (Quebec: A. Côté and Duvernay Brothers 1856), li–89i (per Badgley J.).

97 See Badgley, *Register Offices* (see note 67 above); Registration Ordinance
(see note 6 above). *Register Offices* was mostly a compilation of earlier
newspaper articles by Badgley.

98 See Gibbs, *Debates*, vol. 6, 864; vol. 11, 1762, 1772, 1762; 12 Vict. (1849), c.48
(Can.); 14–15 Vict. (1851), c.93 (Can.).

99 See Gibbs, *Debates*, vol. 9, 126; vol. 11, 3019–20. See also 12 Vict. (1849), c.64
(Can.); 16 Vict. (1853), c.119 (Can.).

100 See generally, J.C., 'De la publicité des Hypothèques dans le Bas-Canada,'
Revue de législation et de jurisprudence 3 (1847), 24; L.R. Lacoste, 'Dissertation de quelques questions sur la section 36ième de l'Ordinance de 1841
sur l'enregistrement,' *Revue de législation et de jurisprudence* 3 (1847), 121; J.
Bonner, *An Essay on the Registry Laws of Lower Canada* (Quebec: John Lovell
1852), 38–138.

101 See, for example, *Delisle v. Richard et Richard* (1856), 6 LCR 37, 38 (*per
curiam*) (S.Ct.); *Morrin et al. v. Daly et al. and Dérousselle* (1857), 7 LCR 119,
120–3 (per Meredith, J. for the court) (S.Ct.); *The Queen v. Comte et al.*
(1857), 2 LCJ 86, 87–9 (per Meredith, J. for the court) (C.A.); *Hillier v. Bentley and Primrose et al.* (1857), 7 LCR 241, 243–4 (per Badgley, J.) (S.Ct.); *Mon-
tizambert v. Talbot dit Gervais* (1860), 10 LCR 269, 275–6 (per Badgley, J.)
(C.A.); *Morland v. Dorion et Sauvé et ux* (1860), 5 LCJ 154 (per Badgley, J.)
(S.Ct.); *Sicotte v. Bourdon* (1864), 15 LCR 40, 41–3 (per Meredith and Mondelet, JJ. for the court) (C.A.); *Desjardins v. Prevost* (1864), 15 LCR 132, 133–
4 (per Badgley, J.) (S.Ct.); *McConnell v. Dixon and Brown and Nivin et al. and
Brown* (1866), 10 LCJ 140 (*per curiam*) (C.A.); *Macdonald et al. v. Nolin* (1869),
14 LCJ 125 (*per curiam*) (C.A.).

102 See, for example, 10–11 Vict. (1847), c.100 (Can.); 14–15 Vic. (1851), c.36
(Can.); 16 Vict. (1853), c.238 (Can.).

103 See, for example, 14 Geo. 3 (1774), c.83 (UK), s.10; 41 Geo. 3 (1801), c.4 (LC).

104 See Gibbs, *Debates*, vol. 9, 901; vol. 10, 838; 14–15 Vict. (1851), c.6 (Can.).

105 See Gibbs, *Debates*, vol. 8, 12, 14, 49, 938; vol. 9, 385, 1332; vol. 10, 476, 672;
vol. 11, 254. See also 13–14 Vict. (1850), c.19 (Can.); 16 Vict. (1853), c.198
(Can.). Compare F.K. Juenger, 'David Dudley Field's Contribution to the
Conflict of Laws,' in J. Erauw, ed., *Liber Memoriales François Laurent, 1810–
1887* (Bruxelles: E. Story-Scientia 1989), 837.

106 See, for example, J.E.C. Brierley, 'Arbitrage conventionnel au Canada et
spécialement dans le droit privé de la province de Québec' (PhD diss.,
Université de Paris 1964), 38–67; Baker, 'Law Practice and Statecraft ...,'
58–60.

107 See, for example, Gibbs, *Debates*, vol. 6, 551; vol. 8, 414, 1007; vol. 10, 480;
vol. 11, 743.

108 See generally, Desjardins, 'Francis Badgley,' 57; R. D. Gidney and W.P.J. Millar, *Professional Gentlemen: The Professions in Nineteenth-Century Ontario* (Toronto: University of Toronto Press 1994), 85–105, 152–79; L.-D. Mignault, 'Histoire de l'École de Médecine et de Chirurgie de Montréal,' *L'Union Médicine du Canada* 55 (1926), 597.

109 See Gibbs, *Debates*, vol. 10, 418, 660, 694, 1333; vol. 6, 329, 715, 1099; vol. 8, 558, 2312; vol. 9, 1414; vol. 11, 1887–8; 14–15 Vict. (1851), c.154 (Can.); 10–11 Vict. (1847), c.26 (Can.); 12 Vict. (1849), c.47 (Can.); 12 Vict. (1849), c.46 (Can.).

110 See, for example, Gibbs, *Debates*, vol. 8, 933, 1376; vol. 10, 764, 920, 956–7; 14–15 Vict. (1851), c.44 (Can.); 12 Vict. (1849), c.195 (Can.).

111 See Gibbs, *Debates*, vol. 6, 406, 478, 497; vol. 9, 1590; vol. 10, 938; 10–11 Vict. (1847), c.57 (Can.); 16 Vict. (1853), c.130 (Can.).

112 Gibbs, *Debates*, vol. 10, 1462. See also vol. 11, 504–6, 3279.

113 Ibid., vol. 11, 504–6; [Badgley], *Account of the Endowments* (note 67 above). See also Gibbs, *Debates*, vol. 8, 558, where Badgley introduced a bill to incorporate the 'Presbyterian Church in Canada.'

114 Compare R.W. Vaudry, *Anglicans and the Atlantic World: High Churchmen, Evangelicals, and the Quebec Connection* (Montreal: McGill-Queen's University Press 2003), 13–38, 97–133; W. Westfall, 'The Doctrine of Expediency: Lord Durham's Report and the Alliance of Church and State,' *Journal of Canadian Studies* 25, no. 1 (1990), 192.

115 For petitions, see, for example, Gibbs, *Debates*, vol. 6, 323 (Clarenceville Academy), 594 (Dunham High School); vol. 11, 250 (Saint Lawrence School of Medicine), 652, 1974 (National School Society of Montreal); and sources cited in note 109 (McGill College). For school-law amendments, see Gibbs, *Debates*, vol. 6, 540, 629, 688. See also 12 Vict. (1849), c.50 (Can.).

116 See 19 Vict. (1856), c.14 (Can.); 19 Vict. (1856), c..64 (Can.). For a good study of analogous developments in the western part of the province that is sensitive to the utilitarian dimensions of what United Canada's legislature was doing, compare B. Curtis, *Building the Educational State: Canada West, 1836–1871* (London: Althouse Press 1988).

117 See McCord-Badgley, box 1, folder 7; NAC Pilot 1–6-1844; D.C. Masters, *Bishop's University: The First Hundred Years* (Toronto: Clarke, Irwin 1950), 41–2.

118 See generally, C. Miller, 'Sir John Joseph Caldwell Abbott,' *DCB*, vol. 12, 4; Mitchell and Slinn, *The History of McMaster, Meighen*, 17–29; Frost, 'The Early Days of Law Teaching at McGill'; S. Normand, 'Profil des périodiques juridiques québécois au XIXe siècle,' *Cahiers de droit* 34 (1993), 161, 171.

119 See M. Nantel, 'Les avocats admis au barreau de 1849 à 1868,' *Bulletin des recherches historique* 41 (1935), 685.

120 See generally, J.K. Johnson, 'John A. Macdonald: The Young Non-Politician,' *Historical Papers* [Canadian Historical Association] 6 (1971), 138–53; H.J. Bridgman, 'William Morris,' *DCB*, vol. 8, 638; J. Friesen, 'Alexander Morris,' *DCB*, vol. 11, 608.

121 See 'Factums of Appeal Cases in the Queen's Bench – Badgley and Abbott' (1858–61), in McGill Arch., MG 4166, container 14, file 00100; *Carignan v. The Harbour Commissioners of Montreal* (1855), 5 LCR 479 (S.Ct.); *Ex Parte Rudolph and the Harbour Commissioners of Montreal* (1856), 1 LCJ 47 (S.Ct.); *City Bank v. Harbour Commissioners of Montreal* (1857), 1 LCJ 288 (S.Ct.); *McGillivray v. Montreal Assurance Company* (1855), 5 LCR 406 (C.A.); *Montreal Assurance Company v. McGillivray* (1858), 8 LCR 401 (C.A.); *McTavish v. Pyke et al.* (1853), 3 LCR 101 (C.A.); *Molson v. Renaud et al.* (1851), 1 LCR 495 (C.A.).

122 See *Doutre v. Montreal and Bytown Railway Company* (1854), 5 LCR 98 (S.Ct.); *L.T. Drummond A.-G. v. Municipality of the County of Two Mountains and the Montreal and Bytown Railway Company* (1855), 5 LCR 155 (S.Ct.). See generally, Mitchell and Slinn, *The History of McMaster, Meighen*, 17–29; P.P. Hutchison, 'Sir John J.C. Abbott: Barrister and Solicitor,' *Canadian Bar Review* 26 (1948), 934.

123 See, for example, *Saint Lawrence and Ottawa Grand Junction Railway Company v. Frothingham* (1855), 5 LCR 140 (S.Ct.); *Frothingham v. Gilbert* (1858), 3 LCJ 136 (C.A.); *Frothingham et al. v. Brockville and Ottawa Railroad Company and Dickinson* (1859), 9 LCR 345 (S.Ct.); *Prevost v. De Lesderniers and Frothingham* (1859), 3 LCJ 165 (S.Ct.).

124 See, for example, Gibbs, *Debates*, vol. 6, 594 (Ross Cuthbert); vol. 8, 2266 (John Munn); vol. 10, 256 (George Moffatt), 335, 480 (Mutual Fire Insurance Company of Missisquoi and Rouville), 518 (Montreal and Lachine Railroad Company), 597 (Montreal and Vermont Junction Railroad Company), 1497 (William Berczy); vol. 11, 12, 1666 (Champlain and Saint Lawrence Railroad Company), 175 (Montreal and Kingston Railway Company), 1650 (Montreal Manufacturing Company), 2201 (Bartholomew Gugy), 2846 (Montreal and New York Railroad Company).

125 Compare 12 Vict. (1849), c.56 (Can.); 13–14 Vict. (1850), c.28 (Can.); 16 Vict. (1852), c.10 (Can.); 16 Vict. (1853), c.124 (Can.); 16 Vict. (1853), c.173 (Can.). See generally, R.C.B. Risk, 'The Nineteenth-Century Foundations of the Business Corporation in Ontario,' *University of Toronto Law Journal* 23 (1973), 270.

126 See, for example, 13–14 Vict. (1850), c.21 (Can.); 14–15 Vict. (1851), c.47 (Can.); 16 Vict. (1853), c.158 (Can.).

127 See *By the King, a proclamation* (London: Mark Baskett 1763); 40 Geo. III
     (1800), c.1 (UC). The classic institutional treatments of those reception
     issues are Morel, 'La réception du droit ...,' and E.G. Brown, 'British Stat-
     utes in the Emergent Nations of North America: 1606–1949,' *American
     Journal of Legal History* 7 (1963), 95.

128 See generally, P. King, *Crime and Law in England, 1750–1840: Remaking Jus-
     tice from the Margins* (Cambridge: Cambridge University Press 2006); J.M.
     Beattie, *Crime and the Courts in England 1660–1800* (Princeton, NJ: Prince-
     ton University Press 1986); L. Radzinowicz, *A History of English Criminal
     Law and its Administration from 1750*, vol. 1 (New York: MacMillan 1948),
     3–493.

129 See 3 Wm. 4 (1833), c.3 (UC); 4–5 Vict. (1841), c.24 (Can.); 4–5 Vict. (1841),
     c.25 (Can.); 4–5 Vict. (1841), c.26 (Can.). See generally, J.D. Blackwell,
     'Crime in the London District, 1828–1837: A Case Study of the Effect of the
     1833 Reform in Upper Canadian Penal Law,' *Queen's Law Journal* 6 (1981),
     528.

130 See, for example, Province of Canada, *The Criminal Statutes of Canada, with
     Notes, and a Copious Index* (Kingston: Derbyshire and Desbarats 1843); J.
     Cremazie, *Les lois criminelles anglaises, traduites et compilées de Blackstone,
     Chitty, Russell et autres criminalistes anglais, et telles que suivies au Canada*
     (Quebec: Fréchette 1842); I. Lewis, *A Class Book, for the Use of Common
     Schools and Families, in the United Canadas, entitled the Youth's Guard Against
     Crime, having embodied in it all the criminal laws of the land* (Kingston: Robert
     R. Smiley 1844); W.C. Keele, *The Provincial Justice, or Magistrate's Manual*
     (Toronto: Upper Canada Gazette 1835); H. Taylor, *Manual of the Office,
     Duties and Liabilities of a Justice of the Peace* (Montreal: Armour and Ramsay
     1843).

131 Discussion of influential imperial reforms, from a variety of interpretive
     perspectives, can be found in R.R. Follett, *Evangelism, Penal Theory, and the
     Politics of Criminal Law Reform in England, 1800–1830* (New York: Palgrave
     2001); K.J.M. Smith, *Lawyers, Legislators and Theorists: Developments in
     English Criminal Jurisprudence, 1800–1957* (Oxford: Clarendon Press 1998),
     55–172; J. Hostettler, *The Politics of Criminal Law: Reform in the Nineteenth
     Century* (Chichester, UK: Barry Rose Law Publishers 1992).

132 See D. Fyson, *Magistrates, Police, and People: Everyday Criminal Justice in
     Quebec and Lower Canada, 1764–1837* (Toronto: University of Toronto Press
     2006), 184–309; D. Hay, 'Legislation, Magistrates and Judges: High Law
     and Low Law in England and the Empire,' in D. Lemmings, ed., *The Brit-
     ish and their Laws in the Eighteenth Century* (Woodbridge, UK: Boydell Press
     2005), 65; L.A. Knafla and T.L. Chapman, 'Criminal Justice in Canada: A

Comparative Study of the Maritimes and Lower Canada, 1760–1812,' *Osgoode Hall Law Journal* 21 (1983), 245.

133 Compare C.M. Wallace, 'Lemuel Allan Wilmot,' *DCB*, vol. 10, 709; J. Phillips, 'The Reform of Nova Scotia's Criminal Law, 1830–41,' in *Proceedings, Canadian Law in History Conference 1987*, vol. 3 (Ottawa: Carleton University 1987), 480; Cook, *The American Codification Movement*, 171–81, 131–53. See also K. Preyer, 'Crime, the Criminal Law and Reform in Post-Revolutionary Virginia,' *Law and History Review* 1 (1983), 53; J.E. O'Connor, 'Legal Reform in the Early Republic: The New Jersey Experience,' *American Journal of Legal History* 22 (1978), 95, 99–109.

134 See generally, J.A. Hostettler, 'The Curious Affair of Lord Cranworth and the Criminal Law Reform in 1853–4,' *Anglo-American Law Review* 13 (1984), 1; R. Cross, 'The Reports of the Criminal Law Commissioners (1833–1848) and the Abortive Bills of 1853,' in P.R. Glazebrook, ed., *Reshaping the Criminal Law: Essays in Honour of Glanville Williams* (London: Stevens and Sons 1978), 5.

135 See Gibbs, *Debates*, vol. 9, 1141.

136 See, for example, 'Editorial,' *Canada Law Journal* 10 (1874), 269; 'Current Events-England,' *Legal News* 1 (1878), 430; 'The English Criminal Code,' *Legal News* 2 (1879), 13; J.B. Perkins, 'The Proposed Criminal Code of England,' *Legal News* 2 (1879), 19, 27 [reprinted from *American Law Review* 12 (1878)]; T.J.J. Loranger, 'Codification des lois criminelles,' *La Thémis* 1 (1879), 269; J.F. Stephen, 'A Sketch of the Criminal Law,' *Legal News* 5 (1882), 209, 219, 225, 230 [reprinted from *Nineteenth Century* 7 (1880), 136]; B.-A.T. de Montigny, 'La codification des lois fédérales,' *La Thémis* 4 (1882), 317; Anon., 'The Consolidation of Statutes,' *Canadian Law Times* 4 (1884), 432.

137 See 55–56 Vict. (1892), c.29 (Can.). See generally, Parker, 'The Origins of the Canadian Criminal Code,' esp. 257–76; Brown, *The Genesis of the Canadian Criminal Code of 1892*, 119–48.

138 S.H. Kadish, 'Codifiers of the Criminal Law: Wechsler's Predecessors,' *Columbia Law Review* 78 (1978), 1098. Compare E. Kolsky, 'Codification and the Rule of Colonial Difference: Criminal Procedure in British India,' *Law and History Review* 23 (2005), 631; K.J.M. Smith, *James Fitzjames Stephen: Portrait of a Victorian Rationalist* (Cambridge: Cambridge University Press 1988), 73–159; G.J. Postema, *Bentham and the Common Law Tradition* (Oxford: Clarendon Press 1986), 264–6, 175–83, 403–52.

139 J.F. Stephen, *History of the Criminal Law of England*, vol. 3 (London: MacMillan 1883), 304.

140 See generally, D.R. Murray, *Colonial Justice : Justice, Morality, and Crime in*

the Niagara District, 1791–1849 (Toronto: University of Toronto Press 2002), 131–216; J.C. Weaver, *Crimes, Constables and Courts: Order and Transgression in a Canadian City, 1816–1970* (Montreal: McGill-Queen's University Press 1995), 23–107; J.-M. Fecteau, *Un nouvel ordre des choses: la pauvreté, le crime, et l'État au Québec, de la fin du XVIIIe siècle à 1840* (Outremont, QC: VLB 1989).

141 See generally, B. Palmer, 'Discordant Music: Charivaris and Whitecapping in Nineteenth-Century North America,' *Labour/Le Travail* 3 (1978), 5; L. Johnson, 'The Gore District Outrages, 1826–1829: A Case Study of Violence, Justice, and Political Propaganda,' *Ontario History* 83 (1991), 109; R. Hardy, 'Le charivari dans la sociabilité rurale québécoise au XIXe siècle,' in R. Levasseur, ed., *De la sociabilité: spécificité et mutations* (Montreal: Boréal 1990), 59.

142 See generally, J. Burgess, 'L'industrie de la chaussure à Montréal, 1840–1870 : Le passage de l'artisanat à la fabrique,' *Revue d'historique de l'Amérique française* 31 (1977), 187; R. Boily, *Les Irlandais et le canal Lachine: la grève de 1843* (Montreal: Leméac 1980); R. Tremblay, 'La grève des ouvriers de la construction navale à Québec (1840),' *Labour/Le Travail* 9 (1983), 243.

143 See generally, M.S. Cross, 'The Shiners' War: Social Violence in the Ottawa Valley in the 1830s,' *Canadian Historical Review* 53 (1973), 1; R. Bleasdale, 'Class Conflict on the Canals of Upper Canada in the 1840s,' *Labour/Le Travail* 7 (1981), 9; J.K. Johnson, 'Colonel James Fitzgibbon and the Suppression of Irish Riots in Upper Canada,' *Ontario History* 58 (1966), 139.

144 See generally, A. Baccigalupo, 'Histoire des administrations municipales québécoises,' in M.J. Palaez, ed., *Papers in Public Law, Public Legal History, Natural Law, and Political Thought* (Barcelona: Catédra de Historia del Derecho y de las Instituciones 1992), 157; J.I. Little, 'Colonization and Municipal Reform in Canada East,' *Histoire Sociale/Social History* 14 (1981), 93; J. L'Heureux, 'Les premières institutions municipales au Québec ou machines à taxer,' *Cahiers de droit* 20 (1979), 331.

145 See generally, M.S. Cross, 'The Laws are Like Cobwebs: Popular Resistance to Authority in Mid-Nineteenth-Century British North America,' *Dalhousie Law Journal* 8 (1984), 103; S. Kenny, 'Cahots and Catcalls: An Episode of Popular Resistance in Lower Canada at the Outset of the Union,' *Canadian Historical Review* 65 (1984), 184; M.S. Cross, 'Violence and Authority: The Case of Bytown,' in D.J. Bercuson and L.A. Knafla, eds., *Law and Society in Canada in Historical Perspective* (Calgary: University of CalgaryPress 1979), 5.

146 See, for example, B.D. Boisery, *A Deep Sense of Wrong: The Treason Trials*

and Transportation to New South Wales of Lower Canadian Rebels after the
1838 Rebellion (Toronto: Dundurn Press 1995), 47–158; F.M. Greenwood
and B. Wright, eds., Canadian State Trials, vol. 2, Rebellion and Invasion in the
Canadas, 1837–1839 (Toronto: University of Toronto Press 2002), 41–159;
F.M. Greenwood and B. Wright, eds., Canadian State Trials, vol. 1, Law, Politics, and Security Measures, 1608–1837 (Toronto: University of Toronto
Press 1996), 323–521.

147 But see I.C. Pilarczyk, 'Justice in the Premises: Family Violence and the
Law in Montreal, 1825–1850' (DCL diss., McGill University 2003); M.-A.
Poutanen, 'Reflection of Montreal Prostitution in the Records of the Lower
Courts, 1810–1842,' in D. Fyson, C.M. Coates, and K. Harvey, eds., Class,
Gender, and the Law in Eighteenth- and Nineteenth-Century Quebec: Sources
and Perspectives (Montreal: Montreal History Group 1993), 99; J. Weaver,
'Crime, Public Order, and Repression: The Gore District in Upheaval,
1832–1851,' Ontario History 78 (1986), 198.

148 But see P.J. Brode, 'Grand Jury Addresses of the Early Canadian Judges in
an Age of Reform,' Law Society Upper Canada Gazette 23 (1989), 130; D.J.
McMahon, 'Law and Public Authority: Sir John Beverley Robinson and
the Purposes of the Criminal Law,' University Toronto Faculty of Law Review
46 (1988), 390; J.M. Beattie, Attitudes Towards Crime and Punishment in
Upper Canada, 1830–1850: A Documentary Study (Toronto: University of
Toronto Press 1977), 1–35.

149 See, for example, J.D. Phillips, 'Educated to Crime: Community and Crim-
inal Justice in Upper Canada, 1800–1840' (PhD diss., University of Toronto
2004); A. Morel, 'Les crimes et les peines: évolution des mentalités au
Québec au 19ième siècle,' Revue de Droit de Sherbrooke 8 (1978), 385; S.
Houston, 'The Impetus to Reform: Urban Crime, Poverty and Ignorance in
Ontario, 1850–1875' (PhD diss., University of Toronto 1974).

150 For prisons, see, for example, P.N. Oliver, Terror to Evil-Doers: Prisons and
Punishments in Nineteenth-Century Ontario (Toronto: University of Toronto
Press 1998), 139–316; J. Laplante, Prison et ordre social au Québec (Ottawa:
Presses de l'Université d'Ottawa 1989); C.J. Taylor, 'The Kingston, Ontario
Penitentiary and Moral Architecture,' Histoire Sociale/Social History 12
(1979), 385. For police forces, see, for example, M. McCulloch, 'Most
Assuredly Perpetual Motion: Police and Policing in Quebec City, 1838–
1858,' Urban History Review 19 (1990), 100; E.K. Senior, 'The Influence of
the British Garrison on the Development of the Montreal Police, 1832 to
1853,' Military Applications 43 (1979), 63; H. Boritch, 'Conflict, Compromise
and Administrative Convenience: The Police Organization in Nineteenth-
Century Toronto,' Canadian Journal of Law and Society 3 (1988), 141.

151 Compare J. Phillips, 'Crime and Punishment in the Dominion of the North: Canada from New France to the Present,' in C. Emsley and L.A. Knafla, eds., *Crime History and Histories of Crime* (Westport, CT: Greenwood Press 1996), 163; R.C. Smandych et al., eds., *Canadian Criminal Justice History: An Annotated Bibliography* (Toronto: University of Toronto Press 1987); V. Masciotra, 'Quebec Legal Historiography, 1760–1900,' *McGill Law Journal* 32 (1987), 712, esp. 719–24.

152 Reported in Brierley, 'Quebec's Civil Law Codification Viewed and Reviewed,' 554–5. See also M.A. Banks, 'An Annotated Bibliography of Statutes and Related Publications: Upper Canada, the Province of Canada, and Ontario, 1792–1980,' in Flaherty, ed., *Essays in the History of Canadian Law*, vol. 1, 358, 377–9; A.H. Manchester, 'Simplifying the Sources of the Law: An Essay in Law Reform – I Lord Cranworth's Attempt to Consolidate the Statute Law of England and Wales,' *Anglo-American Law Review* 2 (1973), 395.

153 Compare J.-L. Halperin, *The French Civil Code*, trans. T. Weir (New York: University College of London Press 2006), 1–15, 53–80, 88–95; G. Birtsch, 'Reform Absolutism and the Codification of Law: The Genesis and Nature of the Prussian General Code (1794),' in J. Brewer and E. Hellmuth, eds., *Rethinking Leviathan: The Eighteenth Century State in Britain and Germany* (Oxford: Oxford University Press 1999), 343; H.E. Strakosch, *State Absolutism and the Rule of Law: The Struggle for the Codification of Civil Law in Austria, 1753–1811* (Sydney: Sydney University Press 1967), 50–215. On the issue of local legal perceptions of European controversy, see generally E. Kolish, *Nationalismes et conflits de droits: le débat de droit privé au Québec, 1760–1840* (Lasalle, QC: Hurtubise HMH 1994); M. Morin, 'La perception de l'ancien droit et du nouveau droit français au Bas-Canada, 1774–1866,' in H.P. Glenn, ed., *Droit québécois et droit français: communauté, autonomie, concordance* (Cowansville, QC: Yvon Blais 1993), 1; F.M. Greenwood, *Legacies of Fear: Law and Politics in Quebec in the Era of the French Revolution* (Toronto: Osgoode Society 1993), 56–138, 193–212.

154 See J. Bentham, 'A General View of a Complete Code of Laws,' in J. Bowring, ed., *The Works of Jeremy Bentham*, vol. 3 (Edinburgh: W. Tait 1843). See also J. Humphreys, *Observations on the Actual State of the English Laws of Real Property with Outlines of a Code* (London: J. Murray 1826); Lord Brougham, 'Speech on the Present State of the Law,' in *Brougham's Speeches*,' vol. 2 (Edinburgh: n.p. 1838), 319; [J. Story], 'Law, Legislation and Codes,' in F. Lieber, ed., *Encyclopedia Americana*, vol. 7 (Philadelphia: Carey, Lea and Carey 1830–33), 581.

155 Compare B. Shapiro, 'Sir Francis Bacon and the Mid-Seventeenth-Century

Movement for Law Reform,' *American Journal Legal History* 24 (1980), 331; L.M. Friedman, 'Law Reform in Historical Perspective,' *St. Louis Law Journal* 13 (1969), 351; G.B. Nourse, 'Law Reform Under the Commonwealth and Protectorate,' *Law Quarterly Review* 75 (1959), 512.

156 Compare M.D. Cahn, 'Punishment, Discretion, and the Codification of Prescribed Penalties in Colonial Massachusetts,' *American Journal of Legal History* 33 (1989), 107; B. Shapiro, 'Codification of the Laws in Seventeenth-Century England,' *Wisconsin Law Review* [1974], 428; G.L. Haskins, 'Codification of the Law in Colonial Massachusetts: A Study in Comparative Law,' *Indiana Law Journal* 30 (1954), 1.

157 See generally, R. Berkowitz, *The Gift of Science: Leibniz and the Modern Legal Tradition* (Cambridge: Harvard University Press 2005), 109–36; H. Schweber, 'The Science of Legal Science: The Model of the Natural Sciences in Nineteenth Century American Legal Education,' *Law and History Review* 17 (1999), 421; M. Reimann, 'Nineteenth-Century German Legal Science,' *Boston College Law Review* 31 (1990), 837.

158 See generally, R.A. Jarrell, 'The Social Functions of the Scientific Society in Nineteenth-Century Canada,' in R.A. Jarrell and A.E. Roos, eds., *Critical Issues in the History of Canadian Science, Technology, and Medicine* (Thornhill, ON: HSTC 1983), 31; S.B. Frost, 'The Natural History Society of Montreal, 1827–1925,' *McGill Journal of Education* 17 (1982), 31; J.J. Talman, 'Agricultural Societies in Upper Canada,' *Ontario Historical Society Papers and Records* 27 (1931), 545. Compare S.J.M.M. Alberti, 'Placing Nature: Natural History Collections and Their Owners in Nineteenth-Century Provincial England,' *British Society for the History of Science* 35 (2002), 309; C. Rosenberg, 'Science and Social Values in Nineteenth-Century America: A Case Study in the Growth of Scientific Institutions,' in C. Rosenberg, ed., *No Other Gods: On Science and American Social Thought* (Baltimore: Johns Hopkins University Press 1997), 135; R.M. MacLeod, 'The X Club: A Social Network of Science in Late-Victorian England,' *Notes and Records of the Royal Society of London* 24 (1970), 305.

159 See, for example, Doucet, *Fundamental Principles of the Laws of Canada*, vol. 2, 1; S.R. Clarke, *A Treatise on Criminal Law as Applicable to the Dominion of Canada* (Toronto: R. Carswell 1872), v; B.A.T. de Montigny, 'Le code criminel en quelques pages,' *La Themis* 1 (1879), 132.

160 See, for example, Chamber of the Association of the Bar, *Report on the State of the Administration of Justice* (Montreal: Louis Perrault, 1842); J.H. Cameron, 'Law Reform,' *Upper Canada Jurist* 1 (1844), 16; [Cartier], 'De la codification des lois du Canada,' 79; G.-E. Cartier, 'Discours sur la codification prononcé le 27 avril 1857 à l'Assemblée législative,' in J. Tasse, ed., *Dis-*

cours de Sir George Cartier, Baronnet accompagnés de notices (Montreal: Eusèbe Senécal et Fils 1893), 129; Ardagh and Harrison, 'Codification of the Laws of New York,' W.D. Ardagh and R.A. Harrison, 'Historical Sketch of the Constitution, Law and Legal Tribunals of Canada,' *Upper Canada Law Journal* 4 (1858), 108; W.D. Ardagh and R.A. Harrison, 'The Work of Legislation,' *Upper Canada Law Journal* 4 (1858), 123; P.C. Van Brocklin, *Proposed Commercial Law* (Toronto: P.C. Van Brocklin 1859); T.J.J. Loranger, 'Le Droit civil du Bas Canada suivant l'ordre du Code,' *Revue Légale* 1 (1860), 1; W.D. Ardagh and R.A. Harrison, 'Codification and Consolidation,' *Upper Canada Law Journal* 6 (1860), 220; Anon., 'Codification of Law in America,' *Upper Canada Law Journal* 6 (1860), 223; F.-M. Bibaud, 'Observations sur le projet de code canadien,' in F.-M. Bibaud, ed., *Exégèse et jurisprudence* (Montreal: F.-M. Bibaud c.1861); T.W. Ritchie, *Some Remarks on the Title 'Of Obligations' as Reported by the Commissioners* (Montreal: J. Lovell 1863); Note, 'The State of English Law: Codification,' *Lower Canada Law Journal* 1 (1865), 17; J. Kirby, 'The Code of Civil Procedure,' *Lower Canada Law Journal* 2 (1866), 25; J. Kirby, 'Proem to Volume the Third,' *Lower Canada Law Journal* 3 (1867), 1; T. McCord, *Civil Code of Lower Canada* (Montreal: Dawson 1867), esp. 1–2.

161 See, for example, C. Warren, *A History of the American Bar* (Boston: Little, Brown 1911), 508–39; R. Pound, *The Formative Era of American Law* (Boston: Little, Brown 1938), 38–80; Cook, *The American Codification Movement*, 17.

162 See R.W. Gordon, 'Book Review,' *Vanderbilt Law Review* 36 (1983), 431; A.J. King, 'Book Review,' *Maryland Law Review* 41 (1982), 329; Miller, *The Life of the Mind in America* ... 239–65.

163 Compare R. Crête, S. Normand, and T. Copeland, 'Law Reporting in Nineteenth-Century Quebec,' *Journal of Legal History* 16 (1995), 147; P. Girard, 'Themes and Variations in Early Canadian Legal Culture: Beamish Murdock and His *Epitome of the Laws of Nova Scotia*,' *Law and History Review* 11 (1993), 101; Normand, 'Profil des périodiques ...,' 118; G.B. Baker, 'The Reconstitution of Upper Canadian Legal Thought in the Late-Victorian Empire,' *Law and History Review* 3 (1985), 219, 223–70; S. Normand, 'Une Analyse quantitative de la doctrine en droit civil québécois,' *Cahiers de droit* 23 (1982), 1009.

164 Compare J. Davies, 'Aspects of Nineteent-Century Legal Literature,' *Cambrian Law Review* 29 (1998), 22; R.A. Macdonald, 'Understanding Civil Law Scholarship in Quebec,' *Osgoode Hall Law Journal* 23 (1985), 573, esp. 577–99; A.W.B. Simpson, 'The Rise and Fall of the Legal Treatise: Legal Principles and the Forms of Legal Literature,' *University of Chicago Law Review* 48 (1981), 632.

165 For historiographic, rather than historical, development of that theme, compare B. Young, 'Overlapping Identities: The Quebec Civil Code of 1866, Its Reception and Interpretation,' in R. Beauthier and I. Rorive, eds., *Le Code Napoléon, un ancêtre vénéré? Mélanges offerts à Jacques Vanderlinden* (Bruxelles: Bruylant 2004), 259; J.-G. Belley, 'Une croisade intégriste chez les avocats du Québec: *La Revue du droit* (1922–1939),' *Cahiers de droit* 34 (1993), 183; S. Normand, 'Un thème dominant de la pensée juridique tradi- tionnelle au Québec: la sauvegarde de l'intégrité du droit civil,' *McGill Law Journal* 22 (1987), 557. For discussion of late-nineteenth and early- twentieth-century nativism at-large, see generally, J. Higham, *Strangers in the Land: Patterns of American Nativism, 1860–1925* (New York: Athenium 1981); C. Berger, *The Sense of Power: Studies in the Ideas of Canadian Imperial- ism, 1867–1914* (Toronto: University of Toronto Press 1970).

166 The leading texts were J. Bentham, *An Introduction to the Principles of Mor- als and Legislation, Principles of the Civil Code, Principles of the Penal Law* (London: W. Pickering 1789) and C. Beccaria, *An Essay on Crimes and Pun- ishment*, trans. E.D. Ingraham (Philadelphia: Philip H. Nicklin 1819).

167 See *Catalogue de la bibliothèque de feu Sir L.-H. LaFontaine* (Montreal: Eusèbe Senécal 1864); *Catalogue of the Library of the Late Hon. Sir James Stuart, Bart., Chief Justice of Lower Canada* (Quebec: Lovell and Lamoureux 1854); *Cata- logue of the Advocates' Library* (Montreal: J. Lovell 1857).

168 See generally, M.H. Hoeflich, 'Translation and Reception of Foreign Law in the Antebellum United States,' *American Journal of Comparative Law* 50 (2002), 753, 769, 771; J. Parrish, 'Law Books and Legal Publishing in Amer- ica, 1760–1840,' *Law Library Journal* 72 (1979), 374–6.

169 See generally, M.T. Maestro, *Cesare Beccaria and the Origins of Penal Reform* (Philadelphia: Temple University Press 1973), 34–45, 125–43; G.M. Beck- man, 'Three Penal Codes Compared,' *American Journal of Legal History* 10 (1966), 148; J. Heath, *Eighteenth-Century Penal Theory* (London: Oxford University Press 1963), 109–40.

170 Compare Livingston, *A System of Penal Law for the State of Louisiana*; G. Roberts, 'Edward Livingston and American Penology,' *Louisiana Law Review* 37 (1976), 1037. See also G.M. Lyons, 'European Response to Edward Livingston's System of Criminal Law,' *Loyola Law Review* 24 (1978), 621.

171 McGill University has two copies of Livingston's *A System of Penal Law for the State of Louisiana*, and one of E. Livingston, *The Complete Works of Edward Livingston on Criminal Jurisprudence; Consisting of Systems of Penal Law for the State of Louisiana and for the United States of America* (New York: National Prison Association of the United States 1873). One of those books

was formerly owned by co-premier LaFontaine, another by mid-nine-teenth-century Montreal lawyer Robert MacKay, and the third by McGill College.

172 See E. Livingston, *Code de réforme et de discipline formant la troisième partie du système de lois pénales préparé pour l'état de la Louisiane* (Quebec: T. Cary 1831); E. Livingston, *Rapport pour servir d'introduction au code de réforme et de discipline des prisons* (Quebec: T. Cary 1831).

173 See J. Bentham, 'Specimen of a Penal Code,' in Bowring, ed., *The Works of Jeremy Bentham*, vol. 1, 164. See also Bentham, *An Introduction* ...; J. Bentham, 'Leading Principles of a Constitutional Code,' in Bowring, ed., *The Works of Jeremy Bentham*, vol. 2, 267.

174 See, for example, J. Bentham, *Codification Proposal Addressed to all Nations Professing Liberal Opinions* (London: Heward, 1830); J. Bentham, 'Papers Relative to Codification and Public Instruction,' in Bowring, ed., *The Works of Jeremy Bentham*, vol. 4, 453, 468, 476, 507, 514. See generally, P.J. King, *Utilitarian Jurisprudence in America: The Influence of Bentham and Austin on American Legal Thought in the Nineteenth Century* (New York: Garland Publishing 1986), 61–336; G.M. Hezel, 'The Influence of Bentham's Philosophy of Law on the Early-Nineteenth Century Codification Movement in the United States,' *Buffalo Law Review* 22 (1972), 239.

175 See generally, M. Franklin, 'Concerning the Historic Importance of Edward Livingston,' *Tulane Law Review* 11 (1937), 163; A.L. Moore, 'William Curtis Noyes,' in D. Malone, ed., *Dictionary of American Biography*, vol. 13 (New York: Scribner 1943), 592; P. Kens, *Justice Stephen Field: Shaping Liberty from the Gold Rush to the Guilded Age* (Kansas: University Press of Kansas 1997); W.B. McCash, 'Thomas Cobb and the Codification of Georgia Law,' *Georgia Historical Quarterly* 62 (1978), 9; M. Bloomfield, 'William Sampson and the Codifiers: The Roots of American Legal Reform, 1820–1830,' *American Journal of Legal History* 11 (1967), 234; W.B. Fisch, 'The Dakota Civil Code,' *North Dakota Law Review* 43 (1967), 485; J.S. Goff, 'William T. Howell and the Howell Code of Arizona,' *American Journal of Legal History* 11 (1967), 221.

176 See generally, Schofield, *Utility and Democracy*, 250–303; L.J. Hume, *Bentham and Bureaucracy* (Cambridge: Cambridge University Press 1981), 55–86, 209–37; N.L. Rosenblum, *Bentham's Theory of the Modern State* (Cambridge, MA: Harvard University Press 1978).

177 See 'Benenaiah Gibb, Ledger E., Judge Badgley' (1852–64), in McCord Museum of Canadian History Archives (Montreal) – Gibb papers, M700, 319; 'W.H. Arnton Account of Sales of Household Furniture and Effects' (6 April 1889), in McCord-Badgley, box 2, folder 16; Mackay, *The Montreal*

Directory; R.W.S. MacKay, *The Montreal Directory* (Montreal: Lovell and Gibson 1849), 19–20; McCord-McCord, 23 September 1852 (see note 22 above); 'Col. William Francis Badgley,' in H.J. Morgan, ed., *The Canadian Men and Women of the Time: A Hand-book of Canadian Biography* (Toronto: William Biggs 1898), 39.

178 Compare Girard, 'Themes and Variations in Early Canadian Legal Culture,' 104–5, 107, 128–35, which suggests that Beamish Murdoch's lack of interest in and treatment of commercial law limited the saleability of his *Epitome of the Laws of Nova Scotia* and thus impaired his anticipated economic mobility. Badgley's commitment to legal integration, land tenure, financial, and other broadly commercial reforms, and their indirect but apparent personal rewards, provides a nice point of contrast. See also P.N. Oliver, *The Conventional Man: The Diaries of Ontario Chief Justice Robert A. Harrison, 1856–1878* (Toronto: University of Toronto Press 2003), 3–118, which links Harrison's publishing success to his concern about economic matters.

179 See generally, A.J. Sebok, *Legal Positivism in American Jurisprudence* (New York: Cambridge University Press 1998), 20–57; R.S. Summers, *Instrumentalism and American Legal Theory* (Ithaca, NY: Cornell University Press 1982), 19–37, 136–75; M.J. Horwitz, *The Transformation of American Law, 1780–1860* (Cambridge, MA: Harvard University Press 1977), 253–66.

180 Badgley's Anglo-American models for code reform were, however, sometimes informed by the continental European developments he shunned. Compare M.H. Hoeflich, *Roman and Civil Law in the Development of Anglo-American Jurisprudence in the Nineteenth Century* (Athens: Univeristy of Georgia Press 1997), 9–102; D.S. Clark, 'The Civil Law Influence on David Dudley Field's Code of Civil Procedure,' in M. Reimann, ed., *The Reception of Continental Ideas in the Common Law World 1820–1920* (Berlin: Dunker and Humblot 1993), 63; G. Dargo, *Jefferson's Louisiana: Politics and the Clash of Legal Traditions* (Cambridge, MA: Harvard University Press 1975), 105–74.

181 Compare E.H. Reiter, 'Imported Books, Imported Ideas: Reading European Jurisprudence in Mid-Nineteenth-Century Quebec,' *Law and History Review* 22 (2004), 445; S. Normand and D. Fyson, 'Le droit romain comme source du Code civil du Bas Canada,' *Revue du notariat* 103 (2001), 87; J.D. Blackwell, 'William Hume Blake and the Judicature Acts of 1849: The Process of Legal Reform at Mid-Century in Upper Canada,' in Flaherty, ed., *Essays ...*, vol. 1, 132. See also P. Girard, 'Married Women's Property, Chancery Abolition, and Insolvency Law: Law Reform in Nova Scotia, 1820–1867,' in P. Girard and J. Phillips, eds., *Essays in the History of Canadian Law: Nova Scotia* (Toronto: University of Toronto Press 1990), 80.

182 On Francis Bacon and inductive legal science, see generally, D.R. Coquillette, *Francis Bacon* (Stanford: Stanford University Press 1992), 275–310, and P.H. Kocher, 'Francis Bacon and the Science of Jurisprudence,' *Journal of the History of Ideas* 10 (1957), 3. On recurrence to scientific metaphors for professional or popular purposes, see generally, D.M. Knight, *Public Understanding of Science: A History of Communicating Scientific Ideas* (London: Routledge 2006), and M. Raff, 'Matthew Hale's Other Contribution: Science as a Metaphor in the Development of Common Law Method,' *Australian Journal of Law and Society* 13 (1997), 73.

183 Compare R.V. Bruce, *The Launching of Modern American Science, 1846–1876* (Ithaca, NY: Cornell University Press 1987); I.B. Cohen, *Revolution in Science* (Cambridge, MA: Harvard University Press 1985), 273–366; C. Berger, *Science, God and Nature in Victorian Canada* (Toronto: University of Toronto Press 1983), 3–27, 53–78.

184 Badgley retired from the fray of legislative law-making in the mid-1850s, and spent two more-or-less uneventful decades on the local Superior Court, the Court of Queen's Bench, and the Court of Appeal. He was removed from judicial office in 1874 by the federal government, ostensibly on the basis of dementia. A cursory review of available public and private records of Badgley's court service suggests that his offenses were more likely bombast, autonomy, and obstinance, traits that he displayed as regularly at age forty as at age seventy. Following his departure from the bench, Badgley carried on an effective law practice for fifteen years and continued teaching at McGill's Faculty of Law for seven years. See generally, J. Swainger, 'A Bench in Disarray: The Quebec Judiciary and the Federal Department of Justice,' *Cahiers de droit* 34 (1993), 59; G.B. Baker, 'Ordering the Urban Canadian Law Office and its Entrepreneurial Hinterland, 1825 to 1875,' *University of Toronto Law Journal* 48 (1998), 175, 186–7, 225; Frost, *McGill University* ..., vol. 1, 277–81.

185 Compare Young, *The Politics of Codification*, 11; Brown, *The Genesis of the Canadian Criminal Code of 1892*; Brisson, *La formation d'un droit mixte*; Normand, 'Une Analyse quantitative ...'; Macdonald, 'Understanding Civil Law ...'; R.C.B. Risk, 'Constitutional Scholarship in the Late Nineteenth Century: Making Federalism Work,' in G.B. Baker and J. Phillips, eds., *A History of Canadian Legal Thought: Collected Essays* (Toronto: University of Toronto Press 2006), 33.

186 Compare Radforth, 'Sydenham and Utilitarian Reform'; Young, 'Positive Law, Positive State'; Curtis, *Building the Educational State*.

187 Compare J.L. McNairn, *The Capacity to Judge: Public Opinion and Deliberative Democracy in Upper Canada, 1791–1854* (Toronto: University of Toronto

Press 2000), esp. 63–115, and P.W. Kahn, *The Cultural Study of Law: Reconstructing Legal Scholarship* (Chicago: University of Chicago Press 1999), 1–6, 128–39, with H.P. Glenn, *Legal Traditions of the World: Sustainable Diversity in Law* (New York: Oxford University Press 2007), 1–30. See generally, D.R. Kelley, *The Descent of Ideas: The History of Intellectual History* (Aldershot, UK: Ashgate Publishing 2002).

9

The Rule of Law and Irish Whig Constitutionalism in Upper Canada: William Warren Baldwin, the 'Irish Opposition,' and the Volunteer Connection

JOHN MCLAREN

The Baldwin family from Knockmore, County Cork, crossed the Atlantic to start a new life in Upper Canada in 1799. It comprised father Robert, a widower with six children, including twenty-four-year-old William Warren Baldwin, the subject of this essay.[1] It was not only the members of the family and their material effects that were transported to the newly founded colony, so were their ideas about government and law – the influence on their thought, values, and practices of the political and legal culture in which they had lived and worked. The Baldwins' departure from Ireland was directly related to the adverse effects of, and personal dangers associated with, the rebellion of 1798. Robert, alarmed by reports of a pending French invasion, had taken steps to fortify his country home and to arm his servants.[2] William Warren, in correspondence from Upper Canada to relatives in Ireland, saw the situation as one of the family being forced from their ancestral home.[3]

This essay seeks to relate the political and legal ideas of William Warren Baldwin – who has strong claim to being the 'father of responsible government' in Upper Canada (Ontario) – to those of Irish Whig constitutionalism.[4] In their infancy, those ideas were represented in the Irish newspaper run by his father Robert and his uncle John in the 1780s. They were later refined and related to the British North American colonial experience by other émigrés from Ireland, most notably lawyer William Weekes and judge Robert Thorpe. The story told here is a tribute to the zest of Peter Oliver, as both an author and general editor, in examining and encouraging the examination of the ideological, professional, and institutional influences on the development of legal cultures within Canada and Upper Canada in particular.[5]

The senior Baldwins had been Irish Volunteers during the late 1770s and early 1780s, a Protestant militia formed to deal with possible French invasion while the regular army was fighting in the American colonies.[6] Like many other Volunteers, they empathized with the struggle of the American patriots, and dreamt of liberty and political and legal autonomy for Britain's earliest and most closely held colony.[7] In the wake of British defeat in the American revolutionary war, these constitutional goals seemed to the Baldwin brothers and other Irish Whigs to have been secured. A Whig administration in London, led by Lord Rockingham, evidently worried by the armed presence of advocates for greater liberty in Ireland, was persuaded to make what looked like fundamental changes in the constitutional relationship between Britain and Ireland in the *Irish Constitution Act* of 1782.[8] The *Declaratory Act* of 1719[9] that embodied a legislative statement of the constitutional subordination of the Irish Parliament to the British executive and Parliament and of the Irish courts to the House of Lords was repealed, and the claims of Westminster to superiority in legislative, executive, and judicial matters dropped. On paper, at least, the Irish constitution was to be independent of that of the rest of Britain, centred on a direct relationship between the monarch as King of Ireland and the Irish people. The term 'Irish people' related at that time to the minority Protestant ascendancy (some 25 to 30 per cent of the total population). However, many of the proponents of the new constitutional and legal order also contemplated the progressive removal of the legal disabilities of the Roman Catholics, at least insofar as they were gentlemen and landowners.[10] The views of the two brothers and Irish Whig sentiment more generally can be gleaned from the newspaper that they co-edited between 1783 and 1785, the *Volunteer Journal of Cork*.[11]

The Irish Whig credo was that the best form of government was that administered by benign aristocrats and gentry who represented 'civic virtue.' In this regard, Irish Whigs shared the values and vision of the Country and Radical Whigs who had constituted an important element in opposition in the British Parliament to the long-standing monopoly of government by Court Whigs, between 1715 and 1760.[12] They stood against corruption and arbitrariness in government. They also believed, with their British counterparts, that the virtue of aristocratic and propertied government could not be taken for granted. The columns of the

Journal stressed that there was a distinction between the aristocratic Whig heroes of the struggle for Irish constitutional independence and both the absentee grandees and those who, although resident in Ireland, opposed and subverted the campaign for political and parliamentary reform. Lord Charlemont, a leader of the volunteers and sympathizer with the American cause, and the Earl of Bristol, the Lord Bishop of Derry, a liberal Anglican divine who championed parliamentary reform, received very favourable press, particularly in accounts of Volunteer conclaves supporting their efforts.[13] By contrast, a gentleman like the speaker of the Irish House of Commons, John Foster, a former Volunteer who had thrown in his lot with the conservative elements of the English ascendancy, was the target of vilification published in the letters column.[14] His advocacy of legislation designed to curb sedition drew a warning, in a letter invoking the Roman author Sallust, about substituting the values of imperial autocracy for those of republican free speech.[15]

The paper could also be very caustic about the aristocratic vice-regents sent to Ireland by British governments, who often came in quick succession, and some of whom betrayed profound ignorance of Ireland and its history. As one report from Dublin suggested, nothing is known of a man and 'in the twinkling of an eye he is qualified to be Viceroy of Ireland.' It added that fortunately the Irish 'are a generous people.'[16] Lord Northington who followed a more popular Lord Lieutenant, Lord Temple, was described by the London correspondent as '[m]ore distinguished as a *bon vivant* than as a man of business,' with the Dublin columnist mentioning 'a love for the bottle.'[17] Northington's successor, the Duke of Rutland, was accused in a letter from 'Lycurgus' of being associated with government corruption, not to mention leading an immoral personal life.[18] 'Philadelphus' accused the English chief secretary in Ireland, Thomas Orde, of 'toadying' to the conservative faction and seeking to divide and conquer by driving wedges between Protestants and Catholics.[19] Writers in the paper sometimes criticised aristocratic rule more generally. The London correspondent of the *Journal* attacked it as being the most unfriendly form of rule to the interests of the people and as having put the Irish for long 'in a state of political insignificance.'[20] A letter from 'WBM' warned readers of the malign power and influence of the unelected Irish House of Lords. He concluded, 'This dangerous infringement, this canker of the Constitution is the more to be dreaded, as 'tis armed with wealth and power which gives't support and consequence.'[21]

The *Volunteer Journal* was launched in a period of high euphoria in

Irish Whig circles. The British Parliament had in the 1782 legislation amended *Poyning's Law* and repealed the *Declaratory Act*, the sources of previous Irish constitutional dependency.[22] It seemed to the most optimistic Irish reformers as though Ireland had become a juridical co-equal with Great Britain with a constitutional compact that recognised the independent existence and jurisdiction of the Irish Parliament and courts.[23] Irish Whigs shared much of the political philosophy of their reformist and radical counterparts in Britain. However, they had, as Nicholas Canny has argued, produced a unique Irish dimension to Whig thought by their assertion of the justice of representative and responsible government for themselves, and by extension the other colonial, settler territories of the British Empire.[24] Since at least the writings of William Molyneux in the late seventeenth century and Jonathan Swift's fourth *Drapier's Letter* in the 1720s, there had been a strain of reformist sentiment in Ireland,[25] reflecting a view amongst Irish Protestants and shared by some in the American and West Indian colonies that they had graduated from the status of colonists to a state of equality with Englishmen.[26] In Ireland during the eighteenth century, the Patriot Party gradually emerged with a voice in the Irish Parliament, promoting the Irish Whig idea that that body should be independent of Parliament at Westminster and answerable to the Irish people.[27] In 1782, in the wake of the victory of American Patriots, it was a combination of Patriot political thought and Volunteer ebullience and enthusiasm for change in the relationship with Britain that persuaded a Whig government in London, worried stiff over Irishmen in arms, to make an apparent concession of legislative independence.[28] The heady mood created was captured in the earlier numbers of the *Journal*, not least in its own statement of purpose. It trumpeted grandiloquently:

We wish, at a humble distance, to keep in view the glorious conduct of the VOLUNTEERS, whose steady loyalty to the King, fervent zeal for constitutional rights, love of order and manly exertion of every public virtue, have excited the admiration of mankind, and crowned them with immortal fame.[29]

Even at the level of more practical political and legal commentary the columns were rife with upbeat references to the reform agenda, which the Irish Parliament was sure to adopt.[30] The agenda was given substance in a report of the resolutions of the Munster Volunteers. This document declared there must be an Irish Bill of Rights to make up for that denied in the 1690s. Rotten boroughs must be abolished, so that members of the House of Commons would truly represent their constituents.[31] Elsewhere, the Dublin correspondent advocated that high levels of taxation should be exacted from absentee landlords and steps taken towards equalization of trade with Britain.[32]

It was a period of hyperexpectancy. And yet, even amidst the rejoicing, there were hints that the way ahead might present challenges and pitfalls. The *Journal* reported at length with implicit approval on the campaign launched by some Irish reformers, led by Henry Flood, to press the British government and Parliament to renounce the *Declaratory Act* rather than, as they had already done, repeal it. The argument here was that merely to repeal legislation gave no guarantee that some corrupt ministry in the future would not reintroduce it.[33] There was anxious discussion to the effect that only through renunciation by Great Britain would it be certain that the Irish courts were masters in their own jurisdiction.[34] The debate on renunciation in the British House of Lords was reported, an account which noted disagreement on the part of some Lords as to whether the renunciation bill would transfer full legislative jurisdiction to Ireland, that is over both external as well as internal affairs.[35] A report from Cork specifically raised the depressing question of 'how Ireland can be said in any just sense to possess legislative independence' when it must depend for the opening and closing of Parliament on the decision of the British ministry.[36]

As early as May of 1783 there was a change in tone, and evidence of an increase in frustration at the lack of action on the reform agenda in the columns of the *Journal*. One senses a dawning appreciation that the assumptions about the independence of the Irish Parliament may have been misplaced. During that month, resistance to the 'junto' of English ministers in Ireland to parliamentary reform was noted in the Dublin report.[37] If this subsists, said the correspondent, 'we must be content to see borough corruption continue to prevail over the true and independent voice of the nation.' In the same edition, a letter from the indefatigable 'WBM' noted the failure of parliamentary reform in Britain. The lesson for Irishmen was to seize the moment and the momentum: 'A new and glorious era is opened to us – Liberty, glorious Liberty is ours; let us then receive this greatest of worldly blessings as we ought: let's up nourish and protest it with the utmost earnest *care* and *affection.*'[38]

By 1784 the emphasis was being laid more clearly on the need to press vigorously for parliamentary reform, for only in this way, as Cork freeholders concluded, would there be resistance to the alarming encroachment by the aristocracy.[39] This was a period when Volunteer organizations came together in convention in Dublin to reaffirm their support for political and parliamentary reform leading to more representative government. However, through misinformation sewn at the behest of Charles James Fox, the British Secretary of State for Ireland, who was increasingly uncomfortable at the influence of armed Volunteers in Irish affairs, disagreement developed among delegates. In the result, Flood's bill to extend representation in Parliament, based on the compromise resolutions at the convention, was soundly defeated in the Irish Commons.[40] Early in 1784, the Volunteer conventions tried again. By May, the *Journal* correspondent in Dublin was reporting the readiness of 20,000 Volunteers to fight for freedom against a corrupt and oppressive ministry.[41] In the same number, 'Rosemount' stressed the legitimacy of resistance if the corruption and abuse in government in Dublin continued.[42] This proved to be so much bravura, and the message fell on a majority of deaf ears in Parliament. A further resolution by Flood to reform the electoral system failed as convincingly as its predecessor.

Early in 1784, the government of William Pitt the Younger replaced that of Lord North and Charles James Fox. Pitt was committed to 'normalizing' constitutional relations between the two nations, in particular by tying commercial concessions to the Irish to an agreement that would see the Irish government contributing to the cost of imperial defence.[43] As resistance to this plan developed among Irish reformers, who saw it as a replay of British intransigence in North America, the tone of some correspondents and contributors to the *Journal* has an almost seditious ring. There were threats of Ireland being torn away from the Empire like the thirteen colonies.[44] Pitt and the Duke of Rutland, the Lord Lieutenant, were accused of suppressing liberty and acting in disregard of 'the constitution of the British Empire.'[45] A toast in Dublin glorying in the prospect of separation was reported as gaining popularity at Patriot tables.[46] Bitter reference was made to government attempts to deny an unjustly imprisoned newspaper man access to counsel.[47] In the same 10 May 1784 issue of the *Journal*, there was a rant against British tyranny that referred to the 'rapacious,' 'extortionate,' and 'unjust' policies of Britain towards its dependencies around the globe, which had produced nothing but loathing in local populations.[48] That same month, it was reported from Dublin that so frustrated were the reformers in the Irish Commons that objections were raised to including a eulogy in the address to the Lord Lieutenant, because of his anti-reform record.[49]

If some of the material published in the *Journal* had a seditious tone, the editors also provided a forum for those opposed to attempts by the Irish ministry to bring in oppressive legislation to curb press criticism. During April 1784, a bill was introduced in the Irish Parliament which, with a fine sense of irony, sought 'to secure the liberty of the press by preventing the abuses arising from the publication of traitorous, seditious, false and slanderous libels.'[50] The bill sought to exercise tight control over newspapers by requiring publishers to provide the Commissioners of Stamp Duties with information on their publications to be kept and used in any trial relating to those newspapers. Publishers were also required to enter into recognizance of £500 per newspaper before printing and to undertake to comply with any regulations or conditions set down. For failure to comply with these requirements, a £100 penalty applied, with half going to any informant. Furthermore, those seeking to secure the publication of 'false and scurrilous libels' or those paying for such material were to be guilty of a high misdemeanour and subject to up to six months' imprisonment. Parties who sold material against which a stop order had been issued or which contained false or libellous statements were liable to be imprisoned on conviction for anywhere from one to three weeks.[51]

There was immediate and vigorous reaction among Irish Whig reformers, including those writing in or to the *Volunteer Journal* in Cork. The report from Dublin on 15 April 1784 exposed the 'Freedom of the Press' bill for what it was, a calculated attempt to suppress press freedom, one striking at 'that great Palladium of liberty.'[52] The fact that it contemplated trial without jury and imposed penalties prior to conviction caused particular outrage as 'trampling on the freedom, liberty and property of the subject, and tearing up, as it were, the constitution by the roots.' Note was taken of the lack of similar legislation in Great Britain which, it was said, had a press that was just as licentious as that in Ireland.[53] The *eminence gris* behind the bill was marked as John Foster, who with his conservative cronies was 'stung by the calumnies of the press.' From Cork itself came charges of British tyranny and oppression and calls for armed resistance to protect 'any little shadow of Liberty ... acquired during the late contest beyond the Atlantic.'[54] There followed a statement that effectively encapsulated in legal terminology the essence of Irish Whig constitutionalism.

The power of the King, Lord and Commons is not an arbitrary power. They are the trustees not the owners of the estate. The fee simple is in US. They cannot alienate, they cannot waste. The power of the legislature is limited, not only by the rules of natural justice and the welfare of the community, but by the forms and principles of our particular constitution.

So vigorous was the opposition to this bill that British ministers intervened to sound the alarm to the Irish ministry, and in May the *Journal* reported that His Majesty had rejected the bill.[55] The latter claim was erroneous. The bill was merely revised to make it less draconian.[56]

By mid-1784, it was becoming apparent that the Volunteers had lost the initiative in Irish politics they had once possessed. Moreover, the Patriot opposition in the Irish Parliament was fragmented and ineffectual. During the summer of 1785, as the paper's debts increased, Robert Baldwin left the partnership and returned to the country.[57] Now labouring under a burdensome stamp tax, the *Journal* struggled on until 1787 when it folded.[58] There were two brief interludes thereafter when it seemed that the reformist agenda might be revived. In 1788–9, during the madness of King George, there were active negotiations by Patriot leader Henry Grattan with the Whigs in London to secure support in Ireland for the regency of the Prince of Wales. Grattan had piloted resolutions through the House of Commons in Dublin supporting the regency in Ireland on generous terms, when the King uncooperatively recovered.[59] Then, late in 1794 as part of a process of coalition building, Pitt was induced by his Whig partners to send their nominee, Earl Fitzwilliam, to Ireland as Lord Lieutenant. Fitzwilliam, after consultation with Grattan with whose views on reform he agreed, began replacing conservative office holders with Irish Whigs and indicated positive movement on Catholic emancipation. Pitt, who had warned the viceroy against such moves, quickly recalled him, and the reform initiative was again lost.[60]

The history of Ireland between 1785 and 1798 was marked by a hardening of positions, increasing tension, and ultimately conflict.[61] The conservative Dublin Castle clique of officials and placemen consolidated their power, becoming more arrogant and impervious to change or concession. Meanwhile, the initiative in opposition politics shifted from the moderate Patriots to the more radical and strident United Irishmen. As the impact of the French Revolution sank in and its rhetoric took hold, this latter group developed a political agenda that included proclaiming independence as a republic. In the process, the middle ground of Irish politics shrank visibly as former Volunteers hewed to one side of the divide or the other. This widening of the political chasm was matched by increasing religious tensions as Orangemen intent on religious cleansing and Roman Catholic defenders clashed. The result was a slide into the Rebellion of 1798, abortive French intervention, and the grim repression by the forces of the Crown, especially the militias, that followed.[62]

Shedding the exaggerated rhetoric that was common in reform newspapers of the late eighteenth century and recognizing that the editors were not to be fixed with the more radical views expressed in their publications, it is still possible to discern in the *Volunteer Journal* the contours of a distinctly Irish reformist notion of liberty and the rule of law. Aristocratic government was supportable, but only if its members were imbued with a sense of civic virtue, eschewed arbitrary and corrupt practices, and worked for the welfare of all the people. The great attraction of the post-1782 Irish constitution to its Whig advocates was that it was designed to bring monarch and his Irish subjects into a direct relationship, which should have meant freedom from British imperial interference and a Parliament that was representative of Irish interests and priorities. In time, it became apparent to Whig reformers that the governance of Ireland was not to be immediately purged of British interference or reactionary Anglo-Irish control. As that reality sank in, emphasis shifted to deploying both Irish and English Whig constitutionalism as a basis for principled opposition to oppressive legislation. The immediate bone of contention was the Irish administration's attempt to curb press freedom in 1784. In the final analysis, however, there was a chastening lesson in the rise and fall of Irish Whig political strategy in Ireland. A reformist opposition that was fractured was no match for either imperial inaction or manipulation, or local conservative elitism and rampant self-interest. There was an associated naivety on the part of the reformers in believing that progress towards a constitutional reordering of the relationship between Ireland and Britain was a *fait accomplit* during a period when powerful British politicians were assessing the impact of the loss of the American colonies and the implications of that loss for Britain's control of the rest of its empire. As time went by and as fears of aggressive republicanism in the United States or more especially in France took hold, it became less and less clear that any imperial reordering that was the result of this soul searching would be marked by a spirit of liberality.[63]

The social, political, and legal values of William Warren Baldwin reflected a firm belief in a balanced constitution, an admiration for aristocracy, and a strong sense of the claim of the propertied classes to provide governance and leadership.[64] He had a personal reputation for being 'aloof and stiff necked' and concerned with his status as both a gentleman and a lawyer.[65] In the legislative assembly of Upper Canada, in which he sat for spells between 1820 and 1830, he was on record as favouring primogeniture. He also spoke in favour of landed property rights and rejected attempts by radical legislators to interfere with the privileges of the members of the Law Society of Upper Canada.[66] This conservative elitism reflected his background. He came from a family of lesser gentry in which his father seems to have played a guiding role.[67] The sense of status may well have been accentuated by the fact that as a class in Ireland these people, including the Baldwins, relied heavily on the largesse of more powerful and wealthy landowners, and often found themselves in financial difficulties.[68] A sense of the tetchiness of Robert Baldwin, the father, about his property is evident in a notice in the *Journal*, early in 1784, advising others to refrain from hunting on his land, so he and his friends could enjoy it for that purpose. He also threatened to prosecute poachers 'with the utmost rigour.'[69]

Soon after the arrival of the Baldwins in Upper Canada, they received elements of the preferment anticipated by their class. Robert who had been Seneschal (Steward) of the Manor of Carrigoline and judge of its Court Leet in County Cork, was appointed a justice of the peace in Durham County and lieutenant of the County.[70] The latter position gave him power of appointment to the local militia to which William was appointed as lieutenant colonel. It was clear, too, that the family arrived with strongly developed notions of the need for political order and social deference. In a letter to his cousin, John, in Cork, in 1801, William made it clear that on first encounter he did not think highly of the American settlers in Upper Canada, whom he described as 'these miserable wretches.' Having, he suggests, been saved from destitution and made independent and comfortable by the colonial government, they repaid that generosity with a desire, had they the chance, 'to overturn the order of things in this country.'[71]

Although William never made it into the ranks of the close advisers to the lieutenant governor or of leading government officials in Upper Canada, he did hold several judicial positions, including those of master in chancery and district court judge.[72] While recognising that a landed aristocracy in the British sense was an impossibility in Upper Canada, the younger Baldwin considered those who were both gentlemen and trained in the high profession of law to be an aristocracy of merit to guide the fortunes of the colony. Within four years of arriving on Canadian shores, he had consciously turned from medicine in which he was trained to reading for and admission to the bar.[73] The advice of both father and Irish friends would no doubt have been crucial here and affected by the tradition of both professional and political service of gentlemen lawyers in Ireland in the late eighteenth century that Philip Girard has noted.[74] In his preparation for the bar, William borrowed a copy of Blackstone's *Commentaries on the Laws of England*, which he seems to have digested with enthusiasm.[75]

Commitment to aristocratic rule did not, however, blind W.W. Baldwin to the fact that 'aristocrats' or their protégés could be both political and legal oppressors. In other words, there were good and responsible elite leaders and leaders who were irresponsible, autocratic, and lacking in civic virtue. This distinction is evident in the calm but scathing letter that Baldwin wrote as treasurer of the Law Society to Attorney General John Beverley Robinson in 1828.[76] This missive criticised Robinson for failing to reprove the young lawyers and articled clerks, some of whom served in the Attorney's chambers, who had taken the law into their own hands and trashed the printing press of William Lyon Mackenzie, a radical newspaper editor, in 1826. Mackenzie was the scourge of the Family Compact, that elite group of conservative, anti-democratic advisers to the lieutenant governor, of which Robinson was a leading member.[77]

The same sense of disappointment at the actions of 'gentlemen of the law' is amply displayed in Baldwin's advocacy in a civil suit on behalf of George Rolph, clerk of the peace for the Gore District where Hamilton, Ontario, is now located. This brother of reformer John Rolph had been tarred and feathered by a group of local Tories dressed in sheets with blackened faces that included lawyers, a magistrate, and a sheriff.[78] As Baldwin put it, these were 'persons holding responsible positions, even occupying the seats of Justice – one of them ... entrusted with the sword of Justice.'[79]

The sentiment of anger and disappointment with corrupt elitism also features in the petition sent by Dr Baldwin and his friends to George IV in 1829. This document complained of the injustice of the removal from office of Justice John Walpole Willis by Lieutenant Governor Peregrine Maitland for upholding the constitution of the colony.[80] Justice Willis had positioned himself, as the colonial executive and its elite local advisers saw it, in opposition to the colonial government. He had gone out of his way to criticise the law officers of the Crown, Attorney General J.B. Robinson, and Solicitor General Henry John Boulton for their failure to prefer criminal charges against Tory hoodlums engaged in acts of personal and group violence and property damage, while at the same time pursuing with gusto sedition prosecutions against radical newspaper editors and other critics of the Maitland regime. Willis had also sent chills up the spines of the conservative elite by consorting with political reformers in the province. The action that constituted 'the last straw' with this troublous jurist was his refusal on constitutional grounds to sit as a member of a two-man Court of King's Bench, while the third judge, Chief Justice Campbell, was on furlough in England.[81] Willis insisted that under the Constitution Act of 1791, the Court of King's Bench was required to sit with a full bench at all times. In each of the instances noted, Baldwin's view was that officers of the colonial government or their minions had acted in arbitrary, if not corrupt, ways and, in the process, had subverted the constitutional and legal order.

Opposition to the government of Upper Canada alleging arbitrary use of power to suppress dissent and punish political enemies was not new. In his first decade in the colony, William Warren had associated with a group of Irish reformers led by lawyer William Weekes and later by Justice Robert Thorpe.[82] This group, the 'Irish Opposition' – which had as its titular head a former administrator of the colony and respected former army officer and councilman, Peter Russell, who had encouraged the Baldwin family to migrate to the colony – lay on the margins of the governing elite.[83] Its members were highly critical of the latter's 'Scotch' monopoly of influence and their mercantile bent.[84] Under the ideological leadership of Weekes, this group had challenged the regime of Lieutenant Governor Peter Hunter for enacting repressive sedition legislation in 1804, which, although it was significantly more draconian than the Irish statute of the mid-1780s, echoed its illiberal sentiments.[85] The act reflected the garrison mentality that afflicted the colony in the wake of the Irish rebellion and the exile of its architects and supporters to North America, in particular the United States, as well as anxieties about the strategic designs of Napoleon Bonaparte.[86] It included provisions that gave the executive as well as the courts summary powers to act against those in the colony who were non-residents or who failed to take an oath of allegiance, on the suspicion of having spread or being about to spread sedition.

Hunter also drew criticism from the group for his land policies that he felt were designed to bring some order and certainty to the process of land settlement, but were resented by those on the receiving end of higher registration fees and pressure brought by the government to take up existing grants.[87] Other owners felt disaffected with the regime at having their land seized for non-payment of debts.[88] Some of these gripes would have come from landholders represented by Weekes, the lawyer. The fact that the lieutenant governor shared in the bounty of fees charged for land registration and made use of funds derived from duties for executive purposes without legislative approval were also seen as examples of the high-handed and arbitrary administration of the colonial government more generally.[89]

With Weekes' premature death in a duel, Thorpe assumed the mantle of leader of the group. Moreover, he ran and was elected in the by-election for Weekes' seat in the legislative assembly.[90] Throwing all caution to the wind, the judge assumed the role of the leader of the opposition in the assembly. Thorpe, who one senses had been previously coached by Weekes in liberal British and Irish Whig thinking, demonstrated in both his words and actions that he possessed a different understanding of the constitution in Upper Canada than the lieutenant governor (now Francis Gore) and his advisers (and, for that matter, the imperial government).[91] At a rhetorical level, Thorpe, who seems to have believed that he had an obligation, real or imagined, to report to the Colonial Office in London his views on life and politics in the colony, sometimes used language similar to that which appeared earlier in the *Volunteer Journal of Cork*. One finds reference to former lieutenant governor Hunter as 'rapacious' and 'guilty of the plunder of Eastern princes,' and his advisers as 'Scotch instruments' and 'reptiles.'[92] Thorpe's less than favourable assessment of Hunter's successor, Francis Gore, was that he was 'imperious, self-sufficient and ignorant, impressed with a high notion of the old system,' and surrounded by the old gang of 'Scotch pedlars.'[93]

Behind the overcharged rhetoric and posturing in Thorpe's correspondence, addresses to juries and comments and partisan actions and language in the assembly, there was an important strand of liberal Whig ideology. In his legal education and training, the judge would have been exposed to the writings of William Blackstone, including in particular those parts of the canon that focused on the glories of the British constitution and the liberty and the rights of 'freeborn Englishmen' that it supposedly guaranteed.[94] Together with his colleagues, Thorpe believed, naively, that the 1791 *Constitution Act*, too, was a liberal document that contemplated a form of governance such as 'the Magna Carta' and 'a Perfect Image and Transcript of the British Constitution,' as the first lieutenant governor of the colony, John Graves Simcoe, had incautiously described it.[95] This, they believed, was reflected in the grant of a full range of legislative organs that matched the British Parliament, as well as a superior court system. There is, moreover, no doubt that Thorpe was fully aware of the tragic events in his homeland as the Irish Whig dream of an independent Irish constitution and Parliament based on a compact between the monarch and the Irish people first faded and was then shattered. He had lived through this period in Ireland, and it was an experience shared with most other members of the Irish opposition in Upper Canada, including William Warren Baldwin.

These various elements of liberal Whig thinking are evident in Thorpe's utterances and writings. When he talked to a grand jury about the glories of the British constitution, when he fulminated in letters to London against what he perceived to be executive corruption and arbitrariness in the colonial executive, when in the assembly he cited the case of Lord Strafford to suggest that colonial servants of the Crown were responsible to the Assembly, and when he warned his fellow assemblymen of the dangers of abdicating control over duties levied by imperial statutes, it was this combination of values and assumptions that his words reflected.[96] In an anonymous tract under the signature 'Canadiensis,' which is thought to have been penned by Thorpe and inspired by Edmund Burke's reference in his *Speech on Conciliation with America* (1775) to the 'Spirit of the Constitution,' the author set out a reading of the relationship between Great Britain and its colonies embodying long-standing Irish Whig beliefs and other elements of reformist British thinking.[97] This reading stressed that colonial legislatures were largely autonomous and linked only by allegiance to the Crown, that the *Constitution Act* of 1791 was declaratory of the common law of empire – a treaty prescribing how constitutional rights were to be exercised and how that government of the Empire was vested conjointly in Westminster and the colonies, with the former exercising power over certain spheres out of necessity but not out of any broader legal prescription. Any imperial law purporting to trench on colonial jurisdiction was void and any judge trying to enforce it would be liable to impeachment. In further reformist vein, the publication considered that colonial executive councils were answerable to provincial legislatures, and argued that councillors should be chosen from local legislatures much in the same way that the cabinet was in Britain and forced to resign following the loss of a majority in Parliament. Here in essence are the pieces of what would later be described as responsible government.

This reformist liberal philosophy of the constitutional relationship between Great Britain and its colonies was thoroughly ill timed, given the prevailing political attitudes in both London and York. Moreover, several senior members of the Irish Opposition group paid the price of their activism in pressing the cause. Thorpe was dismissed from judicial office in 1807 by the secretary of state for the Colonies, Lord Castlereagh, after Gore had earlier 'amoved' him.[98] Another member, Joseph Willcocks, a distant cousin of William Warren Baldwin, and sheriff of York, had already been removed from office by Gore for his colourful criticism of the administration. He then founded and edited the first opposition newspaper, *The Upper Canadian Guardian* or *Freeman's Journal*, and continued the battle against the executive as an assembly member. In the War of 1812, Willcocks went over to the American side, thus severing any further active connection with Upper Canadian politics.[99]

The survivor of the group was William Warren Baldwin, who seems by and large to have kept his counsel during this tumultuous period.[100] He did not receive the preferment in the colonial administration that he and some of his supporters felt was merited, such as the clerkship of the legislative council or that of crown and pleas.[101] However, he was appointed, in sequence, a master in chancery, the registrar of the Court of Probate, and a district court judge.[102] Moreover, Baldwin seems to have been able, unlike the more senior members of the 'Opposition,' to keep on the right side of Lieutenant Governor Gore despite the latter's view of him as an 'Irishman, ready to join any party to make confusion.'[103] In 1812, he was involved in a controversial and uncharacteristic drama, an ill-considered attempt at a duel with John MacDonnell, a rising star of the conservative legal establishment who, Baldwin alleged, had slandered him in court. Happily, neither party shot, as McDonnell declined to raise his pistol and his opponent's honour was satisfied by that gesture.[104] William Warren settled down to a life centred on family and a law practice, in which he had considerable financial success, and in consolidating and managing significant land holdings and the wealth they generated.[105]

It was in 1820 that Baldwin first entered provincial politics as the member for York and Simcoe in the legislative assembly. As I have already noted, his position on social, proprietary, and professional issues was conservative.[106] He opposed legislation to abolish primogeniture, decried fees and taxes on land and praised the benefits of hierarchical and aristocratic government. In opposing the primogeniture bill, he worried that 'aristocracy, upon which the *happy, happy* Constitution of

Great Britain rested, would be destroyed.' He added that he wished to see the aristocracy 'supported in this Colony to preserve the constitution ... and not to run into a scheme of Democracy by establishing new fangled laws.'[107] Alongside these conservative traits there were reformist elements in Baldwin's view of law and governance. The most evident example of this in his early years in the assembly, was his commitment to the repeal of the *Sedition Act*. This enactment had been invoked recently to silence and get rid of Robert Gourlay, a Scottish radical and activist.[108] In 1821, Baldwin advised the chamber that, as long as the act remained in force, Upper Canadians were 'without a constitution; at least a free one.' The statute, he continued, 'remained in force not only in the face of Magna Carta, but directly in the face of all the statutes made for the liberty and protection of the subject.'[109] In making these arguments, he drew heavily from Blackstone's renderings of the glories of British constitutional and English legal history, as well as the resistance of his Irish Whig forbears to the censorship of the press and attempts to bridle political opposition.

Robert Fraser in seeking to explain Baldwin's political and legal credo, perceptively suggests that it was not only Blackstone's view of British constitutionalism that he drew upon. His views also matched in some ways the liberal strain of English constitutionalism represented in political opposition in the British Parliament in the mid-eighteenth century:[110]

Baldwin was a whig constitutionalist whose ideas on law and politics were similar to those of the pre-war opposition of Thorpe and Wilcocks and the post-war opposition initiated by Nicol. His emphasis on limited government, retrenchment of expenditures, the independence of the constitution's respective parts and the civil rights and liberties of subjects was consistent with the country tradition in English politics.[111]

But, as Fraser also discerns, there was a distinctive Irish influence in Baldwin's politico-legal makeup. His Irish Whig heritage was most pronounced when he talked of the constitutional relationship between Great Britain and Upper Canada and the sovereignty of colonial legislatures.[112] Here, his beliefs increasingly accorded with those of the author of the 'Canadiensis' tract.[113] In 1821, William Warren spoke out against the view propounded by a joint committee of the assembly and council on commercial intercourse with Lower Canada that it was not open to the colonial legislature to impose duties on imports, that being the exclusive power of the imperial Parliament. Commenting that this amounted to 'an incapacity in ourselves to govern ourselves,' he added that to accept such a principle was 'subversive of everything Valuable in our constitution,' which could not be repealed except by the consent of the colonists.[114] As he was to assert in 1823, in opposing a proposed union of the Canadas, the *Constitution Act* of 1791 granted to the inhabitants of Upper Canada 'the right to make laws for their peace order and good government, reserving certain powers to the King and Parliament ... to legislate in particular circumstances.'[115] In that same speech, Baldwin went on to argue that 'the imperial parliament could not constitutionally alter *this* law without our consent; for, if so, we had no constitution at all.' What we have in essence here is the Upper Canadian version of Irish Whig compact constitutionalism refracted through the influence of Weekes and Thorpe during the first decade of the nineteenth century.

Having lost his seat in 1824, Baldwin directed his attention to partiality in the administration of justice in the colony, representing radicals and reformers who had been prosecuted for their dissenting and allegedly subversive opinions or were suing for or defending libel actions.[116] In the process he developed a clear antipathy to the regimes of Sir Peregrine Maitland and Sir John Colborne and their Family Compact advisers. Elected as treasurer of the Law Society of Upper Canada for a third term (1824–8), William took a strong interest in the affairs of the legal profession and in preserving its privileges.[117] Here, he found it easy to make common cause with conservative lawyers like the Attorney General, John Beverley Robinson.[118] Where he parted company with Robinson and his ilk was in his belief in the need for lawyers and judges to uphold the rule of law that for him meant not only judgment according to law and legal processes but a broader obligation to preserve rights and well-fought-for liberties in English and then British history. This strongly held commitment induced Baldwin both in and out of court to speak out against the governing elite's perversion of the rule of law by resorting to or condoning by inactivity Tory-inspired vigilante justice against radical or reformist critics, and refusing to prosecute friends and supporters, while relentlessly pursuing their enemies and seeking to ensure their conviction in sedition prosecutions.[119]

Successful in the 1828 election in the riding of Norfolk, William became the effective leader of the reform group in the assembly, recognized by his more radical colleagues as having the 'gentlemanly' qualities and impeccable Anglican and professional credentials for leadership.[120] In this role, Baldwin took the lead in public protests against the removal of Justice John Walpole Willis. In both his address to a constitutional meeting on 5 July 1828 and in the petition to George IV, decrying the removal from office of Willis and more generally the subversion of constitutional and legal values in the province by the colonial government and Family Compact, William Warren was to demonstrate some movement beyond his earlier constitutional views and some shifting from his implicit faith in aristocracy as the best form of government.[121] These were almost certainly influenced by his more radical colleagues, lawyers John Rolph and Marshall Spring Bidwell.[122] Blended with his already well-formed views on compact constitution-alism was now a clear commitment to responsible government. Baldwin advocated an executive responsible to the elected assembly, and a reformed, although not an elective, legislative council. For him it was important to free the council of the influence of 'placemen and pension-ers who depended on the Executive for a living,' men who did not rep-resent 'an independent gentry.' Another important plank in his agenda was an independent colonial judiciary, appointed during good behav-iour rather than at pleasure. Baldwin also asserted that colonial judges had no business serving on executive or legislative bodies.[123]

After being defeated in the 1830 election, William Warren Baldwin withdrew from involvement in provincial politics and from an active law practice, although he maintained the views that he had developed on the colonial constitution and the law.[124] In 1836, as the colony tee-tered on the brink of open conflict between the supporters of the Family Compact and the radicals led by William Lyon Mackenzie, Baldwin was lured back into active political debate in the cause of moderate reform-ism in the Constitutional Reform Society and the Toronto Political Union.[125] Although the aging statesman was accused by Lieutenant Governor Sir Francis Bond Head of being a 'republican' and of being aware of Mackenzie's plans for insurrection, the evidence is to the con-trary.[126] Clearly dispirited by the slide to open conflict and the 'rash insurrection,' as he dubbed the Rebellion of 1837, William Warren retired from further involvement in constitutional politics.[127] However, he did meet briefly with Lord Durham, together with his son Robert, to whom the mantle of active political support for responsible government had now shifted.[128] Moreover, both Baldwins wrote at length to Durham setting out their views on responsible government, as well as the causes of disaffection in the colony.[129] It seems likely that the recom-mendations of the *Durham Report* advocating the restructuring of the relationship between Great Britain and its remaining North American colonies and the introduction of responsible government were influenced by them.[130]

William who engaged in increasingly acerbic reflection on the recent political and constitutional history of the province was not to experience personally the establishment of responsible government in Upper Canada.[131] He died in 1842. Because of the initial resistance of London to Durham's recommendations on a new colonial constitution, responsible government was not granted until 1848, after extensive lobbying by colonial reformers, including his son Robert and Joseph Howe of Nova Scotia.[132] William Warren would have taken posthumous pleasure from knowing that the first government under the new constitutional order, applicable to the province of Canada, was the Lafontaine-Baldwin regime co-led by Robert.[133] The Irish Whig vision of compact constitutionalism – with its emphasis on a direct relationship between the Crown and the local populace and on local autonomy in governance – together with a reformist commitment to responsible government pressed by Robert Thorpe and his friends, and later espoused by the Baldwins, had finally become a reality.

Conclusion

Graeme Patterson has argued that, while W.W. Baldwin may have derived his ideas on constitutionalism in part from his Irish Whig heritage, it also reflected Blackstonian values picked up during his self-education as an aspirant to the bar in Upper Canada.[134] For his part, Robert Fraser has suggested that although Dr Baldwin's constitutional discourse reflects the strong influence of Irish Whig thinking, his aversion to arbitrary and oppressive government was based firmly upon English Whig ideology, buttressed by his reading of Blackstone on liberty.[135] What I have sought to do in this chapter is to refine those positions and to press the claims of the Irish connection in greater detail than earlier writers. I have argued that Baldwin's political, social, and legal views represented a melange of conservative and progressive ideas that evolved and changed over time. They included an attraction to the ordered constitution and hierarchical society so prized by Blackstone, while also being affected later by the ongoing process of English reform politics, particularly as refracted through its champions in Upper Canada in the 1820s.

I stress here that the discernible third element, that of Irish Whig thought, was perhaps more indelible than has been suggested. As an Irishman, William Warren would have had a keen knowledge of Irish history. Moreover, through his father, with whom he had a close and positive relationship and who lived until 1816, he would have been presented with a clear, even vivid sense of the rapid rise and fall of the late-eighteenth-century Irish constitution and the sense of frustration, if not betrayal, felt by Irish Whigs at its demise. From that tragic story, it would have been evident to him that governing aristocratic elites produce their share of power mongers, manipulators, jobbers, and sycophants. He would also know that governments that are not responsible to the local communities they serve are often highly insensitive to local problems and issues. William Warren would have appreciated, too, that imperial imperatives can subvert local priorities, and that corrupt members of the elite and the governments they control or influence can and will in their own self-interest manipulate the constitution and trample on individuals' rights, especially of those who dissent and oppose them politically. Certainly, there is abundant evidence in the *Volunteer Journal* that father Robert and Robert's brother John and their correspondents understood these features of the Irish constitutional story. Finally, parallels between these critical features of Irish political life and similar problems in Upper Canada clearly affected young Baldwin as a relatively silent associate of the Irish activist group comprising Weekes, Thorpe, and Joseph Willcocks, who constituted a political opposition to what they saw as arbitrary government during the years 1804–12.[136]

The Irish Whig experience in Ireland had provided a chastening lesson, that enthusiasm for the cause of reform was no guarantee that the cause would succeed, especially when faced with powerful and manipulative opponents. Moreover, those events spoke to the merit of careful and deliberative readings of the tenor of the times by those who advocated colonial constitutional reform. Robert Thorpe and the excitable group of Irishmen of which he was a member failed to recognise this lesson and its corollary in the early years of the nineteenth century. They suffered the consequences by being cast into political and legal oblivion by a reactionary imperial system. Of Thorpe and his friends, however, it may be said that they set the scene for change in the sort of vivid and irreverent tones whereby professional burial was hastened but ideological resurrection was assured. It was William Warren Baldwin and later his son Robert who, through perseverance and by adopting a calmer and more deliberative approach, ultimately secured the desired constitutional changes. Through their efforts they were able to persuade the

British authorities that colonial constitutional reordering was both necessary and inevitable. In the process, they kept alive and refined the Irish Whig ideology of William Warren's father, Robert, his uncle, John, and that earlier group of Upper Canadian activists so that it became an acceptable manifesto for responsible government.

NOTES

1 See W.W. Baldwin, 'Account of Life of his Father, Robert Baldwin' (unpublished, 29 December 1816), 13–16, Metro Toronto Reference Library (MTR), Baldwin Room, William Warren Baldwin Papers, L12.

2 Robert Fraser, 'William Warren Baldwin' [hereinafter 'WWB'] in Robert Fraser, ed., *Provincial Justice: Upper Canadian Legal Portraits* (Toronto: Osgoode Society for Canadian Legal History and University of Toronto Press 1992), 201–2.

3 Ibid., 202.

4 In part the inspiration for this work is the richer body of literature in the United States relating to the influence of the republican United Irishmen in that country to which a number migrated or were exiled, during part of the same period. There is, in Canada, no work to match David A. Wilson's comprehensive study of these immigrants, *United Irishmen, United States: Immigrant Radicals in the Early Republic* (Ithaca, NY: Cornell University Press 1998), or recent scholarship on the early civil rights litigation of William Sampson, United Irishman, New York lawyer, and civil rights activist. See Walter Walsh, 'The First Free Exercise Case,' *George Washington University Law Review* 73 (2004), 1, and Professor Walsh's forthcoming book on Sampson, based on his 1997 S.J.D. thesis at Harvard, *Postcolonial Radical: The Life and Thought of William Sampson, 1764–1836*.

5 See the introduction to this volume.

6 On the Volunteers and their role, see Thomas Bartlett, '"This Famous Island Set in a Virginian Sea": Ireland in the British Empire, 1690–1801,' in P.J. Marshall, ed., *The Oxford History of the British Empire*, vol. 2, *The Eighteenth Century* (Oxford: Oxford University Press 1998), 253, 265–8. The involvement of the brothers Baldwin is traced in R.M. and J. Baldwin, *The Baldwins and the Great Experiment* (Don Mills: Longmans 1969), 17–22.

7 See Maurice O'Connell, *Irish Politics and Social Conflict in the Age of the American Revolution* (Philadelphia: University of Pennsylvania Press 1965), 25–9; R.B. Macdowell, *Irish Public Opinion, 1750–1800* (1944; reprint, Westport, CT: Greenwood Press 1975), 43–8.

8 On the constitutional history of Ireland before 1800, including the constitutional changes of the 1780s, see Alan J. Ward, *The Irish Constitutional Tradition: Responsible Government and Modern Ireland, 1782–1992* (Washington, DC: Catholic University of America Press 1994), 15–29.

9 *The Declaratory Act* (1719) 6 Geo. 1, c.5. The act had confirmed and extended the effects of *Poyning's Law* passed by the English Parliament in the reign of Henry VII, which had subjected bills of the Irish Parliament to approval by Westminster, so that there could no doubt that the English Parliament could legislate for Ireland. The act also allowed appeals of decisions of Irish superior courts to the House of Lords in London.

10 See *Resolutions of the Dungannon Convention of the Ulster Volunteers*, February 1782, from Francis Dobbs, *History of Irish Affairs from 1779–1782*, 1783, reproduced in *Grattan's Parliament: Historical Documents* (Dublin: National Library of Ireland 1982), Document 7.

11 On the founding of the paper, see R.M. and J. Baldwin, *The Great Experiment*, 22–3. This newspaper should not be confused with the *Volunteer Journal* published in Dublin, which was the leading and most aggressive Volunteer publication in Ireland. It is likely that one of its employees was the Dublin correspondent of the Cork paper. On the politicisation of the Irish press during and after the American War of Independence, see Brian Inglis, *The Freedom of the Press in Ireland, 1784–1841* (London: Faber and Faber 1954), 19–23.

This essay is part of larger project designed to analyse the interrelation of understandings of liberty and the rule of law as constitutional values within and among British colonial territories in the late eighteenth and early nineteenth centuries. Elsewhere, I have traced the influence of conflicting ideas about liberty and the rule of law from mid-eighteenth-century Britain to the Thirteen Colonies, thence back to Britain itself, but more especially to Ireland. In that work I have begun to trace the impact of the diffusion of these ideas about law, politics, and the subject on the remaining British North American colonies and New South Wales in the period after the American War of Independence.

12 On the ideology of English Country and Radical Whigs in the mid-eighteenth century, see H.T. Dickenson, *Liberty and Property: Political Ideology in Eighteenth-Century Britain* (London: Methuen 1977), 163–92.

13 See *Volunteer Journal of Cork* (*VJC*) 2, no. 43 (29 May 1783), 4, for a favourable report of Lord Charlemont's review in the Phoenix Park, Dublin of the Cavalry and Infantry of the Irish Volunteers; see *VJC* 3, no. 16 (23 February 1784), 1, for an address to Earl of Bristol by the Bill of Rights Battalion, and from a meeting of 'Gentlemen, Clergy and Freeholders' of the County of

Mayo. On Charlemont's role in the Volunteer movement, see Maurice J. Craig, *The Volunteer Earl: Being the Life and Times of James Caulfield, First Earl of Charlemont* (London: Cresset Press 1948).

14 On the life and times of John Foster, especially his resistance to the reforms championed by the Irish Volunteers and Patriot MPs, see A.P.W. Malcolmson, *John Foster: The Politics of the Anglo-Irish Ascendancy* (Oxford: Oxford University Press 1978), 32–77.

15 *VJC* 3, no. 38 (10 May 1784), 2.

16 *VJC* 2, no. 37 (8 May 1783), 2.

17 Ibid.

18 *VJC* 3, no. 28 (17 May 1784), 1. Rutland was accused of nocturnal revelry and inebriation, lewd recreations of a brothel, and ignoring his wife for feasting upon 'the meretricious arms of some fallacious nymph.'

19 Ibid.

20 *VJC* 3, no. 20 (10 April 1783), 1.

21 *VJC* 2, no. 47 (12 June 1783), 1.

22 See footnote 8.

23 Bartlett, '"This Famous Island ...,"' 267.

24 Nicholas Canny, *Kingdom and Colony: Ireland in the Atlantic World 1560–1800* (Baltimore: Johns Hopkins University Press 1988), 122. Canny suggests that in applying English radical political thought to their own situation, the Irish Whigs produce 'an original contribution to political debate, a contribution which had more appeal to radical leaders in the British overseas colonies than it did in England.' He also notes that '[t]he essential link that Ireland contributed to the development of a radical chain of thought has been identified by Caroline Robbins, and she was also correct in representing Irish constitutional thinking as more advanced than in any other dominion of the English Crown during the early decades of the eighteenth century.' The reference here is to Caroline Robbins, *The Eighteenth-Century Commonwealth Man* (Cambridge, MA: Harvard University Press 1959), 134–76.

25 On Molyneux's tract, *The Case of Ireland's Being bound by Acts of Parliament in England, Stated*, published first in 1698, see Robbins, *The Eighteenth-Century Commonwealth Man*, 122–3. Although this appeal for greater independence was quickly forgotten, it resurfaced from time to time, not least in relation to the status of the American colonies before and during the Revolution (ibid., 123–4). On the contribution of Dean Swift's views, see J.C. Beckett, *The Making of Modern Ireland 1603–1923* (London: Faber and Faber 1966), 165–6. Beckett notes that Swift, 'in the letter, addressed to the whole people of Ireland' states his position openly. He denies that the people of Ireland are 'in some state of slavery or dependence different from those of En-

gland.' Both kingdoms alike depend directly on the Crown, and England
has no right to make laws for Ireland. His purpose is, he declares, to show
his readers 'that by the laws of god, of nature, of nations, and of your own
country, you are and ought to be as free a people as your brethren in
England' (ibid., 166).

26 Canny, *Kingdom and Colony*, 125–6.

27 Beckett, *The Making of Modern Ireland*, 187–206.

28 Alan Ward, *The Irish Constitutional Tradition*, 18–20.

29 *VJC* 1 (14 November 1782), 1. The publishers were originally John Baldwin,
Robert's brother, and Phineas Bagnell, who had previously edited the *Cork
Evening Post*. Bagnell retired from the partnership after six weeks. John,
having purchased the latter's share, brought Robert in to replace him. See
R.M. and J. Baldwin, *The Great Experiment*, 23.

30 *VJC* 2, no. 38 (12 May 1783), 1, report from the Dublin Correspondent.

31 *VJC* 2, no. 20 (13 March 1783), 1.

32 *VJC* 2, no. 38 (12 May 1783), 1. It is also noted that the outgoing lieutenant
governor, Lord Temple, has been on record as favouring an absentee landlord tax, and the hope was expressed that 'his successors my possess the
same liberal sentiments.' *VJC* 2, no. 42 (26 May 1783), 3, Report from Dublin.

33 *VJC* 1, no. 9 (30 January 1783), 2–3, with an extract from *Dublin Evening
Post*. The question of whether repeal or renunciation was the appropriate
strategy caused a permanent rift between the Patriot leaders, with Grattan
espousing the former and Flood the latter. As relations between the two
men deteriorated, they agreed upon a duel as the way to resolve the ongoing dispute. Both were arrested on route to the duel venue and bound over
to keep the peace. See National Library of Ireland, *Grattan's Parliament*,
Document 10, Cartoon of the parliamentary exchange between Grattan and
Flood with excerpts from text of speeches (from a print in the British
Museum).

34 *VJC* 2, no. 20 (13 March 1783).

35 *VJC* 2, no. 32 (24 April 1783), 2–3. The Duke of Richmond argued for ple-
nary jurisdiction, while the Earl of Abingdon would have restricted Irish
legislative autonomy to internal matters.

36 *VJC* 2, no. 38 (12 May 1783), 2.

37 *VJC* 2, no. 43 (29 May 1783), 2.

38 Ibid., 3. Emphasis in original.

39 *VJC* 3, no. 5 (15 January 1784), 2–3.

40 R.M. and J. Baldwin, *The Great Experiment*, 29–31. The authors note that the
Patriots in the Irish Parliament were divided, because Lord Charlemont

and Henry Grattan had been alienated, the former because of fears of an open break with Britain, and the latter on the question of Catholic emancipation, which he supported. Flood for his part was only interested in an expanded Protestant legislature.

41 *VJC* 3, no. 37 (6 May 1784), 1.

42 Ibid., 2.

43 Bartlett, '"This Famous Island ...,"' 268.

44 *VJC* 3, no. 37 (6 May 1784), 3.

45 *VJC* 3, no. 38 (10 May 1784), 1.

46 Ibid. The text went: 'Confusions to the Ins and Outs in England, such a time being the only one opportunity for us to wrest concessions from the fangs of our tyrannical sister.'

47 Ibid., 2. This was a reference to Matthew Carey, the publisher of the *Volunteer Journal* of Dublin, who was arrested on the orders of the speaker of the House of Commons, John Foster, imprisoned, and charged with sedition. The *Journal* had been engaging in increasingly heated and colourful criticism of the Irish administration and its members. See Inglis, *The Freedom of the Press in Ireland*, 23–38.

48 Ibid.

49 *VJC* 3, no. 39 (17 May 1784), 2.

50 Reported in the *VJC* 3, no. 31 (15 April 1784).

51 Ibid., 2, for the text of the bill.

52 Ibid., 3.

53 Ibid. Report on parliamentary proceedings and vigorous debate that had occurred.

54 Ibid. One assumes that this was penned either by one of the Baldwins or by someone in their employ or otherwise very close to them.

55 *VJC* 3, no. 37 (6 May 1784), 1, and no. 38 (10 May 1784), 2.

56 For the background to this legislative initiative and its fate, see Inglis, *The Freedom of the Press in Ireland*, 38–46. Inglis suggests that in the result the legislation was not nearly as detrimental to the Patriot press as the stamp duty legislation passed the following year.

57 R.M. and J. Baldwin, *The Great Experiment*, 32.

58 Ibid., 32–3.

59 See James Kelly, *Henry Grattan* (Dublin: Historical Association of Ireland 1993), 24–5.

60 Ibid., 32–3.

61 For a helpful overview of this period in Irish history, see Robert Kee, *The Green Flag*, vol. 1, *The Most Distressful Country* (Harmondsworth, UK: Penguin Books 1972). Several of the leaders of the United Irishmen had previ-

ously been Volunteers. A good example of a Volunteer who chose the credo of law and order was Robert Day, recorder of Dublin, and, from 1796, justice of the Irish Court of King's Bench. In that capacity he sentenced rebels to hang or to be transported during and after the Rebellion. He was a life long friend of Henry Grattan, although they separated politically. Day was one who reacted unfavourably to the excesses of the French Revolution. His conversion was completed by the Rebellion of 1798. See Ella B. Day, *Mr. Justice Day of Kerry, 1745–1841* (Exeter: William Pollard 1938), foreword by Stephen Gwyn, xi–xii. A collection of Day's charges to juries are collected in bound volumes held by the Royal Irish Academy. I am indebted to Dr Ruan O'Donnell of the Department of History, University of Limerick, for this lead.

62 As 1998 was the bicentenary of the Irish Rebellion of 1798, there was an outpouring of national and local histories dedicated to the subject. An engaging month by month account of the conflict is provided in Ruan O'Donnell, *1798 Diary* (Dublin: Irish Times Books 1998).

63 John Manning Ward, *Colonial Self-Government: The British Experience 1759–1856* (Toronto: University of Toronto Press 1976), 4–20.

64 Christopher Moore, *The Law Society of Upper Canada and Ontario's Lawyers, 1797–1997* (Toronto: University of Toronto Press 1997), 71–6.

65 Ibid., 72.

66 On these aspects of William Warren Baldwin's social and political conservatism, see Robert Fraser, "'All the Privileges which Englishmen Possess": Order, Rights and Constitutionalism in Upper Canada' and 'WWB' in Fraser, ed., *Provincial Justice*, xlii–xlvii, 208–210, respectively. Christopher Moore suggests that while Baldwin shared many of the political and social predilections of men such as John Beverley Robinson, who were among the governing elite of the colony, he differed in two respects. First, he recognized the propertied classes in Upper Canada as encompassing a wide range of land owners, from the humble to the great. Secondly, he seems to have seen the importance of upholding the independence of the Law Society as in part related to its capacity to harbour and protect lawyers with reformist beliefs. See Moore, *The Law Society ...*, 75–7.

67 W.W. Baldwin, *Account of Life of his Father*, 6. The younger Baldwin refers to his father as being a 'peacemaker' in family disputes.

68 This was true of Robert Baldwin who experienced bankruptcy in 1788 and financial difficulties thereafter, until the family left Ireland. His principal creditor in 1788 and economic mentor in the wake of insolvency was Sir Robert Warren, a kinsman and more substantial landowner. Warren was Robert's uncle by marriage. See ibid., 10–3.

69 *VJC* 3, no. 9 (29 January 1784), 1.

70 W.W. Baldwin, *Account of Life of his Father*, 6–9, 22.

71 Letter from W.W. Baldwin to John Baldwin, Attorney, Cork, 24 October 1801, Baldwin Family Correspondence, Metro Toronto Library, L12.

72 Fraser 'WWB,' 203.

73 On the circumstances surrounding this decision, see R.M. and J. Baldwin, *The Great Experiment*, 60–3.

74 Philip Girard, *Patriot Jurist: Beamish Murdoch of Halifax, 1800–1875* (PhD diss., Dalhousie University 1998), 83–105. In this section of the thesis, Girard examines through the early career of Murdoch's mentor, Richard John Uniacke, the legal profession in late-eighteenth-century Dublin. William Warren would have been aware of the reputations and role of the leading lawyer Patriots of that era, including Henry Grattan, Henry Flood, and John Philpott Curran.

75 Fraser, '"All the Privileges which Englishmen Possess,"' xl. See William Blackstone, *Commentaries on the Laws of England*, 4 vols. (Oxford: Clarendon Press 1765). Baldwin would have had access to a later English edition.

76 Draft letter from W.W. Baldwin to John Beverley Robinson, 21 May 1828, W.W. Baldwin Papers, Metro Toronto Library. See also Paul Romney, 'Very Late Loyalist Fantasies: Nostalgic Tory "History" and the Rule of Law in Upper Canada,' in W. Wesley Pue and Barry Wright, eds., *Canadian Perspectives on Law and Society: Issues in Legal History* (Ottawa: Carleton University Press 1987), 196, 131–2.

77 On the 'Family Compact,' see Jane Errington, *The Lion, the Eagle and Upper Canada: A Developing Colonial Ideology* (Kingston: McGill-Queen's Press 1987), 89–96; Graeme Patterson, 'An Enduring Canadian Myth: Responsible Government and the Family Compact,' *Journal of Canadian Studies* 12 (1977), 3–16.

78 Paul Romney, *Mr. Attorney: The Attorney General for Ontario in Court, Cabinet, and Legislature, 1791–1899* (Toronto: Osgoode Society for Canadian Legal History and the University of Toronto Press 1986), 109–14; Fraser, 'WWB,' 211. On the broader pattern of Tory-inspired violence in Upper Canada in the 1820s, see Carol Wilton, '"Lawless Law": Political Violence in Upper Canada, 1818–1841,' *Law and History* 13 (1995), 111.

79 Fraser, 'WWB.'

80 Dr Baldwin and others, Petition to King George IV on the case of Justice Willis ('Baldwin Petition'), 1828, CIHM 41338. See also Romney, *Mr. Attorney*, 141–53; Fraser, 'WWB,' 213–14.

81 For a biographical entry on the controversial Willis who subsequently became a member of the New South Wales Supreme Court and was again

removed from office in 1843, see Alan Wilson, 'John Walpole Willis,' in Fraser, ed., *Provincial Justice*, 195–8.

82 Fraser, '"All the Privileges which Englishmen Posses,"' lv–lviii, lx.

83 On Russell and his record of service in the colony, see Edith Firth, 'Peter Russell,' *Dictionary of Canadian Biography*, vol. 5, 1801–20, available online from www.biographi.ca/EN/index.html.

84 On the contribution of this group, especially Thorpe, to political and legal ideology in Upper Canada and the stir it caused, see Douglas Brymner, *Report on the Canadian Archives, 1892* (Ottawa: Queen's Printer 1893); Graeme Patterson, 'Whiggery, Nationality, and the Canadian Reform Tradition,' *Canadian Historical Review* 56 (1975), 25; John McLaren, 'The King, the People, the Law ... and the Constitution: Justice Robert Thorpe and the Roots of Irish Whig Ideology in Early Upper Canada,' in Jonathan Swainger and Constance Backhouse, eds., *People and Place: Historical Influences on Legal Culture* (Vancouver: UBC Press 2003), 11–24.

85 *An Act for the better securing this Province against all Seditious Attempts or Designs to disturb the Tranquility thereof, Statutes of Upper Canada* 1804, c.1. The text is set out in F. Murray Greenwood and Barry Wright, eds., *Canadian State Trials: Law, Politics, and Security Measures*, vol. 1, *1608–1837* (Toronto: Osgoode Society for Canadian Legal History and University of Toronto Press 1996), 660–4.

86 See *Journals of the Upper Canada House of Assembly and Legislative Council*, February–March 1804, 6th Report of the Bureau of Archives for the Province of Ontario (Toronto: Bureau of Archives 1911), and Barry Wright, 'Migration, Radicalism and State Security: Legislative Initiatives in the Canadas and the United States, c. 1794–1804,' *Studies in American Political Development* 16 (2002), 48–60.

87 On Hunter's land policy, see In Collaboration, 'Peter Hunter,' *Dictionary of Canadian Biography* vol. 5, 1801–20, available online from www.biographi. ca/EN/index.html. Hunter had been military governor of Wexford in the wake of the Irish Rebellion of 1798.

88 A majority of the Court of King's Bench had in *Bliss v. Street* in 1799 decided that land could be seized for indebtedness. Justice Henry Allcock had dissented on the ground that such a decision would be ruinous to the small farmers of the colony. He made this opinion clear to Lieutenant Governor Hunter when, in 1801, the latter was considering legislation to enshrine the court's decision. See Paul Romney, *Mr. Attorney*, 77–8.

89 In Collaboration, 'Peter Hunter.'

90 McLaren, 'The King, the People, the Law,' 12–13. Thorpe was aware that at that time some judges sat in Parliament at Westminster (including Irish

judges and the Master of the Rolls) and in colonial legislatures (chief justices often sat in legislative councils and a predecessor of Thorpe on the Upper Canadian bench, puisne justice Henry Allcock, has been elected to the Assembly in 1802 only to have his election nullified because of the importuning of his agent, one William Weekes). See on Thorpe's views on the propriety of him sitting in the assembly, undated letter from Thorpe to Lieutenant Governor Gore, Brymner, *Report on Canadian Archives*, 93. On the Allcock election, see Patterson, 'Weekes,' 285–6.

91 On Weekes' influence on Thorpe and how he seems to have stage-managed Thorpe's contact with assize juries, see McLaren, 'The King, the People, the Law,' 16–17.

92 Letters from Justice Thorpe to Edward Cooke, Under-Secretary, Colonial Office, 24 January 1806 and 1 April 1806, Brymner, *Report on Canadian Archives*, 39, 46–7.

93 Letter from Thorpe to Sir George Shee, Under-Secretary, Colonial Office, 1 December 1806, ibid., 52.

94 Blackstone, *Commentaries on the Laws of England*, vol. 1, 117–41.

95 For the persuasive thesis that the *Constitution Act of Upper Canada* (1791) was in reality a counter-revolutionary document designed to give the British government close control of this colony (as well as of its sister colony, Lower Canada), see John Manning Ward, *Colonial Self-Government*, 1–3, and Fraser, '"All the Privileges which Englishmen Posses,"' xxviii–xxix. For the text of Simcoe's statement, see J.M. Bliss, ed., *Canadian History in Documents, 1763–1966* (Toronto: Ryerson Press 1966), 34.

96 Patterson, 'Whiggery, Nationality and the Upper Canadian Reform Tradition,' 31–2.

97 Ibid., 32–5. Fragments of the tract were published in an anonymous letter to the *Upper Canadian Herald*, 14 October 1829. The text of that letter is appended to K.D. McRae, 'An Upper Canadian Letter of 1829 on Responsible Government,' *Canadian Historical Review* 31 (1950), 288–96, 291–6.

98 Letter from Castlereagh to Gore, 18 June 1807, Brymner, *Report on Canadian Archives*, 85–6. Gore had requested Thorpe's removal from office by letter to William Windham, a short-lived Secretary of State for the Colonies, 13 March 1807, ibid., 61–4. The letter is accompanied by a series of documents relating to Thorpe's impropriety. Also McLaren, 'The King, the People, the Law,' 18.

99 Elwood Jones, 'Joseph Willcocks,' in Fraser, ed., *Provincial Justice*, 432–42.

100 Fraser, 'WWB,' 203–4, indicates that, while Baldwin was ready to and did support his friends when they needed it, 'he avoided any overt demonstration of his political sympathies.'

101 Ibid., 203. Peter Russell and Robert Thorpe were respectively Baldwin's sponsors for these positions.

102 Ibid.

103 Ibid.

104 Ibid., 204. See also R.M.and J.Baldwin, *The Great Experiment*, 88–90, and J. Phean, 'A Duel on the Island,' *Ontario History* 69 (1977), 237.

105 Ibid., 'WWB,' 205–6; R.M. and J. Baldwin, *The Great Experiment*, 97–101. Baldwin did share the view that the 'Scotch' continued to have a stranglehold on the colony's administration. Fraser, 'WWB,' 207.

106 See note 66.

107 *Kingston Chronicle*, 11 January 1822, 1–2, Proceedings of the House of Assembly.

108 On the use of the act against Gourlay, see Barry Wright, 'The Gourlay Affair: Seditious Libel and the Sedition Act in Upper Canada, 1818–1819,' in Greenwood and Wright, eds., *Canadian State Trials*, vol. 1, 487–504, and documents, 697–702.

109 *Kingston Chronicle*, 21 December 1821, 2, Proceedings of the House of Assembly.

110 H.T. Dickinson, *Liberty and Property*, 121–94.

111 Fraser, 'WWB,' 209.

112 Ibid., 209–10.

113 See McRae, 'An Upper Canada Letter,' 291–6; Patterson, 'Whiggery, Nationality, and the Upper Canadian Reform Tradition,' 25–44.

114 Fraser, 'WWB,' 209–10.

115 *Kingston Chronicle*, 7 March 1823, 3, Proceedings of the House of Assembly.

116 Ibid. On the abuses of the justice system during this period, see Fraser, '"All the Privileges which Englishmen Possess,"' lxviii–lxix.

117 Baldwin had already been treasurer for the years 1811–15 and 1820–1 and would serve again from 1832–6.

118 Fraser, '"All the Privileges which Englishmen Possess,"' xliii–xlvii.

119 Ibid., lxviii.

120 Fraser, 'WWB,' 213.

121 See Petition by Dr Baldwin and others to King George IV on the case of Justice Willis (Baldwin Petition) 1828, CIHM No. 41338. The speech is reported in the *Canadian Freeman*, 12 July 1828.

122 See G.M. Craig, 'John Rolph,' *Dictionary of Canadian Biography*, vol. 9, 1861–70, and G.M. Craig, 'Marshall Spring Bidwell,' *DCB*, vol. 10, 1871–80, available online from www.biographi.ca/EN/index.html.

123 Baldwin Petition. Fraser, '"All the Privileges which Englishmen Possess,"' lxxi–lxxii.

124 Fraser, 'WWB,' 217–18.

125 Ibid., 218.

126 For evidence of Bond Head's antipathy to W.W. Baldwin and his tarring of him as a member of the 'Republican Party,' see Sir Francis Bond Head, *A Narrative* (1839; reprint, Toronto: McClelland and Stewart 1969), 61–2, 86, 108–13. This apologia contains significant excerpts from the lieutenant governor's correspondence with the Colonial Office.

127 Ibid., 218–19.

128 Ibid., 219.

129 Ibid.

130 Gerald M. Craig, ed., *Lord Durham's Report* (Toronto: McClelland and Stewart 1963), xi, 139–45.

131 Fraser, 'WWB,' 218–19.

132 For an account of British resistance to Durham's advocacy of responsible government and Joseph Howe's classic rejoinder to it, see Lord John Russell, 'Objections to Responsible Government,' and Joseph Howe, 'Letters,' in Bliss, ed., *Canadian History in Documents, 1763–1966*, 63–9.

133 See J.M.S. Careless, *The Union of the Canadas: The Growth of Canadian Institutions* (Toronto: McClelland and Stewart 1967), 113–31.

134 See Patterson, 'Whiggery, Nationality and the Upper Canadian Reform Tradition,' 41.

135 Fraser, 'WWB,' 209.

136 One wonders whether Baldwin, a younger man than most other members of the group and perhaps more judicious by nature, saw some virtue in distancing himself from the more extreme conduct of its members. It is difficult to suppose that either he or his father would have approved of flags with an uncrowned harp being used in Thorpe's election campaign. See McLaren, 'The King, the People, the Law,' 12–13.

PART FOUR

New Directions in Legal History – Private Law, International Law, Low Law, and Informal Law

10

Diplomacy, International Law, and Foreign Fishing in Newfoundland, 1814–30: Revisiting the 1815 Treaty of Paris and the 1818 Convention

RAINER BAEHRE

A recent study of nineteenth-century international law and state transformation notes that 'treatises of international law were on every diplomat's reference shelf.'[1] In the writing of Canadian legal history, however, we know very little about the role of international law and its application, except in relation to Aboriginal issues. In particular, nobody has examined at any length the diplomatic and legal context of two important treaties: the Treaty of Paris of 1815[2] and the Convention of 1818. The former (hereafter the Treaty of Paris) established peace and economic relations between Britain and France. The latter (the Convention) was signed between Britain and the United States, and constituted the third stage in the return to peace and normalization of relations after the War of 1812. It was preceded by the Treaty of Ghent of 1814, which ended hostilities between the two countries; the earlier Commercial Convention of 1815, under which trade resumed; and the Rush-Bagot Treaty of 1817, which demilitarized the Great Lakes. All were 'legally binding instruments with established enforcement mechanisms,'[3] yet, as with all treaties, their negotiation, content, and implementation were shaped by a variety of factors, including the effect of war on previous treaties, the ability to enforce the terms, and interpretations of the language.

The Treaty of Paris and the Convention included clauses on French and American fishing rights in Atlantic Canada, particularly in Newfoundland and Labrador, and attempted to resolve some long-standing disputes.[4] The protracted struggle between France and Britain for dominance in North America was rooted in the seventeenth century, continued during the War of the Spanish Succession between 1702 and 1713, and culminated in a series of treaties widely known as the Treaty of Utrecht. Under this treaty, France ceded Acadia, lands around Hudson's Bay, and Newfoundland to Britain. However, under Article 13, it retained fishing rights from Cape Bonavista to Point Riche, a stretch of coastline often referred to as the old French Shore, upon which France could raise various temporary physical structures to conduct the fishery but not fortifications or settlements.[5]

When conflict resumed between Britain and France three decades later, finally concluding with the Seven Years' War and the complicated and global Treaty of Paris of 1763, which incorporated seventeen previous treaties, the issue of French fishing rights again emerged.[6] Under Article 5, the Treaty of Utrecht's terms regarding the island of Newfoundland were 'renewed and confirmed,' giving French subjects 'the liberty' of fishing along the previously designated coastline, though French fishing was restricted to fifteen leagues off the coast in parts of the Gulf of St Lawrence, Cape Breton, and Nova Scotia. Also, under Article 6, the islands of St Pierre and Miquelon off Newfoundland's south coast were ceded to France but only to provide 'a shelter to the French fishermen.'

The next diplomatic episode involving the Newfoundland fishery came during the War of American Independence, which France supported, when both French and traditional American fishing rights were negated, only to be renewed and confirmed under the Definitive Treaty of Peace of 1783.[7] Article 3 stated that 'the people of the United States shall continue to enjoy unmolested the right to take fish of every kind on the Grand Bank and on all the other banks of Newfoundland, also in the Gulf of Saint Lawrence and at all other places in the sea, where the inhabitants of both countries used at any time heretofore to fish,' with the 'liberty to take fish of every kind on such part of the coast of Newfoundland as British fishermen shall use, (but not to dry or cure the same on that island).' Article 13 of the Treaty of Utrecht was adopted under a Declaration of His Britannic Majesty, and Britain applied 'positive' law to ensure non-interference with the French fishery, including prohibiting settlement by either party upon the French shore and overwintering, but allowing French fishers to build temporary scaffolding and coming into shore to repair their vessels. St Pierre and Miquelon remained a place of 'real shelter' only, and fishing between them and the island of Newfoundland was to be limited to the middle of the channel.[8] In turn, the French government declared that it was 'fully satisfied' with the provisions governing its use of the Newfoundland fishery.

Although the Treaty of Paris of 1815 and the Convention of 1818 are part of a historical continuum going back to the Treaty of Utrecht, this essay suggests that the diplomatic and legal context during the negotiations was also markedly different from their predecessors. British concessions to France and the United States in the Newfoundland fishery had a significant impact upon the island's economic history. These concessions led to the return of the French fishery along large sections of the north-east and western coastline of the island, establishing a new French Shore, and extended American fishing rights along the south and the west coast, or 'the American Shore,' which overlapped large sections of the French shore, and extended along the Labrador coast. [9]

As well, these treaties and their implementation[10] illustrate early-nineteenth-century conflict resolution over geopolitical and economic issues – how nation states attempted to avert confrontation and possible war.[11] As one author has argued, 'the political discourse surrounding peace negotiations often sheds more light on the structural and legal context within which a treaty has to be considered than contemporary [legal] doctrine.'[12] This essay examines that discourse, as well as the diplomatic and legal arguments arrayed, in the negotiations, and also looks at both the language of the treaties and at how compliance was effected. While the antecedents and successors of the Treaty of Paris (for example, the Treaties of Utrecht and of Washington) and the Convention (the Reciprocity Treaty) have received considerable attention, little work has been done on these two treaties or on how they influenced British, French, and American relations during the 1820s and, in turn, shaped Newfoundland's history. The purpose of this essay is thus to add a further international legal dimension to our understanding of important topics in Newfoundland's history.

The French Shore

Historians have viewed the Anglo-French treaties of 1814 and 1815 largely as extensions of earlier treaties,[13] suggesting that the renewal of French and American fishing in Newfoundland after 1815 constituted, in part, a form of prescriptive or historic right to fishing grounds based on traditional usage and previous agreements. Contemporary British,

French, and American officials and their lawyers have often referred to the rights defined in the Treaty of Utrecht (1713), the Treaty of Paris (1783), and others. Yet there was also universal agreement at the beginning of the nineteenth century that war suspended, if it did not negate, all past treaties,[14] and thus the fishing provisions of the Treaty of Paris cannot be seen as axiomatic; they were the product of contingent choices, negotiation, and understandings of international law.

The original French Shore had been established under the Treaty of Utrecht when Britain gave France 'concurrent' fishing rights along Newfoundland's coast, and were reaffirmed in the Treaty of Paris of 1763. After 1763, France argued that it had an 'exclusive' claim to the Newfoundland fishery – a position Britain then rejected, though it did give France fishing privileges. French rights were again lost when France and the United States signed the Treaty of Amity and Commerce (1778) during the American Revolution. France renegotiated the rights under the Treaty of Versailles (1783), though on a different coastline, the 'new French Shore.' Fishing rights were taken away once more in 1793, except for a brief hiatus after the Treaty of Amiens (1802). Following Napoleon's abdication and the 1814 Treaty of Paris, French fishing rights were restored, only to be suspended during Napoleon's Hundred Days return and then reaffirmed in the second Treaty of Paris. The absence of a French Shore for most of the years between 1793 and 1815 is significant in Newfoundland's history because its English fishery enjoyed boom years as a result, and many British fishers and settlers moved into what many considered to be a rich, if not the richest, fishery on the island.

Under existing international law Britain was under no obligation to restore France's fishery in 1815. It did so largely in the interests of a lasting peace. British victory had ensured it supremacy of the seas, but its continuing security was threatened by French political instability in the post-Napoleonic world. The purpose of the Treaty of Paris, as well as the Congress of Vienna and the Concert of Europe, was 'a just balance of power in Europe' to ensure peaceful relations among remaining European powers. There were serious differences among the victors in how to deal with France. For instance, Prussia viewed the Treaty of Paris (1815) as not hard line enough because of Napoleon's return. While France complained that the treaty was 'not moderate enough,' forcing it to accept pre-1793 boundaries, a war-weary Britain took the middle road, offered France concessions, and sought to consolidate its global hegemonic status by reducing the chances of war. To this end,

Foreign Secretary Castlereagh employed a pragmatic strategy of cooperation and conciliation.[15] Consequently, the Treaty of Paris was less a matter of redistributing political and military power to restore international order than of establishing 'a legal and moral balance, an *équilibre des droits.*'[16] This was a position consistent with 'the international law of the civilised nations,' under which sovereign states were recognised as having equal rights and obligations and the duty to act on the basis of good will rather than on Machiavellian diplomacy.[17]

The nineteenth-century Newfoundland nationalist historian D.W. Prowse bitterly denounced Britain for sacrificing the island's fishery to France. He condemned Castlereagh's rationale as 'the flimsiest and most paltry excuse for a great diplomatic blunder.'[18] Now, however, historians generally concede that British diplomats genuinely believed that they needed to keep republicanism and revolution at bay in order to achieve a lasting peace. As Prince Metternich, the key Austrian diplomat at the Vienna Congress emphasised, 'a fresh war would bring alarming chances of danger and revolution.'[19] Castlereagh knew well that nationalism and continuing ideological divisions among republican and Bourbon supporters were an ever-present danger, and 'that a peace which humiliated France would unite royalists and Bonapartists in pressing for an active foreign policy to restore French pride and reaffirm the greatness of France.'[20] The answer was to find a political equilibrium through conciliation and concession, which firmed up a constitutional monarchy and appeased nationalist sentiment. The Newfoundland fishery served a role in advancing this equilibrium of rights and reducing France's sense of humiliation. The Grand Banks, St Pierre and Miquelon, and the French Shore, all traditionally a nursery for the French navy where fish bounties had been used to ensure that 'enrolled fishermen' would be easily drafted,[21] reflected France's imperial ambitions and symbolised its former glory.[22] France viewed British domination of the seas as a threat to the balance of power in Europe. To counteract this supremacy, it heavily subsidized its fisheries for economic reasons and to sustain a nursery for seamen in Newfoundland and elsewhere to advance its naval power.

British diplomats also appreciated that concessions in the Treaty of Paris would not alone protect France's new rulers. A return to economic normalcy was also needed, and in this the French Shore was important, for in the 1780s, upwards of ten thousand French fishers had worked there.[23] The number of ships from Bayonne and St-Jean-de-Luz alone in the mid-1780s increased to twenty-four vessels of 45 to 205 tonnes from St Pierre and Miquelon and another seven ships, mostly over 200 tonnes, out of Port au Choix and Cape Ray. The signing of the Treaty of Amiens of 1802 saw the return of 109 French sailing ships and 3,000 fishers for that one fishing season. The reacquisition of St Pierre and Miquelon and a return of the French Shore were therefore important in helping France in its economic recovery while also yielding political benefits.

Nevertheless, the return of the French Shore was not inevitable, nor was it business as usual. Newfoundland merchants, supported by Governor Richard Keats,[24] strongly argued against handing over the coastline.[25] Merchants supplied the British government with a wealth of information outlining how planters and fishers had been working and building expensive establishments along the former French shore since 1793. Keats warned the government *prior to the treaty's signing* of 'the very serious consequences to be apprehended,' should France (and the United States) be granted fishing privileges again, especially for landing and curing fish. In anticipating British concessions, however, Keats asked that, should France be given new concessions, the French be restricted to the Gulf of St Lawrence coastline, a less desirable area than the north-east coast from Cape Norman to Cape St John, which was 'very plentifully supplied with fish,' and would serve as compensation for losses suffered by soon-to-be dispossessed planters and fishers. He also recommended that Britain keep St Pierre and Miquelon to reduce smuggling, though France might be given access to meet the needs of its migratory fishery. Keats also urged concurrent rather than exclusive rights, allowing British fishers to fish alongside the French, as well as time to dispose of their buildings and property, 'at their leisure,' in the event that they were denied the use of them.[26]

The home government, however, was unmoved, and secretary of state for the Colonies Lord Bathurst informed Castlereagh that he was 'not particularly pugnatious [*sic*] as to what we are to give up.'[27] As a result, Article 8 of the Definitive Treaty of Paris (1814) called for the restoration of 'the Colonies, Fisheries Factories, and Establishments of every kind which were possessed by France on the 1st of January, 1792, in the Seas and on the Continents of America, Africa, and Asia,' while Article 13 stated, that '[t]he French right of fishery upon the Great Bank of Newfoundland, upon the coasts of the island of that name, and of the adjacent islands in the Gulf of St Lawrence, shall be replaced upon the footing on which it stood in 1792.'[28]

Britain showed some willingness to protect Newfoundland and its fishery when Napoleon unexpectedly returned. For example, Bathurst suspended the treaty and left intact all British possessions on the soon-to-be restored French Shore. Also, during the Hundred Days, when France requested the right to import American timber into St Pierre and Miquelon for the purpose of rebuilding its possessions, a flurry of diplomatic correspondence followed, and Britain consented to France's request only after receiving assurances from the French minister of the marine as to the exact nature of the goods and number of vessels.[29] In a separate incident during December 1814, when the French fishing fleet appeared off the Grand Banks, Keats sent troops to protect Newfoundland's outports against treaty violations, such as taking wood from its coast.[30] In short, at this stage, Britain was willing to defend its sovereignty, even if conflict resulted. In 1815, however, after the final defeat of Napoleon, Newfoundland residents watched helplessly as St Pierre and Miquelon were returned, France's fishing rights were restored, and the settlement of unauthorized residents restricted on large portions of the coastline.

In the past, the legal enforcement of French treaty and fishing rights had often proven difficult. Prior to 1783, Newfoundland governors were explicitly ordered not to allow French officers to exercise authority over British subjects. But to appease France and minimize conflict, Britain had directed settlers on this coast to remove themselves, or risk ejection. French fishers were also prevented from settling and overwintering, and often had to rely on Newfoundland residents, or *gardiens*, to protect their property during long winter absences.[31] Occasionally, removals were ruthlessly carried out by both French and British authorities who destroyed British fishing stations and forcibly relocated illegal settlers.[32] After 1783, France began to dominate the regulation of the French Shore, in part because there were few British vessels to do so.[33] While insisting that there was no loss of sovereignty, and that this remained a 'concurrent' fishery, Britain nevertheless thus gave France, a foreign power, control over British subjects and by doing so unwillingly gave support to France's claims of an 'exclusive' right. To complicate matters, when, after 1793, France left the region, a growing number of fishers, furriers, and salmoniers from eastern and northeastern Newfoundland moved into the French Shore region.[34]

In 1814, Britain insisted once more that the French Shore fishery remain 'concurrent,' though British fishers were expected to keep their distance from the French, subject to arrest and penalty for illegal fishing and settling. The Newfoundland residents who had established themselves previously were therefore asked to leave. Occasionally, French and British authorities destroyed British fishing stations along the French shore, and forced them out.[35] In 1819, for example, British planters hired by the Rennie Stewart company of St John's went to St George's Bay to fish cod and herring, only to find that 'in several instances [they were] driven away from the Fishery Ground by the French there at the time, who claimed an exclusive right to the Fisheries of that Bay.'[36] When the company's agent asked Governor Hamilton of Newfoundland[37] whether France's rights were indeed exclusive, he was told that they were not – they were a common right based on King William's Act (10 and 11 Wm. 3, c.25) – but that pursuant to the Treaties of Utrecht and Paris (1783) no one was allowed to settle, and English fishers must 'not interrupt or disturb' French fishers.[38] Newfoundland chief justice Francis Forbes also confirmed that 'an exclusive privilege' had not been granted to the French;[39] it remained a concurrent fishery, with fishers of either nation allowed to catch their fish and use the land to erect stages and huts, as necessary, for the drying process.

Despite the British view that the fishery had stayed concurrent after 1815, tensions mounted. In 1820, English settlers at St George's Bay were accused of destroying the flakes and nets of two French settlers in nearby Liver's Bay.[40] In the following year, Joseph Bird Jr of the firm T.S. Bird of Sturminster Newton and Poole, was confronted by a French sloop of war, *La Diane*, which forced him to abandon Bonne Bay, his father's 'settlement' of thirteen years, and then forced 'many English' engaged in the salmon fishery out of the Bay of Islands. When Britain remonstrated, France agreed to allow the company's employees to fish salmon, though not cod, along the French Shore.[41]

In other incidents French huts on the Petit Nord at Quirpon were pillaged and burnt by British fishers and sealers on their way to Labrador, prompting the governor to offer a reward of £20 for apprehending the perpetrators,[42] and a murder was committed at nearby Conche.[43] Captain Nicolas, the British naval officer acting as the governor's surrogate, was sent to investigate and enforce the law. He reported back: '[T]he French people represent that the crimes committed at Quirpon are only a part of the many which are annually committed by British subjects in each succeeding fall, and more particularly in each succeeding spring on that part of the Coast of Newfoundland assigned to the French fisheries.' However, Nicolas could find sufficient evidence only to prosecute the Quirpon case.[44] He also found two French sloops of war, *La Diane* and *La Charrante*, at anchor at Croque, where Captain Venancourt questioned Nicolas' legal authority, informing him that France had an exclusive right over the fishery, and that Croque was a French port.

By 1822 these confrontations prompted Governor Hamilton to issue a proclamation, as several Newfoundland governors had done in the past, in favour of France's 'full and complete enjoyment of the fishery within the limits and boundaries in the manner they are entitled to enjoy the same under the said Treaty of Utrecht.'[45] Two years later, when Newfoundland received its royal charter as a colony, this proclamation became embedded in the *Fisheries Act*.[46]

In the years following 1815, Britain's position continued to be that the French Shore constituted a temporary right.[47] French vessels could fish there undisturbed and use the coast, but not reign over it. In contrast, France claimed that Britain had acknowledged a *de facto* exclusive right to the French Shore.[48] This issue of an 'exclusive' as opposed to a 'concurrent,' or common, right on the French Shore soon caused serious differences, not only with Britain but also with the United States, because the 'American Shore,' as defined by the Convention, overlapped the French Shore. French authorities continued to insist on claiming their shore as a *droit exclusive*,[49] even when in 1829 Britain sent the warship *Hannah* to Quirpon to press its position. Later, France's determination to secure exclusive rights was reflected in its placing Codroy Island, a fishing station on the west coast, 'as much under its control as either St. Pierre or Miquelon,' and in issuing a permanent title for Red Island near Cape St George to Companie Générale Maritime de France.[50] This polarity of views resulted in long-standing frictions, and only in 1904 with the signing of the *Entente Cordiale* did France fully relinquish its position.[51]

The American Shore

The first and most important article of the Convention between Britain and the United States related to the Atlantic fishery, especially in Newfoundland and Labrador. It was termed a 'convention' rather than a 'treaty' because various clauses other than fishing rights involved agreements-in-progress. Like the Commercial Convention of 1815, it fell under the framework of 'friendship, commerce, and navigation treaties,' and represented 'a serious legal undertaking both in international and domestic law.' Under the American constitution, the agreement was to be treated 'like a Federal statute,' or the 'supreme Law of the Land.'[52] It was also incorporated into British statute law.[53]

The American fishing and whaling fleets had long been active on the Newfoundland banks. During the eighteenth century, they moved into the Gulf of St Lawrence, up the Labrador coast, and into the Canadian Arctic, only to see their activities interrupted by the American Revolution. In the wake of American independence, Britain took a conciliatory course and restored American fishing rights in the Treaty of Paris (1783). In part, Britain conceded these rights because it wanted peace, but in any event the region was sparsely settled, its fishery 'inexhaustible,' and the American fishery did not impinge upon British fisheries. After 1783, an estimated 300 to 400 American vessels fished annually on the Newfoundland banks, the Gulf of St Lawrence, and Labrador. The numbers increased even more after the turn of the century. In 1804, 1,360 American vessels from Cape Cod, Boston, and Plymouth arrived with 10,600 fishers, a number which increased the following year to 1,500 vessels, each carrying ten to twelve crew members.[54] By 1807, British merchants thought that over 2,000 American fishing schooners and least 15,000 personnel had come, roughly two-thirds of them fishing off the Labrador coast.[55] They also argued that much of this catch was reshipped to European and West Indian markets, making American exports of salt fish to the West Indies three times as high as Newfoundland's, and more valuable to the United States than an annexation of the Canadas.[56] This American fishery ended for a time with the *Embargo Act* of 1807, when American ports were closed to British vessels and Britain prohibited American fishing, but resumed when the ports were reopened between May 1809 and the War of 1812.

During these years, New Brunswick, Nova Scotia, and Newfoundland often complained that American vessels breached customs laws and treaty restrictions. In 1803, for example, George Leonard, the superintendent of trade and of the fishery for the Maritime colonies,[57] protested illicit American trade in the Bay of Fundy and at Canso, and recommended using a naval vessel and more effective legislation to guard against smuggling.[58] A decade later, American vessels were caught in Newfoundland for putting into Quirpon to cure their fish and two vessels were seized. Admiral Erasmus Gower also confiscated the catch to be sold at public auction.[59] This, however, was an isolated success; most violators were never caught.

In 1814, Governor Keats provided the most comprehensive list of complaints and described how the American fishers could enter the

Gulf of St Lawrence earlier than Newfoundlanders and took the best harbours, because the annual spring ice pack in the Straits of Belle Isle often blocked access from the north-east tip. The Americans allegedly caused a scarcity of fish for others because they threw their offal overboard, polluted the waters to the detriment of the salmon, and interfered with the capelin stocks needed for bait. They were also accused of cutting competitors' nets, stealing goods from sealing posts, and setting the woods on fire adjacent to harbours to prevent the island's fishers from building and repairing their flakes and stages. In defiance of the Treaty of Paris (1783), they also illegally caught salmon, 'a river fishery,' by setting their nets across river mouths and preventing an estimated half of the annual salmon stock from spawning. At Labrador Harbour, Red Bay, and Cape Charles they illegally used coastal residents to cure their fish, smuggled in provisions for sale, and lured away indentured boatkeepers. In so doing, the Americans undermined the rights and profits of Newfoundland merchants and deprived the government of custom duties.[60]

The War of 1812 suspended the Convention and American rights under it, and thereafter, during the negotiations leading to the Treaty of Ghent. The fishery was so valuable[61] it let U.S. President Madison to adamantly assert, 'Our right to the fisheries, to the full extent of our territory as defined by the Treaty of 1783 with Great Britain ... are of course not to be relinquished.'[62] But the British commissioners were told by their government not to bend and that the fishing rights and privileges of the United States had been terminated with the war.[63] That the fisheries were left unmentioned in the Treaty of Ghent did not reflect their secondary status, but their considerable importance. As the negotiations for the Treaty of Ghent went on, Britain refused to compromise and prohibited Americans from fishing in its colonial waters.[64] Not until the 1818 Convention was the America Shore restored.

The importance of this fishery to the United States is amply demonstrated in comments made by American diplomats. During negotiations for the Convention, John Quincy Adams contended that American fishing rights were firmly stipulated in the Treaty of Paris (1783). He stated that the United States would not only 'have protested against' any attempt to prevent American fishers from frequenting the British North American coast but would have 'reserved the right of recovering the whole by force whenever we should be able.'[65] Following the Convention's signing, he argued that excluding the Americans would result in 'perpetual war between Great Britain and the United

States.'[66] Similarly, Richard Rush, the chief American negotiator of the Rush-Bagot Treaty and the Convention, wrote that 'although not first in the order of discussion, [the fisheries] came first in the convention. The points of misunderstanding had not risen to much height, practically; but it is scarcely going too far to say, that they menaced the peace of the two countries.'[67] In particular, he noted that the agreement represented matters of 'great magnitude' for the United States: 'besides affording profitable fields of commerce, they fostered a race of seamen, conducive to the national riches in peace, as to defence and glory in war.'[68]

The initial failure to settle the fisheries issue between 1814 and 1818, however, resulted in heightened international tension, especially when the Royal Navy seized American fishing vessels in disputed waters.[69] In July 1815 the sloop of war *Jaseur* warned an American vessel not to come within sixty miles of the coast. Believing that war had abrogated American fishing rights, Rear Admiral Griffith was intent on protecting Nova Scotian inhabitants from the 'violence, outrage, and chicanery' practised by the American fishers. However, once notified over this course of action, Anthony Baker, secretary of the British delegation, called upon the navy to observe the laws of maritime jurisdiction, which defined the coastline on the basis of a cannon shot, or one marine league from shore,[70] and, in turn, told the Americans that this action had been unauthorised and would not reoccur.[71] The American government responded decisively, Adams asserting that the *Jaseur*'s action was 'incompatible' with a desire for 'amicable relations' and risked undoing the peace established by the Treaty of Ghent.[72] When the navy forced another vessel out of the Gulf of St Lawrence, Castlereagh placed new restrictions on any interference with the American fishery. As a result, when American vessels made their way to Labrador through the Gut of Canso, Griffiths 'cautioned the captains against using violence' unless they discovered illegal entry, such as ships going into British harbours.[73]

As negotiations dragged on, however, British officers were again told to protect the fisheries and seize and detain all illegal fishing vessels. Several such violations occurred in Nova Scotia during 1816 when American ships entered coastal waters in search of bait, wood, and water.[74] This led to the detention of eight vessels by HMS *Portia*, with Rear Admiral Griffith's approval. Their crews were arrested and sent before a Halifax magistrate,[75] but Attorney General Richard Uniacke could find no grounds upon which to prosecute them, except perhaps under the *Hovering Act*, which prevented foreign vessels from entering British waters.[76] The British government responded by ordering that no American vessels be seized or detained for taking and drying fish in unsettled parts, but for only one fishing season or until the matter was resolved. The navy was directed to 'distinctly warn' American vessels that this was a temporary arrangement.[77]

Despite repeated warnings, American violations in British waters continued into 1817. Rear Admiral Milne now called upon his officers to use 'every means in your power' to protect the fisheries against encroachment and trespass, unless the ship was clearly distressed. By late June, the HMS *Dee* had seized twenty fishing schooners near Shelburne, Nova Scotia, for catching bait, cleaning fish, taking wood and water, 'tampering' with British fishers, and conducting themselves in a 'riotous' manner while present in coastal harbours. The violators were taken to Halifax for prosecution.[78] In turn, the American government again voiced its disapproval over these 'wholly unprovoked' seizures and claimed that the vessels had been driven into the coast because of a storm, with their crews now in danger of losing their catch and livelihood.[79] The British authorities, the Americans said, had acted 'in violation of humanity and the established usages of nations.'[80]

The British position became unhinged when the Nova Scotia Attorney General, the Lieutenant Governor, the Lords of the Admiralty, and the foreign secretary consulted one another and realized that no legal provisions existed to seize vessels or fine violators, even under local colonial legislation. There were fishing regulations in Newfoundland and for colonial ports, but the British government's legal advisers warned that, as the law stood, no legal proceedings could be instituted.[81] On 29 September 1817, Michael Wallace, judge of the Vice-Admiralty Court at Halifax, decreed that no law allowed naval or colonial authorities to seize the American vessels or to take their catch. While recognizing this case to be of 'great national importance,' Judge Wallace pointed out that without a positive law he could not rule on a clear penalty or forfeiture of property. He therefore ordered, subject to an appeal to a superior court, that crew, seized vessels, and property were to be returned to their American owners.[82] Rear Admiral Milne, who had authorized the seizures, supported Judge Wallace's main conclusion.[83]

The law officers of the Crown in London also concurred 'that the judgment of the Court ... was right,' after they had reviewed statutes going back to *King William's Act* (10 and 11 Wm. 3, c.25) and the Treaty of Utrecht; there was simply no mention of a penalty. To complicate matters further, they also concluded that 'the limits of the seas in or about Newfoundland' remained undefined as to whether or not 'seas' constituted creeks, harbours, and coasts, and this risked opening the door for American fishers to use the island's coast at will. Parliament, they argued, had to provide legislation, legalize the penalty of confiscation, and clarify its intentions before there could be further proceedings.[84]

Consequently, at the opening of the 1818 fishing season, the British government ordered its navy to suspend operations[85] 'in order to avoid any unpleasant collision.'[86] However, when the United States still continued to delay the negotiations for the Convention, and despite the previous year's legal rulings, the Admiralty carried out another round of vessel seizures. HMS *Syren* captured six vessels in the Bay of Fundy. American newspapers now attacked British 'encroachments on the freedom of the seas,' and proclaimed the seizures to be a matter of 'national concern.'[87] The British hard line was short lived; the captured vessels were soon released and the government worked towards a compromise 'on the ground of practical accommodation towards a friendly Power.'[88] To avert war, President James Monroe also instructed his plenipotentiaries to find an agreement.

The discussions leading to the Convention concerned three principal issues: what constituted customary rights, the original intent of the Treaty of Paris (1783), and what constituted a nation's 'territorial waters' (and thus what other area was 'international waters.') The last of these issues was unresolved in the eighteenth and early nineteenth centuries, although theorists, including Grotius and Bynkershoek, had discussed it.[89] In 1783, the British government had demanded that American vessels respect a boundary of three leagues, or nine nautical miles, off the British North American coast (with the exception of Cape Breton, where the distance was set at fifteen leagues), but the Americans rejected the idea.[90] Taking its lead from Scandinavian countries, the American government introduced a provisional and uniform three-mile limit in 1793 to define its coastline, 'for the purposes of neutrality,' which became statute law a year later.[91] This was based on Bynkershoek who had proposed that territorial sovereignty might be determined on the basis of a cannon shot from shore, or 'the cannon-shot rule.' In 1796, Britain had tentatively agreed to a three-mile coastline for North America in unsuccessfully seeking a commercial agreement, but then pulled back from its position. In 1814, Monroe refused Britain's request for an extended coastal limit.[92] The three-mile rule, as the 'neutrality zone,' was finally accepted by Britain in the Convention and became the maritime standard on the continent, though remaining an issue elsewhere.[93]

A more difficult issue in the fisheries' negotiations was whether the Americans' long-standing rights to the fishery were necessarily restored by the cessation of hostilities. The American government made two main arguments based on principles of international law. First, the government adverted to the principle of *uti possidetis*, which stated that all possessions should be returned intact unless otherwise determined by treaty. Second, the government used the general principle of *status ante bellum*, that called for a return to a state of affairs which existed prior to war. On both grounds, American negotiators insisted that all agreements were to remain in place regardless of the outcome of war, that 'the principle of a mutual restoration of whatever territory may have been taken by either party' was to prevail.[94]

The Americans linked these ideas to the fishery by arguing that fishing rights were long-standing customary rights that survived the war. They argued that before the American Revolution, all of British North America had been 'the common property of all British subjects.' John Quincy Adams, for example, stated that his country's access to Newfoundland waters was 'a right,' because Americans had uniformly enjoyed the right to fish 'on the whole Coast of North America from the first settlement of the Country.' It was a prescriptive right based on custom and long usage.[95] Further, American colonists had been instrumental in defeating the French and securing this fishery during the Seven Years War. The Treaty of Paris in 1783 had not changed this; indeed it stated that American citizens 'shall continue to enjoy unmolested the right to take fish of every kind' on the Newfoundland banks, the Gulf of St Lawrence, and 'all other places in the sea, where the inhabitants of both countries used at any time heretofore to fish.'[96] The treaty also gave the United States 'the liberty to take fish of every kind on such part of the coast of Newfoundland as British fisherman shall use (but not to dry or cure the same on that island),' and elsewhere on the 'unsettled' parts of British territories. It had also been given the 'liberty to dry and cure fish in any of the unsettled bays, harbors and creeks of Nova Scotia, Magdalen Islands, and Labrador,' until they too were settled, after which it would be considered 'not lawful' to do so, 'without a previous agreement' from those who owned the land.[97]

Adams also appealed to the 'Law of Nature,' or moral law. Reflecting a late-Enlightenment view that 'true diplomacy consisted of the application of rules that were aimed at common happiness,'[98] and a 'new conception of active diplomacy founded on the progress of the law of nations,'[99] he called upon Britain to see not only the justice of the American argument but also its mutual benefits, such as peace and prosperity. In particular, he argued that many American fishers relied entirely on the fishery and would face economic hardship if these fishing grounds were removed, forcing them into rely on factory work, which would create unwanted competition.[100]

The American position differed markedly from existing European views and represented an attempt to remake international law. A few years later a similar argument was upheld by the Supreme Court of the United States in the case of *Society for the Propagation of the Gospel in Foreign Parts v. The Town of Newhaven* with the court deciding that post-war treaties did not *ipso facto* extinguish earlier agreements but only suspended them.[101] At the time of the fishery negotiations, however, this position was not shared by Britain, which asserted that war ended all previous agreements. Secretary of State Bathurst pointed out that Britain's own legal experts, and some French supporters of the United States, were long agreed that 'by every principle of international law' the American Revolution had extinguished any common right to the fishery. Likewise, any pre-existing American right or liberty had disappeared with the War of 1812, and there was 'no exception to the rule that all treaties are put an end to by a subsequent War between the Parties.'[102] Consequently, there was also no 'necessary connexion [*sic*]' between the American claim of national independence and a continuation of fishing rights. Indeed it was illogical for the Americans to equate 'the nature of the liberty to fish within British Limits, or to use British territory' with their 'Right to Independence.'[103] While Britain recognized 'the right' of Americans to fish in international waters, like the Newfoundland banks or the Gulf of St Lawrence, it had only given the Americans the 'liberty' or the 'privilege' rather than the 'right' to fish on the coast of Newfoundland and Labrador, and had only granted the 'liberty' of drying and curing of fish in 'unsettled' coastal parts of Atlantic Canada and Labrador, entirely as 'concessions strictly dependent on the Treaty itself.'[104]

As noted above, the British negotiators wanted to limit the American right to dry and cure fish on shore[105] because, in the past, American fishers had carried out unfair fishing practices and illegal trade, such as smuggling, 'to the great injury of the British Revenue.'[106] Consequently, Britain was determined to make concessions only 'in a way which shall effectually protect her own subjects from such obstructions to their lawful enterprises as they too frequently experienced immediately previous to the late war and which are from their very nature calculated to produce collision and disunion between the two states.' In 1817, there were offers and counteroffers of which areas could be used by American fishers, but no agreement. Britain then informed the Americans that its fishers would be excluded from the region unless the issue was resolved, 'in order that any unpleasant collision may be avoided.'[107] That year, Britain strictly enforced its sovereignty in British North American waters, including the seizure of the aforementioned twenty American vessels, and when the United States negotiators continued to delay, British naval cruisers seized and condemned another two schooners. In denouncing the seizures, the American government also delayed further negotiations on the grounds that it needed more information about the coastline Britain was offering. Charles Bagot, however, speculated that Monroe's delays were more politically motivated. Most of the eastern states had voted against the newly elected president, and he was now 'appearing to consult their wishes and receive their instructions upon a subject so intimately connected with one of their chief interests.'[108]

During this hiatus, and in a gesture of good will, Castlereagh ordered the temporary end to any seizures or detentions of American vessels taking and drying fish in unsettled parts of British waters, though for one fishing season only.[109] The back and forward of negotiations finally produced a Convention in 1818, ratified by the Senate the following year and implemented on the British side by an Act of Parliament.[110] The Convention consisted of four main parts, and its main focus was the restoration and extension of American fishing rights on the banks of Newfoundland, the Gulf of St Lawrence, and the Labrador coast.[111] Article 1 gave American fishers the 'liberty' of carrying out concurrent fishing on the coast of Newfoundland. It included the right of Americans 'to take, dry, and cure Fish' in unsettled areas on the south coast of Newfoundland between Cape Ray and the Ramea Islands; on the western and northern coasts from the shores of the Magdalen Islands and Cape Ray to the southern coast of Labrador through the Straits of Belle Isle; northwards 'indefinitely' to the areas controlled by the Hudson's Bay Company; and along the northern peninsula of western and northeastern Newfoundland down to the Quirpon Islands. Significantly, then, the American fishery was given access to the south coast of Newfoundland for the first time. These curing and drying privileges would end once these areas became settled, unless the inhabitants agreed otherwise.[112] Equally significantly, Britain conceded that the fishing rights themselves were a 'liberty for ever.'

The Convention's terms were quickly implemented in practice. Naval officers, acting as the governor's surrogates, enforced the new agreement and acted to prevent smuggling.[113] On 19 June 1819, the *Egeria* was sent to Cape Charles in Labrador to collect 'the fullest information' on the American presence, then to Croque Harbour and other parts of White Bay between Quirpon and Cape St John to make sure that the French fishing was 'suitably performed.'[114] Also, the *Drake* left on a month's voyage for the Burin Peninsula to report on American (and French) fishing vessels, ensure compliance with the law, and protect 'their respective fisheries,' before it went on to Harbour Breton in Fortune Bay.[115] The *Carnation* was directed to the coast of Labrador to visit various fishing establishments from fifty-five degrees north and to observe and inform on American fishing vessels, before sailing along the north side of the Gulf of St Lawrence to overview French and American fishing there.[116] In this way, the entire coastlines of Newfoundland and Labrador were monitored and regulated by the Royal Navy.

There was similarly vigorous enforcement of American rights. Governor Hamilton drew attention to the Convention by issuing a Proclamation on 21 June 1819, after the naval vessels had received their orders, and gave 'notice to all His Majesty's subjects' not to interfere with the American fishery. While Hamilton directed naval commander-in-chief LeGeyt and his officers to strictly enforce the law against Newfoundland residents, they were to do so with 'the most conciliatory line of conduct.'[117] The thirty-nine magistrates of all eleven judicial districts were simultaneously informed.

It was once argued that the Convention 'sensibly diminished' former American rights by prohibiting its fishers to enter within the three-mile limit of the British colonial coast, except in Newfoundland and Labrador.[118] However, at the time, the Americans were very pleased with the provisions.[119] James Gallatin, secretary to his father and plenipotentiary Albert Gallatin, believed that 'England has been most generous in every way.' His father had 'done his best to conciliate all – Lord Castlereagh has worked in perfect accord with him.'[120] In his view, American negotiators had struck a good deal, for although the United States was now prevented from fishing within three miles of Nova Scotia, this mattered little; all principal fishing grounds were in international waters, and quite accessible. In addition, Gallatin boasted, the American fishery had unexpectedly acquired 'extensive fishing rights on the best coasts and generous areas for curing, including Newfoundland beaches from which the treaty of 1783 excluded Americans.'[121] Fellow plenipotentiary Richard Rush also believed that overall the agreement had 'gone beyond' the Treaty of Paris (1783) to the Americans' advantage, and he thought this the product of American hard bargaining and Britain's desire to avoid continuing friction. This view was in accord with British commentators. As the biographer of one of the British plenipotentiaries, Henry Goulbourn, noted, 'The successful arrangement of several long-festering disputes had placed British-American relations on a more secure foundation, and the price in concessions had not been particularly high.'[122]

Clearly Castlereagh had sacrificed future growth in the Newfoundland fishery to a lasting peace. 'We thought it of less moment which of the parties gained a little more or lost a little more by the compact,' he told Rush, 'than that so difficult a point should be adjusted, and the harmony of the two countries ... be made secure.' There were likely also economic considerations that shaped these British concessions. The United States had become a principal exporter of food and cotton to Britain, and the single largest importer of British manufactured goods.[123] The Convention as a whole ensured the continuation of trade: 'Britain seemed willing to sacrifice her colonies in order to enlarge her international commerce.'[124] Moreover, ensuring peace would reduce government military expenditures – two-thirds of government spending and a significant contributor to the national debt.[125] Within this fiscal context, it is no surprise that Newfoundland's call for fish bounties and increased naval protection would have found little political resonance.

Richard Rush also offered some insights into the reasons for Britain's strategy based on informal conversations he had with unidentified people whom he claimed had inside knowledge. These people suggested that Britain was willing to give up part of the Newfoundland coast because the fishery was not doing well. As long as the government pursued policies like restricting settlement and leaving intact the colony's legal and institutional structures and thereby reducing the island's population, it would continue to struggle.[126] In addition, Rush's sources told him that the Americans were better positioned than British merchants in the provisions trade for the Newfoundland fishery, for the United States possessed 'the means superior' to provide salt for the fishery and to export its fish in the western hemisphere. These advantages were irreversible, so the British-based fishery had begun directing its energies towards European markets where it could still undersell its rivals. There was also a growing British interest in an expanding the Icelandic fishery, where the cod catch brought up to $5 more per quintal than Newfoundland fish. In short, British merchants were losing interest in Newfoundland.

Aftermath of the Treaty and the Convention

For Newfoundland, the Treaty of Paris and the Convention were consummated at the worst of times. After several years of unprecedented wartime prosperity and comparatively high immigration, the island's fishing-based economy entered a deep and long-lasting post-war recession, with high unemployment and a profusion of bankruptcies.[127] In 1816, St John's merchants pleaded with Britain to do something about the French shore and called for a protective bounty as compensation for the loss of rich and fishing grounds.[128] In 1817, Poole merchants told the Select Committee on Newfoundland Trade that prices in foreign markets had become so low that any further reduction would result in losses, and their capital would be 'by degrees withdrawn' from the Newfoundland trade. George Garland, a witness at the committee hearings, added, 'By no means the least cause' for this 'serious and alarming depression' was 'growing competition of the French Newfoundland trade.'[129] Overcapacity and overproduction in the fishery now contributed to fierce international competition, especially in Mediterranean markets, and while France and the United States offered protection to their fisheries in the form of bounties, Britain refused to follow suit.[130] To worsen matters, the once bustling mercantile centre of St John's experienced four major fires between 1816 and 1819, and its property losses reached well over £500,000 – an amount exceeding all claims for Upper Canadian losses during the War of 1812.[131]

The island's economic woes were further complicated by a welter of internal political, social, and legal difficulties. Administered as 'a fief of the Admiralty' and 'a moveable fishery'[132] with an increasingly ineffectual system of naval government, some Newfoundland residents called for their own legislature to solve local problems manifested in the demise of the migratory fishery, a growing resident population, serious unemployment, destitution, and reports of starvation.[133] Some critics claimed that a sizeable portion of the island's unemployed were persons forced off the French Shore and unable to find work in the depressed fishery of eastern Newfoundland.[134] Despite giving some latitude to its governors to deal with these issues, by and large the British government continued to decide its affairs from afar. The Treaty of Paris came just at the beginning of this recession and the Convention was enacted in its midst. They became part and parcel of a series of unfortunate events.

Of course, negative public reaction in Newfoundland to the signing of the Convention was entirely predictable,[135] for fishing merchants, planters, and servants were now shut out of nearly two-thirds of what had constituted the Newfoundland fishery between 1793 and 1815, but concerns were also voiced in England. *The Times* condemned British concessions to the United States as reaching a 'frightful magnitude' and risking the ruin of the island.[136] The press also cited critics on 'the unfavourable state of their trade ... and the ruinous policy of extending to citizens of the United States any further privileges in that fishery.' It explained that during the negotiations leading to the Convention fishing merchants had expected the British government to provide them with bounties of 3 shillings per quintal for all fish cured on the island, as compensation for losing the French Shore.

The British government did respond to Newfoundland's complaints. On 22 April 1819, a few months after the Convention was ratified, the Committee of the Privy Council for Trade wrote to the recently appointed Newfoundland governor Sir Charles Hamilton[137] that, after consulting with the treasury, they could not justify asking Parliament to grant a bounty on fish. Instead, as compensation, the committee offered a temporary suspension of all duties of Newfoundland products exported to the United Kingdom and on imported British goods. Meanwhile, 'no practicable means' would be left untried to see duties reduced on Newfoundland fish in Spain and Italy.[138] This proved little consolation.

The 'failure' of the fishery in 1821 again brought hard times and destitution to St John's and to every outlying district. One hundred and fifty-six signatures were affixed to a petition from St John's, including those of the Attorney General and other prominent figures, to forward a 'faithful account' of the island and its 'great distress' to the governor.[139] The petition blamed the 'Treaties with Foreign Nations' and the attendant loss of 'the finest parts of our Coast' for the troubles.[140] The concessions wrought by the Treaty of Paris and the Convention were the primary causes of Newfoundland's continuing economic crisis, and the failure of the British government to counteract foreign fish bounties had exacerbated this recession, caused a flight of capital, removed rich sources of cod, and adversely affected the island's ability to recover economically.

While Newfoundland struggled, France and the United States continued to enjoy the benefits of these agreements. In 1828, the New-foundland government sent 'an experienced and intelligent officer' to survey the French fishery in Newfoundland. He recorded 313 large French vessels with 12,520 men who used 2,253 small boats to fish, with roughly 80 per cent working the north-east coast; there were very few Anglo-Newfoundlanders.[141] Newfoundland fishers were increasingly forced to fish on the Labrador coast, competing with an estimated 15,000 American fishers and 1,500 vessels on that coast. Taken together, the size of the French and American fishery outnumbered Newfound-land's by nearly five to one.

St John's merchants were hardly alone in viewing these treaties as unjust.[142] Nova Scotia, New Brunswick, Prince Edward Island, and Lower Canada also objected to them.[143] Even a full generation later, a Nova Scotia committee of the House of Assembly summed up the Treaty of Paris (1783) as 'a fatal Treaty' and the Convention as 'inconsiderate ... (to speak of it in the mildest terms).' The colony was 'still galled' by the Treaty of Paris of 1814, had been 'lulled into submission' by Britain's promises of fish bounties that never came, and was a victim of endless violations by the American fishery -'those invaders of our rights' - which the navy was unwilling to prevent.[144]

The return of American fleets to parts of the French Shore also initiated some international tension, when France tried to press its claim to an exclusive fishery. In 1820 and 1821, French war ships ordered American fishers away from their fishing stations along the west coast.[145] When, in 1822, one Captain Nicholls confronted Captain Venancourt at Quirpon, he was told that the French fleet 'now uniformly send the American fishing vessels away wherever they find them without using the slightest ceremony towards them.'[146] France's interference with American vessels raised the ire of the American government. Aware of Hamilton's 1822 proclamation, it recognized that Britain was willing to abandon a concurrent fishery on the French Shore and remove British residents; this, however, was not 'a primary and indispensable obligation' but rather an exercise of its decision to secure peace by making practical concessions which served its own interests.[147] The French fishery depended on British willingness to compromise and accommodate rather than any principle of international law.[148] Extensive arguments about the effect (or nullification) of prior agreements such as the 1778 Treaty of Alliance between the two ensued, but they did not resolve the problem,[149] and the United States resorted to increasingly strong language. The 'forcible means' used by France were labelled 'an aggression.'[150]

This conflict between France and the United States came early in the year in which the Monroe Doctrine, a defining moment in American foreign policy, was promulgated. The doctrine asserted that European intervention in the American hemisphere would not be tolerated by the United States, including any colonisation initiatives.[151] Monroe's announcement was aimed at Spanish efforts to regain its South American colonies from independence movements, but the tensions over fishing rights in Newfoundland had a minor role to play in shaping American foreign policy, especially after France forced American ships to leave the French Shore.[152] No further confrontations between the French navy and American fishers are recorded in the Newfoundland records from this period, but the issue of American fishing rights in Newfoundland was never fully settled until the award of the Hague Court of Arbitration of 1910.[153]

The question of whether the French Shore fishery was exclusive or concurrent also did not disappear from Anglo-French relations in the 1820s. In 1828, for instance, French treaty violations and reports of interference by British fishers once more reached crisis proportions, to the point that Governor Cochrane feared that Newfoundland fishers were gathering arms to defend themselves. Britain, however, remained reluctant to enforce a concurrent fishery with war vessels, because it continued to avoid confrontation. In practice, this meant that preventing British encroachments on the French Shore was left to the French navy, but nobody knew clearly whether France had the legal right to seize British fishing vessels along the French Shore. Yet France was left to try to do something about the problem because, despite repeated requests from St John's merchants and the Chamber of Commerce, Cochrane decided not to protect British fishing vessels. French authorities felt helpless in dealing with angry British fishers and sealers, 'ill disposed persons employed in the British fishery,' who committed acts of violence against French fishers and destroyed French property. Similarly, neither the Newfoundland governor nor the colony's courts were clear about their legal rights to deal with French violations. Foreign vessels could be seized and their goods confiscated, but there was uncertainty over whether the subjects of another country could be prosecuted and what penalties might be exacted.

In an ironic twist, the French and British governments eventually agreed to circumvent the legal obstacles by allowing each other to arrest, but not to try, the other's treaty violators and criminals. Thereafter, French naval authorities were to bring British treaty violators on the French Shore to St John's to stand trial in a British court. Likewise, the British took French transgressors to St Pierre and Miquelon. In a further effort to reduce tensions, Newfoundland's governor issued, with British approval, yet another proclamation that prohibited unauthorized persons from fishing on the French Shore and interfering with the French fishery, thereby creating a *de facto* exclusive fishery.

In closing, one is reminded that law is 'an expression of social power.'[154] Such use of the law becomes readily apparent when one observes how Britain used the Treaty of Paris and the Convention to conciliate France and the United States. These British concessions may have reduced the risk of war and promoted its broad imperial interests,[155] but they represent an exercise of political, economic, and social power that between 1814 and 1830 severely hampered the recovery of the struggling Newfoundland fishery. This hegemonic imperial agenda also fostered deep feelings of injustice and contributed to calls for political reform and local control, and the treaties served to create an important set of cultural referents about Newfoundland's survival in the face of historic adversity.[156]

The British government's attitude, in part, was a cultural expression of the contemporary legal world where France, the United States, and Britain were considered 'equals' and belonged to the 'community of civilized states,' and Newfoundland remained dependent and unequal, belonging to those peoples, 'not civilized enough to guarantee adequate moral, legal and political standards.'[157] However, not all British politicians entirely shared this *mentalité*. For example, in 1830, reform-minded members of the House of Commons called for a select committee to inquire into the state of Newfoundland. During the debate, they drew attention unsuccessfully to the despised treaties, suggested revisiting them, and demanded to know whether the French Shore fishery was concurrent or exclusive. Their motion was defeated 82 to 29,[158] and signalled the continuance of a political and diplomatic discourse that would for another eighty years preoccupy British, French, American, Canadian, and Newfoundland lawyers and politicians.

NOTES

1 R. S. Horowitz, 'International Law and State Transformation in China, Siam, and the Ottoman Empire during the Nineteenth Century,' *Journal of World History* 15 (2004), 446.

2 This treaty is actually two treaties, though called one: the Definitive Treaty of Paris of 1814 (May 30) and the Treaty of Paris of 1815 (November 20). Their full text can be found at www.napoleon-series.org/research/government/diplomatic/c_paris1.html and www.yale.edu/lawweb/avalon/paris763.htm.

3 C. Bell, 'Peace Agreements: Their Nature and Legal Status,' *The American Journal of International Law* 100 (2006), 384.

4 Other outstanding issues regarded the boundary between the United States and British North America from Lake Superior to the Rocky Mountains, and compensation for refugee slaves in British North America.

5 *Traite de paix entre la France et l'Angleterre conclu à Utrecht le 11 avril 1713* is available online at www.canadiana.org/ECO/PageView/41706/0006?id=24c0d7af4af04347. See Article 13, 59–60.

6 'The definitive Treaty of Peace and Friendship between his Britannick Majesty, the Most Christian King, and the King of Spain. Concluded at Paris the 10th day of February, 1763. To which the King of Portugal acceded on the same day.' Retrieved 18 April 2008 from www.yale.edu/lawweb/avalon/paris763.htm.

7 The Definitive Treaty of Peace 1783 is available online from www.yale.edu/lawweb/avalon/diplomacy/britain/paris.htm.

8 *Declaration of His Britannic Majesty*, Versailles, 3 September 1783 and *Counter Declaration of His Most Christian Majesty*, Versailles, 3 September 1783, cited in F. Thompson, *The French Shore Problem in Newfoundland: An Imperial Study* (Toronto: University of Toronto Press 1961), 192.

9 On the region's fishing economy, see D. Alexander, 'Newfoundland's Traditional Economy and Development to 1934,' and S. Ryan, 'The Newfoundland Salt Cod Trade in the Nineteenth Century,' both in J. Hiller and P. Neary, eds., *Newfoundland in the Nineteenth and Twentieth Centuries* (Toronto: University of Toronto Press 1980), 18–39 and 40–66; K. Matthews, *Lectures on the History of Newfoundland, 1500–1830* (St John's: Maritime History Group 1973); J. Candow, 'An Overview of the Northwest Atlantic Fisheries, 1502–1904,' retrieved 18 April 2008 from www.stm.unipi.it/Clioh/tabs/libri/1/11-Candow(22).pdf.

10 J. Hiller, *The Historical Background to the Canada–France Maritime Boundary*

Decision (London: Canada House 1993); P. Neary, 'The French and American Shore Questions as Factors in Newfoundland History,' in Hiller and Neary, eds., *Newfoundland in the Nineteenth and Twentieth Centuries*, 95–122; Thompson, *The French Shore Problem in Newfoundland;* H. Innis, *The Cod Fisheries: The History of an International Economy*, rev. ed. (Toronto: University of Toronto Press 1954), esp. chap. 10; A. McLintock, *The Establishment of Constitutional Government in Newfoundland, 1783–1832: A Study of Retarded Colonization* (London: Longman's, Green 1941).

11 Bell, 'Peace Agreements,' 374–5.

12 'Introduction,' in R. Lesaffer, ed., *Peace Treaties and International Law in European History: From the Late Middle Ages to World War One* (Cambridge: Cambridge University Press 2004), 5; A. Osiander, 'Talking Peace: Social Science, Peace Negotiations and the Structure of Politics,' in ibid., 289–315.

13 A recent overview is O. Janzen, 'The French Shore Dispute,' in J. Hiller and C. English, eds., *Newfoundland and the Entente Cordiale 1904–2004, Occasional Publication No. 1* (St John's: Newfoundland and Labrador Studies 2007).

14 F. Wharton, *Digest of International Law of the United States*, vol. 3 (Washington, DC: GPO 1886), 242.

15 On post-war British policy, see W. Hinde, *Castlereagh* (London: Collins 1981), 232; C. Bartlett, *Defence and Diplomacy: Britain and the Great Powers 1815–1914* (Manchester: Manchester University Press 1993), 8–15; T. Otte, '"It's What Made Britain Great": Reflections on British Foreign Policy, from Malplaquet to Maastricht,' in T. Otte, ed., *The Makers of British Foreign Policy From Pitt to Thatcher* (London: Palgrave 2002), 8–9.

16 P. Schroeder, 'Did the Vienna Settlement Rest on a Balance of Power?' *American Historical Review* 97 (1992), 697.

17 M. Bélissa, 'Peace Treaties, *bonne foi* and European Civility in the Enlightenment,' and H. Steiger, 'Peace Treaties from Paris to Versailles,' both in Lesaffer, ed., *Peace Treaties and International Law in European History*, 66–7, 248.

18 D. Prowse, *A History of Newfoundland* (1895; reprint, St John's: Boulder Publications 2002), 408.

19 R. Metternich, ed., *Memoirs of Prince Metternich, 1773–1815*, vol. 2 (New York: Howard Fertig 1970), 561.

20 J. Derry, *Castlereagh* (London: Allen Lane 1976), 178–9.

21 M.H. Perley, *Memorandum of Information Relative to the French Fisheries at Newfoundland* (London: Colonial Office 1857), 16.

22 See Schroeder, 'Vienna Settlement,' 691.

23 See 'Etat des Bâtiments Expédiés à Bayonne et à Saint-Jean-De-Lux Pour Aller Faire La Pêche De La Morue Pendant Les Années 1784, 1785 et 1786,' in E. Ducérée, *Rechèrches Historiques sur La Pêche De La Morue et al Découverte*

de Terre-Neuve par les Basques et les Bayonnais (Pau: Imprimerie-Stéréotypie Garet 1893), 65, 119–20; C. de la Morandière, *The French Cod Fishery in Newfoundland from the Sixteenth Century to the Present: Its Economic, Social and Political Significance* (St John's: Centre for Newfoundland Studies 2005), 95 (this is an abridged translation of *Histoire de la pêche française de la morue dans l'Amerique septentrionale* [Paris: G. Maisonneuve et Larose 1962–6]); L. Soublin, *Cent Ans de Pêche à Terre-Neuve*, vol. 1, 1815–67 (Paris: Henri Veyrier 1991), chap. 1.

24 P. O'Flaherty, 'Keats, Sir Richard Goodwin,' *Dictionary of Canadian Biography* (hereafter *DCB*) retrieved 18 April 2008 from www.biographi.ca/EN/ShowBio.asp?BioId=37072&query=keats.

25 Henry Hunt to Earl Bathurst, 28 April 1814, in Colonial Office Series [hereafter CO] 194, Newfoundland. Original Correspondence. Secretary of State, vol. 55, 182–5.

26 Bathurst to Castlereagh, 26 April 1814. Enclosure. G. Keats to Lord Melville, 1814, Castlereagh Papers, Public Record Office of Northern Ireland [hereafter PRONI], D/3030/3983. Thanks to archivist Anne Craig for these documents.

27 Bathurst to Castlereagh, 26 April 1814. Enclosure. Keats to Lord Melville, undated, Castlereagh Papers, PRONI, D/3030/4022.

28 July 1814, in CO 194, vol. 55, 49; 30 July 1814, in CO 194, vol. 55, 51–3; 28 October 1814, in CO 194, vol. 55, 55–6.

29 Comte de Jaucourt to Duke of Wellington, 19 November 1814, in CO 194, vol. 55, 324; Wellington to de Jaucourt, 21 November 1814, in CO 194, vol. 55, 326; W. Hamilton to Major. Gen Bunbury, 25 November 1814, CO 194, vol. 55, 320; Ducérée, *Rechèrches Historiques sur La Pêche De La Morue et al Découverte de Terre-Neuve par les Basques et les Bayonnais*, 65.

30 Keats to Earl Bathurst, 29 December 1814, in CO 194, vol. 55, 95–104.

31 C. Sanger, 'The Evolution of Sealing and the Spread of Permanent Settlement in Northeastern Newfoundland,' in J. Mannion, ed., *The Peopling of Newfoundland* (St John's: ISER 1977), 136.

32 O'Flaherty, *Old Newfoundland*, 102–5.

33 McLintock, *The Establishment of Constitutional Government*, 113.

34 See P. Thornton, 'The Demographic and Mercantile Bases of Initial Permanent Settlement in the Strait of Belle Isle,' and Mannion, 'Settlers and Traders in Western Newfoundland,' in Mannion, *The Peopling of Newfoundland*, 152–83 and 234–74.

35 Sanger, 'The Evolution of Sealing,' 136.

36 A. Jack to Hamilton, 13 April 1820, in D'Alberti Papers, Centre for Newfoundland Studies, Memorial University of Newfoundland, typewritten

copies of the handwritten transcripts of the Newfoundland material obtained from the Colonial Office Records in the Public Record Office, London, for the Privy Council arbitration on the Labrador Boundary Dispute in 1927.

37 P. Buckner, 'Hamilton, Sir Charles,' *DCB*, retrieved 18 April 2008 from www.biographi.ca/EN/ShowBio.asp?BioId=37548&query= charles%20AND%20hamilton.

38 Hamilton to A. Jack, 22 April 1820, in D'Alberti Papers.

39 Francis Forbes to Hamilton, 23 April 1823, in D'Alberti Papers.

40 Hamilton to Mon. Begon Delarouzière, St John's, 13 November 1820, in D'Alberti Papers.

41 Joseph Bird Jr, Forteau, to Captain Nicolas, HMS *Egeria*, 7 August 1821, in CO 194, vol. 65, 314. He was the son of Joseph Bird of the English firm Joseph Bird and Thomas Street. See Mannion, 'Settlers and Traders in Western Newfoundland,' 244–5, and Thornton, 'Demographic and Mercantile Bases of Settlement,' 161.

42 C. Hamilton, St John's, to Capitaine de Venancourt, Croque Harbour, 13 August 1821, CO 194, vol. 64; Hamilton to C. LeGeyt, 13 August 1821, in CO 194, vol. 64, 149.

43 J. Toup Nicolas, Croque Harbour, to Hamilton, 6 September 1821, in CO 194, vol. 64, 145.

44 Nicolas to Hamilton, 8 September 1821, in CO 194, vol. 64, 145–6.

45 Thompson, *The French Shore Problem*, 23.

46 (U.K.) *Newfoundland Fisheries Act* (4 and 5 Geo. 4, 1824), c.51, s.12.

47 (U.K.) 28 Geo III, c.35 (1788), cited in Thompson, *The French Shore Problem*, 19.

48 The French legal position as it developed during the nineteenth century is summarized by Thompson, *The French Shore Problem*, 29.

49 Ibid., 22–4, and Mannion, 'Settlers and Traders,' 248.

50 Perley, *Memorandum of Information Relative to the French Fisheries at Newfoundland*, 8–10.

51 P. Rolo, *Entente Cordiale: The Origins and Negotiation of the British-French Agreements of 8 April 1904* (London: Macmillan 1969); McLintock, *The Establishment of Constitutional Government*, 113.

52 Thompson, *The French Shore Problem*, 1, 4. Also see Committee on Foreign Relations United States Senate, *Treaties and Other International Agreements: The Role of the United States Senate* (January 2001), 276, available online, at http://purl.access.gpo.gov/GPO/LPS11656.

53 'An Act to enable His Majesty to make Regulations with respect to the taking and curing Fish on certain parts of the Coasts of *Newfoundland, Labrador,*

and His Majesty's other Possessions in *North America*, according to a Convention made between His Majesty and the United States of America.' The treaty became statute law as (U.K.) 59 Geo. 3, c.38 (14 June 1819) and appeared in various colonial statutes in Nova Scotia, New Brunswick, and Prince Edward Island.

54 S. Ryan, 'Fishery to Colony: A Newfoundland Watershed, 1793–1815,' *Acadiensis* 12 (1983), 34.

55 Memorial of the Committee of Merchants interested in the Treaty, Navigation, and Fisheries of the Island of Newfoundland, the Gulf of St Lawrence and on the Coast of Labrador, in No. 10, London, July 29, 1814, in *Correspondence respecting the British North American Fisheries: 1803 to 1851* (1873), 18 (hereafter *Correspondence*).

56 Memorial of the Committee of Merchants trading from London and different ports of the kingdom with the Island of Newfoundland and its Dependencies, No. 4, January 11, 1814, in ibid., 7–8. Also see T. Hodgins, *British and American Diplomacy Affecting Canada, 1782–1890* (Toronto: Rowsell-Hutchison Press 1900), 12–13.

57 A. Condon, 'Leonard, George,' *DCB*, retrieved 18 April 2008 from www.biographi.ca/EN/ShowBio.asp?BioId=37088&query=george%20AND%20leonard.

58 S. Cottrell to G. Hammond, Office of Committee of Privy Council for Trade, Whitehall, 31 March 1803, *Correspondence*, 1.

59 C. Head, 'Gower, Sir Erasmus,' *DCB*, retrieved 18 April 2008 from www.biographi.ca/EN/ShowBio.asp?BioId=36546&query=sir%20AND%20erasmus%gower; E. Gower to Earl Cambden, 25 October 1804, *Correspondence*, 3.

60 Background on the American fisheries and their presence in the Gulf of St Lawrence can be found in Innis, *The Cod Fisheries*; F. Landry, *Laboureurs du Golfe* (Quebec: Le Mateloire 1985), 92; C. Elliott, *The United States and the Northeastern Fisheries* (Minneapolis: University of Minnesota Press 1887).

61 J. Stagg, 'James Madison and the Coercion of Great Britain: Canada, the West Indies, and the War of 1812,' *William and Mary Quarterly* 38 (1981), 29. The Convention of 1818 is also seen as part of the extended peace settlement following the War of 1812 in Jon Latimer, *1812: War with America* (Cambridge, MA: Belknap Press of Harvard University Press 2007), 404; Mark Zuehlke, *For Honour's Sake: The War of 1812 and the Brokering of an Uneasy Peace* (Toronto: Vintage Canada 2006), 385–6.

62 October 1814, *Diplomatic Correspondence*, 221; Charles Francis Adams, ed., *Memoirs of John Quincy Adams*, vol. 3 (1874–77; reprint, Freeport: Books for Libraries Press 1969), 60–1.

63 J. Thompson, *Memorandum on Points of Law Connected with the Fisheries* (London: n.p. ca. 1887), 3–4. Retrieved 18 April 2008 from www.canadiana.org/ ECO/ItemRecord/9_01969?id=76f667e15c6e56ca.

64 American historians, though not Canadian historians, have noted the importance of these negotiations. For example, see B. Perkins, *Castlereagh and Adams: England and the United States, 1812–1823* (Berkeley: University of California Press 1964), chap. 14.

65 Ibid., and Adams, ed., *Memoirs of John Quincy Adams*, vol. 4, 97–8.

66 Adams, ed., *Memoirs of John Quincy Adams*, vol. 4, 95.

67 Rush, *Memoranda of a Residence at the Court of London*, 389.

68 Rush memorandum, 10 November 1818, cited in Perkins, *Castlereagh and Adams*, 273.

69 V. Golladay, 'The United States and British North American Fisheries, 1815–1818,' *American Neptune* 33 (1973), 247. The issue of vessel seizure was closely related to the matter of impressment and the British seizure of American vessels, which were among the causes of the War of 1812.

70 No. 25, Baker to Rear-Admiral Griffith, 19 July 1815, *Correspondence*, 5.

71 No. 28, Baker to Castlereagh, 15 September 1815, *Correspondence*, 39.

72 No. 27, Adams to Bathurst, 25 September 1815, *Correspondence*, 35.

73 Edward Griffith to Anthony Baker, Halifax, 18 June 1815, *Correspondence*, 33.

74 Captain Wilson to Rear Admiral Griffith, No. 35, 28 May 1816, *Correspondence*.

75 Griffith to the Secretary to the Admiralty, No. 35, 20 June 1816, *Correspondence*, 57; Wright and Campbell to the Commissioners of Customs, No. 36, 29 May 1816, *Correspondence*, 58.

76 (U.K.) 4 Geo. 3, c.15, s.33, and s.34. The Attorney General for the Province of Nova Scotia to Captain Wilson, No. 36, 23 May 1816, *Correspondence*, 59.

77 Bathurst to Admiralty, 10 May 1817, No. 42, *Correspondence*, 68.

78 Orders addressed to Captain Chambers, No. 47, 12 May 1817, *Correspondence*; Bagot to Castlereagh, No. 47, 30 June 1817, *Correspondence*, 73; Captain Chambers to Rear Admiral Sir D. Milne, 8 June 1817, No. 47, *Correspondence*, 74.

79 Extract of a Letter from the Collector of Customs at the Port of Boston, dated 30 June 1817, No. 49, *Correspondence*, 79.

80 Bagot to Castlereagh, No. 49, 8 August 1817, 78; Rush to Bagot, No. 49, 11 August 1817, *Correspondence*, 78.

81 C. Robinson to Castelreagh, 28 July 1817, *Correspondence*, 73. Nineteenth-century treaties had 'no provisions either for the peaceful settlement of disputes or about the execution of the treaties.' See Steiger, 'Peace Treaties from Paris to Versailles,' 91–2.

82 Extract from a Halifax paper of 6 October 1817, No. 50, *Correspondence*, 81.
83 Milne to the Secretary to the Admiralty, No. 51, 1 October 1817, *Correspondence*, 82–3.
84 The Law Officers of the Crown to Viscount Castlereagh, 17 December 1817, Enclosure 52, *Correspondence*, 83–4.
85 Bagot to Milne, Enclosure 2, No. 53, 23 March 1818, *Correspondence*, 86.
86 Castlereagh to Bagot, No. 54, 9 June 1818, *Correspondence*.
87 Extracts from the *Daily National Intelligencer*, No. 62, 15 July 1818, *Correspondence*, 92.
88 Private and Secret. Castlereagh to Bagot, No. 55, 9 June 1818, *Correspondence*, 86. Shortly afterwards, several newly captured American vessels in the Bay of Fundy were freed. Bagot to Castlereagh, No. 62, 24 July 1818, *Correspondence*, 91.
89 H. Grotius, *Mare Liberum* (1609; reprint, Indianapolis: Liberty Fund 2004); C. van Bynkershoek, *De dominio maris dissertation* (1702; reprint, New York: Carnegie Endowment for International Peace 1923).
90 T. Balch, 'The American-British Atlantic Fisheries Question,' *Proceedings of the American Philosophical Society* 48, no. 193 (1909), 321.
91 Act of 5 June 1794, c.50. Cited in B. Heinzen, 'The Three-Mile Limit: Preserving the Freedom of the Seas,' *Stanford Law Review* 11, no. 4 (1959), 614–15.
92 J. Adams to Mr Oswald, 30 November 1782. Cited in Foreign Office, July 1875, Memorandum by Mr Rothery on the British North American Fisheries Question. Rough Draft (Not completed), 2 [CIHM 902319].
93 Heinzen, 'The Three-Mile Limit,' 618. Heinzen points out that the British government had begun leaning towards the three-mile limit by 1806–7. Also see R. Gushue, 'The Territorial Waters of Newfoundland,' *Canadian Journal of Economics and Political Science* 15 (1949), 344–52.
94 American Plenipotentiaries to the British Plenipotentiaries, Ghent, 24 October 1814, *Correspondence*, 22.
95 Thompson, *The French Shore Problem*, chap. 1.
96 Memorandum on Points of Law Connected With the Fisheries, 1.
97 Treaty of Paris (1814), Article 3.
98 See Bélissa, 'Peace Treaties ...,' 248.
99 American diplomats were in the vanguard in advancing this strategy. See ibid., 253.
100 The United States Congress, *The New American State Papers: Commerce and Navigation*, vol. 4 (Wilmington, DE: Scholarly Resources 1973), 350–5. On the role of the law of nature, or legal philosophy, see Hueck, 'The Discipline of the History of International Law,' 200–1.

101 Balch, 'The American-British Fisheries Question,' 324–5.
102 Bathurst to John Quincy Adams, 30 October 1815, in *Diplomatic Correspondence*, 747–9.
103 Ibid., 750.
104 Ibid., 750–1.
105 Ibid., 19 September 1815.
106 Ibid., 752. Adams denied ever having heard of 'any such complaints' and thought that careful regulation would solve them.
107 Castlereagh to Bagot, 22 March 1817, No. 38, *Correspondence*, 65.
108 Bagot to Castlereagh, 3 June 1817, No. 45, *Correspondence*, 71.
109 Bathurst to the Lords Commissioners of the Admiralty, Downing Street, 10 May 1817, No. 42, *Correspondence*, 68.
110 (U.K.) 59 Geo. 3, c.38 (1819).
111 'Convention Respecting Fisheries, Boundary and the Restoration of Slaves,' in *Treaties, Conventions, International Acts, Protocols and Agreements between the United States of America and Other Powers 1776–1909*, Part I (1910; reprint, New York: Greenwood Press 1968), 631–3.
112 For the full text of Treaty of Paris (1783), see www.yale.edu/lawweb/avalon/diplomacy/britain/paris.htm. For the Convention of 1818, see www.yale.edu/lawweb/avalon/diplomacy/britain/conv1818.htm.
113 (U.K.) 26 Geo. 3, c.26 (1786).
114 Hamilton to Rowley, 19 June 1819, D'Alberti Papers.
115 Hamilton to Glascock, 22 July 1819, D'Alberti Papers.
116 Hamilton to Gordon, 11 June 1819, D'Alberti Papers.
117 Hamilton to LeGeyt, 13 August 1819, D'Alberti Papers.
118 A. Fraser, 'Fisheries Negotiations with the United States, 1783–1910,' in S. Saunders, ed., *Newfoundland: Economic, Diplomatic, and Strategic Studies* (Toronto: Oxford University Press 1946), 354.
119 Golladay, 'The United States and British North American Fisheries, 1815–1818.'
120 Count Gallatin, ed., *The Diary of James Gallatin, Secretary to Albert Gallatin, A Great Peace Maker 1813–1827* (1914; reprint, Westport, CT: Greenwood Press 1979), 133.
121 Ibid., 263–4.
122 Jenkins, *Henry Goulburn*, 114.
123 Perkins, *Castlereagh and Adam*, 228–9; W. Galpin, 'The American Grain Trade to the Spanish Peninsula, 1810–1814,' *American Historical Review* 28, no. 1 (1922), 24–44.
124 W. MacNutt, *The Atlantic Provinces: The Emergence of Colonial Society, 1712–1857* (Toronto: McLelland and Stewart 1965), 170.

125 K. O'Rourke, 'The Worldwide Economic Impact of the French Revolution-
    ary and Napoleonic Wars, 1793–1815,' *Journal of Global History* 1 (2006),
    123–49; John D. Post, 'The Economic Crisis of 1816–1817 and Its Social and
    Political Consequences,' *Journal of Economic History* 30 (1970), 248–50. Also
    Bartlett, *Defence and Diplomacy*, 16–17; P. Harling and P. Mandler, 'From
    "Fiscal-Military" State to Laissez-Faire State, 1760–1850,' *Journal of British
    Studies* 32 (1993); 44–70; A. Lambert, 'Preparing for the Long Peace: The
    Reconstruction of the Royal Navy 1815–1830,' *Mariner's Mirror* 82 (1996),
    41–54.
126 Richard Rush to John Quincy Adams, 14 April 1819, *Diplomatic Correspon-
    dence* 1, 905.
127 P. O'Flaherty, *Old Newfoundland*, 126–32, and his 'The Seeds of Reform:
    Newfoundland, 1800–1818,' *Journal of Canadian Studies* 23 (1988), 39; C.
    English, 'The Official Mind and Popular Protest in a Revolutionary Era:
    The Case of Newfoundland, 1789–1819,' in F. Greenwood and B. Wright,
    eds., *Canadian State Trials*, vol. 1, *Law, Politics, and Security Measures 1608–
    1837* (Toronto: The Osgoode Society 1996), 313–16; S. Cadigan, *Hope and
    Deception in Conception Bay: Merchant-Settler Relations in Newfoundland,
    1785–1855* (Toronto: University of Toronto Press 1995); Prowse, *History of
    Newfoundland*, 402–11; J. Hatton and M. Harvey, *Newfoundland* (Boston:
    Doyle and Whittle 1883), 78–86.
128 William Haynes to Pickmore, 26 November 1816, D'Alberti Papers.
129 Britain, House of Commons, Report and Minutes of Evidence, Select Com-
    mittee on the Newfoundland Trade, 19 June 1817, George Garland, 3, 5–6.
130 J. Hiller, 'The Newfoundland Fisheries Issue in Anglo-French Treaties,
    1713–1904,' *Journal of Imperial and Commonwealth History* 24 (1996), 1–23,
    and his 'Utrecht Revisited: The Origins of Fishing Rights in Newfound-
    land Waters,' *Newfoundland Studies* 7 (1991), 23–39; J-F. Brière, 'Pêche et
    politique à Terre-Neuve au XVIIIe siècle: la France véritable gagnante du
    traité d'Utrecht?' *Canadian Historical Review* 64 (1983), 168–87; C. Cole, 'The
    St Pierre and Miquelon Maritime Boundary Case and the Relevance of
    Ancient Treaties,' *Canadian Yearbook of International Law* 31 (1993), 265–81.
131 See G. Sheppard, *Plunder, Profit, and Paroles: A Social History of the War of
    1812 in Upper Canada* (Montreal: McGill-Queen's University Press 1994),
    123.
132 Debate on the state of the island of Newfoundland in the House of Com-
    mons, on Tuesday, 11 May 1830, including the speeches of Mr Robinson,
    Sir George Murray, Mr Bernal, Mr Labouchere, Mr Hume, Mr Warburton
    (London: The Mirror of Parliament 1830), 3–4. [CIHM 9_07141]
133 Legal developments of this period are described in C. English, 'The Legal

Historiography of Newfoundland,' in C. English, ed., *Essays in the History of Canadian Law*, vol. 9 *Two Islands: Newfoundland and Prince Edward Island* (Toronto: Osgoode Society for Canadian Legal History and University of Toronto Press 2005), 19–38; and his 'From Fishing Schooner to Colony: The Legal Development of Newfoundland, 1791–1832,' in L. Knafla and S. Binnie, eds., *Law, Society, and the State: Essays in Modern Legal History* (Toronto: University of Toronto Press 1995), 73–93; J. Bannister, *The Rule of the Admirals: Law, Custom, and Naval Government in Newfoundland, 1699–1832* (Toronto: University of Toronto Press 2003), esp. chap. 8; S. Cadigan, 'Seamen, Fishermen and the Law,' in Colin Howell and Richard J. Twomey, eds., *Jack Tar in History* (Toronto: Acadiensis Press 1991), 105.

134 Keats to Bathurst, 15 April 1816, in CO 194, vol. 57, 21–39; Pickmore to Bathurst, 11 December 1816, in CO 194, vol. 57, 132–9.

135 A petition and summary of St John's merchant views on the treaties is contained in Hamilton to Bathurst, 5 December 1821, in CO 194, vol. 64, 165–6.

136 *The Times* (London), 1 and 4 March 1819.

137 P. Buckner, 'Hamilton, Sir Charles.'

138 22 April 1819 the Committee of Privy Council for Trade wrote the recently appointed Governor Duckworth, 89.

139 Hamilton to the Respective Magistrates of the several districts in Newfoundland, 29 October 1821; Hamilton to Stephen Lawler, 5 November 1821, in D'Alberti Papers.

140 Petition of the People of St John's, 6 May 1822, in CO 194, vol. 65, 26.

141 'A Statement of the French Fishery on the Coast of Newfoundland 1829,' in CO 194, vol. 78, 111.

142 See 'Memorandum on the Canadian Fisheries Question' (Foreign Office: London, 1870). [CIHM 9_02305] The nineteenth-century American position is presented in C. Isham, *The Fishery Question: its Origin, History and Present Situation* (New York: Putnam and Son's 1887) and J. Jay, *The Fisheries Dispute: A Suggestion for its Adjustment* (New York: Dodd, Mead 1887).

143 French claims to exclusivity were also addressed much later in Quebec. See *La pêcherie de Terreneuve: droits de la France: exposés aux assertions de l'Institute colonial* (Quebec: n.p. 1876). [CIHM 24133]

144 Appendix No. 4. Enclosure in Sir C. Campbell's Despatch, 23 May 1837, no. 77, 31. Report of the Committee of the House of Assembly of Nova Scotia, on the subject of the Fisheries. Extracted from the Journals – 1837, in *Papers relative to the fisheries of British North America* (London 1852), 276–9. Interestingly, the United States also viewed the agreement as unsatisfac-

tory. See 'Editorial Comment. The Newfoundland Fisheries,' *American Journal of International Law* 1 (1907), 144–8.

145 Gallatin to Chateaubriand, Paris, 22 January 1823, in CO 194, vol. 73, 213.

146 Vanancourt to Nicolas, 6 September 1821, in CO 194, vol. 64, 149.

147 Ibid., 23–8.

148 Ibid., 15.

149 Gallatin to Chateaubriand, Paris, 22 January 1823, in CO 194, vol. 73, 213; Chateaubriand to Gallatin, Paris, 28 February 1823, in CO 194, vol. 73, 215–17; Gallatin to Chateaubriand, 14 March 1823, in CO 194, vol. 73, 219–26; Gallatin to Chateaubriand, 2 April 1823, in CO 194, vol. 73, 229; Chateaubriand to Gallatin, 5 April 1823, in CO 194, vol. 73, 227–8.

150 Gallatin to Chateaubriand, 15 April 1823, in CO 194, vol. 73, 231–2.

151 G. Dangerfield, *Defiance to the Old World: The Story Behind the Monroe Doctrine* (New York: Putnam 1970); E. May, *The Making of the Monroe Doctrine* (Cambridge, MA: Belknap Press of Harvard University Press 1975).

152 W. Robertson, 'The Monroe Doctrine Abroad in 1823–24,' *The American Political Science Review* 6 (1912), 546–63.

153 See N.a., 'The North Atlantic Coast Fisheries Arbitration,' *Columbia Law Review* 11 (1911), 1–23.

154 Bannister, *The Rule of the Admirals*, 275–7.

155 See B. Messamore, 'Diplomacy or Duplicity? Lord Lisgar, John A. Macdonald, and the Treaty of Washington, 1871,' *Journal of Imperial and Commonwealth History* 32 (2004), 48.

156 Innis, *The Cod Fisheries*, 309; Neary, 'The French and American Shore Questions ...'

157 Steiger, 'Peace Treaties from Paris to Versailles,' 67.

158 Debate on the state of the island of Newfoundland in the House of Commons, on Tuesday, 11 May 1830, 27.

11

Social Workers, Courts, and the Implementation of the *Children of Unmarried Parents Act,* 1921–69

In 1921, legislation was passed in Ontario that was ostensibly intended to mitigate the worst social and economic consequences of illegitimacy for children. Lauded internationally as an advanced and humane approach to child welfare, Ontario legislation served as a model for reform in other provinces and in several American states. Surprisingly, however, the legislation has not been studied by historians; this essay is part of a larger project that fills this lacuna.[1] After outlining the reforms of 1921, this essay uses case files amassed by the Children's Aid Society to explore the implementation of reform measures. While the case files illustrate that the legislation failed as a child welfare measure, my focus is not on this failure or the experiences of women, but on the exercise of discretionary power by social workers and the courts. The role of administrators under various forms of welfare law is as yet a little studied subject in Canadian legal history. In this essay, I highlight the importance of case files and the records of social workers and bureaucratic organisations in order to understand the role of law in everyday people's lives, a reality that is often obscured when only law reports are studied.[2]

Illegitimacy in Law

At common law, the child born to an unmarried mother was a child of nobody and, although *de facto* custody was often with the mother, no one was obligated to support an out-of-wedlock child.[3] Although the fiscal responsibility of the father for his non-marital child was gradually expanded in Britain starting in 1576,[4] all liability of the father was eliminated by the English *Poor Law Amendment Act* of 1834, under which an illegitimate child was to be maintained solely by his or her mother. If the mother's parish became responsible for the child's support, the parish, but not the mother, could sue the father for reimbursement. The mother's evidence as to paternity had to be corroborated by a third party.[5]

Upper Canada, while sharing punitive attitudes towards illegitimacy, excluded England's poor laws from reception. This left the colony without a system of public relief for paupers, and without affiliation proceedings. Upper Canadian legislators made fathers potentially responsible for the support of their illegitimate children in 1837 through the *Seduction Act*.[6] Anyone who furnished necessaries for an illegitimate child could sue the putative father of the child for the costs of such support. However, the mother's evidence regarding paternity had to be corroborated by a third party. In cases in which women were successful in affidavits of affiliation, the liability imposed on the father lasted until the child reached his or her majority.[7] The next substantive reform to the law regarding illegitimacy was the legislation of 1921.

The first act in this child welfare package, the *Legitimation Act*, allowed for the subsequent legitimation of children, born outside of lawful wedlock, whose biological parents later married.[8] The second act, the *Adoption Act*, provided a mechanism for the permanent adoption of children either by strangers or by kin.[9] In cases of illegitimacy in which marriage was not possible, relinquishment for adoption was believed to be in the best interest of the child. Reformer J.J. Kelso, whose work had been central to the creation of the Children's Aid Society (CAS) and to the passage of child protection laws, argued that 'the experience of the ages has proved conclusively that no unmarried mother can successfully bring up her child and save it from disgrace and obloquy. (But) the child, if adopted young by respectable, childless people, will grow up creditably, and without any painful reminders of its origins.'[10]

The third act in this legislative package, the *Children of Unmarried Parents Act*, provided a mechanism by which unwed mothers could obtain financial support from the putative fathers of their children. The act eliminated the common law assumption that the mother was the *de facto* guardian of her illegitimate child. Instead, it provided that 'the provincial officer may upon his own application be appointed guardian of a child born out of wedlock either alone or jointly with the mother of such child.'[11] Under existing child welfare legislation, the CAS had the right to remove children from the custody and control of unfit parents, to make such children Crown wards, and then to release them for adoption without parental consent to relinquishment.[12] This power was expanded under the Act which provided that when 'the mother ... through lack of means is unable, or through misconduct is unfit to have the care of the child, the child may, with the consent of the provincial officer, be dealt with as a "neglected child."'[13] The state, not the mother, had the primary right to claim child support from the putative father, but court proceedings were a choice, not an obligation; unless social workers were convinced of paternity and the likelihood of success in court, proceedings would not be initiated.[14] The mother, or 'any person who has custody of a child born out of wedlock,' could also apply for support from the putative father of the child, but such applicants had to bear the cost of the proceedings themselves.

In court, the judge could only make an affiliation order 'on sufficient evidence,' a standard that was also not defined. The judge could declare 'the person named to be the father' and could order the father to pay 'reasonable expenses for the mother' resulting from the pregnancy and during her recovery and 'a sum of money weekly towards the maintenance of the child.' The sum to be awarded was to be based, not on need, but on the father's 'ability to provide and (his) prospective means.' Enormous discretionary power was delegated to local Children's Aid Societies to decide which mothers would and would not receive government assistance in seeking child support from the fathers of their children.[15] The question for the historian is how such discretion was exercised.

Illegitimacy and the Law Reports

Little evidence regarding the implementation of the act can be gleaned from the provincial law reports. Information about a case was first taken by a social worker in the offices of the CAS, and a determination was made whether or not to proceed to court. Mothers and CAS workers then appeared before the magistrate or family court judge, but decisions in these courts were not routinely reported. For this reason, the majority of decisions available in public documents were cases on appeal. Between 1921 and 1969 only twenty cases involving the legislation appear in the *Ontario Journal* and the *Ontario Reports*. Three of these cases involved technicalities of law; fifteen were cases in which fathers challenged child support orders that had been imposed by lower courts; and in two cases mothers appealed the rejection of their claims.[16]

In ten of the fifteen cases in which putative fathers sought to challenge the decisions of a lower court, they were unsuccessful. Although this ratio would suggest that men had limited success on appeal, the conditions under which appeals by putative fathers were denied deserve examination. Two cases were leave to appeal decisions and in both leave to appeal was denied; in one case the putative father had failed to contradict the evidence provided by the mother, and refused to enter the witness box,[17] and in the other he had corroborated her story to a third party.[18] Of the thirteen other cases, eight appeals were denied. In one case the appeal occurred after the death of a mother in childbirth.[19] Two others also involved very limited costs to the putative fathers as one child had been adopted[20] and another had been stillborn.[21] In the other five cases in which the appeal was denied, evidence of paternity was overwhelming. Two fathers had signed detailed voluntary agreements for support in which they admitted paternity.[22] The third father had written extensive love letters confirming the nature of his relationship with the mother of the child, and these letters had been entered into evidence at trial.[23] The fourth father had admitted paternity to several third parties.[24] In the final case, the court stated that the decision of a lower court should not be overturned where 'the learned trial judge is satisfied that there is corroborative evidence.'[25]

In five cases, putative fathers were successful and orders for support were vacated. In one case, the mother was legally married at the time of conception and had failed to provide evidence of non-access by her husband,[26] but the remaining four cases reveal important hints regarding the difficulty that women faced in providing legally acceptable corroboration of their stories of pregnancy. One appeal was granted on the basis that the mother's claims of keeping company with the putative father, and the resemblance of the baby to him, did not constitute proof of paternity.[27] In another case, evidence of the mother's alleged promiscuity was fatal to her claim. She admitted that she had had sexual relations with two men. Although the other relationship had been over long before the period relevant to conception, the judge argued that he could 'not escape the conclusion that the evidence falls short of amounting to proof sufficient to support a judicial determination.'[28]

Another appeal was allowed on the assertion by the high court that any 'doubt – reasonably entertained – should, as in any penal proceeding, have inured to the benefit of the accused.'[29] This was despite the fact that the proceedings were civil, not criminal, and that the standard of proof should have been the balance of probabilities, not the criminal requirement of proof beyond a reasonable doubt. Moreover, there was no discussion of the ease with which such doubts might be created by defamation of the character of the unwed mother. In an ironic admission, while granting the appeal of another putative father, the court asserted in 1921 that, despite the ostensible purpose of the legislation as a child welfare measure, 'the new Act in many of its terms (was) more onerous' than the regime that had preceded it.[30]

Only two cases in which mothers challenged the dismissal of their claims were reported. One of these cases was dismissed and in the other the mother was vindicated. In the first, the report provides no indication why the judge determined that the mother's claim was fraudulent.[31] In the case in which the mother's appeal was granted, her evidence was accepted as sufficient to prove that 'she did not keep company with any other man during the year or more she and the defendant were continually going about together.' Perhaps more importantly, 'the defendant's staying out of the witness box and omitting to give any explanation of a series of circumstances so suspicious as to call for explanation' was fatal to his case.[32]

The reported cases suggest that few women challenged lower court decisions and that they were held to a high burden of proof. The law reports, however, raise more questions than they answer; these cases were, after all, appeals. Not only is it unclear what proportion of cases were determined in favor of women at the lower court level, but also negotiations and struggles that preceded the arrival of cases in court are rendered invisible. To fully understand the procedures to which women were subjected, case files amassed by social workers are essential.

The Case Files

The central sources for this essay are case files created under the act between 1921 and 1969. The files contain standardised questionnaires given to unwed mothers, transcripts of court proceedings, CAS notes from interviews with mothers and with putative fathers, letters from mothers and children to the CAS, and miscellaneous evidence amassed by mothers to corroborate their claims of paternity.[33] These case files are a rich source for historical inquiry, but need to be treated with caution. The unwed mother's case was interpreted, mediated, filtered, constructed, and reconstructed through the eyes of social workers and judges in county and family courts across the province.[34] As Margaret Little argues in her study of the *Ontario Mothers' Allowance Act*, case files 'enable us to examine how this new relationship between social worker and client was established.'[35] Imbalances of power permeate these records, and the files illustrate the extent, and precise contours, of administrative discretion.

The cases used in this study represent a cross section of the province geographically, with records available from Algoma, Bruce, Frontenac, Grey, Huron, Kent, Waterloo, Wentworth, and York Counties, but with the preponderance of evidence drawn, not surprisingly, from the City of Toronto. Although the sample is large and geographically and chronologically diverse, it does have obvious limitations. Most importantly, the extant cases represent a small proportion of the women and children processed under the legislation, and an even smaller proportion of women pregnant out of wedlock. The reason for starting the study with files from 1921 is obvious. The end date of 1969 is more arbitrary. Affiliation proceedings were abolished on 31 March 1978,[36] and the designation 'illegitimate' was formally removed from Ontario law in 1980.[37] Despite these later changes, in many ways 1969 marked the end of an era. The decriminalisation of birth control in that year, and the partial decriminalisation of abortion, provided women with increased reproductive control and opened new debates about women's right to reproductive freedom. The expansion of welfare benefits under the *Canada Assistance Plan* of 1966 and the *Ontario Family Benefits Act* of 1967 meant that unwed mothers were no longer singled out as undeserving of social assistance. A 1969 Supreme Court of Canada decision, *Re Mugford*,[38] gave notice to social workers that many of the practices outlined in this essay were unacceptable. By the late 1960s the case files on which this research is based were becoming less common;[39] the case files for later years also decline dramatically in detail. Until the late 1960s, however, very little change was evident in the treatment meted out to unwed mothers by the CAS and the courts. In part, this reflected the fact that popular attitudes towards unwed mothers remained punitive. In part, it reflected the fact that CAS workers and magistrates often served long terms and reappeared in cases across decades.

Two distinct groups of women sought the assistance of the state under the auspices of the *Children of Unmarried Parents Act*. As Linda Gordon concludes, young women who 'had become pregnant and had neither an abortion nor a marriage' were very different from older women, 'often married and separated, who often had some legitimate children.'[40] Of the 4,023 women whose case files are extant, 2,031 had cohabited with the fathers of their children, and 1,992 were truly single. The legislation had been designed with only the second group of women in mind, and it is to the experiences of these 1992 women that we now turn. How was the discretionary power of the CAS exercised? Under what circumstances did women go to court seeking child support? How did judges and magistrates respond to the needs of single mothers? Ultimately, how 'just' was administrative justice?

Intake Proceedings at the Children's Aid Society

The unwed mother was required to report her pregnancy to the local CAS and it was 'the duty of the provincial officer, by inquiry through Children's Aid Societies, to obtain all information possible with respect to every child born out of wedlock.'[41] Young women arrived at the offices of the CAS seeking assistance in obtaining financial support for their children. Before any help would be forthcoming, however, the unwed mother had to convince the CAS worker that proof of paternity was overwhelming. The process of interrogation to which women were subjected replicated what Foucault and others have described as 'the ritual of the confessional.'[42] Without the opportunity to consult lawyers, young women were subjected to intense questioning and forced to complete standardized questionnaires. Basic demographic information – age, employment status, place of residence, religious affiliation and sometimes ethnicity – was collected. Women had to describe in detail the circumstances under which they had become pregnant, naming the putative fathers of their children and outlining any previous sexual history. The questionnaire also solicited information about smoking, drinking and attendance at dance halls and moving picture houses, a fact that illustrates the links that were drawn between illegitimacy and other socially unacceptable behaviours.

There is no doubt that these interviews were often unpleasant for unwed mothers. Of more importance, however, is the power that social workers had to determine women's access to court proceedings. If a woman's story was believed, the putative father would be sought for questioning. If, however, social workers determined that the woman was untruthful, that she was promiscuous and therefore could not prove paternity, if she was unable to provide contact information for the putative father of her child, or if she was believed to be unworthy and incapable of being a proper mother, no further action would be taken on the case. Of the 1,992 women who had not cohabited with the fathers of their children, 508 saw their cases dismissed informally at intake. This failure to believe women did not decline significantly over time, and condemnation of the unwed mother remained pervasive.

Corroborating the Woman's Story

If the social worker believed that the woman's story was plausible, the next step in the process of affiliation proceedings was to determine whether or not the woman had sufficient evidence to corroborate her claim. The act stated that 'no order of affiliation shall be made upon the evidence of the mother of the child unless her evidence is corroborated by some other material evidence.'[43] A mother could bring her friends, family, and work associates into the CAS office to provide evidence of intimacy between the parties or public admissions by the father of his role in the pregnancy. Evidence that would be considered by the CAS was explicitly listed by one social worker when interviewing a recalcitrant (and very obviously dishonest) putative father:

[H]ow are you going to establish you are not the father. We have the evidence now first from the mother of the child who says you are the father. You had relations with her from time to time. There is corroboration from her mother, discussions you had with her, promises to marry, the arrangements for the marriage, setting the dates, the fact you bought her that ring after the child was born, you paid her money after the child was born. These things would indicate you are likely to be the father of the child.'[44]

Ultimately, however, the evidence of the mother (and her friends and family) was not enough. CAS workers sought corroboration from putative fathers themselves. In cases that proceeded beyond intake, the CAS would attempt to locate and interview the putative father. Many, however, disappeared before they could be interviewed. As CAS workers noted in one case, 'it looks as though our bird has flown the coop ... we have been informed that he quit his job and nobody knows where he is.'[45] If a judge felt that a man was at risk of disappearing, he could be 'detained as a material witness,'[46] but in practice, men who wanted to disappear did so long before cases proceeded to court, and before such procedures could be invoked. Of 1,992 non-cohabiting fathers, 401 could not be located for interviews. Putative fathers also seem to have been aware that orders could not be enforced against those who resided outside Ontario. One sarcastic putative father taunted his former girlfriend with this fact in a letter that he wrote to her after fleeing to Vancouver: 'Since I am now residing in Vancouver, it will be impossible for me to appear on May 3. I would appreciate a more convenient time and place.'[47] When they could find putative fathers, CAS workers tried to convince them to enter into voluntary agreements for the support of children, and ultimately 291 of 1,992 non-cohabiting men admitted they were fathers.

Of the 1,083 cases that were not dismissed at intake and in which men did not disappear, in 409 men denied paternity during informal interviews, and sought to impugn the reputations of former girlfriends.[48] The informality of interviews with the CAS rewarded the most recalcitrant, irresponsible, and dishonest of men. Men were not under oath when they spoke to social workers at the CAS. Despite the fact that they had a financial interest in disproving paternity, their veracity was rarely questioned. Men were not subjected to the standard questionnaire, and even those who were described as 'unreliable'[49] or who had 'never been known to be steadily employed'[50] were not thereby judged as likely to be dishonest. Informal discussions with the CAS, while putting women on the defensive in having to explain their 'promiscuity,' provided men with ample opportunity to humiliate their girlfriends and to impugn their reputations. Ultimately, the CAS would not go to court unless a man admitted responsibility.

If a mother was denied access to court proceedings at the CAS, she still had the right to go to court at her own expense. This, however, was a remote possibility for most working-class women. The disincentives to such action were enormous since 'an unmarried mother may make a private application but must pay the costs if they are not recovered.' W.H. Bury, the provincial officer in charge of the Department of Public Welfare, Children's Division, put government policy on this issue bluntly in 1953: 'An application for an affiliation order is usually made by the Provincial Officer [Section 8 (g) C.U.P.A.] acting through the Superintendent of a Children's Aid Society, who is the representative of the Provincial Officer. As the Provincial Officer is liable in the first instance for the costs of the action, including court and solicitor's fees, the P.O. will authorize an application for an order only where a mother's claims can be fully corroborated.'[51] Only in thirty-one cases did women, or their parents, fund petitions to the court challenging the refusal of the CAS to support their applications.

This does not mean, however, that women were unaware of the unequal terms under which they negotiated with putative fathers and the CAS. But they had little power to protest. If unwed mothers criticised the CAS, all services to them could be withdrawn. It was standard practice, when women were deemed uncooperative, to refuse them further representation. As one CAS worker put it in a letter to a young woman 'no further services would be available' for the simple reason that the woman had 'been very critical of our handling of this case.'[52] A minimum of thirty-seven non-cohabiting women were sent letters threatening that if they were not more cooperative, services to them would cease; it is impossible to know how many times such verbal threats were made. As the Social Planning Council of Toronto admitted in 1960, 'legal counsel to unmarried mothers is very limited and the laws protecting children give Children's Aid Societies extraordinary power and authority.'[53] Of 1,992 mothers, 1,318 were denied any help from the CAS because they were disbelieved (before or after interviews with putative fathers) or because putative fathers disappeared.

Determining the Future of the Child

Not only were the vast majority of women denied the opportunity to seek child support from the fathers of their children, but also, because of the simultaneous legal and social powers of the CAS, they were pressured to marry men against their wishes and/or to release their children for adoption. Under the act, it was the responsibility of social workers in the CAS not only to determine which paternity cases would advance to court, but also to help the mother formulate a plan for the child. As some social workers began to recognise by the late 1960s, 'there are grave implications when one organization acts in both social and legal capacities.'[54] In the opinion of CAS workers, the obvious and most desirable solution in cases of unwed pregnancy was marriage. Given the legal disadvantages and social opprobrium attendant upon illegitimacy, it was not unreasonable for CAS workers to recommend marriage to the mother and the putative father as the best solution for the child, particularly given the passage of the *Legitimation Act*. The hope that many couples would marry, however, was misplaced. Only 56 of 1992 couples married.

Given the emphasis of social workers on marriage as the best solution to unplanned pregnancy, it is ironic that a minimum of eighty-seven men were not free to marry. Marriage was not advocated if it would necessitate a divorce. In fact, CAS workers and the court often went out of their way to ensure that wives would be protected from knowledge of their husbands' sexual indiscretions and to encourage separated men to reconcile with legal wives. Men, it appears, could be expected to 'sow a few wild oats,'[55] and their future and family life should not be jeopardised by such behaviour. Unwed mothers, however, had no such protection from social sanction or poverty, and vehemently denounced men who had deceived them by feigning bachelorhood. One woman ended her affair when she learned that her lover was already married. By this time, however, she was pregnant. When he then claimed to the court that he could not afford to pay child support because of his obligation to his legitimate wife and children, she expressed scorn and anger. He had 'thought nothing of spending large sums on treating her' and he had 'represented himself as a single man when they were going together, and spoke of marriage to her when he knew very well he was married.' She asserted, to the court and to the man's wife, that the man would simply use this spending money to 'get another girl in trouble.'[56] Although women expressed anger with men who had deceived them, CAS workers were contemptuous of women who had engaged in affairs with married men and such behaviour was taken as evidence of a woman's promiscuity, not of a man's dishonesty, a fact that clearly reflected the sexual double standard.

CAS workers also cajoled and pressured women. Women who did not want to marry the fathers of their children, who asserted that 'we fought like cats and dogs every time I saw him,'[57] or that 'he never got a steady job or settled down and he would not be a good prospect as a husband,'[58] were perceived to be irresponsible and undeserving of financial support. CAS workers would not invoke court proceedings against any man who offered to marry his girlfriend. As was asserted in one case by the social worker, 'I have pointed out to the woman that her marriage now with H would legitimize the child and relieve him for the rest of his life of a handicapping stigma. She, however, persists in her refusal to marry H and insists on keeping the child.'[59] Despite the fact that the man in this case was domineering and abusive,[60] the CAS determined that the only correct option for the mother was to accept his offer of marriage. When she refused to do so, they decided that her case would receive no further attention. Although her parents, with whom both she and the baby were living, hired a lawyer and funded a petition to the court, the judge concurred with the CAS, asserting that 'he is quite willing to marry the woman or to take the child and maintain it at his own expense. She quite stubbornly refuses either of these proposals ... Under the circumstances I do not think that he should be tied up to a periodic payment.'[61]

In most cases, marriage was not possible, and social workers had to help mothers to formulate other plans for their babies. The possibility of adoption, with its limited financial implications for putative fathers, was always suggested to mothers and was part of the informal negotiations carried out by the CAS with unmarried fathers. In fact, social workers seem to have introduced the possibility of adoption into negotiations with putative fathers even when mothers were adamant that they did not want to relinquish their children. The informality of negotiations with putative fathers indirectly empowered men to influence the decisions of mothers with regard to the futures of their children, despite the fact that legally, the mother of an illegitimate child was the only parent required to sign consent to relinquishment papers.[62] In 203 of the 1,992 cases involving non-cohabiting women, putative fathers admitted paternity informally to the CAS and agreed to pay costs pending adoption, but refused to provide a formal admission of paternity and threatened to force the issue into court if the mother wanted long term support. As one father asserted to a CAS worker in 1952, 'he was not going to do anything more than this $200. If the girl did not take that, he would just live outside of the Province of Ontario and she could not collect anything.'[63] Another man threatened his pregnant ex-girlfriend and the CAS. 'If Miss K is prepared to place her child for adoption he would be prepared to enter into an agreement for confinement expenses and maintenance from the date of the child's birth until placement. He stated that if Miss K wished to keep the child that he would be prepared to have the matter brought before the court.' She was unemployed, unable to speak English, and as a recent immigrant, had no local family to help her, and it is not surprising that ultimately she accepted her former lover's offer of $120 and gave her child up for adoption.[64] Shockingly, CAS workers did not use such admissions against men in court, but seem to have assumed that men would carry through with threats to abscond or to deny paternity and that it was therefore a waste of time and money to pursue support for mothers.

Women themselves, however, recognised the power of putative fathers in negotiations; as one mother lamented, 'he is trying to force me to place the baby for adoption so he can evade payment.'[65]

Going to Court

With the attrition of cases through the disbelief of the mother by CAS workers, the disappearance of fathers, their informal denials of paternity, and the pressures surrounding marriage and adoption, few cases advanced even to the level of the magistrate or family court. Only 291 cases advanced to court proceedings and in all cases fathers had admitted paternity; proceedings, ironically, were precipitated by non-payment. In 203 of these 291 cases, men who had initially admitted responsibility for pregnancies used the opportunity of court proceedings to rescind admissions, thus putting women on the defensive. In 160 of 203 cases men succeeded in having women's claims dismissed.

Paternity suits, as one contemporary observer noted, were 'barbaric in terms of consideration for human dignity ... [the mother had to describe] in open court in very explicit terms how, when, and where the male defendant's penis [had] entered her vagina. The entire procedure implicitly indicates that the court regards her as a whore, and that the court listens to her at all only for the sake of the taxpayers.'[66] Technically, these should have been civil proceedings in which the standard of preponderance of the evidence was to apply in reaching a verdict. In practice, however, because the mother was assumed to lie, she had to prove her case beyond a reasonable doubt. In fact, confirmation that the civil, not the criminal, burden of proof applied in affiliation cases did not come in Ontario until 1976.[67] It is not surprising that he said/she said contests produced transcripts that bear a remarkable resemblance to those in rape cases.[68] Judges routinely allowed invasive, highly personal, and condescending questioning to continue unabated, even when such questions were obviously irrelevant to the issue of paternity.

Putative fathers attempted to convince the court that, as one man put it, although he did not know of any specific men who had been sexually active with his ex-girlfriend, she had slept with him on their first date and therefore 'it would have been easy for any guy.'[69] Another putative father asserted that it was relevant that his ex-girlfriend had 'had sexual relations with other men prior to her association with him' and that 'she was, at the very least, an exceedingly flirtatious woman.' He suggested that this proved that her word could not be trusted. The woman's lawyer, whom she had hired when the CAS refused to take her case to court, countered that 'it is noteworthy that he calls not a single one of these persons (with whom he claims she may have been involved) to the stand, some of whom were personal friends of his.'[70] The lawyer representing another defendant asserted that 'it is important to show persons with whom she had intercourse because normally once a woman has intercourse with a man, as a matter of normal probative value, she will enjoy intercourse with that man and he will be able to call upon her from time to time in the future.'[71] Such erroneous and damaging stereotypes went largely uncorrected by the bench.

At times, the libelous nature of the testimony of putative fathers and their friends was painfully obvious. In a case that came before the court in Toronto in 1959, a father admitted intercourse at the material time, but had a close friend testify that he too had been sexually active with the woman. During cross-examination by the CAS, however, glaring inconsistencies emerged in the friend's testimony. He claimed to have picked the girl up at her apartment and to have had intercourse with her both there and in his car, yet he was unable to describe the apartment in question, claiming that it was on the second floor of an old house. In an unusual acknowledgement of the dishonesty of some witnesses, the presiding judge dismissed the witness from the stand with a warning that he had committed perjury at the completion of the following tirade by the representative of the CAS: 'I'm going to introduce evidence that Miss R. lived in a basement apartment with the entrance at the back, so you can start making your excuses right now. If you know so little about these things, such as the house, I could cross-examine you for 2 days with regard to the intercourse and you'd be mired completely. We've had this happen before.'[72] Ironically, however, the evidence of other witnesses (most of whom were also friends of the putative father) was considered to disprove paternity, and the woman in this case did not receive support.

Even under the most extreme and compelling of circumstances, women could be disbelieved and denied support. As one forthright Ontario judge put it in 1942, the court was inherently 'doubtful of her [the mother's] veracity.'[73] For example, a woman who had borne an illegitimate child in 1952 had charged the father of the child with rape. He had been acquitted, however, when his wife, after initially refusing to do so, provided him with an alibi. Physical evidence provided strong proof that the rape had indeed occurred. The woman claimed that she had been 'previously chaste' and several witnesses came forward to attest to her 'good character.' The CAS supported her claim throughout the proceedings and described the putative father in extremely unflattering terms. In his initial contact with the CAS the putative father had admitted paternity, yet the judge asserted that he was 'not certain that this woman was entirely truthful.'[74] She did not appeal.

Another woman claimed to have consented to intercourse only upon a promise of marriage. When she became pregnant, the putative father provided her with medicine intended to produce a miscarriage. She became violently ill, ending up in emergency care. The boyfriend was then charged with administering drugs to induce an abortion, and was given a suspended sentence. Despite his admission of paternity in the attempted abortion case, and in his initial dealings with the CAS, when called to court in the affiliation hearing he denied responsibility for the pregnancy. The judge dismissed the case with the following denigrating commentary about the unwed mother: 'She admits that she was quite willing for the intercourse. No blood was produced by the intercourse. The witness, W (a friend of the accused) swears that the girl told him that if he would come out with her she would rob him of his purity. Considering these doubts cast upon the previous chastity of the girl I find myself unable to conclude in any satisfactory way that M was the father of this child. The application is therefore dismissed.'[75] At no point in the proceedings had it been suggested that the mother had had intercourse with anyone other than the putative father at a time material to conception. Her alleged promiscuity was adequate evidence to prove that her 'veracity could not be trusted,' despite the fact that all so-called evidence of promiscuity had been obtained from friends of the putative father. Again evidence should have been overwhelming; again the CAS supported the woman's claim throughout the proceedings; again she failed to appeal.

In another instance, a judge dismissed a case which had been supported by the CAS, asserting that 'any one of the men named could have provided the vital sperm and would have been permitted to do so at any time ... at 15 the applicant was a potential tramp and now has fully realized that potential.' All evidence regarding the young woman's alleged promiscuity had been provided by friends of the accused, but the woman did not appeal. Not surprisingly, however, the CAS worker described her departure from the court as 'marked by tears.'[76] The same judge, as late as 1966, dismissed another case in which evidence from the woman's roommate provided corroboration that the putative father had 'pretty much lived with them for the last year,' and that no-one else had been intimate with the mother. The judge, however, argued that such living arrangements revealed the promiscuity of the mother, that young women 'shouldn't live unchaperoned' and that he therefore 'just cannot believe it.'[77] Young women could, and did, face hostility and doubts regarding their veracity, not only in the offices of the CAS, but also in the court.

Conclusion

The law reports render invisible the procedures that preceded (and often precluded) court proceedings and that were humiliating for the unwed mother. Women pregnant outside the context of cohabitation were extraordinarily vulnerable; of 1,992 women in such circumstances, 508 were dismissed at intake, 401 saw boyfriends (or attackers) disappear, 409 had their cases dismissed once CAS workers had interviewed putative fathers, 56 married their lovers (sometimes under duress), and in 203 cases fathers were willing only to pay costs pending adoption; only 291 men admitted paternity. In 124 cases, proceedings failed to advance to court, but evidence in the case files is inadequate to understand and categorise the reasons why, and at what stage of the proceedings, cases were not pursued. After the attrition of cases at the CAS, 88 fathers continued to admit paternity, but 203 denied responsibility in court, and in 160 of these cases they were successful in overturning agreements for support. In 31 cases women challenged the dismissal of their cases by the CAS through the court process, but only in 2 cases were such appeals successful. Men could disappear, lie in the offices of the CAS, and when these strategies failed, could further challenge orders in court, and were likely to be successful. In total, therefore, of 1,992 non-cohabiting women who sought support through the auspices of the CAS, only 133 were successful in obtaining agreements or orders for child support (and this did not guarantee that they would receive any of the money owed to them).

The case files amassed by social workers provide incontestable evidence that unwed mothers were humiliated, insulted, and disbelieved at all stages of the proceedings mandated by the *Children of Unmarried Parents Act*. Subjected to intense questioning by CAS workers, they were far too often denied the right to pursue the fathers of their children in court. Instead, they were pressured to marry the fathers of their children, or to release their children for adoption. When cases did proceed to court, the humiliation of women continued unabated. Yet, because of poverty and other difficult life circumstances, women had few alternatives but to seek aid from the CAS. One observer, arguing for reform, asserted in 1966 that 'the cruelty of the law (was) most intense in its treatment of unwed mothers.'[78] Even this cogent remark, however, missed the fact that much of the cruelty meted out to unwed mothers was through informal, quasi or extra-legal (low law) discretionary procedures; the majority of unwed mothers, after all, did not ever appear in court. In illustrating the magnitude, frequency and specific contours of the mistreatment of unwed mothers, the CAS case files are essential. Administrative mechanisms, despite their relative invisibility in legal history, are central to the rule of law. Without explicit procedures for appeal, administrative discretion had potentially devastating consequences for those regulated under legislation such as the *Children of Unmarried Parents Act.*

NOTES

1 For a more detailed and extensive critique of the legislation, see Lori Chambers, *Misconceptions: Unmarried Motherhood and the Ontario Children of Unmarried Parents Act, 1921–1969* (Toronto: University of Toronto Press and the Osgoode Society for Legal History 2007). This article is a more focused version of the book's second chapter.

2 As I have argued in earlier work, law reports are often a limited source for historical inquiry because of the discretionary nature of reporting, See Lori Chambers, *Married Women and Property Law in Victorian Ontario* (Toronto: University of Toronto Press and the Osgoode Society for Legal History 1997). As this study illustrates, they also obscure the reality of law as experienced by real people if the records of those with discretionary administrative power are not also considered. Douglas Hay makes a similar argument with regard to what he refers to as the high law/low law distinction in *Masters, Servants and Magistrates in Britain and the Empire, 1562–1955* (Durham: University of North Carolina Press 2004).

3 As William Blackstone asserted, 'The incapacity of a bastard consists principally in this, that he cannot be heir to any one, neither can he have heirs, but of his own body. Being *nullius filius*, he is therefore kin of nobody, and has no ancestor from whom any inheritable blood can be derived.' See William Blackstone, *Commentaries on the Laws of England* (London: Kerr 1857), 485.

4 Under the statute of 1576, either parent could be charged for the support of

the child and committed to jail on default of a support order, *An Act for Setting the Poor on Work*, 18 Elizabeth c.3. The next legislative enactment, passed in 1609, was more severe. The mother of the illegitimate child who became a charge on the parish could now be imprisoned for a full year. In 1662, it was enacted that the goods and income of the mother and the putative father could be seized for the support of the illegitimate child. A statute of 1733 provided that a single pregnant woman could charge any man with being the father of her child. In 1809 this statutory scheme the putative father was made liable for the expenses of the birth and for the costs of his own arrest and affiliation proceedings. See Alan MacFarlane, 'Illegitimacy and Illegitimates in English History,' in Peter Laslett, Karla Osterveen, and Richard Smith, eds., *Bastardy and Its Comparative History* (London: Hodder and Stoughton 1980), 75, and Harry D. Krause, *Illegitimacy: Law and Social Policy* (New York: The Bobbs-Merrill Company 1971).

5 Martha Bailey, 'Servant Girls and Masters: The Tort of Seduction and the Support of Bastards,' *Canadian Journal of Family Law* 10 (1991), 152.

6 *Statutes of Upper Canada*, 7 William 4, c.8. The mother had to swear an affidavit as to the child's paternity within six months of its birth. Peter Ward, 'Unwed Mothers in Nineteenth-Century English Canada,' *Canadian Historical Association – Historical Papers* (1981), 41.

7 The first part of the act amended the common law by making it possible for a father to sue his daughter's employer for the daughter's seduction. Previously, only an employer had been able to sue someone who had seduced, and rendered unproductive through pregnancy, a woman in his employ. In 1877, the two parts of the original statute were severed. The civil remedy remained and a new criminal offence of seduction was created. Ontario's *Seduction Act* was finally repealed in 1978. Bailey, 'Servant Girls and Masters,' 154. For further information on seduction, see Constance Backhouse, 'The Tort of Seduction: Fathers and Daughters in Nineteenth-Century Canada,' *Dalhousie Law Journal* 10 (1986), 45–80.

8 *An Act respecting the Legitimation of Children by the Subsequent Intermarriage of Their Parents*, Statutes of Ontario [hereafter S.O.] (1921) c.53.

9 *An Act respecting the Adoption of Children*, S.O. (1921) c.55. Until 1921, adoption was available in Ontario only through a private member's bill in the provincial legislature.

10 As quoted in A.E. Jones and L. Rutman, *In the Children's Aid: J.J. Kelso and Child Welfare in Ontario* (Toronto: University of Toronto Press 1981), 156.

11 *An Act for the Protection of the Children of Unmarried Parents*, S.O. (1921) c.54, s.10.

12 *An Act for the Prevention of Cruelty to, and the Better Protection of Children,*

S.O. (1893). As Dorothy Chunn illustrates, the statutes passed at the end of the nineteenth century sanctioned 'unprecedented intervention into deviant or potentially deviant families': Dorothy Chunn, *From Punishment to Doing Good: Family Courts and Socialized Justice in Ontario, 1880–1940* (Toronto: University of Toronto Press 1992), 44.

13 *Children of Unmarried Parents Act*, S.O. (1921), c.54, s.11. The *prima facie* right of the mother to the custody of her illegitimate child was only firmly established by the Supreme Court of Canada in 1950. See *Re: Baby Duffell, Martin et al. v. Duffell* [1950] S.C.R. 737, [1950] 4 D.L.R. 1.

14 *Children of Unmarried Parents Act*, S.O. (1921), c.54, s.18. For the summary of the act in the rest of this paragraph and the next, see ibid., ss.13, 18, and 25.

15 The CAS was a unique institution. It assumed responsibility for a wide range of child welfare legislation and was empowered to claim custody of children as well as to enforce the acts of 1921. The CAS operated as a private agency run by its own boards at the local level. Although enforcing state policies, the CAS experienced only minimal government regulation and financial support, rendering each institution dependent upon community charity and ensuring that little cash was available to support single mothers (or to cover the costs of other child welfare programs facilitated by the CAS). Only in 1965 did the provincial government commit itself fully to paying for child welfare services for unmarried mothers provided through the CAS. *Child Welfare Act*, S.O. 1965, c.14, s.12. For further discussion of the funding provided to the CAS, see N. Trocme, 'Child Welfare Services,' in R. Barnhorst and L. Johnson, eds., *The State of the Child in Ontario* (Toronto: Oxford University Press 1991).

16 Of the twenty higher court cases that appear in the law reports, three (15 per cent) were purely about technicalities in the interpretation of the legislation and provide little insight into the impact of legislation on women, putative fathers, or children. *Grawburger and Moyer (Re)* [1929] Ontario Journal [hereafter O.J.] No 96; *Hilton v. Tassman* [1944] O.J. No. 337; and *Duckworth v. Skinkle (R)* [1924] O.J. No. 18.

17 *Re Yeo and Benner* [1926] O.J. No 339.

18 *Carleton v. MacLean* [1953] O.J. No. 275.

19 *Leskey v. VanHorne* [1954] O.J. No. 346.

20 *M.G. (Re)* [1943] O.J. No. 270.

21 *Kirkpatrick and Moroughan (Re)* [1927] O.J. No. 58.

22 *Power (Re)* [1952] O.J. No. 336, and *Adrian and McGuire (Re)* [1925] O.J. No. 449.

23 *Walker v. Foster* [1923] O.J. No. 23.

24 *Wicks v. Armstrong* [1928] O.J. No. 160. This was also a particularly disturb-

ing case as the young woman, who worked for the putative father as a domestic servant, asserted that the putative father had 'compelled her to have intercourse with him.'

25 *C.S. v. M.R.* [1954] O.J. No. 281. This case may reflect more the weariness of the court with appeal cases based only on a retrial of the facts (rather than technicalities of the law and procedures) at the high court.

26 *Brown and Argue (Re)* [1925] O.J. No. 50.

27 *Re Eisenmenger and Doherty* [1924] O.J. No. 558.

28 Gwyllt (Re) [1944] O.J. No. 85.

29 *Re Nunn v. Featherstone* [1927] O.J. No. 173.

30 *Hunt v. Lindensmith (Re)* [1921] O.J. No. 50.

31 *Gabel v. Bolander* [1943] O.J. No. 162.

32 *Middleton v. Bryce* [1931] O.J. No. 234.

33 Although extensive details regarding the sexual and social experiences of pregnant women are available through these case files, women fashioned their answers to the probing questions of social workers under circumstances which may have inhibited complete honesty. This issue makes the interpretation of personal details in the case files difficult. This essay explicitly excludes personal details, and focuses exclusively on the discretionary interpretation of the act by the CAS and the court.

34 The sources on which this study is based were written in a context which assumed the privacy of documents and the protection of the client – and the social worker – from public exposure. The identities of women, their children, families and friends, and of putative fathers and social workers have been disguised to respect both the privacy of the living and the dead and to meet the conditions of access to documents. Although a specific box number for the archival source is provided to reflect the date and region of each case, the numbering of cases is arbitrary.

35 Margaret Jane Hillyard Little, *No Car, No Radio, No Liquor Permit: The Moral Regulation of Single Mothers in Ontario, 1920–1997* (Toronto: University of Toronto Press 1998), xxii.

36 Diana Dzwiekowski, 'Casenotes: Findings of Paternity in Ontario, *Sayer v. Rollin,*' *Canadian Journal of Family Law* 3 (1980), 318–26. Instead, fathers can now sign voluntary declarations of paternity, or mothers can require blood tests of them.

37 *Family Law Reform Act*, R.S.O. (1980), c.152, s.1(a).

38 *Re Mugford* [1970] 1 O.R. 601.

39 While for all years until 1967 the number of extant cases found at the archives was reasonably stable, with an average of 83.8 cases per year and no fewer than 71 or more than 94 (a fact made even more significant by the

chance nature of the sample); for 1967, only 45 cases are extant, 37 for 1968, and 23 for 1969.

40 Linda Gordon, *Pitied but Not Entitled: Single Mothers and the History of Welfare, 1890–1935* (New York: The Free Press 1994), 22.

41 *Children of Unmarried Parents Act,* S.O. (1921), c.54, s.7.

42 Michel Foucault, *The History of Sexuality: An Introduction,* vol. 1, trans. Robert Hurley (New York: Pantheon Books 1980), 45.

43 *Children of Unmarried Parents Act,* S.O. (1921), c.54, s.25.

44 Archives of Ontario [hereafter AO], box 24–2–3–2, case 538, Wentworth, 1960.

45 AO, Box 24–2–3–4, case 221, Wentworth, 1958.

46 *An Act for the Protection of the Children of Unmarried Parents,* R.S.O. (1921) c.54, s.24.

47 AO, box 24–2–3–3, case 15, Wentworth, 1966.

48 In 124 cases the outcome of the case is unclear; in 56 cases couples were married and proceedings therefore were halted; and in 203 cases men signed limited agreements for costs pending adoption, but without formally admitting paternity.

49 AO, box 66-3-3–14, case 104, Wentworth, 1953.

50 AO, box 66-3-3–14, case 110, Wentworth, 1956.

51 AO, box 27–9-1–1, case 303, Middlesex, 1953. In this case the mother, after finding the CAS to be unreceptive to her claims, had hired a lawyer for herself and this letter by Bury was in response to queries by the lawyer regarding court procedure. This letter provides confirmation of the practical problems created for lawyers by the paucity of reported cases regarding the application and interpretation of the *Children of Unmarried Parents Act.*

52 AO, box 11–26–4-17, case 2362, York, 1963.

53 Social Planning Council of Metropolitan Toronto, *A Report on Maternity Homes in Metropolitan Toronto* (Toronto, 1960), 51.

54 Ibid.

55 AO, box 27–9-1–1, case 301, Middlesex, 1952.

56 AO, box 24–2–3–3, case 69, Wentworth, 1956.

57 AO, box 411–1-4–1, case 433, York, 1959.

58 AO, box 66–4-4–6, case 190, Wentworth, 1947.

59 AO, box 512–2–3–4, case 1025, Algoma, 1927.

60 Family members and friends testified that he had been jealous and possessive and that they supported the woman's decision to refuse the offer of marriage.

61 AO, box 512–2–3–4, case 1025, Algoma, 1927.

62 Until the 1980s, even cohabiting fathers had no explicit legal right to partic-

ipate in this decision. The only exception occurred when biological parents subsequently married. *Re G., G. et ux v. C. et ux* [1951] 3 *Dominion Law Reports* [hereafter D.L.R.], 138. By the 1980s, putative fathers were challenging their exclusion from this decision-making process as unconstitutional.

63 AO, box 411–1-3–11, case 501, York, 1947.
64 AO, box 411–1-3–9, case 397, York, 1955.
65 AO, box 411–1-3–12, case 2050, York, 1950.
66 Robert Viet Sherwin, 'The Law and Sexual Relationships,' *Journal of Social Issues* 22, no. 2 (1966), 113–14.
67 *Panaccione v. McNab* [1976] O.J. No. 1690, par. 6.
68 For further information on the nature of rape trials, see Carolyn Strange, 'Patriarchy Modified: The Criminal Prosecution of Rape in York County, 1880–1930,' in Jim Phillips, Tina Loo, and Susan Lewthwaite, eds., *Essays in the History of Canadian Law: Crime and Criminal Justice* (Toronto: The Osgoode Society 1994), 207–51; Constance Backhouse, 'Nineteenth-Century Rape Law, 1800–1892,' in Jim Flaherty, ed., *Essays in the History of Canadian Law* (Toronto: The Osgoode Society 1988), 200–47; T. Brettel Dawson, 'Sexual Assault Law and Past Sexual Conduct of the Primary Witness: The Construction of Relevance,' *Canadian Journal of Women and the Law* 2 (1987–88), 310–34.
69 AO, box 411–1-4–2, case 703, York, 1954.
70 In this case, an agreement was reached as the child died during the court proceedings and payments were therefore finite. AO, box 24-2-3–4, case 223, Wentworth, 1967.
71 AO, box 411–1-4–6, case 2295, York, 1964.
72 AO, box 411–1-4–1, case 452, York, 1959.
73 AO, box 66–3-3–14, case 89, Wentworth, 1942.
74 AO, box 24–2-3–2, case 599, Wentworth, 1952.
75 AO, box 512–2-3–4, case 1039, Algoma, 1935.
76 AO, box 411–1-4–6, case 2420, York, 1961.
77 AO, box 11–26–4-20, case 2553, York, 1966.
78 Sherwin, 'The Law and Sex Relationships,' 118.

12

The David Fasken Estate: Estate Planning and Social History in Early Twentieth-Century Ontario

C. IAN KYER*

When David Fasken died on 2 December 1929, after a lengthy illness, his death was front-page news. 'David Fasken, KC, Dies at Home After Long Illness'[1] said the *Globe*. 'David Fasken, Wealthy Mining Magnate Dies'[2] reported the *Toronto Daily Star*. Each noted his many achievements as a lawyer and managing partner of an important law firm, as president of the Excelsior Life Insurance Company, the Nipissing Mining Company Limited, the Northern Ontario Light and Power Company Limited, and the Northern Canada Power Company Limited, and as a major benefactor of the Salvation Army and the Toronto Western Hospital.

On 4 and 5 December his funeral was again front-page news,[3] including pictures of many of Toronto's leading citizens who not only attended the funeral at his home on University Avenue but also drove through deep snowdrifts to his gravesite in Elora.[4] Included were business leaders like Colonel Edward Albert Gooderham, Edward Rogers Wood and Sigmund Samuel, court of appeal judges like William R. Riddell and Cornelius A. Masten, prominent doctors like John Ferguson, and the leading architect Edward James Lennox, many of whom acted as honorary pall-bearers. Later, on 3 January 1930, on the probating of his will, the newspapers yet again gave his affairs extensive front-page coverage. Relying on his will and the probate documents, the *Toronto Daily Star* reported that he had left an estate of nearly $2,000,000.[5]

The newspaper coverage, extensive as it was, underestimated the size of his estate and missed its real significance. The report of his estate 'of nearly $2,000,000' is quite misleading because it fails to take into account a series of estate planning steps that he had taken over the decade or so preceding his death.[6] David Fasken was far wealthier. He was one of Canada's wealthiest men. He had accumulated many assets during his life that were not referred to in his will or listed for probate purposes, assets that had a much greater value, many millions of dollars more, than the $1,792,328.11 shown for Ontario probate and succession duty purposes.[7] David's assets were in fact so valuable that they would ultimately make his grandson, David Fasken Jr, a billionaire. The news reports also missed or chose to ignore the significance of some of the things that David did and did not do in his will, final decisions that give us insight into the personal life of one of Canada's most important business lawyers.

This essay is both a social history and a case study of how a wealthy Canadian lawyer with access to the very best legal advice in the first quarter of the twentieth century chose to deal with his assets in anticipation of his death.[8] It will provide insights into the tools and techniques of estate planning in the early days of Canadian estate taxes. David Fasken undertook his estate planning within a decade of the introduction of income tax in 1917[9] and within thirty years of Ontario enacting legislation in 1892 to collect succession duties.[10] Because estate planning is by its very nature one of the most personal acts of a business person (choosing how his or her accumulated wealth will be distributed to family, friends, causes, and institutions), this study also provides a window into Fasken's personal life. Rarely do we have an opportunity to glimpse this side of a leading Canadian business lawyer.[11]

Fasken's estate planning was quite extensive, involving *inter vivos* gifts[12] and discretionary trusts,[13] charitable donations, foreign investments, a form of estate freeze, and a skillfully prepared will. His planning reflected a desire to reduce succession duties and taxes but even more a wish to ensure that his wealth was used to fund projects that he supported and to help family members in need. Fasken abhorred the *Succession Duty Act*. 'He didn't see why the Governments should be able to gobble up most of his wealth when he died, so he decided to do something about it,' wrote his second cousin and family biographer.[14] Tax planning was certainly a motivating factor in his estate planning, but the steps that he took also reflect his fervent desire to do his duty to his family, both nuclear and extended, while at the same time keeping the control of his assets out of the hands of his wife whom he disliked and his son whom he did not trust.

One cannot understand estate planning without knowing what assets the deceased had accumulated during his lifetime and what people and causes he wanted or had an obligation to support. This essay shall therefore start with David Fasken the businessman and lawyer to understand the sources and nature of his wealth. I then turn to David Fasken the man to understand his relationship with his immediate and extended family and with such institutions as the Methodist Church, the Salvation Army, and the Toronto Western Hospital, and I look briefly at the Ontario *Succession Duty Act*. Once we have an understanding of how this statute worked, we can better understand his last will and testament and the inventory of the assets it addressed and the steps that he took in the 1920s outside of his will to deal with his enormous wealth. I conclude with a brief review of the court challenges taken by the Canadian federal government as well as the Governments of Texas and Ontario in an effort to claim some of his wealth.

David Fasken, Lawyer and Businessman

David Fasken was first and foremost a talented lawyer.[15] After graduating from the University of Toronto in 1882 with a BA, he articled with Beatty, Chadwick, and Blackstock,[16] the law firm that served the needs of the Gooderham and Worts family businesses.[17] On his call to the bar in 1885, he practised with that firm. William Henry Beatty, the managing partner of the firm, was so impressed with the work ethic of 'this raw lad from the farm' that he suggested that his son emulate him.[18] As one biographer would later say, 'His outstanding traits were a capacity for sustained and concentrated effort, close attention to detail, and absolutely unprejudiced weighing of facts.'[19] By 1902 David Fasken had become Beatty's administrative assistant at the firm. Beatty was then president of Confederation Life and was assuming an increasing role in the Gooderham and Worts family ventures. He left the day-to-day management of the firm to Fasken. In September 1906, Fasken became managing partner of the firm. By 1915 the firm name was changed to Fasken, Cowan, Chadwick, and Rose, and it was relocated in the newly completed Excelsior Life Building at 36 Toronto Street, which, like Fasken's first custom-built house on Queen Street East, was designed by Toronto's leading architect, E.J. Lennox.[20]

The revenue that Fasken drew from the law firm, however, would never have, in and of itself, allowed him to accumulate immense wealth. Under the 1906 partnership agreement,[21] David Fasken and William R. Riddell, respectively the leading business and litigation lawyers in the firm, each received $8,500 of the net annual profits up to $30,000 and 35 5/6 per cent of the profits between $30,000 and $45,000. Assuming a profit of about $45,000 per year, Fasken received approximately $13,500, a very good wage for the day but not enough to make him a millionaire.

If the practice of law did not give Fasken the capital he needed, it did give him access to people of wealth and influence and to business opportunities. Fasken exploited that access and those opportunities to make his money as an investor and a businessman. His principal business activities were in insurance, mining, hydroelectric power, and land development. Shortly after the incorporation of the Excelsior Life Insurance Company in the late 1880s Fasken bought up many of its shares and encouraged the law firm's largest client, the Gooderhams, to do so. Their shares together with his own gave him control of the company.[22] On 13 February 1900, he was elected president, a position that he was to hold until his death.[23] Working on its affairs in his spare time, he built the insurance company into a very successful and profitable business, increasing its annual revenue from $3 million, when he first invested, to $100 million, at the time of his death.[24]

Three years after becoming president of Excelsior Life, Fasken seized another opportunity to combine his energy and talents with his clients' money to their mutual benefit. When, during the construction of what is now the Ontario Northland Railway, cobalt, nickel and silver were discovered at Long Lake (now Cobalt, Ontario),[25] Fasken put together an investors group consisting of Ellis P. Earle and other New York-based investors. They formed the Nipissing Mining Company Limited and secured claims covering over 846 acres.[26] The *Cobalt Daily Nugget* would report in 1910 that the company that Fasken put together 'occupies the very centre of the Cobalt Camp. It is, in fact, the centre.'[27] The centre of what the *Provincial Geologist* reported in 1908 to be 'the world's largest producer of silver' and the region that 'controls the market for cobalt.'[28] In addition to serving as Nipissing's president and one of its directors, he became a director and substantial shareholder of both La Rose Consolidated Mines Limited and Trethewey Silver Cobalt Mine Limited, each of which had mines at Cobalt.[29]

Fasken also acquired three power plants which supplied much-needed hydroelectric power to the Cobalt workings and later to the discoveries at Porcupine and Kirkland Lake. In 1911, Fasken merged the power plants he had acquired to form the Northern Ontario Light and Power Company Limited of which he was president. He also organized the Northern Canada Power Company Limited.

David Fasken, who was spending time in the Temagami area, saw other opportunities in the fact that investors in the Cobalt mines needed accommodation and transportation. David, his brother Alex and their client William George Gooderham financed hotels, steam-ships, and general stores at the new lakeside village of Temagami. Of his investments, however, this proved the least successful.[30]

Morris Zaslow has said that, 'Cobalt was the opening victory in the long campaign waged by Canadians to wrest mineral wealth from the Precambrian Shield.'[31] David Fasken played a key role both in that opening victory and also in the 'long campaign,' financing numerous other mining initiatives. In 1909 the *Montreal Star* listed him among the seventeen Canadians and eight Americans whom Cobalt had turned into millionaires.[32] Fasken became a part of a group of wealthy Canadi-ans and Americans who formed the Canadian Mining Exploration Company, a venture that in 1912 was said to have 400 properties under consideration.[33]

David and his brother Alex were also key members of the syndicate in 1914–15 that grubstaked the Flin Flon mine in Manitoba. In 1915, the two brothers actually visited the site in northern Manitoba, travelling at times by oxen and by canoe. They later formed part of the Toronto-based investors syndicate that optioned these claims. While the others sold their interest before the Flin Flon mine was developed, David Fasken hung on. W.F. Currie, one of the original grubstakers, noted in 1927: 'We got out and were quite satisfied to do so. Only David Fasken was left and I hear he's made a very good thing out of sticking to the end.'[34]

After 1915, Fasken spent much of his time at a ranch that he had pur-chased in 1913 near Midland, Texas.[35] Fasken's 'C' Ranch was enor-mous – 226,000 acres. Although he purchased the ranch with the thought that he would subdivide the property for farming, he found it almost useless for traditional farming because it lacked sufficient water.[36] Having invested over a million dollars in it, however, he did not give up on the property. In 1917, he moved his nephew Andrew Fasken down to manage the property. They tried dry farming with crops like cotton on a model farm. To support the would-be-purchasers of farms, Fasken founded a small town with a school, stock pens and a hotel, which he called Fasken, Texas,[37] and he built a 66-mile railroad, the Midland and Northwest, to the site.[38] Some lots were sold but few people moved in and Fasken, Texas, died in the 1920s.[39] Andrew Fasken, however, proved a good manager and was able to turn the property back into a prosperous cattle ranch.

As we shall see, Fasken had to fight a legal battle with the State of Texas to keep the property, but keep it he did. Fasken would never know, however, that this was the best investment he ever made – in the 1930s after his death, a vast oil reserve was found on the property, making his grandson David Jr one of the wealthiest men in the world.

David Fasken, The Man

David Fasken's professional life may have been very successful, but his personal life was problem filled. He did not have a good relationship with his wife or his son. He did, however, value his extended family.[40] David was the fifth of ten children of Robert Fasken and Isabel Milne. In 1837, Robert, then seventeen, had come with his family from Scotland. In 1844, Robert and his brother George[41] purchased 100 acres in Pilkington Township near Elora, 'facing the Grand River and about two miles from the farm of his parents,'[42] and cleared the land for farming. The two brothers had built back-to-back houses on the farm which they both worked. David's family lived in the front house and his uncle's family lived in the back house. On 31 December 1860, David was born in the front house. As a youngster, brothers, sisters, and cousins surrounded David. He worked around the farm and fished in the Grand River that ran along the back of the farm property. He worshiped at Bethany Methodist Church and attended a one-room school with his many brothers, sisters, and cousins. Both the church and school were a short walk from the farm. He had a much longer walk (about three miles) when he attended the Elora High School.

After graduating from Elora High School, he and his cousin George were able to convince their parents that they should be the first in the family to go to university. They enrolled at the University of Toronto and moved to Toronto. The family provided a small allowance for Fasken, but there was nothing left for sports or concerts or even transportation. Fasken walked everywhere.[43] Although he had trouble with French, he graduated from the university in 1882 and began his articles of clerkship. In 1885 he was called to the bar and joined the Beatty firm. His cousin George also graduated and became pastor of St Paul's Methodist Church.

During those early years in Toronto, he boarded with two sisters who were much older than he was.[44] Although engaged to Nellie Bye in Elora, he had an affair with Alice Winstanley, one of his landladies. Unfortunately, she became pregnant. Fasken did not love her, but duty and honour dictated that he marry her, which he did in 1891. The baby, Mary Isabel, was born on 24 February 1892. Regrettably, the baby died just over three months later on 4 June. Fasken found himself in a love-less marriage, mourning the death of his first child. Fasken and his wife did have another child in 1893, a son, Robert Alexander, but this son was to bring Fasken little joy.

Robert was to be a regular source of trouble and concern for his father. As soon as the child was born, Fasken enrolled him in Toronto Model School, but Robert did not do well in school and Fasken soon realized his son was not likely to follow in his footsteps.[45] Robert's first marriage brought more concerns.[46] Fasken maintained a cottage in the Temagami region. The Ferland family had a cottage nearby. When in his late teens, Robert met and fell in love with May Ferland. She was a student at the Toronto Conservatory of Music and a Roman Catholic. When Mrs Fasken learned of the relationship, she promptly took her son on an extended visit to Europe. If she hoped that the infatuation would fade, her plan did not work. On his return from Europe, Robert learned that May had gone to Boston for further study. He found an excuse to visit Boston and, in 1913, the couple were married there in a Roman Catholic service. Fasken seems to have accepted the marriage. He increased his son's allowance and gave the couple a honeymoon in Europe. Fasken's wife, however, was not as forgiving.

Robert did not have a job, so he and May moved into his parents' home on University Avenue in Toronto. Although a large house, it was not big enough for mother and daughter-in-law. When Fasken's grand-son, David Jr, was born on 22 April 1915 and baptised as a Catholic, matters became even worse. May found the stress of dealing with her mother-in-law too much and she had a nervous breakdown. She went to a sanatorium in Barrie, leaving her baby in the care of her husband and mother-in-law. After a time, she returned to the Fasken home in Toronto, but nothing had changed and she again had a breakdown. This time she was advised to spend time with her family up north. Her husband agreed to let her go, but insisted on having his mother look after the baby.

When May left, Mrs Fasken decided to move with her son and grand-child to Texas, where Fasken had purchased the 'C' Ranch. Mrs Fasken, her son and grandson, however, did not live on the ranch. They moved into a house Fasken bought for them in the nearby town of Midland. David Fasken and his wife never again lived together.

May would not learn where her husband and son had gone until she received notice in 1917 that her husband had filed for divorce in Texas.[47] May successfully defended the 1917 divorce action, which Robert unscrupulously brought on the grounds of her abandonment of him. May's lawyer successfully argued that there had been no abandonment and that Robert's residence in Texas was not bona fide but was just to qualify to bring a divorce action that would not have been permitted under Canadian law. Robert and his mother filed for divorce again in 1919 and, when once again were unsuccessful, they filed yet again in a different town in Texas in 1920. The 1920 trial lasted four days. May alleged that David Fasken had tried to buy her off with an offer of $50,000. Fasken stated that he simply did not want to see his son's wife dependent on anyone else no matter what the circumstances. (Robert had provided no support to his wife for the last four years.) Fasken also stated that he had no objection to her religion. 'Lots of my friends and business associates are Catholics.'[48] For him the problem lay elsewhere. 'Two families ought not to live under the same roof. I am talking of two wives and husbands. Two young people and two old people should not, do not fit in the same house.'[49] This time the court granted Robert his divorce and gave him custody of the child for nine months of the year. May was granted custody for the summer months, but only on condition that she not take the child out of Texas. Being unable to support herself in Midland, she returned to Toronto and never saw her son again.

This whole affair put an even greater distance between Fasken and his wife and son. Mrs Fasken and Robert moved to Ross, California, near San Francisco where Robert married Inez Ratcliffe. They would have a daughter Mary Isabel (known as Inez Jr) in 1925. Unfortunately, the girl would die in 1945.

Fasken, meanwhile, had turned for companionship to his niece Ellen Maria 'Nellie' Wallace. She was thirty years younger. Like Fasken, Nellie's life involved personal tragedies and failed relationships.[50] In 1906–7, Nellie had become the centre of a personal legal drama played out in the Toronto papers and the Ontario legislature. She was the daughter of Fasken's brother William (known as Bud) and Mabel Bye, the sister of young Nellie Bye who had earlier been engaged to Fasken. Fasken's niece attracted the attention of Harry Parr who worked on her father's farm. Although Nellie knew that her parents would not approve, the young couple asked the rector of the Anglican church to secretly marry them, which he did on 19 April 1906. Both were under age. Nellie did not tell her parents of the marriage, but within a week her parents knew. They sought help from David Fasken.[51] He thought the marriage invalid. The couple was under age and the marriage had not been consummated. There was, however, no procedure to seek a court declaration of invalidity. What happened next seems incredible. Fasken approached friends in the Ontario legislature to pass a law creating such a procedure. An amendment to the Ontario *Marriage Act* was included in the 1907 *Statute Amendment Act*.[52] Marriage, of course, is a federal matter, as the federal government reminded Ontario Attorney General Foy in August 1907. Nevertheless, the legislation permitted an application to be made seeking a declaration that an unconsummated marriage between two underage people was not valid under federal law. Bud Fasken applied on his niece's behalf. The *Toronto Daily Star* correctly noted that the legislation seemed to have been passed especially to permit this very application.[53] On the morning of 9 August 1907, Mr Justice James P. Mabee, formerly a lawyer in Fasken's firm, made the declaration.[54] The marriage was said by the *Toronto Star* to have been annulled, but according to the legislation, it is more proper to say that the court declared that no valid marriage had ever been effected.

Nellie's parents, however, could not forgive her.[55] The next year she married Donald Wallace, a marriage brokered by David Fasken who gave the young couple a fifty-acre farm as a wedding present. Despite or perhaps because of Fasken's help, the marriage did not last. After a few years, Donald left Nellie. Uncle David helped Nellie sell the farm and eventually obtain a divorce. More importantly, he offered her room, board and a job. She moved in with Fasken and his wife in Toronto and she became his personal secretary. For the last decade of his life Nellie was 'his constant companion.' 'They travelled extensively on the Continent, throughout the USA; to and from the city of New York repeatedly, and throughout Canada, often stopping at famous hot springs in the USA.'[56]

Nellie became one of the five people that Fasken trusted and relied upon. The others were his youngest brother, Alex, his nephews Charles Q. Parker and Andrew Fasken, and his cousin Sam Fasken. Alex was a lawyer in the Fasken firm.[57] Disliked by many, he had sound business judgment and a strong work ethic.[58] He assisted David in the management of the firm and in most of his business ventures. Andrew Fasken, the son of David's older brother Robert,[59] was born about 1890. He was the person to whom Fasken turned for help with his ranch in Texas. A farmer, he and his wife went to Texas with his uncle to run Fasken's ill-fated farming operation. He was pivotal in turning that operation into a successful cattle ranch. Charles Q. Parker, his other nephew, was an investment manager.[60] Sam Fasken operated Fasken's two farms. He was a cousin, being the son of George Fasken, Fasken's uncle. Sam had been born in the back house on the family farm the year before David.[61] The first of Fasken's farms was in fact the 100-acre family farm on which they had both grown up, and Sam and his family lived in the back house in which Sam had been born. Fasken, meanwhile, reno-vated the front house where he had grown up.[62] The second was a his-toric 300-acre farm in Clarkson (Mississauga), overlooking Lake Ontario and the Credit River.[63]

The *Succession Duty Act*

Fasken had amassed a substantial fortune. He had homes in Toronto, Clarkson, Elora, Temagami, Ontario, and in Midland, Texas, several of which were situated on large farm or ranch properties. He also had shares in mining and power companies and an insurance company. Fasken's plans for dealing with these assets were shaped in large part by the Ontario *Succession Duty Act*.

According to the preamble to the statute, it had been passed in 1892 to raise funds to pay the 'very large sums [expended] annually for asy-lums for the insane and idiots, and for institutions for the blind and for deaf mutes and for the support of hospitals and other charities.'[64] It had been re-enacted and amended several times before Fasken's death to close perceived loopholes and to broaden its scope.[65] Essentially, it was a tax imposed on the beneficiaries of a will or other instrument that passed title to property on or in contemplation of death. The estate itself was not the taxpayer, although it had an obligation to pay the duty on behalf of the beneficiaries within eighteen months of the testa-tor's death.[66] Succession duty was not a tax on the value of the estate but rather on the value of any property that beneficially passed to one or more beneficiaries.[67] The rate of duty was determined by the rela-tionship between the testator and the beneficiary, with parents, spouse, and children enjoying a lower rate.

The key elements were that there had to be both a beneficiary and what the original act had referred to as a passing of property or what the act in force at Fasken's death called a disposition of an interest in property or in the income from it.[68] The act allowed deductions for bona fide debts of the testator and did not apply to charitable donations or gifts for educational or religious purposes.[69] Someone wishing to avoid the application of the act might think that the way around the act was to give property away during their life time. Gift tax, as such had not yet been implemented, but the act was drafted to close off this loophole. The act applied to all *inter vivos* gifts whether or not made in contemplation of death.[70] If property was sold or otherwise transferred for value, there was no gift and the transaction was exempted. Being an Ontario statute, however, the act applied only to property situated in the province.[71]

A Fateful Step

One of Fasken's key estate planning moves, albeit not originally taken to avoid succession duty, was to invest in property outside of Ontario, namely, the Texas 'C' Ranch. Fasken's investment in the 'C' Ranch also gave him some experience in structuring his asset holding and management to achieve a specific legal result. Texas law provided that non-residents could not hold or have an interest in real property in the state.[72] Fasken retained the best lawyers he could find to help him structure his land deal in a way that permitted the purchase but complied with the law. He was advised that a farm company should be incorporated because farm companies could acquire and hold the land for resale. This suited his purpose well because he had bought the land for sale as farms. Midland Farms Company was formed. Fasken, acting through an *inter vivos* trust, loaned the money the company needed for the purchase. The 'C' Ranch was purchased and title to the ranch was conveyed to the Midland Farms Company in exchange for 2,997 of the company's 3,000 shares. The remaining shares were for director's qualifying shares. As the company improved the land and built the railroad from the mainline of the Texas and Pacific Railroad to the ranch, Fasken loaned the company more money through the trust. At the time of his death, the value of the debt held by the trust was $2,374,461.99.

By 1920, Fasken realized that it was unlikely he could sell the ranch as farms. He knew that if he retained any personal interest in it whatsoever, he might be faced with a claim for succession duty. He also knew that his continued ownership, even if indirect, might run afoul of the

Texas law prohibiting foreign ownership. As part of his estate plan, Fasken decided to relinquish any personal connection with the Texas property and loans. He ceased to be a shareholder, director, or officer of Midland Farms. The shares of Midland Farms Company were transferred to Robert, his son, who had become a U.S. citizen.[73] This was the equivalent of what today we call an estate freeze. Robert received the shares of the company, but those shares were of limited value because Midland Farms acknowledged the debt then held for David Fasken in trust by its three trustees, Alexander Fasken, Charles Q. Parker, and Andrew Fasken. The trustees in turn acknowledged the terms under which they held the debt. One of these terms was that 8 per cent interest should be paid to David Fasken. Under this arrangement, Robert owned the Midland Farms Company but would benefit only from future growth in the value of the ranch in excess of 8 per cent per year. Then in 1924 the interest entitlement was also transferred to Fasken's wife, Alice.

Fasken had not bought the foreign property to avoid Ontario succession duty nor had he set up the elaborate ownership structure for that purpose. As a part of his 1920 estate plan, he did, however, transfer the ownership of the shares and the benefit of the interest in the debt. The net effect was that a very valuable asset, worth more than $2 million dollars, would not form part of his estate for income tax or succession duty purposes. The property was located outside of Ontario, so arguably it was not subject to Ontario succession duty. In any event, Fasken did not own the ranch nor was the $2,374,461.99 loan owed to him. Neither would be listed in his assets on the probating of his will.

The Will and His Statement of Assets

Let us now turn to Fasken's will, prepared on 17 November 1924. He was a man with a strong sense of duty as well as social and family responsibility. Ironically, his ties to his extended family were much stronger than to his immediate family. He was effectively, if not legally, separated from his wife who was living in California with their son. His relationship with his son was neither close nor trusting. I am sure that he had hopes for his grandson, but he seems to have had little contact with David Jr. He did, however, have many brothers and sisters, nieces and nephews with whom he tried to maintain contact. He was especially close to his brother Alex, his niece Nellie, and his nephews Andrew and Charles Parker.

For probate purposes, Fasken listed his assets as per table 12.1.

Table 12.1: David Fasken's assets at probate

Household goods and furniture	$300.00
Farm implements	$700.00
Horses	$800.00
Horned cattle	$2,800.00
Sheep and swine	$450.00
Money secured by mortgage	$74,216.80
Money secured by insurance	$7,217.30
Stocks	$377,424.75
Securities for money	$1,229,170.99
Cash on hand	$1,288.87
Cash in the bank	$9,709.40
Farm produce	$1,600.00
Boats etc.	$150.00
Real estate	$86,500.00
Total	$1,792,328.11

In preparing his will and the *inter vivos* trusts that he established before and after making his will, Fasken had three guiding principles. First, he wished to keep his wealth intact for the benefit of future generations. His will made no specific bequests of property. All of his property on his death was to be held in trust for specific purposes. Second, he wished no one to receive more than what he deemed that they needed to live comfortably but not lavishly. Thirdly, he wished all investment decisions to be made by or to be at least strongly influenced by the small circle of people in whom he reposed trust.

His will named four executors and trustees – his wife Alice, his son Robert, his brother Alex, and his nephew Charles Parker. These four trustees clearly divided into two groups – his wife and son who were to be the principal beneficiaries of the trusts established under the will had a personal interest in its administration, and his brother Alex and his investment manager and nephew Charles Parker who had professional experience and judgment. This division between family and professional is reflected in the trustee replacement provisions. If his son should die or be unable or unwilling to serve the other trustees were to choose a replacement, preferably from his next of kin. If Alex or Charles Parker should die or be unable or unwilling to serve, the Toronto General Trusts was to be appointed. By appointing four, he was assured that decisions could not be made by his wife and son, neither of whom he trusted, without the concurrence of Alex and Charles Parker or other professional money managers.

All of his estate was to be held by the four trustees on the following trusts:

1 to pay his debts,
2 to maintain the family burial plot in Elora,
3 to permit his wife the use of his household goods in his homes in Toronto, Clarkson, Elora, and Temagami as well as the use of his cars and boats,
4 to permit his wife the use and occupation of his homes in Toronto, Clarkson and Temagami provided she paid for taxes, repairs, and insurance,[74]
5 to retain any of his investments they chose but otherwise to convert the remainder of his assets into money,
6 to invest $500,000 and to pay his wife quarterly for the rest of her life the net income derived from such investment,
7 to invest $10,000 and to pay the two children of his deceased cousin Rev. George Fasken for the rest of their lives the net income derived from the investment,
8 to pay any succession duties owing on the specific bequests made, and finally
9 to retain and invest all other monies in a capital fund, including the capital invested under 6 and 7 above when no longer required for the stated purposes.

The provisions dealing with the capital fund are very extensive. Essentially, the capital fund was first to be used to ensure that his son received $30,000 in income each year of his life. To the extent that Robert had income from other sources, the amount paid from the capital fund was to be reduced. On Robert's death, the capital fund was to be divided into separate capital funds for each of Robert's children or their issue, then living. Each such fund was to be used in the discretion of the trustees to give such child $10,000 per year. The amount could be increased at the discretion of the trustees on marriage of the child or on their starting a business. On the death of each such child their separate capital fund would go to their children in equal shares or otherwise as the deceased child had directed by will or living declaration. The capital fund was to be maintained for the maximum period allowed under the *Perpetuities Act*, namely, the life of the last surviving child of Robert born before Fasken's death plus twenty-one years less a day. At that point the fund would be distributed in accordance with the appointment made by the last surviving child or, on the failure of a declaration, to the next of kin of David Fasken as if he had died intestate.

Clearly, Fasken did not want Robert, his son, to inherit his millions. In fact, he seems to have intentionally denied Robert more than 'an allowance,' something he had been giving him for years. Robert lived less than five years after his father, dying on 25 September 1934. He received only four annual amounts of no more than $30,000. Neither did Alice Fasken inherit her husband's fortune. She had the use of three of the homes, and the household goods from four homes but she was then living in California and thus drew little benefit from these. She also did not live long, dying in 1935. She received only the income on the $500,000 set aside to fund her payments. Assuming a return on investment of 8 per cent (the rate Fasken had collected on his Texas loan), she would have received $40,000 a year for five years, or $200,000.

Thus, the bulk of the estate was not paid out and continued to accumulate in the capital fund. On Robert's death, two capital accounts were created, one each for David Jr and his half-sister Inez. She, however, died in 1945 at the age of nineteen, leaving no issue. During the ten years after Robert's death, neither David Jr nor Inez married or started a business. Only $20,000 a year would have been paid out. The annual increase in the capital fund at this point would have been in the hundreds of thousands of dollars. After 1945, David Jr became the sole beneficiary of the income from the capital fund. He, of course, was only receiving $10,000 a year.

One can imagine how much the capital fund had accumulated by 1952 when a dispute arose over the legality of the capital fund provisions. The *Accumulations Act* prohibited a period of accumulation of more than twenty-one years from the death of the testator.[75] This meant that in 1950 the annual increase in the fund had to be paid out. The question was, to whom? The will had provided a default of Fasken's next of kin. Robert's wife Inez sought the money on behalf of Robert's estate, David Fasken Jr argued he was the proper recipient, and two of David Sr's sisters and thirty-three nieces and nephews collectively argued they were his next of kin.

Mr Justice Fred Barlow, the trial judge, sided with David Jr. Noting that David Fasken had been 'a barrister and solicitor of this court with a wide knowledge of the law,' he stated that it was clearly Fasken's intention to leave his estate to his direct descendants.[76] Fasken had chosen the words next of kin because those words were widely settled to mean direct descendants.

When Fasken's sisters, nieces, and nephews appealed, the majority of the Ontario Court of Appeal panel (Henderson and Gibson JJ.A.) disagreed with Justice Barlow (Roach J.A. dissenting) and found for them.[77] The majority held that 'next of kin' should be given the meaning found in the *Devolution of Estates Act*,[78] which defined 'next of kindred' as 'the father and the mother and the brothers and the sisters of the intestate [who] shall be deemed of equal degree but there shall be no representations admitted among collaterals after brothers' and sisters' children.' Justice Roach would have upheld the trial decision on the basis that paragraph 18 (the default provision) was an attempt by the testator to avoid an intestacy of his estate and, thus, 'next-of-kin' should be taken to mean those who would take on an intestacy and should include lineal descendants. David Jr took the matter to the Supreme Court of Canada where a panel of five judges – Justices Kerwin, Rand, Kellock, Locke, and Cartwright – overturned the Court of Appeal and reinstated the trial judgment.[79] David Jr alone was to get the annual surplus.

In 1961, David Fasken Jr, by this point a very wealthy oil man, sought a declaration that his grandfather's collateral next of kin (the children of Fasken's brothers and sisters) had no claim to the residue of the estate. Mr Justice Gale noted that the dominant purposes of David Fasken's will were to pass assets on to descendants and to circumvent the rule against perpetuities.[80] In light of this, he held that David Fasken Jr validly had the power to appoint the residue of David Fasken's estate which he did to the Prairie Foundation (a charitable Texas corporation), meaning that the collateral next of kin had no claim to the residue of the estate.[81]

Assets Not in the Estate

We have already seen that Fasken's estate for probate purposes did not include the value of the Texas ranch (or the loan made to purchase it). There were many other assets not included in the estate because of steps taken by Fasken before his death. Those other amounts include the $402,000 reported by the *Toronto Daily Star* to have been given by Fasken to family and friends while he was alive, as well as the approximately $500,000 he gave to the Toronto Western Hospital and the other substantial amounts he gave to the Salvation Army, Upper Canada College, the Toronto Infants Home, and other charities. It also did not include the many trusts that he established in the last years of his life for various family members and for the Elora Methodist Church and the Bethany Methodist Church. We shall look at each category of excluded assets in turn.

The period from 1920 to 1925 was when Fasken put much of his estate planning into action. He established a series of trusts in 1920, the trust for the Texas loan in 1924, and a trust for Nellie Wallace and his grandson in 1925. In 1920, he set up a series of discretionary trusts for his extended family, including a discretionary fund for relatives who might need financial assistance from time to time for health or other reasons.[82] We have some evidence of how Fasken structured the trusts for his extended family by virtue of an application made in 1959[83] for an interpretation of trust deeds made by Alex Fasken as trustee in furtherance of two of the trusts established by David Fasken in 1920 – those for David Williams and Isabel Richmond, children of David Fasken's sister Mary Williams.[84] Each was to receive income from an investment of $6,000 (increased in 1925 to $15,000) at the discretion of the trustee Alex Fasken. It seems safe to assume that similar terms applied to the trusts that Fasken set up in 1920 for all of his brothers, sisters, nieces, and nephews.[85]

He also established trusts for the churches he had worshipped at as a youngster. Today, when you visit Bethany United Church at the intersection of Side Road 10 and 4th Line East in Pilkington Township near Elora you find a wonderfully maintained rural church. That is in part due to a trust that Fasken established for this church and the Elora Methodist Church in the 1920s. There is a modest plaque in the Bethany United Church thanking David Fasken for his generous gift.[86]

Fasken did not leave any money or property to Nellie in his will. He did, however, set up a trust fund for her and his grandson. We can assume it was substantial not only because it was for his constant companion and his grandson but also because more than sixty years later its residue would be the subject of a court action.[87] Nellie was eligible to receive the net income from the trust property until her remarriage or death. David Jr was eligible until his death, provided he openly and publicly professed the Protestant religion. This requirement is somewhat startling in light of David Fasken's protestations at his son's divorce hearing in Texas that he had no objection to his daughter-in-law's religion. There is no evidence that his wife influenced any of Fasken's estate planning, so we have to assume that it was his choice to include this religious condition.[88] Surprisingly, this aspect of the trust attracted no judicial comment whatsoever from Madam Justice Louise Arbour in 1990 when she was asked to rule on other aspects of the trust. She simply noted that it was not an issue between the parties because David Jr had remained a Protestant.[89]

It is worthy of note that in 1925 when Fasken set up this trust, he did not make either his wife Alice or his son Robert a trustee, even though his grandson was a beneficiary. Instead, he chose Nellie and Charles Parker as trustees. Clearly, he used the same approach as with his testamentary trusts – one trustee who had a personal interest in the trust and the other who was a professional adviser. With this trust he also satisfied two of his concerns. He gave his companion, Nellie, money to sustain her lifestyle, and he ensured that his grandson had a source of income independent of and inaccessible by his father. Unfortunately, we do not have many details about the trust.[90]

Money Given Away

Fasken gave substantial amounts for the building and upkeep of the Western Hospital and its nurses' home in Toronto. His biographer Marion MacKenzie believed that '[t]hat was his real baby.'[91] He first came to support the hospital in 1906, because one of its founders, Dr John Ferguson, was a founder of Excelsior Life Insurance, of which Fasken was the president and controlling shareholder.[92] Fasken was one of the hospital's earliest and most important supporters. He provided the funding for the first 1906 addition to the modest original building. In 1911 he funded the Bathurst Street Building (and convinced his friend and architect E.J. Lennox to do the design without charge).[93] A few years later, he financed the building of a nurses' home known as the Edith Cavell Memorial Nurses' Home.' The hospital trained many of Fasken's relatives, including Jean Fasken, later Mrs Cleveland Porrett; Isabel Fasken, later Mrs Floyd Dyer; Jean Card who became Mrs (Dr) Garbutt; Isabel Fasken who became Mrs Roy Banbury; Marion Fasken, later Mrs Jack Morris; and Gloria Fasken.[94] These donations had all been made before Fasken turned his mind to any estate planning. He did, however, make two large donations during the 1920s when he was implementing his estate plan. In 1923, he donated money to permit another extension of the hospital and, in 1924, he made a matching grant when a citywide appeal raised $200,000.

The *Toronto Daily Star* tells us that Fasken donated 'about $500,000' to the hospital,[95] but his biographer Marion MacKenzie wrote of 'the millions he poured into [its] building and up-keep.' We do not know what he actually donated, but one comment in a brief history of the hospital prepared in the 1950s suggests that MacKenzie may be closer to the truth. It states that Fasken was '[b]y nature a quiet, unassuming man, who did not desire public recognition or even knowledge of his many generous acts.'[96] These words echo a remark made by his good friend Reverend Andrew Robb in Fasken's funeral oration. Fasken 'had amassed a great fortune but he had spent liberally ... on others, not himself. He had given away hundreds of thousands of dollars unknown to the world at large, unknown even to all but a few of his closest friends. In all his giving he abhorred publicity.'[97]

Another charitable organization that Fasken supported was the Salvation Army.[98] As was often the case with Fasken, his support for this organization had a link to his family. Two sisters had joined the Salvation Army, Mary Fasken, an older sister, and Margaret Fasken, a younger sister (born about 1862).[99] Margaret became an officer and moved to Vancouver as a captain.

Application of the *Succession Duty Act* to the Fasken Estate

The scheme of the *Succession Duty Act* lets us see why Fasken structured his estate and created his testamentary trusts in the way that he did. First, there would have been no succession duty on the extensive grants of money to the Toronto Western Hospital or the Salvation Army or on his trusts for Bethany Methodist Church and the Elora Methodist Church. Those were expressly exempt from duty. Second, he prepared the will to avoid, to the fullest extent possible, the two requirements of the act – a transfer of property and a beneficiary. Fasken did not direct his trustees to pay succession duties on the value of his estate but rather only on his specific bequests. There was no transfer of property on the settling of the testamentary trusts because there was no transfer of a beneficial interest and therefore no triggering event for succession duty purposes. There was also no clear beneficiary of the bulk of his estate, the capital fund. He talks of 'the specific legacies hereinbefore directed to be paid, and ... the sums hereinbefore directed to be set aside.' These are references to the fact that he granted his wife and the two children of his deceased cousin a life interest in the income of certain investments. There would have been a present valuing of that interest and duty would have been paid on that value. This would clearly have applied to the grant of income on the $500,000 in investments that Fasken granted to his wife Alice. That life interest in this income would have been valued and the appropriate percentage (ranging from 1½ per cent to 14 per cent) would have been paid by the trustees. The grant of the revenue from a $10,000 investment to the two children of his cousin would also have been valued.

The wording of the trust to pay succession duty strongly suggests that Fasken did not expect to pay any succession duty on the capital fund or on the provision for his son. The capital fund was not set aside for any particular beneficiary. Certain amounts up to $30,000 per year were to be paid to his son Robert, but there was no certainty as to the amount. This would mean that, even if succession duty were to be paid, a discount would have been applied in determining present value of the income stream because of the potential reduction of that amount if Robert had other income. Fasken likely expected his son to have little if any other income, so this was a way to save succession duty with no practical effect to Robert. The grant to Robert's children of the $10,000 a year on Robert's death was also discretionary and would have had a heavy discounting, because it could be expected that this grant would not become effective for many years. Robert was only thirty-seven when his father died. The act stated that such an interest would be valued based on mortality tables, which presumably would have contemplated that Robert would live to more than age sixty. The trustees would thus have been valuing a right to receive $10,000 a year in about twenty-five years.

The trustees of the capital fund could increase these future payments to Robert's children if, in the discretion of the trustees, it was warranted and they could withhold on a bankruptcy of one of the beneficiaries. There was no certainty to such future increased payments, either as to when or if they would be paid and as to the amount. There was thus no basis for a present valuation. The net effect was that Fasken's estate paid relatively modest succession duty on the almost $2 million of his probated estate and no succession duty at all on the Texas ranch or his extensive charitable donations.

For succession duty purposes, the *inter vivos* trusts for his relatives were characterised as gifts and they likely represent at least part of the

$402,000 in gifts that Fasken is said to have made to his relatives. The likelihood, however, is that the estate also paid little on the these *inter vivos* trusts because almost certainly they were discretionary trusts. This conclusion is supported by the evidence we have about the trusts established for David Williams and Isabel Richmond. Each was to receive income from an investment of $6,000 (increased in 1925 to $15,000) at the discretion of the trustee Alex Fasken. Succession duty would have been payable on each such *inter vivos* trust under the act, but the present value was reduced by virtue of the use of a discretionary trust.

Court Challenges

During his lifetime, David Fasken was no stranger to litigation over his personal and business affairs. The purchase of the Texas property, for example, led to much litigation. When Fasken discovered that he had been misled as to the presence of water on the property, he contemplated legal action against his business agent William Harvey who had arranged the purchase.[100] He also found himself defending an action by W.J. Moran, who claimed to have brought the property to the attention of Harvey and to be owed a real estate commission on the purchase. To Fasken, the Moran litigation was adding insult to injury. He had never intended to purchase and operate a ranch in Texas. This had been intended simply as a land development deal whereby he sold the serviced land as farms. To be unable to sell because there was no water (something he had expressly told Harvey to be sure of) and to then be sued for a commission on the purchase was galling to him. Nevertheless, while working with Andrew Fasken to make his investment worthwhile, he defended and won this action. The supreme insult, however, came in the form of an action by the Texas government to seize the land as having been illegally acquired. Fasken knew when he bought the land that there was a prohibition against foreigners owning Texas land, but he had been informed that there would be no problem if a farm company was formed to purchase and resell the land. The flaw in this strategy was that the land was not resaleable as farms. Fasken, therefore, found himself as the indirect owner of a Texas ranch property. As we have seen, he had transferred his indirect holding to his son Robert who had become a U.S. citizen, but that did not insulate the 'C' Ranch from the Texas seizure action in the view of the Texas government. Fasken fought this action through most of the last years of his life, ultimately succeeding at the U.S. Supreme Court in 1927 on the argument that the Texas law was contrary to public policy being in contravention of the U.S. treaty with Great Britain under which each country had agreed to grant reciprocal treatment to the subjects of the other. Since Great Britain (of which Canada was still a colony) permitted U.S. citizens to hold land in Canada, it was inappropriate for the U.S. not to do likewise. Had the case arisen less than a decade later after the Treaty of Westminster, perhaps the result would have been different.

Given this lengthy period of litigation and the publicity it generated, it is not surprising that the Ontario government learned of the extensive land holdings Fasken had acquired in Texas. They likely heard as well that oil had been found in the region in 1927 and on the 'C' Ranch in the early 1930s. In any event, they brought an action against the estate and its trustees to collect unpaid succession duty. By their calculation they were owed about $500,000.[101] Initially, the province brought its case before Mr Justice Garrow in Assize Court, but he died before rendering a judgment. On 17 October 1934, the case reopened before Mr Justice McEvoy.[102] I.A. Humphries, the Deputy Attorney General, and J.B. O'Brien appeared for the province. Two future chief justices of Ontario, R.S. Robertson and J.W. Pickup, both partners in the Fasken firm, appeared for the Fasken estate. At issue was whether the $2,374,461.99 debt that had been owed to David Fasken by the Midland Farms Company qualified as 'property' under the *Succession Duty Act*.[103] If it did, a succession duty ought to have been applied to it and paid in 1930. Under section 19 of the act the original duty was collectible together with a 50 per cent penalty and 8 per cent interest per year, and this amount was collectible from the estate and the trustees of the debt personally.[104]

The definition of property in the act was very broad. It extended to every form of property real or personal that was capable of being passed or bequeathed to another.[105] Section 8 stated that the act applied to the transfer of all property in Ontario. The province argued that the declaration of trust of 1924, whereby the three trustees held the acknowledgment of the debt, was an Ontario document. It had been prepared and signed by two of the three trustees in the Fasken firm offices in Toronto (Andrew had signed in Midland, Texas). This had the effect of making the debt Ontario property, they argued.

On 9 January 1935, the court held that the province had only the power to impose direct taxes in the province. Here the property in question was a contract debt situated outside of Ontario. In any event, it had been transferred by David Fasken during his life and no interest passed on his death. No succession duty was found to be owing.

The province appealed. The appeal was heard quickly by a panel of five judges.[106] Shockingly, W.R.R. Riddell, a long-time partner of David Fasken and an honorary pallbearer at his funeral,[107] and Cornelius A. Masten J.A., another friend of David Fasken who had attended his funeral, sat on the appeal panel.[108] The relationship of Riddell and Masten to Fasken was well known, yet the case report does not note any objection by the province nor any suggestion of impropriety. Perhaps the addition of two judges to the usual panel of three was intended to offset this obvious bias. The province attacked the trial judge's finding that the contract debt was situated outside Ontario. They argued that the acknowledgment had been signed under seal in Ontario, that the trust was created in Ontario by an Ontario settlor, and that it had originally two and now three Ontario trustees. Further, they argued that David Fasken had retained full control over the debt, notwithstanding the purported trust and gift. Robertson and Pickup stressed that David Fasken had signed nothing. He had no interest in the trust. The beneficiaries were in the United States and substantial amounts had been paid to them since the trust had been established. No one in Ontario had received anything.

Mr Justice Middleton, who merely reiterated what the trial judge had said, wrote the majority opinion. Under Texas law at the time, the acknowledgment of indebtedness created a simple contract debt that was situated in Texas. There was no property in Ontario and no power to tax property outside Ontario. Mr Justice Masten wrote a longer concurring judgment. In addition to the points made by the majority, he noted that although there was the power to tax individuals resident in Ontario, here no such residents benefited from the acknowledgment of indebtedness or the trust. He also noted that the trust was not an Ontario trust because it had been created in Texas when David Fasken gave his directions to the Midland Farms Company to acknowledge that the debt was being held by the three trustees.

The David Fasken estate was not yet finished its battles with Canadian governments. In 1944, the federal income tax authorities reassessed Fasken's income tax returns for the years 1925 to 1929. In 1948, the federal minister of national revenue brought an action under the *Income War Tax Act* 1917 to collect income tax that they claimed was owing for those years as a result of the transfer of the right to receive income from the debt repayment from Fasken to his wife, Alice.[109] Under section 4(4) of the act, a person who sought to reduce his or her tax by transferring property to a spouse was liable for tax on that amount. That section had been amended in 1926 to include transfers of income from property. The section was stated to apply to the years 1925 and following.[110]

The judgment of Mr Justice Thorson in the Exchequer Court notes that on 31 December 1924, Midland Farms acknowledged the debt to David Fasken, and Fasken's three trustees (Alexander Fasken, Charles Q. Parker, and Andrew Fasken) acknowledged the terms under which they held the debt. One of these terms was that the interest should be paid to David Fasken's wife, Alice. She had received $10,000 in 1925, $5,000 in 1926, $11,000 in 1927, $15,000 in 1928, and $20,000 in 1925.

The court held that the right to receive the interest payable on the indebtedness was property for the purposes of the tax act. There was also a valid transfer of property from husband to wife. While the property was transferred due to an act by the trustees, this was but an indirect way of transferring the property, and what mattered was the result of the transfer, not whether the transfer was done directly or indirectly. However, in the end, the court held that no tax was, in fact, payable since the tax in question only applied to transfers after 1925, and in this case the date of the transfer was 1924 (when the trustees acknowledged the interest owed to Mrs Fasken).

Fasken's estate had dodged the last bullet. During his life time Fasken knew that the U.S. courts had upheld his right to retain the Texas ranch and to structure his holding as he had done. After his death, both the Ontario and Federal Courts had refused challenges to how he had structured his estate planning.

Conclusion

I began my review of David Fasken as a businessman by noting that '[h]is outstanding traits were a capacity for sustained and concentrated effort, close attention to detail, and absolutely unprejudiced weighing of facts.'[111] This study of his estate planning gives credence to that assessment. He built up vast wealth through his entrepreneurship and he carefully planned to ensure that it was dealt with as he wanted it to be. He took many carefully chosen steps in anticipation of death to reduce succession duties and taxes and to exercise some level of control over how his wealth was distributed and used after his death. He had very definite views about how he wished his wealth to be used, namely, not only to fund projects like the Toronto Western Hospital and the Salvation Army, to help with the upkeep of the churches that he had attended and the family gravesite but also to support and to help family members in need, including his many brothers and sisters and their children. In planning how to achieve these goals, he gave careful attention to taxing statutes like the Ontario *Succession Duty Act* and thus reduced the amounts that he paid to the Ontario government. But it would be wrong to think that he avoided tax out of any selfish motives or any lack of a sense of social responsibility. His charitable donations and his help for his family make it abundantly clear that he had a strong sense of both family and social responsibility.

If there is one sad aspect to the story, it centres on his poor relationship with his wife and son. He did not treat them badly. They did not receive millions but they received a substantial income for that time. It is clear, however, that Fasken did not trust them to use his wealth wisely and for the purposes for which he wanted it used. This is where the discretionary trust served Fasken very well.[112] It had the effect of reducing succession duty, but it also gave him a flexible mechanism to maintain and grow his capital while funding needs as they arose. The key, of course, was having a small group of people in whom he could repose complete trust. Alex Fasken, his brother, led that group and served Fasken well as trustee and investment adviser. Charles Q. Parker assisted. Andrew Fasken, who had proven so valuable to Fasken during his life in turning what Fasken saw as his worst investment of his life into an acceptable one, also helped for a time. To Alex Fasken, however, must go the kudos for turning that acceptable investment into the best investment that Fasken had ever made, and for using Fasken's wealth as he wanted it used.

In seeking to control his wealth after his death through discretionary trusts and foreign investment, Fasken was a Canadian pioneer in tax-efficient estate planning. His pioneering efforts led to a series of court challenges which brought his tools and techniques to the attention of the legal and accounting communities. Those cases also gave Canadian courts the opportunity to opine on numerous estate, trust and tax matters.[113] Fasken's will and his *inter vivos* trusts and the cases that they engendered for a period of more than sixty years are an important part of his legacy.

NOTES

* I wish to thank Howard Carr of the estates department of Fasken Martineau DuMoulin LLP [hereafter FMD] for reviewing a draft of this essay. Gabriel Stern, a student at FMD and Olga Calivjnaia, a student at the University of Toronto, researched the caselaw. In preparing this essay, I have not reviewed any materials in the files of FMD that are subject to solicitor–client privilege.

1 *Globe* (Toronto), 3 December 1929, 1.

2 *Toronto Daily Star,* 3 December 1929, 1.

3 'Many attend funeral of the late David Fasken,' *Toronto Daily Star,* 4 December 1929, 1, and *Globe* (Toronto), 5 December 1929, 1.

4 'Fasken Funeral Struggles through Snow-bound Roads,' *Toronto Daily Star,* 5 December 1929, featuring a picture of a 'motor car here being pulled out of the snow by a motor truck.'

5 'Estate of David Fasken Totals Nearly $2,000,000,' *Toronto Daily Star,* 3 January 1930, 1.

6 Bruce Ziff makes a similar comment on the value for succession duty purposes of the Reuben Wells Leonard estate in, *Unforeseen Legacies: Reuben Wells Leonard and the Leonard Foundation* (Toronto: Osgoode Society and University of Toronto Press 2000), 47.

7 The Surrogate Court inventory of his assets dated 13 December 1929 is in the Provincial Archives of Ontario.

8 We are fortunate to have a series of judgments of the Ontario courts between 1951 and 1990 interpreting his 1924 will or the various *inter vivos* trusts that he had established in 1920 and 1925. See *Re Fasken* (trial) [1952] Ontario Reports [hereafter OR] 802; *Re Fasken* (appeal) [1952] OR 802 (at 807); *Fasken, Jr. v. Fasken et al.* [1953] 3 Dominion Law Reports [hereafter DLR] 431; *Re Fasken* [1961] OR 891; *Re Fasken* 19 DLR (2d) 182; *Canada Trust Co. v. Fasken* 69 DLR (4th), 575. There are also judgments in the actions brought by the Ontario government in 1935 to collect additional succession duties (*The Attorney-General for Ontario v. Fasken et al.* (trial) [1935] OR 115 and *The Attorney-General for Ontario v. Fasken et al.* (appeal) [1935] OR 288) and by the federal government in 1949 to collect additional income taxes from his estate (*Fasken v. Minister of National Revenue* [1949] 1 DLR 810). These relatively dry narratives are brought to life for us by a chatty, well-informed and very extensive unpublished family history by his second cousin, Marion Fasken MacKenzie. See Marion Fasken MacKenzie, 'Chronological Family Tree of "THE HARDSCRABBLERS" of "HARDSCRABBLE,"' unpublished manuscript 1959 (hereafter, Marion

MacKenzie). A copy was given to the FMD Toronto office archives [here-
after FMD Archives] by Ann MacKenzie, her niece, in March 2004. Marion tells us 'like all people over seventy' she became 'acquainted with
'BOREDOM,' which comes to all who 'DON'T HAVE TO do anything in
particular.' She knew many of the people personally, but she also did
extensive newspaper research (unfortunately, seldom noting the source of
news clippings). She prepared the extensive text herself. 'Now, my eyes
are playing havoc with me, so I am typing the finish of this section of it
without the aid of specs, except to hold them up to my eyes occasionally
to make corrections.' She tells us that 'David Fasken died at the age of
sixty-nine years, which was ten years younger than I soon will be.' Marion MacKenzie, chap. 19.

9 *Income War Tax Act, 1917 Statutes of Canada* [hereafter S.C.] 1917 c.28.

10 *Succession Duty Act, Revised Statutes of Ontario* [hereafter RSO] *1927*, c.26.
Ontario had enacted legislation in 1892 to collect succession duties.

11 There are few biographies of leading business lawyers. One notable exception is Barry Cahill, *The Thousandth Man: A Biography of James McGregor
Stewart* (Toronto: Osgoode Society and University of Toronto Press 2000).
Cahill also edited Frank Manning Covert, *Fifty Years in the Practice of Law*,
ed. Barry Cahill (Montreal: McGill-Queen's University Press 2004). There
are also the collected essays edited by Carol Wilton, *Essays in the History of
Canadian Law*, vol. 4, *Beyond the Law: Lawyers and Business in Canada, 1830–
1930* (Toronto: Osgoode Society and University of Toronto Press 1990),
especially the chapters by John Honsberger on E.E.A. DuVernet and by
James Gunn on Robert Home Smith. There is even less written on estate
planning by a wealthy Canadian professional. There is a brief description
of the will and charitable bequests of a professional engineer and businessman, Reuben Wells Leonard. See Ziff, *Unforeseen Legacies*, 46–8. Interestingly, Leonard was born in the same year as Fasken and also made his
money from the Cobalt silver mines in northern Ontario.

12 Gifts and trusts are categorised as *inter vivos* and testamentary. An *inter
vivos* trust is created and comes into effect during the life of the person settling the trust. A testamentary trust is created during the life of the person
settling the trust in his or her will and comes into effect on that person's
death.

13 A discretionary trust involves some element of discretion or judgment on
the part of the trustee. The discretion is often when, how, if, or to whom the
trust property is distributed.

14 Marion MacKenzie, chap. 21.

15 See my biographical sketch of 'David Fasken' in *Dictionary of Canadian Biography* (*DCB*) (Toronto: University of Toronto Press 1966), vol. 15.

16 The firm is now known as Fasken Martineau DuMoulin LLP. See my 'New Light on an Old Firm,' *Law Society of Upper Canada Gazette* 18 (1984), 205–9, and 'The Transformation of an Establishment Firm: From Beatty Blackstock to Faskens 1902–1915,' in C. Wilton, ed., *Inside the Law: Canadian Law Firms in Historical Perspective* (Toronto: University of Toronto Press and Osgoode Society for Canadian Legal History 1996). See also my biographical sketches of 'William Henry Beatty' and 'Edward Marion Chadwick,' its two founders, in *DCB* vols. 14 and 15.

17 William Henry Beatty was the son-in-law of James Gooderham Worts and the confidant and chief adviser of George Gooderham. Under Beatty, the firm served the legal needs of both the Gooderham and the Worts families and their businesses. There are two very detailed contemporary accounts of the Gooderham and Worts businesses: 'Annual Review of the Trade of Toronto for 1861,' *Globe* (Toronto), 7 February 1862, and 'Canadian Manufactures No. IV, One of the Largest Distilleries in the World, Gooderham & Worts, Toronto,' *Mail*, 23 April 1872. See also 'Messrs. Gooderham and Worts,' in *The Canadian Biographical Dictionary and Portrait Gallery of Eminent and Self-Made Men* (Toronto: American Biographical Publishing Company 1880–1), 62–70, and my article 'The Incorporation of Gooderham and Worts: A Case Study in Nineteenth-Century Business Organization,' in J. Phillips and B. Baker, eds., *Essays in the History of Canadian Law*, vol. 8 (Toronto: Osgoode Society and University of Toronto Press 1999).

18 In a letter to his son, C.W. Beatty, 3 August 1892, W.H. Beatty said, 'You could never give [him] too much to do – always ready for more.' Copy in FMD Archives, original in possession of a family member.

19 *A Standard Dictionary of Canadian Biography 1875–1933*, vol. 2 (Toronto: TransCanada Press 1934), 149.

20 For a description and picture of the Fasken home, the Excelsior Life Building and the hospital wing, see M. Litvak, *Edward James Lennox: 'Builder of Toronto'* (Toronto: Dundurn Press 1995).

21 The agreement in the FMD Archives was dated 1 September 1906 and was between William Henry Beatty, Edward Marion Chadwick, David Fasken, William R. Riddell, Thomas P. Galt, Harper Armstrong, Alexander Fasken, Hugh E. Rose and Melville Ross Gooderham.

22 On the relationship between Fasken and the Gooderhams and control of Excelsior Life, see *Report of the Royal Commission on Insurance Minutes of Evidence*, vol. 1 (Toronto, 1907), 1287. On the circumstances surrounding the

commission and its hearings and findings, see *The Canadian Annual Review 1906* (Toronto, 1907), 215.

23 Obituary notice prepared by the Excelsior Life Insurance Company on the death of David Fasken in December 1929 in FMD Archives.

24 *The Excelsior Life Banner* 18, no. 1 (January 1930), 9, states that he took the company from $3 million in business to $100 million.

25 See Robert J. Surtees, *The Northern Connection: Ontario Northland Since 1902* (Toronto: Captus Press 1992), especially chap. 2, 'The Cobalt Bonanza and Beyond.'

26 *The Monetary Times*, quoted in H.V. Nelles, *The Politics of Development: Forests, Mines and Hydro-electric Power in Ontario 1849–1941* (Toronto: Macmillan of Canada 1974), 147–8, noted that the 'president of the Nipissing Mines Company [David Fasken] is understood to have paid $250,000 for the properties which were chiefly of prospective value. The sellers thought that they had outwitted a Yankee [presumably a reference to Fasken's U.S. investors]. Now, probably, they are assuring themselves that they were foolish to part with so great a property at so small a price.'

27 *Cobalt Daily Nugget*, September 1910.

28 S.A. Pain, *Three Miles of Gold: The Story of Kirkland Lake* (Toronto: Ryerson Press 1960), 3. *The Cobalt Daily Nugget* of September 1910 reported Nipissing's production from 1905 to halfway through 1910 at a value of $8,375,541.58, with aggregate dividends paid of $5,040,000 plus $400,000 to the syndicate. It also reported for the period 1904–9 aggregate ore shipments, value of ore shipments, and dividends paid by Cobalt mines as 78,487.58 tonnes, $32,840,906 and $14,347,969 (or 43.7 per cent of value shipped, respectively).

29 At Fasken's funeral, his long-time client and business partner, E.P. Earle stated, '... from the beginning Mr. Fasken's guidance and cooperation had much to do with the success of the Company. In the early days of Cobalt when at times engineers were doubtful of the permanency of the camp, Mr. Fasken never lost faith and he showed his courage by investing large sums of money in the development of Hydro Electric for the Camp. Subsequently, Mr. Fasken continued his cooperation in the development of power for Porcupine and Kirkland Lake. Probably no one man did as much toward the development of the north country as did Mr. Fasken.' *Toronto Daily Star*, 4 December 1929, 1.

30 This did not prove as good an investment as it seemed, and they sold out in 1914. See Bruce Hodgins and James Benidickson, *The Temagami Experience* (Toronto: University of Toronto Press 1989), 119, 186.

31 Morris Zaslow, *The Opening of the Canadian North 1870–1914* (Toronto: McClelland and Stewart 1989), 185.
32 *Montreal Star*, 14 April 1909, 12.
33 *The Canadian Annual Review 1912*, 644.
34 A review of the history of the Flin Flon mine and David Fasken's role appeared in the *Mail and Empire*, 10 December 1927, 17 complete with pictures of David Fasken with his Aboriginal guides canoeing and riding a large ox.
35 J.B. Robinson Memoirs in FMD Archives states, 'He had a large office in the firm's Toronto Street premises, but he only came to Toronto for a few days each year.' The acquisition is outlined in *Fasken v. Minister of National Revenue* [1949] 1 DLR, 810, 812–14.
36 In a letter dated 30 October 1913 on his law firm stationary, David wrote to G.W. Kerr, the agent trying to sell the property that David had had 'no report of a good well on the property ... I feared that we merely had a ranching proposition on our hands.' The purchase agreement and related correspondence are in the Nina Stewart Haley Memorial Library, Midland, Texas. I am currently writing a book about the Texas transaction entitled *The Reluctant Rancher*.
37 See 'Fasken, Texas,' in Wallace Prescott Webb, *The Handbook of Texas*, vol. 3 (Austin, TX: State Historical Association 1952–76), 293.
38 There are several Texas historical plaques on the 'C' ranch one of which, erected in 1967, describes the Midland & Northwestern Railroad as a 'standard gauge 66-mile line built by David Fasken Sr.' It operated from 1916 to 1920, when it was washed out and abandoned. See also the *Midland Reporter-Telegram*, 15 March 1959, 6, and 14 October 1968, 4B, as well as the *San Antonio Standard-Times*, 19 January 1966, Section B.
39 *Handbook of Texas*, vol. 3, 293.
40 Marion Mackenzie notes that Fasken 'loved more than anything to gather with his former farm neighbours and old friends and poor as well as wealthy relatives, and the poor were more plentiful than the rich.' He made it a point to attend the funerals of old friends and relatives and at such events to join the men gathered in the yard talking of their crops. 'He was genuinely interested in everyone rich and poor.' Fasken was 'the most Clannish Members of the Fasken Clan.' Marion MacKenzie, chap. 21.
41 John Robert Conon, *The Early History of Elora Ontario and Vicinity* (reissued and with an introduction by Gerald Noonan) (Waterloo: Wilfrid Laurier University Publications 1975), 42. See also the materials in the Wellington County Museum and Archives, A2001.163 and A2001.99.

42 Marion MacKenzie, chap. 7.

43 Marion MacKenzie stresses that as rich as he became, Fasken was always very careful with his money. He 'learned the hard way the value of EVERY COPPER.' She quotes him as saying, 'I walked when others rode.' 'At home he had learned how to do without and live on a minimum; while an apprentice he had continued learning it even more so, and as a Graduate Lawyer, even after he became a very wealthy one, the same practice was followed.' She illustrates her point by telling a story. Fasken, the multi-millionaire, while travelling by train from New York to Toronto, wanted a cup of coffee. He went to the dining car and asked what a coffee would cost. When told it would cost 35 cents, he tried to bargain with the waiter, arguing that no coffee was worth 35 cents. The waiter explained that that was the price that he was required to charge. Fasken left without the coffee, refusing to pay more for something than it was worth.' Marion MacKenzie, chap. 20.

44 Marion MacKenzie, chap. 19.

45 Marion Mackenzie and her mother visited Fasken at his law office, 'and as soon as his Dad introduced him to Mother and me, I knew that Bob would be of no help to his Dad at any time as a lawyer or as a Business Man.' Marion MacKenzie, chap. 21.

46 Marion MacKenzie, chap. 21.

47 Marion MacKenzie, chap. 22. She has with her history several unidentified newsclippings hand-dated 2 and 9 November 1921, whose headlines read 'Robert Fasken Seeks Divorce: Wife Wins in Texas Court' and 'Robt. Fasken Awarded Divorce: Wife Will Enter an Appeal.' Given the ongoing interest of the *Toronto Daily Star* in David Fasken, they may well be from that paper.

48 Ibid.

49 Ibid.

50 Marion MacKenzie, chap. 22. Marion taught Nellie in the local school.

51 Marion MacKenzie, chap. 21. She has with her history an unidentified newsclipping, 'Young Wife Seeks to Annul the Marriage.' This was from the *Toronto Daily Star*, 6 August 1907, 1.

52 *Statutes of Ontario* [hereafter S.O.] *1907*, c.23, s.8.

53 'Declared the Marriage Null,' *Toronto Daily Star*, 9 August 1907, 6. See also 'Marriage Null and Void: So Declares High Court,' *Toronto Telegram*, 9 August 1907, 13.

54 Mabee would soon be appointed chairman of the Railway Commissioners for Canada. See *The Macmillan Dictionary of Canadian Biography*, 4th ed. (Toronto: Macmillan of Canada 1978), 480.

55 Marion MacKenzie, chap. 21.

56 'He tried to give her a life full of thrills and excitement which she had always loved, and great parties were held for her benefit to which the most eligible young men were invited but she would have naught to do with any of them ... She would trust herself to no one but her Uncle Dave.' Marion MacKenzie, chap. 21.

57 Alex, the youngest of the Fasken children, had joined the Beatty Blackstock firm in 1899. He had been born on 27 June 1871, on the family farm. After graduating from Elora High School, he had attended the University of Toronto and Osgoode Hall Law School. He had articled with Cassels and Standish and been called to the bar in 1894. Initially, he opened a practice in Fergus, Ontario, but after five years he acceded to his brother's request and joined him in Toronto.

58 Marion Mackenzie tells us that 'Alex, being the youngest of the family, soon became the baby tyrant of the family, for he had three or four older sisters who waited on him hand and foot and he carried this tyrannical characteristic with him throughout the rest of his life, demanding to his very last day immediate and complete obedience to his every whim from associates, family and all business firms with which he had dealings.' Marion MacKenzie, chap. 22.

59 Robert Fasken, David's older brother, was born on 30 April 1856. He and his son were farmers. Marion MacKenzie, chap. 7. Mitchell Andrew is regarded as a pioneer of Midland, Texas, as is David. See *Pioneers of Midland Texas* (Midland, Texas: n.p., n.d.).

60 Although I have not been able to trace the family connection, he is referred to in the *Toronto Daily Star* as his nephew. He was a pall-bearer at Fasken's funeral with five other family members, four of Fasken's brothers, and with Andrew Fasken, a nephew. The other thing that supports Charles being a relative is that Fasken seldom went outside of his family for key advisers and aides. As Marion MacKenzie has said, David was the most clanish of the clan.

61 Conon, *The Early History of Elora Ontario*, 42–3.

62 Marion MacKenzie tells us that Fasken was only able to spend a weekend or two at the farm each year. 'By that time Dave was quite wealthy, so he had [his] section of the quite large house furnished according to his wealth, and that caused a rift between him and the neighbouring farmers.' Marion MacKenzie, chap. 21.

63 There is a picture of the stately home on the farm together with a brief history of it in the *Mail and Empire*, 2 August 1930, under the heading, 'Historic Country Estate Sold to Businessman.' It was a historic site, being part of the land grant given in 1820 to Colonel P. Adamson for his services in the Pen-

insular War. Adamson had built a large stone house on the property, which Fasken renovated.

64 Preamble to 55 Vict. c.6.

65 A history of the statues and its many amendments can be found in *Ontario Statute Annotations R.S.O. 1970* edition (Toronto, 1974), 719. It was passed as 55 Vict. c.6. and then re-enacted in 1907 as 7 Edwd 7 c.10 and again in 1909 as 9 Edwd 7 c.12. Provincial succession duty legislation in Canada was repealed in the 1970s, with Ontario being last in 1979. This was done in part because Alberta refused to implement such legislation, making it a 'death tax haven,' and in part because of the federal taxation of estates and the desire to avoid double taxation. See Wolfe D. Goodman, 'DeathTaxes in Canada, in the Past and in the Possible Future,' *Canadian Tax Journal* 43 (1995), 1360–76.

66 *Succession Duty Act, RSO 1927*, c.26, s.19.

67 See the discussion of the difference between succession duty and estate tax in Ralph R. Loffmark, *Estate Taxes* (Toronto: Carswell 1960), 1–2.

68 See F.E. LaBrie, 'Property Taxable under the Estate Tax Act and the Ontario Succession Duty Act,' *LSUC Special Lectures 1964* (Toronto: Law Society of Upper Canada 1964), 263–87.

69 55 Vict. c.6, s.3, later in *RSO 1927*, c.26, s.6.

70 It was held initially that despite the words of the statute that the gift had to have been made within a year of the death of the giver, but the Ontario Court of Appeal in *Re Roach* (1905) 10 Ontario Law Reports 208 found no basis for such a finding.

71 55 Vict. c.6, s.4, later in *RSO 1927*, c.26, s.3.

72 See *Fasken v. Minister of National Revenue* [1949] 1 DLR 810, 812–4.

73 Cited in *Fasken v. Minister of National Revenue* [1948] Ex.C.R. 580.

74 The family home in Elora was not included. The Toronto and Temagami homes were not to be sold without her consent. If they were sold she could have an equivalent house built for her.

75 *The Accumulations Act, RSO 1950*, c.9.

76 [1952] OR 802.

77 [1952] OR 807.

78 *RSO 1950*, c.4.

79 [1953] 3 DLR 431.

80 [1961] OR 891.

81 The Prairie Foundation still exists. An Internet Google search reveals that today it supports the United Way of Midland, Big Brothers and Sisters of Midland, CASA (court approved special advocates for children), and the greening of the plains.

82 Marion MacKenzie, chap. 20, says that '... he didn't salt away his money in

vaults, but used it to better the lives of his nearest relatives, especially the older members of the Fasken Clan who had not been able to acquire too many of this world's comforts. To each of them was paid a monthly instalment, sufficient to ensure them comfortable lives as long as they lived, and arrangements were made legally to ensure that no matter what happened to him nor when, that money would be forthcoming ... as long as they should live ... He also had a Trust Fund set up whereby such of his relatives who should ever really need any financial aid that they were unable to provide for themselves, should get as much help as his Trustees decided was necessary.' She added that, in 1959, 'the 'Trust Fund is still active. But, any relative who can earn or who has enough to manage on comfortably without such help gets nothing from the Trust Fund.'

83 *Re Fasken* (1959) 19 DLR (2d) 182.
84 See Marion MacKenzie, chap. 7, for a description of her family.
85 In concluding that David provided a trust for all of his nieces and nephews, I have been influenced by the fact that Mary Fasken, David's older sister, had ten children and did not die until 31 August 1939, aged eighty-six. Why would David have established a trust during her lifetime for only two of her ten children and why for only her children and not those of his other siblings? The names of her children were Isabel, Robert, Richard, Griffith, Owen, Sarah, Margaret, David, Mary, and Ella.
86 The plaque was put up years later at the suggestion of Sam Bowman, a local Mennonite farmer turned township Reeve. I spent a wonderful day in the summer of 2001 with Sam and our mutual friend Hugh Laurence as Sam showed us the original homestead of David's grandfather, the Fasken family farm where David was born, the Bethany Methodist Church as it was known in David's day, the one-room school house David attended (now a family home), the family gravesite in Elora, and the Wellington County Museum and Archives. Sam, now deceased, was a source of much knowledge and insight.
87 *Canada Trust Co v. Fasken* (1990) 69 DLR (4th) 575.
88 On the legal treatment of similar conditions in the Leonard Foundation scholarships, see Ziff, *Unforeseen Legacies*. Ironically, 1990, the year of the Fasken estate litigation, was the very year that the Ontario Court of Appeal ruled that the Leonard scholarship conditions, also administered by Canada Trust, were unlawful and unenforceable. *Canada Trust v. The Human Rights Commission* (1990) 69 DLR (4th) 321.
89 *Canada Trust Co v. Fasken* (1990) 69 DLR (4th) 575.
90 It is described very briefly in *Canada Trust Co v. Fasken* (1990) 69 DLR (4th) 575.
91 Marion MacKenzie, chap. 20.

92 *The Toronto Western Hospital,* pamphlet, Archives of Toronto Western Hospital no. 978.208. A copy is also in the FMD Archive.

93 See Litvak, *Edward James Lennox.*

94 Marion MacKenzie, chap. 20.

95 *Toronto Daily Star,* 3 December 1929, 1.

96 *The Toronto Western Hospital,* pamphlet, 13.

97 Marion MacKenzie has with her history an unidentified newsclipping hand-dated 5 December, that summarizes the oration. From its text it seems to be from a local Elora paper.

98 Marion MacKenzie, noting that Staff Captain McCoy of the Salvation Army had attended Fasken's funeral, tells us that 'Dave had been a special friend of the Salvation Army helping them in their work with the needy, with his money, of which no one knew anything about except the Officers of the Army.' Marion MacKenzie, chap. 22.

99 Marion MacKenzie, chap. 8.

100 Harvey, in his sworn examination for discovery in the Moran lawsuit tells us that he first met David Fasken when Harvey was an articling clerk in the Beatty firm. Harvey had then gone west to Manitoba and had become Fasken's agent in land deals in Manitoba and Alberta. When Harvey learned the 'C' Ranch in Texas was for sale, he came to Toronto to convince Fasken to buy it. Relying on Harvey and insisting that there must be water on the property, Fasken agreed. *W.J. Moran v. Midland Farms Company, et al.,* District Court of Midland County No. 1724 in the Nina Stewart Haley Memorial Library.

101 Unidentified newsclipping dated 1935 in the Marion MacKenzie manuscript and entitled 'Province Losses Suit for $500,000 in Taxes.'

102 *Toronto Daily Star.*

103 *The Attorney-General for Ontario v. Fasken et al.* [1935] OR 115.

104 The trustees for the debt had been Alex Fasken, Andrew Fasken, and Charles Parker. According to corporate minutes in the FMD Archives, in 1931 Andrew and Alex had had a falling out over the appropriateness of drilling for oil on the 'C' Ranch and Alex had removed Andrew from his position as manager of the Texas property. At the same time, he had replaced Andrew as trustee of the loan with James ('Jimmy') Aitchison, another of Fasken's nephews and a lawyer in the Fasken firm.

105 *Succession Duty Act, RSO 1927,* c.26, s.1(g).

106 *The Attorney-General for Ontario v. Fasken et al.* [1935] OR 288.

107 On Riddell and his personality, see Hilary Bates Neary, 'William Renwick Riddell: Judge, Ontario Publicist and Man of Letters,' *Law Society Gazette,* vol. 11 (1977), 148.

108 *Toronto Daily Star,* 4 December 1929, 1.

109 *Fasken v. Minister of National Revenue* [1949] 1 DLR 810 or [1948] Ex.C.R. 580.

110 S.C. 1927 c.10, s.12.

111 *A Standard Dictionary*, vol. 2, 149.

112 D.W.M. Waters states that the discretionary trust did not become common in Canada until the late 1960s and early 1970s. See his comments in *The Law of Trusts in Canada* (Toronto: Carswell 1974), 369–70.

113 The Fasken litigation is cited in most Canadian texts on estate planning and estate taxes. Several of the cases, for example, are cited in Loffmark, *Estate Taxes*. The Federal income tax case of 1949 was cited by Culltity and Forbes in their 1978 text on *Taxation and Estate Planning* (Toronto, 1978), 309–16, as a leading case on spousal transfers that attract attribution. The case on the power of appointment that Fasken gave his grandson was cited by Waters, *The Law of Trusts in Canada*, 66.

13

Squatters' Rights and the Origins of Edmonton Settlement

BRUCE ZIFF AND SEAN WARD*

As long as Canada is a free country every Canadian has an inherent right to a share of the public domain, for his own use, whether he obtains it by conforming with the ordinary government regulations or by squatting on it in advance of survey, and it will be a dark day for the North West and for Canada when the exercise of that right is prohibited.[1]

Possession, it must be remembered, is nine points of the law ...[2]

The 1931 Academy Award–winning epic *Cimaran* begins with a re-enactment of the extraordinary Oklahoma land rush of 1889. At the outset, thousands of would-be settlers, on horseback, in wagons, or on foot, restlessly gather on the wide-open plains. At the appointed hour, the blare of a bugle and the firing of shot by the cavalry announce the official opening of a vast frontier. The mad race that ensues rapidly degenerates into a tangle of confusion and chaos until all of the available quarter-sections are spoken for.

The first-occupancy strategy of frontier development was common, even if most such efforts were not undertaken with the dramatic flair adopted in Oklahoma. However, the wisdom of allocating land in this way remains a subject of debate. Criticism has emerged, in part, because the rush to secure land came at a cost. Given that parcels were offered at a nominal cost, and not at market rates, homesteaders may have been induced to develop and clear some regions prematurely. Homesteading in more remote areas was, arguably, inefficient whenever access to markets and supplies was difficult and costly.[3]

Moreover, many settlers simply refused to play by the rules. Land acquisition by illegal occupation – squatting – has a long though ignoble history in the settler colonies within the British Empire and elsewhere. It became commonplace for pioneers, hungry for lush, arable, or otherwise valuable realty, to set out ahead of the governmental systems designed to facilitate orderly settlement. What was seen as unclaimed wilderness beckoned the hearty and resolute. In doing so, the many Aboriginal communities that were, in fact, first in time on these lands were treated as invisible or irrelevant. On the ground, the settlers barely took notice of their presence. This was recently acquired Crown land, formerly the massive land empire of the Hudson's Bay Company. No earlier provenance seemed to matter. Although Aboriginal nations were typically absent from narratives of frontier settlement, it must be remembered that disputes over squatters' rights inevitably assumed, or resulted in, Aboriginal dispossession.[4]

Some common features characterize these squatter episodes. After settlers ventured out, staking claims that had no initial legal standing, conventions developed to determine entitlements *inter se.* Informal institutions, such as vigilante organizations, emerged to provide a measure of protection and stability. Attempts were made by government to dislodge these 'wilful freebooters'[5] and to prevent others from following in their tracks. A predictable by-product was the bubbling up of animosity between squatters and the state. Almost always, the authorities eventually capitulated, according recognition to unlawfully acquired rights in some way. Over and over again, in the development of the (now) developed world, rights sprouted up in this fashion.

The Australian story is well known. In New South Wales, squatters acquired the lands, mainly for grazing, west of Sydney during the 1830s and 1840s, though there was also squatting in the preceding decade. Where sparsely vegetated lands were involved, large tracts of land were occupied to sustain the sheep and cattle runs. In due course, officialdom abandoned its hopes for its planned development of a society of farmers, and sanctioned the pastoralists' shaky titles. Certain half-measures were initially offered, including licenses of various sorts, but the squatters held out for, and won, far more. As of 1847, they were entitled to obtain pastoral leases for up to fourteen years, and were permitted to purchase the freehold over these lands, at its unimproved value, during or at the end of the lease term.[6] Meanwhile, squatting continued apace elsewhere, particularly in Queensland.[7] The upshot was the creation of a wealthy squattocracy, as it came to be called.

In the United States, the process was comparable in scope.[8] Squatters were taking up lands in Massachusetts in the first half of the seventeenth century. The practice spread to Maryland, Vermont, Maine, and other colonies along the eastern seaboard. Elaborate conventions arose to define and perfect claims, some of which migrated as the western frontier was opened up. In the West, claims clubs and other settler associations were created to protect the interests of those on the land from the challenges of claim jumpers and speculators. Vigilantism was common, with violence and other acts of reprisal being carried out, or threatened, as a means of enforcing the established ownership norms. The sundry efforts of Congress to curb the tide fell short. In fact, the system of land sales adopted in the late eighteenth century almost certainly served to fuel illegal occupations, for the prices sought were simply too high for the market. Land theft was far preferable.

As in Australia, the ultimate capitulation of the state occurred in stages. A host of pre-emption statutes were passed in the early part of the nineteenth century, leading to legislation in 1841, under which Congress conferred pre-emptive rights of purchase for those in occupation of surveyed federal property. Later on, the scope of that pre-emption law was expanded to include unsurveyed land. Twenty years later, the *Homestead Act* of 1862 provided for acquisition of land on payment of a fee of $10. As a condition of the grant, the land had to be occupied for a minimum of five years and improved during that time.

In a recent study of the undulating courses of frontier settlement, John Weaver describes and assesses at length both government policies and the squatter phenomena in relation to European settlement in Australia, South Africa, the United States, New Zealand, Argentina, and Canada. However, his treatment of illegal land-grabbing in Canada in general, and in Western Canada in particular, is quite limited.

The Canadian experience, as described by Weaver, was a fairly tame affair. Although both squatting and illegal timber stripping were prevalent in Upper and Lower Canada, the process of land acquisition was less turbulent than that occurring at roughly the same time on the American frontier. The rugged individualism found in Canada was not quite as rugged, for there was more deference to authority among the Canadian settlers. The acquisition of land for grazing played a major role in the American West, but was far less significant in Canada, especially in the East. Land was used principally for farming, and the holdings, whether lawfully acquired or not, tended to be small. [9]

The last major region to experience a land rush was the Canadian West. That process began in earnest following the acquisition of Rupert's Land from the Hudson's Bay Company in 1870. The bulk of the Company's vast territories in Western Canada were transferred to the federal government. At the time of the transfer, there was virtually no settlement in Rupert's Land outside of the Company's trading posts. The *Dominion Lands Act* (1872),[10] allowed a would-be settler to acquire a quarter-section at a nominal price, coupled with the right to purchase additional lands below market value. In return, the land had to be cleared and developed.

By the time that settlement of the West was undertaken, many of the mistakes and oversights affecting the formal settlement procedures that had occurred elsewhere in North America, relating to such matters as surveying and land dispersal, had been addressed. It was in the Canadian West, uniquely, that there was both time and money to carry out the planned settlement.[11] Still, some squatting did take place. Most is thought to have involved small acreages near river valleys, where the land was mainly used for hunting and fishing.[12] Squatters clustered in small communities in such places as Prince Albert, St Albert, along the Souris River, and in the Qu'appelle region. Much of the central area of what is now the City of Edmonton was unilaterally appropriated by settlers within a year of the region having been acquired by Canada. Dozens of homesteads in the outlying lands near Edmonton were obtained in the same fashion.[13]

In this essay, our focus will be on the curious sequence of events that occurred in and around Edmonton Settlement in the 1870s and 1880s.[14] The Edmonton experience is absent from John Weaver's otherwise masterly account, and seems never to have been placed within the meta-narratives of frontier development. We will attempt to demonstrate that the squatting period, though brief, reflects the major themes and ideologies that characterise frontier squatting. They emerge here in microcosm.

The Emergence of Edmonton Settlement

The 1898 Supreme Court of Canada ruling in *Brown & Curry v. Town of Edmonton*[15] concerned whether the dedication of a public way was subject to a pre-existing obstruction, and whether compensation must be paid for removal of the obstruction by a municipal authority. The so-called obstruction was a log building that had several years earlier been built on – not near, not adjacent to, but on – an old trail and the planned route for Jasper Avenue, then as now an important commercial thoroughfare in Edmonton. The new delineation of Jasper Avenue called for the relocation of the building some forty feet to the north. John Brown and Duncan Steel Curry had been operating a general store on those premises for several years. They refused to budge, and turned down a handsome settlement offer.[16]

By the time the matter came to trial in 1892, Messrs Brown and Curry had been the patented owners of the land for five years, though the building had been constructed earlier, when they were mere squatters. Their counsel asserted that the pre-existing structure took precedence over the dedication of the trail as a highway, even though the dedication took place in 1886, before Brown and Curry obtained their patent. They lost at trial, and again on appeal to the Supreme Court of the Northwest Territories sitting *en banc*.[17] An appeal to the Supreme Court of Canada was likewise unsuccessful. In writing for the Court, Mr Justice John Wellington Gwynne concluded a detailed and measured judgment with the sharp-edged comment that to uphold the defendants' assertion would be 'a perversion of common sense.'[18]

Of course, Justice Gwynne was right: to assert a claim against the Crown based on an earlier act of privateering was audacious. But, then, the Edmonton Settlement had been born of audacity. At the time of the litigation, a land inventory would have revealed that about half of the privately owned lots in Edmonton had been initially acquired by the brazen acts of a handful of squatters. Holding on tenaciously to their ill-gotten parcels, they bullied their way through bureaucratic resistance, eventually acquiring sanctioned titles. Brown and Curry may have lost their claim to the land on which the highway was routed, but the property they retained was adjacent to what became the town's main street, and it was (and remains) fairly lucrative real estate.

Edmonton Settlement was informally founded in 1871, a few months after Rupert's Land was sold to Canada by the Hudson's Bay Company. Under the terms of the transfer, the HBC retained significant landholdings (approximately 7 million acres of fertile terrain), and was entitled to reserve up to 3,000 acres around established trading forts. There had been a fort in Edmonton since 1795, and the full 3,000 acres was reserved there. The rest of the land in the vicinity was essentially left vacant.

The vacuum created by the withdrawal of the HBC was soon filled. Homestead legislation was not introduced until 1872, and although the reserve area was surveyed in 1873, the surrounding lands were not. Within a year of the sale, settlers began staking claims, mainly east of the reserve lands. The first two claims were taken by the Reverend George McDougall, for a Methodist mission and a parsonage. A string of easterly claims followed along the crest of the North Saskatchewan River valley. There was one large claim to the west of the reserve, as well as a cluster of sizable parcels south of the river. A number of these original squatters were former HBC employees, including Richard Hardisty, who had served as the chief factor in Fort Edmonton. A consensus appeared to develop at an early stage that squatters could claim up to a 200-yard frontage for the highly prized river lots.[19]

By 1880 there had still been no official survey, and no patents had been issued for lands along the river. However, there was a bustling community of about 300 souls, with shops, woodframe houses, and a coalmine. By 1874, the great westward trek of the North-West Mounted Police had been completed, so there was a police presence nearby. And beginning in 1880, the *Edmonton Bulletin* conveyed the news from the East and chronicled local events. The *Bulletin* was owned and edited by Frank Oliver, who arrived in the settlement in 1876. It operated on lands that Oliver had purchased from an original squatter. The paper became, in essence, the voice of the squatters. By the early 1880s, the push had begun for the transformation of the *de facto* land rights into *de jure* titles, and all of the important moments in that struggle were narrated weekly in the *Edmonton Bulletin*.

The most notorious of such moments occurred in early 1882. The rights to the river grants being founded on occupancy only, it was quite predictable that attempts to claim-jump might ensue. By 1882, trouble had been 'brewing, as the settlers became thicker and the land became more valuable.'[20] The first confrontation of that year involved one of the earliest lots to be staked, which had been transferred three times over the previous ten years. As of February 1882, the lot belonged to a group of investors, who had acquired it from one John Sinclair. Prior to that transfer, Sinclair had leased part of the property to A. McDonald & Co. for use as a store. However, no one was residing on the land, and to some it seemed ripe for the picking. Indeed, various people in the settlement had been 'casting a longing eye'[21] at this large plot, believed to be valued at between $5,000 and $10,000.

In early February 1882, an American working in Edmonton as a store clerk, and referred to simply as L. George in the *Bulletin* account, arrived on the lot, drove in boundary stakes, and with the help of several hired hands began building a small (10′ x 20′) frame house. News of these events circulated like wildfire. In the afternoon, one of the owners arrived at the scene and demanded that the workers stop at once. This fell on deaf ears. George pitched a tent inside the framing (for that was all that had been completed), and slept there Saturday and Sunday in order to maintain his *de facto* occupation.

There was a mounting apprehension that a chain reaction of claim jumping might ensue, and that this was a test case of the durability of the squatter claims. On Monday afternoon matters came to a head. By around 4 o'clock, a crowd of about 150 men – a loosely organised vigilante group – had gathered in the vicinity of the property. George was given an ultimatum: remove the building immediately or it would be removed for him. He refused outright, then drew a revolver, brandishing it at those in the throng who happened to be closest to him. He was summarily disarmed. There was a further war of words between the proprietors and George; this produced a stand-off. The gang then efficiently relocated the frame to the bottom of the river valley, 200 feet below, at which point the firearm was returned to George, as was the tent and bedding that had been removed from the frame before it was dragged over the cliff.

The creation of the vigilante group was ad hoc, but that evening a meeting was held, the purpose of which was to create a more permanent organisation; a mutual protection society of some form was envisioned. About 100 people assembled at McDougall's Hall to discuss just what such an organisation might entail. The upshot of the rather spirited debate was the formation of a vigilance committee. It was to operate as a secret society (whatever that might mean), so as to allow its members 'greater freedom of action,' in carrying out its stated functions.[22] Terms of reference and an oath were prepared, and by the time of adjournment, forty-seven men had joined as founding members.[23]

It was not long before the committee was pressed into service. On 21 February a second claim-jump was attempted, this time by one Joseph McKay Bannerman, who happened to be the brother of a Member of Parliament for an Ontario constituency.[24] The parcel at issue was the mission property, part of the Methodist Church holdings, and one of the first to be staked. For over a decade it had been used as a parsonage. There being no minister or missionary in residence for some time, the mission house had been leased to Matthew McCauley during the proceeding eight months. In return, he was obliged to maintain the property, and presumably also to secure the claim.[25]

On the morning of 21 February, workers were seen building a structure behind the mission house. Later that day, Bannerman, by letter to the newly formed vigilance committee, declared his intentions:

Dear Sir: – I beg to inform you that I am about to locate and homestead the claim adjoining the HBC Co.'s town plot on the east, and by doing so I must say that I am not infringing any local rule that may have been framed by the vigilance committee, from the fact that I am duly authorized to do so by the Minister of the Interior. Any doubt upon the subject may be removed by calling upon me for such proof.

I am yours truly, J.M. Bannerman[26]

The vigilance committee met that evening and resolved to protect the mission claim and to 'apply the necessary persuasion'[27] to ensure that the claim jump did not pre-empt a decision by the authorities as to the mission's right to receive a patent for that property. At the agreed hour they arrived, making no attempt to conceal their identities or purpose. Oliver, who had refused to join the vigilance committee because he preferred it to be an open association, was nevertheless front and centre during the confrontation. Following a brief verbal exchange, the group mobilised for action. They were well prepared for the task at hand. The dwelling was hoisted by rope onto two bobsleighs, then drawn by a team of horses for a quarter of a mile to a spot near Brown and Curry's store. There, Bannerman's unfinished shanty suffered the same fate as George's wood frame.[28] Whether the chosen route was necessitated by the need to reach the precipice, or was designed to visit a little rough music on Bannerman through a very public display, is not clear.[29]

In the aftermath of the first claim-jump attempt, George had threatened legal action, but nothing came of it.[30] However, following this second encounter, there were legal repercussions. Several men, including Matt McCauley and Frank Oliver, were charged with the offence of malicious injury to property. A preliminary inquiry held in early March led to six of the nine accused being committed to trial. Several weeks later, a civil suit was also filed.

Community support was decidedly in favour of the defendants. In a public lecture held several weeks later, the Reverend Canon Newton drew from scripture to resolve the moral ambiguities imbricated in illegal squatting, claim jumping against initial wrongdoers, and the remedy of violent self-help. Abraham, the audience was reminded, had used honest money to pay for land to secure a burial site for his family in the land of Canaan, even though God had promised Abraham that he would inherit those lands. That ought to serve 'as an example to be followed by all those who wish to acquire lands already in the occupancy of others.' Secular law was also invoked: 'it was laid down as an axiom by Blackstone that the first occupant of unclaimed land was in fact the owner.'[31]

A jury of six men was empanelled. Among them was Malcolm Groat, who had staked a large claim west of the HBC reserve. The trial was held on 15 June, before Hugh Richardson, a stipendiary magistrate. The accused were unrepresented. Several witnesses were called to place in evidence the sequence of events that took place on the mission property. In the end, the jury returned a verdict of not guilty. The defence was premised in part on the protection of the church's prior property rights to the land where the mission house had been built.[32] Likewise, in the civil action it was held that the pre-existing claim, even if adverse to that of the Crown, was superior to Bannerman's. That outcome accords with long-established common-law doctrine.[33] The plaintiff did recover a judgment of $40 against one of the vigilantes, McCauley, for the destruction of the building materials. Soon afterwards, Bannerman left for Calgary.

While tensions were mounting in the river lot area, another major event of 1882 was occurring within the confines of the Hudson's Bay Company reserve. The company had decided that the time had come to subdivide and sell off portions of the reserve lands. Some, but only some, of the lots were put up for sale in the initial offering. A similar approach, that is, maintaining demand above supply, had been adopted for the equally large reserve lands at Winnipeg, where real estate sales had been a robust success. In Edmonton, the location was 'high and dry,' and the prices and terms were attractive. As expected, there was an extremely strong demand for the properties, and over the span of just a few days about 400 lots were sold. Sales grossed $12,000, or about $25 to $30 per lot. Once the company suspended the sales, a number of the lots that had been sold in this initial flurry fetched much higher prices in the secondary market that quickly emerged.

While squatters were selling river lots, and the HBC was developing its own land market, there was another regime, in fact the main system of land allocation, in operation. The Macdonald government was aggressively promoting westward expansion as part of its National Policy. Following closely on the heels of the purchase of Rupert's Land, a homesteading system drawn extensively from the 1862 American homestead legislation was implemented. Most of Rupert's Land was surveyed under a township system that created mile-square sections (640 acres) bordered on all sides by road allowances. By virtue of the *Dominion Lands Act*, settlers could acquire quarter-sections (160 acres) for a nominal fee, with a pre-emptive right to purchase additional land. In 1882, the pre-emption prices for quarter-sections ranged from $320 and $400 (or $2.00 to $2.50 per acre).[34]

While it may have seemed to Oliver and others that the government was doing very little to address the land rights question, in fact there was considerable work afoot. In 1878, William King did some preliminary survey work in the vicinity for the Department of the Interior, and in 1881 some of the locals hired the surveyor who had created the plat for the Hudson's Bay reserve to establish boundary lines for the river lots. In July 1882, that is, not long after the court cases concerning the mission property, the department dispatched a team of surveyors to lay out the township lines in the Edmonton area.

Another surveyor, Michael Deane, was sent west with orders to collect data on Edmonton Settlement. Deane's instructions were to create an inventory of improvements and to determine the extent of cultivation occurring in the area. He was not supposed to set out lot lines, for there were concerns that by doing so he would be placing an imprimatur of legitimacy on the claims and their delineation.[35] Perhaps predictably, he succumbed to local pressure to do just that, and, as feared by Ottawa, the resulting cadastre was viewed by the settlers as possessing some ill-defined air of legitimacy. Figure 13.1 shows the Deane survey; it is, in effect, Edmonton's first published work of fiction.

By early 1883, the surveying of lands in the Edmonton district was well underway. At a public meeting called to consider political action in relation to lands in the settlement, that important first step was applauded. Resolutions were passed calling for the removal of timber levies, and the relocation of an Aboriginal community to the 'Indian farm at Peace Hills.' A further resolution was designed to call to attention the fact that rights had been granted by the federal government to a colonization company over approximately half of the area of Edmonton Settlement. It was pointless, the motion stated, to grant land in

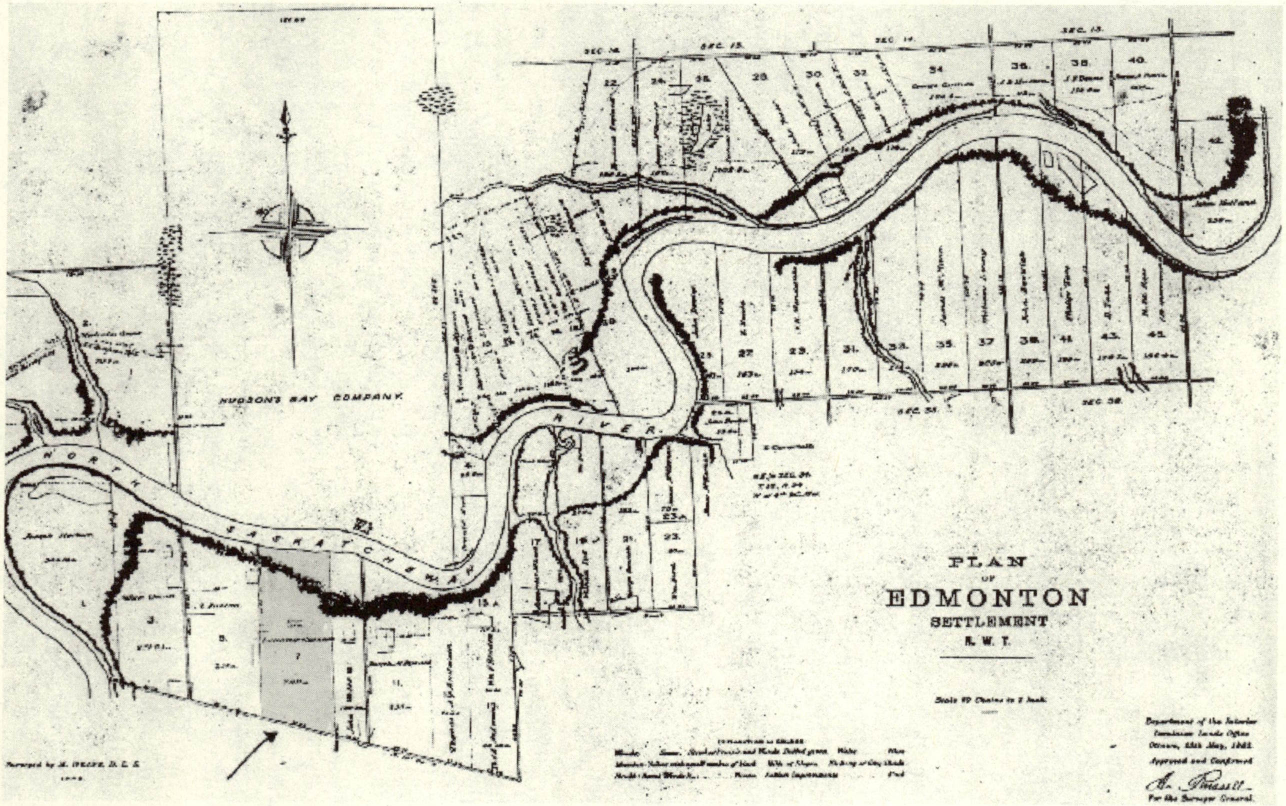

Figure 13.1: Plan of Edmonton Settlement, NWT (1883)

order to promote settlement when these areas had been 'thickly settled' for years. Consequently, the government was urged to annul the grant as being injurious to the existing occupiers and contrary to the spirit of the enabling legislation.[36]

In Ottawa there was both a desire to resolve the squatting question as well as support for the squatters' claims.[37] In consequence, in 1883 the federal government made major concessions. Amendments to the homesteading legislation recognized claims to specified lands. A settler who was in *bona fide* occupation, and had made improvements prior to survey on lands designated for homesteading would be granted a pre-emptive right to obtain free homestead entry.[38] That provision did not cover all squatting and almost certainly not the lands in the centre of Edmonton Settlement, which was never rendered into quarter-sections in accordance with the general land policy. Nonetheless, at the very least, the 1883 amendments held great practical and symbolic significance for those occupying the river lots. In the same year, the Department of the Interior acceded to requests from delegates from several settlements to recognize their land rights. 'Justice has been guaranteed the original river settlers,' announced the *Bulletin* triumphantly.[39]

In the wake of these developments, the final step was to confirm entitlements on the ground, a task that fell to William Pearce, a senior civil servant.[40] Arriving in the Edmonton area in 1884, he was required to deal with some 240 disputes, the lion's share pertaining to pre-survey homesteading in the outlying vicinity. These were routine claims, and as a general rule, homestead rights were conferred. About two dozen files concerned boundary disputes, mainly within Edmonton Settlement.

Faced with the Deane survey and the sense of entitlement that had congealed around it, Pearce elected to preserve the status quo whenever possible; hence, only three deviations were made to the Deane plat. Shortly afterwards, a protocol was established for the issuance of letters patent for the Edmonton Settlement claims. Among other things, title would be granted on the payment of a $10 fee, the same as that levied for homestead entry.[41] Certain disputes dragged on, such as those relating to pre-emption prices for additional quarter-sections,[42] and to squatter claims in the outlying areas, HBC properties, Aboriginal reserves, and school and railway lands.[43] However, the main fight over the lots of Edmonton Settlement had been won.

Edmonton Settlement and the Broader Themes of Frontier Development

As suggested at the outset, several features characterized the process of frontier development throughout the British Empire and the United States: settlement was messy, government procedures proved inadequate to the task, and informal rule systems arose which eventually led to legally recognized titles. These elements were all present in Edmonton and environs. Pioneers pressed forward in advance of the official system, taking land before it was surveyed or before it was officially released for homestead entry. Local informal laws quickly emerged to provide a measure of stability. At the earliest moments, a convention appeared to develop regarding the acceptable measure of entitlement: a frontage of 200 yards. Moreover, apart from some exceptional cases, the Deane survey and the Pearce commission were undertaken with little local turmoil.[44]

Over this period there was a brooding resentment of the government in Ottawa, a recurring theme in Alberta politics that can fairly be said to have been born at this point. Requests had been made for pre-emptive rights for squatters *à la* American homestead law, and prior to that some sought the implementation of quasi-formal rules for establishing boundaries applicable to squatters *inter se*. The prevalence of squatting in the region was blamed on the Department of the Interior, which was criticised for its inability to keep abreast of the demand for land by those willing to pioneer the West. Moreover, Frank Oliver's editorials complained that the bureaucratic delays in resolving squatters' rights were inducing Canadians to leave in search of greener pastures south of the border.[45]

Squatter narratives often focus on the tensions that existed between *de jure* and *de facto* orders. Oliver's attack on the authorities typifies that kind of discourse. Squatting is itself defined by reference to distinction between legal and unlawful settlement, and this divide is what makes these moments especially noteworthy. Yet it is arguably just as important to understand the ways in which these protagonists shared a set of aspirations and ideals. There was a synergy between the needs of the squatters in places such as Edmonton Settlement and the policies being pursued by the Government of Canada. Settlement was a cornerstone of the National Policy. Rupert's Land had not been created to serve as a colonial plantation. Though it had been under British control for 200 years, there was virtually no settlement infrastructure except within the confines of the trading fort palisades and the odd failed settlement experiment. From the 1870s onwards, Canadians were lured westward with grandiose promises of the good life.[46] Accordingly, what the squatters did in Edmonton and surroundings was wholly consistent with the needs of the newly formed federal government. Oliver played up this synchrony:

The squatter who strikes out ahead of his fellows and seeks new fields is the man who deserves well of his country. He answers for geological and meteorological observatory. He injures no one inasmuch as he takes up land where no one else would have it before, and it is only right that he should receive every advantage that his enterprise brings him, and when the government tries to displace him for any cause, they are working themselves as much injury as they are to him.[47]

Despite the concerns expressed from time to time that the government would let them down, the squatters had in fact little reason to fear. The earlier American experience, in which squatter claims were eventually recognised by the government, were a matter of record, and may well have affected settler conduct in the Northwest Territories. In addition, in Upper Canada it had become accepted usage that, in disposing of Crown lands, preference was afforded to squatters who had already defined, cleared, and cultivated a plot.[48] Land was plentiful, and it had to be filled in some way. It was simply pointless (not to mention futile) to try to uproot the squatters. Granted, they refused to play fair, but they were really more akin to queue-jumpers than outright thieves.

Most important of all, both the original inhabitants of Edmonton Settlement and the authorities which they chose to defy shared an ideological point of view. Both believed to their bones in what John Weaver has labelled the doctrine of improvement.[49] The movement West represented in palpable ways a march of progress. The West was destined to be tamed and made productive; and it was to be marked, confined, divided, and memorialised on cadastres. In more general terms, a rough-hewn version of possessive individualism was the dominant theme of westward expansion in North America. It was Lockean virtually from top to bottom.[50] As is well known, John Locke's theory of property rights is founded on entitlements derived from labour and desert. Locke's defence of property rights starts with a depiction of the state of nature in which all property was held in common. God having commanded man to labour, he was, in return, entitled to those earthly goods which had become imbued – mixed – with his labour, so long as he took only so much as would not be wasted, and provided also that enough and as good was left for others. As labour accounts for the greatest element of value of an object (be it land or goods), one who contributes labour deserves to acquire the fruits of one's efforts.

Locke drew upon the American experience to support this analysis. America, vast and bountiful, was to him the modern manifestation of the state of nature. As he put it, 'in the beginning all the world was America.'[51] He suggested that although the North American continent was rich in natural resources, 'for want of improving it by labour,'[52] it provided few of the decorous comforts of life enjoyed in England. These ideas align with the main premises of the Canadian and American homesteading laws. Entitlements were granted to settlers for a nominal fee, but the land had to be developed. This same cult of improvement and desert underscored the entitlements asserted by the river lot settlers in Edmonton Settlement, as narrated via Frank Oliver's editorials in the *Bulletin*.

Reading the history of illegal western occupation largely in terms of a contest about the rule of law not only underplays the existence of this common ideological reference point, it also obscures some significant social fissures. There were many constituencies on the Canadian prairies, and the conflicts that erupted among them involved far more than the occasional dispute over claim-jumping or the correct placement of boundary markers.

As Robert Williams has shown, the conception of the American frontier as a wasteland, Locke's state of nature, rendered the territories fully available for appropriation and improvement.[53] Adopting a similar perspective, in 1832 the Nova Scotia lawyer and treatise writer Beamish Murdoch described the new world as one inhabited by 'wild animals and hunters almost as wild ... [who held no] idea of property (of an exclusive nature) in the soil, before their intercourse with Europeans.'[54] To European eyes, the prairies were a pristine wilderness, available for the taking. Such readings allow Aboriginal communities to be pushed to the margins, or ignored altogether.[55] Such was the case, it seems, among the earliest white settlers in the Edmonton area. It was not until 1877 – some six years after the first squatter claims were staked – that the Papaschase Cree agreed to adhere to the terms of Treaty 6, and were promised reserve lands in what is now southeast Edmonton.[56]

Again, Locke's writing is instructive. In arguing that labour provided the greatest part of the value of land, Locke advanced a hypothetical illustration involving an acre of fertile land in both England and America. He supposed that the benefit to humankind in one year would, in the former case, be equal to £5. In contrast, the American yield would amount to one penny. However, and here lies the key aspect, he added that 'if the Profit an Indian received from it were to be valued, and sold here; I may truly say, [it would be worth] not 1/1000.'[57]

There were also severe divisions among the European settlers. The accounts presented in the *Bulletin* portrayed the squatters as on the moral (and mainly the literal) high ground. They were not land thieves but valuable, though undervalued, trailblazers. So, in an 1882 editorial Frank Oliver described the squatters in the Northwest as 'the scouts, the pickets, the advance guard of Canadian settlement.' By contrast, the land speculator, long the whipping boy of American settlement politics, attracted Oliver's acid criticism, along with the railways ('the great public swindle')[58] and the colonisation societies.[59] These interests had received 'million upon millions of acres'[60] from the federal government.

Speculative purchasers and speculative (i.e., non-resident) squatters also abounded. But Oliver was far less troubled by this latter cohort. Almost all speculating squatters (99 per cent, Oliver opined)[61] were settlers who intended to remain in the territories, and ultimately to make a living by working the land. At all events, such people were to be distanced from the *bona fide* squatter. True, they were speculators of a sort, since it was expected that their holdings would appreciate as new waves of homesteaders arrived in search of the best parcels. However, their rights to the land had been earned by virtue of the settlement on, and improvements made to, the very lands they claimed.[62]

Squatters' rights were said by Oliver to belong to Canadians, though the term Canadian took on a distinct, coded meaning in his writing. Oliver was advocating on behalf of native-born Canadians, or for men from countries who had 'thrown in their lot completely with Canada' and who therefore had the same entitlements as those born on Canadian soil. Expressly excluded were 'Mennonites ... Jews, or chinamen, or any foreign nation or strange class.'[63] Moreover, the failure of the government to promote Canadian settlement competently had induced others to settle in the territories. Hence, he maintained that 'every hindrance possible is thrown in the way of [Canadians] coming to the North-West, while special encouragement is given to Jews and heathens, paupers and criminals, hypocrites and swindlers from other countries to come in and possess the land.'[64] In brief, a distinct hierarchy of worthiness was being manufactured.

Conclusion

In recent years, increased attention has turned to the history of frontier settlement. One thread of modern development theory stresses the importance of establishing secure *de jure* titles as a means of promoting growth in developing nations and former Soviet states. The best-known exponent of that theory is the Peruvian economist Hernando de Soto. In *The Mystery of Capital*,[65] de Soto seeks to illustrate the importance of validating extra-legal titles, and the futility of policies that run against that grain. In doing so, he draws back to the American frontier experience. It is quite possible that, had de Soto been aware of the early history of Edmonton, he would have appreciated that it produced a superb setting in which to compare the dynamics occurring within *de jure* and *de facto* land markets.

Consider again the events of 1882, and in particular the decision by the Hudson's Bay Company to sell off lots within its reserve. A plan of subdivision was drawn, and titles to the lots sold there were rock solid. Following the initial sales, a brisk secondary market soon emerged. Directly to the east of the HBC reserve were most of the squatter-owned river lots, all existing on a legal no-man's land. These properties were also subdivided, and secondary sales were not uncommon. These two markets, literally side by side, created laboratory conditions – a kind of real estate petri dish – under which one can assess the degree to which security of title affected the value of land.

Hudson's Bay lots that originally sold for $25 at the beginning of 1882 were going for $300 just a few months later.[66] The Edmonton Settlement lands also sold well, often at prices far in excess of the reserve land sales (owing to the size and location of the river lots). Even so, it was appreciated that the river-lot transactions were being conducted under a cloud, since 'not a line was surveyed or the remotest prospect of a deed ever being given or received was in view.'[67] Likewise, 'as the original settlers held no titles they were afraid to sell lest their rights to the balance of their claims should be prejudiced and buyers were, of course, afraid to invest in more than they actually needed for present use.'[68]

Still, it is mistaken to imagine, as de Soto appears to have done, that the circumstances in places such as Edmonton Settlement circa 1880 can somehow be compared to the impoverished peri-urban squatter communities found today.[69] The inhabitants there are on the periphery of society in all possible ways. The squatters of the great land rushes often were, or in short order became, integral members of mainstream society. Many ascended to positions of power, as in the case of the Australian squattocracy.[70] In Edmonton, Frank Oliver was elected as the Member of Parliament for the region, and during his political career served as minister of the interior. Matthew McCauley, erstwhile vigilante, became the first mayor of Edmonton. A number of city districts in Edmonton (Oliver, Groat Estates, Garneau, Hardisty, and so forth) are named after squatters. To miss that squatting was primarily a quest to become part of a new propertied elite is to overlook an important aspect of the saga.

NOTES

* This is a revised version of a paper first presented at the Biennial Property Law Conference held in Reading, U.K., in March 2006. The conference paper can be found in B. Ziff and S. Ward, 'De Soto Discovers the Prairies: Of Squatters and the Canadian West,' in E. Cooke, ed., *Modern Studies in Property Law*, vol. 4 (Oxford: Hart 2007), 219.

1 'Squatters and Squatting,' *Edmonton Bulletin*, 5 May 1883.

2 'Claim Jumping,' *Edmonton Bulletin*, 24 January 1883.

3 See further C. Southey, 'The Staples Thesis, Common Property and Homesteading,' *Canadian Journal of Economics* 11 (1978), 547. In K. Norrie and D. Owram, *A History of the Canadian Economy*, 2nd ed. (Toronto: Harcourt Brace 1996), 231, the authors regard this reasoning as elegant but as yet unsubstantiated. See also T.J. Anderson and P.J. Hill, 'The Race for Property Rights,' *Journal of Law and Economics* 33 (1990), 177; R.L. Stroup, 'Buying Misery with Federal Land,' *Public Choice* 57 (1988), 69. For a defence of American settlement policies, see D.W. Allen, 'Homesteading and Property Rights; Or, How the West was Really Won,' *Journal of Law and Economics* 34 (1991), 1.

4 An account of that process of dispossession is beyond the scope of this essay. See further S.L. Haring, *White Man's Law: Native People in Nineteenth-Century Canadian Jurisprudence* (Toronto: Osgoode Society and University of Toronto Press 1998), chap. 11.

5 J.C. Weaver, *The Great Land Rush and the Making of the Modern World, 1650–1900* (Montreal: McGill-Queen's University Press 2003), 21.

6 B. Kercher, *An Unruly Child: A History of Law in Australia* (St Leonards, NSW: Allen and Unwin 1995), 122.

7 See S.H. Roberts, *The Squatting Age in Australia, 1835–1847* (London: Cambridge University Press 1964).

8 See further P.W. Gates, *Landlords and Tenants on the Prairie Frontier* (Ithaca, NY: Cornell University Press 1973).

9 Weaver, *The Great Land Rush*, 265.

10 *Statutes of Canada*, 1872, c.23.

11 Weaver, *The Great Land Rush*, 251.

12 Ibid., 252.

13 Glen Grismer's work on rural Saskatchewan is one of the few studies of squatters on the prairies. Grismer found that the first waves of squatters chose moderately forested areas over plains, a pattern that was later altered when settlers sought land more suited to agricultural development. Predictably, squatters sought out locations with ample water supply. Valley locations were popular, though generally speaking topographical extremes were avoided. Although some settlement preferences were seemingly influenced by the anticipation of surveys, locations were chosen in the absence of institutional structure and guidance. See G. Grismer, 'Early Squatting Holdings in Saskatchewan, 1878–1886,' in Regional Geographical Studies, *Some Current Research on the Canadian Plains* (Regina: University of Regina 1980), 22.

14 For earlier accounts, see also E.A. Mitchner, 'The North Saskatchewan River Settlement Claims, 1883–84,' in L.H. Thomas, ed., *Essays on Western History* (Edmonton: University of Alberta Press 1976), 129, and J.F. Gilpin, 'The Edmonton and District Settlers' Rights Movement, 1880 to 1885,' in R.C. Macleod, ed., *Swords and Ploughshares: War and Agriculture in Western Canada* (Edmonton: University of Alberta Press 1993), 149.

15 The decision in this case was rendered on 1 May 1894, but 'was unfortunately mislaid and therefore not reported.' *Heiminck v. Town of Edmonton, Supreme Court Reports* [hereafter S.C.R.] 28 (1898) 501, 510 (*per* Gwynne J.). A four-paragraph summary of the case appears at S.C.R. 23 (1894) 308. The mislaid judgment in *Brown* came to light much later; it is found reported in its entirety by means of a footnote in *Heiminck*, 510*ff*.

16 See further T. Cashman, *The Best Edmonton Stories* (Edmonton: Hurtig 1976), 145–8.

17 *Territories Law Reports* 1 (1893) 454 (Supreme Court).

18 *Brown v. Town of Edmonton*, as quoted in *Heiminck v. Town of Edmonton*, 519n.

19 'The Land,' *Edmonton Bulletin*, 11 February 1882.

20 'On the Jump,' *Edmonton Bulletin*, 11 February 1882.

21 Ibid.

22 'The Vigilance Committee,' *Edmonton Bulletin*, 18 February 1882.

23 'The Vigilantes,' *Edmonton Bulletin*, 11 February 1882.

24 William Bannerman, Sr (1841 to 1914), MP for Renfrew South, Ontario, 1880–2.

25 'The Church Property,' *Edmonton Bulletin*, 4 March 1882.

26 'Next!,' *Edmonton Bulletin*, 25 February 1882.

27 Ibid.

28 'Court,' *Edmonton Bulletin*, 17 June 1882.

29 During the court proceedings described below, it was later claimed that the original plan was to relocate the building on Bannerman's lot and that Bannerman had rejected that proposal. See 'The House Moving,' *Edmonton Bulletin*, 4 March 1882.

30 George filed a complaint with the federal government seeking $10,000 in damages. The *Bulletin* offered that this was 'not a bad price for a hundred dollar shanty.' *Edmonton Bulletin*, 18 February 1882.

31 'Sunday Lecture,' *Edmonton Bulletin*, 18 March 1882.

32 'Court,' *Edmonton Bulletin*, 17 June 1882.

33 See, for example, *Asher v. Whitlock* (1865), 1 *Law Reports Queen's Bench*, 1.

34 'The Very Latest,' *Edmonton Bulletin*, 4 March 1882.

35 Compare Frank Oliver's description of Deane's mandate: 'His general instructions are to, as far as possible, prevent claim jumping on the one hand and claim sprouting on the other. The lines will run due north and south, and twenty chains frontage by one mile in depth will be allowed wherever practicable. Broken sections in rear of the river lots will be divided among the holders of the river claims so as to give homesteads of the full size – 160 acres – and pre-emptions if possible. He will commence work on the claims adjoining the H.B. Co. reserve. He will not run the lines through but will put in the boundary stakes at the front and rear of the claims. Where there are no settlers on the river the township surveys will govern. Claims with river frontages will not be allowed as homesteads to parties holding homesteads elsewhere. Quit claim deeds from one actual occupant to another will hold good.' 'River Surveys,' *Edmonton Bulletin*, 29 July 1882.

36 'Public Meeting,' *Edmonton Bulletin*, 27 January 1883.

37 See, for example Malcolm Cameron, MP for Huron West, *House of Common Debates (Canada)*, 30 January 1884, 75–6.

38 *Dominion Lands Act, Statutes of Canada* 1883, c.17, s.28. Once the Province of Alberta acquired authority over public lands in the province, it put an end

to this legal indulgence. Section 16 of the *Provincial Lands Act, Statutes of Alberta* 1931, c.43, provided that 'the occupation of land, without entry as provided by this Act, gives to the occupant no right thereto and the occupant may be ejected as a trespasser and any improvements made by him shall thereupon be forfeited to the Crown.' That provision forms the basis of the current law. *Public Lands Act, Revised Statutes of Alberta* 2000, c.P-40, s.4.

39 'The Answer,' *Edmonton Bulletin*, 28 July 1883.
40 Largely unsung, William Pearce (1848–1930) had a storied career aiding development in the West, especially in Alberta. See further, E.A. Mitchner, 'William Pearce and Federal Government Activity in Western Canada 1882–1904' (PhD diss. University of Alberta 1971).
41 And in 1884 a land office to process homestead applications was finally opened in the region. 'Homestead Rights,' *Edmonton Bulletin*, 4 October 1884.
42 '$1 An Acre,' *Edmonton Bulletin*, 31 October 1885.
43 'Claims,' *Edmonton Bulletin*, 13 June 1885.
44 Oliver was, however, deeply displeased with some of Pearce's rulings. 'Land Decisions,' *Edmonton Bulletin*, 28 March 1885.
45 'The numbers of Canadians who leave their country and settle in the States has long been and is yet a subject of remark and wonder. Had this human tide been flowing into the North-West, Canada would no doubt occupy now a prominent position among the nations ...' 'The Last Land Act,' *Edmonton Bulletin*, 10 June 1882.
46 See generally D. Owram, *Promise of Eden: The Canadian Expansionist Movement and the Idea of the West, 1856–1900* (Toronto: University of Toronto Press 1992).
47 'Speculative Squatting,' *Edmonton Bulletin*, 12 January 1884.
48 In *Cosgrove v. Corbett* (1868) 14 *Grant's Chancery Cases* 617 (Ont.) 620, this practice is acknowledged.
49 Weaver, *The Great Land Rush*, especially 81ff.
50 Although these themes were not Locke's alone. Weaver credits the spread of the doctrine of improvement to the work of the Englishman Arthur Young. Weaver, *The Great Land Rush*, 84.
51 J. Locke, *Two Treatises of Government, Second Treatise* (1690; reprint, New York: Mentor 1960), paragraph 49.
52 Ibid., paragraph 41.
53 R.A.Williams, *The American Indian in Western Legal Thought: The Discourses of Conquest* (New York: Oxford University Press 1990), 246–9.
54 B. Murdoch, *Epitome of the Laws of Nova Scotia*, vol. 2 (Halifax: Joseph Howe 1832–3), 57.

55 See further Weaver, *The Great Land Rush*, especially 135–41.
56 See further *Papaschase Indian Band No. 136 v. Canada (Attorney General)*, *Alberta Law Reports* [hereafter Alta. L.R.] 4th ed. 43 (2004) 41 (Queen's Bench), reversed Alta. L.R. 4th ed. 66 (2006) 243 (Court of Appeal).
57 Locke, *Two Treatises of Government, Second Treatise*, paragraph 43.
58 'The Last Land Act,' *Edmonton Bulletin*, 10 June 1882.
59 'Squatters and Squatting,' *Edmonton Bulletin*, 5 May 1883. See also 'The Answer,' *Edmonton Bulletin*, 28 July 1883.
60 'Speculative Squatting,' *Edmonton Bulletin*, 12 January 1884; 'Speculative Squatting,' *Edmonton Bulletin*, 26 April 1884.
61 Ibid., 26 April 1884.
62 See further, 'Squatters and Squatting,' *Edmonton Bulletin*, 5 May 1883. See also Robert Watson, MP for Marquette, *House of Commons Debates (Canada)*, 28 February 1883, 86.
63 'The Last Land Act,' *Edmonton Bulletin*, 10 June 1882.
64 Ibid.
65 H. de Soto, *The Mystery of Capital: Why Capitalism Triumphs in the West and Fails Everywhere Else* (New York: Basic Books 2000).
66 'Dry Facts,' *Edmonton Bulletin*, 29 April 1882.
67 'The Boom,' *Edmonton Bulletin*, 4 February 1882.
68 Ibid.
69 Elsewhere we have outlined in greater detail the contextual differences that undermine de Soto's claim that the American experience is akin to event unfolding in the states of the former Soviet Union and in the developing world. See Ziff and Ward, 'De Soto Discovers the Prairies.'
70 See Kercher, *An Unruly Child*, 120–1.

Contributors

Constance Backhouse holds the positions of Distinguished University Professor and University Research Chair at the Faculty of Law, University of Ottawa. She has published three books on legal history with the Osgoode Society, included *Colour-Coded: A Legal History of Racism in Canada, 1900–1950* (1999), which was awarded the 2002 Joseph Brant Award, and *Petticoats and Prejudice: Women and the Law in Nineteenth-Century Canada* (1991), which was awarded the 1992 Willard Hurst Prize in Legal History by the Law and Society Association.

Rainer Baehre is a member of the Historical Studies and Social/Cultural Studies programs at Sir Wilfred Grenfell College, Memorial University of Newfoundland. In addition to *Outrageous Seas: Shipwreck and Survival in the Waters Off Newfoundland, 1583–1893* (McGill-Queen's UP 1999), he has published various writings on Canadian legal, criminal justice, and social/cultural history.

G. Blaine Baker is Professor of Law at McGill University. He has written extensively about the history of Canadian legal thought and Canada's legal professions, and was awarded the Surrency Prize by the American Society of Legal History in 1986. He has co-edited two Osgoode Society volumes and has been a contributor to five.

Joseph Ashley Berkovits holds a PhD (history) and a JD from the Uni-

versity of Toronto, is a Member of the Bar of Ontario, and is an adjudic-
tor at an administrative board in Ontario.

Patrick Brode practises law in Windsor, Ontario, and is the author of
five books on legal history, four published by the Osgoode Society. The
most recent was *Courted and Abandoned: Seduction in Canadian Law*
(2002).

Loir Chambers is Professor of Women's Studies at Lakehead University
in Thunder Bay. She is the author of two Osgoode Society books: *Married Women and Property Law in Victorian Ontario* (1997) and *Misconceptions: Unmarried Motherhood and the Ontario Children of Unmarried Parents
Act, 1921–1969* (2007). Her current research project is a study of the legal
treatment of co-habitants in Canada.

Paul Craven teaches in the Social Science Division, York University,
and writes legal, labour, and industrial history. His essays have
appeared in three previous volumes of this series. He was editor of
Labouring Lives: Work and Workers in Nineteenth-Century Ontario (Ontario
Historical Studies Series 1995) and co-editor (with Douglas Hay) of *Masters, Servants and Magistrates in Britain and the Empire, 1562–1955* (2004).
He is currently completing a book about low law in colonial New Brunswick.

Philip Girard is University Research Professor and Professor of Law,
History, and Canadian Studies at Dalhousie University in Halifax,
Nova Scotia. He is co-editor of two Osgoode Society volumes and the
author of *Bora Laskin: Bringing Law to Life* (Osgoode Society 2005). He
continues to research, write, and teach in the area of Canadian legal
history.

C. Ian Kyer is a senior partner in the Toronto office of Fasken Martineau
DuMoulin LLP. He has a doctorate in medieval and early modern Euro-
pean history and is co-author of *The Fiercest Debate: Cecil A. Wright, the
Benchers and Legal Education in Ontario, 1923–1957*, published by the
Osgoode Society in 1987, and has contributed two previous articles to
the Society's *Essays in the History of Canadian Law* series.

John McLaren is Emeritus Professor of Law at the University of Victoria. He researches in both Canadian and comparative colonial legal

history. He is currently engaged in a major research project on judicial appointment, accountability, and independence in the colonies of the nineteenth-century British Empire. He was co-editor (with Hamar Foster) of *Essays in the History of Canadian Law*, vol. 6, British Columbia and the Yukon (Osgoode Society 1996).

R. Roy McMurtry was founder of the Osgoode Society in 1979 and has been its president for many years. His other appointments have included Attorney General of Ontario, Canadian High Commissioner to the United Kingdom, and Chief Justice of Ontario.

Jim Phillips is Professor of Law and History at the University of Toronto. He has co-edited five volumes published by the Osgoode Society, and is the author or editor of three other books. He is editor-in-chief of the Osgoode Society.

John T. Saywell is University Professor Emeritus of York University. Among other books he has published *'Just Call Me Mitch,'* a biography of Premier Mitchell Hepburn (University of Toronto Press 1991), and *The Lawmakers: Judicial Power and the Shaping of Canadian Federalism* (Osgoode Society 2002).

Jonathan Swainger is Professor and chair of the history program at the University of Northern British Columbia. He has published a book on the history of the Department of Justice in the post-Confederation years and edited three collections on western Canadian legal history, including most recently a history of the Alberta Supreme Court.

Sean Ward is a graduate of the Faculty of Law at the University of Alberta. He articled with the Court of Queen's Bench of Alberta and is currently a member of the Law Society of Alberta.

Bruce Ziff is Professor of Law at the University of Alberta. His research interests centre on property law and legal history. He is co-editor (with P.V. Rao) of *Borrowed Power: Essays on Cultural Appropriation* (Rutgers UP 1997), and author of *Principles of Property Law*, now in its fourth edition. *His Unforeseen Legacies: Rueben Wells Leonard and the Leonard Foundation Trust* was published by the Osgoode Society in 2000.

PUBLICATIONS OF THE OSGOODE SOCIETY FOR
CANADIAN LEGAL HISTORY

2008   Constance Backhouse, *Carnal Crimes: Sexual Assault Law in Canada, 1900–1975*
Jim Phillips, R. Roy McMurtry, and John T. Saywell, eds., *Essays in the History of Canadian Law, Volume X: A Tribute to Peter N. Oliver*
Greg Taylor, *The Law of the Land: Canada's Receptions of the Torrens System*
Hamar Foster, Benjamin Berger, and A.R. Buck, eds., *The Grand Experiment: Law and Legal Culture in British Settler Societies*

2007   Robert J. Sharpe and Patricia I. McMahon, *The Persons Case: The Origins and Legacy of the Fight for Legal Personhood*
Lori Chambers, *Misconceptions: Unmarried Motherhood and the Ontario Children of Unmarried Parents Act, 1921–1969*
Jonathan Swainger, ed., *The Alberta Supreme Court at 100: History and Authority*
Martin L. Friedland, *My Life in Crime and Other Academic Adventures*

2006   Donald Fyson, *Magistrates, Police, and People: Everyday Criminal Justice in Quebec and Lower Canada, 1764–1837*
Dale Brawn, *The Court of Queen's Bench of Manitoba, 1870–1950: A Biographical History*
R.C.B. Risk, *A History of Canadian Legal Thought: Collected Essays*, edited and introduced by G. Blaine Baker and Jim Phillips

2005   Philip Girard, *Bora Laskin: Bringing Law to Life*
Christopher English, ed., *Essays in the History of Canadian Law, Volume IX: Two Islands: Newfoundland and Prince Edward Island*
Fred Kaufman, *Searching for Justice: An Autobiography*

2004   Philip Girard, Jim Phillips, and Barry Cahill, eds., *The Supreme Court of Nova Scotia, 1754–2004: From Imperial Bastion to Provincial Oracle*
Frederick Vaughan, *Aggressive in Pursuit: The Life of Justice Emmett Hall*
John D. Honsberger, *Osgoode Hall: An Illustrated History*
Constance Backhouse and Nancy Backhouse, *The Heiress versus the Establishment: Mrs Campbell's Campaign for Legal Justice*

2003   Robert J. Sharpe and Kent Roach, *Brian Dickson: A Judge's Journey*
Jerry Bannister, *The Rule of the Admirals: Law, Custom, and Naval Government in Newfoundland, 1699–1832*
George Finlayson, *John J. Robinette, Peerless Mentor: An Appreciation*
Peter Oliver, *The Conventional Man: The Diaries of Ontario Chief Justice Robert A. Harrison, 1856–1878*

2002   John T. Saywell, *The Lawmakers: Judicial Power and the Shaping of Canadian Federalism*

W.H. Morrow, ed., *Northern Justice: The Memoirs of Mr Justice William G. Morrow*

Beverley Boissery, *A Deep Sense of Wrong: The Treason, Trials, and Transportation to New South Wales of Lower Canadian Rebels after the 1838 Rebellion*

1994   Patrick Boyer, *A Passion for Justice: The Legacy of James Chalmers McRuer*

Charles Pullen, *The Life and Times of Arthur Maloney: The Last of the Tribunes*

Jim Phillips, Tina Loo, and Susan Lewthwaite, eds., *Essays in the History of Canadian Law, Volume V: Crime and Criminal Justice*

Brian Young, *The Politics of Codification: The Lower Canadian Civil Code of 1866*

1993   Greg Marquis, *Policing Canada's Century: A History of the Canadian Association of Chiefs of Police*

Murray Greenwood, *Legacies of Fear: Law and Politics in Quebec in the Era of the French Revolution*

1992   Brendan O'Brien, *Speedy Justice: The Tragic Last Voyage of His Majesty's Vessel Speedy*

Robert Fraser, ed., *Provincial Justice: Upper Canadian Legal Portraits from the Dictionary of Canadian Biography*

1991   Constance Backhouse, *Petticoats and Prejudice: Women and Law in Nineteenth-Century Canada*

1990   Philip Girard and Jim Phillips, eds., *Essays in the History of Canadian Law, Volume III: Nova Scotia*

Carol Wilton, ed., *Essays in the History of Canadian Law, Volume IV: Beyond the Law: Lawyers and Business in Canada, 1830–1930*

1989   Desmond Brown, *The Genesis of the Canadian Criminal Code of 1892*

Patrick Brode, *The Odyssey of John Anderson*

1988   Robert J. Sharpe, *The Last Day, the Last Hour: The Currie Libel Trial*

John D. Arnup, *Middleton: The Beloved Judge*

1987   C. Ian Kyer and Jerome Bickenbach, *The Fiercest Debate: Cecil A. Wright, the Benchers, and Legal Education in Ontario, 1923–1957*

1986   Paul Romney, *Mr Attorney: The Attorney General for Ontario in Court, Cabinet, and Legislature, 1791–1899*

Martin L. Friedland, *The Case of Valentine Shortis: A True Story of Crime and Politics in Canada*

1985   James Snell and Frederick Vaughan, *The Supreme Court of Canada: History of the Institution*

1984   Patrick Brode, *Sir John Beverley Robinson: Bone and Sinew of the Compact*

David Williams, *Duff: A Life in the Law*

1983 David H. Flaherty, ed., *Essays in the History of Canadian Law, Volume II*

1982 Marion MacRae and Anthony Adamson, *Cornerstones of Order: Court-houses and Town Halls of Ontario, 1784–1914*

1981 David H. Flaherty, ed., *Essays in the History of Canadian Law, Volume I*